Namibia

The travel guide

Footprint Handbook

**Nick Santcross , Gordon Baker &
Sebastian Ballard**

*Only the desert has a fascination – to ride
alone – in the sun in the forever unpossessed
country – away from man. This is the great
temptation.*

DH Lawrence

Hilltop house, Windhoek   1
Sam's Giardino, Swakopmund   3
    Turnstone tours
Terrace Bay   1
Etendeka Camp, Damaraland 2
    (16a)
Halali, Etosha   3
Namutoni, Etosha   2
Okonjima   2

Namibia Handbook
Third edition
© Footprint Handbooks Ltd 2001

Published by Footprint Handbooks
6 Riverside Court
Lower Bristol Road
Bath BA2 3DZ. England
T +44 (0)1225 469141
F +44 (0)1225 469461
Email discover@footprintbooks.com
Web www.footprintbooks.com

ISBN 1 900949 91 1
CIP DATA: A catalogue record for this
book is available from the British Library

Distributed in the USA by
Publishers Group West

Credits

Series editors
Patrick Dawson and Rachel Fielding

Editorial
Editor: Tim Jollands
Maps: Sarah Sorensen

Production
Typesetting: Emma Bryers, Leona Bailey
and Davina Rungasamy
Maps: Robert Lunn, Claire Benison and
Maxine Foster
Colour maps: Kevin Feeney
Cover: Camilla Ford

Design
Mytton Williams

Photography
Front cover: gettyone Stone
Back cover: Pictor
Inside colour section: Gordon Baker,
James Davis Travel Photography, Robert
Harding Picture Library, Images of Africa
Photobank, La Belle Aurore

Print
Manufactured in Italy by LEGOPRINT

Every effort has been made to ensure
that the facts in this Handbook are
accurate. However, travellers should still
obtain advice from consulates, airlines
etc about current travel and visa
requirements before travelling. The
authors and publishers cannot accept
responsibility for any loss, injury or
inconvenience however caused.

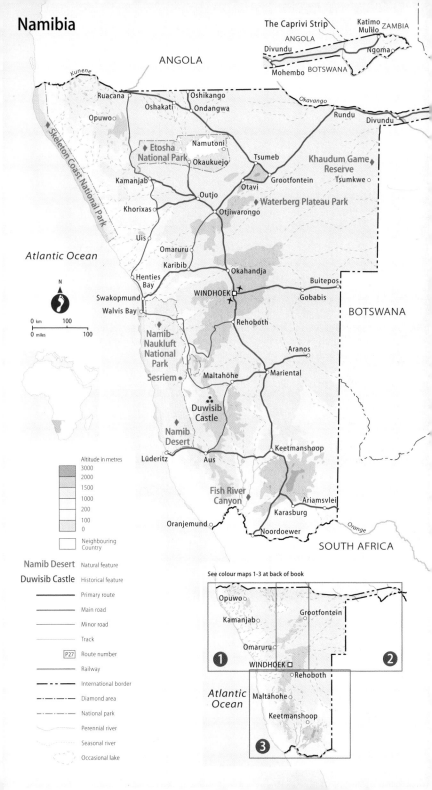

Contents

A foot in the door

Right: Taking a hot air balloon ride at dawn from Sesriem provides stunning views of the magnificent dunes at Sossusvlei.
Below: Driving through Etosha National Park, where 114 mammal, 110 reptile and over 300 bird species can be found.
Previous page: An elegant, 300-m high dune in the Namib desert at Sossusvlei.

Above: Lonely shipwrecks litter the Skeleton Coast. The elements which led to its name are now its biggest attraction: desert, isolation and solitude.
Right: The Fish River Canyon, enclosed on both sides by sandstone, shale and lava deposited there over a 1000 million years ago – the four-day, 85-km hike through the canyon is a rugged but rewarding challenge for the self-sufficient and hardy.

Highlights

Since gaining independence from South Africa in 1990, Namibia has been growing in popularity as a tourist destination. Superb wildlife, vast expanses of silent, unspoilt wilderness and a fascinating colonial history challenge the visitor to choose what to leave out of the adventure. While Sossusvlei, Swakopmund, Etosha National Park and the Fish River Canyon are the most popular destinations, there are almost limitless opportunities to enjoy the wild beauty of this empty, ancient land.

Deserts

Point your car in either an easterly or westerly direction from Windhoek, the capital, and it won't be long before you find yourself in one of Namibia's two great deserts. The red sand of the Kalahari Desert, to the east, is the last home of the fabled Bushmen, superb trackers and hunters, who have lived in harmony with nature in southern Africa for thousands of years. To the west lies the 80 million-year-old Namib, with its endless, seemingly lifeless sand dunes, its sharp, barren coastal border and its uniquely adapted plants and animals that survive thanks to the nightly, life-nourishing fog that rolls inland off the cold southern Atlantic Ocean.

Etosha – and much more

As a safari destination, Namibia can boast all of the 'Big Nine' game attractions. Etosha National Park is one of the great African game parks, its central feature the huge, flat Etosha Pan. The best time to visit is the dry season (July to early October) when time spent at one of the waterholes is like watching a wildlife play unfold, with a cast of animals emerging herd by herd out of the haze and down to the water to drink. At night, after a typical Namibian braai in one of the park's three camps, sit up by the floodlit waterhole and enjoy the unforgettable sounds of the wild African night. If you prefer seeing your game on foot, then head for Damaraland in the northwest of the country and visit one of the bush lodges that offers walking safaris led by experienced trackers – you might be lucky and catch a glimpse of the last free-roaming black rhinos in the world, as well as herds of uniquely adapted desert-dwelling elephants which survive by following ancient migration routes between waterholes. Namibia is also the last stronghold of the cheetah, with an estimated 3,000 animals, living predominantly on the country's commercial ranchlands.

Fish River Canyon

According to early Bushman legend, Africa's second largest canyon was carved out of the sandstone rock by a mighty serpent, Kouteign Kooru, as he slithered off into the desert to escape chasing hunters. True or not, this huge 300 million-year-old gash in the earth forces the Fish River to wind tortuously through the towering sandstone rocks before eventually flowing into the Orange River and the sea. Drive to the observation point near Hobas to witness the spectacular view and then head down into the depths of the canyon to enjoy the hot springs at Ai-Ais. Alternatively, for the fit and the adventurous, there is a four-day, 85-km hike through the canyon, and numerous other walks from a private lodge further upstream.

Adventure sports

Throughout Namibia, there are plenty of opportunities for the the the serious hiker, from the mountainous Naukluft trail to the hike along the sandy, ephemeral Ugab River. If the sky is your thing, you can try paragliding, gliding or parachuting in the clear desert skies, followed by a spot of quad-biking or sandboarding down some of the highest dunes in the world. Leisurely canoe trips on the Zambezi River may be a little more to some people's taste, while the incorrigible adrenaline junkie should head for the rapids on the Kunene or Orange Rivers.

People and a way of life

The tiny Namibian population of around 1.8 million comprises 11 ethnic groups, each of which contributes to the rich tapestry of customs, languages and way of life that make the country unique. Namibia's peoples include ancient hunter-gatherers and semi-nomadic livestock herders, Bantu-speaking farmers, herders and fishermen, the descendants of white missionaries, traders and hunters, and mixed-race farmers and white settlers who arrived in search of land to graze their cattle herds.

Rural and urban

However, Namibia is also a blend of the rural and the urban, a land divided between the old and the new. At the same time as some still practise the ancient traditions of hunting, gathering and livestock herding, others pursue modern urban lifestyles of salaried work, with cell phones and satellite television. While the majority still dwell in traditional homesteads across the north of the country, more and more Namibians are moving to towns in search of employment, better healthcare and education and all the other trappings of the modern world.

The last refuge of the Bushmen

The oldest inhabitants of Namibia are the Bushmen, or San, who migrated here thousands of years ago, and whose delicate, vivid cave paintings are visible in their ancient resting places all over the country. Regarded as semi-human by both white settlers and the Bantu-speaking tribes, the Bushmen were hunted down like animals and slaughtered. Today, Botswana and Namibia are the last refuge of these ancient and fragile tribes, struggling to keep a sense of identity in the modern world.

Cultural blend

The soulful choirs of the Nama and the colourful, long dresses and headgear of the Herero women reflect the blend of European and African cultures that have thrived in Namibia. But while the Herero, Bantu-speaking people who brought the traditions of cattle-herding with them from east Africa, are rapidly entering the formal sector of the economy, their cousins, the Himba, still wear traditional leather clothing in the remote and wild Kaokoveld, the last nomadic, herding peoples in southern Africa.

Owambo-speaking peoples

The largest single group in Namibia, the Owambo-speaking peoples, are centred in the far north, near Angola. As such they bore the brunt of the bush war during the struggle for independence. Traditionally, they were cattle herders and farmers living in homesteads protected from wild animals by thick wooden-spiked fences. Today, the Owambo represent the backbone of the new Namibia, no longer just poorly paid migrant labourers, but working in government ministries, schools and hospitals and modern offices in Namibia's cities. However, ties with tradition are still strong and, at weekends and during the holidays, Windhoek's pick-up trucks and buses are piled high with people and goods for the long trek back to the villages in the north.

Independence and the future

The white community, too, is seeking a balance between its voortrekker and colonial past and the demands and ways of the modern world at the start of a new millennium. White businesses dominate urban areas and white farmers own the majority of the commercial ranchland in the country. Despite the legacy of advantage over their countrymen, tough economic and political realities affect the white tribes of Namibia just as they do their fellow black countrymen. Indeed, recent struggles for land in neighbouring Zimbabwe reflect the broader struggle for economic and social equity between black and white Africans everywhere. While peaceful cooperation and endeavour hold the key to a prosperous future for all Namibians, there remain some powerful underlying forces of resistance that threaten to destabilize the positive efforts of the majority.

Left: Goerke House, in the remote seaside town of Lüderitz, which offers visitors a perfectly preserved glimpse of Namibia's German colonial heritage.
Below: Shopfronts in the Kavango region, often as colourfully named as they are painted, and often the sole providers of goods and entertainment for the communities they serve.
Next page: The Quiver Tree Forest, one of the main attractions of southern Namibia. A type of aloe, the Quiver tree owes its name to the former practice of the San and Nama peoples of using the hollowed-out braches as arrow quivers.

Above: A Herero woman in Windhoek defies the heat and western concepts of fashion by wearing her traditional Victorian dress.
Left: Many Himba women still wear the dress of their ancestors, red ochre is rubbed into their skin and their hair is styled with mud.

Essentials

2

Essentials

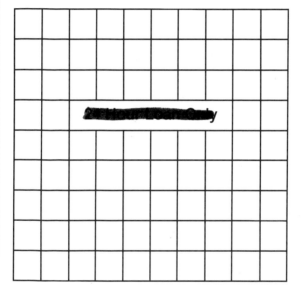

CUNARD

THE MOST FAMOUS OCEAN LINERS IN THE WORLD ™

Planning your trip

Where to go

Namibia is a vast country, almost four times the size of the UK, with its attractions greatly spread out. A full visit to the country will require a month or more with a car, which involves a considerable initial outlay for car hire. But the flexibility and access of your own transport will be key to your appreciation of the country. Furthermore, economies can be made during your visit by camping in some of the picturesque sites. Careful research into which of the great range of activities and destinations most appeal is an important stage of your trip preparation. Beware setting yourself too ambitious an agenda as distances are significant. Try to arrange stops of two to four days in each location or region to fully appreciate what there is to offer; rather than cram in too much, decide instead to return some time in the future. Being in a rush through Africa is the surest way of coming to grief.

Depending on how much driving you are prepared to do, you may wish to focus more on the north or south of the country. On the other hand, if you are driving through Namibia en route to Zimbabwe, Botswana or South Africa you will have the chance to sample a bit of all the country, including the Kavango and Caprivi regions. While we highly recommend visiting these areas, we have not included them in specific itineraries below because of the time and distance involved in reaching them.

Below are three suggested routes of 10, 14 and 21 days respectively, which seek to take in the main places of interest for those pressed for time. They do not include special interest activities such as the Fish River Canyon hike, a canoe trip down the Orange River or a safari in Kaokoland, each of which requires four or five days. Depending also on whether you are more interested in a general cultural visit or a more wildlife oriented trip you may prefer to skip places such as Swakopmund or Lüderitz, and focus more on Etosha, Sossusvlei, the Naukluft Mountains and a private game lodge.

The fourth tour is for lottery winners and anyone else wishing to see Namibia at its best. Much of this tour could be arranged in advance with a specialist Namibia travel agent such as *Sunvil Africa* (or others, see Tours and tour operators below.)

Day	Activity	Overnight	Route 1:
1 & 2	Sightseeing, preparing for trip, visit Daan Viljoen Game Park	Windhoek	**10 days**
3	Drive to Etosha – Namutoni	Mushara Lodge	
4	Game drives	Okaukuejo Camp	
5	Northern Damaraland	Twyfelfontein	
6	Brandberg/Spitzkoppe	Swakopmund	
7	Welwitschia Drive/Desert Tour/Dolphin Cruise	Swakopmund	
8	Drive via Kuiseb Canyon to Sossusvlei	Sesriem	
9	am early visit dunes at Sossusvlei, pm into Tsaris Mountains	ZebraRiver Lodge	
10	Drive to Windhoek	Windhoek	

Day	Activity	Overnight	Route 2:
1-8	As above		**14 days**
9	am early visit dunes at Sossusvlei, pm drive to Duwisib Castle	Duwisib Rest Camp or local guestfarm	
10	Drive to Lüderitz via Helmeringhausen and Aus	Lüderitz	
11	Kolmanskop tour, Coast tour	Lüderitz	

Essentials

12	Drive to Fish River Canyon or Cañon Roadhouse	Fish River Lodge
13	Drive to Keetmanshoop: visit Quiver Tree Forest & Giant's Playground	Keetmanshoop
14	Early start to Windhoek via Brukkaros volcano	Windhoek

Route 3: 21 days	Day	Activity	Overnight
	1 & 2	Sightseeing, preparing for trip, visit Daan Viljoen Game Park	Windhoek
	3	am drive to Waterberg pm short walks around and up to Plateau	Waterberg
	4	Drive to Etosha, visit Hobas Meteorite, and Otjikoto Lake	Namutoni Camp
	5	Game drives	Halali Camp
	6	Game drives	Okaukuejo Camp
	7	Drive to Damaraland for Twyfelfontein, Organ Pipes, Burnt Mountain	Twyfelfontein or Damaraland Camp
	8	Drive via Brandberg (White Lady) to game farm near Omaruru	Erongo Wilderness Lodge
	9	Game drive and walks	As above
	10	Drive to Swakopmund, sightseeing	Swakopmund
	11	Adventure sports, Welwitschia drive, desert tour/dolphin cruise	Swakopmund
	12	Drive through Namib Desert (Kuiseb Canyon) to Sossusvlei	Sesriem
	13	am visit dunes at Sossusvlei pm drive to Duwisib Castle	Duwisib
	14	Drive to Lüderitz via Helmeringhausen & Aus	Aus or Lüderitz
	15	Kolmanskop tour, coast tour	Lüderitz
	16	Drive to Fish River Canyon	Fish River Lodge
	17	Horse-riding, 4WD or hiking in Canyon	Fish River Lodge or Cañon Roadhouse
	18	Drive to Keetmanshoop, sunset visit to Quiver Tree Forest/Giant's Playground	Keetmanshoop or Quiver Tree Forest

Suggested tours

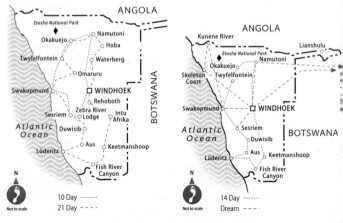

19 & 20	Either: drive to Intu Afrika Game Lodge	Intu Afrika	
	Or: drive to Lake Oanob Resort	Rehoboth	
21	Return to Windhoek	Windhoek	

Day	Activity	Overnight	Dream tour
1 & 2	Preparing for trip; visit Daan Viljoen Game Park	Hotel Heinitzburg	
3	Fly to the Skeleton Coast on private safari	Khumib River base camp	
4	Explore the Skeleton Coast with guides on foot	As above	
5	Fly up to the Kunene River (Epupa Falls) for the day	As above	
6	Fly to Swakopmund, sightseeing, adventure sports	Swakopmund Hotel & Entertainment Centre	
7	Explore the town or join a tour to Walvis Bay	As above	
8	Day tour to the Namib Desert/ Welwitschia Drive	As above	
9	am to yourself; pm to railway station, board train	Desert Express	
10	Arrive Windhoek 1000; pm explore town	Windhoek Country Club	
11	Fly to Etosha National Park; pm game drive	Mushara Lodge	
12	Game viewing in Etosha Park; lunch at Okaukuejo	As above	
13	Fly to Victoria Falls; pm visit the falls	Victoria Falls Hotel	
14	Explore the town; fly over the falls; pm sundowner cruise on Zambezi	As above	
15	Fly to Katima Mulilo, transfer to Mudumu National Park	Lianshulu Lodge	
16	Early am bush walk; pm boat trip on Kwando River	As above	
17	am game drive; pm transfer to airport, fly to Windhoek	Windhoek Country Club	
18	am fly to Sossusvlei; pm visit Sesriem Canyon, evening walk in dunes	As above	
19	early am flight/ballooning over dunes pm activities at Wilderness Camp	As above	
20	Fly to Windhoek and catch flight home		

Essentials

When to go

There is no bad time to visit Namibia, but depending upon what you wish to see and do there are certain months which are better than others. August and December are the busiest months for tourism, be sure to book your car hire and accommodation in advance. Outside the winter months of June-September, the heat can spoil your holiday. This is not to say don't come in the summer; after all, summer in Namibia coincides with winter in Europe and the United States. But it can get very hot, particularly in Windhoek and the south. For the two weeks around Christmas and the New Year there is a mass exodus, for those who can afford it, to the coast where temperatures are significantly cooler. During school holidays, local families often book the national parks accommodation in advance.

Namibia is essentially an arid country. If you are keen on game viewing then the dry winter months of May-October are the best months to visit. This is when most wild animals congregate around the natural and man-made waterholes. During the 'rainy' season (November-March) many roads in rural areas can be closed to saloon cars for several days. Birdwatching is best after the rains when there are numerous flooded depressions which attract migrant species. Much of the countryside is totally unrecognizable after the rains, when the landscape is green and many unusual flowering plants can be enjoyed. Hiking should not be attempted during the hot summer months; in fact the Fish River Canyon trail is closed between 15 September and 15 April, because of temperatures in excess of 45°C.

There are a number of colourful festivals that are worth enjoying while you are in the country. While none of them is significant enough to base your entire trip around, should you be in the area at the time they do provide an interesting insight into the heritage of the different tribes of this cosmopolitan country (see page 48).

Tours and tour operators

UK & Ireland *Abercrombie & Kent Travel*, Sloane Square House, Holbein Place, London SW1W 8NS, T020-7730 9600, F020-7730 9376, www.abercrombiekent.co.uk *Africa Exclusive*, Hamilton House, 68 Palmerston Rd, Northampton NN1 5EX, T01604-628979, F639879, www.africaexclusive.co.uk High budget, small group holidays for those with £3,000 to spend on a two-week trip. *Africa Travel Centre*, 21 Leigh St, London WC1H 9QV, T020-7387 1211, info@africatravel.co.uk, www.africatravel.co.uk Taylor-made itineraries. *Art of Travel*, The Travel House, 51 Castle Street, Cirencester, Gloucestershire GL7 1QD, T01285-650011, www.artoftravel.co.uk *Dragoman*, Camp Green, Debenham, Stowmarket, Suffolk IP14 6LA, T01728-861133, F861127, www.dragoman.co.uk *Exodus Travels*, 9 Weir Road, London SW12 0LT, T020-8772 3822, www.exodus.co.uk

Explore Worldwide Ltd, 1 Frederick Street, Aldershot, Hants GU11 1LQ, T01252-760000, F760001, www.exploreworldwide.com ***Guerba***, T01373- 826611, F858351, www.guerba.com Trekking and adventure travel specialists, offering combined Namibia family adventure with trip to Victoria Falls. ***Kumuka Expeditions***, 40 Earls Court Rd, London W8 6EJ, T020-7937 8855, F020-7937 6664, www.kumaka.com ***www.namibia-safaris.co.uk*** UK-based safari provider with good destination information. ***www.rainbowtours.co.uk/namibia*** Aimed at luxury end. ***Safari Drive***, Wessex House, 127 High St, Hungerford, Berkshire, RG17 0DL, T01488-681611, F685055, www.safaridrive.com Self-drive safaris in Africa. ***Sunvil Africa***, Sunvil House, Upper Square, Old Isleworth, Middlesex, TW7 7BJ, T020-8232 9777, F8568 8330, Africa@sunvil.co.uk, www.sunvil.co.uk The leading tour operator to Namibia, up-to-date advice and plenty of guidance when planning a route; informative website. ***Trailfinders***, 194 Kensington High Street, London W8 7RG, T020-7938 3939, F7938 3305, www.trailfinders.com ***Travelbag Adventures***, 15 Turk Street, Alton, Hampshire GU34 1AG, T01420-541007, F541022, www.travelbag-adventures.co.uk ***Wildlife Worldwide***, 170 Selsdon Road, South Croydon, Surrey, CR2 6PJ, T020-8667 9158, F8667 1960, www.wildlifeworldwide.com

North America

David Anderson Safaris, 30 West Mission Street, Santa Barbara, CA 93101, T800-9274647, F805-5637953, www.davidanderson.com ***Goway***, 5865 South Kyrene Rd, Tempe AZ 85283, T800-3878850, F6654432, www.goway.com ***Himalayan Travel***, 8 Berkshire Place, Danbury, CT 06810, T800-2252380, F203-7978077, www.gorp.com/himtravel ***On Safari***, 182 Sound Beach Avenue, Old Greenwich, CT 06870, T800-70036777, F203-6376813, www.onsafari.com ***Travel Cuts***, 187 College St, Toronto, Ontario M5T 1P7, Canada, T416-9792406, F9798167, www.travelcuts.com

Namibia Tourism offices

Head Office
Namibia Tourism, Private Bag 13346,
Windhoek, T061-2842366, F221930,
www.tourism.com.na
Regional offices
Keetmanshoop Southern Tourist
Forum (STF), 5th Avenue, T0631-221166,
F223818, munkhoop@iafrica.com.na
Lüderitz Lüderitz Foundation,
Bismarck Street.
Omaruru Namib-i,
Main Street, T064-570261.

Oujto Etosha Information Bureau,
PO Box 78, T/F067-313072.
Swakopmund Namib-i,
corner Roon & Kaiser Wilhelm Street,
PO Box 1236, T064-402224, F405101.
Tsumeb Travel North Namibia,
OMEG Allee, PO Box 799, T067-220728,
F220916.
Windhoek 7 Post Street Mall (close to
the Gibeon Meteorites), T061-220640;
Continental Building, Independence
Avenue, T061-2842111.

Essentials

Australia &
New Zealand
Africa Wildlife Safaris, Melbourne T3-9696 2899, F9658 6055. *Goway*, 350 Kent Street,
Sydney NSW 2000, T2-92624755, F92901905, www.goway.com *Jet-Age Marketing*,
Travel House, 6 Walls Road, Penrose, Auckland, New Zealand, T9-5252360, F5252227,
www.jetage.co.nz

Rest of Europe
& Israel
ABC Afrique, www.abcafrique.com *Best of Africa*, www.best-of-africa.com *HoGaTourS*
GmbH Reisebüro, 76646 Bruchsal, Germany, T7251-55011, F55045, www.ilk.de/hgts/
index.html Specialize in southern Africa, their Namibian offerings are with Jacana Tours
for general adventure travel and Pinder Reisen who organize golf trips to Namibia.
Iwanowski's Individuelles Reisen GmbH, Büchnerstrasse 11, 41540 Dormagen, Ger-
many, T2133-260300, F260333, iwanowski@afrika.de, www.afrika.de Tailored holidays,
everything from chauffeur-driven safaris, 4WD trips, guestfarms, wilderness trips, two
weeks in the desert, all types of adventure holidays. *Jedek Reisen*, Doblinger Haubstrasse
23, 1190 Wien, Austria, T1-3696622, F3696605, jedek.reisen@telecom.at Karawane
Reisen, Schorndorfer Strasse 149, 71638 Ludwigsberg, Germany T7141-284830,
F284838, www.karawane.de *Makila Voyages*, www.makila.fr *Namibia Safaris &*
Spezialreisen, Schottenstr 75, 78462 Konstanz, Germany, http://home.t-online.de/
home/namibia.travel *Rotunda Tours*, Weisenstrasse 10, CH 8008, Zurich, Switzerland,
T1-386466, F3864688, www.rotunda.ch *Thika Travel*, Kerkplein 6, 3628 AE Kockengen,
Netherlands, T346-242526, F242525, thika@knoware.nl *Travelshop*, www.travelshop.
de/afrika *Travel Worldwide*, Hermelijnlaan 23, B-2900 Schoten, Belgium, T03-6583702,
F6850636. *Windrose Fernreisen* GmbH, Neue Gronstraáe 28, 10179 Berlin, Germany,
T030-2017210, F20172117, www.windrose.de Good deals for organized luxury tours.
World Wide Adventures, Valkyrigaten 15, 0166 Oslo, Norway, T022-609920, F569766.

South Africa
Look under **local tour operators** in the web listings below for Namibian and South
African operators. These can all be booked from outside Namibia, and may be cheaper
and better informed than travel agents in your home country – and with web searches
and email, it needn't be that time-consuming or expensive.

Finding out more

Tourist offices
are listed in the
directory section of
individual towns
A good way of finding out more information for your trip is to contact the **Namibian
Tourism** office in your country or to consult their website (see box for contact details).
There are also, literally, hundreds of websites covering travel in Namibia. Listed below
are some that provided useful information in September 2001 – worth a look before
you travel.

Namibia Tourism overseas offices

Germany *42-44 Schillerstrasse, 60313 Frankfurt, T69-1337360, F13373615, www.namibia-tourism.com*

South Africa Cape Town *Main Tower, Standard Bank Centre, Adderley Street, PO Box 739, Cape Town 8000, T21-4193190, F4215840, info@ct.namtour.com.na*

Johannesburg *11 Alice Lane, 3rd Floor, East Wing, Standard Bank Building, PO Box 78946, Sandton City, Johannesburg 2146, T11-7848024, F7848340, namtour@ citec.co.za, www.iwwn.com.na/namtour*

Spain *Representative: Alberto Ruiz Thierry, Juan Hertado de Mendosa 5, 28036 Madrid, T1-3501532, F3501810.*

UK *6 Chandos Street, London, WIG 9LU, T020-7636 2924/28, F7636 2969, info@namibiatourism.co.uk, www.namibiatourism.co.uk*

USA *Representative: Kartagener Associates, 12 West 37th Street, New York, NY 10018, T1 -212 4650619, F212 2688299, kainyc@worldnet.att.net*

Essentials

News & views portals

Namibian portals
www.africaonline.com.na Easy to use, useful, interesting Namibian portal, part of the Africa-wide portal.

www.iwwn.com.na/iwwn Internet World Wide Namibia site, good for tourist information, operates as a portal for Namibians, with links, bulletin boards and chat rooms.

www.namibweb.com Multilingual, hugely informative online travel agent and information source. Useful links and details of internet cafés.

News
www.namibian.com.na The country's independent newspaper online, with useful classifieds. News also at **www.namibianews.com** and **www.allafrica.com/namibia**

Dedicated to tourists
www.tourism.com.na Namibia's Ministry of Environment and Tourism homepage.

www.travelnews.com.na and **www.holidaytravel.com.na** Locally maintained sites providing topical information, travel stories and links to local travel services. Run by company responsible for the free, bi-monthly *Travel News Namibia* tourist publication.

Other
www.africanconservation.com/namibia Ongoing conservation projects.

www.fco.gov.uk UK's Foreign Office site, for the 'official' latest on the political situation (their UK travel advice unit can be reached on T020-7008 0232).

www.lonelyplanet.com/destinations/africa/namibia For recent traveller comments, see 'postcards'.

www.africanbirdclub.org and **www.sabirding.co.za** Birding opportunities in Namibia. See also **www.natmus.cul.na/birds/birdlist.html** for a list of all birds identified in Namibia.

www.africanwildliferesources.org Internet directory, virtual library, research tool and resource centre, promoting sustainable wildlife practices.

www.downhilladventures.co.za Information on sandboarding in southern Africa.

www.felixunite.com The original and best canoe operator on the Orange River, also offer a fabulous Kunene trip, taking in the highlights of northern Namibia on the way (5 days on the river).

www.gorp.com Popular US outdoor pursuits site, search under Destinations.

www.tara.org.uk/namibia1.htm For African rock art information.

Special interest sites

www.afroventures.com Fly-in safaris across Africa, with virtual tours on their site.

www.chameleonsafaris.com Wide range of safaris, Windhoek-based.

www.horizon.fr/namibia.html Independent travel 'guide' in French and English.

Local tour operators

www.inshore.com.na Based in Walvis Bay, with Damaraland, Kaokaland and Skeleton Coast expertise.

www.kidigo-safaris.de Tailored to German visitors.

www.namibian.org A good site for the budget traveller, from the *Cardboard Box* hostel in Windhoek.

www.oryxtours.com.na Offer scheduled, tailor-made and self-drive tours, fly-in, adventure safaris, specialist services for disabled travellers, and can provide for large functions, arrange chauffeurs etc where a personalized touch required.

www.resafrica.net Excellent online booking system (with photos and descriptions) for accommodation, car hire, flights and tours.

www.scadventures.co.za Offers a 'Relics of the Past' and other Namib desert drives, based in Springbok, South Africa.

www.trans-namibia-tours.com Provide for those interested in natural history and culture.

Also try www.namibia-tours.com; www.namibiatravel.com; www.orusovo.com /sksafari, for Skeleton Coast safaris; **www.safarishop.co.za**, a Johannesburg-based safari agent with good selection and toll-free number from the US; and **www.swasafaris.com.na**, a specialist operator in the region since 1954.

Language

For some simple opening phrases in each of the common languages, see page 381

Although English is the official language, Afrikaans is still the lingua franca in the central and southern parts of the country. In the north, the majority of people are Oshiwambo speakers with English as second choice. Afrikaans is spoken in the Kavango with English most common in the Caprivi Strip. Visitors who speak German will find that many white-owned businesses in the tourist industry are owned and run by German-speaking people.

In remote areas, and during your encounters with locals, your welcome will improve immeasurably if you take time with a few pleasantries before plunging in with demands or requests. A handshake is almost always welcome (man to man); you will quickly master the three-grip handshake. Before asking whatever it is you want of a person in the street or a shopkeeper, take a moment to ask how they are, etc. While this may seem unnecessary, it greatly improves the likelihood and accuracy of the response. Be sensitive to cultural issues, particularly when entering traditional villages; if in doubt, ask.

Disabled travellers

Most buildings in Namibia are unlikely to be disabled friendly but because most accommodation will be bungalow style, negotiating stairs etc is rarely a problem. Many roads, even in towns, are gravel and very few outside Windhoek have pavements, reducing mobility for wheelchairs. As far as activities are concerned, anything active involving the desert or bush is likely to prove difficult in Namibia, but sightseeing by car in Etosha or in the desert need not be a major problem. *Oryx Tours* (www.oryxtours.com.na) have dedicated services for disabled travellers; they are a good first port of call for information, and offer tailored tours in consultation with travellers. It is also worth visiting the www.geocities.com site. Their Global Access - Disabled Travel Network Site is dedicated to providing information for 'disabled adventurers' and includes a number of reviews and tips for members of the public.

Gay and lesbian travellers

The climate is not particularly welcoming for lesbian and gay visitors. There is a gay rights support group, the Rainbow Project, with over 1000 members. In April 2001, protesters took part in a Gay Rights march in Windhoek after President Nujoma threatened to outlaw homosexuality, arrest gay Namibians and deport gay foreigners. In a speech at the University of Namibia in March 2001, he declared, 'The Republic of Namibia does not allow homosexuality or lesbianism.' In fact, there is no such law; conversely, there is a law against discrimination. Also in March 2001, a bizarre incident was reported in which soldiers of the President's Special Field Force were apparently ordered to apprehend men wearing earrings and forcibly remove the jewellery from their ears. Overall, however, discrete visitors should encounter no problems.

Student travellers

Namibia is a nation of young people and in this respect is a good place for students to travel. Similarly, there are many volunteers (VSO, Peace Corps, Operation Raleigh etc) working in the country, so you are likely to find good company when you travel. While the cost of camping or staying in backpackers hostels is not prohibitive on a student budget, the cost of car hire is. Hitch-hiking (see page 41) is certainly possible and it is common to see groups of young Namibians hiking (as it is locally called), particularly at weekends. However, given the high death rate on Namibian roads it is not advisable to do so unless unavoidable. You will typically be asked to pay the same rate as a shared taxi fare, so rather use these services where possible.

Travelling with children

In the main towns with supermarkets, you will find plentiful supplies of all you need to feed and look after your little ones. Hygiene throughout the country is of a good standard; stomach upsets are rare and the tap water everywhere is safe to drink. Most of the guest lodges will be happy to welcome families with young children, although it is advisable to call ahead; game drives may be deemed unsuitable for the very young. Be sure to cover your children against the intense sun's rays, and be aware of the potential dangers of wild animals, snakes and insects in the bush.

Flying with kids
Visit:
www.babygoes2.com

Inform the airline in advance that you are travelling with a baby or toddler and check out the facilities when booking as these vary with each aircraft. British Airways now has a special seat for under 2s; check which aircraft have been fitted when booking. Pushchairs can be taken as hand luggage or stored in the hold. Skycots are available on long-haul flights. Take snacks and toys for in-flight entertainment and remember that swallowing food or drinks during take-off and landing will help prevent ear problems

Women travellers

Women, both local and foreign, do travel by themselves or in pairs around Namibia, and generally speaking Namibia is safe enough in daylight hours. However, newspapers report frequent incidents of domestic violence and rape, albeit mostly confined to the townships. Women travellers unfamiliar with the area are therefore advised to avoid walking around by themselves at night. As in any country, there are risks associated with single women travellers, however these are no greater in Namibia than elsewhere. In fact, given the lack of big cities and the low population density perhaps the risks are lower. Two or more women travelling together are likely, at some point, to meet with some unreconstructed male chauvinism, but are unlikely to encounter anything more serious. Women travelling alone by car should be aware that, if driving by themselves, they should expect to have to change at least one tyre during their stay.

Working in the country

Most foreign workers in Namibia are employed through embassies, development or volunteer agencies or through foreign companies. For the most part these people will have been recruited in their countries of origin. Teachers – especially of maths, science and English – could try their luck with the local Ministry of Basic Education and Culture office in each regional centre. Other possibilities are to seek work in the tourist industry: those with languages and experience will stand the best chance of finding work. In all cases, foreigners require work/residence permits and these are fairly easily obtained with the help of the relevant officials but note that it is very difficult to upgrade a tourist visa to a working visa once inside Namibia. Given the high unemployment rate in the country and the low cost of labour, those seeking to work unofficially are unlikely to find conditions to their liking, and might also reflect upon the ethics of taking away scarce work from local people.

Before you travel

Getting in

Visas & immigration
All visitors must be in possession of a passport which is valid for a minimum of six months from their date of entry. At present, visitors from Angola, Austria, Belgium, Botswana, Canada, France, Germany, Ireland, Italy, Japan, Luxembourg, Netherlands, Moçambique, Russia, Singapore, South Africa, Switzerland, Tanzania, United Kingdom, United States of America and Zimbabwe can stay in the country for a period of 90 days with a permit issued on arrival at point of entry. Extensions have to be applied for from the Ministry of Home Affairs, Independence Avenue, Windhoek, T061-2929111. Tourist visas can also be obtained from Namibian Embassies overseas. Work and study visas must be applied for from your home country and granted before you depart.

Insurance
Always take out travel insurance before you set off and read the small print carefully. Check that the policy covers the activities you intend or may end up doing. Also check carefully what your medical cover includes, ie flight cancellations and baggage loss, ambulance, helicopter rescue or emergency flights back home. Also check the payment protocol. You may have to cough up first (literally) before the insurance company reimburses you. It is always best to dig out all the receipts for personal effects like jewellery and cameras. Take photocopies of these items and note down all serial numbers.

You are advised to shop around for insurance. *STA Travel* and other reputable travel organizations offer good value policies. Young travellers from North America can try the International Student Insurance Service (ISIS), which is available through *STA Travel*, T1-800-7770122, www.sta-travel.com Older travellers should note that some companies will not cover people over 65 years old, or may charge higher premiums. Some of the best policies for older UK travellers are offered by *Age Concern*, T0845-6012234.

If you have failed to make insurance arrangements at home and need to arrange cover locally, contact *TourMed Namibia*, T061-235188; who offer 24-hour countrywide emergency medical rescue specifically for tourists, plus medical advice over the telephone (24 hour, with a specific expertise on poisons, as they put it, 'ingested, inhaled or absorbed') as well as evacuation, admission to hospital, treatment and repatriation of mortal remains (!). Clearly, this is a medical rather than financial insurance service; you might find that your home contents insurance covers the great majority of your possessions at home and abroad. Check before you travel, and take with you a photocopy of the relevant sections of your policy outlining procedures to follow when things go wrong.

Namibian embassies and consulates

Belgium *Avenue de Tervuren 454,*
1150 Brussels, T2-7711410, F7719689.
Botswana *Gaborone Sun Hotel, Room 412,*
P Bag 0016, Gaborone, T35111, F302555.
France *80 Avenue Foch 17,*
Square de l'Avenue Foch, Paris,
T1-4417 3265, F4417 3273.
Germany *Mainzer Strasse 47,*
Bonn 53179, T346021, F346025.
South Africa *Tulbach Park, Eikendal Flat*
Suite 2, 1234 Church Street, Colbyn,
Pretoria 0132, T3423520, F3423565.

Sweden *Luntmakargatan 86-88, 11122,*
PO Box 26042, S 100 31, Stockholm,
T6127788, F6126655.
United Kingdom *6 Chandos Street, London*
W1M 0LQ, T020-7636 6244, F7637 5694.
USA *1605 New Hampshire Avenue, NW,*
Washington DC 20009, T202-9860540,
F9860443.
Zambia *6968 Kabanga Road, Rhodes Park,*
PO Box 30577, Lusaka, T252250, F252497.
Zimbabwe *31A Lincoln Road, Avondale,*
Harare, T304856, F304855.

Essentials

Customs

Duty free There are no restrictions for travellers from South Africa. Overseas visitors: 400 cigarettes or 50 cigars or 250 g of tobacco, 50 ml of perfume and 250 ml of toilet water, 2 litres of wine and 1 litre of spirits, gifts up to the value of N$50 000 are allowed to be imported duty free. All hunting rifles must be declared on arrival; permits are issued when entering of the country. Temporary import of vehicles: contact Namibia Customs, T061-2099111.

There is a small duty free shop at Hosea Kutako airport for outbound travellers, but the choice is limited. Remember to use up your currency (Namibian dollars are not transferable once overseas) and buy any souvenirs before you reach the airport. Failing that, Air Namibia has a limited stock of goods for sale in the air. Bona fide tourists to Namibia are exempt from paying sales duty or excise duty on luxury items such as jewellery or Swakara fur garments. The General Sales Tax (GST) is 8% on almost all goods, and VAT of 15% is included in the prices you pay (unless stated) for accommodation and goods.

Export restrictions

The CITES Convention made illegal the trade in products derived from endangered species, such as elephant ivory, sea turtle products and the skins of wild cats. Restrictions have been imposed on the trade in reptile skins, coral, and certain plants and wild birds. Special import and export permits are available for some products but it is best to ask before you buy. The restricted animal products that tourists are most likely to encounter in Namibia are ivory, biltong made from protected species such as elephant or endangered antelope, and wallets, shoes, and handbags made from kudu, crocodile or snake skins. While these products may be freely available for the domestic market, and you would not be breaking any laws if you were to buy such an item as a gift for a local resident or someone in South Africa, be aware that each purchase effectively ends the life of another animal.

Within the country, be aware that as you travel from the Far North, Caprivi or Northwest regions across the Red Line (veterinary fence) to the South, you are not permitted to transfer any animal products. This includes souvenir animal horns and skins, ostensibly to prevent the spread of disease, without prior clearance from a vet.

Namibia is making a concerted effort to promote export businesses and has significant tax incentives in place. Information for import/export businesses is available from the Namibia Investment Centre and Offshore Development Company, T061-2837335, F061-220278, www.grnnet.gov.na or www.mti.gov.na

Vaccinations
For detailed health advice and information, see page 55

Neither smallpox nor cholera vaccination certificates are required by visitors to Namibia but those travelling from other (especially Central and West) African countries do require yellow fever certificates. Vaccinations against infectious hepatitis, polio, tetanus and typhoid are recommended – see Health section for further details.

What to take

Essentials

Clothing
Namibian fashions are similar to those in Europe or the US

Day wear tends to be casual and most people on holiday wear shorts, sandals and a T-shirt. If you intend to do any game viewing clothes in green, muted browns and khaki colours are best and these colours are less likely to attract mosquitoes at dawn and dusk. It is always advisable to dress in clean smart clothes: dressing down and looking scruffy is not appreciated by anyone in Namibia. People are expected to sport more formal clothes in the evenings in restaurants and bars; trainers, sandals, jeans and shorts are not appreciated. Long trousers, shirts and a good pair of leather shoes are acceptable.

Night-time temperatures in winter can get very low. If you are camping, a fleece jacket or a thick sweater are essential. By the coast, the wind can really blow; bring a windproof top of some kind. By day, sunstroke and sunburn can be a serious problem and a wide brimmed hat, long sleeved cotton shirts, high SPF sunscreen and sunglasses are vital for protection from the sun. It is a good idea to bring two basic sets of clothes, one set of sturdy cotton outdoor clothes and one set of evening wear, appropriate for the surroundings you expect to find yourself in.

Deserts are very cold by night

Footwear should be as well ventilated as possible for the hot weather; sandals or canvas trainers are recommended. European style leather walking boots are too heavy except perhaps for the Fish River Canyon or the Waterberg Plateau hikes, when a good pair of comfortable and sturdy boots are essential. Lightweight hiking boots (no need for fabulous waterproofing in this climate) are popular. In Windhoek and Swakopmund you can buy a good range of local handmade leather (kudu hide or seal skin) desert boots. While these are usually excellent, check that they are properly stitched and remember they will need time to break in.

Checklist
Always take half as many clothes as you think you will need and twice the amount of money

Everybody has their own list. Obviously what you take depends on where you are intending to go and how you plan to travel. Backpackers will want to travel light as lugging a heavy pack around in the heat is not much of a holiday. Laundry services are readily available (and clothes dry in minutes), so there is no need for many clothes. If you have arranged to hire a car from the airport, you will be able to be more generous with luxuries, books and camping gear. Virtually anything you require is available in Namibia, but be aware that outside Windhoek the choice reduces dramatically – and outside the larger towns it dwindles to essentials (and beer) only. Dust will get into everything you take, so particularly sensitive equipment such as computers and digital cameras should be looked after carefully or left behind.

Before you leave, send yourself an email with details of such things as travellers' cheques, passport, driving licence, credit cards and travel insurance numbers. Be sure that someone at home also has access to important details

Strong shoes/boots; **sandals**; **windproof top**; **swimming costume**; small **towel** (look out for the new lightweight ones that you can wring out after use); **hat**, wide brimmed to protect your exposed neck; large **water bottle**; Swiss Army **penknife**; **torch** (flashlight), gadget lovers and Italians will require head torches, but a standard AA battery hand torch is fine; for any electrical goods, you'll need an **adaptor** available from Windhoek supermarkets or hardware stores, but you are advised to bring US:Euro or UK:Euro adaptors as Namibian:Euro adaptors are often the only ones available (another option is to buy a plug on arrival and rewire, not advised for cellular phone chargers); a **camera** with UV filter to offset the bleaching effect of the midday sun, plus dustproof bag and lens cleaner, and waterproofing and silica gel in rainy season – good film and batteries are available in all towns; **binoculars** are essential on safari, wonderful for stargazing, and generally useful to keep handy as there is game and birdlife all along the road; **earplugs** and an airline-type **eye mask** to help you sleep in noisy and poorly curtained rooms.

In addition to the useful medicaments and first aid kit supplies given in the Health section (page 56), we recommend: **high SPF lip salve**; **high SPF sunscreen** and '**After Sun**' cream; **pre-moistened wipes** (such as 'Wet Ones') for lunches on the road; **toilet** paper; **insect repellent** , with high DET percentage; **fabric plasters** (band-aids); **condoms** and **tampons**, although both are found in towns; **face wash and moisturizing cream**, as the sun and dust will wreak havoc on even a rugged European complexion; **eye drops**; **travel sickness pills**, particularly if you plan to enjoy an early morning flight over the dunes or a trip to see the seals off Lüderitz ; **dental floss**, for backpack repairs and fishing in addition to its traditional use (your diet will probably be heavily meat based); **contact-lens solution** can be difficult to find outside large cities.

Campers will find the following useful, and not a burden if they are taking a car (if so, don't forget your driving licence). All are available in Namibia, although the range (particularly of tents and sleeping bags) is limited and imported items fairly expensive: **tent with built-in mosquito net**; **sleeping bag**; **mattress** – Thermarest are the best; portable gas **stove and lamp**; **cool bag/box**; **pans and lightweight barbecue grate**; **cutlery and crockery**; **condiments** (sugar, powdered milk, salt and herbs, packed in portable airtight containers); **washing-up liquid and sponge**; **lighter**. Off-road enthusiasts may find the services of a **GPS** useful. There are good maps available in the main regional centres, particularly the Shell publications.

Camping equipment

Essentials

Money

The Namibian dollar is pegged one to one with the South African rand. Outside Namibia the local currency is not convertible, so remember to change any surplus Namibian dollars back into your own currency before your departure. This is a straightforward transaction which can be completed at any bank so long as you have a coupon proving your original purchase of Namibian dollars.

There is no black market for currency

In 1993 Namibia issued its first set of bank notes, prior to which the South African rand had been legal tender (which it still is). At first, only three notes were issued: N$10, N$50 and N$100. In 1996 the N$20 note and N$200 note were introduced to complete the series. The famous Nama chief, Hendrik Witbooi, features on all the notes. There are few forged Namibian notes in circulation.

Currency

   Notes N$10, N$20, N$50, N$100 and N$200. **Coins** 5c, 10c, 50c, N$1 and N$5. As South African rand is still legal tender you will certainly come across notes and coins, particularly in national parks and in the south where you encounter a higher frequency of South African visitors. If your return flight is via Johannesburg, you might want to stash some rand away for a meal, drink, duty free or souvenirs on the way home (the choice is poor at Hosea Kutako).

Currency is not transferable outside Namibia

   Warning Many of the soldiers fighting in Angola were paid off in US dollars. There has been a problem with forged US$100 notes for some time; do **not** accept any US currency, especially in the north, except from a bank. All the banks have equipment to detect forged notes supplied by the US treasury to combat the worldwide problem.

All three major banks – *First National Bank*, *Standard Bank Namibia* and *Bank Windhoek* – are connected to the Cirrus and Plus global cash systems, meaning that, as long as you have your card and PIN, you can use ATMs as easily as at home. Equally, you can use your credit card if you have a PIN. The amount you can withdraw seems to vary between systems and cards, but you should be able to take out up to N$1,000 on each occasion. Remember to keep your receipt in case you need to change currency back.

ATMs
Probably the most efficient way to access your funds

The following are the main branches of the high street banks, each of which offers foreign exchange services: *Bank Windhoek*, T061-2991122, F2991287, www.bankwindhoek.com.na; *First National*, T061-2992222, F2992214,

Banks

Exchange rates: November 2001

Currency	Namibian Dollar (N$)	Currency	Namibian Dollar (N$)
US $1	9.62	French Franc 1	1.32
UK £1	14.00	Aus $1	4.84
Euro 1	8.66	Yen 100	7.86
DM 1	4.43	South Africa Rand 1	1.00
Dutch Guilder 1	3.93	Botswana Pula 1	1.64
Swiss Franc 1	5.89	Zimbabwe $10	1.80

www.fnbnamibia.com.na; *Commercial Bank*, T061-2959111, www.c-bank.com.na; *Standard*, T0800-028000, T061-2949111, www.standardbank.com.na Some small branches may close for an hour over lunch. All branches should be able to sell you foreign currency (ie South African rand or US dollar) should you need the cash for continuing your travels in southern Africa or elsewhere after Namibia. You will need to prove your foreign national status and source of funds outside Namibia (eg ATM receipt) if not withdrawing directly with a credit card. Interestingly, *First National Bank* has a single branch network across South Africa and Namibia, while all the others are separate legal entities; this may make access to funds easier for South Africans.

Credit cards

Credit cards are rarely accepted at petrol stations but are very helpful for car hire and accommodation

A credit card is very useful. It is a convenient way to cover large transactions and purchase foreign exchange. It offers the most competitive (wholesale) rate when withdrawing cash from an ATM. It allows you to book accommodation in advance (particularly useful in national parks). It allows you to leave a deposit for a hire car or cellular phone without having to hand over cash. In most shops (although not petrol stations), Visa, Mastercard/Eurocard, American Express and Diners Club are accepted, although some shops charge extra for Amex due to the high service cost to them. Transactions can take up to 10 minutes or longer to gain authorization as they all go via the central credit computer in South Africa and there are occasional communication breakdowns. Once approval is granted, the shopkeeper will be casual about the accuracy of your signature so be sure to cancel lost/stolen cards quickly.

Credit card agencies

American Express, T061-249037, F224417, and in Johannesburg T11-3901233, www.amex.co.za; *Diners Club* and *MasterCard*, contact the *Standard Bank of Namibia*, T061-2942143, F2942199; *Visa Card*, contact the *First National Bank of Namibia*, T061-2292213, F226676.

Travellers' cheques

One advantage of travellers' cheques is that if you lose them there is a relatively efficient system of replacement which should not cost the customer anything. For this reason, make sure you keep a full record of their numbers and value, separate from themselves; sending yourself a detailed email (to a web-based service) can be useful for this purpose. One drawback with travellers' cheques is that only the banks in Windhoek are likely to be able to issue replacement cheques. See the instructions provided with your travellers' cheques for specific telephone numbers.

A major disadvantage of travellers' cheques is the time it takes to cash them and the commission charged by the bank. Different branches of the same bank tend to raise their commission as the distance from major banking centres increases. Bank commission ranges between 0.2% and 0.5%. The most widely recognized cheques are American Express, Citicorp, Thomas Cook (they have a local partner, Rennies, T061-229667) and Visa. US dollar and sterling travellers' cheques can be exchanged at banks throughout the country. Eurocheques can be cashed at banks.

Western Union, T061-246986, have a network of offices to which money can be trans- **Wiring money**
ferred. Fees range from 4% to 10% depending on the amount involved. Check with your
bank before you depart, especially if you plan to be away for a long time, you may be able
to leave specific instructions concerning your bank accounts. To transfer money to someone in Namibia, pay cash and give the receiver's passport number (or password). The
receiver should be able to collect from the international division in the Namibian bank
minutes later. International funds transfers using the SWIFT payments system are also
possible. Funds can be transferred overnight, although if you have lost your ID and bank
cards you may have to make special arrangements in order to gain access to them.

If you are travelling independently and propose to hire a car, you will need to budget **Cost of**
N$200-800 per day, depending on season and type of vehicle – a considerable outlay. **travelling**
The cost of fuel is similar to that in the US, about half what Europeans are used to, but
distances travelled can be considerable so be prepared for a hefty fuel bill. Accommodation will represent your other principal daily outlay. If staying in simple B&Bs and
hotels, budget N$250 per couple per night. By camping, you can bring this down to
N$30, on average, per person per night. Food and drink is good value and an evening
meal with wine will cost under N$200 for two people.

Getting there

Air

International flights from Europe arrive at **Hosea Kutako International Airport** outside Windhoek. If you are coming from another southern Africa country it is possible to
fly into a small town on one of Air Namibia's regional flights before visiting Windhoek.
For example, there are three flights a week between Victoria Falls in Zimbabwe and
Katima Mulilo in the Caprivi Strip; or you could fly on the Cape Town to Windhoek flight
but get out in Lüderitz before reaching the capital. The majority of charter, private and
Air Namibia internal services fly from **Windhoek – Eros Airport**.

Air Namibia, www.airnamibia.com.na   For latest timetable information,
Windhoek T061-2996000, reservations T061-2996333, Hosea Kutako airport
T062-640315; Eros airport T061-238220; Frankfurt T61-7240660; UK T01293- 596654;
Paris T1-42975588; New York T212-4650619; Rome T6-59602148; Cape Town
T21-216685; Johannesburg T11-9701767.

Air Namibia is currently the only scheduled airline flying direct from Europe to **From Europe**
Windhoek, with four flights a week: on Monday and Thursday from Frankfurt via
Munich, on Saturday from London via Frankfurt, and on Tuesday from Frankfurt via
Nairobi. Expect to pay £450-650 for a return economy ticket, although there are occasionally deals (down to £250) in low season. The main problem is seat availability, particularly in July/August; book as far ahead as you can, and turn up three hours before
take off (both on the way out and coming home) to ensure you get on. The airline is in a
terrible financial state; its long-term viability is in doubt after the latest N$300 million
bail-out by the government prompted the sacking of most of the management team
and a major operational investigation. *KLM* are looking at taking a significant share of
the ownership and management responsibility, so hopefully financial and operational
conditions will improve and the service's long term viability will be ensured. The fleet is
expected to continue to fly under the *Air Namibia* banner.

Lufthansa cancelled its service in April 2001, but a German charter company *LTU*
flies on Tuesdays and Fridays from Düsseldorf via Münich to Windhoek. Münich,
T089-97591916; Düsseldorf, T0211-941029; Windhoek, 141 Stuebel St,

☞ Discount flight agents

Australia and New Zealand

Flight Centres, 82 Elizabeth St, Sydney, T13-1600; 205 Queen St, Auckland, T09-3096171. Also branches in other towns and cities.

STA Travel, T1300-360960, www.statravelaus.com.au; 702 Harris St, Ultimo, Sydney, and 256 Flinders St, Melbourne. In NZ: 10 High St, Auckland, T09-3666673. Also in major towns and university campuses.

Travel.com.au, 80 Clarence St, Sydney, T02-92901500, www.travel.com.au

UK and Ireland

Council Travel, 28a Poland St, London W1V 3DB, T020-7437 7767, www.destinations-group.com

STA Travel, 86 Old Brompton Rd, Londfon SW7 3LH, T020-7437 6262, www.statravel.co.uk They have other branches in London, as well as Brighton, Bristol, Cambridge, Leeds, Manchester, Newcastle and Oxford and on many university campuses. Specialists in low-cost student/youth flights and tours, also good for student IDs and insurance.

Trailfinders, 194 Kensington High St, London, W8 7RG, T020-7938 3939, www.trailfinders.com

Usit Campus, 52 Grosvenor Gardens, London, SW1 0AG, T0870-2401010, www.usitcampus.co.uk Student/youth travel specialists with branches also in Belfast, Brighton, Bristol, Cambridge, Manchester and Oxford. The main Ireland branch is at 19 Aston Quay, Dublin 2, T01-6021777.

North America

Air Brokers International, 323 Geary St, Suite 411, San Francisco, CA94102, T01-800-8333273, www.airbrokers.com Consolidator and specialist on RTW and Circle Pacific tickets.

Council Travel, 205 E 42nd St, New York, NY 10017, T1-888-COUNCIL, www.counciltravel.com Student/budget agency with branches in many other US cities.

Discount Airfares Worldwide On-Line, www.etn.nl/discount.htm A hub of consolidator and discount agent links.

International Travel Network/Airlines of the Web, www.itn.net/airlines Online air travel information and reservations.

STA Travel, 5900 Wilshire Blvd, Suite 2110, Los Angeles, CA 90036, T1-800-7770112, www.sta-travel.com Also branches in New York, San Francisco, Boston, Miami, Chicago, Seattle and Washington DC.

Travel Cuts, 187 College St, Toronto, ON, T1-800-6672887, www.travelcuts.com Specialists in student discount fares, IDs and other travel services. Branches in other Canadian cities.

Travelocity, www.travelocity.com Online consolidator.

T061-238205. **Angola Airlines** have a weekly service from Paris and Lisbon, via Luanda. But by far the most frequent service is via South Africa, using either **South African Airways** (SAA) or your national carrier, and adding the final hop with a local provider. **SAA**, www.saa.co.za, has two flights per day to Johannesburg from both Frankfurt and London, four per week from Paris and one per week from Copenhagen. **British Airways**, www.britishairways.com, has two overnight flights to Johannesburg and one to Cape Town every day, and daily (except Tuesdays) they connect from Johannesburg to Windhoek.

From North America **SAA** and **American Airlines** run daily direct flights from New York to Johannesburg. **SAA** also flies daily from Atlanta via Fort Lauderdale. Once in South Africa there are regular connections from Johannesburg or Cape Town to Windhoek. For direct flights into Windhoek it will be necessary to fly to Frankfurt or Munich in Germany.

Border opening times

With Angola		With South Africa	
Oshikango	0600-1800	Hohlweg	0600-2200
Ruacana	0600-1800	Rietfontein	0600-2200
Rundu	0600-1800	Ariamsvlei	24 hours
		Noordoewer	24 hours
With Botswana		Oranjemund	Permit holders only
Buitepos	0600-2300	Velloorsdrif	24 hours
Impalila Island	0700-1700		
Mohembo	Sunrise-Sunset	**With Zambia**	
Ngoma Bridge	0600-1800	Wenella	0600-1800

Essentials

Unless your travel agent can offer a particularly good alternative, the best route to Namibia is via Johannesburg or Cape Town in South Africa and then make your own arrangements for an onward flight with *SAA* or *Air Namibia*. A return ticket from Johannesburg to Windhoek should cost about US$200-300, a little more from Cape Town.

From Australia & New Zealand

Qantas fly from Auckland and Sydney to Johannesburg for roughly A$3,000 return. *MAS* tend to offer the cheapest flights to Johannesburg and Cape Town departing from Melbourne and Sydney, however they do involve a stopover in Kuala Lumpur. *SAA* fly from Sydney via Perth to Johannesburg four times a week; from Johannesburg there are regular connections to Windhoek.

South African Airways fly twice daily between Windhoek and Johannesburg. *Air Namibia* operate 11 flights a week between Cape Town and Windhoek, as well as 10 flights to Johannesburg each week. There are also flights to Lusaka (Tuesday), Harare (Tuesday), Victoria Falls (Monday, Tuesday, Wednesday and Sunday) and Maun (Tuesday and Wednesday). All of these are comparatively expensive routes, however *SAA* and *Air Namibia* offer a regional discount fare scheme for non-residents. With the **Air Namibia Travel Pass** there are considerable savings to be made on domestic and regional flights between Namibia and Victoria Falls, Harare, Maun, Johannesburg and Cape Town (for details see Getting Around section below).

From southern Africa

Road

The principal road crossing is between **Oshikango** and **Santa Clara**. See table for border opening times. It is possible to cross this border on a day trip, however we would strongly advise against travelling further into Angola at present.

From Angola

| From Botswana | The main border crossings between Botswana and Namibia are at **Buitepos** and **Ngoma Bridge**. Both of these border posts are in remote country but newly completed tarred roads mean that both routes are easily navigable in an ordinary car. |

From Botswana

The main border crossings between Botswana and Namibia are at **Buitepos** and **Ngoma Bridge**. Both of these border posts are in remote country but newly completed tarred roads mean that both routes are easily navigable in an ordinary car.

From South Africa

Intercape Mainliner, one of the major South African coach companies, runs a service linking Windhoek with Cape Town and Johannesburg (via Upington). If you want to spend a few days in Cape Town before entering Namibia then the coach journey up the West Coast offers fine views, although it is a long day (see timetable on page 382).

The three main border posts (each open 24 hours) between Namibia and South Africa are at **Rietfontein**, **Noordoewer**, and **Ariamsvlei**.

From Zambia

There is one border post, Wenella, which involves a ferry across the Zambezi. The bridge is still under construction, the road on the Zambian side of the border is notoriously bad; we advise that you cross from Zambia to Zimbabwe at Victoria Falls and travel through Botswana before entering Namibia via Ngoma Bridge.

Touching down

Airport information

Hosea Kutako International Airport

For those anxious about arriving in chaotic third world capital cities, have no fear. Hosea Kutako is calm, clean and free from thieves and hawkers, which is an appropriate introduction to the country. Travellers are deposited on the tarmac, where they follow an orderly queue towards the terminal, past an unusual sign announcing 'You are entering a yellow resident area'. As a rough guide, a Boeing 747 empties (including baggage collection) in about 30 minutes and, should you be fortunate enough to be met, your welcoming committee can wave to you as you make your way towards immigration, through the glass 'fish bowl' walls of *Nelson's café*.

Bring some cash to change at the airport

In 2001, the arrivals hall was undergoing major refurbishments. There is a helpful tourist information kiosk and a selection of official money changers but no ATMs or banks in the arrivals building. The commissions charged average 1% for credit card advances and travellers' cheques. **Avis**, **Budget**, **Europcar**, **Hertz** and **Imperial** have desks, although pretty much any car hire company you have booked (which you should have done in advance, if you are planning to drive yourself) will be able to collect you or bring your car to the airport. There was no indication as to what new offering was expected once the renovations were completed.

Take the shuttle to town

On leaving the terminal you will be approached by taxi drivers offering their services. They are legitimate and reliable; expect to pay N$200-250 to central Windhoek, but be sure to fix the price in advance. There is no public bus or rail service but there's an efficient N$50-70 shuttle service (eg Euro Airport Shuttle, T061-234698, T081-1275825 (mob)) that will wait until it has two or more passengers and transport you to your chosen downtown destination just as quickly as a taxi. Journey time to downtown Windhoek is roughly 30 minutes. You will pass through a police checkpoint; no need for alarm, they are only on the lookout for shabby vehicles and drunk, unbelted or unlicenced drivers. Enjoy your first glimpse of the straight roads and the camelthorn trees, and keep an eye out for kudu, warthogs, meercats, baboons, foxes and squashed snakes.

Be at the airport early for all departures

Make a note at this stage to be in very good time (three hours or more) for your return flight, particularly in peak season. The flights (especially those of *Air Namibia*) are often overbooked and seats are allocated on a rigid first come, first served basis. Of course, if you aren't in a hurry to get home and fancy a couple of days in a hotel, turning up 90 minutes before departure may get you a couple of free nights in four-star luxury.

Touching down

Hours of business

Banks Monday-Friday, 0800-1530;
Saturday, 0800-1000.
Businesses Monday-Friday, 0800-1730;
Saturday, 0800-1300.
Government offices Monday-Friday,
0830-1630. Most shut for lunch 1300-1400.
Post Offices Monday-Friday, 0830-1600;
Saturday, 0800-1200.
Shops and supermarkets
Monday-Friday, 0800-1800;
Saturday, 0800-1300.

Official time

Winter Time: GMT + 1 hour (6 April –
6 September); Summer Time: GMT + two
hours (7 September – 5 April).

Voltage 220/240 volts AC at 50 Hz,
using three-point, round-pin (one
10 mm and two 8 mm prongs), 15 amp
plugs. Check supermarkets and
hardware stores in Windhoek for
adaptors. Hotels usually have two
round-pin sockets for razors and
hairdryers. Travel with a battery razor as
many of the small town hotels will not
have a suitable socket.

Weights and measures The metric
system is used: speed limits are in kmph;
food is weighed in kilograms and grams;
petrol is sold in litres.

Essentials

Airport tax will be included in your ticket price. There are no further taxes to pay on
your arrival or departure, whether domestic or international. **Airport tax**

Tourist information

In general, Namibia is fairly well provided with tourist information. Most towns have
dedicated staff and offices. Failing that, lodge owners are a reliable and informative
source, often layered with a good degree of opinion as well – aren't we all! Where you
have a choice between a private information centre and the government one, the private one will tend to have more helpful and knowledgeable staff. The bi-monthly
Travel News Namibia publication is certainly helpful, and provides good colourful studies (biased of course) of selected areas, as well as a tourist news update (new lodges,
closures, HAN award winners etc). Information offices are also your best bet for discovering if there is any local 'colour' (festivals, etc) that you can enjoy during your visit.

*Lodge owners are
your best bet for
information*

Local customs and laws

There are numerous customs relating to behaviour when visiting tribespeople in their
rural environment. These are identified in the body of the text. In 'normal' urban environments, there are no obvious differences from Europe/North America in dress,
behaviour or customs. In conversation, it is customary to engage in a few pleasantries
before asking for help or a service.

Behaviour

If you are travelling from so-called 'liberal' countries, be prepared for the occasional
uncomfortable conversation with 'unreconstructed' males. The immigrants from
South Africa and Germany (mostly white) tend to be staunch conservatives, with
old-fashioned lifestyles and opinions.

Sustainable or Eco-Tourism has been described as: " … ethical, considerate or informed
tourism where visitors can enjoy the natural, historical and social heritage of an area
without causing adverse environmental, socio-economic or cultural impacts that com-
promise the long-term ability of that area and its people to provide a recreational
resource for future generations and an income for themselves … " Namibia is a beatiful,
dramatic and wild country but also a living, working landscape and a fragile and vulnerable place. By observing the simple guidelines outlined above and behaving

**Responsible
tourism**

Essentials

How big is your footprint?

- *Where possible choose a destination, tour operator or hotel with a proven ethical and environmental commitment – if in doubt, ask.*
- *Spend money on locally produced (rather than imported) goods and services and use common sense when bargaining – your few dollars saved may be a week's salary to others.*
- *Use water and electricity carefully – travellers may receive preferential supply while the needs of local communities are overlooked.*
- *Don't give money or sweets to children – it encourages begging – instead give to a recognized project, charity or school.*

- *Learn about etiquette and culture – consider local norms and behaviour – and dress appropriately for local cultures and situations.*
- *Protect wildlife and other natural resources – don't buy souvenirs or goods made from wildlife unless they are clearly sustainably produced and are not protected under CITES legislation.*
- *Always ask before taking photographs or videos of people.*
- *Consider staying in local, rather than foreign owned, accommodation – the economic benefits for host communities are far greater – and there are far greater opportunities to learn about local culture.*

responsibly you can help to minimise your impact and protect the natural and cultural heritage of this unique country.

Tipping Waiters, hotel porters, stewards, chambermaids and tour guides expect 10%; don't be overgenerous with surly service. It is common practice to tip petrol pump attendants, depending on their service – up to N$5 for a fill up, oil and water check and comprehensive windscreen clean. When leaving tips make sure they go where you intend, there is no guarantee that kitty money gets to everyone. Photographing local tribespeople should be followed by a tip of some kind. Non-payment is not something you can get away with lightly.

Religion Christianity is the dominant religion, among blacks and whites, and church-going is fairly common. Smart dress is the norm in church ('Sunday best').

Prohibitions Marijuana is fairly prevalent around Namibia, but remains firmly **illegal**, as are all narcotics.
Do be aware of the restrictions on access into the restricted **Diamond Areas**. The authorities take a dim view of trespassers, even if it is strictly a mistake. Note that because of the very hot summers, access to the **Fish River Canyon** is prohibited from September to April each year.

Safety

Generally speaking, Namibia is a safe country in which to travel, although there are of course some exceptions. It is important to stress that although Namibia borders South Africa, crime and personal safety conditions are not the same and there is nothing in Namibia to compare with South Africa's urban danger.

Cities
Beware pickpockets on Independence Ave, Windhoek
As with all larger towns and cities in the world, care should be taken with valuables such as wallets and expensive jewellery when walking in the streets. Obvious rules like putting money safely away before leaving the bank and not leaving purses or wallets on tables in outdoor restaurants/cafés apply in Namibia as much as anywhere else. Pickpockets operate in the busy shopping areas of Windhoek by day. Recently, there have been isolated incidents where tourists have been mugged. Travellers should

therefore exercise caution, particularly at night and at weekends, when the central shopping districts of all towns generally become deserted and a lone traveller might be unlucky. Overall, common sense precautions will be sufficient to ensure that your holiday is not spoiled by any unpleasant incidents.

All central and southern Namibian towns have townships, the largest being Khomasdal and Katutura in Windhoek. While by no means out of bounds to tourists, it would not be wise to wander into a township by yourself. On the other hand, if you know a local or have friends living and working in Namibia who know their way around, a trip to a township market or nightclub can be an interesting and rewarding experience. If you do have the chance to spend some time in a township, it will undoubtedly give you a different picture of the way a very large number of urban Namibians live (see page 73 in Windhoek section).

Townships

Essentials

Where to stay

Until a few years ago, accommodation in most Namibian towns was a choice between a characterless hotel and a municipal campsite. Visitors with their own transport made their way to isolated guest lodges and game farms. In the past five to ten years, the standard and range of accommodation has improved enormously. Many hotels have been refurbished and a number of new top-end options have appeared. At the other end of the price range, there has been an improvement in cheap accommodation for the budget traveller. Many of the regional centres now have some form of backpacker hostel as well as a campsite. While it has not been possible to visit every establishment in the country, for each location in the book there is a list of places to stay, with recommendations where appropriate.

See inside front cover for our accommodation price guide, based on the price for two sharing a double room

Apart from camping, these hostels provide the cheapest accommodation in Namibia. Budget up to N$50 for a dorm bed and N$200 plus for a double room. The facilities offered vary widely, from hostels that look like chaotic student squats to clean, well-run communal houses. There is usually a well-stocked kitchen (with utensils, stove, fridge, cupboards, etc), a range of rooms including a dormitory, bar, lounge with library and TV, and often at least a notice-board for travellers if not someone who can arrange budget safari tours and car hire, book local restaurants and advise on entertainment. For independent travellers, these places are the best source of information, companionship, parties and advice.

Backpacker hostels
Stock up on the latest advice at the town's busiest hostels

The down side is that hostels are often noisy until the small hours, can be unsafe (for your belongings, not yourself), and usually provide a wholly unrepresentative impression of a country. If far away from home, you may be tempted to remain within the isolated 'comfort' of a hostel; do not succumb, you came to Africa for more than this!

Once confined to Windhoek, the B&B concept has really begun to take off in the past two to three years. Most B&Bs operate along conventional lines, providing a full cooked breakfast, while others will have small kitchens where you can make your own. As with all B&Bs you will be staying in someone's home, which can be a good way to meet local (white) people and gain some insight into their lives and sentiments. As they represent an ill-defined category, in most sections of the book B&Bs are not separately identified – take a look at the **B&B Association of Namibia**'s website at www.bed-breakfast-namibia.com for details.

Bed & breakfast

For the visitor on a limited budget who wishes to see as much of the country as possible, staying in campsites and using the money saved towards hiring a car is probably

Camping & caravan parks

your best bet. Camping is not a neglected end of the market as a good number of domestic and South African tourists spend their annual family holidays in caravans or large tents. In the most popular game reserves, even the tent and caravan pitches get booked up to a year in advance, so if you are in Namibia during the school holidays (see page 48 for dates) don't automatically assume there will be space at a campsite.

The popularity of camping has meant that there are good facilities at many parks, and most game farms have their own private campsites. Even the most basic site will have a clean washblock, many with electric points, lighting and hot water. For a small extra fee you can use electricity points at your site, particularly useful for caravans (see above under What to Take for advice on adaptors). Many will also have self-catering rooms, of varying quality and facilities, ranging from a single room with a couple of beds to chalets with several rooms and fully equipped kitchens.

Be sure to stock up with provisions in major cities

Camping equipment can be bought in Windhoek and Swakopmund; look for Cymot, in particular, although supermarkets often stock useful supplies. Some items are rather dated and can seem heavy and cumbersome when compared to the latest hi-tech products from the USA and Europe. We would recommend you bring at least your own tent and sleeping bag. A bit of advance reading about the areas you plan to visit will help in deciding what else to bring. The cooking side of camping is the most awkward for the overseas visitor. Much can be brought with you, but don't be afraid to ask your car hire company in advance for bulky items such as tables, chairs and cool boxes – some might require a small additional payment, others might throw them in with the cost of the car. Failing that, buy the necessary equipment and try to sell it on to a fellow traveller when you leave. The major car rental companies stock four-wheel drive vehicles fully equipped for camping and if cost is no concern you can hire one with a built-in refrigerator, water tank, solar-heated portable shower, roof tents, long-range fuel tanks and all the smaller items necessary for a successful and safe journey into the bush. To save time **do not** leave the hire of a vehicle and camping equipment until you arrive in Namibia, you could easily have to wait for several days at the busiest time of year. Arranging everything in advance will enable you to head straight off from the airport, not wasting a minute in town.

Arrange car hire in advance

Just about all the car hire companies will hire four-wheel drive vehicles equipped with camping equipment. Additionally, try the following for **camping equipment hire** *Camping Hire Namibia*, PO Box 80029, 12 Louis Raymond Street, Windhoek, T061-251592, F252995. *Gav's Camping Hire*, PO Box 80157, 76 Sam Nujoma Drive, Windhoek, T061-220604, F220605. *Le Trip*, PO Box 5408, Wernhil Park, Windhoek, T/F061-233499.

Somewhat surprisingly, the **Namibia Wildlife Resorts**' sites do not necessarily work out that cheap as visitors pay for entry for themselves (N\$20 per person) and their vehicles (N\$20) and then pay for the site (N\$75-140) on top. Expect to pay N\$30-60 per person in private campsites depending on location and facilities.

Game farms & guestfarms
Aim to spend at least two nights in a working game or guest farm to enjoy the hospitality and expereince

Before independence, most visitors to Namibia originated from South Africa and visiting a working farm or game ranch was confined to those who knew the owner in some way or another. Over the past decade, roughly 200 guestfarms have sprung up all over the country. Some were farmers noting a gap in the market, and now offer riding, hiking, good food and relaxation in a tranquil, rural setting. Other farmers and entrepreneurs jumped on the bandwagon, looking simply to make easy money from passing tourists. Still others, hard hit by drought, looked at it as a lifeline for survival. There is now a fantastic range of excellent guest and gamefarms which, although not all cheap, offer a superb opportunity to experience the bush first-hand, with guides who know their land and everything that lives on it intimately. Government statistics show relatively low occupancy rates (30% in 1999), so you should have no trouble finding accommodation, particularly outside the August peak season.

NAMIBIA IN ALL ITS GUISES
- *from CC Africa*

Namibia is a land of mesmerizing contrast and changeability. CC Africa presents it to you in many shapes and forms, from the sheer luxury of the country's premier lodge to the thrills of an adventurous camping safari with its tour operating division, Afro Ventures.

Merging into the red ochre dunes, hewn of mountain rock and glass, *Sossusvlei Mountain Lodge is an altar to boundless space, stillness, solitude and the world's oldest living desert, the Namib.

Here, in southern Africa's largest private reserve, the painstakingly reclaimed NamibRand Nature Reserve, your relaxation is total. Accommodating only 20 guests at one time, there are few to invade your privacy.

Expert rangers will lead you to an intriguing array of desert-adapted creatures and plants. You can venture out on all-terrain, four-wheeled motorcycles, visit the Sesriem Canyon, or spend a day at Sossusvlei.

Your evening entertainment is the star-filled sky. View it through the powerful telescope in our own observatory, or, when you retreat to your private Desert Villa, through your ceiling skylight.

If you're the adventurous type, try the alternative - an Afro Ventures mobile safari. Choose a basic or luxury safari, a set itinerary or one personalised just for you, along with a guide conversant in your own language. Enjoy confidence in a company with 30 years experience and a reputation for quality.

From canyons to game parks to ghost towns – they're all on the Afro Ventures menu of enthralling destinations. It's the ultimate way to experience the lure of Africa.

*Nominated by Conde Nast Travelers' 2001 Hotlist as "one of the coolest places to stay" and winner of the Ivanowski Golden Award 2000 "Newcomer"

CC Africa
conservation corporation africa

tel: (+27)(11) 809 4447 fax: (+27)(11) 809 4400 email: information@ccafrica.com
www.ccafrica.com

Reawaken your soul

If you are coming from Europe, it is easy to be misled by the word 'farm'. In fact, most Namibian farms are vast tracts of land, typically as large as 10,000 ha (10 km x 10 km) used predominantly for livestock farming. The basic difference between a guestfarm and a game farm is that the former will usually be a working commercial farm offering visitors the chance to experience it at first hand. There may be hiking or horse-riding trails, there will usually be a swimming pool, and often the opportunity for a tour around the farm. Although most guestfarms will usually have some game such as springbok, gemsbok and warthogs, the 'game drives' offered will tend to be scenic, rather than wild, experiences.

A game farm or ranch on the other hand will usually have been especially stocked with wild game such as elephant, rhino, the carnivorous cats and the antelope on which they feed. Here the emphasis will be on game-viewing drives and possibly guided hikes in the bush, offering a firsthand view of the bush, the 'spoor' (footprints and droppings) and the animals themselves. A stay at a good game ranch does not come cheap but is well worth the expense for the unique experience it offers visitors.

There are also a number of farms where licensed trophy hunting is carried out, strictly regulated by the government. Whatever your views about hunting, most Namibians see it as normal and acceptable; the meat is used to make biltong or eaten fresh and hunting is seen as part of the process of wildlife conservation and game management. We have tried to identify such places in the text. On the whole, these lodges are happy to take non-hunting groups; they will avoid having mixed groups (tourists and hunters), but it is worth checking in advance.

Most guestfarms cater for a limited number of visitors and provide an intimate, personable service. Generally your hosts will be very friendly, and will be happy to discuss any and everything about Namibia with you; on the other hand it is worth noting that a small number of farms are predominantly German speaking and not really geared for the non-German speaking visitor. If you fall in the latter category you may prefer to avoid such places; calling in advance is the best way to ensure all is in order.

Guesthouses These tend to be a cross between a hotel and a B&B and are generally found in Windhoek, Swakopmund and the towns of the central and southern regions. Guesthouses generally offer en-suite twin rooms, sometimes with phone and TV, and usually with a small swimming pool. A hearty cooked breakfast is usually included in the price which will range from N$130 to N$300 per person.

Guesthouses usually do not have bars or restaurants, although there may be a small fridge in your room and it may also be possible to arrange an evening meal by calling ahead. Smaller than your average hotel, guesthouses tend to offer a more personal service which some people enjoy; while others prefer the relative anonymity of a hotel where they can come and go unnoticed.

Hotels Every medium sized town has at least one small hotel, often providing the only comfortable bar and restaurant in town. Many of these hotels are family run and have been so since they were built. Under these circumstances the owners are not always that susceptible to any form of criticism about the way things operate. As more visitors from overseas stay in Namibia so many of the small hotels are improving their facilities and image. All hotels are classified by the Hospitality Association of Namibia (HAN) under a star rating of one to four related to the services provided rather than the quality of those services. More usefully, perhaps, HAN also awards regional and national prizes for the best accommodation each year, which we have tried to reflect in the relevant sections.

Most small country hotels fall into the two-star category, offering basic, clean rooms, a restaurant serving three meals a day and a bar. Prices will generally range between N$150 and N$300 per person and usually include a full cooked breakfast. For such places it is usually not necessary to book in advance, although during school holidays it is possible that places en route to Etosha and in Swakopmund will get crowded.

NACOBTA

The Namibia Community Based Tourism Association is a non-profit membership organization that supports local communities in their efforts to develop tourism enterprises and thereby gain income and employment. In their own words, they are 'taking indigenous people and their environment seriously and adapting to local circumstances without feeling isolated or lost'.

NACOBTA was established in 1995. The central body not only provides source funding for new ventures, but takes care of marketing and lobbying for each enterprise, and provides training in guiding and tourism, business advice and reservations and admin systems. Essentially, the central body aims to free the local communities to concentrate on providing local, people-focused services.

The NACOBTA projects are, to a greater or lesser degree, managing to bring some of the income generated by you and me travelling to Namibia to the local community. Without them, most tourists would have no direct contact with non-whites, as virtually all lodges are owned and managed by whites. While this is largely a result of individual energy and expertise, it also highlights the division of wealth (land and capital) and opportunity (education and training) that exist in the country over a decade after independence. NACOBTA is one institution attempting to rebalance this situtation.

A separate, but equally important, point is that without local communities benefiting from tourism, it will be very difficult to encourage them to 'preserve' their wildlife, let alone the trees and habitat that supports it. NACOBTA is, quite literally, turning poachers into gamekeepers. Further information: PO Box 86099, Windhoek; T061-250558, F061-222647, www.nacobta.com.na

Karas Region (South)
Bruckaros Campsite
Kunene Region (Northwest)
Anmire Traditional Village
Purros Traditional Village

Aba-Huab Campsite
Kunene Village Restcamp (Opuwo)
Okarohombo Campsite
Ongongo Campsite
Purros Campsite
Erongo Region (Northwest)
Brandberg Mountain Guides
Spitzkoppe Restcamp
Daureb Craft, Uis
Khomas Region (Windhoek)
Katatura Face-to-Face tours
Penduka Craft Cooperative
The North Central Region
Nakambale Museum and Restcamp
Otjozondjupa Region (Tsumkwe, the North)
Nyae Nyae Conservancy
Omatako Valley Restcamp
Caprivi Region (Northeast)
N//goabaca Campsite
Salambala Campsite
Kubunyana Camp
Mashi Craft Centre
Caprivi Arts Centre

Other

Omaheke San Trust *aims to preserve the traditions and culture of the !Xoo, !Naro and !Twa San communities and build their self reliance, while at the same time ensuring that such things as their right to education and health care are preserved. Located in the remote east of Namibia, near the Botswanan border, it aims to have a campsite and craft shop in operation by the end of 2001. T062-564073, ost@iafrica.com.na*

Tsumeb Cultural Village *is an open air museum, established with the help of the Namibia Association of Norway, set up to give tourists an insight into the different tribes living in Namibia. They have a representative family living in traditional style in the village, producing crafts for sale and providing entertainment and services (including meals and accommodation, if booked in advance). T067-220787).*

Essentials

☞ ## Accommodation prices for national parks and resorts

Admission fees (NAM residents less 50%, and less 25% on accommodation)
General: Adults N$20; Children (6-16) N$2; Cars N$20.
Etosha, Skeleton Coast and Sossusvlei: Adults N$30; Children (6-16) N$2; Cars N$20
Central reservations: T061-236975, www.namibiawildliferesorts.com

Ai-Ais Hot Springs

Lux Flat (2 bed)	N$320
Flat (4 bed)	N$275
Hut (4 bed)	N$190
Camping	N$95

Duwisib Castle

Camping	N$85

Daan Viljoen

Lux suite (4 bed inc breakfast)	N$500
Bungalow (2 bed inc breakfast)	N$260
Camping	N$95

Etosha National Park:
Okaukuejo

Lux Suite (4 bed)	N$690
Lux Bungalow (4 bed)	N$380
Bungalow (4 bed)	N$335
Bungalow (3 bed)	N$310
Bungalow (2 bed)	N$230
Std Room (2 bed)	N$295
Camping	N$140

Halali

Lux Suite (4 bed)	N$545
Lux Bungalow (4 bed)	N$335
Econ Bungalow (4 bed)	N$315
Standard Room (2 bed)	N$285
Camping	N$140

Namutoni

Lux Suite (4 bed)	N$585
Lux Flat (4 bed)	N$380
Std Chalet (4 bed)	N$335
Std Flat (4 bed)	N$320
Standard Room (2 bed)	N$295
Economy Room (2 bed)	N$200
Camping	N$140
Fort Room (2 bed)	N$120

Gross Barmen Hot Springs

Lux Suite (4 bed)	N$495
Std Bungalow (5 bed)	N$280
Std Bungalow (5 bed)	N$170
Econ Bungalow (2 bed)	N$160
Room (2 bed)	N$140
Camping	N$75

Hardap Dam Recreational Resort

Lux Suite (4 bed)	N$410
Lux Bungalow (4 bed)	N$285
Std Bungalow (5 bed)	N$275
Econ Bungalow (2 bed)	N$200
Econ Dormitory (12 bed)	N$200
Camping	N$95

National parks accommodation
Full details of the facilities and alternatives are included under the separate entries for the parks and reserves; prices are given in the box above

Namibia Wildlife Resorts (NWR) is responsible for management of all the services at the Ministry of Environment and Tourism's 20 declared game reserves and parks across Namibia. These range from the totally untouched Mamili National Park to the fully developed Gross Barmen Hot Springs Resort, complete with accommodation, restaurant and conference facilities. Most of the parks and resorts have some form of accommodation, which can be booked up to 18 months in advance. The accommodation is a mix of self-catering bungalows with two to six beds, well-serviced campsites and simple camps with overnight huts. Payment must be made in full if the accommodation is to be taken up less than 25 days from the date of the reservation. Visitors from overseas can organize their accommodation by fax and pay in advance by credit card. This is worth considering, particularly for Etosha National Park, if you are going to be in Namibia during school holidays.

Hobas & Fish River Canyons

Camping	N$95

Khaudum Game Reserve

Econ Hut (4 bed)	N$105
Camping	N$85

Lüderitz (Shark Island)

Lux Suite (5 bed)	N$480
Std Bungalow	N$275
Camping	N$65

Namib-Naukluft Park:
Sossusvlei/Sesriem

Camping	N$140

Naukluft

Camping	N$85

Namib Desert Park

Camping	N$75

Popa Falls Rest Camp

Lux Hut (4 bed)	N$210
Std Hut (4 bed)	N$190
Camping	N$85

Reho Spa Recreational Resort

Lux Bungalow (3 bed)	N$285
Econ Bungalow (6 bed)	N$260

Econ Bungalow (5 bed)	N$200
Econ Bungalow (4 bed)	N$180
Camping	N$85

Skeleton Coast Park:
(North of Ugab River – permit holders only)

Terrace Bay
(all inc 3 meals per day)

Lux Suite (8 bed)	N$2000
Single	N$440
Double (pp)	N$305

Torra Bay

Camping	N$95

West Coast Recreational Area:
Mile 14, Mile 72, Mile 108 & Jakkalsputz

Camping	N$95

Von Bach Recreational Resort

Econ Hut (2 bed)	N$95
Camping	N$75

Waterberg Plateau Park

Lux Suite (5 bed)	N$430
Lux Bungalow (5bed)	N$325
Std Bungalow (3 bed)	N$310
Std Room (2 bed)	N$295
Camping	N$95

On the whole, the accommodation is clean and in good working order, although some are in need of minor repair and almost everywhere could be made significantly more attractive with a coat of paint or an overhaul using local, natural materials. Overall, they represent reasonable value and in most cases the camps have been located in beautiful positions.

The *NWR* reservations office in Windhoek is in the Kaiserliche Landesvermessung building on the corner of John Meinert and Moltke streets, more or less opposite the Kudu Statue in Independence Avenue. Open for information: Monday-Friday, 0800-1700; for reservations 0800-1500; T061-236975/6/7/8, F224900, www.namibiawildliferesorts.com

Getting around

Air

Internal flights
Travel details including car hire can be found under individual towns' transport sections

Internal flights are the quickest way to get around the country. Most destinations are within two hours' flying time of each other. *Air Namibia* serves all the regional centres, while private operators and tour companies will fly visitors into remote regions, game parks and private guestfarms with landing strips. All internal flights arrive/depart from Windhoek's **Eros Airport**, which is next to the *Safari Court Hotel* complex, a 10-minute drive south from the city centre.

Be sure to get a window seat to fully enjoy the landscape

Visitors who flew with *Air Namibia* from Europe can take advantage of a special coupon scheme for regional flights. You must book within 14 days of your arrival within Namibia to take advantage of the **Air Namibia Travel Pass**. If planned carefully, this can represent a considerable saving of time and money. The pass works on the basis of coupons which you purchase for each leg of your route up to a maximum of six. A two-flight coupon costs US$146, plus just over US$100 per additional leg. This represents a considerable saving for longer flights (Windhoek-Harare), but is not good value between, say, Windhoek and Swakopmund (economy single is N$300). Coupons are valid for up to three months and you are not permitted to travel any route twice. They can be used for any internal destination listed below, plus Luanda and Johannesburg, and are also valid on flights offered by neighbouring countries' carriers, including internal flights in South Africa and Botswana. There is a US$100 surcharge for Victoria Falls in Zimbabwe. Check with *Air Namibia* for details and to make arrangements, telephone numbers (all 061) as follows: central reservations T2996333, F2996146; Hosea Kutako airport T2996600; Eros airport T2996500; town office under the *Kalahari Sands Hotel* on Independence Avenue, T2996444, F2996168; flight operations T2996911.

Air Namibia's internal flight schedule changes regularly with demand. Currently, there are daily direct flights from Windhoek to Swakomund, Walvis Bay, Sesriem, Tsumeb and Mokuti Lodge (for Etosha). There are two Windhoek-Ondangwa flights each weekday, one on Saturday. Four flights per week go to Cape Town via Lüderitz and Oranjemund, five to Katima Mulilo and Victoria Falls, and three to Lianshulu Lodge (Eastern Caprivi) and Maun.

Charter flights
Private air safaris, charters or scenic flights can be arranged through any local travel agent. There are a number of small companies offering flights over the dunes, down to the Fish River Canyon, along the Skeleton Coast, out to the Kalahari for a 'Bushman experience', or to Victoria Falls and Eastern Caprivi, with or without stopovers; they will tailor a trip to your interests, and advise what is possible and what is over-ambitious. The main charter companies (telephone code 061 unless specified otherwise) are *Atlantic Aviation*, T064-404749, F405832, www.natron.net/tour/aviation; *Bush Pilots*, T248316, F225083, bushpilots@mweb.com.na; *Comav*, T227512, F245612, www.resafrica.net/comav; *Desert Air*, T228101, F254345, deserta@iafrica.com.na; *NatureFriend Safaris*, T234739, F259316; *Sunbird Tours*, T272090, F272091, sunbirdt@iafrica.com.na; *Westair*, T223038, F232778, charters@westwing.com.na who also run a scheduled daily Windhoek-Tsumeb service; and *Wings over Africa*, T/F255001, wrld@iafrica.com.na

Road

Bus
Compared to the trains, Namibia's long-distance buses are marginally more comfortable, somewhat more expensive and much quicker, but still very limited in terms of destinations offered. *Intercape Mainliner*, T061-227847, F228285,

Local travel

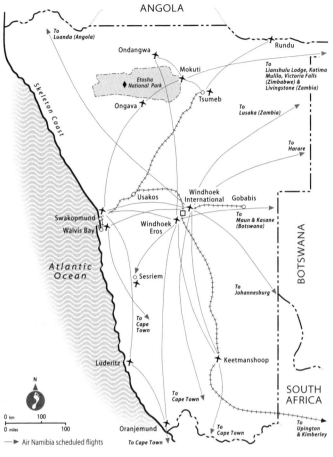

— ► Air Namibia scheduled flights

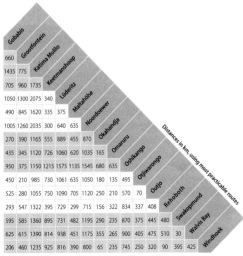

Distances in km, using most practicable routes

Gobabis	Grootfontein	Katima Mulilo	Keetmanshoop	Lüderitz	Maltahöhe	Noordoewer	Okahandja	Omaruru	Oshikango	Otjiwarongo	Outjo	Rehoboth	Swakopmund	Walvis Bay	Windhoek
660															
1435	775														
705	960	1735													
1050	1300	2075	340												
490	845	1620	335	375											
1005	1260	2035	300	640	635										
270	390	1165	555	889	455	870									
435	345	1120	726	1060	620	1035	165								
950	375	1150	1215	1575	1135	1545	680	635							
450	210	985	730	1061	635	1050	180	135	495						
525	280	1055	750	1090	705	1120	210	210	570	70					
293	547	1322	395	729	299	715	156	322	834	337	408				
595	585	1360	895	731	482	1195	290	235	870	375	445	480			
625	615	1390	814	938	451	1175	355	265	900	405	475	510	30		
206	460	1235	925	816	390	800	65	235	745	250	320	90	395	425	

www.intercape.co.za is a South African company that runs luxury buses between Windhoek, Victoria Falls and South Africa, stopping at any town of reasonable size en route. See the timetable on page 382. For the budget traveller, this service is only of value for long journeys. Coaches are air conditioned, have toilets, some show videos and the crew will serve tea and biscuits.

Ekonolux, T064-205935, runs a Walvis Bay to Cape Town service, leaving 0730 on Fridays only (via Windhoek, depart 1300) for N$365. Most locals are unaware of the timetable or existence of these services, so you will have to hunt fairly hard to find bus stops and other information, which we have included where found.

Car hire

We cannot over-emphasize that driving at night is dangerous

Most independent visitors to Namibia choose to drive themselves around the country. This provides maximum flexibility and is often the only way to cram your itinerary into the time available without resorting to specialist travel agents and flights. There is a good choice of car hire companies, particularly in Windhoek, and it is worth comparing the rates of a few before committing yourself. A two-wheel drive car will cost you N$200-400 per day depending on season and length of hire, a four-wheel drive (only necessary if travelling to remote areas) anything up to N$900 in peak season with a roof tent and camping equipment included. The distances to be travelled are massive, and must be done during daylight hours, so plan your overnight stops carefully. Fill up when you can and remember that gravel roads behave like icy ones when you travel at speed.

Don't forget your driving licence and credit card

You will need a driving licence, passport and credit card to hire a car in Namibia. To a driver accustomed to European roads, the traffic is virtually non-existent, but the roads are not without their dangers. It is not by accident that credit card deposits for damage and collision run into the thousands of Namibian dollars. Third-party insurance is included in the hire price but drivers are advised to take out extra insurance for 100% collision damage and loss waiver. The dangers of unexpected people/animals, poor roads and bad driving are considerable. If you are planning on visiting the remote areas, you would be wise to take a four-wheel driving course before leaving home, or at least watch a video or buy a book to enhance your awareness.

When collecting your vehicle, as well as checking it for bumps and scratches it is worth taking 10 minutes to familiarize yourself with it. Check the spare tyre (two are preferable) and how to use it. Is there a puncture repair kit and a pump? Do you know how to use them? What sort of fuel does it take? Do you have sufficient clearance for the terrain you are planning to cross? You don't want to be discovering a problem for the first time in an emergency, in the middle of nowhere.

Driving is on the left side of the road and speed limits range from 60 kph in town and built-up areas to 120 kph on the main tarred highways. By law, you must wear a seat belt in the front seats at all times and have your driving licence and passport available for inspection. The police are very strict on drink driving and checkpoints and speed traps with on-the-spot fines are employed. Useful numbers are the *Automobile Association of Namibia*, T224201, available 24 hours, with offices in Windhoek at the corner of Independence Avenue and Peter Müller Street and the *Car Rental Association of Namibia* (CARAN), www.natron.net/tour/caran/carane.htm for registered rental agencies.

Finally, be sure that you have enough fuel to cover the distance you are planning to travel, there are often no petrol stations between main towns. Also, no petrol stations accept credit cards, so you will have to budget sufficient cash for fuel as part of your day-to-day needs. On the whole, petrol stations are clean and efficient, often with a takeaway attached to them. An attendant will fill up your car while you fill up on provisions; a small tip is expected for efficient service (which does include cleaning your windscreens but does not include spilling a cupful of fuel on the tarmac).

If you plan to stay in the country for a while, buying your own car may be a sensible **Buying your** option. With the dry climate, most cars will be free from rust but, with the great dis- **own car** tances to be travelled and rough gravel roads, even young cars may be a little tired and scratched. Windhoek (or, better still, Johannesburg or Cape Town) is the best place to buy or sell. Dealerships are concentrated around the John Meinert Street and Independence Avenue junction. Check the local press for private sales. Be sure to discuss the possibility of selling back to your dealer, assuming that you don't take the jalopy he sells you to the end of the proverbial road.

Chances are that the only European bikers you will see will be bearded, tanned, **Motorbike** trans-Africa adventurers, but for the tourist with a motorbike licence and talent at handling gravel roads it is possible to hire a bike for your holiday transportation. *Gravel Travel Motorbike Adventures*, T061-250147, www.gravel-travel.de offer guided safaris (or straight bike hire) on their desert-modified Yamaha XT600Es. If you fancy a burn on a Harley, try *www.333.com.na* based in Walvis Bay. See box page 161 for potential pitfalls.

For the budget traveller, the best way to see the principal tourist attractions – albeit in **Safaris** a way, with a crowd and at a pace that may not be optimal – may be with one of the safari companies that operate from Windhoek and Swakopmund. See relevant websites on page 16 or tour companies in the Windhoek and Swakopmund sections. *Wild Dog Safaris*, T061-257642, www.wilddog-safaris.com are recommended, or choose after discussion with travellers in the tourist offices and backpacker hostels once you arrive. Compare prices and itineraries carefully as you may spend the great majority of your time squeezed into a minibus.

In the absence of a public transport network, entrepreneurs have stepped in with vehi- **Shared taxi** cles of greater or lesser safety, size and comfort. They are almost without exception serving the non-white market and run from town centre to town centre rather than to the tourist spots. Given this limitation, you are advised to make the most of their services and then hitchhike the final stages, remembering of course that you may be in a remote spot and might have to wait a while for your lift. Whatever happens, start your day early; we would certainly not recommend getting into any stranger's vehicle after dark.

The price demanded for a journey will vary according to the quality of the vehicle, the distance travelled and, occasionally, the amount they think you can be 'taken for a ride'. Our experience indicated a fare of between N$10-30 per 100 km. The best method, of course, is to check out what your fellow travellers are paying and agree to pay exactly that amount, **on arrival**. If you don't get to your destination, chances are you will have to hitch the remaining journey. While this is up to you, you should not feel compelled to pay the proportion of the journey achieved; after all, you agreed to pay for a trip to, say, Rundu, not somewhere hundreds of kilometres short of it, to be deposited after dark, with no food and no realistic chance of getting there that day.

While not generally recommended, this is the only way to get to many of the interest- **Hitch-hiking** ing corners of the country without your own transport and can provide the adventurous traveller with rewarding insights into and contact with local people. At its best, hitching can open doors to more than just a ride but it is a risky method of travelling, particularly if you are alone, in a hurry, or inexperienced. If you do decide to give it a try, it is a good idea to walk or take a taxi to the edge of town (perhaps the last petrol station on the main road) and start hitching from there. The major problem facing most travellers is the lack of traffic rather than security or the willingness of Namibians to give lifts. As a general rule, a sign stating your destination is a good idea ('Timbuktoo' can work wonders, although it *does* exist, so beware if you start crossing borders). So too is standing at a junction or fuel station in full view, so that your hosts can give you a once over from close range before committing and having time to brake safely. Whatever the case, be sure to take some food and plenty of liquids with you, and warm clothes for those rides through the night on the back of a truck. In most rural areas, there is no public transport. You may well be asked to contribute for a lift in remote areas where private transport can often end up as a taxi service as well. Establish the fair price from others (either passers-by or fellow passengers) and pay this amount only when you have reached your destination.

Train

For Transnamib's timetable, see page 383 Few tourists use the Namibian railway service (**Transnamib**) because it is slow and serves few centres of interest to the overseas visitor. Once you have completed one journey by train you are likely to choose a bus for your next leg. The passenger trains that do run, however, are very cheap. Trains stop everywhere along the way (thus their slow progress) and, given their main use is freight haulage, there can be a good deal of noise and shunting, often in the small hours of the morning.

Luxury trains In an effort to tap into the luxury market made popular by South Africa's highly regarded Blue Train, Transnamib runs two luxury services from Windhoek. The **Desert Express** runs to Swakopmund and back twice a week. It in fact won the HAN award for 'Best Hotel with fewer than 50 beds' in 2000. The experience doesn't come cheap at N$1330-1500 (depending on season) per person, sharing, one way. A new service to Etosha, the **Northern Desert Express**, started in 2001. It leaves Monday at 0900, with a long afternoon stop (and wine-tasting tour) at Omaruru, overnight on the train and arrival in Tsumeb at 0900 Tuesday. Transfer by bus to Mokuti Private Reserve, afternoon game drives, overnight at Mokuti Lodge, morning game drive, lunch and back to Tsumeb at 1400 on Wednesday. Arrival Thursday 1500 in Windhoek. Price from N$2500-3200 per person, sharing, for the round trip, depending on season. Reports have all been positive. For further details, see Windhoek travel section, page 92, and Etosha National Park, page 126. Reservations: Windhoek T061-2982600, Swakopmund T064-400372, www.transnamib.com.na/dx

Keeping in touch

Communications

Internet Internet cafés are opening in many towns, details are given where available in the relevant sections. Access is often painfully slow. While it can be useful (and comforting) to contact those back home, try to remember you haven't travelled all this way to wait 20 minutes for Hotmail to appear on an ancient computer screen. Go outside! The websites and email addresses included in this book are best used from overseas to help you gather information and make reservations without incurring international phone charges. Once you are here, you are better off using the phone.

Post Post offices are open weekdays 0830-1600, Saturday 0800-1200. For poste restante services, encourage your friends and family to make sure mail is labelled clearly, with the surname first and underlined to speed the process of discovery. Internal mail can be very slow – up to three weeks. Expect letters to take a minimum of 10 days to get to Europe. Postcards cost N$2.60 to the USA and N$2.50 to Europe, and letters cost that amount per 10 g. The post office will allow international calls on a meter and sends faxes overseas at roughly N$3 a page. There are efficient overnight parcel services, main offices: **DHL** T061-263161, **Fedex** T061-264777 and T064-2012333 (Walvis Bay), as well as **TNX** (via rail) to South African destinations within three days, T061-2982666.

Regional dialling codes

Country code: 264. When dialling a number in Namibia from abroad drop the first 0 in the area code.

Major dialling codes
061 Windhoek
063 Keetmanshoop
063 Lüderitz
064 Swakopmund
064 Walvis Bay
064 Omaruru

066 Katima Mulilo
066 Rundu
067 Otjiwarongo
067 Tsumeb

Local codes in rural areas have been included with the listed telephone number since it is not always obvious which exchange a remote guestfarm or game reserve may be connected to.

Essentials

Telephone

Namibia has an efficient telephone system which was originally installed by the South Africans. Most numbers are on digital exchanges and have a three-digit area code (06x) followed by a six-digit number. The remainder are dialled by calling the local exchange, where an operator answers and puts you through manually. Beware calls from hotel phones; as anywhere, they can be very expensive.

Telecards Telecards are sold for N$10, N$20 and N$50, divided into 20 cent units. They are obtainable at post offices, dealers and teleshops. These are normally the type that you insert into the phone, although there are cards with a PIN that you dial. Local calls are good value.

International enquiries T1025. International calls are expensive. There is one price band no matter what time of day you make the call.

Local enquiries T1188.

Cellular phones Namibia's **Mobile Telecommunications Company** (MTC, www.mtc.com.na) provides a reliable but limited-range GSM system for cellular phones. A cellphone can be very useful, both for booking ahead and keeping in touch with your loved ones. Overseas visitors are able to use their phones in the country provided they have arranged to do so with their service providers at home. Not only are outgoing calls (both local and interantional) expensive, beware high charges for receiving calls under these arrangements. A better value alternative is to hire a phone and/or SIM cards (for those with snazzy phones already) through **Get Smart Mobile**, gsmrent@iafrica.com.na, who have offices at Hosea Kutako airport, T062-540101; in the Mutual Platz shopping centre (next to Edgars) in Windhoek, T061-245225; in Swakopmund, T064-400042; and in Walvis Bay, T064-206082. You will need a credit card as deposit, but rental and domestic calls are good value and incoming calls and voicemail are free. Telephone numbers can be pre-booked, so that you can tell everyone at home your number before you travel. Reception coverage includes all the main towns, and along the tarred roads from Windhoek as far as the coast, Rehoboth and Gobabis. Outgoing international calls are expensive: check how the billing system works or you could be in for a shock. In 2001, phone rental was N$13 per day (or N$6 for just the SIM card), although if you rent through *Budget*, *Imperial* or *Europcar*, you will get a discount.

Bring your own mobile phone, you can hire SIM cards cheaply for local calls

   MTC provides a list of useful numbers: customer services is T120 (or +26481-120 from overseas), emergencies T112 and the police, countrywide, T10111.

Media

Newspapers If it's local scandal, crime and debate that you're after, head straight for the newspaper stand. *The Namibian* is the country's only English-language, independent daily, with some international news; you can get a year's subscription sent to Europe, or perhaps better value to check www.namibian.com.na from time to time. Others are the *Observer* on Saturday and *Tempo* (multilingual) on Sunday; *Republikain* (daily, Afrikaans); *Mail* and *Guardian* (weekly South African and international news). For tourists, *Travel News Namibia*, bi-monthly, provides relevant updates; you can subscribe T061-225665, tnn@iafrica.com.na, www.holidaytravel.com.na German visitors will enjoy the monthly *Tourismus* publication.

Radio The government encourages free speech and there are lively oral debates and phone-ins on the radio each day. As well as the *Namibian Broadcasting Corporation (NBC)* , available almost everywhere throughout the country, in English, there are five commercial radio stations in Windhoek. *Radio 99* and *Radio Energy* are recommended. Don't expect much reception (other than NBC) out of urban centres.

Short Wave Radio If you are not familiar with short wave radio read the notes in the manual about reception; a simple attachment can greatly enhance the quality of your signal. Digital tuning makes finding weak frequencies considerably easier. Signal strength varies throughout the day, with lower frequencies generally better at night. For programme listings contact BBC, PO Box 76, Bush House, London.

British Broadcasting Corporation (BBC). These bands cover the whole region from Namibia to Moçambique, as well as different times of the day. 90m band: 3255 kHz; 49m band: 6005 kHz, 6190 kHz; 25m band: 11860 kHz, 11940 kHz; 19m band: 15400 kHz; 16m band: 17885 kHz; 13m band: 21470 kHz, 21660 kHz.

Voice of America (VoA). 25m band: 11920 kHz; 22m band: 13680 kHz; 19m band: 15580 kHz; 16m band: 17895 kHz; 13m band: 21485 kHz.

Television The state broadcaster, *NBC*, broadcasts one television channel in English. The South African paying channel, *M-Net*, is available in most hotels and backpacker hostels. Most subscribers tend to take this service for the films and the sport. Football fans will have no trouble keeping in touch with events back in Europe, as there is a weekly summary of Italian, German and Spanish football and an overall look at European football. To top it all you can watch three live Premier League football matches from England each week. Namibian youths are well informed on all the results and stories back in Europe. To make room for American sports such as basketball and baseball there are two dedicated sports channels, Supersport One and Two, also broadcast from South Africa. A digital satellite service is also growing in popularity, offering up to 40 channels of film, music, sport and light entertainment.

Food and drink

Cuisine Carnivores should lick their lips, as the meat is plentiful, excellent and very cheap (by European standards). Everywhere, German and Afrikaans influence prevails and you will soon realize why so many of them have that distinctive 'thick-set' physique. Supermarkets and butchers sell a wide range of sausages, kebabs, ribs and choice cuts (the 'sosaties' are delicious), often prepared in the traditional way, and self-caterers are spoilt for choice in the variety of prepared meats. Restaurants tend to serve large, good value if fairly simple meals, with menus revolving around steak, chicken and schnitzel, plus good, fresh seafood (and shellfish, in season) by the coast. Meals taken in

Namibian braai recipes

Be ambitious about your braai cuisine and you will look forward to each evening with relish. Before you travel, you could search for inspiration on the web (try www.geocities.com/ pete_in_za/recipes.html#Recipes) and we would definitely recommend that you bring a simple braai cookbook with you or buy one on arrival. Here are a few starter recipes.

Butternut Soup

1 butternut, small, cut in 1 inch squares
1 teaspoon ginger, ground (if fresh, crushed)
1 teaspoon salt
1 teaspoon curry powder
1 cup cream, evaporated milk or full-cream milk
Cover butternut with water and boil, together with all ingredients except cream, until soft. Mash. Return to the heat for a couple of minutes, before adding cream and allowing to heat through. Serve hot.

Chicken potjie *(serves 2)*

500g chicken
oil
1 onion, chopped
1 clove garlic, crushed
carrots, diced
sweet potatoes, cubed
celery
dried peaches
1 cup white wine, ½ cup water
seasoning
Fry chicken with oil, onion and garlic until brown. Add (in order) layers of carrots, sweet potato, celery, peaches and seasoning, pour in wine and stock, cover and leave to simmer gently for one hour. Do not stir, the layering is important. Serve with rice. This dish has long been the local method of using up whatever leftovers and produce that is available, so be bold and perfect (even name!) your own potjie, using your choice of meat and whatever (within reason) vegetables you have to hand: chillies, mushrooms, tomatoes, squash, parsley, leeks, apple, dried fruit, etc

Stuffed potatoes

Wrap clean potatoes in foil (shiny side in) cook deep in the coals of the fire for one hour, remove, unwrap, scoop out some flesh and refill with your favourite filling.

Fillings suggestions:

Tuna and mayonnaise, mixed with a shredded carrot, onion, curry powder, paprika and lemon juice

Ham cubes and cottage cheese, with black pepper
Home made sour cream (lemon juice mixed with long-life cream) mixed with tinned oysters or mussels and black pepper
Fish (preferably smoked) mixed with cocktail sauce and lemon juice

Ratatouille *(serves 2)*

1 onion, chopped
1 green pepper, chopped
1 clove garlic, crushed
oil
½ small carrot, diced
1 tin chopped tomatoes
1 courgette, sliced
salt and seasoning
Fry onion, pepper and garlic until soft, add the rest and simmer until tender. You may have to add a little water.

Quick braai sauce/marinade

½ cup ketchup
1/4 cup Worcester Sauce
1 tbspn chutney
1 tspn mustard powder
½ cup vinegar
1 tbspn oil
1 clove garlic, crushed
1 tbspn sugar
½ cup cream
Mix all ingredients together and simmer for five minutes; use as a marinade for any meat dish.

Cowboy dampers

250g self raising flour
1 tsp baking powder
pinch salt
little water
30 g margarine
Work all ingredients into a sticky dough. Whittle a stick (multi-pronged if you want multi-feeding) to get a clean end. Wrap a fingerful around the end of the stick and bake over the fire. Serve with jam as a simple and entertaining 'dessert'; also nice with savouries (see potato fillings above) as a starter.

guestfarms, lodges and houses are always plentiful and usually excellent. As just about everything is grown organically in this land (imported fertilizers being beyond the budget of most farmers) and levels of hygiene and standards of preparation are good, we advise being adventurous with dishes you may be unfamiliar with, particularly the local game specialities. While gastronomes may be disappointed outside the main towns of Windhoek and Swakopmund, we have tried to point visitors to what we found were the best eateries in the relevant sections. On the downside, fresh produce can be hard to find in smaller towns, so vegetarians should stock up when they can; even in restaurants, the choice is limited.

The braai One of the first local terms you are likely to learn will be 'braai', which quite simply means barbecue. The braai is incredibly popular, part of the Namibian way of life, and every campsite, picnic spot and lay-by has a braai pit. Given the excellent range of meat available, learning how to cook good food on a braai is an art that needs to be mastered quickly and is part of the fun of eating in Namibia. Once you have established a core of heat using firelighters and wood or charcoal (charcoal is more eco-friendly and less smoky but wood makes for a wonderful fire), wrap up potatoes, sweet potatoes, squash, butternut etc in *heavy-duty* foil and cook them in the coals for an hour or so. Set beside a good piece of meat, with a sauce and a cold beer, you will be living the Namibian dream.

An extension of the braai is the 'potjie' (pronounced 'poy-kee'), literally a cast-iron pot with legs that sits on top of coals. This is the traditional cooking vessel of many tribes and is wonderfully simple to use. Just brown your meat and throw in any vegetables and leftover meat, together with fruits, dried fruit, stock, chutneys and herbs and leave the pot to simmer away on the coals. Once prepared, apart from occasionally replenishing the coals, the dish requires no attention whatsoever. Allow to cook slowly so that all the flavours blend. A chicken potjie might take up to two hours to cook, lamb two to three, and oxtail perhaps six hours to reach its best. Most Namibian bookstores will have sections devoted to braai and potjiekos ('kos' is food in Afrikaans).

Drink The lager in Namibia is excellent, as you would expect given the German heritage. Windhoek Lager won a gold medal (and Windhoek Light a bronze) at the 2001 International Beer and Cider Competition. Germany's famous Beck's beer has been brewed under licence in Namibia since 2000. A 330ml bottle will cost you no more than N$4 from a bottle store and not much more in most bars. Wine is imported from South Africa and is reasonably easy to find, except in smaller stores. The Afrikaans influence means that low-grade brandy is available everywhere (ask for a Klipdrift and Coke in a bar and see how you go). The only local label is the reasonably palatable wine from the Kristall Kellerei; to sample it you will have to visit the farm outside Omaruru.

The standard shop selling alcohol is known as the '**bottle store**', open daily except Sunday, 0900-1800. With few exceptions, you are unable to buy drink from shops in the evening. At the end of each month you will see queues of Namibians withdrawing their wages and going straight to the bottle store. Alcohol abuse is a serious problem in the country. Drink driving is also a major problem, so take extra care over the last weekend of the month.

Shopping

Further details can be found under individual towns African art and curios are of widely varying quality and can be surprisingly expensive. Sculptures, baskets, ceramics and other souvenirs start as curios sold at roadside stalls but as the quality and craftsmanship improves these products are reclassified as art with prices to match. Animal products made from ivory and reptile skins are on sale in Namibia but if you take them back home you could well fall foul of CITES regulations.

There are a number of excellent craft and curio shops in Windhoek, but don't expect any bargains when looking at the quality products.

The exceptional wool of Namibia's hardy, desert-reared karakul sheep is woven into clothing and carpets, often with attractive local and animal designs. There are furriers in Windhoek and Swakopmund, and weavers in Dordabis, Karabib and Lüderitz . Each weaver keeps a good range of output for sale on the farm and, if you have the ability to carry your purchases, you are advised to buy there rather than wait until you return to Windhoek. Further information on the industry is available from the *Karakul Board*, T061-237750, F236122, agrapels@agra.com.na

There are four main regional handicrafts centres in the country, produce from all of which can be found at reasonable prices in Windhoek in the cooperative gallery next to the Warehouse Theatre (Tal Street). In the south, Gibeon is a centre for embroidery, producing attractive black-backed cotton embroidery work. The Bushmen of remote east Bushmanland produce colourful and intricate beadwork. Baskets, woodcarving and simple pots are produced in the Kavango and Caprivi regions, with the greater abundance of palms, wood and clay (go to the Caprivi Arts Centre in Katima Mulilo for the country's best selection). In the northwest, centred on Opuwo and Epupa, the Himba have learned to adapt their traditional costumes and jewellery into attractive and intricate designs, using leather, metal, plastic and wood.

Entertainment and nightlife

Namibians enjoy watching sport. Most whites are passionate about rugby, and the majority are loyal supporters (with satellite dishes) of the neighbouring Springboks. The rest of the country takes a keen interest in football, and there are fairly regular matches played in Windhoek. Ask at tourist information centres for fixture details.

On the whole, Namibia is not the place to come to for the nightlife. Outside Windhoek and Swakopmund, your best bet will typically be a hotel bar with a pool table that will only do reasonable business on weekends (particularly after pay day). You will be surprised at how quiet towns become at weekends, as the majority of the population returns home to their families. However, when the party does start, there are no rules or regulations threatening to end it and you may find yourself carrying on into the small hours, witnessing consumption of huge volumes of alcohol. We have tried to identify the best spots in each town in the relevant sections.

Cinema Only Windhoek and Swakopmund have large, comfortable cinemas which show international releases and South African films. The main cinema in Windhoek, *Ster-Kinekor* (three screens), is located in the Maerua Park complex; the cinema in Swakopmund is the *Atlanta* (three screens). Admission is around N$20 per person. There are smaller cinemas ('Paradiso') in Ondangwa and Oshakati as well.

Performing arts The larger towns often have shows, jazz and local dance performances. They rarely publish a schedule more than a month in advance and usually restrict performances to weekends. Ask at local tourist information centres or consult the town's monthly magazines for details. Latest details of theatre, movies, music and art are posted on the website www.backstagenewz.com   In Windhoek, there are regular performances at the National Theatre of Namibia (NTN) on Robert Mugabe Avenue, involving the Windhoek Symphony Orchestra and African music groups, as well as ballet and plays. Additional events are hosted by the Franco-Namibian Cultural Centre at the College for the Arts in Peter Muller Street, as well as at the Warehouse in the Old Breweries Building on Tal Street.

Essentials

Nightlife Outside Windhoek, this is restricted to a few hotels and only really gets going at weekends and on the major holidays. The locals mostly rely on TV and early nights. Windhoek has a few bars worth exploring and a couple of night-clubs. Again, check www.backstagenewz.com for the latest offering.

Holidays and festivals

Festivals **April:** *Namibian International Trade Fair;* **April/May:** *Windhoek Carnival* (last week of April and first week of May); *Rundu Barge Carnival.* **June:** *Holiday and Travel Expo* **October:** *Agricultural and Industrial Show* (first week of October). *Oktoberfest.* **November:** *Enjando Street Festival* (a Saturday in November).

Public holidays There are 12 public holidays. **1 January:** New Year's Day; **21 March:** Independence Day; **20 March:** Good Friday; **1 April:** Easter Monday; **1 May:** Workers' Day; **4 May:** Cassinga Day; **9 May:** Ascension Day; **25 May:** Africa Day; **26 August:** Heroes' Day; **10 December:** Human Rights Day; **25 December:** Christmas Day; **26 December:** Goodwill Day.

Public holidays for 2002 are listed above. Those for 2003 are the same with three exceptions: Good Friday 18 April; Easter Monday 21 April; Ascension Day 29 May.

School holidays While seemingly trivial, the dates of Namibian and South African school holidays can have a significant bearing on your visit. Not only are prices often higher, but most of the popular destinations become fully booked. In Swakopmund over Christmas there simply won't be anywhere to stay if you have not made an advance reservation. This also applies to national parks accommodation in late August, in particular the three camps in Etosha National Park.

School holidays take place from mid-December to mid-January; mid-April to early May; and early August to early September – see www.natron.net for precise dates.

Sport and special interest travel

Ballooning With virtually year-round clear blue skies and warm sunshine, Namibia is an ideal place to go ballooning. A one-hour trip over the desert at Sossusvlei is a favourite with many people, and there are a number of guestfarms which also offer balloon safaris. The only drawback is the expense – a one hour trip costs around N$1800 per person, champagne breakfast included. (See page 284 for a description of a balloon trip over Sossusvlei.)

Canoeing Whether it's a casual 30-minute paddle on the Zambezi or a fully-fledged expedition down the Kunene or Orange rivers, a canoe trip on one of Namibia's perennial rivers is great fun. For wildlife enthusiasts, gliding down the river in a canoe is an excellent way of getting a close look at birds and game without frightening them away. A number of organizations (see below) offer the chance to shoot the rapids along the Kunene and Orange rivers (see page 333, Orange River Canoe Adventure). Prices are reasonable, with a four- or five-day trip starting at around N$1250 all inclusive.

All operators of Orange River canoe safaris are headquartered in Cape Town: *Felix Unite* T+2721-6836433, www.felixunite.co.za, the original and best, also offers a fabulous Kunene trip, taking in the highlights of northern Namibia on the way (five days on the river). The competition is led by *River Rafters*, T+2721-725094, www.riverrafters.co.za, but take a look also at www.rafting.co.za, www.riversinc.co.za and www.wildthing.co.za

Scuba-diving is run through the ***Namibian Underwater Federation (NUF)***, **Diving &**
T061-238320, theo@schoemans.com.na, who recommend that all divers are experi- **caving**
enced, as sea temperatures are low (9-17°C). There is some fascinating diving available
in Otjikoto Lake, near the eastern gate to Etosha, where a retreating German army
dumped much of its weaponry in 1915. The lake bed has been declared a national
monument. Some of the items have been landed and are shown in the Tsumeb
museum, but there is a great deal still underwater. Additionally, the Dragon's Breath on
Haruchas Farm (between Grootfontein and Tsumeb) is thought to be the world's largest underwater lake. Groups must organize their own gear, transport and permission
and, needless to say, should be highly experienced.

There are numerous charter companies and air taxi operators that will happily take **Flying**
paying guests on scenic flights over the dunes and mountains, along the coast to the
inaccessible wrecks and adapted wildlife that live there. Details of some are given on
page 38 but a local pilot can usually be arranged through any upmarket lodge or hotel.
Most pilots train in South Africa, and there are no formal facilities for overseas visitors to
learn the trade within Namibia; rather, you will be enjoying the services of a local pilot
and his machine.

Extremely popular with Namibians, fishing trips can be organized either from Walvis **Game fishing**
Bay or Swakopmund. The cold, clean waters of the South Atlantic provide rich feeding
grounds for a wide range of species (refer to the Swakopmund section for specific fishing excursions and tour operators). Be aware that there are hundreds of regulations
restricting location, season, methods, species and catch sizes, with significant penal-
ties imposed on those who contravene them. Information is available from the local
tourist and MET offices. The angling season on the Zambezi, Linyati and Okavango
rivers is August to December.

Namibia is reputed to be one of the best **Gliding**
places in the world for gliding due to near
perfect atmospheric conditions. Near
Mariental is the ***Bitterwasser Flying Centre and Lodge***, T063-265300, F265355,
www.bitterwasser.com which caters
expertly for proficient gliders (and can
arrange transport of equipment from
Europe). During the season (November to
February), you will be lucky to find
accommodation on site. You may be able
to occupy the passenger seat for a fee
(although you'll need a strong stomach).
Peak season is December to January, longer if the rains are late. At this time, the
Centre fills up with European enthusiasts.
Numerous '1000 km triangles' are flown,
the challenge for 2002 is 1250 km.

Golf may not be an adventure sport in **Golf**
many people's eyes, but played in the
searing heat, off the desert sand, with
endless dunes in the background, must
be one of the more unusual rounds to
play, so it gets our vote. The two best

Special interest detours and diversions

Like rambling on and on? There are three trails at Daan Viljoen (including one overnight); Waterberg four-day trails (guided and unguided); scenic hikes in the Triangle from Ghaus Lodge; game walks from lodges outside Etosha, but not in the park; three-day trails at Brandberg and Spitzkoppe with guides; Tsaris Mountain trails; desert walks (guides available) at Sossusvlei; the Naukluft Trail, Brukkaros Volcano; numerous trails from Klein Aus Vista; and the four-day Fish River Canyon hike.

Feeling adventurous? Adventure sports are centred on Swakopmund (all coast, aerial and dune activity), but with pockets of riverborne activity on the Fish, Kunene, Okavango and Zambezi Rivers; gliding near Mariental; ballooning and flying from Sesriem; scuba diving for experts near the Triangle.

Wacky about wildlife? It's worth extending your stay at Etosha and, for those who can afford it, stopping at a nearby guest lodge (Ongava, Mokuti); Okonjima and CCF near Otjiwarongo are good for big cats; guided walks at Sossusvlei will give you a new perspective on desert fauna; Damaraland camps track elephant and black rhino on foot; Waterberg Plateau scenic/game drives are available; birders should head straight for the parks in the Caprivi.

Seeking the best 4x4 routes by far? This is the right country. Experienced, well prepared enthusiasts will be heading for Kaokoland and Bushmanland; the rest will probably find the gravel roads challenge enough. For a taster of the tough stuff try the Naukluft Trail, around Gamsberg Mountain (southwest of Windhoek), or the dunes north of Lüderitz.

Water, water, everywhere? Namibia's perennial rivers are few and far between: try one-to-four-day whitewater canoe trips on the Orange and Kunene, angling (particularly the Zambezi but also on dams), game watching; scuba for the experienced in underground lakes and sinkholes; all seaside and offshore activities require hardiness and experience due to the cold Benguela current.

Starry, starry nights? The Gamsberg area expects clear skies 340 nights a year and is a mecca for stargazers the world over. But just about everywhere, outside the rainy season, you can expect a gleaming canopy to cover you as you sleep.

Culture vulture? German colonial history is the most evident as you travel around, particularly Windhoek, Swakopmund and Lüderitz. The isolated Baster community has settled in Rehoboth, and well preserved examples of traditional homesteads are evident in the far north (Owambo), northeast and northwest (Himba).

known courses are at the **Windhoek Country Club**, T061-2055116, and, near Swakopmund, the **Rossmund Golf Course**, T/F064-405644, originally built for use by mineworkers, but now open to visitors. These are the only two grassed 18-hole courses (although another is planned for Otjiwarongo) – both are challenging, clubs can be hired, there is a club house with bar and restaurant. Other courses (many in poor condition) are detailed in the relevant sections.

Hiking
See under individual hikes for further details

For those visitors interested in experiencing the bush at first hand, there are excellent bush hikes in Namibia, whatever your experience and level of fitness. For the uninitiated, walking in the bush is an excellent way of getting a close look at Namibia's diverse flora and fauna, and whether you walk for an hour or a day, you are sure to see something new and interesting. Most parks and many guestfarms have well marked trails suitable for inexperienced walkers. For a more in-depth experience, enquire locally about guides, who can fill in the detail on plants, birds and game in what might be a new and unfamiliar environment. A useful source of information is the Hiking Federation of Namibia, T061-230896, F230856.

For the experienced hiker there is the challenge of the Fish River Canyon (see page 327), Ugab River (page 249) and Naukluft Hiking Trails (page 276), all of which require high levels of fitness, and a willingness to carry everything necessary with you on your back. At an intermediate level there are fantastic hikes in the Naukluft Mountain Park (page 278), at the Waterberg Plateau Park (page 121) and in the south near Aus for the Namib Feral Horse Hiking Trail (page 314). Finally, for those people not wishing to get too serious, there are rewarding but manageable hikes at Daan Viljoen Game Park near Windhoek (page 94) and easy trails around the base camp at Waterberg Plateau.

As experienced walkers will know, good preparation is the key to a successful and enjoyable hike. It is also important to remember that, however short or easy a walk may appear to be, walking in the bush is not like going for a stroll in the park – a few basic steps should be followed. Below is a short checklist of equipment and guidelines to hiking in the bush:

Day hikes Good walking boots or shoes; sunhat; minimum of 2 litres of water per person; first aid kit; penknife; trail snacks (peanuts, biltong, dried fruit); binoculars, camera and birdbook/gamebook; toilet paper and matches to burn paper.
Additional overnight gear Sleeping bag; fleece or equivalent top, even in summer; torch; lightweight camping stove (it is not always permitted to collect firewood); matches/lighter/firelighters; dehydrated food, eg pasta, instant soups etc.

Tips
- ■ Don't leave litter or throw away cigarette butts
- ■ Leave everything as you find it – don't pick plants or remove fossils or rocks
- ■ Stick to marked trails especially in the bush – it's easy to lose your way!
- ■ Camp away from waterholes so as not to frighten game away
- ■ Never feed the animals
- ■ Remember, in the southern hemisphere the sun goes via the north not the south.

Horse riding & camel safaris

Reitsafaris Namibia, T061-217940, F256300, www.reitsafari.com offer a 12-day, 400 km ride that they have completed dozens of times. The route runs from Ganab and competent horsemen and women can undergo the 'experience' on horse or camel. They offer shorter trails in the Brandberg region. There are also plenty of horse-riding opportunities on the many privately-owned guestfarms, where an experienced hand will guide you as part of a multi-day safari or a simple scenic/game ride. We have tried to highlight the farms that offer this in the text, but even if you are just passing through it is worth asking at any farm should you be interested in a ride.

Hunting

Although certainly not to everyone's taste, hunting is a part of Namibian life and is often used by farmers as a necessary control on game numbers within individual farms. The season runs during the winter months, generally June to August. There are a number of registered guestfarms specializing in guided hunting trips and; for those with the cash and the inclination, these are the places to head for. The *Namibian Professional Hunters Association (NAPHA)*, T061-234455, F222567, www.nat-ron.net/napha has a new head office on Sam Nujoma Drive, on the road to/from the airport. NAPHA produces regular publications and is your best bet for information on guestfarms, species, guides, safaris, regulations, books, taxidermy, shipping, etc. Also try *Safari Club International*, the international membership body for 'sport hunting, conservation and rural development'. Their *African Chapter* is based in Pretoria, South Africa, T+2712-6638073, F6638075. The *African Sporting Gazette* is published

Essentials

quarterly in South Africa and is posted worldwide, F+2711-8032022. Taxidermy is readily available for trophies (including one just by Hosea Kutako airport) and freight companies are accustomed to shipping these prizes back to Europe.

Microlighting Microlighting, whether as an experienced pilot or first timer, is available for the brave and provides a fantastic opportunity to see game and nature from a new perspective. Try *Scenic Flights* based in Windhoek, T081-2424000 (mob), or *Action Safaris*, T064-570185 (Omaruru), www.actionsafaris.com.na

Off-road driving This is one of the most popular pastimes in a country that offers varied and challenging terrain, stunning landscapes, uncharted expanses, remote wilderness campsites, isolated rural communities and plentiful game. As well as the four-wheel drive tours arranged by nearly all of the car hire companies, we recommend *Uri Adventures*, T061-231246, F227575, www.namibweb.com/uri.htm, for an opportunity to take specialized, Namibian-made, two-wheel drive, off-road vehicles (known as 'Uris') along riverbeds, rocky ground and stretches of dune desert, in multiple day tours. Their most popular routes travel from Windhoek to Swakopmund, taking three to four days across the mountains and desert. But they have itineraries up to 14 days, taking in the main sites and covering considerable ground.

Paragliding Namibia has some of the clearest conditions and best thermals in the world. In order to fly legally in Namibia you must get temporary membership of the *Namibia Hang Gliding and Paragliding Association (NAHPA)*. This can be obtained by sending a copy of your current hang gliding or paragliding licence plus a fee of N$30 to the NAHPA contact in Namibia prior to your arrival. You will be issued with a temporary licence, valid for three months. You must also have insurance against paragliding accidents, including full *air rescue* as one often flies in very remote areas. *Aeromed* insurance provides this degree of cover (see page 55). NAHPA advises visitors to be fit and hold a valid Class 4 medical certificate. Conditions are extreme and temperatures can be as high as 40°C in the air. Restricted air space must be respected. There is only one tour operator organizing winching and general flying trips: contact Christo Pieterse for more details at T064-400209 or T081-1294026 (mob).

Local NAHPA clubs will be able to provide details of site regulations. Upon arrival in Windhoek, contact Piet Steenkamp, T061-2835110 (work), T259353 (home), T081-1277493 (mob), piet.steenkamp@bon.com.na or Chris Lotter T061-226450 (work), T081-1299908 (mob). See also www.paragliding.co.za

Quad-biking Quad-biking trips through dry river beds are full of incidents and accidents. Understand your machine before heading out, or your Yamaha Blaster 200cc with manual six-speed gearbox will up-end you more surely than any bucking bronco. Again, *Action Safaris,* T064-570209 (Omaruru), www.actionsafaris.com.na are a good start. They will arrange multiple day safaris, centred on quad-biking and microlighting but with game drives, four-wheel drives, wave jumping etc included in your high-adrenalin trip.

Safaris

Game viewing The majority of game viewing in Namibia's national parks is undertaken independently. With the exception of Etosha in peak season, the reserves are uncrowded and have an extensive network of gravel roads which are laid out to provide access to waterholes, hides and the various different ecosystems within a park.

See under individual national parks and reserves for further details As visitors are left to their own devices to such a great extent it is a good idea to buy some of the wildlife identification books which are available in bookstores and camp shops. Best viewing is early in the morning and late in the afternoon. The midday heat is usually too intense for the animals, who rest up in thickets for most of the day. The best season for viewing is winter (July-October) when the lack of surface water forces animals to congregate around rivers and waterholes. The height and thickness of vegetation is much less at this time of year, making it easier to spot wildlife. The disadvantage of winter viewing is the relatively weak condition of the animals and harshness of the landscape. Summer weather, from November to January, when rain is expected, is the best time of year for the animals. They will be in good condition after feeding on the new shoots and there are chances of seeing breeding displays. In late February and March there is a chance of seeing new offspring in green and lush surroundings,

National parks & reserves

Essentials

1 Bwabwata Game
Reserve (East & West)
2 Daan Viljoen Game Park
3 Etosha National Park
4 Fish River Canyon
5 Hardap Dam
Recreational Resort &
Game Park

6 Khaudum National Park
7 Mahango Game
Reserve
8 Mamili National Park
9 Mudumu National
Park
10 Namib-Naukluft
National Park

11 National West Coast
Tourist Recreational
Area
12 Popa Falls National Park
13 Skeleton Coast National
Park
14 Waterberg Plateau Park

N

0 km   50
0 miles   50

but the thicker vegetation and the wider availability of water mean that the wildlife is more evenly spread throughout the park and therefore more difficult to spot.

Driving around endlessly searching for animals is not the best way to spot many of these creatures. While speed limits are often 60 kph, the optimum speed for game viewing by car is around 15 kph. Drives can be broken up by stops at waterholes, picnic sites and hides. Time spent around a waterhole out of your car gives you an opportunity to listen to the sounds of the bush and experience the rhythms of nature as game moves to and from the water. The areas where you are allowed out of your car are specifically designated; never get out of the car unless it is at a designated area, not only are you liable to be prosecuted and thrown out of the park, but you may well be seriously injured or killed.

Namibia's game reserves are well organized; following the few park rules will ensure an enjoyable stay. Most parks are only open to visitors during daylight hours, the camp leaflets will give you the details of seasonal changes, so it is important to plan your game-viewing drive so that you can start at first light and return before the camp gates shut just before dark.

Within the park it is forbidden to feed the animals, as they will develop a dependency on humans as a source of food. Once animals such as elephants learn that food is available from humans they can become aggressive and dangerous when looking for more and will eventually have to be shot. Litter is not a serious problem within the parks; throwing rubbish out of your car will spoil other people's enjoyment of nature. Keep your litter inside the car and dispose of it when you reach a camp or, better still, a town.

If your car breaks down while you are in the park, do not leave the car in search of help. Stay inside your car until a park ranger comes to your rescue. Chances are that other visitors will be using the same roads as you and you will be able to pass a message on to the park authorities through them. If the worst happens and night falls before you are rescued, remember that the park keeps a record of all the cars that have entered each day. If your car has not returned before dark, the park rangers will know you are missing and send out a search party. While game viewing in some of the larger parks, remember that the weather can be hot and dusty. It is a good idea to take water bottles and fruit juice with you, as well as snacks in case of emergency.

Travelling on gravel roads means that the car and passengers inside will be covered in dust before the end of the trip. The only sure way of avoiding this is to travel with the windows rolled up and the air conditioning unit on full. Expect dust to get into everything that is not locked in air-tight containers. Wear comfortable old clothes, preferably in dull greens or khakis.

Don't forget your binoculars and spare film

Invaluable for game viewing is a good pair of binoculars. The wildlife is not always conveniently close to the car and binoculars will help you pick out animals and features at a range that leaves your subjects undisturbed. It is a good idea to buy your binoculars before you reach Namibia as they are imported here and will be more expensive. When you are buying a pair of binoculars don't just consider the strength of magnification, much of the best game viewing is done when light levels are low so a large aperture letting in more light can be as useful as high magnification. Consider also weight; a compact pair is much more comfortable on game walks.

Game reserve accommodation

Once you have reserved your accommodation in a game reserve (see page 36), you will be able to move in anytime after midday until the camp gates shut at nightfall. The camps in Etosha have a shop, restaurant and bar, but overall visitors will find them fairly basic. Shops typically sell a range of relevant books as well as maps, leaflets and food. At the camp office you register and can enquire about available game walks and drives. Most accommodation is self-catering, so you may well find that there is no restaurant – be sure to check ahead and plan accordingly. The camp shops usually sell some pots and pans, utensils and food but the range tends to be limited. In most reserves (including Etosha and all of Sossusvlei to the 2WD car park by the dunes), road conditions between camps are good; well maintained gravel roads are navigable by saloon car, a four-wheel drive is not necessary.

There are numerous safari companies operating out of Windhoek which can arrange accommodation and game-viewing trips as part of a wider tour. The cost of tours varies: there are good budget options as well as more expensive luxury safaris. In fact, given Namibia's limited public transport and the need for a car while game viewing, these companies often offer the cheapest access to game reserves. Typically, a 10-25% mark-up is charged for their efforts, which may well be worthwhile, given the economies of scale and expertise bought.

Safari companies

Essentials

Health

Staying healthy in Namibia is straightforward. Taking simple precautions, you should keep as healthy as you are at home. Most visitors return home having experienced no problems at all. However there are health risks in Namibia, depending on how and where you travel. The country has a mixed sub-tropical and desert climate, so the range of health problems differs from those elsewhere in sub-Saharan Africa. In particular, the cities are clean and the standard of medical facilities is high. There are under-developed areas of course and infectious diseases predominate in the same way as they did in the West decades ago. Clearly, the business traveller in smart hotels will encounter fewer risks than the backpacker trekking through rural areas, but there are no hard and fast rules to follow; often the best source of advice (beyond your own judgement) is that of lodge owners, shopkeepers and residents in the area.

See the directory under individual towns for information on local and medical facilities

Medical care is expensive in Namibia. There are two private hospitals in Windhoek, each with fully equipped intensive care units. Medical facilities in rural areas are limited. In rural areas and game parks both infectious and insect borne diseases still occur. Diseases such as Schistosomiasis (Bilharzia) still occur, HIV infection is very much on the increase and Tuberculosis is still widespread. **NB** Taking a **malaria** prophylactic (preventative) is recommended, especially between November and March (rainy season) for travellers visiting the north and east. Check with a specialist before you travel for the recommended drugs and dosage. See page 61 for further advice.

Medical facilities

Before you go

Take out medical insurance and check it carefully to ensure it includes the possibility of medical evacuation by air ambulance both to Windhoek and back to your own country. One of the greatest risks is road accidents, many of which occur in remote regions; the quickest/best route to hospital is by air, even for non-critical conditions; you don't want to be left to pick up the bill. The Namibian *Aeromed* has links with Europ Assistance, the largest medical assistance network in the world. Contact them at 1 Merensky Street, Windhoek, T061-231236 or 249777 in emergency. There are regional offices in Otjiwarongo (T067-303776) and Rehoboth (T062-522091). *Namibia Medical Care (NMC)* provides emergency rescue services throughout Southern Africa. They operate from the Sanlam Building on Independence Avenue, Windhoek, T061-2947111, F2947454, www.nhca.com.na Emergencies: Namibia T0800-000001, South Africa T08000-111261, elsewhere in southern Africa T+2711-4524611.

You should have a dental check up, obtain a spare glasses prescription, a spare oral contraceptive prescription and, if you suffer from a chronic illness (such as diabetes, high blood pressure, ear or sinus troubles, cardio-pulmonary disease or nervous disorder) arrange for a check up with your doctor, who can at the same time provide you with a letter explaining the details of your disability. If you are on regular medication, make sure you have enough to cover the period of your travel.

Medicines Drugs and medicines are generally of high quality. This means you do not have to carry a whole chest of medicines with you, but remember that the shelf life of some items, especially vaccines and antibiotics, is markedly reduced in hot conditions. Buy your supplies at the better outlets where there are more refrigerators, even though they may be more expensive; check expiry dates. Immigration officials occasionally confiscate drugs (Lomotil is an example) if they are not accompanied by a doctor's prescription.

Children A degree of care is required when travelling to remote areas with babies and young children, where health services are primitive. Children can become ill more rapidly than adults (equally, they often recover more quickly). Diarrhoea and vomiting are the most common problems, and need to be acted on rapidly and intensively. Wet wipes are useful for keeping clean and clearing up messes and can be found in the major towns, as can disposable nappies. Breastfeeding is best and convenient for babies; powdered milk is available in the cities, as is baby food. Bananas and other fruits are all nutritious and can be cleanly prepared. The treatment of diarrhoea is as for adults, but should start earlier and be continued with more persistence. Children get dehydrated very quickly in hot countries and can become drowsy and uncooperative unless cajoled to drink water or juice plus salts. Upper respiratory infections, such as colds, catarrh and middle ear infections are also common and if your child suffers from these normally take some antibiotics against the possibility. Outer ear infections after swimming are also common; antibiotic eardrops will help.

Medical supplies Consider taking the following items with you: water purification tablets (Pota Agua is recommended); malaria prophylactic tablets; anti-infective ointment (eg Cetrimide); talcum powder containing fungicide; antacid tablets for indigestion; rehydration salts plus anti-diarrhoea preparations; painkillers/anti-inflammatories such as Ibuprofen or Aspirin; a course of antibiotics for diarrhoea etc.

First Aid Kit – small pack containing a few sterile syringes and needles and disposable gloves. The risk of catching hepatitis etc from a dirty needle used for injection is very low, but some may be reassured by carrying their own supplies – available from camping shops and airport shops. Be aware that overzealous customs officials may regard ownership of syringes in a negative light.

Vaccination & immunization Smallpox vaccination is no longer required anywhere in the world and cholera vaccination is no longer recognized as necessary for international travel by the World Health Organization – it was not very effective. Namibia requires yellow fever vaccination certificates from travellers who have entered from other (especially Central and West) African countries or from infected countries. Vaccinations against the following diseases are recommended.

Infectious Hepatitis Less of a problem for travellers than it used to be because of the development of two extremely effective vaccines against the A and B form of the disease. It remains common, however, in rural areas. A combined hepatitis A & B vaccine is now licensed, one jab covers both diseases.

Polio Despite its decline in the world this remains a serious disease if caught and is easy to protect against. There are live oral vaccines and in some countries injected vaccines. Whichever one you choose it is a good idea to have a booster every three to five years if visiting developing countries regularly.

Tetanus One dose should be given with a booster at six weeks and another at six months and 10 yearly boosters thereafter are recommended.

Typhoid A disease spread by unsanitary preparation of food. A number of new vaccines against this condition are now available; the older TAB and monovalent typhoid vaccines are being phased out. The newer, eg Typhim Vi, have fewer side effects, but are more expensive. For those who do not like injections, oral vaccines are available.

Other vaccinations Children should already be properly protected against diphtheria, polio and pertussis (whooping cough), measles and Hep B all of which can be more serious infections than at home. Measles, mumps and rubella vaccine is also given to children throughout the world, but those teenage girls who have not had rubella (German measles) should be tested and vaccinated. Hepatitis B vaccination for babies is now routine in some countries. Further vaccinations might be considered in the case of epidemics, eg meningitis.

Further information

Further information on health risks abroad, vaccinations etc, is available from your local travel clinic. If you wish to take specific drugs with you, such as antibiotics, these are best prescribed by your doctor. Be aware that not all doctors are experts on the health problems of remote countries. More detailed or more up-to-date information than local doctors may provide is available from various sources.

In the UK there are hospital departments specializing in tropical diseases in London, Liverpool, Birmingham and Glasgow. The Malaria Reference Laboratory at the London School of Hygiene and Tropical Medicine provides free advice about malaria, T020-7636 7921, F7436 5389. In the USA, contact the local Public Health Services or obtain information centrally from the Centre for Disease Control (CDC) in Atlanta, T404-3324559, www.cdc.gov The World Health Organisation, www.who.int/ith/ provides malaria and other information for travellers.

There are additional computerized databases which can be accessed for destination-specific, up-to-the-minute information. In the UK there is MASTA (Medical Advisory Services for Travellers Abroad), www.masta.org, a private company from whom you can obtain a health brief tailored to your journey by calling T01276-685040 and answering a telephone questionnaire. Be warned that calls are charged at premium rates (currently 60p per minute) so this can work out expensive. A good alternative is to consult www.fitfortravel.scot.nhs.uk

There are many travel clinics now providing these specialized services; check your local telephone directory for details. In the UK, the **British Airways Travel Clinic** provides inoculation advice and treatment at its clinic in Victoria Place, London SW1, T020-7233 6661. Try also **Trailfinders Travel Clinic**, 194 Kensington High Street, London W8, T020-7938 3999.

The 'bible' on medical problems overseas is by Richard Dawood (Editor) – *Travellers' Health, How to Stay Healthy Abroad*, Oxford University Press. We strongly recommend this, especially to the intrepid traveller heading for the more out of the way places. General advice is also available in the UK in *Health Information for Overseas Travel* published by the Department of Health and available from HMSO and *International Travel and Health published by WHO Handbooks on First Aid*, produced by the British & American Red Cross and by St. John's Ambulance (UK).

On the road

For most travellers, a trip to Namibia means a long air flight. From Europe and South Africa there is little or no time difference, however, if you are travelling from North America or Asia, then jetlag can be a problem. Your body's biological clock will be out of sync with the real time at your destination. The main symptoms are tiredness and a tendency to wake up in the middle of the night wanting breakfast. Most find that the problem is worse when flying in an easterly direction. The best way to get over jetlag is to try to force yourself into the new time zone as strictly as possible. This may involve, on a westward flight, trying to stay awake until your normal bedtime and on an eastward flight forgetting that you have lost some sleep on the way out and going to bed relatively early but near your normal time the evening after you arrive. The symptoms of jetlag may be helped by keeping up your fluid intake on the journey, but not with alcohol. Some travellers swear by the hormone melatonin but it is not currently licensed in Europe.

On long-haul flights, remember to stretch your legs and flex (tighten and relax) your muscles (particularly legs) regularly, this will lessen risks of blood clot development and deep vein thrombosis (DVT). Drinking plenty of non-alcoholic fluids will also help.

Staying healthy

Intestinal upsets The thought of catching a stomach bug worries visitors to Namibia but there have been great improvements in food hygiene and most such infections are preventable. Travellers' diarrhoea and vomiting is usually caused by eating food which has been contaminated by food poisoning germs, drinking water is rarely the culprit. However, it is possible to be infected by contaminated sea or river water. As a general rule the cleaner your surroundings and the smarter the restaurant, the less likely you are to suffer.

Foods to avoid Uncooked, undercooked, partially cooked or reheated meat, fish, eggs, raw vegetables and salads, especially when they have been left out exposed to flies. Stick to fresh food that has been cooked from raw just before eating and make sure you peel fruit yourself. Wash and dry your hands before eating; disposable wet-wipe tissues are useful where this is not possible.

Shellfish eaten raw are risky and at certain times of the year some fish and shellfish concentrate toxins from their environment and cause various kinds of food poisoning. The local authorities notify the public not to eat these foods at these times. Ignore warnings at your peril.

Heat treated milk (UHT, pasteurized or sterilized) is becoming more available as is pasteurized cheese. On the whole, matured or processed cheeses are safer than the fresh varieties. Unpasteurized milk from whatever animal can be a source of food poisoning germs, tuberculosis and brucellosis. This applies equally to ice-cream, yoghurt and cheese, so avoid these home-made products – the factory made ones are probably safer.

Tap water throughout the country is chemically treated (you can often taste it) and safe to drink. If in doubt buy bottled mineral water which is available from most shops.

Travellers' diarrhoea Infection with various organisms can give rise to travellers' diarrhoea. They may be viruses, bacteria, eg Escherichia coli (probably the most common cause world-wide), protozoa (such as amoebas and giardia), salmonella or cholera. The diarrhoea may come on suddenly or rather slowly. It may or may not be accompanied by vomiting or by severe abdominal pain and the passage of blood or mucus when it is called dysentery. If you can time the onset of the diarrhoea to the minute ('acute') then it is probably due to a virus or a bacterium and/or the onset of dysentery. Treatment, in addition to rehydration, is the antibiotic Ciprofloxacin 500 mg every 12 hours; the drug is now widely available and there are many similar ones.

If the diarrhoea comes on slowly or intermittently ('sub-acute') then it is more likely to be protozoal, ie caused by an amoeba or giardia. Antibiotics will have little effect; you are advised to visit a doctor, as for any outbreak continuing for more than three days. Sometimes blood is passed in amoebic dysentery and for this you should certainly seek medical help. If this is not available then the best treatment is probably Tinidazole (Fasigyn), one tablet four times a day for three days. If there are severe stomach cramps, the following drugs may help but are not very useful in the management of acute diarrhoea: Loperamide (Imodium) and Diphenoxylate with Atropine (Lomotil). They should not be given to children.

Any kind of diarrhoea, whether or not accompanied by vomiting, responds well to the replacement of water and salts, taken as frequent small sips, in some kind of rehydration solution. There are proprietary preparations consisting of sachets of powder which you dissolve in boiled water or you can make your own by adding half a teaspoonful of salt (3.5 g) and four tablespoonfuls of sugar (40 g) to a litre of boiled water.

The lynch pins of treatment for diarrhoea are rest, fluid and salt replacement, antibiotics such as Ciprofloxacin for the bacterial types and special diagnostic tests and medical treatment for the Amoeba and Giardia infections. Salmonella infections and cholera, although rare, can be devastating diseases and it would be wise to get to a hospital as soon as possible if these were suspected! Avoid fasting, peculiar diets, alcohol, milk and chillies!

Rest, fluid and salt replacement are key to recovery

Essentials

Diarrhoea occurring day after day for long periods of time (chronic diarrhoea) is notoriously resistant to amateur attempts at treatment and warrants proper diagnostic tests (cities with reasonable sized hospitals have laboratories for stool samples). There are ways of preventing travellers' diarrhoea for short periods of time by taking antibiotics, but this is not a foolproof technique and should not be used other than in exceptional circumstances. Doxycycline is possibly the best drug. Some preventatives such as Enterovioform can have serious side effects if taken for long periods.

Paradoxically **constipation** is also common, probably induced by dietary change, inadequate fluid intake in hot places and long bus journeys. Simple laxatives are useful in the short-term and bulky foods such as rice, beans and plenty of fruit are also useful.

There are a number of ways of purifying water in order to make it safe to drink. Dirty water should first be strained through a filter bag (camping shops) and then boiled or treated. Bringing water to a rolling boil at sea level is sufficient to make the water safe for drinking, but at higher altitudes you have to boil the water for longer to ensure that all the microbes are killed.

Purifying water

There are sterilizing methods that can be used and there are proprietary preparations containing chlorine (eg Puritabs) or iodine (eg Pota Aqua). Chlorine compounds generally do not kill protozoa (eg Giardia).

There are a number of water filters now on the market available in personal and expedition size. They work either on mechanical or chemical principles, or may do both. Make sure you take the spare parts or spare chemicals with you and remain sceptical of the manufacturer's promises.

Full acclimatization to high temperatures takes about two weeks. During this period it is normal to feel a bit apathetic, especially if humidity is high. Drink plenty of water (up to 15 litres per day are consumed by labourers in the tropics), use salt on your food and avoid extreme exertion. Tepid showers are more cooling than hot or cold ones. Large hats do not cool you down, but do prevent sunburn. Remember that, especially at higher altitudes, there can be a large and sudden drop in temperature between night and day, so dress accordingly. Sporting and outdoor clothing manufacturers are using materials designed to wick moisture away from the skin during the heat of the day and also provide insulation against night-time cold; these are worth trying out.

Heat & cold

While mosquitoes are carriers of potentially serious diseases, these are more of a nuisance than a hazard and you can usually prevent yourself entirely from being bitten. Sleep off the ground and use a mosquito net or some kind of insecticide. Preparations containing pyrethrum or synthetic pyrethroids are safe. They are available as aerosols

Insects
Mosquito repellent is a must

Essentials

or pumps and the best way to use these is to spray the room thoroughly in all areas (follow the instructions rather than the insects) and then shut the door for a while, re-entering when the smell has dispersed. Mosquito coils release insecticide as they burn slowly. They are widely available and useful out of doors. Tablets of insecticide plugged into a wall socket are highly effective, but you'll need access to electricity. They fill the room with insecticidal fumes in the same way as aerosols or coils.

You can also use insect repellents, most of which are effective against a wide range of pests. The most common and effective is diethyl metatoluamide (DET). DET liquid is best for arms and face (take care around eyes and with spectacles, DET dissolves plastic). Aerosol spray is good for clothes and ankles and liquid DET can be dissolved in water and used to impregnate cotton clothes and mosquito nets. Some repellents now contain DET and permethrin, an insecticide. Impregnated wrist and ankle bands can also be useful.

If you are bitten or stung, itching may be relieved by cool baths, antihistamine tablets (take care with alcohol or driving) or mild corticosteroid creams, eg hydrocortisone (take great care: never use if any hint of infection). Careful scratching of all your bites once a day can be surprisingly effective. Calamine lotion and cream have limited effectiveness and antihistamine creams are not recommended – they can cause allergies themselves.

Bites which become infected should be treated with a local antiseptic or antibiotic cream such as Cetrimide, as should any infected sores or scratches. If they are failing to dry up in a humid environment, consider using *Savlon Dry*, an aerosol medication that seals up the infected area while letting it heal.

When living rough, skin infestations with body lice (crabs) and scabies are easy to pick up. Use whatever local commercial preparation is recommended for lice and scabies.

Crotamiton cream (Eurax) alleviates itching and also kills a number of skin parasites. Malathion lotion 5% (Prioderm) kills lice effectively, but do avoid the use of the toxic agricultural preparation of Malathion, more often used to commit suicide.

In some parts of Africa, the jigger flea commonly burrows its way into people's feet causing a painful itchy swelling which finally bursts in a rather disgusting fashion. Avoid these by not going barefoot or wearing sandals and if they do become established have someone experienced winkle them out with a sterile needle. Similarly, certain tropical flies which lay their eggs under the skin of sheep and cattle also occasionally do the same thing to humans with the unpleasant result that a maggot grows under the skin and pops up as a boil or pimple. The best way to remove these is to cover the boil with oil, vaseline or nail varnish so as to stop the maggot breathing, then to squeeze it out gently the next day.

Other afflictions

Athlete's Foot While unlikely in the dry climate, this and other fungal skin infections are best treated with Tolnaftate or Clotrimazole.

Prickly Heat This very common, intensely itchy rash is avoided by frequent washing and by wearing loose clothing. It is cured by allowing skin to dry off through use of powder or by spending a couple of days in an air conditioned hotel!

Sunburn The burning power of the Namibian sun, especially at altitude, is phenomenal. Always wear a wide brimmed hat and use some form of sunscreen lotion. You will need to use high protection creams designed for use in the tropics, and by mountaineers and skiers (SPF 15 or above). Glare from the sun can cause conjunctivitis, sunglasses are recommended.

Ticks Usually attach themselves to the lower parts of the body often after walking in areas where cattle have grazed. They take a while to attach themselves strongly, but swell up as they start to suck blood. The important thing is to remove them gently, so that they do not leave their head parts in your skin because this can cause a nasty allergic reaction some days later. Do not use petrol, vaseline, lighted cigarettes etc to remove the tick, but, with a pair of tweezers remove the beast gently by gripping it at the attached (head) end and rock it out in very much the same way you might extract a tooth.

Other risks and more serious diseases

Remember that rabies is endemic throughout Africa, so avoid dogs. If you are bitten by a domestic or wild animal, do not leave things to chance: scrub the wound with soap and water and/or disinfectant, try to have the animal captured (within limits) or at least determine its ownership, where possible, and seek medical assistance at once. The course of treatment depends on whether you have already been satisfactorily vaccinated against rabies. If you have (this is worthwhile if you are spending lengths of time in developing countries) then some further doses of vaccine are all that is required. Human diploid vaccine is the best, but expensive: other, older kinds of vaccine, such as that derived from duck embryos may be the only types available. These are effective, much cheaper and interchangeable generally with the human derived types. If not already vaccinated, anti rabies serum (immunoglobulin) may be required in addition. It is important to finish the course of treatment whether the animal survives or not. Dogs and other domestic animals also carry hydatid disease – keep away from them. A pocketful of stones to throw at attacking animals is useful where you suspect danger. **Rabies**

AIDS in Namibia is mainly spread by heterosexual intercourse. Men and women are about equally infected. The same precautions should be taken as when encountering any sexually transmitted disease, namely avoiding sexual contact of any kind, and wearing latex condom contraception to avoid the exchange of any fluids. The AIDS virus (HIV) can be passed via unsterile needles which have been previously used to inject an HIV positive patient, but the risk of this is very small indeed. It would, however, be sensible to check that needles have been properly sterilized or disposable needles are used. The chance of picking up Hepatitis B in this way is more of a danger. Be wary of carrying disposable needles. Customs officials may find them suspicious. The risk of receiving a blood transfusion with blood infected with the HIV virus is greater than from dirty needles because of the amount of fluid exchanged. Supplies of blood for transfusion are supposed to be screened for HIV in all reputable hospitals so the risk should be small. Catching the virus which causes AIDS does not necessarily produce an illness in itself; the only way to be sure if you feel you have been put at risk is to have a blood test for HIV antibodies on your return to a place where there are reliable laboratory facilities. However the test does not become positive for over three weeks. **AIDS**

Africa is facing an enormous challenge with the AIDS epidemic which has long been forecast and is only now starting to be borne out by evidence. But there are many lesser but very real risks associated with sex. Ranging from the mildly embarrassing and uncomfortable to the horrifically ugly and seriously threatening, STDs should at once be presented to a specialist. Often, once diagnosis has been achieved, treatment will be easily available, but on rare occasions, more serious solutions may be required. For a full listing and description of the known STDs, visit *www.sexeclinic.com* That should be enough to put you off any late night encounters while abroad. **Other sexually transmitted diseases**

Malaria occurs in Northeast Namibia with the highest risk area being the Caprivi Strip. There is a much lower risk around Etosha National Park and the east of the country, but the risk is still there. It increases markedly after heavy rains. Malaria remains a serious disease and you are advised to protect yourself against mosquito bites as above and to take prophylactic (preventative) drugs if you are entering a malarial area. Typically, visitors start taking the tablets a few days before exposure and continue to take them six **Malaria** weeks after leaving the malarial zone. Remember to give the drugs to babies and children, pregnant women also.

Before you travel you must check with a reputable clinic or doctor the likelihood and type of malaria in the areas which you intend to visit. Take note of advice on prophylaxis but be prepared to receive conflicting advice. It is still possible to catch malaria even when taking prophylactic drugs, although it is unlikely. If you do develop symptoms (high fever, shivering, severe headache) seek medical advice *immediately*. The risk of contracting the disease increases the further you move into rural areas with primitive facilities and standing water.

Infectious Hepatitis (Jaundice) The main symptoms are pains in the stomach, lack of appetite, lassitude and yellowness of the eyes and skin. Medically speaking there are two main types. The less serious, but more common, is hepatitis A for which the best protection is the careful preparation of food, the avoidance of contaminated drinking water and scrupulous attention to toilet hygiene. The other, more serious, version is hepatitis B, which is acquired usually as a sexually transmitted disease or by blood transfusion. It can less commonly be transmitted by injections with unclean needles and possibly by insect bites. The symptoms are the same as for hepatitis A. The incubation period is much longer (up to six months compared with six weeks) and there is a greater likelihood of complications.

Hepatitis A is protected against by the Havrix vaccination, which is certainly useful for travellers living rough, who should have a shot just before leaving. Immunity lasts up to 10 years, after which boosters are required. Havrix monodose is now widely available, as is junior Havrix. The vaccination has negligible side effects and is extremely effective. If not found, Gamma globulin injections (lasting six months) can be a bit painful, but it is cheaper than Havrix and may be more available in some places.

Hepatitis B can be effectively prevented by a specific vaccine (Engerix) – three shots over six months before travelling. If you have had jaundice in the past it would be worthwhile having a blood test to see if you have developed immunity to either type, and thereby avoid the necessity and cost of vaccination or gamma globulin. There are other kinds of viral hepatitis (C, E etc) which are fairly similar to A and B; vaccines are not yet.

Typhus Can still occur, carried by ticks. There is usually a reaction at the site of the bite and a fever. Seek medical advice.

Intestinal worms These are quite common and the more serious ones such as hookworm can be contracted from walking barefoot on infested earth or beaches. Some cause an itchy rash on the feet 'cutaneous larva migrans'.

Snake, spider & scorpion bites This is a very rare event indeed for travellers but if you are unlucky (or careless) enough to be bitten by a snake, spider, scorpion or sea creature, first, don't panic, second try to identify the creature, without putting yourself in further danger. Snake bites in particular are very frightening, but in fact rarely poisonous – even venomous snakes bite without injecting venom. What you can expect if bitten are: swelling, pain and bruising around the bite and soreness of the regional lymph glands, perhaps nausea, vomiting and a fever. Signs of serious poisoning would be the following: numbness and tingling of the face, muscular spasms, convulsions, shortness of breath or a failure of the blood to clot, causing generalized bleeding. Victims should be taken to a hospital or a doctor without delay. Commercial snake bite and scorpion kits are available, but are usually only useful for the specific types of snake or scorpion. Most serum has to be given intravenously so it is not much good equipping yourself with it unless you are used to making injections into veins. It is best to rely on local practice in these cases: the particular creatures will be known about locally and appropriate treatment can be given.

Treatment Reassure and comfort the victim frequently. Immobilize the limb with a bandage or a splint or by getting the person to lie still. Do not slash the bite area and try to suck out the poison because this sort of heroism does more harm than good. If you know how to use a tourniquet in these circumstances, you will not need this advice. If you are not experienced, do not apply a tourniquet.

Precautions Simple precautions involve not walking in snake territory in bare feet or sandals – wear proper shoes or boots. If you encounter a snake stay put until it slithers away, and do not investigate a wounded snake. Spiders and scorpions may be found in the more basic hotels. If stung, rest and take plenty of fluids and call a doctor. The best precaution is to keep beds away from the walls and look inside your shoes and under the toilet seat every morning.

Certain fish and shellfish may inject venom into bathers' feet, which can be exceptionally painful. If such creatures are reported, avoid being stung by wearing shoes of some description. The pain can be relieved by immersing the foot in extremely hot water for as long as the pain persists.

Stings, bites & other insects

Dengue fever This is a growing problem in Namibia. It can be completely prevented by avoiding mosquito bites in the same way as malaria. No vaccine is available. Dengue is an unpleasant and painful disease, typified by a high temperature and body pains. There is no specific treatment – just pain killers and rest.

Filariasis causing such diseases as elephantiasis occurs in Namibia. It is also transmitted by mosquitoes.

Leishmaniasis causing a skin ulcer which will not heal occurs in Namibia. It is transmitted by sand flies.

Schistosomiasis (Bilharzia) is a parasite harboured by snails which live in fresh water lakes. The parasites enter through the skin and are responsible for serious, ongoing disease in the gastrointestinal tract or bladder. Do not swim in freshwater lakes which are known to harbour the disease.

Trypanosomiasis (sleeping sickness). This disease, essentially a brain infection causing drowsiness, is transmitted by a large, tenacious insect - the tsetse fly. This is a fly not always repelled by DET but very susceptible to Pyrethroid fly spray and Permethrin. The main risk is in game parks where these rather aggressive flies are common.

First-time exposure to countries where sections of the population live in poverty can cause odd psychological reactions in visitors. Simply be prepared for this and try not to over-react. Adjusting to your new surroundings inevitably takes time, and may be exacerbated by jet lag, fatigue and homesickness. If you are feeling worn out or miss home after travelling for a long time, you may find that the company of countrymen, spoiling yourself with a couple of nights in a hotel, a trip to the cinema or a meal in a luxurious restaurant raises your spirits.

Psychological disorders

When you return home

Remember to continue taking your antimalarial tablets as prescribed (usually four more weeks). If you have had attacks of diarrhoea it is worth having a stool specimen tested in case you have picked up amoebas. If you have been living rough, blood tests may be worthwhile to detect worms and other parasites. If you have been exposed to

Essentials

schistosomiasis by swimming in lakes etc check by means of a blood test when you get home, but leave it for six weeks because the test is slow to become positive. Report any untoward symptoms to your doctor and tell the doctor exactly where you have been and, if you know, what the likelihood of disease is to which you were exposed. Early symptoms of malaria are not dissimilar to flu; be sure to go to your doctor immediately should you feel poorly on your return. Malaria takes roughly three weeks to incubate before you will feel properly ill.

The above information has been compiled for us by Dr. David Snashall, Senior Lecturer in Occupational Health at the Guy's, King's & St. Thomas' Hospitals in London and until recently Chief Medical Advisor of the British Foreign and Commonwealth Office. He has travelled extensively in Central and South America and the Caribbean, worked in Peru and in East Africa and keeps in close touch with developments in preventative and tropical medicine.

Further reading

Below is a list of a few books on the country and its people to give you a flavour before you travel, accompany you as you go or help fill in the gaps when you return. There are numerous pictorial 'visual souvenir' books available, but getting hold of anything else, either before you leave or in Namibia, can be a battle. Check websites before you go (eg www.amazon.com). Browsing bookstores in Windhoek on arrival is probably your best bet. If you have tried to find the books locally and failed, a good publisher and distributor of natural history, with newsletter and catalogue, is Russel Friedman Book, PO Box 73, Halfway House 1685, South Africa, T+2711-702 2300, www.rfbooks.co.za

Fiction **Jones, Hennie**; *The Moon's on Fire*. Story of the lives, experiences and spirituality of Bushmen living by the Skeleton Coast. **Slaughter, Carolyn**; *Dreams of the Kalahari*. Coming of age story of colonial girl in Namibia. **Smith, Wilbur**; *Burning Shore*. Typically racy drama from the South African born 'master storyteller', guaranteed to excite the young bucks in your party ahead of the trip.

Non-fiction adventure **Augustinus, Paul**; *Desert Adventure*. A year's diary of a trip through the wilds of Namibia and Botswana, enlivened with excellent sketches and photographs. **Buckley, David**; *Grains of Sand*. A desert lover's personal journey through the Namib, as part of a series of trips to all the deserts of the world. **Degre, Alain and Robert, Sylvie**; *Tippi of Africa*. Two French photographers' account of their daughter growing up in the Kalahari wilderness with animals for friends. **Denker, Kai-Uwe**; *Along the Hunter's Path*. Confessions of a passionate professional hunter. **Jenkins, Geoffrey**; *A Twist of Sand*. Boy's own WWII thriller set in the Namib. **Owens, Mark and Delia**; *Cry of the Kalahari*. Documenting seven years of survival while studying indigenous lions and hyenas. **Lush, David**; *Last Steps to Uhuru*. English journalist's personal account of the years immediately preceding Independence. **Martin, Henno**; *The Sheltering Desert*, Creda Press. Adventures and reflections of German geologists hiding in the Namib Desert during WWII. Recommended. **van der Post, Laurens**; The *Lost World of the Kalahari*, the classic tale of his search for the Bushman in the 1950s. There is a sequel too, *The Heart of the Hunter*, and a fictional period novel *A Story Like the Wind* (also published with photos by David Coulson).

Non-fiction **Crandall, David**; *The Place of Stunted Ironwood Trees*. A year in the lives of the cattle-herding Himba. **Taylor, Jane**, with **Laurens van der Post**; *Testament to the Bushmen*. Detailed history with supporting photos. **Gewad, Jan-Bart**; *Herero Heroes*. A look at the key figures at an important time in the tribe's history, 1890-1923. **Heywood, Annemarie**; *The Cassinga event*, National Archives of Namibia. Detailed investigation into the Cassinga massacre.

Jacobsohn, Margaret; *Himba - Nomads of Namibia*. Descriptions of the lives and predictions for the future of this beautiful tribe. Jafta, M et al; *An Investigation of the shooting at the Old Location on 10 December 1959*, Discourse/Msorp. Investigation of forced removals of black population to townships. Katjavivi, Peter; *A History of Resistance In Namibia*, UNESCO. Concise history of Namibia. Lau, Brigitte; *Hendrik Witbooi Papers*, National Archives of Namibia. Personal letters and papers of influential 19th century Namibian leader. Lau, Brigitte; *Namibia in Jonker Afrikaner's Time*, Windhoek Archives. Detailed account of central and southern 19th century Namibian history. Lau, Brigitte; *Trade & Politics in Central Namibia 1860-64* (Charles John Andersson Papers Vol 2), Windhoek Archives. Personal diary of 19th century hunter, trader and explorer. Lewis Williams, JD (Ed.); *Stories that Float from Afar*. Bushman folklore. Leys, Colin, *Namibia's Liberation Struggle*. Scrupulous study of SWAPO, published in 1995. Liebenberg, Louis, *The Art of Tracking*. An insight into the Bushman's extraordinary abilities, in the context of the evolution of science. Malan, JS; *Peoples of Namibia*, Rhino Publishers. Concise anthropology of Namibian people. Mossolow, Dr N; *Otjikango or Gross Barmen*, John Meinnert. History of first Rhenish Mission Station in Namibia. Pool, Gerhard; *Samuel Maherero*, Gamsberg McMillan. Biography of late 19th and early 20th century Herero leader – covers 1904-1907 Namibia-German war. Sylvester, Jeremy; *My Heart Tells Me That I Have Done Nothing Wrong*, Discourse/Msorp. The Fall of Owambo King Mandume Ndemufayo.

Visual souvenirs Coulson, David; *Namib*. Compiled over 15 years of travel and photography by this rock-art expert. Johnson, Peter and Bannister, Anthony; *Okavango - Sea of Land, Land of Water*. Johnson, Peter and Bannister, Anthony; *The Bushmen*. Detailed pictorial study of their lives and habits. Lambrechts, Hans; *Namibia - A Thirstland Wilderness*. Mead, Colin; *Shadows of Sand - Photodocument of the Namib Desert Dunes*. Stunning desertscapes. Schoeman, Amy; *Skeleton Coast*. Study of the inhabitants, topography, shipwrecks, flora and fauna of this inhospitable region. Tingay, Paul, *Wildest Africa*. The *Desert* chapter in particular.

Reference Bridgeford, P&M; *Touring Sesriem and Sossusvlei*. Detailed factual information on this popular region. Craven, Patricia and Marais, Christine; Waterberg Flora. Sketchbooks identifying regional flora, also *Namib* and *Damaraland*. Joubert, Jan; *4x4 – a Practical Guide to Off-Road Adventures in Southern Africa*, Struik Publishers. An excellent handbook to prepare for the rigours of the road ahead. Lindsay, Gordon; *Robert's Birds of Southern Africa*. The standard (although large) reference guide for the region. Also one for mammals. There are numerous similar, but lighter weight publications. Pager, Shirley-Ann; *A Walk through Prehistoric Twyfelfontein*. Informative guide to the local rock-art. Schnieder, Ilme; *Waterberg Plateau Park*, Shell Guide. Detailed guide to history, flora and fauna of Waterberg Plateau Park. Seely, Mary; *The Namib*, Shell Guide. Detailed natural history of the Namib Desert. Tooley, RV; *Collectors' Guide to maps of the African Continent and Southern Africa*, Carta Press. A must for map buffs. van Dyk, Rita; *The 4x4 Cookbook*, Struik Publishers. For inspiration before you depart, to ensure at least one tank is always full.

Film Videos can provide the thousands of words that you may not have had time to read, and can be an excellent appetizer ahead of your trip. Sadly, the selection is fairly thin (animals and more animals) and what titles there are can be difficult to get hold of. The Discovery Channel was filming in Bushmanland in 2001, creating a fictional story of a plane-crash survivor who is adopted by locals, taught their ways, and who then makes the long walk back to 'civilization', encountering game, etc. Along with countless mothballed BBC treasures, we can only sit, wait and consult the television listings in hope. The titles that we did find (either in curio shops in Namibia or in the UK through a video directory) available from most video stores are listed below.

Elephants - Giants of Etosha; National Geographic Films. An introduction to the park and its largest attraction. *Kalahari;* Prowler Press, November 1996. *Lost Horses of the Namib,* with Richard Goss. *Okavango - Jewel Of The Kalahari;* Revelation Films, October 1996. Two hours of stunning natural history, underlining the importance of water to the animals of the area. *Savage Season - A Long Dry Winter In The Kalahari,* Laserlight, July 2000. 60 minutes of beautifully filmed harshness at the edge of the Kalahari desert, thankfully (although perhaps not for one orphaned baby elephant) free from Walt Disney's sentimental meddling. *Shrinking Waters,* Peter and Kathy Jacobson and Mary Seely. Natural historians look at the disappearing rivers and the fragile ecosystem. *Skeleton Coast Safari – Coast of Loneliness.* A South African made film of this bleak coastline, including footage of lions feeding on washed up carcasses of seals and whales. *Wild Wild World Of Animals - Wolf/Coyote/African Wild Dogs. The Zimbabwe, Botswana & Namibia Experience,* Lonely Planet and Pilot Productions, 1995. 50 minutes of backpacker adventuring with a high-spirited Australian and his cameraman, covering Vic Falls, the Okavango and a short 20 minutes through Ovamboland, Sossusvlei, Swakopmund, Fish River, Lüderitz and Kolmanskop.

Maps   A 1998 government map is provided free of charge by the tourist offices and car rental companies, which is perfectly adequate for navigation, distances and road numbers for those with cars. Greater detail of specific regions is provided by the excellent *Shell* series of maps, particularly the Kaokaland area. *Namibia Breweries* sponsored a map of the Caprivi region published in 2000, with informative descriptions and very clear detail in large scale, of the national parks in the region.

    Trekkers will find good maps of the Fish River Canyon, Naukluft Park and Waterberg Plateau are available from the shops in the national parks and nearest towns.

www.footprintbooks.com
A new place to visit

Windhoek

3

Windhoek

Windhoek, Namibia's capital city, is located at an altitude of 1,646 m in the country's central highlands, with the Auas Mountains to the southeast, the Eros Mountains to the northeast and the hills of the Khomas Hochland rolling away to the west. Lying more or less in the geographical centre of the country, the city and surrounding suburbs are spread out over a series of picturesque valleys which lie at the crossroads of all Namibia's major road and rail routes. Although relatively small for a capital city by international standards, and despite talk about decentralization, Windhoek remains the political, judicial, economic and cultural centre of the country.

Although many tourists choose to spend little time in the capital, Windhoek, with its mix of distinctive, colonial German architecture and post-modernist, new buildings is a place worth spending a few days looking around before setting off to view the game of Etosha or the sand dunes of the Namib.

The numerous street cafés and outdoor restaurants lining the side streets running into Independence Avenue are pleasant places to sit, eat and drink and watch people going about their business. The streets themselves are generally busy without being intolerably crowded, even at the end of the month when long queues of Windhoekers form at the banks waiting to cash their pay cheques before going off on the monthly spending spree. Traffic pollution has yet to become a serious issue, and gridlock is, for the time-being, unheard of.

Windhoek

★ Things to do in Windhoek

- Explore Namibia's colonial past and its liberation struggle at the **National Museum** in the Alte Feste overlooking the city.
- Feel the bush close up by taking a **hike in Daan Viljoen Park** and see how close you can get to the antelopes and baboons.
- Have a sundowner on the terrace at **Heinitzburg Castle** as the mountains of the Khomas Hochland turn purple, orange and gold.
- Eat a gourmet meal at the **Gourmet Inn** washed down by the best of South African wines.
- Go dancing until dawn to the kisomobo rhythms of Angola at **Kuddisanga nightclub**.

Ins and outs

Getting there

Phone code: 061
Colour map M1,
grid C5
Population: 220,000
Altitude: 1,646 m

There are two airports serving Windhoek, which can confuse first time visitors. However, all the International flights arrive at Hosea Kutako airport out of town, whilst internal flights and some regional flights use the smaller Eros airport in the southern suburbs. There is no regular transfer service between the two airports.

Hosea Kutako International Airport is 45 km east of the town centre and it is used for flights to/from Europe and South Africa and Air Namibia flight to **Victoria Falls** departs from here. For years the airport has consisted of just a single terminal building with the left end is for departures and the right end for arrivals, however a new terminal currently under construction should soon be completed.

Inside the airport there is a bank, post office, car hire offices and a mobile phone hire bureau as well as facilities for making international calls. The departure lounge has a small duty free shop and a bar which also serves snacks. Change any remaining Namibian dollars at the bank by the arrival point, you cannot exchange the currency once you have cleared exit formalities.

Transport to/from airport: *Intercape*, the long distance coach company, run a bus between the airport and the Grab-a-Phone terminal taxi stand opposite the Kalahari Sands Hotel (N$40pp). The service connects with all international flights. As with all airports the taxi fare is comparatively high, expect to pay in the region of N$200 to go to hotels in the centre of town.

Eros is the smaller airport. It is used by *Air Namibia* for domestic flights, by tour operators, charter companies and private flights. The airport is next to the *Safari Court Hotel*, 3 km south of the town centre. There is no public transport at the airport, and you have to telephone for a taxi to come and collect you. If you are travelling with very little luggage you could walk the 400 m to the *Safari Court Hotel* complex, and then either ask the hotel reception to call for a taxi, or use their complementary town centre transfer service, a mini bus which runs every 10-15 mins to the Grab-a-Phone office on Independence Ave. Here you will always find waiting taxis.

Intercape coaches for Swakopmund and South Africa arrive and depart from the parking area in front of 'Grab-a-phone' at the junction of Müller St and Independence Av (see page 382 for timetable).

Windhoek train station is situated close to the town centre at the northern end of Mandume Ndemufayo St. All passenger services depart from here, so too does the luxury **Desert Express** train.

Getting around

The most obvious feature of the city centre is its size – or lack of it. The central district consists of Independence Avenue running from south to north, and a series of well-ordered streets laid out on a grid around it. It is easy to walk around. The main shops, banks, Post Office, tourism offices and larger hotels are all found along Independence Avenue, so it doesn't take long for the visitor to feel comfortable getting around. **Zoo Park**, with its lawns and palm trees, lies on Independence Avenue right at the heart of the city, and offers a green and shady place used for some Windhoekers to relax at lunchtimes. There is also a café, **The Zoo Park Cafe,** open 0800-1700 every day of the week offering baked goods, a choice of eating indoors our outdoors with good service. Adjacent to the park there is a small open-airrural crafts market specializing in excellent baskets from the north and wood-carvings from the Kavango – with the 2 m tall giraffes the stars of the display! **Post Street Mall**, the main shopping area, is close by with its department stores and traditional arts and crafts street market; at the far end lies the main Werne Hill Shopping Mall.

Greater Windhoek

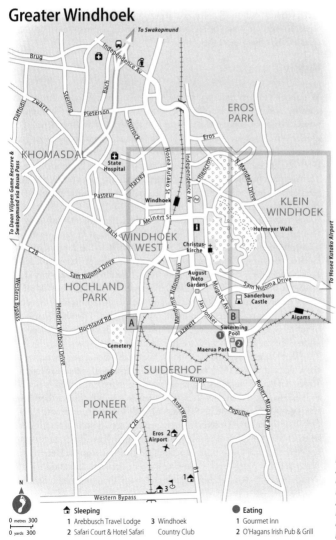

Related maps
A Windhoek centre, page 83
Independence Avenue, page 75
B Klein Windhoek and Ludwigsdorf, page 84

🛏 **Sleeping**		🔴 **Eating**
1 Arebbusch Travel Lodge	**3** Windhoek	**1** Gourmet Inn
2 Safari Court & Hotel Safari	Country Club	**2** O'Hagans Irish Pub & Grill

0 metres 300
0 yards 300

N

First impressions The drive into town from Hosea Kutako International Airport takes you through a typically empty Namibian landscape of rolling hills of dry scrub savannah, until almost without warning you're in a distinctly Western-feeling city. It's easy to be disoriented by the turn-of-the-century German architecture, the well maintained roads, the continental style street cafés and the surrounding mountains into thinking that you're in a medium-sized Bavarian or Austrian town. If you're expecting a bustling, chaotic West African-type city then you're likely to be disappointed.

If you venture into the suburbs close to the centre of the city, you'll get a good idea of the very pleasant lifestyle that white Namibians created for themselves before independence and which are now also enjoyed by the new black élite. In areas such as Klein Windhoek or Eros Park, most houses are spacious bungalows with attractive gardens, many with their own swimming pools. Here, wealthy Windhoekers relax and barbecue as they enjoy the average 300 days of sunshine a year. The high barbed wire fences, alarm systems and guard dogs are the other side of the coin.

History

Windhoek's history reflects the movements of different peoples through the country, and in particular offers the visitor an insight into the past hundred years of colonial conquest, apartheid and struggle for independence. Originally Windhoek was known by the Khoikhoi or Nama people as *Ai-gams* (steam or fire-water) and by the Herero people as *Otjomuise* (place of smoke) due to the hot water springs found in what is now the Klein Windhoek district. These springs had been used for centuries as watering holes by the Bushmen (San) and Khoikhoi (Nama), nomadic and semi-nomadic peoples who trekked through the area with their animals.

The roots of today's city, however, lie in the settlement established by the Oorlam leader Jonker Afrikaner in the 1840s and 1850s at *Ai-gams*, stretching along the ridge of the Klein Windhoek valley. In 1836 Jonker urged the British explorer Sir James Alexander, who called the settlement Queen Adelaide's Bath, to organize a missionary for him. In 1842 the Rhenish missionary Hahn arrived to find a well-established settlement, which he called Elberfeld after a centre of the Rhenish mission in Germany. He was so impressed by the settlement that he was drawn to comment, 'The location of Elberfeld is superbly beautiful ... seeing the extensive thorntree forest with its delicious green and curious forms, the lovely gardens, and the beautiful greensward ...'.

Jonker himself, in an 1844 letter to the Wesleyan Mission Station, referred to the settlement as *Wind Hoock*, and despite much speculation that he named the settlement after *Winterhoek*, his ancestral home in the Cape, there is no solid evidence to suggest this. However, it is certain that Windhoek was the original name given by Jonker and his followers when they settled here around 1840.

Under Jonker, the settlement flourished and served both as a trading station between the Oorlam/Namas and Herero, as well as a headquarters from which Jonker and his commandos launched cattle raids on the Herero living north of the Swakop River. Following Jonker's death at Okahandja in 1861, Windhoek was temporarily abandoned until the missionary Schröder installed himself in the remains of the original buildings in the 1870s.

In 1890 the Germans, under Curt von François, were still not well established in Namibia, and having been effectively driven out of Otjimbingwe and Tsaobis by the Nama leader Hendrik Witbooi, made a strategic retreat to Windhoek. This move neatly coincided with the death of Herero leader

Townships

Most people with a rudimentary knowledge of South Africa have heard about the Johannesburg township Soweto, usually in the context of violent crimes like 'necklacing' or civil unrest between rival ANC and Inkatha Freedom Movement urban guerrillas. What is perhaps less well-known is that all towns in South Africa and Namibia, from the smallest dorp to the largest city, have their own townships. Usually far from the town centre and well hidden from the white suburbs, the townships are home to the vast majority of black and coloured Namibians in the central and southern regions.

In keeping with the apartheid policy of separateness, it was not sufficient to merely reserve the most desirable parts of town for whites, a policy of divide and rule required that the black and coloured communities also be separated. On the apartheid scale of civil rights, the coloured community enjoyed better educational and employment opportunities than the black community. The construction of separate townships for the two groups in the late 1950s and 1960s was a further expression of the divide and rule strategy of apartheid.

Towards the end of the 1950s the white community in Windhoek decided that the 'non-whites' were living too close for comfort, and so the black and coloured communities were evicted from the 'Old Location' on the western side of the city centre, and relocated further away to the W and NW. Resistance to the forced removals was mobilized by the then two recently formed liberation movements, Swanu and Swapo, and culminated in the Dec 1959 uprising when police shot dead 13 protestors and wounded many others. In the Namibian context this massacre signalled a landmark in the liberation struggle comparable to the events that were to take place in Sharpeville, South Africa a few months later.

Two new townships were built, Khomasdal for the coloured community, and Katutura (variously translated as 'we have no dwelling place' or 'the place where we don't want to stay') for the black community. The black township was itself divided along tribal lines with different sections for the Damara, Herero, Owambo and so on. Whilst no expense was spared when it came to providing facilities for the white community, the opposite applied to the creation of Katutura. Thousands of uniform shoe-box houses were built, lining the dirt and dust roads of the township, and until the late 1970s black people were not even entitled to own property and businesses in their own communities!

After the scrapping of this legislation and of the Group Areas Act restricting freedom of movement, Katutura saw both an influx of newcomers from rural areas and an upsurge in black-owned businesses. This emergent class of business people were soon profiting enough to build themselves some fancy houses in areas such as Soweto and Wanaheda.

Although nowadays, in theory, anyone can live where they want, the fact remains that the overwhelming majority of black Windhoekers live in Katutura in cramped, poor quality accommodation, little changed since independence. Furthermore, Namibia has a rapidly expanding population, 70% of whom are under 25 years old, and an estimated adult unemployment rate of over 40%. This has resulted in a continuing influx of people from the regions to the capital placing further pressure on the limited housing stock. Contrast the average street in one of the former white-only suburbs with Katutura and you have a vivid picture of the combined legacies of apartheid and colonialism.

Windhoek

Maherero, and by the time his successor Samuel Herero sent envoys to Windhoek a few weeks later, the Germans were already half-way through the completion of the original fort. This served as the headquarters for the **Schutztruppe** (colonial troops) and is known as the **Alte Feste** (Old Fort). It now houses the historical section of the State Museum and is the oldest surviving building in Windhoek.

The German colonial settlement of Windhoek emerged around the Alte Feste and the springs surrounding it. The settler John Ludwig established substantial vineyards and fruit and vegetable gardens which fed the small settlement; the modern suburb, Ludwigsdorf, is named after him. The Klein Windhoek valley continued to be agriculturally productive until the beginning of the 1960s with the hot springs below the Alte Feste 'smoking away'.

With the completion in 1902 of the railway to Swakopmund on the coast, the settlement was able to expand and develop as the economic and cultural centre of the colony. In 1909 Windhoek became a municipality and this period saw the construction of a number of fine buildings, including the **Tintenpalast**, the present site of Namibia's Parliament, and the **Christuskirch** with its stained glass windows donated by Kaiser Wilhelm II.

During the 1960s the South African government pursued a policy designed to incorporate Namibia into South Africa as the fifth province, and this period saw a further era of rapid development and growth, not just in Windhoek but in the country as a whole. In Windhoek, the government started forcible movements of people from the 'Old Location' in 1959, and as the black population was gradually obliged to settle in Katutura, the white suburbs of Hochland Park and Pioneer's Park were developed on the western side of the city.

The period since independence has seen further growth characterized by some distinctly post-modern buildings in the city centre. The still very much low level skyline is dominated by the Kalahari Sands Hotel and the Namdeb (formerly CDM) building, but new office blocks, the new Supreme Court Building and other Ministry buildings recently completed are quickly changing the face of the city.

On a more modest scale, the last five years have seen a rapid explosion of medium to low cost housing developments around the western and south-eastern outskirts of the city. These new developments have helped to extend the city far beyond its old boundaries and are bringing Namibians of all races together, as upwardly mobile young black and coloured Namibians seek to move out of the townships and young white Namibians, no longer able to afford property in the expensive former white suburbs, look elsewhere.

Sights

As virtually all the sites of interest are in the city centre, the most obvious way to see them is on foot. One full day will allow the visitor with limited time the opportunity to see the more than a dozen old German colonial buildings sprinkled around the city, and visit a couple of the museums. For people with two or three days to spare, a fairly thorough exploration of the city will be possible. Here follows a walking tour.

Clock tower & Zoo Park A good place to start a walk around the city is by the **clock tower** on the corner of Independence Avenue and Post Street. The tower itself is modelled on that of the old Deutsch-Afrika bank built in 1908, but now long-since gone. Cross the road, turn right and walk along Independence Ave as far as **Zoo Park**. Before walking into the park itself, look back across the road and you will see three buildings designed by Willi Sander, a German architect responsible for the design of a number of Windhoek's original colonial buildings.

The **Erkrathus Building**, the furthest right of the three, was constructed in 1910 and is typical of buildings of the period, incorporating business premises

Independence Avenue

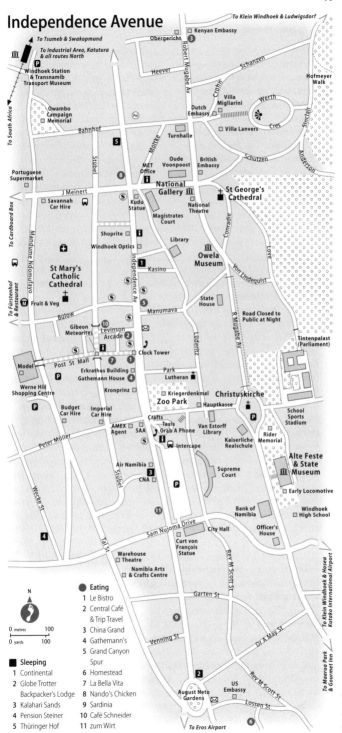

Windhoek

To Klein Windhoek & Ludwigsdorf

To Tsumeb & Swakopmund

To Industrial Area, Katutura & all routes North

Windhoek Station & Transnamib Transport Museum

To South Africa

Owambo Campaign Memorial

Portuguese Supermarket

To Cardboard Box

Savannah Car Hire

J Meinert

Shoprite

Windhoek Optics

St Mary's Catholic Cathedral

To Fürstenhof & Restaurant

Fruit & Veg

Bütow

Gibeon Meteorites

Levinson Arcade

Model

Post St Mall

Werne Hill Shopping Centre

Budget Car Hire

Imperial Car Hire

Peter Müller

AMEX Agent

SAA

Air Namibia

CNA

Wecke St

Stübel

Tal St

Sam Nujoma Drive

Warehouse Theatre

Namibia Arts & Crafts Centre

Garten St

Venning St

August Neto Gardens

To Eros Airport

Obergericht

Kenyan Embassy

Heever

Robert Mugabe Av

Crohn

Schanzen

Schanzen

Werth

Hofmeyer Walk

Smuts

Villa Migliarini

Dutch Embassy

Villa Lanvers

Cres

Anderson

Bahnhof

Stübel

Monte

Turnhalle

Schützen

MET Office

Oude Voonpoost

British Embassy

National Gallery

St George's Cathedral

Kudu Statue

National Theatre

Magistrates Court

Corradia

Library

Owela Museum

Love

Von Lindequist

Kasino

Independence Av

State House

Manumava

R Mugabe Av

Road Closed to Public at Night

Tintenpalast (Parliament)

Luderitz

Gathemann House

Erkrathus Building

Kronprinz

Clock Tower

Park Lutheran

Kriegerdenkmal

Zoo Park

Hauptkasse

Christuskirche

School Sports Stadium

Crafts

Taxis Grab A Phone

Van Estorff Library

Kaiserliche Realschule

Rider Memorial

Intercape

Supreme Court

Alte Feste & State Museum

Early Locomotive

Bank of Namibia

Windhoek High School

City Hall

Officer's House

Curt von François Statue

Rev M Scott St

Dr A May St

US Embassy

Lossen St

To Klein Windhoek & Hosea Kutako International Airport

To Maerua Park & Gourmet Inn

Eating

1 Le Bistro
2 Central Café & Trip Travel
3 China Grand
4 Gathemann's
5 Grand Canyon Spur
6 Homestead
7 La Bella Vita
8 Nando's Chicken
9 Sardinia
10 Café Schneider
11 zum Wirt

Sleeping

1 Continental
2 Globe Trotter Backpacker's Lodge
3 Kalahari Sands
4 Pension Steiner
5 Thüringer Hof

N

0 metres 100
0 yards 100

Related maps
Windhoek centre, page 83
Greater Windhoek, page 71
Klein Windhoek & Ludwigsdorf, page 84

War memorials

All over Windhoek there are memorials, dating back to the early German colonial occupation, which remember German losses during wars with the different Namibian peoples. Among these are the Kriegerdenkmal in Zoo Park, the plaques on the walls in the Christuskirche, the Rider Memorial outside the Alte Feste and the Owambo Campaign Memorial next to the railway station. As with all such memorials the victors have commemorated their own dead without any acknowledgment of those conquered or defeated. Since independence a debate has raged about what should be done with these relics of the country's colonial past, and in particular with the war memorials. Some argue that these symbols of oppression and occupation have no place in a free, independent Namibia and should be removed. Others maintain that these statues and memorials are part of history and therefore should remain. Inevitably these conflicting opinions reflect the different emotions and views of the descendants of those involved in the wars. Nevertheless, whilst wandering around Windhoek it is worth keeping in mind what the monuments represent to the majority of Namibian citizens.

downstairs and living quarters upstairs. Two buildings to the left is **Gathemann House**, commissioned by the then Mayor of Klein Windhoek, Heinrich Gathemann, and now home to Gathemann's restaurant. The stepped roof was of European design intended to prevent the roof from collapsing under the weight of a build-up of snow! The third building bears the inscription **Kronprinz**, the name of the hotel which occupied the building until 1920, and the date of its completion in 1902 can also be seen carved in the stone. The photo shop here has a fine collection of turn-of-the-century photographs of Windhoek, which can be bought as souvenirs.

Walk into the park about 20 m and you will see a **sculptured column** depicting scenes of a prehistoric elephant kill believed to have taken place some 5,000 years ago on this site. The fossilized remains of two elephants and a variety of Stone Age weapons were found when the park was reconstructed in 1962, evidence that the hot springs were already attracting game to the area in pre-historic times. A message to that effect is carved into the side of the column. On top of the column is part of a fossilized elephant skull, however the rest of the bones and tools were removed to the State Museum's research collection in 1990. Also in the park is the **Kriegerdenkmal**, unveiled in 1907, a memorial to the German soldiers killed between 1893-94 whilst fighting the Namas led by Hendrik Witbooi.

Peter Müller Street Continuing up Independence Avenue the first road on the left is Peter Müller Street. On the opposite corner by the taxi rank there is a small **craft market** selling carvings and baskets. At the top of this steep hill on the corner of Lüderitz Street is the **Hauptkasse**, the former home of the German colonial government's finance section. The building now serves the Ministry of Agriculture's Directorate of Extension Services. Directly opposite is **Ludwig Van Estorff House**, named after the former Schutztruppe commander who, between campaigns, lived here from 1902-10. Over the century it has housed senior officers, a hostel and a trade school until the National Reference Library, usually referred to as the Van Estorff library, moved here in 1984. It is now the **Namibian German Foundation Goethe-centre** in affiliation with the British Council, a centre of cultural exchange with multi-media facilities open to the public. On the far side of the library stands the **Supreme Court Building**, opened in October 1997, that looks down over the parking area and over to the Kalahari Sands Hotel.

At the top of the hill on an island in the middle of the road is one of **Christuskirche** Windhoek's striking landmarks, the Christuskirche often called the fairycake **& Rider** church. Designed by Gottlieb Reddecker, the church's foundation stone was **Memorial** laid in 1907 and the building itself finally consecrated in 1910. The church was built by the Germans to commemorate the 'peace' between the Germans and the Nama, Herero and Owambo peoples, and inside there are seven plaques bearing the names of German soldiers killed during the wars. Of the Nama, Herero and Owambo dead there is no record.

This Lutheran church was constructed from local sandstone and its design is an interesting mix of neo-Gothic and Art Nouveau styles. As the sun moves across the sky, the colours on the church walls also change to reflect the colours on the mountains of the Khomas Hochland to the southwest. The church looks most striking at sunrise and sunset which are probably the best times to take photographs. The stained glass windows were donated by Kaiser Wilhelm II and the altar bible by his wife Augusta, and although not particularly impressive looking from outside, are well worth climbing up the steps to the balcony to get a better look at. The **key** to the church is available to visitors during working hours from the **church offices**, at 12 Peter Müller Street just down the hill.

The walk along Robert Mugabe Avenue, running south from the church, takes you towards the whitewashed walls of the **Alte Feste**, the Old Fort which has looked over central Windhoek for the past century. Before reaching the steps leading up to the fort's entrance one can't fail to notice the enormous Reder Denkmal, **The Rider Memorial**. The statue of a mounted soldier depicts General von Trotha, the German Commander who succeeded in 'pacifying' the rebellious Herero and Nama peoples during the 1904-1907 uprising. These victories allowed the colonizers to consolidate their control over Namibia and in turn subjugate the indigenous Namibians.

The Old Fort itself was built as the headquarters of the first Schutztruppe to **Alte Feste area** arrive in Namibia in 1889 and is Windhoek's oldest surviving building, an impressive sight shimmering in the sunlight on top of the hill. The plaque on the wall outside the entrance states that the fort was built as a 'stronghold to preserve peace and order between the rivalling Namas and Hereros'. This statement was a convenient justification for the colonization and subjugation of Namibia, and typical of the European rhetoric of the time.

The Alte Feste now houses the **State Museum's Alte Feste Display and Education Centre** which is well worth a visit. The first room has an exhibition of photographs depicting significant events in Namibia over the whole of this century, and includes photographs of important Namibian leaders such as Hendrik Witbooi, Maherero, and current President Sam Nujoma. One of the most powerful photographs is of Owambo King Mandume Ndemufayo's dead body being recovered by South African troops in 1917. One story has it that the South Africans cut off his head and took it to Windhoek to serve as a warning to other 'rebellious' leaders.

In other rooms there are displays of the early household implements, tools and musical instruments of the first missionaries and European settlers. Arranged alongside these are similar objects used by the different ethnic Namibian peoples, making for an unorthodox, but nevertheless interesting, display.

The Independence Exhibition contains photographs, flags, uniforms and other memorabilia of the transition period from South African colonial rule to independence, monitored by the United Nations Transitional Assistance

Group (UNTAG). In addition there are interesting sections looking at the various sectors of the economy and their respective roles in Namibia's future development. One prominent section focuses on SWAPO, Namibia's governing party since independence. Climb the turret before leaving and you'll be rewarded by a splendid view of Windhoek and the hills of the Khomas Hochland to the west.

Windhoek High School is next to the fort and across the road opposite the school is the old **Officer's House** built in 1906-1907, now serving as the Office of The Ombudsman. The highly decorative and rather attractive brick-work is a recreation of Putz architecture which was fashionable in Germany at the time. The architect, Gottlieb Redecker, designed the building after returning from a year's visit to Germany, and this was the first building of its style in Namibia. Walking back in the direction of the Christuskirche one passes the former **Kaiserliche Realschule**, which opened in 1909 as the first German high school in Windhoek. After the Second World War the building became an English-medium school and now functions as the administrative part of the National Museum.

Robert Mugabe Avenue Walk back in the direction of the Christuskirche and down Robert Mugabe Avenue until you see some gardens on your right. These gardens were laid out in the 1930s and contain an olive grove consisting of 100 trees and a bowling green. More significantly, they surround the home of Namibia's Parliament, the **Tintenpalast**, an impressive yellow and white double-storied building with a verandah running around it. This building was also designed by Gottlieb Redecker, and first opened for business in 1914 as the German colonial government headquarters. It reputedly acquired its name, The Ink Palace, from the amount of paper work that went on here. Over the course of the century the Palace has housed successive governments, before being renovated at independence, in preparation for its role as the home of an independent **Namibian Parliament**.

Further down Robert Mugabe Avenue you will find **State House** on your left hand side. Currently home to President Nujoma this grandiose building was formally the official residence of the South African Administrator- General.

Owela Display This section of the state museum is located just below State House and houses the ethnology hall. The exhibition consists of a series of diaromas intended to give the visitor a picture of the life-styles of the inhabitants of the country within their various environments. They include depictions of the cultivation of omahangu (millet), fishing in the Kavango, the Kalahari Bushmen (San) and the Owambo *oshanas* (water pans). The foyer of the museum has an ever-changing temporary display.

In contrast to the plethora of German inspired architecture, **St George's Cathedral** in Love Street offers a taste of rural England with its solid brown brickwork and exposed beams inside. It is the smallest functional cathedral in southern Africa and is the spiritual home of the Anglican community in Namibia. Designed by GHS Bradford and dedicated in 1925 the bell tower houses a bell cast in 1670, one of a set made for St Mary's Church in Northwall, Canterbury. Love Street starts opposite the Owela Display next to the Engen garage. On Werth and Sinclair streets round the corner from the Cathedral are a pair of fine houses, **Villa Migliarini** and **Villa Lanvers**, both dating back to 1907.

The **National Theatre of Namibia (NTN)** building lies at the bottom of Robert Mugabe Avenue on the corner of John Meinert Street. Turn left at the corner onto John Meinert Street and walk past the **Art Gallery**, and cross over

The Turnhalle Conference

In 1973, South African Prime Minister Vorster made a gesture of granting civil rights to the black population in Namibia by creating a 'native council'. Remarkably, this event happened to coincide with SWAPO being granted observer status at the UN. A constitutional conference was summoned, from which all political parties were banned, and charged with the task of writing a constitution for an independent Namibia.

Delegates were strictly divided along ethnic lines into 11 groups, and the agenda was still fundamentally racist; the first draft which appeared in Mar 1977

was a model for an ethnically segregated country and unsurprisingly was condemned by the group of five western members of the Security Council. However, the meeting was significant, since it was the first time that members of all the different ethnic groups in Namibia had sat down together to talk about their country's future. Although in the end the conference failed to bring Namibia closer to independence, it did inspire the creation of a new political party – the Democratic Turnhalle Alliance or DTA – which today is Namibia's main opposition party.

Lüderitz Street where the Magistrate's Courts are located until you find yourself back at Independence Avenue. The bronze statue of a kudu on the corner is a familiar Windhoek landmark, commemorating the kudu which died during the 1896 rinderpest epidemic. Opposite the kudu is the **Oude Voorpoost**, formerly the survey offices and now home to the National Theatre's offices, with a fire-proof archives room. Next to this building are the offices of Nature Conservation, a classic piece of colonial architecture dating from 1902.

The **Owambo Campaign Memorial**, a stone obelisk in the garden next to the railway station in Bahnhof Street, is reputed to have the head of King Mandume buried beneath it. Another war memorial is the **Cross of Sacrifice** on Robert Mugabe Avenue.

You can't miss the **Gibeon Meteorites** or **Meteor Fountain**, claimed to be the largest collection of meteorites anywhere in the world. Fashioned into a series of sculptures sitting on top a series of steel columns set around a fountain, they dominate the middle of **Post Street** right in the heart of Windhoek. The meteorites get their name from the area in which they were found, southwest of Mariental, and are believed to have belonged to the world's largest ever meteor shower which took place some 600 million years ago. Although they look like fairly ordinary rocks, the meteorites are in fact made from solid metal, mostly iron, with nickel and some smaller amounts of cobalt, phosphorus and other trace elements. The average weight of the meteorites is an impressive 348.5 kg and in total 77 rocks were originally recovered of which a total of 33 are on display here.

Other sights of interest

The **Crafts Market**, running most of the way down Post Street is an enjoyable place to wander around, whether you're planning on buying any souvenirs or not. If you do decide to buy be prepared to bargain over the price. You should be able to pick up some objects at considerably lower prices than in the boutiques around town.

The **Namibia Crafts Centre** is located in the old breweries building next to the Warehouse Theatre. This is a small indoor market on two floors, selling a variety of Namibian carvings, pottery, basket, leatherwork, jewellery and artwork. It also houses an earthy cafe frequented by tourists as well as some of Windhoek's artsy crowd. Recommended. ■ *40 Tal St, Mon-Fri 0900-1730, Sat 0900-1330.*

If you're interested in African arts and crafts **Bushman Art**, a trendy boutique on Independence Avenue opposite the park is worth a visit as it has probably the best selection of souvenirs anywhere in Windhoek. In the back of the store there's an interesting display of carvings, metalwork, jewellery and pottery from all over the continent.

Other buildings of interest around Windhoek are the **Roman Catholic Cathedral** on the corner of Stübel and Bülow streets, the **Turnhalle Building** on Bahnhof Street which played a role in the process of Namibian independence, and the **Railway Station** itself.

The **Windhoek Conservatoire** on the corner of Peter Müller and Stübel streets, built in 1911-12, was formerly the Regierungsschule (Governement School), and has an impressive ornamental weather vane perched on top of its pyramidal tower.

The **statue** of **Curt von François** stands outside the Windhoek Municipality on Independence Avenue, and was unveiled in 1965 on the 75th anniversary of the 'founding' of the city.

A short distance from the city centre sitting atop a series of hills to the east are Windhoek's three elegant castles, **Schwerinburg**, **Heinitzburg** and **Sanderburg**. All three were designed by the architect Willi Sander, the first for Graf Schwerin in 1914, and the second for his wife as her residence. The design of Schwerinburg incorporates an original stone structure built by Curt von François and used as a lookout post in the early days of the Schutztruppe's presence in Windhoek. Sander designed the third castle for himself in 1917.

Heinitzburg Castle on Heinitz Strasse is open to the public as a luxury hotel; however anyone can go and have coffee on the terrace which offers one of the best views of central Windhoek and the mountains of the Khomas Hochland to the west. The terrace coffee shop is open from 1000-1800 and it is well worth the effort of walking up from the city centre to enjoy the views. Sanderburg Castle is privately owned and Schwerinburg Castle, which used to house the Italian Embassy, was recently sold for an undisclosed sum.

The **Hofmeyer Walk** takes about an hour, and if you're feeling moderately energetic is worth the effort for the views it offers of the Klein Windhoek valley. The best time for the walk is March/April when a variety of aloes are in bloom. You can start the walk either in Sinclair Street or at the upper end of Uhland Street.

Avis Dam, on the eastern outskirts of the city on the way to the international airport, is a popular spot for birdwatchers particularly just before the first summer rains fall, when more than a hundred different species have been reported in a day.

City drive

If you have a car you might be interested in taking a drive around the city to get a feel for the residential areas. The Shell map of Namibia has a good map of Windhoek which also covers Katutura and Khomasdal. With this you can plan a route to take you round the city, or you can follow the signs from the city centre towards **Daan Viljoen Game Reserve** until you reach the **Western Bypass**. Take this road north and on your right between Pioneer's Park and Hochland Park you will see the site of the **Old Location**, lying cleared of its former buildings but never subsequently developed. Continue on towards **Khomasdal** which will be on your left hand side, and before you reach **Katutura** you should join **Independence Avenue**; depending on how you feel about being a wealthy foreigner and voyeur in the township, you could choose to drive into Katutura down Independence Avenue and take a walk around the covered market. Alternatively, you might choose to follow the signs back towards the city centre. If on the other hand you should find someone to act as your guide, a walk through Katutura is interesting and worthwhile, not least when one bears in mind that this former township is now larger than the main part of the city, and additionally is a melting pot for Namibians from all parts of the country.

Back in town, drive down **Nelson Mandela Avenue** past the Indian High Commission on your right hand side, and before reaching the **Quba Mosque** turn left and drive up any one of a series of extremely steep hills and you will find yourself in **Ludwigsdorf**, probably the most exclusive part of the city. Mansions here come fully equipped with swimming pools, gyms and even squash courts in some cases. Rejoin Mandela and turn right onto **Sam Nujoma Drive** which will take you back into the centre of town. Alternatively meander up the streets to the south of Sam Nujoma Avenue for a closer look at the castles. From there make your way back into town.

Museums and galleries

Alte Feste Display & Education Centre Houses the historical section of the **State Museum** and is an interesting place to go to get a feel for both Namibia's colonial heritage and her fight for independence. ■ *Robert Mugabe Avenue. Mon-Fri 0900-1800, Weekends 1000-1300 and 1500-1800.*

Owela Museum Natural history museum with dioramas of traditional village life. Also has a permanent cheetah exhibition which seeks to educate people about Africa's most endangered cat, the largest population of which is found in Namibia. ■ *Robert Mugabe Avenue next to State House. Mon-Fri 0900-1800, weekends 1000-1300 and 1500-1800, closed public holidays.*

National Gallery Houses a permanent display reflecting a spectrum of both historical and contemporary Namibian art, including the work of well-known artist John Mufangeyo. ■ *Corner of John Meinert Street and Robert Mugabe Avenue. Mon-Fri 0900-1700, Sat 0900-1100, closed Sun.*

Transnamib Transport Museum Housed upstairs in the **Old Railway Station Building** has well laid out and extensive collection depicting the history of rail and other transport in Namibia over the past 100 years. ■ *Bahnhoff Street. Weekdays 0900-1300 and 1400-1700, closed weekends and public holidays. N$5 adults, N$3 children (under 18).*

Tours

As long as you are up to walking around the city there isn't really any need to sign up for an organized tour of Windhoek. Most of the tour companies (see Essentials) offer one-day game-viewing and sundowner tours to guestfarms around Windhoek and if you're really pressed for time you might well want to consider opting for one of these. If you're in the country on business for a few days, then a day in the bush with a knowledgeable guide followed by a Sundowner and optional braai makes for a good break and is well worth it. Elena Travel Service, PO Box 3127. T244443. They also organize day trips to Arnhem Cave and the Ibenstein Weavery. Namibia Breweries, T262915, have tours and beer tasting at their factory in the northern industrial area.

Essentials

Phone code: 061

As a general rule two people sharing a double room get a much better rate than one person on their own as most places don't actually have single rooms

Windhoek offers a good range of hotel and guesthouse accommodation, from the 4-star luxury of the *Windhoek Country Club* to dormitories for backpackers at the *Cardboard Box*. Unless you need to be near either of the airports there is no need to look for accommodation outside the city centre whilst you are in Windhoek. The larger hotels, apart from the *Safari Hotel* by Eros Airport, are all either on or close to Independence Avenue, whilst most guesthouses are found in suburbs close to the city centre.

Making a choice between staying in a hotel or a guesthouse is less about price than about atmosphere. Broadly speaking the guesthouses, many of which are run by German-speaking Namibians, tend to be smaller and more personal than the hotels, but offer similar facilities, with en suite bathrooms and televisions available in most. One major difference is that although all guesthouses listed here offer breakfast, they generally do not have restaurants or bars, so meals need to be eaten out. Room service also tends not to be on offer in the guesthouse, so if you prefer to remain relatively anonymous but still enjoy being waited on, then a hotel will be a better choice.

Sleeping

Hotels

■ *on maps, pages 71, 75, 83 and 84*
Price codes: see inside front cover

A *Windhoek Country Club*, Western bypass, located south of the town centre just beyond Eros airport. Regular bus transfers to city centre, T2055911, F252797, hrwccr@ stocks.com.na 152 a/c luxury rooms (all spacious and comfortable). Two quality restaurants, poolside snack bar, casino. This is the best of its kind in Namibia but it may not suit someone planning a quiet holiday. Nevertheless this is the ideal place from which to start and finish your visit. Located next to an 18-hole golf course. Recommended. **A-B** *Kalahari Sands Hotel*, Independence Av, T222300, F222260. A/c, TV, restaurants, pool, gym, casino and roof-top pool, a Windhoek landmark right in the centre of the city, all you'd expect of a 4-star hotel, very popular with both local and overseas business people, good views over Windhoek. **B** *Hotel Heinitzburg*, Heinitzburg Strasse, T249597, F249598. Stylish old world style rooms with all mod cons in this turn of the century castle, with magnificent views over the city, swimming pool. Recommended. **B-C** *Safari Court & Hotel Safari*, Rehoboth Weg (B1 S), well placed for Eros Airport, T240240, F235652/223017. Offers 2 hotels in one with a/c, TV, restaurants, pool and free transport 0700-1900 into city centre. **B-D** *Continental Hotel*, Independence Av, T237293, F231539. Right in the middle of town has a variety of rooms from standard to luxury which includes en suite bathroom, a/c, TV, minibar, room service, the hotel also has a sauna, 2 bars, disco and restaurant. **C** *Hotel Fürstenhof*, T237380, F228751, Bülow St. Well known for the quality of its continental style restaurant, comfortable rooms, a/c, TV, bar, secure parking, within easy walking distance of the city centre. **C** *Thüringer Hof Hotel*, Independence Av, T226031, F232981. Known for its beer garden is a comfortable old-style hotel close to the city centre, the staff are friendly and the rooms have en suite bathrooms, a/c, TV. Recommended.

Guesthouses

Price generally including cooked breakfast

B *Villa Verdi*, Verdi St, T221994, F222574. Within easy walking distance of the city centre, offers tasteful African theme rooms with TV, phone, pool, comfortable lounge and secure parking. Recommended. **B-C** *Charlotte's Guesthouse*, 2A John Ludwig St, T/F228846. Luxury suites set around a lush courtyard. A very comfortable start and finish to your stay in Namibia. Recommended. *Ekundu Guesthouse*, 10 Johann Albrecht St, T253440, F230729. 8 twin rooms with ensuite bath and t.v. Secure parking on premises. 5 min walk from town. Conference facilities. Recommended. **C** *Kleines Heim*, Volans St, T248200, F248203. Acquired its name from its function as a maternity home during the days of the 'Old Location', smart English cottage style rooms with showers,

TV, phone, bar, conference facilities built around small pool. Recommended. **C** *Pension Cela*, Bülow St, T226294/5, F226246. Centrally located, has rooms with en suite showers, phone, mini bar, TV, laundry service and secure parking. Recommended. **C** *Pension Moni*, Nesser St, T228350, F227124. 12 double rooms, swimming pool. Makes a pitch for the 'budget-conscious traveller' with good cooked breakfasts.

Windhoek centre

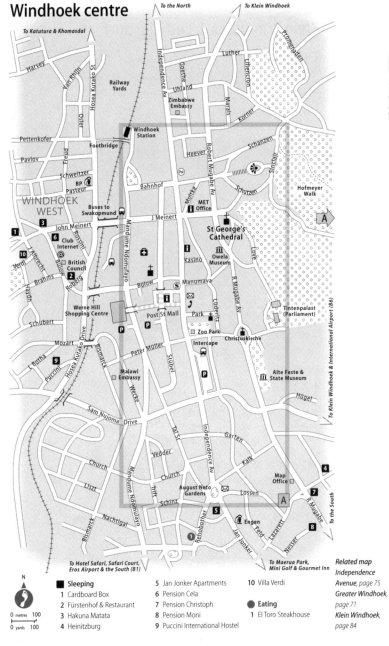

Sleeping
1 Cardboard Box
2 Fürstenhof & Restaurant
3 Hakuna Matata
4 Heinitzburg
5 Jan Jonker Apartments
6 Pension Cela
7 Pension Christoph
8 Pension Moni
9 Puccini International Hostel
10 Villa Verdi

Eating
1 El Toro Steakhouse

Related map
Independence
Avenue, page 75
Greater Windhoek,
page 71
Klein Windhoek,
page 84

C *Pension Christoph*, corner of Henitzburg St and Robert Mugabe Av, T240777, F248560. Close to the city centre, 12 double rooms with showers, fans, TV, phone and swimming pool. An excellent small, family run, pension. The author's favourite, and judging from the amount of repeat trade, the same applies for most guests. Nearly always full – book well in advance to avoid disappointment. **C** *Hotel Pension Steiner*, 11 Weckerstrasse, T222898, F224234. Clean en suite rooms, swimming pool, braai area, lounge. Recommended. **D** *Hotel-Pension Alexander*, 10 Beethoven St, T240775.

Klein Windhoek & Ludwigsdorf

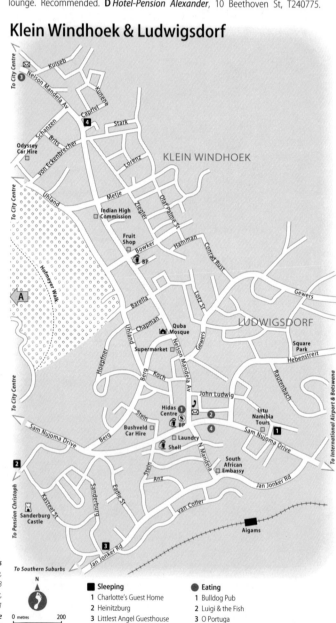

Related maps
Windhoek centre,
page 83
Greater Windhoek,
page 71
Independence
Avenue, page 75

N

0 metres 200
0 yards 200

■ **Sleeping**
1 Charlotte's Guest Home
2 Heinitzburg
3 Littlest Angel Guesthouse
4 Roof of Africa

● **Eating**
1 Bulldog Pub
2 Luigi & the Fish
3 O Portuga
4 Yangste

Behind the Werne Hill Park shopping centre close to the city centre, has en suite rooms, some with baths, TV, parking and TV lounge.

E *Littlest Angel Guesthouse*, 106 Jan Jonker Weg, T231639. 5-min drive from town has **Bed &** rooms in the family house with basic cooking facilities, telephone and en suite bath- **breakfast** rooms. Popular with volunteers. **E-F** *Marie's Guesthouse*, 156 Diaz St, Suiderhof, T251787/251766, F252128. 10-min drive from the city centre, variety of rooms and self-catering flats, guests can use the pool and braai area.

A few years ago Windhoek was poorly served but now there are at least 10 places to **Backpacker's** choose from. This is good news for the budget traveller as the standard of service **hostels** should continue to improve and hopefully more backpackers will have the opportunity to enjoy the country. If you are not happy with your choice, move on. If this is the case please let us know so we can continue to provide useful tips and information. **D-F** *Globetrotter Backpacker's Lodge*, Independence Av, August Neto Gardens, T223249, F227698. Centrally located and offers secure parking, 10 en suite twin rooms and 3 rooms with 6 beds, popular with Overlanders, bookings advisable especially for groups, can be noisy at night. **E-F** *Cardboard Box*, 15 Johan Albrecht St, T228994, F256581. Long-time first choice with backpackers, is close to town and has double rooms and dorms, weekly rates also available, TV, bar, swimming pool, cooking facilities, car hire is one of the cheapest around, notice board with travellers' information. Over-subscribed by the younger set but still very popular. **E-F** *Chameleon Backpackers*, 22 Wagner St, T/F247668. Lies at the top of a steepish climb past the polytechnic, 10-15 mins from city centre, rooms and four 6-bed dorms with communal kitchen and common room with TV, phone/fax, pool, secure parking and car hire also available, popular with mature travellers. **F** *Backpacker Unite*, 5 Grieg St, T/F259485, mobT081-1298093. Room for up to 22 people, dorms and double rooms, kitchen, TV lounge, swimming pool, sauna. Run by Hermann and Erica. Good value tours to the desert can be organized from here. **F** *Hakuna Matata*, 78 John Meinert St, T/F245444. Look out for the blue and yellow wall. Dorms, kitchen, TV, laundry, swimming pool, secure parking. **F** *Puccini International Hostel*, 4 Puccini St, T/F236355. Dorm, double rooms, camping, rates include breakfast. Kitchen, laundry, secure parking, lockers, swimming pool, sauna. Close to city centre. **F** *Roof of Africa*, 124 Nelson Mandela Av, corner with Gusinde St, T254708, F248048, 081-1244930 (mob). A neat, new, setup in the northern areas of Klein Windhoek. Dorms, double rooms and camping (tents provided), a well equipped kitchen, bar, lockers, secure off street parking, e-mail facilities. Free pick-up from town centre. Recommended.

C *Jan Jonker Holiday Apartments*, 183 Jan Jonker Weg, T221236, F238794. Fully **Self-catering** equipped modern flats, cooking facilities, phone, TV, video, secure parking, close to city centre. Recommended.

C-F *Arebbusch Travel Lodge*, Rehoboth Weg (B1 S), on the outskirts of town. 2 and 5 **Camping** bed bungalows, en suite double rooms, and camping/caravan sites, bar, shop, laundrette and pool, closest camping to centre of town. Recommended. **F** *Daan Viljoen Game Park*. Caravan and campsite, maximum 8 people, 2 vehicles, 1 caravan or tent per site, communal ablution blocks, field kitchens.

C *Auas Game Lodge*, T240043, F248633. Follow B1 23 km south of Windhoek, turn **Guestfarms** onto D1463 for 22 km to farm. 16 large double rooms, swimming pool, tennis court, golf, hiking, stocked farm with giraffe, wildebeest, eland, blesbok, dam for birdwatching, including breakfast.: **C** *Düsternbrook*, T232572, F257112. Follow B1 towards Okahandja, after 30 km take D1499, follow for 10 km and then follow sign for

Windhoek

farm. 4 doubles, 2 singles in old Geman colonial farmhouse, restaurant, swimming pool, stocked game farm with giraffe, eland, wildebeest, leopard for game viewing, bird-watching, hiking trails, all inclusive. **C** *Eagle Rock Leisure Lodge*, T/F234542. Follow C28 towards Swakopmund for 38 km, take D1958 for Wilhelmstal, turn off at sign for Eagle's Rock. 4 double bungalows, 1 family unit, restaurant, swimming pool, TV, video, hiking trails, horse riding, game drives in Khomas Hochland close to Daan Viljoen, all inclusive. **C** *Midgard Guestfarm*, T0621-503888, F503818. Follow B6 towards Gobabis for 20 km, turn onto D2102 for 60 km. En suite double bungalows, organic dining under poolside lapa, tennis, volleyball, badminton, hiking, horse riding, game drives in Otjihavera Mountains, rather large and impersonal though. **C** *Weissenfels*, T0628 (Friedental) 1213, F061-226999. Follow C26 towards Gamsberg Pass for 114 km, follow signs to farm. 5 en suite rooms, pool, hiking, horse riding, game viewing, birdwatching in Gamsberg Mnts.

Other guestfarms in the area *Corona* T0628(Friedental)-1330, F061-251084. *Elisenheim*, T/F264429. *Finkenstein*, T234751, F238890. *Hochland*, T232628, F238890. *Hope*, T0628(Nina)-3202, F061-223899. *Kamab*, T/F0621-503708. *Karivo*, T560028, F238486. *Kuzikus Game Ranch*, T0628(Nina)-3102, F061-225000. *Mountain View Game Lodge*, T560008, F560009. *Niedersachsen*, T0628(Hochland)-1102, F061-225820. *Okapuka Ranch*, T234607, F234690. *Okatore Lodge*, T/F232840. *Ondekaremba*, T0626-40424, F40133. *Rooisand Desert Ranch*, T0628(Friedental)-1302. *Silversand*, T06202-1102, F061-235501. *Sundown Lodge*, T232566, F232541. *Swarfontein*, T0628(Namibgrens)-1112, F061-226999.

Eating

● on maps, pages 71, 75, 83, and 84 There are plenty of places to eat out in Windhoek, however many restaurants offer the same meaty fare of steak, ribs, schnitzel and hamburgers. There are a small number of restaurants offering a more varied menu, but vegetarians are unlikely to find anything to write home about, as the vast majority of Namibians are serious carnivores. If you do like your meat there are some interesting game dishes on offer, gemsbok steak, kudu kebabs and crocodile tail being a few of the delicacies you can try. Prices are reasonable by European/North American standards, from around N$120 for 2 for a light meal with drinks up to N$350 for a serious meal and wine in one of the better establishments. **NB** Most restaurants close by 2300, after which sausage and chips from the nearest garage takeaway will be your only option.

Continental *O'Portuga*, Eros, T272900. Great Portuguese cuisine, good wine. *Homestead Restaurant*, 53 Feld St by August Neto Gardens, T221958/221990. Interesting and varied menu with pleasant seating outside on terrace or inside, friendly though rather slow service amply compensated by the quality of the food, worth making a reservation on weekends and at the end of the month. Recommended. *Fürstenhof Hotel*, Bülow St, T237380. Renowned for its high quality food and good service, worth making a reservation and dressing semi-smart for. Recommended. *Gourmet Inn*, 195 Jan Jonker Weg and corner of Centaurus St, T232360. Excellent and very popular restaurant with a varied menu including fresh sea food and a range of vegetarian dishes, good service, relaxed atmosphere, bookings essential. Recommended. *Gathemann's Restaurant*, Gathemann Building, 139 Independence Av, T223853. Upstairs dining with terrace overlooking the street, busy, smartish German restaurant specializing in hearty meat dishes and expensive wines, bookings recommended for the evening. *La Bella Vita*, Kaiserkrone Building, Post Street Mall, T230141, formerly known as Marco Polo, serves a basic range of Italian food as well as the more recognized, meaty Namibian specialities. Pleasant outdoor courtyard seating in an historic building plus comfortable relaxed indoor section, and a separate 'fast' lunchtime menu to cater for central Windhoek business crowd. *Luigi & The Fish*, Sam Nujoma Drive, T256399. Bar and restaurant with a sundowner deck. Sardinia, 39 Independence Av close to August Neto Gardens, T225600. Good value Italian family run café/restaurant specializing in great pizzas, pasta and a small number of traditional Italian dishes, excellent espresso, cappuccino and ice creams in the café at the front, dining in the popular restaurant at the back. Closed Tue. Recommended. *Abyssinia*, Lossen Str, T254891. Tasty ethnic Ethiopian food, interesting place but a touch costly. *Africa Restuarant*, Alte Feste, T247178. Novelty African dishes and a great spot for sundowners.

Yang Tze Restaurant, Sam Nujoma Drive, just after the Klein Windhoek crossing, T234779. Closed Sun and Mon lunchtime. Newly relocated but well-established restaurant catering for both the western and eastern palates. If you want authentic Chinese, ask for the other menu – recommended. *China Grand Restaurant*, Kenya House, Robert Mugabe Av, T225751. Authentic mainland Chinese cooking and decor, large portions, friendly service. Recommended. **Chinese**

These are generally the most popular eating places in Windhoek and many are chain restaurants. They all serve more or less the same type of food for similar prices with the odd speciality here and there. The portions tend to be generous, the meat good quality, the service American style and the atmosphere relaxed and informal. Some are also popular drinking holes with young (white) Namibians and get pretty crowded and loud later in the evenings. Overall if meat's your thing then the following offer good value. **Steakhouse restaurants**

Grand Canyon Spur, 251 Independence Av, T231003. Good value steaks and hamburgers as well as a variety of spicy Mexican dishes. *Dros*, Post Street Mall, T242740. Nice steaks with nice prices. Saddles, T233292, Maerua Park, Centaurus Rd, next door to the cinema. *O'Hagan's Irish Pub and Grill*, corner of Robert Mugabe and Jan Jonker streets, access via Centaurus St, T234677. Pub lunches, evening grills, popular evening drinking hole. *El Toro Steakhouse*, Snyman Circle, 4 Rehobother Weg, T226093. Spanish style steakhouse, huge portions, good service – the best in Windhoek. Recommended. *Restaurant zum Wirt*, 101 Independence Av, T234503. Aryan in food and atmosphere.

Le Bistro, corner of Post Street Mall and Independence Av, popular spot in the heart of town with seating inside and out under umbrellas, offering good cooked breakfasts, pizzas, pasta, gyros for lunch and supper, after work drinking spot for young Windhoekers. *Central Cafe*, Levinson Arcade, Independence Av. Busy breakfast and lunchtime spot, schnitzels, bratwurst, plus takeaway rolls and coffee. *Cafe Schneider*, Levinson Arcade, Independence Av, T226304. German style restaurant popular at lunchtimes, look out for daily specials. *Gert's Klause Restaurant*, Sanlam Building. Popular lunchtimes for snacks and light meals. *Golden Gate Coffee Bar*, Maerua Park Mall, Centaurus St. Has an excellent variety of salad lunches, as good as anywhere in Windhoek, as well as a wide range of fresh coffees. **Cafés**

There are numerous fast food outlets all over central Windhoek, including *Kentucky Fried Chicken*, *King Pie* and *Nando's Chicken*. In addition most Portuguese corner shops and many garages also have fried chicken, sausages and chips to takeaway. **Fastfood**

Bars

During the day most of the cafés mentioned also serve as bars. In the evening there is not a massive choice of drinking places, and many double as nightclubs/disco bars (listed under nightlife) charging between N$5-10 admittance. Since in Namibia a liquor license is required before a gambling permit is issued, small bars often have slot machines lining the walls. Opening hrs are variable, but all are open until late. **Bulldog Pub**, Hidas Centre, Nelson Mandela Av. **Joe's Beer House**, Eros Shopping Centre, Nelson Mandela Av. A very popular spot complete with mock olde worlde interior with barbecue and bar area. For many residents this is their favourite good value venue. **The Factory**, Tal St. Popular with the Afrikaner crowd. **The Plaza Café Bistro Bar**, Maerua Park Mall, Centaurus St, is popular as an after cinema drinking spot with trendy young Windhoekers. **The Royal Hotel**, Independence Av, Aussppanplatz. Erstwhile Irish pub, now converted into a sports bar with cable TV, pool tables on one side, and all-white country music bar on the other, entrance via the car park at the back.

Entertainment

Art galleries The National Art Gallery, Robert Mugabe Av and John Meinnert St, exhibitions and permanent display of Namibian and other African art.

Cinema Sterkinekor, Maerua Park Mall, Centaurus St, T248980, 3-screen cinema with showings from midday until 2200. Wed tickets are less than half price so you need to buy them early as it gets crowded fast.

Gambling There are numerous bars with slot machines as well as book makers covering horse racing from South Africa. In 1995 casinos were legalized and there has been a steady development of venues. The larger and smarter casinos are found at the **Windhoek Country Club Resort**, Western Bypass, T205911. **Kalahari Sands Hotel**, Gustav Voigts Centre, Independence Av, T222300 and the **Hotel Safari**, on the B1 heading south towards Rehoboth.

Health clubs **Virgin Active**, Maerua Park, Centaurus Rd, T234399. Is the largest and best equipped gym in Windhoek with indoor swimming pool, squash courts, a full range of weights machines, aerobics classes and saunas and a warm pool all year round, their cheapest deal is a monthly fee of N$99. **Nucleus Health and Fitness Centre**, 40 Tal St, T225493. Is smaller but has a good range of weight machines and also has aerobic classes.

Nightlife **The National Theatre of Namibia**, Robert Mugabe Av, T/F237966. Stages plays, opera, dance, mime. **The College of Arts**, Peter Müller St, T225841, F229007. Has classical music concerts, ballet and modern dance. **The Warehouse Theatre**, 42 Tal St. Is the most popular live music venue in Windhoek featuring rock, jazz and African bands from Africa and Europe, excellent atmosphere, late bar, recommended, check local press for details. **The Woofer**, Kelvin St, in the Southern Industrial Area is popular with the 'in' young white crowd and has a disco and late night drinking. **Kuddisanga**, Bahnhof St. Mixed, young crowd, kizomba (Angolan music), rap, hip-hop, rave, Wed, Fri, Sat all night. **Club Thriller**, Katutura. Plays a mixture of the latest club sounds and African dance music, with the occasional band outside in the courtyard, open until very late, a taxi is the best way to get there or a local guide recommended. **Club Pamodze**, Antiochie St, Wanaheda, Katutura. Plays up-to-date dance music until late, again you'll need to take a taxi or a local guide to find it.

Sports

Spectator: Football and rugby are played at their respective Independence Stadia just off the B1 heading south. Check local press for match details. **Swimming**: the municipal pool is located at Maerua Park, Centaurus St.

Festivals

Apr/May *Windhoek Carnival*, a 2-week traditional German festival culminates with a parade down Independence Avenue. During the festival there are various cabaret evenings and an all night masked ball. Check press for details.

26 Aug *Herero Day* in Okahandja commemorates fallen war heroes and involves a parade through town to the graves of former leaders.

Oct Festival is held at the end of the month with beer and 'oompah' bands. Organized by Sportklub Windhoek, T235521.

1-8 Oct *Windhoek Industrial and Agricultural Show*.

Nov *Enjando St Festival* takes place towards the end of the month in Independence Av with traditional music and dance. Information from Windhoek Information and Publicity, T2902050.

Shopping

African Curiotique, Gustav Voigts Centre, Independence Av. *Crafts Centre*, Tal St, next to the Warehouse Theatre. *Craft Shop*, corner of Independence and Garten St, no name on front of shop! *Master Weaver*, Werne Hill Shopping Centre, stocks wide range of southern African carpets, wall hangings and other crafts. *Namibia Crafts Centre*, 40 Tal St. *Namos & Tameka Crafts Shop*, Gustav Voigts Centre, Independence Av. *Oshiwa Workshop*, 8 Sinclair St, mornings only. *Post Street Mall outdoor market*. *Rogel Souvenirs*, delivers world wide, 177 Independence Ave.
Arts & crafts

Books are unfortunately expensive in Namibia, subject as they are to 15% value added tax (VAT). Until recently most reading on Namibia history and culture was only available in the form of the excellent DISCOURSE/MSORP publications available in most bookshops. However, in the last two or three years there has been a steady growth in up-to-date, informative books on different aspects of Namibia. *Bücher Keller*, Peter Müller St. *CNA*, Gustav Voigts Centre, Independence Av and Werne Hill Shopping Centre. *New Namibia Books*, Post Street Mall, especially good for books on Namibia and Southern Africa. *The Book Den*, Frans Indongo Gardens, Bülow St.
Books, magazines & newspapers

Nitzsche-Reiter, corner of Peter Müller and Independence. *Photo World*, Independence Av opposite Bülow St.
Camera equipment

Cymot, 60 Mandume Ndemufayo Av. *Ernst Holtz Safari Land*, Gustav Voigts Centre, Independence Av, wide range of hiking and safari clothes. *Trappers Trading Co*, Post Street Mall, wide range of outdoor clothes and camping equipment. *Safari Den*, 8 Bessemer St, Southern Industria.
Camping

Edgars, Post Street Mall. *Foschini*, corner of Independence and Peter Müller. *Markhams*, corner of Independence and Peter Müller. *Model Woolworths*, Werne Hill Shopping Centre, end Post Street Mall. *Otto Mühr Mens' Outfitters*, Independence Av. *Truworths*, Levinson Arcade.
Clothes

Hamm Pelze Furs, Gustav Voigts Centre, Independence Av. *Nakara*, Kronprinz Building, Independence Av, high quality karakul leather clothes. *Pelz Haus*, corner of Daniel Munamava and Independence Av, karakul leather and furs.
Furs & leather

G Leiten, Gustav Voigts Centre, Independence Av. *Namib Jewellers*, Kronprinz Building, Independence Av. *Rocks and Gems*, corner of Post St and Independence, semi-precious stones and jewellery.
Gems & jewellery

Maps Detailed maps are available from the Surveyor General's office on Robert Mugabe Av. The office is a short walk from the junction with Lazarett St. All types of maps can be bought here. The 1:50,000 are useful if you plan on doing some hiking. The 1:250,000 are useful for the remote areas where some of the road signs can be confusing.

Supermarkets *Model*, Werne Hill Shopping Centre, end Post St Mall. *Checkers*, Gustav Voigts Centre, Independence Av. *Shoprite*, Independence Av.

Tour operators There is a bewildering array of tour companies offering safaris in Namibia and southern Africa, by plane, by 4WD, and on foot. If you plan to book an organized tour from your own country, the best bet is to locate a travel agent with a link to a tour company in Namibia, as they will probably be able to get you the best deals. Alternatively, if you prefer top have everything arranged before you arrive it is worth contacting a Namibia specialist travel agency in Europe – such as *Sunvil Africa* (see Planning your trip, page 18). Below is listed the main tour companies and the specialities they offer.

There are a multitude of tour operators in the country offering everything from fly-in safaris to the Skeleton Coast and Okavango Delta, hiking tours of Damaraland and canoe safaris down the Kunene River. Many companies offer guided trips to the remoter parts of the country for small groups. With some you have to come as a ready made group, with others you can join up with an existing group. As most have offices in the city centre they're easy to get to, and it's worth visiting a few in person to discuss the various options and to compare prices.

Adozu Tours, 6 Erikson St, T236634, F235453, will arrange off-road safaris and camping trips. *Baobab Tours*, 7 Willan St, Cultural and Environmental Tours, T224017, F232314. *Chameleon Safaris*, T/F247668, chamnam@chameleon.com.na, www.millennia.co.za/chameleon, offer camping safaris. *Crazy Kudu Safaris*, T/F222636. *Eden Travel Consultancy*, 6 Andraditstrasse, Eros Park, T/F234342, arranges fly-ins to neighbouring countries. *Enyandi Car Hire & Safaris*, 135 Krupp St, T255103, F303892. Car hire and B&B for guests. *Gondwana Tours* in Keetmanshoop, T0631-23892, will organize trips to the Fish River Canyon and Namaqualand. *Karibu Safaris*, 53 Krupp St, Suiderhof, T251661, offer guided off-road driving and hiking trips in the bush. *Makalani Safaris*, T233101, F233102, can arrange personalized off-road safaris. *Mola Mola Safaris* in Walvis Bay, T064-205511, F207593, offer ski boat fishing and dolphin viewing trips off the Namibian coast. *Namib Pappot Safaris* in Maltahöhe, T0663-3042, F3180, arrange tours of the Namib Desert, Damaraland and Kaokoland. *Namib Sky Safari Adventures* in Maltahöhe, T0663-25703, specialize in balloon trips above the dunes of Sossusvlei. *Namibian Tourist Friend*, T249408, F233485, arrange fly-drive safaris over Windhoek, the Namib and as far as Lüderitz in the south. *Ondese Travel & Safaris*, Kunene Court, Heliodore St, T220876, F239700. *Oryx Tours*, 11 Van der Bijil St, Northern Industrial Area, T217454, F263417, are of the larger tour companies offering coach tours around Namibia. *Pasjona Safaris*, T/F223421, give guided tours. *Ritz Reise Travel Agency*, 250 Independence Ave, T236670, F227575. *Southern Cross Safaris*, 10 TV More St, T221193. *SWA Safaris*, 43 Independence Ave, T221193, F225387, another large coach tour company. *Trip Travel Agency Independence Ave*, T236880, F225430, offer some of the best deals around. *Trans Namibia Tours*, 414 Independence Ave, T221549, F230960, also specialize in eco-tourism. *Welwitschia Travel*, Post St Mall, T225710, are a reliable company. *WTS Travel Service*, 6 Peter Müller St, T237946, F225932.

Transport

Windhoek is in the centre of the country, all the surfaced highways and railways radiate out from here. The pattern of the road network makes it difficult to do a circuit of the country without having to return to Windhoek at some point – unless you want to spend a lot of time driving on gravel roads of variable condition.

It is 1,218 km to Katima Mulilo, 482 km to Keetmanshoop, 850 km to Lüderitz, 533 km to Namutoni (Etosha NP), 786 km to Noordoewer (South Africa border), 435 km to Okakuejo (Etosha NP), 350 km to Swakopmund, 1435 km to Victoria Falls (via the Caprivi Strip).

Car hire: More and more visitors are choosing to tour the country in their own vehicle. There is a lot of competition, but the best car hire rates will be fixed if you make a firm booking several months in advance. If you leave car hire until you arrive in Namibia you may find it difficult to get a car and the rates will be high. Expect to pay between N$250-400 per day for a saloon car. For 4WD prices usually start around N$800 per day. *Andes*, 25 Voigt St, T256334, F228552. *Asco Car Hire*, 10 Diehl St, Southern Industrial Estate, T233064/5, F232245. *Avis*, *Safari Hotel*, Aviation Rd, T233166, F233072. *Budget*, 72 Mandume Ndemufayo Av, T228720, F227665. *Camping Car Hire*, corner of Mandume Ndemufayo Av and Edison St, Southern Industrial Area, T237756, F237757. *Champion Four-Wheel Drive Hire*, 165 Diaz St, Suiderhof, T251306, F251620. *Enyandi Car Hire & Safaris*, 135 Krupp St, T255103, F303892. *East End Land Rover Hire*, 335 Sam Nujoma Drive, T233869. *Imperial*, 43 Stübel St, T227103, F222721. *Kessler*, PO Box 20274, Windhoek, T/F256323, kessler@iafrica.com.na, www.kessler.com.na. *Odyssey*, 23 Schanzenweg, T223269, F228911. *Pegasus Car and Camper Hire*, 53 Bülo St, T251451. *Savanna*, corner John Meinert and Mandume Ndemufayo streets, T227778, F223292 a/h T252060. Probably the best deal in Windhoek. Limited cars, so book well in advance.

Local

Air International: There are currently no major European airlines flying directly into Windhoek's Hosea Kutoko International Airport. This means that the only practical alternative route is to fly into Johannesburg or Cape Town (there are plenty of flights every day from Europe) and then transfer to a *South African Airways*, *British Airways* (Com Air) or *Air Namibia* flight to Windhoek.

Air Namibia serves the following towns from Windhoek: Swakopmund, Lüderitz , Oranjemund, Keetmanshoop, Katimo Mulilo (Mpacha), Mokuti, Ondangwa, Luanda (Angola), Victoria Falls and Harare (Zimbabwe), Lusaka (Zambia), Johannesburg and Cape Town (South Africa). Check when booking which airport your flight departs from. Most domestic flights fly from Eros Airport. *Comair*, T248528, F248529 **Johannesburg** (2½ hrs). *LTU*, T237480, flights to **Munich** and **Düsseldorf**. LTU also fly from **Cape Town** to Munich and Düsseldorf. *South African Airways*, T231118, operate direct flights to Cape Town and Johannesburg, from these two towns there are onward connections to all major towns in South Africa as well as Zimbabwe, Botswana, Malawi and Moçambique. **Cape Town** (2 hrs), **Johannesburg** (1½ hrs).

Long distance

Domestic flights from Eros A variety of private and charter companies fly from here, if you have booked on a safari which starts with a flight out of Windhoek make sure you check which airport they are using. *Air Namibia* have at least 1 local flight a day from here. **Keetmanshoop** (95 mins), **Lüderitz** (2½ hrs), **Mokuti, Ondangwa** (2½ hrs), **Ongava** (2 hrs), **Rundu** (2½ hrs), **Swakopmund** (45 mins), and **Tsumeb** (1 hr).

Road *Intercape*, T061-227847, see timetable on page 382. The coaches from South Africa and Swakopmund direction all terminate by the taxi rank and information booth on the corner of Independence and Müller streets, close to the *Kalahari Sands Hotel*. The service no longer runs to Tsumeb. **Cape Town** (21 hrs), via Rehoboth, Mariental and Noordoewer (border post), Mon, Wed, Fri, Sun, 1800. **Keetmanshoop** (5 hrs), Mon, Wed, Fri, Sun, 1900. **Swakopmund** (3½ hrs), Mon, Wed, Fri, Sat, 0700. **Upington** (10

Reservations must be made 72 hrs before departure

Windhoek

hrs), Mon, Wed, Fri, Sun, 1900. **Victoria Falls**. **Walvis Bay** (4 hrs), Mon, Wed, Fri, Sat, 0700. **Swakopmund**: a cheap (N$70) minibus service departs from the Caltex Garage by Rhino Park Hospital. You may have to wait 2-3 hrs for the bus to fill up. They might be fun and cheap, but they are dangerous. We do not advise using the service.

Train Gobabis (7½ hrs), Tue, Thu, Sun, 2200. **Keetmanshoop** (11 hrs), via Rehoboth and Mariental, daily except Sat, 1900. **Swakopmund** and **Walvis Bay** (9 hrs), daily except Sat, 2000. **Tsumeb** (16 hrs), via Omaruru and Otjiwarongo, Tue, Thu, Sun, 1800. See also timetables on page 383.

The Desert Express: bookings at the Railway Station. T2982600, F2982601. This is Namibia's answer to luxury train travel. There are two classes, the *Starview Sitter* and the *Spitzkoppe Sleeper*. A superb service with cuisine and care to match. En route the train stops for a couple of local excursions for the passengers. Departs Windhoek Tue, Fri and Sun; departs Swakopmund Mon, Wed and Sat. Good value when compared with similar luxury trains in the region. Expect to pay in the region of N$2,200 for a double sleeper, all inclusive.

Directory

Airline offices For Eros Airport enquiries T238220, Hosea Kutako International Airport T0626-40229. *Aeroflot*, Ground Floor, Sanlam Centre, Independence Ave, T229266/229120, F220007. *Air Namibia*, Gustav Voigts Centre, Independence Ave, T299630, F228763, central reservations, T2982552, F221382, Fares dept T2982340. *Comair*, T248528, F248529. *LTU*, 141 Stübel St, T237480. *South African Airways*, Carl Lis Building, Independence Ave, T231118. *TAAG* (Angolan Airline) Sanlam Building, Independence Ave, T226625, F227798.

Banks There are 4 main banks in Namibia, *Standard Bank*, *Bank Windhoek*, *Commercial Bank* and *First National Bank*, all of which have a number of branches in central Windhoek which change money.

Communica- *Windhoek Post Office*, Independence Ave, T2019311. Open 0800-1600 for parcel ser-
tions vice round the side on Munamava St as are phones. Phone cards can be bought in the main hall of the post office. *Grab A Phone*, Independence Ave and Peter Müller St, T220708, F220820. Facilities for international calls and faxes. **Internet café**: *Tourist Junction*, 40 Peter Muller St, T231246, F231703, info.ritztours@galileaosa.co.za, coffee shop, telephones, internet access, bus reservations, bookings.

Cultural *Franco-Namibian Cultural Centre*, 118 Robert Mugabe St, T225672, F224927,
centres fncc@mweb.com.na Exhibitions and film shows, check press for details.

Embassies & *Angola*, 3 Ausspan St, T220302. *Botswana*, 101 Nelson Mandela, T221941. *Brazil*, 52
consulates Bismarck St, T238560. *British High Commission*, 116 Robert Mugabe Ave, T223022. *P R China*, 13 Wecke St, T222089. *Finland*, 5th Flr, Sanlam Building, Independence Ave, T221355. *France*, 1 Goethe St, T229022. *Germany*, 6th Flr, Sanlam Building, Independence Ave, T273100/33. *Ghana*, 5 Nelson Mandela, T220536. *India*, 97 Nelson Mandela, T226036. *Italy*, Anna/Gevers St, T228602. *Kenya*, 5th Flr, Kenya House, 134 Robert Mugabe Ave, T226836. *Malawi*, 56 Bismarck St, T221391. *Netherlands*, 2 Crohn St, T223733. *Nigeria*, 4 Omuramba Rd, Eros, T232103. *Norway*, 5th Flr, Sanlam Building, Independence Ave, T227812. *Portugal*, 28 Garten St, T228736. *Russia*, 4 Christian St, T228671. *South Africa*, Nelson Mandela/Jan Jonker St, T229765. *Spain*, 53 Bismarck St, T223066. *Sweden*, 9th Flr, Sanlam Building, Independence Ave, T222905. *USA*, 14 Lossen St, T221601. *Zambia*, 22 Curt von Francois, T237610. *Zimbabwe*, Independence Ave/Grimm St, T226859.

Public Library, 18 Lüderitz St, T224163. | **Libraries**

Medicity Windhoek, Private Hospital, Heliodoor St, Eros, T222687, is the best and most expensive hospital in Windhoek. *Central State Hospital*, Florence Nightingale St, T2039111. *Roman Catholic Hospital*, 92 Stübel St, T237237. *Rhino Park Clinic*, Rhino Park, Hosea Kutako Drive, T225423. *Medrescue Namibia*, 24-hr evacuation service, T230505. **Emergencies:** T211111. | **Medical services**

Catholic Cathedral, Stübel St. *Anglican*, Love St. *Mosque*, Nelson Mandela Ave, Klein Windhoek, *Baha'i Centre*, Cladius Kandovazu St, Katutura. | **Places of worship**

7 Post St Mall, T220640. Continental Building, Independence Ave, T2842111, F221930, www.iwwn.com.na/namtour | **Tourist offices**

Useful addresses **Immigration:** Department of Civic Affairs, Cohen Building, Kasino St, T2929111. **Police:** Main station, Bahnhoff St. Emergencies: T211111.

West from Windhoek

Daan Viljoen Game Park

The park is a fabulous resource, with walks through pretty hills and past dams with game and abundant birdlife. It is a wonderful spot to enjoy nature, amazing so close to Windhoek. Recently, however, the park has obtained a reputation for being run down, expensive, noisy (particularly the campsite) and generally 'complacent'. As with almost all the NWR sites, investment in facilities over the past few years has been low, but it is clean, the hot water and electricity work and there is a reasonable restaurant and bar with nice twinkling views of Windhoek in the distance. Remember, you are here to enjoy nature; get a good fire going, watch the sun set by the Augeigas Dam and enjoy the tranquillity of the spot. | *Colour map 1, grid C5*

Getting there 24 km west of Windhoek on the **C28**. Simply find Sam Nujoma Drive and follow the signposts which take you all the way to the park's entrance. The road is a scenic meander through seemingly endless hillocks. If you continue along the road it will take you further into the Khomas Hochland and eventually down into the Namib desert via the Spreethoogte Pass, just about the steepest in Namibia. **Getting around** A 6 km gravel circuit is designed to take the visitor to where the animals are and there are a few nicely positioned viewpoints that should be enjoyed. On the tar road from the entrance gate to the main office there are also a couple of viewpoints, also worth a pause. The real beauty of Daan Viljoen is that there is no big game, so the area can be safely explored **on foot**. The walking trails will probably reward you with better game sitings, and certainly gives you more of a feeling of being in the bush. | **Ins & outs**

The park is situated at an altitude of about 1,700 m in the Khomas Hochland, a landscape of rolling hills scarred by river valleys and ancient erosion. This 3,953 ha park was proclaimed in 1962 and is a very pleasant introduction to the 'bush experience' for first time visitors. Formerly a reserve, and home to a group of Damara people, the park is named after Daan Viljoen, the former South African administrator to South West Africa. | **Background**

The vegetation in the park is typical of that of the central highlands area, with an abundance of thorn trees such as blue, mountain and red umbrella, and thorn

Windhoek

bushes such as trumpet and honey thorn. After the summer rains the hills are covered with new grass, but as the months pass they turn from green to yellow and then become barren just before the next rains. The views over the highlands and Windhoek itself are spectacular whatever the time of year.

Wildlife The park is well stocked with various species of antelope and other medium-sized game. Chances of seeing mountain zebra, blue wildebeest, springbok, gemsbock, kudu, red hartebeest and impala are good. Smaller mammals such as baboons and rock dassies can also be seen. There is an abundance of birdlife in the park including the colourful rollers and bee-eaters, hornbills and weaver birds. By the small Augeigas Dam there is a fantastic assortment of waterbirds.

Hiking trails There are three hikes that can be undertaken. The 3 km **Wag-'n-bietjie** (wait a while) trail is undemanding provided you don't set off in the middle of a summer's day; it is suitable for anyone, whatever their level of fitness. The 9 km **Rooibos** (Red Bushwillow) trail is more demanding, but for anyone who is in reasonable shape it's a very enjoyable experience. The first part of the trail takes the hiker steadily uphill to a triangulation point at 1,763 m, before descending into a river-bed which meanders back to the main camp area by way of a final, particularly vicious hill.

The 32 km two-day unaccompanied **Sweet Thorn Trail** is supposedly for groups of 3-12 people, although unaccompanied couples reported their enjoyment (and difficulty in locating the path) in the visitors book. This trail should be booked in advance if possible, and costs N\$65 per person. A 0900 start from the main office is advised. Ask ahead regarding water; you must be self-sufficient for the overnight stop at a picturesque shelter. These trails are a good introduction to walking in the bush for those who intend to take on the more strenuous walks such as the Ugab River, Fish River Canyon or Naukluft Park Trails. It's important to have decent walking shoes, at least 2 litres of water per person per day, and adequate sun protection for all walks. Poor quality photocopied maps are all that the office will provide. It is certainly possible to get lost on any of these walks, so it is worth having a chat with the staff before you set out, and keeping alert on the way.

Essentials
Bring warm clothes and sleeping equipment, as the temperature drops sharply at dusk

The park is open year round and is very popular with both Windhoek residents and travellers passing through the area who don't wish to stop in Windhoek. It's a relaxing place to come and swim (in the summer), braai and enjoy a few cold beers; at weekends and on public holidays the campsite and braai areas are busy. If the dams are full enough, join the birds and try your hand at fishing, permits obtainable from the office. The entrance gate is open until midnight for those with reserved accommodation, and until sunset for everyone else. Out of season, just turn up, or book through Central Reservations Windhoek, see page 36. Entrance fee, applicable to all guests, N\$20 adults, N\$2 children, N\$20 cars, per day.

Daan Viljoen Game Park

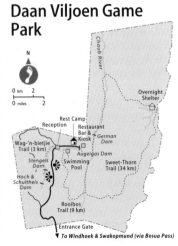

Sleeping and eating   **B/C** *4 bed luxury suites*, in 2 en-suite rooms, with fridge, kitchen, kettle, stove, cutlery and crockery. **D** *2 bed bungalows*, including breakfast, fridge, hot plate, wash basin, braai pit, communal toilets, and showers, ask for view over dam, all are in fairly poor condition. **F** *caravan & campsites*, grassed, no privacy, lights, braai pit, electricity, max 8 people, 2 vehicles per site, communal ablution blocks, field kitchens. The restaurant serves decent meals 0730-0830, 1200-1330, 1900-2030. There is a charge for each picnic site, although it is on your conscience to pay, as no one checks. A small kiosk, open 0900-1700, sells soft drinks, snacks, some braai supplies and firewood.

North from Windhoek

The B1 north out of Windhoek leads first to Okahandja (68 km) where it branches into the B2 for Swakopmund (350 km) and the B1 north for the Waterberg Plateau, Otjiwarongo and the 'triangle' towns of Otavi, Tsumeb and Grootfontein.

For the first 15 km the road is an impressive four-lane highway but then, just before the turn-offs for Döbra and Brakwater, it slims down to a more modest two lanes. As well as being the main route to Swakopmund and the north, this road is a commuter route between Windhoek and Okahandja. It therefore gets very busy during daily 'rush' hours and on Friday and Sunday afternoons with traffic leaving and returning to Windhoek. Care should be exercised when driving this stretch.

The light industry surrounding Windhoek is soon left behind and the road then snakes its way through the attractive mountainous Khomas Hochland, with cattle ranches and guestfarms situated on either side of the road. About 10 km before Okahandja the road passes the Osona Military Base and soon after on the right is the turn-off for **Von Bach Dam**. Just before the turn-off for Okahandja itself, the road passes over the Okahandja River, a dry, wide sandy river-bed with some market gardening practised along its banks.

Okahandja

The small town of Okahandja is one of the oldest established settlements in Namibia and is the administrative centre of the Herero-speaking people, with a number of its former leaders buried here. A yearly procession through the town to the Herero graves commemorates Herero dead during various wars against the Nama and the Germans. As a crossroads between the routes west to the coast and north to Etosha, Okahandja is a busy, bustling place with a railway station, shops, petrol stations and two large outdoor crafts markets.

Phone code: 062
Colour map 1, grid C5

The last couple of years have seen a growth in light industry in the town and the relocation of the research arm of the Ministry of Education as part of the decentralization process in the country. A new diamond cutting factory opened here in 1998 and together with the increasing number of people choosing to live in Okahandja and work in Windhoek, the town is set to continue growing.

Okahandja was known to the Nama as *Gei-keis* meaning 'big sandy plain', a term which aptly describes the wide sandy river bed by the town. The missionary Heinrich Schmelen visited the area briefly in 1827 and for a number of years during the first half of the 19th-century the settlement was known as Schmelen's Hope by Europeans; this name never stuck. Oral tradition

History

Windhoek

suggests that Herero-speaking peoples have been living in the vicinity of Okahandja since the end of the 18th century, coinciding with their migration south from the Kaokoland from circa 1750 onwards.

During the 1840s the Herero chiefs Tjamuaha and Katjihene both established themselves at Okahandja, having moved away from Oorlam leader Jonker Afrikaner's base in Windhoek, and in 1850 missionary Kolbe established a mission station here. The establishment of this mission ran contrary to the wishes of Jonker Afrikaner, at the time the most powerful leader in central Namibia, as he felt that European influence over the Herero would interfere with his self-declared rights over Herero cattle. In August 1850 he raided the settlement, destroying the mission and killing men, women and children indiscriminately. The site where most of the atrocities took place was named **Moordkoppie** or **Blood Hill** in memory of those who fell there. Jonker Afrikaner himself settled at Okahandja in 1854, using the settlement as a base from which to launch his cattle raids in Hereroland, and lived here until his death in 1861. The site is just west of town.

During the turbulent 1860s, Herero chief Maherero moved his base away from Okahandja to the more secure location of Otjimbingwe, but in 1868 he moved back again – ostensibly to be near the grave of his father, Tjamuaha. In 1870 the missionary Reverend Diehl built another mission station and house for himself, the latter surviving until 1990 when it was demolished. Maherero's sons, Willem and Samuel, each built himself a house in Okahandja and Samuel Maherero, who succeeded his father as the senior Herero leader in 1890, remained at Okahandja until the Herero uprising of 1904.

The official founding of Okahandja is deemed to be 1894, despite the fact that the Herero had already been living here for about 100 years. This reflects the increasing power and influence of the German colonial presence in Namibia. Gradually, the rich grazing land around Okahandja was appropriated by white settlers, and today only a fraction of the land around the town is for communal grazing. The period of German rule saw the construction of a number of fine buildings still standing today, these include the present day library, the railway station and the riding club. Nevertheless, Okahandja still remains an important centre to the Herero-speaking peoples and the graves of many of their former leaders lie here.

Okahandja

To Otjiwarongo & Reit Club
Caltex
To Swakopmund
Mose
Curios
Water
Brand
Engen
Kataazu
Walden
Ossmann
Hoof
Dentist
Ulispan
Heroes
ENB
Kaiser
A Doeseb
Biltong
Football Ground
Standard
Windhoek
To Blood Hill & Hospital
Bahnhof
Dinter
Koedoe
Pharmacy
Old Fort
Tennis Club
Voigts
Herero Graves
Swimming Pool
To Gross Barmen
Library
Spar
B Templin
Total
M Neb
Eerste
Biltong
Rhenish Mission
Dr Vedder House
Heroes
Kolbe
Church of Peace
To Windhoek
To Windhoek
Experimental Tobacco Station

N

0 metres 100
0 yards 100

● Eating
1 Backerei Dekker
2 Bürgerstübchen
3 Café Spitze
4 Purple Blues Pub

There are a number of attractive turn-of-the-century buildings scattered **Sights**
around the town, unfortunately none of them have yet been turned into a
museum, and apart from a casual glance, there is not much to see. The **Old Fort**,
situated just along from the post office on Martin Neib Street was started in
1894, the year Okahandja was officially founded, and served for many years as
the police station. It now lies empty and rather forlorn and the various schemes
to put it to use (perhaps as a museum) have so far come to nothing.

At the northern end of Kerk Street just after Voigt Street by the tennis
courts, is the turn-off for the **Herero Graves**. It is not possible to go into the
graveyard, but this is where on 26 August the annual march to commemorate
Herero war heroes ends up. Located here is the communal grave of the 19th
century leader Maherero and his son Samuel Maherero, who led the Herero
into exile in Botswana in 1904 after a final pitched battle against the Germans
at the Waterberg Plateau (see History section, page 337).

There is a cluster of buildings at the southern end of Kerk Street, including
the **Rhenish Mission Church** containing the grave of Willem Maherero, the
eldest son of the late 19th century Herero leader Maherero. Opposite is the
Church of Peace, consecrated in 1952, which contains the graves of three
influential Namibian leaders: the 19th-century Oorlam leader **Jonker Afrikaner**, who died in 1861; Herero leader **Chief Hosea Kutako**, widely credited
as the leader of post Second World War resistance to South African rule in
Namibia; and Chief Clemens Kapuuo, Kutako's successor and former Democratic Turnhalle Alliance (DTA) President, who was assassinated in 1978.

Behind the Church of Peace is the former house of **Dr H Vedder**, a pioneer
in linguistic studies and oral history in Namibia during the first half of this
century, viewed by some as an important Namibian historian and by others as
an apologist of white, colonial rule in the country. Just round the corner from
here is the old **Experimental Tobacco Station** where in 1906 the planting of
tobacco and making of cigars was started. Although quite an attractive building it is now overgrown and stands empty.

Across the railway line at the end of Bahnhof Street is the **Library**,
another attractive early 20th century building, constructed for the first district official Fromm.

Leaving town north on Voortrekker Street, next to the National Institute
for Educational Development, stands the **Reit Club** with its old-fashioned
green corrugated iron roof. Originally the 1909 home of Dr Fock, the first
Mayor of Okahandja, today the house and grounds serve as a stables, with one
large and impressive building and spacious courtyard forming the Horseshoe
Bar and Grill, a pleasant lunch stop on your way north.

Every year on 26 August, **Heroes Day**, the Herero gather to honour their
forefathers and those fallen in battle. The procession (numbering perhaps a
couple of hundred) begins on the outskirts of town, and women in traditional
Herero dresses and men in military uniforms march to the graves of their former leaders to pay their respects. It is a colourful ceremony, but fairly low key.

Entertainment (for your children, really) is available 2 km north out of town, **Excursion**
turn left onto D2110. The *Ombo Show Ostrich and Crocodile Farm* is still in its
infancy, with a 30-minute tour of a few young Nile crocodiles and trained
ostriches (N$25 per person), a good curio shop with ostrich egg items, restau-
rant/coffee shop (0830-1700), small Herero and Himba rural life display.
Next door are the *Okakango Widlife Gardens*, T503280, principally a plant
nursery, but with some animals (giraffe, zebra) and a kids play area, a nice
leafy lunch spot and good curio shop.

Sleeping

There is a bewildering array of accommodation in and around Okahandja; pick your price bracket, and check the location twice, there are some nice places just off the main roads

In/near Okahandja The *Okahandja Hotel* is a fleapit, not recommended. If you want to stay in/near town, your best bet is the **B/C** *Okahandja Lodge*, T504299, F502551, okalodge@africaonline.com.na, opened in late 2000, with 22 thatched en-suite doubles and 2 family rooms, all with fan (TVs to be added), tastefully decorated in African style, restaurant, bar, conference facilities, swimming pool, game drives available. Self-catering accommodation planned for 2002. **F** camping, located 2 km north of town on the B1, at N$40pp with good shared ablutions, cooking facilities under construction. Very nicely done, but lacking in intimacy due to size. **C/D** *Horseshoe Bar and Grill*, located next door to the Riet Haus on the B1 about 2 km north of town, has one 4 bed and one 2 bed room, shared ablutions with the **F** basic camping with electricity. The bar gets lively at night. **D** *Ferienhaus/Villa Nina*, 327 Peter Brand St, T503205, F502497, www.ferienhaus-namibia.de offers one, pretty guesthouse with kitchen, 2 bathrooms, satellite TV and swimming pool, preferably for a stay of longer than one night. **D** *Sylvanette B&B*, 311 Hoogenhout St, T501213, F501079, T081-1273759 (mob), 2 en-suite doubles, s/c, lovely shaded garden, swimming pool, secure parking, located 2 blocks west of the railway line, between Kaiser and Peter Brand Streets. Comfortable and pleasant, fairly central. **E/F** *Okahandja Rest Camp*, T504086, has 9 rondavels/chalets with fan, kettle, sink, with or without full bathroom, each has outdoor braai area, table and seating. Campsite is N$60 per site, with good comunal ablutions and camp kitchen, and individual sites with braai area, table and seating, light and electricity. Bar and simple restaurant planned. Clean, nicely laid out with established shade trees, the best value option, located opposite the Shell station at the B1 turn off for town (immediately north of the bridge over the Okahandja River).

Guestfarms in the area **AL** *Otjisazu*, T501259, F501323, otjisazu@iafrica.com.na Follow D2102 southeast from Okahandja for 27 km. 12 en-suite doubles, 2 family units, swimming pool and thatched poolside lapa, horseriding, mountain bike trails, game drives, hiking trails in former mission station, all inclusive. **A** *Otjiruze*, T/F503719, bushsaf@iafrica.com.na Follow the B1 south and D2102 southeast for 27 km, turn left on the D2170, signposted after 17 km. 10 spacious en-suite rooms, restaurant, bar, swimming pool, tennis court, thatched lapa, 4WD drives and walking trails. Smaller Bush venture camp has been built for 'natural' experience, with 6 tents. **A** *Wilhemstal North*, T/F503977, silkefas@mweb.com.na 63 km west from Okahandja (49 km east of Karabib) just off the B2, turn off at the Khan Rivier sign, and again just after you cross the railway line. Poorly signposted. A hunting lodge, the host a professional hunter, with 13 beds most with en-suite bathroom. Old-fashioned feel, heavy with skins and trophies, small bar and dining room, swimming pool, caters for 'tourists' as well, call ahead.

B *Ovita Game Lodge*, T503881, F503882. Take B1 north from Okahandja, turn west onto D2110 for about 60 km, follow signs. 5 en-suite doubles, swimming pool, excellent food and hospitality, wide range of game including 17 species of antelope, giraffe, elephant and predators such as leopard and cheetah. Game drive and overnight hiking trail staying in bush camp, guided by knowledgeable and friendly owner. All inclusive, recommended. **B** *Ozombanda*, T503870, F503996, ozambanda@natron.net or ozombanda@iafrica.com.na Follow B2 west, 28 km from Okahandja. Has 3 thatched en-suite double bungalows, half board, swimming pool, game drives, hiking trails and game viewing from blinds, all inclusive. **B** *Moringa*, T/F503872, moringa@iafrica.com.na Follow B2 44 km west, turn south, following signs for 20 km. Has 3 en-suite bungalows with minibar and kitchen, small dining room, lounge, bar, swimming pool, well established garden with shade trees, cacti and succulents, plentiful game (as for *Oropoko*, minus rhino) mingled happily with cattle, easily seen on game drives, landing strip, intimate and peaceful, that is, if you aren't hunting; they run hunting trips too (which seems absurd, game is so plentiful). **B** *Oropoko*, T503871, F503842, www.namibia-travel.com Drive 44 km west of

Okahandja on the B2, turn south, follow signs for 18km. Room for 30 couples/pairs and 3 families in tastefully built, thatched, en-suite bungalows, each with a/c, bar, safe and telephone. A fabulous resort on a granite outcrop with commanding views over game-stocked plains. 15 rhino are in a 1,000 ha adjacent area and can be viewed from the restaurant terrace with binoculars. Other game includes giraffe, oryx, kudu, eland, springbok, game drives (they have 11,000 ha in all, and parts are so well stocked it's like visiting a zoo). Bar, large restaurant (buffet and a la carte), TV room and library. Almost recommended, but lacking intimacy; call ahead, they occasionally fill up with a busload of tourists. **B** *Rock Lodge*, T503840, F503170, rocklodg@iafrica.com.na, www.k7.namib.com/rocklodge.html Just off the B2, 11 km west of Okahandja. Has 16 en-suite doubles, many with fine views of the 'Rock', good conference facilities, attractive wooden and stone walkways, game walks, drives and a motorbike trail.

B/C *Khan Rivier*, T503883, F503884, www.khanrivier.com.na Drive 63 km west on the B2, then 20 km north, follow signs. 5 very comfortable en-suite rooms with private terrace, a HAN award winner, swimming pool with poolside dining lapa and bar. Recommended. **B** *Midgard*, T503888, F503818, www.namibsunhotels.com.na South on the B1, then take D2102 for 56 km. Has 46 en-suite doubles in thatched bungalows, organic dining under poolside thatched lapa, tennis, volleyball, badminton, hiking, horse riding, game drives in Otjihavera Mountains, rather large and impersonal. *Okomitundu*, T503901, F503902, www.okomitundu.com 63 km west on the B2, 35 km south on the D196. Has 5 en-suite doubles, a HAN award winner, with 11,000 ha offering game drives, swimming in a heated pool and stargazing. **B/C** *Matador*, T518363, F518362. 42 km north, off the B1. En-suite rooms with good food, local game and birdwatching, garden with large palm trees. A hunting farm, book ahead. **C** *Okowiruru Sud*, T/F549080, F549086, okowi@namib.com 132 km east of Okahandja on the D2170, just east of the junction with D1435.3 doubles on this working cattle/game farm, collection from Hosea Kutako possible.

Backerei Dekker, Martin Neib St, pleasant bakery serving fresh rolls, pies, cakes and coffee. *Bürgerstübchen*, Post St, T501830, small restaurant with outdoor terrace offering steaks, game, schnitzel, reasonably priced, friendly service. Recommended, closed Sun evening. *Café Spitze & Bakery*, Voortrekker St. Shady terrace and a/c dining room, serving variety of pies and hamburgers with chips, licensed. For a drink, try *Purple Blues*, Martin Neib St, or the *Horseshoe Bar and Grill*, an active late night spot, with big screen TV for sports and reasonable food, 1 km north on the B1. **Eating**

Biltong *Closwa*, Vortrekker St, sells excellent biltong and dried wors, ideal for car journeys; also *kewcor*, Martin Neib St. **Souvenirs** There are 2 outdoor craft markets in town. The bigger one is on the corner of B1 as you turn into town from the south, opposite the Shell Ultra: the *Namibian Carvers Association* specializes in carvings of animals, masks and drums. The smaller is on Voortrekker St by railway crossing, good quality, and bargains to be had, but beware of crafts from Zimbabwe being sold at inflated prices. Ask for locally crafted goods to get a feel for what is produced where in the country. **Shopping**

Municipal tennis courts and swimming pool (summer only), both a little run-down but functional and cheap. **Sports**

Road For *Intercape* coaches to Swakopmund, Walvis Bay and Windhoek, see timetable on page 382. All bus transport starts and finishes at the Shell Ultra, by the B1 entrance to town from the south, taxis can be taken here or at the junction of Voortrekker and Martin Neib streets. **Train** For trains to Swakopmund, Tsumeb, Walvis Bay and Windhoek, see timetable on page 383. **Transport**
68 km to Windhoek
278 km to Swakopmund

Windhoek

Directory **Banks** *Standard Bank*, Martin Neib St, *First National Bank*, A Doeseb St, *Bank Windhoek*, Martin Neib St. All change money and have ATMs. **Communications** Post Office: Martin Neib St, Mon-Sat 0800-1600, Sat 0800-1100. **Internet:** Slow, daytime only, corner Voortrekker and Bahnhof streets. **Tourist offices** *Information Centre* in the Municipality Building, Martin Neib St, is not worthy of the name: they had no information, no maps, and no idea there was a bus service. **Police**: B Templin St.

Von Bach Resort Recreation Area
5 km south of town signposted off the B1

The dam is the main water supply for Windhoek. For residents it is a reasonably popular place for fishing, water sports (BYOB, bring your own boat) and picnics; sadly there are no walking trails. Apart from swimming in the blue water and bird watching, the dam offers little for the overseas visitor. The dam and surrounding reed beds attract large numbers of **birds**, in particular water birds such as moorhens, teals and coots. There are also large numbers of Monteiro's hornbill, lilac-breasted rollers and crimson-breasted shrikes with their distinct black and crimson markings. Benches on the edge of the dam are excellent places from which to twitch.

There are camping facilities and two bed huts (with shared cooking facilities, ablutions blocks, no power points, **F**) if you do decide to visit and wish to stay over. It costs N$10 adults and N$1 children, and N$10 car.

Gross Barmen Hot Springs Resort

Background
Colour map 2, grid C1

Gross Barmen was known by the Herero as Otjikango, meaning 'a weak spring running over rocky ground', an apt description for the hot spring which bubbles up here and leaves its salty residue around the resort. The main reasons for visiting the resort are these hot spring baths and the outdoor swimming pool, both supplied by the thermal spring (although the outdoor pool is still quite chilly in winter).

In 1844 Hugo Hahn and Heinrich Kleinschmidt established a mission station here, the first amongst the Herero-speaking people, and named the station *Neu Barmen* after Barmen, the headquarters of the Rhenish Missionary Society in Germany. Kleinschmidt and his wife left soon after to establish the mission station amongst the Swartbooi Namas at Rehoboth.

The first church was completed in December 1847 and consecrated early the following year. Growing numbers of impoverished Herero came to settle by the new church at Gross Barmen and the mission station also became a trading post. In 1849 Hahn wrote: 'Who would have thought that at the very beginning – yes, even two years ago – that this station would become such a market place! Sometimes, the Herero come here from places several days' journey distant to trade.'

During the turbulent 1860s the station was abandoned and resettled a number of times, following attacks by the Afrikaner Oorlams under Jan Jonker Afrikaner. At the beginning of the 1870s, the 'decade of peace', a new, larger church was consecrated, and the mission station flourished first under missionary Brinker and then missionary Meyer.

Following the German occupation of Namibia in the 1880s, a military garrison was established at Okahandja in 1894 and a substation established at Gross Barmen. This consisted of a double-storey fort with watchtower, which allowed the soldiers to survey a 600 m radius. In 1902 the fort was enlarged but the mission station itself was dying. Reverend Hammann commented, 'As regards Gross Barmen, it is interesting to note that almost all the Herero have moved away from there. Only four to six families remain...'.

Following the 1904-1907 Herero-Nama uprising against the German occupation of Namibia, the colonial government approved the sale of land to white settlers, and in 1907 Gross Barmen was sold off. The Hot Springs Resort was opened in 1966 and is popular with locals as a weekend getaway. Gross Barmen is a good place to relax for a day en route to the coast or after a dusty trip in the north.

The indoor thermal hall consists of a large sunken bath and artificial fountain, somewhat out of date and tired now, but still a good place for a relaxing soak during the cooler winter months (June-August). The water temperature is roughly 50°C. The outdoor swimming pool and children's pool are shaded by large palm trees, there are picnic sites, braai pits, a restaurant and drinks/ice cream kiosk; the area gets quite animated on summer weekends. **Hot springs**

Although no trails have been laid out, there are some enjoyable walks along paths and dry river-beds around the resort, where it is possible to see kudu, warthogs and baboons. As always, keep an eye out for snakes. A prominent rocky outcrop offers views back over the resort and across the arid plains. The salty spring itself, by the campsite, makes an interesting geography lesson for the kids. **Hiking**

The resort is open all year, direct T501091 or through Windhoek central reservations. The resort has 2 tennis courts, a children's play area, a well-stocked shop, restaurant and petrol station. **Essentials**

Sleeping **D-E** *Luxury Suites, Standard and Economy Bungalows*. Well equipped, varying degrees of luxury but all with military barracks 'feel'; all with fridge, cooker, kettle and reveille at 0600 (only joking). **F** *Caravan & campsites*. 16 good, large sites with communal ablutions, braai areas, laundry and ovens. Entrance to resort N$10 adults, N$1 children under 16, N$10 cars. Entrance to thermal baths N$10 adults, N$5 children under 16.

Transport Turn off the B2 near Okahandja onto the C87. Follow the road for 25 km to resort entrance; keep an eye out for the enormous ant heaps, as tall as small trees.

East from Windhoek to Botswana

The main road, **B6**, east out of Windhoek passes through the suburb of Klein Windhoek before it starts to weave its way through the Eros mountains and out onto the plains past Hosea Kutako and on to Botswana. After passing under the railway bridge there is a curio shop and working taxidermist **Eharui**, 20 km from Windhoek, T232236, open Mon-Fri, 0700-1900, for those who have left their shopping until the last minute. It is geared towards the hunter, but does have some videos, books and a good selection of carvings and hunting souvenirs. The airport has almost nothing, so rather spend your final pennies here, if you have time.

Traffic is only heavy on the B6 when there is an international flight arriving or departing from the airport, 45 km out of town. Drive carefully along here, especially at dusk, there are often loaded taxis who will overtake on blind stretches in a mad rush to the airport. The airport was built here because of the need for level land and a clear approach for larger aircraft (Air Namibia's one Boeing 747, for example), closer to Windhoek there are too many mountains.

Sleeping & eating **Between Windhoek and airport C** *Airport Lodge*, T2314919, F236709, T081-1245923 (mob), airportl@mweb.com.na offers 7 thatched self-catering chalets with TV and mini-bar, conference facilities, swimming pool. It is one of the few lodges in the country not run by whites, and offers pleasant views of the surrounding hills. A good bet if you don't fancy staying downtown. Just further on towards the airport is a camp/caravan site **D-F** *Trans-Kalahari Caravan Park*, T222877, F220335, www.mietwagonnamibia.com, run by the wonderfully named Grundela Grimm, with 5 en-suite chalets. She may offer you a cheap (N$55) bed in one of their camper vans if they have failed to hire it out. It does seem to lure the trans-continental bunch, and can be an interesting spot to view the weird and wonderful vehicles your fellow travellers are using. The last place before the airport is **C** *Heja Game Lodge*, T257151, F257148, heja@namib.com, 25 en-suite twin chalets with a/c and TV, game drives, horse riding, walking trails, swimming pool by dam with spit braai area, can cater for big groups, weddings, etc, also more remote chalets far from the restaurant and bar. Transfers to/from the airport at N$50. Has a nice rural feel, despite proximity to town.

After passing the airport the road is a dull straight drive to Gobabis. Keep your eyes peeled for warthogs, baboons, antelope (including kudu) and birds of prey. There are rest stops every 10 km or so for a picnic or to relieve boredom or yourself. Sadly, there is evidence at most that you are not the first visitor. The terrain is relatively flat and, as you near Witvlei, there are few trees. Most of the country is owned by large commercial cattle and sheep farmers. After good rains the countryside turns a beautiful green, but for most of the year it is a dull burnt brown covered with scrub vegetation.

You'll go past Seeis in the blink of an eye and **Witvlei** is a God-forsaken, dusty place in the dry season, but it does have a petrol station and a biltong factory; the latter is opening up a factory shop with good value dried beef, kudu and gemsbok as well as fresh farm produce. There are bottle stores and small shops, the train stops here, and there is a police station and clinic.

Next door to the petrol station, there is a new B&B with pretty Cape Dutch style gables, **D** *Die Broeihuis*, T062-570079, 570063, broeihys@iway.na with 6 en-suite doubles, which used to be an ostrich egg hatchery. They plan to replace the tin roof with thatch, which will make it all the more attractive. Dinner is N$45, book ahead. Over the road is the **E** *Doll's House*, T062-570120, a decrepit truckers' halt. Open around the clock, but not recommended, rather choose one of the guestfarms along the way (book ahead for all of them) or push through to Gobabis, the border or Windhoek. **Gobabis**, the regional centre, is the last settlement of any note before you reach the Botswana border. There are cheap hotels, pleasant guest houses, banks and a good range of shops. If you are planning on exploring the Kalahari in Botswana this is the best place to stock up with supplies.

Dordabis

Colour map 2, grid C2 Dordabis is a tiny settlement, but offers an interesting detour for those inclined to learn about or purchase the output of the **karakul** carpet weavers. **Ibenstein Teppiche**, T/F062-573524, www.ibenstein-weavers.com.na just south (ie left at the T-junction) of the village (don't be confused by the private farm of the same name) offers tours of the farm and weavery, Monday-Friday, 0700-1230, 1430-1800. They produce a range of animal and African designs in varying sizes. They don't come cheap; as a measure, a metre square rug will cost you roughly US$100, but it will certainly last your lifetime.

A *Eningu Clayhouse Lodge*, T062-573580, F062-573577, www.natron.net/ **Sleeping**
tour/eningu Located 1 km southwest of the D1471/D1428 junction, just off the C51,
65 km from Hosea Kutako airport. A superb guest lodge which blends into the dry landscape, built by the owners using local clay bricks, 5 en-suite doubles, attractive decorative designs enhance this peaceful location, central dining and lounge area,
solar-heated swimming pool, outdoor whirlpool, ideal for hiking and birding plus some
game viewing, curio shop. Recommended. **B** *Auas Game Lodge*, T061-240043,
F061-248633, auas@iafrica.com.na Look for the sign on the C23, perhaps 40 km from
the B6, then it's 14 km to the lodge; they can collect from the airport for N$265. Has 7
en-suite chalets and one suite, all with a/c, with an attractive swimming pool/braai area
looking out over unspoilt country. Full board adds N$200 per person, or you can self
cater. They offer game drives and have some caged cheetahs. A lovely spot to open
your itinerary. **B** *African Kirikara – Guestfarm Kiripotib*, T062-573319, 061-223617,
www.natron.net/tour/kirikara Located 160 km southwest of Windhoek: take the B6
east for 28km, turn south on the C23 for 63 km to Dordabis, take the MR33 for
Uhlenhorst for 55 km and follow signs for 10 km from the turning onto the D1488. A
colourful, multi-faceted jewellery workshop, spinning/weaving factory, working sheep
farm and guestfarm with 5 en-suite doubles, en-suite tents, swimming pool, good
home cooking, bar, hiking trails, informative, friendly hosts.

Take the B6 from Windhoek for the airport, after 24 km turn right on the C23 to **Transport**
Dordabis. 66 km of gravel road brings you to Dordabis. A *Star Line* bus runs via Dordabis
every Mon and Fri, 0800, the journey takes about 1 hour. You can return to Windhoek
on the same service in the afternoon at 1600. Journey time is 2 hours each way. There is
a store/bottle store and petrol station (sunrise to sunset).

If you have plenty of time or are particularly interested in caves and bats then a **Arnhem Cave**
detour to Arnhem Cave can be recommended. The cave is situated on a pri-
vate farm in the Arnhem hills south of the B6. Contact Jannie Bekker,
T/F062-573585, arnhem@mweb.com.na in advance. He drives groups to the
entrance at 1000 each day (given demand). The farm is 4 km (signposted)
from the junction of the D1506 and D1808. Entrance to the cave is N$50 per
person (reductions for guests of the restcamp), with helmets and torches
available for hire.

The cave system is 4,500 m long, making it the longest in Namibia. It is a dry
cave and thus there are few of the typical cave formations such as stalagmites.
After it was first discovered in 1931 by Jannie's grandfather, it was exploited as
a source of bat guano, today the cave remains a home to five different species of
bat: the Egyptian slit-faced bat, giant leaf-nosed bat, horseshoe bat, leaf-nosed
bat and the long-fingered bat. The best time to visit is just after the first summer rains, when the insect eating mammals are at their busiest; sitting by the
cave entrance overnight is a spectacular experience.

Sleeping and eating **D-F** *Arnhem Cave & Restcamp*, details above, 4 chalets with 2
or 4 beds, fully equipped for self-catering, plus a campsite and swimming pool, excellent meals are available on request. About 40 km towards Witvlei from here is
B *Okambara*,T062-560217, T081-128 0669 (mob), www.okambara.de A luxury
10,000 ha game farm with elephants, rhino, leopard and cheetah. Christian and Uschi
Schmitt have literally built the place from nothing over the past 10 years. There are 3
en-suite chalets and 3 doubles in the main house, an impressive thatched fort. Full
board, with excellent home cooking, they hunt for meat (and take in occasional groups
of hunters). Advance booking required. It is not signposted, so call for directions.

Windhoek

Gobabis

Phone code: 062
Colour map 2, grid C3
Altitude: 1,442 m

Gobabis is a typical Namibian town; it is the capital of the Omaheke region, surrounded by important cattle country, an area that is only just waking up to its tourist potential. Gobabis itself has little to recommend it beyond its pretty churches (the greatest density in Namibia). It is a place for stocking up on supplies en route to Botswana or using as a base for exploring the surrounding farms, which offer Bushman art and 'experiences': game viewing on foot, challenging hunting (for trophies, birds and biltong) and, for those interested, cattle ranching.

Background The region, although arid, has excellent grazing (and browsing for small game) and stock levels have replenished after a few years of good rains. The town's name is derived from a Nama word meaning 'the place where people had quarrelled', although there is stronger local support for the derivation being from a different word 'Goabbes' – 'the place of the elephants', which is plausible, as a white hunter's cache of tusks was found nearby. For visitors driving across the Kalahari from Botswana this will be your first introduction to urban Namibia. Afrikaans is the very much the spoken tongue, and despite some inter-racial mixing in the hotel bars, the white clientele is very conservative in its outlook. There is little of interest for the tourist, and nightlife is limited. On the way through, a quick stop at the churches and a glimpse of Herero women and their 'traditional' costumes, will probably suffice. The main attractions of the region are the lodges, farms and rural communities out of town.

The first Europeans to settle in the district were Rhenish missionaries, in August 1856 Amraal Lambert decided to move to Gobabis and build a church and small school. For many years the settlement was a popular stop-over point for hunters and traders travelling between Walvis Bay, Omaruru, Rietfontein, Ghanzi and Lake Ngami. Some of the great adventurers of the period were attracted to the region: Baines, Green, Chapman, Hahn and McKiernan. But once all the profitable wild animals had been killed the trade and interest moved elsewhere.

In 1895, following skirmishes with local tribes, the Germans built a military post to patrol the eastern borders of their colony. Unfortunately this fort was demolished after sustaining considerable damage in the 1934 floods. But it was still difficult to persuade people to come and settle in this dusty region on the

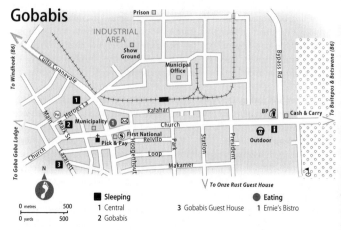

Gobabis

Sleeping
1 Central
2 Gobabis

3 Gobabis Guest House

Eating
1 Ernie's Bistro

edge of the Kalahari. The rinderpest outbreak in 1897 killed more than 50% of the cattle in the area making the region even less attractive to potential settlers. In an effort to stimulate development the first four farms were sold to former members of the Schutztruppe in 1898, the first civilian to buy a farm was Carl Ohlsen in 1899. The post office opened in August 1898, but by 1913 there was still only a full mail service twice a month. The future of the town was only secured when the railway service was opened in November 1930, this greatly facilitated the export of cattle from the district to Windhoek and South Africa.

Modern Gobabis is probably best known as a cattle centre, producing a third of Namibia's red meat; visitors might find the monthly stock sales interesting, at the kraal on the left of the B6 as you approach from Windhoek. A meat processing plant built in 1983 has never been used, it is known locally as the 'Blue Elephant'. The mayor is hoping that planned investment in goat's milk processing and mushroom canning factories will reap better return. Since 1998, First National Bank, Bank Windhoek and Pick and Pay have moved in, and a Shoprite is expected to open in late 2001. There are plans for a new building for Gobabis Museum, 144 Elephant Street, T562489, where there is an open-air display of farming equipment and a school wagon.

The prosperity of the town and region is buoyed by the Trans-Kalahari Highway, which has greatly increased the number of tourists, hauliers and businessmen visiting the town. There are plans to extend the railway alongside the road all the way to Johannesburg, allowing bulk goods to be transported from Walvis Bay to land-locked Botswana and onto Johannesburg.

Essentials

In town E *Gobabis Hotel*, Mark St, T562568, F562641, 17 rooms with satellite TV, shower, a/c or fan, clean and airy but very square, shaded courtyard, restaurant, bar, pool tables, swimming pool, off road parking. This is the focus of most activity for the local white community, particularly at weekends. Around the corner is **E** *Central*, Heroes Lane, T562094, F562092, 15 rooms with satellite TV, restaurant, bar, rooms not quite so comfortable as the *Gobabis*, but little to choose between the two. Neither can be recommended for more than an overnight stop.

Sleeping

A little more expensive but less impersonal are the guest houses in town. The best (and a HAN 2000 award winner) is **C/D** *Goba Goba Lodge*, Elim St (follow signs), T564499, F564466, goba-goba@iafrica.com.na with 7 en-suite doubles, a/c, TV, a decent tennis court, big swimming pool, and plenty of africanalia such as dugout canoes and carvings dotted around. It's in the Nossob river-bed, they are buying some game for the waterhole visible from their hide. **D/E** *Gobabis Guest House*, Lazerette St, T563189, gghnam@iafrica.com, 11 en-suite rooms, cable TV, a/c or fan, B&B, tasty dinner available on request (it has to be steak, really) or **D/E** *Onze Rust Guest House*, Rugby St, T562214, F565060, www.natron.net/tour/onzerust, facilities as above, but with braai area.

Guestfarms in the area There are some lovely farms in the district which welcome visitors. In addition to providing a peaceful overnight stop, these farms give an insight into life on the arid fringes of the Kalahari desert. **NB** Trophy hunting is a popular and lucrative pastime in this region; if you don't wish to share the dinner table with hunters, call in advance. Some of the following are a considerable distance from Gobabis.

B *Harnas Wildlife Foundation and Guestfarm*, T568788, F568738, www.harnas.org Take the B6 for the border, turn north on the C22, it's a further 94 km, follow signs. Stone and wooden chalets with en-suite bathrooms, fans and braai pits, camping with ablutions, restaurant, swimming pool, trampoline, volleyball. The focus of the Foundation is reha-bilitating injured and orphaned game, and they have many tame predators that arrived as cubs, which they allow adults to 'play' with. Recommended by visitors, although not as impressive as Okonjima. **B** *Ohlsenhagen*, PO Box 434, T562330, F563536. On the C22, 20 km north of Gobabis. 5 double rooms, small conference room, swimming pool, hunting, game viewing. **B/C** *Kalahari Bush Breaks*, T568936, F569001, www.kalaharibushbreaks.com On the B6, 26 km before the border. Aimed at the high-budget hunter. The architect owner and his wife (who leads the game drives) have built a fabulous 3-storey thatched lodge with 5 doubles, dining room and bar. Full board, plunge pool, Bushmen paintings nearby, hides for bird/game watching, even one that can be camped in overnight for a wilderness thrill. Also good value **F** tented camp with electricity, braai pits and clean, thatched ablutions block. Camping available at N$15 pp, with open air ablutions. Recommended. **C** *Zelda Game and Guest Farm*, PO Box 75, T560427, F560431, zelda.guestfarm@iafrica.com.na On the D6, 23 km before the Bot-swana border. Picturesque place that caters for larger groups, including overlanders. Rooms with or without en-suite bathroom, camping, swimming pool, volleyball, aviary, trampoline, dinner for N$60, bar that gets busy when overland buses deposit their thirsty pilgrims. They can arrange for walks dancing with Bushmen, in groups of 10 or more. **D/E** *Quinta*, T/F568911, quintas@iway.na 5 en-suite doubles decorated in African style, 2 self-catering flats under construction, with campsite planned for 2002, swimming pool, shared TV, lounge. Peaceful retreat (book ahead), good value.

If you are interested in seeing Bushmen, James Chapman (great grandson of his name-sake, the first white man to walk the breadth of Namibia, in the 1850s) organizes an interesting and fairly discrete excursion for 2-8 people from his cattle farm **B** *Good Hope Country House*, T/F563700, www.sanworld.com.na To get there, take the B6 for the border, turn left after 36 km on the D1601, after 10 km turn left, follow signs for 14 km along the sandy farm track. The aim is to provide as genuine a Bushman 'experience' as possible. There are 4 en-suite doubles with a/c, a small plunge pool, full board. A recommended game walk with James and a Bushman brings the flora and fauna to life and there are displays of traditional dancing put on in the evening. You might argue that these Bushmen are not the 'real thing', as they live in houses and wear jeans, but they still have their traditional knowledge and skills. Visitors' comments tell of a rewarding experience. Hunting (with a seasoned local pro) and bird shooting trips also available. Advance booking essential, each group gets exclusive use of the place during their stay. Recommended.

Eating If you don't wish to eat in or cook yourself try *Erni's Bistro*, Church St, centrally located with a bar and some tourist information.

Shopping If you are travelling towards Botswana this is a good place to stock up with fresh pro-duce and Namibian beer. On the Botswana side of the border you will only come across village stores until you reach Ghanzi. There is a good selection of chemists, supermar-kets and petrol stations, a hardware store and a large cash and carry on the main road as you leave town for the border.

Sports The *Gobabis Golf Course* charges N$15 for 9 holes, but they have no clubs for hire. Keep an eye for the faded sign 1 km east of town, on the B6, turn south opposite the cash and carry. There are also dilapidated *tennis courts* in the center of town.

Transport
Windhoek, 330 km
Botswana, 122 km

If you are trying to hitch into Botswana you would be best advised to wait for a through lift as far as the border, if not Ghanzi. **Bus** *Star Line* buses run several services to outly-ing villages, Epukiro and Leonardville, as well as a weekly bus into Botswana.

Reservations, Windhoek T061-2982032. **Train**   See timetable on page 383, a very slow service which more or less follows the main road all the way into Windhoek.

See timetable on page 383

Banks The big three all represented, with ATMs. **Private hospital** T563980, F562084, visiting times 1100-1200, 1500-1600 and 1900-2000. **Tourist offices** *Omaheke Information Centre*, T562551, is almost useless, except to collect the few flyers they stock of local guest houses. They did not know where the museum is (to be fair, nor did anyone in town). Better information can be obtained in cyberspace at www.omaheketourism.com.na **Useful addresses** Police: T10111.

Directory

The road to the Botswana border is tarred and in good condition. The road is straight and dull all the way to the border, with a good number of guestfarms and rest camps to tempt the weary, many of which will provide a decent lunch, or indeed breakfast.

Buitepos-Mamuno Border

Traffic volume has increased considerably with the opening of the Trans-Kalahari Highway (tarred all the way) and with travellers to northern Botswana wary of the trouble in the Caprivi area. Just before you arrive at the border there are a couple of garages and on your left, **D-E** *East Gate Service Station*, where you can camp or stay in three-bed bungalows. This is a pleasant spot and a surprise in such a desolate region, they sell braai packs (meat) and firewood; basic provisions are available at the petrol station. If you wish to drive through to Maun in one stretch then it is advisable to spend the night here and cross the frontier as soon as it opens.

At the border   Open 0600-2300. The Namibian office closes for an hour at lunchtime. A Cross Border Certificate is required to take vehicles **not** registered locally out of Namibia, obtained from the police station. All foreign vehicles entering Botswana are charged a small (10 Pula) road tax. Vehicles registered outside the Southern African Common Customs Area (SACCA) are required to obtain third party insurance, this can be purchased at the border post.

Onward into Botswana By starting your journey early you will be able to make good progress before the heat becomes a factor. The first comfortable accommodation is the **B-D** *Kalahari Arms Hotel* in **Ghanzi** which has chalets and space for camping, there is also a swimming pool to help you cool off and a menu that will warm the carnivore's heart.

The roads on the Botswana side have all been upgraded as part of the Trans-Kalahari Highway. It is now possible to drive all the way to Johannesburg via Kang, Sekoma and Lobatse on tarred roads. At present there are only a few petrol stations along the Botswana stretch, so make a point of filling your tank at the border.

Windhoek

The North

4

The North

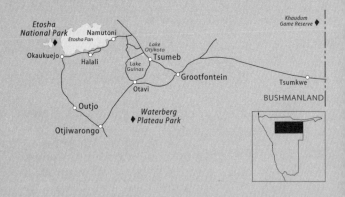

The north of Namibia houses some of its principal attractions, and is an almost inevitable feature of any tour, due to the irrepressibly stunning landscapes and abundant wildlife at Etosha National Park. Visitors should be sure to allow at least a couple of days of game viewing at this magnificent park, it will be one of the highlights of any trip. As well as comfortable accommodation within the park, a number of the country's most luxurious lodges are located on its perimeter, providing the well-heeled with an unforgettable, upmarket bush experience.

The two other game reserves in the region should not be overlooked; Waterberg Plateau Park offers some excellent hiking (if booked ahead) in a well stocked park, across an unusual limestone geography. And to the northeast is the remote Khaudum Game Reserve, one of Africa's more remote wilderness areas, deep in the flat and dry wilderness known as Bushmanland.

The towns in the region are well served with tarred roads, plentiful service stations, supermarkets and a good supply of accommodation at all price levels. Consider these towns useful restocking centres and pass on to your destination: Etosha, Damaraland, Kaokoland, the Kavango and Caprivi are all within reach of the open savannah of Namibia's north.

As there is no fuel on the 174 km drive on the B1 to Otjiwarongo, fill up before leaving Okahandja.

Otjiwarongo

Phone code: 067
Colour map 1, grid B5

The town of Otjiwarongo is a fast growing commercial centre, strategically located in the centre – north of Namibia, serving the farming communities in the surrounding area. It is also a regular stopping-off place for people travelling to Etosha and the Waterberg Plateau, with a wide range of reasonably priced accommodation and ambitious plans for development of its own tourist potential. Otjiwarongo's tourism bodies are aiming to make their town a destination rather than transit stop by appealing to tourist's interest in carnivorous cats, in particular the cheetah. They are to establish a 'Meet a Cheetah' trail of artistically designed sculptures strategically placed in a route through town. There will be tightened links with the Cheetah Conservation Fund outside town and a new mini-reserve just southwest of town alongside a new golf and leisure development.

History

Otjiwarongo means 'place of the fat cattle' or 'beautiful place' in Herero. Given the central role that cattle play in their culture, both meanings are appropriate

The town is officially deemed to have been founded in 1906 upon the arrival of the narrow-gauge railway linking the important mining centre of Tsumeb with the coast. However, as with elsewhere in many parts of Namibia, there is evidence that Bushmen were living in the area thousands of years ago. It is believed that groups of Damara settled in the area in the late 14th century where they lived as hunter gatherers until the arrival of the Herero in the early part of the 19th century. The land was ideal for cattle grazing and the Herero gradually forced the Damaras off the land and into the surrounding mountainous areas.

In 1891 the Rhenish Mission Society secured the agreement of Herero Chief Kambazembi, and a mission was established, opening the way for adventurers and traders to move further north. The Herero 'revolt' of 1904 and their eventual retreat from the German troops into the Omaheke sandveld, where thousands died of thirst and hunger, provided the colonial authorities with the opportunity to take control of the land in the area. German (and later Afrikaner) cattle farmers were the principal benefactors.

Sights

Otjiwarongo Heritage Exploratorium

Two major developments are underway to encourage bypassing tourists to stay in town. The Otjiwarongo Heritage Exploratorium is expected to be complete in January 2002, the centrepiece will be a museum (history and telecommunications), laser show, theatre, curios, coffee shop and conference area. On the lawn will be the **Narrow Gauge Locomotive 'No. 41'**, which until late 2001 will sit outside the railway station. A luxury carriage used by numerous foreign dignitaries in its heyday will be coupled to it. The locomotive is one of three manufactured by Hensel & Son in Germany in 1912 for Namibia's original narrow gauge railway and remained in commission until 1960 when the track was widened from 600 to 1067 mm. The carriage is being reappointed and will offer luxury overnight accommodation.

Adjoining the complex will be a modern walkway, the central shopping precinct and the **Crocodile Ranch**, which is unique in Namibia and a family business started in 1985, primarily rearing the beasts for their skins. These are exported to Europe and North America for use in making expensive leather shoes, wallets and briefcases. Following the sale of a number of the 'youngsters', a new breeding programme is being initiated. A tour takes about 30 minutes. ■ *T303121, Mon-Fri 0900-1600, Sat and Sun 1000-1300, N$15 adults, N$10 children.*

The second major development is slightly out of town (south west), centred geographically on a new 18-hole grassed **golf course**, adjoining three large fenced areas set aside for cheetah and game, with a background of an attractive natural rock feature called the 'whale rock'. A separate area, centred on a sewage works is to be developed for bird watching, with hides. Further plans for quad-biking, go-karting, horse riding, paintball, a swimming pool and target range are in the offing. A *Joe's Beerhouse* will headline the refreshments on offer.

Golf

The North

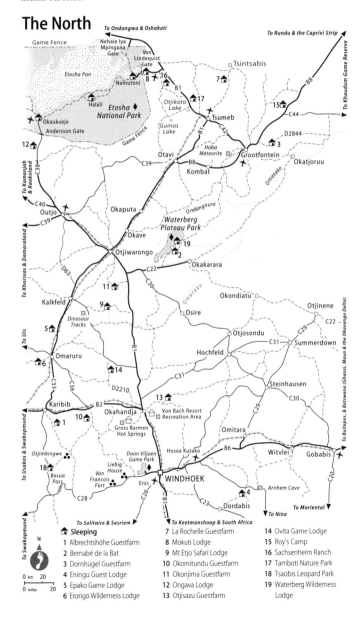

The North

Sleeping

1 Albrechtshöhe Guestfarm
2 Bernabé de la Bat
3 Dornhügel Guestfarm
4 Eningu Guest Lodge
5 Epako Game Lodge
6 Erongo Wilderness Lodge
7 La Rochelle Guestfarm
8 Mokuti Lodge
9 Mt Etjo Safari Lodge
10 Okomitundu Guestfarm
11 Okonjima Guestfarm
12 Ongava Lodge
13 Otjisazu Guestfarm
14 Ovita Game Lodge
15 Roy's Camp
16 Sachsenheim Ranch
17 Tamboti Nature Park
18 Tsaobis Leopard Park
19 Waterberg Wilderness Lodge

★ **Things to do in the North**

- Treat yourself to an educational and luxurious stay at **Okonjima** – predators never seemed so cuddly or awe-inspiring.
- Join the masses watching elephants in Etosha National Park come to drink their sundowners at Okaukuejo's **floodlit watering hole**; bring your book, beer and binoculars and watch the show unfold.
- Remind yourself of your frailty with a **midnight stroll** inside the Namutoni camp perimeter fence, but keep an eye out for snakes.
- Have a **sundowner beer** at the escarpment edge on the Waterberg plateau, overlooking the endless plains below.
- Sleep in *Hotel Thousand Stars* at Hohenfels campsite, on the way to Waterberg.
- Take the **Bushman painting** walk/scenic drive from the beautifully located *Ghaub Guest Farm*.
- Drive the meandering back roads of the **Otavi Mountain Conservancy**.

The North

Cheetah The central theme throughout the town will be the cheetah, Namibia has the largest population of wild cheetahs in the world, 90% of which live outside established game reserves on livestock ranches. This is not a cynical marketing ploy to tourists, it is hoped that raising awareness of the value of these animals to the country will encourage people to take pride in the existence of these animals and serve to protect the species in the wild.

Distributed through Otjiwarongo will be numerous weird and wonderfully painted and sculpted cheetahs, linked to form a 'Meet a Cheetah' trail. The walking trail will take visitors to all the interesting parts of town and whet their appetite for a visit to the Cheetah Conservation Fund at Elands Vreugde Farm, 40 km out of town. The **Cheetah Conservation Fund** (CCF), T/F306225, www.cheetah.org is a non-profit organization, begun in 1990, engaged in cheetah conservation, research and education. Among other things, the CCF monitors numbers and keeps an up-to-datea health/gene pool database, it advises on predator management and relocation techniques, and works with all parties to promote awareness of their sleek protégés. They have large numbers of enthusiasts through their 8 chapters in the USA, and indeed in 2001 President Nujoma sent 10 cheetahs to US zoos as a present.

Other carnivores On the subject of wild cats, the guestfarm at **Okonjima**, www.okonjima.com, just south of Otjiwarongo, is home to the **Africat Foundation**, www.africat.org, a non-profit making organization dedicated to the conservation and protection of Namibia's wild carnivores. Currently, visitors must be overnight guests at Okonjima; the only day visitors permitted are school children on educational tours. There are plans to offer a day visitor agenda in future; call for an update. Overnight guests have a full, informative agenda, including viewing and feeding carnivores, particularly leopard and cheetah. The foundation is a multi-faceted operation, working in partnership with farmers, who traditionally have regarded the cats as pests, to find ways in which to preserve the wild cheetah population, as well as housing and attempting to reintroduce, where possible, orphaned, injured or captured carnivores. In summer 2001, they released their first three rehabilitated cheetahs (collared, for monitoring purposes) into the a large area of near wilderness. School groups may book directly with Africat, otherwise, all bookings are through Okonjima. Read more on Okonjima below, under Sleeping.

Other attractions in the area include walks in the *Waterberg Plateau*, historical **Other sights** tours of the Herero-German **war sites**, **Dinosaur Tracks** near *Mount Etjo Guest Lodge* southwest of town and the huge **Omaue Rock** with bushman art (at Farm Rüppell) and popular goat's cheese operation at the farm. Visitors with the time and geological/mineralogical interest might visit the Okoruso **fluorspar mine** in an extinct volcano. These are all more or less open to tourists, ask when you reach town, either at the information centre on Second St, or at *Bush Pillow Guest House*.

Essentials

In town C *C'est Si Bon*, Swembad St, T301240, F303208, sibon@iafrica.com.na, is the nicest accommodation downtown, laid out like a leisure complex with 20 large, en-suite doubles in thatched bungalows, a central grassed courtyard with swimming pool, tennis courts by the car park, a cosy restaurant over two floors, bar. TV, telephone and a/c in each room. Immaculately tended, friendly welcome, tasty a la carte food; the only issue is the price. **D** *Out of Africa Lodge*, T303397, F304383, levaneck@iafrica.com.na, on the B1 on the southern edge of town, expected to open in late 2001, with 10 en-suite doubles, swimming pool, lounge bar and coffee shop. If the B&B of the same name on Tuin St (built and run by the same friendly couple) is anything to go by, this will be the best lodge in/near town, and good value, too. **D** *Hamburgerhof Hotel*, Bahnhof St, T302520, F303607, www.namibsunhotels.com.na, is a characterless, stark town hotel, with clean and spacious en-suite rooms with a/c and TV, restaurant, fairly popular bar with draught beer. **D** *Bush Pillow B&B*, Son St, T303885, F301264, artworks@iafrica.com.na, www.bushpillow.hypermart.net, is run by Neville Neveling and his wife, Neville is heavily involved in the Otjiwarongo's tourist promotion effort and is very knowledgeable about the town and area; 7 en-suite rooms with fan and TV; welcoming lounge with leather seats, small library, drinks, food and fabrics for sale, restaurant and bar, small swimming pool, secure parking. **D** *Pension Bahnhof*, Bahnhof St, T304801, F304803. 17 en-suite

Sleeping
You are spoilt for choice in Otjiwarongo, which has probably the best choice of accommodation outside Windhoek and Swakopmund, and at more affordable rates

The North

Otjiwarongo

To Tsumeb & Etosha National Park

To Waterberg Plateau & Windhoek (B1)   To Out of Africa B & B

0 metres 200
0 yards 200

■ **Sleeping**
1 Bush Pillow B & B   3 Falkennest   5 Haus Blumers
2 C'est Si Bon   4 Hamburgerhof   6 Pension Bahnhof

● **Eating**
1 Café Carstensen
2 Prime Rib & Flintstone Pub

rooms with a/c, TV, kettle and phone, B&B, small dining area; has the unwelcoming feel of an overnighting truckers' halt, but the rooms are unexpectedly nicely done with African touches, 24 hr reception, secure parking. **D/E** *Falkennest*, 21 Industria St, T/F 302616, otjbb@iafrica.com.na has 6 tidy but simple rooms with TV, a/c, phone, communal kitchen and braai area for self catering in the evening, B&B, small pool in well-tended garden with interesting cacti, decoration and aviary, secure parking. **D/E** *Out of Africa B&B*, 94 Tuin St, T303397, F304383, levaneck@iafrica.com.na is an immaculate guesthouse with a total of 21 newly decorated, en-suite rooms with TV, fridge, writing desk and comfortable chairs. Friendly hosts, well focused on tourists' needs and willing to answer your questions. Dining room serves breakfast only, lounge, 2 swimming pools, family flat, overnight parking attendant. They also run a car hire company and lodge of the same name. Recommended. **E** *Haus Blumers*, T303887. Has 4 large en-suite doubles in an old, slightly delapidated townhouse with thin mattresses, cigarette smoke hanging in the air and plenty of character, central, clean, friendly, the cheapest beds in town. **Camping   F** *Acacia Park*, T302121, F302926 is the municipal campsite, which means it's cheap and central but ugly, and potentially unsafe (crime). However, new management has properly fenced it and is doing its best to add attractive touches, each site has electricity and light, communal ablutions.

Guestfarms in the area   L *Okonjima*, T304563, F304565, www.okonjima.com Located 48 km south of Otjiwarongo on the B1, 24 km along private road, well signposted. Has 10 luxurious en-suite rooms with ornate and tasteful locally crafted furniture and decoration, gourmet food, indoor and outdoor dining areas and bar, lounge and library, swimming pool, game drives, birdwatching, hiking trails, animal and vulture feeding, all inclusive. Separate camp with 8 large luxury thatched rondavels opened Aug 2001 with similarly lavish facilities and full agenda. An excellent, informative experience for a worthwhile cause, the highlight of many visitors' time in Namibia. Recommended. **A/AL** *Oase*, T309010, F309011, oase@iafrica.com.na, 46 km from the B1 on the D2804. A regular HAN award winner, 6 en-suite doubles around colourful garden courtyard with pool. Friendly hosts, a good place to unwind for a couple of days in comfortable surroundings; little to do beyond informative farm drives, commune with the tame ostrich or soak up the tranquillity by the pool, somewhat overpriced. **C** *Otjibamba Lodge*, T303133, F304561, bamba@iafrica.com.na, 3 km south of town on the B1. Has 21 large en-suite doubles with TV, a/c, telephone and veranda, swimming pool, the main building houses a lounge, restaurant and bar popular with locals. A gentle introduction to the 'wild', with maps and flora/fauna identification charts available for self-guided walks (up to 3 hrs) through the 220 ha fenced game park, with numerous antelope and abundant bird life. Swiss owner; clean, welcoming and good value, if a little square and lacking in African feel. **C/D** *Otjiwa*, T306667, F306670, www.namibsunhotels.com.na is a large, impersonal place with 68 beds in (fixed) mobile bungalows located 38 km south of Otjiwarongo on the B1. Enclosed, grassed, swimming area, game viewing of large white rhino population in surrounding farm, short walks to animal hides, game drives available. Not your romantic picture of Africa, but worth stopping in for lunch at the decent restaurant, and to enjoy the rhino and pool on the way past. **D** *Aloe Grove*, T306231, 302580. Signposted 20 km north of Otjiwarongo on the B1, a further 18 km along the rutted and winding farm track, P2438. Simple en-suite accommodation with fan in tranquil spot on working farm, fruit trees, swimming pool and pleasant outdoor lapa; tame zebra, lion feeding (not part of the same activity), s/c facilities (again, not connected); possibly more effort to get to than it's worth. **E-F** *Nordland*, T306661. Drive 9 km north on the B1, then 4km on the D2433, and a further 3km along a farm track. Opened in 2000, large, old-fashioned, thin-walled, musty bungalow with 3 s/c rooms, available at N$75pp, very good value if you're lucky enough to get the whole place to yourself; plus cheap camping with braai area and light but basic ablutions.

Camping F *Hohenfels*, T304885, T081-2503252 (mob). Off the B1 (28 km south of Otjiwarongo), take the D2476 (towards Waterberg) 5 km, then follow sign down farm track for 3 km. Individual grassed sites with tables, seating and fabulous views from the hillside, braai pits and lights, swimming pool, bar and dining area for eating your meals and communing with your fellow campers. Well located for Waterberg, with better facilities and greater intimacy than camping in the park. Recommended. **F** *WesRand Farm*, T304108, T081-1245606 (mob). Take the C33 for Kalkfeld, turn right after 10 km, follow signs. 6 grassed sites with electricity, lights, free firewood, fridge.

Others   You may see signs for *Wabi Game Lodge*, and *Okaputa*, neither has been included as they are both very much private hunting farms.

C'est Si Bon lives up to its name. The restaurant at *Otjibamba Lodge*, 4 km south of town on the B1, has been recommended, although the kitchen closes at 2100. *Prime Rib and Flintstone Pub*, serves good meaty dinner. *Café Carstensen*, St George's St is a good place to stop for coffee, cakes and light snacks. So is the *Koffeeschtübe* by the Shell station on Hage Geingob St (south).   **Eating**

Main shopping centre situated at the eastern end of St George's St, expansion planned as part of the Heritage Exploratorium. Omaue Namibia (T303830), also St. George's St sells gemstones and minerals, plus curios, with tourist information available. Plein Square is due to be transformed from a dusty, littered gathering place to a thriving market with stalls selling locally made embroideries and carvings.   **Shopping**

It is 249 km to Windhoek; 190 km Okaukuejo (Etosha); 375 km to Swakopmund. **Road**   For *Intercape* coaches to Windhoek via Okahandja and north to Katima Mulilo, see timetable on page 382. Well served by **shared taxis** on the Windhoek-Oshakati route, limited service towards Outjo. **Train**   For trains to Windhoek, Tsumeb, Swakopmund and Walvis Bay, see timetable on page 383.   **Transport**

Banks   *First National*, St George's St. *Bank Windhoek*, Hage Geingob St. *Standard Bank*, Hage Geingob St. All have ATMs and change money. There is an FNB ATM in the Shell station on Hage Geingob St (south). **Communications** Post Office: Van Riebeeck St, Mon-Fri 0800-1630, Sat 0800-1130. **Medical services**   *The State Hospital*, T302491, Hospital St (!) on the eastern outskirts of the town. *Medicity Otjiwarongo Private Hospital*, T303734/5, Son St, is a costlier option. **Useful addresses**   Tourist info: Second St, in *Omaue Namibia* (T303830) minerals and curios shop, helpful ex-geologist shopkeeper. **Police:** St George's St, T10111.   **Directory**

Waterberg Plateau Park

Known to the Herero-speaking people as Oueverumue or 'narrow gate' between the Kleine and Grosse Waterberg, the Waterberg Plateau is Namibia's only mountain game park. The plateau rises up to 200 m above the surrounding plain, extending some 50 km by 16 km. The sharp barrier of the plateau presents a stark contrast to the monotonous, scrubby, bushveld plain below, and has operated as a game sanctuary for endangered species since 1972.   Colour map 1, grid B6

Today, it is of interest to naturalists and geographers for it's rare animal populations, atypical flora and striking sandstone topography, as well as being the scene of an historic encounter in the German and Herero troops.

The North

Ins and outs

Getting there Turn off B1 22 km south of Otjiwarongo onto C22. Follow this road for 41 km before turning left onto the D2512. Follow this for a further 27 km to Bernabé de la Bat Rest Camp, the entrance to Waterberg Plateau. There is no public transport to the park and once off the main road, there is little local traffic and hitchhiking may involve a long wait.

Getting around Open-top **game-viewing vehicles** set off early morning and mid-afternoon from the rest camp, and provide the opportunity for those unable or unwilling to hike on the plateau with the chance to see game. The tours stop at game-viewing hides, often well frequented with game. Bookings should be made at the camp office, wrap up in winter. N$50 adults, N$20 children. Book on arrival since this is a popular drive, lasting 3 hrs and taking you to an area of the plateau that is closed to the public.

Background

Originally part of a much larger plateau which extended as far southwards as Mount Etjo, the sediments which make up the Waterberg were originally laid down in Karoo times (290-120 million years ago). The break-up of the super-continent Gondwanaland 150 million years ago caused an upswelling of lava which compacted underlying sediments into rocks. At the same time, the huge pressure caused by the break-up of the continent caused uplifting of Africa's edges.

This uplifting started an erosion cycle visible today at Waterberg, Mount Etjo and Omatako, which are remnants of the old land surface, and which are slowly being eroded down to the level of the surrounding plain. Finally, in the late Karoo period, a thrust fault on the northwest side of Waterberg covered part of the plateau with debris, thereby protecting it from further erosion. This part, the Okarakuvisa Mountains, is the highest part of the plateau today.

Vegetation on the plateau is lush-green, sub-tropical dry woodland, with tall trees, grassy plains and a variety of ferns on top. This is in stark contrast to the acacia savannah at the base of the plateau, against which aggressive ant-bush

Waterberg Plateau Park

Related map
A Waterberg
Unguided Trail,
page 122

encroachment measures are being taken. The mixture of very sandy soils and the Etjo sandstone cause the plateau to act like a sponge, absorbing any water that falls. The water is sucked into the soil until it reaches a layer of impermeable stone, from where it runs off underground to emerge on the southeast side of the plateau as springs. It is from the springs that the plateau gets its name.

History

In 1873, two missionaries from the Rhenish Mission Society, G Beiderbecke and H Brincker, established a mission station at the largest fountain at the Waterberg, although they had been instructed only to assess the situation. Their congregation consisted of Herero, Damara and Bushmen, described by the missionaries as living in mutual distrust. In 1880 during a dispute between Damara and Herero groups, the mission station was looted and burned to the ground, and lay deserted until 1890, when Missionary Eich was sent to resurrect it. Over the next 10 years a school, church, trading post and post office were established.

However, events elsewhere in Hereroland were leading to a major confrontation between the Germans and the Herero. Unscrupulous traders encouraged and forced Herero-speaking people to buy goods against credit, and when the latter couldn't pay, the traders took land to cover these debts. Certain Herero chiefs, such as Samuel Maherero of Okahandja and Zacharias of Otjimbingwe sold off large tracts of tribal land to meet their growing desires for European manufactured goods and alcohol. Both promised their people that the land would be recovered at a later date.

In January 1904, facing increasing pressure to take action over the lost lands, or to stand down as Paramount Herero Chief, Samuel Maherero gave the order to drive the Germans from Herero land. Initial Herero attacks were successful, but following the appointment of General von Trotha as German commander in the middle of the year, the tide started to turn against the Herero. As a growing number of Herero men, women and children retreated to the Waterberg with their cattle, the scene was set for the crucial battle of the war.

Throughout 11 August, skirmishes took place between the German and Herero forces. The Germans had a total of about 1,500 men, as well as 30 cannons and a dozen machine guns. Estimates of the strength of the Herero forces range from 35,000-80,000 with between 5,000 and 6,000 guns at their disposal. As the day progressed, the battle moved deeper into the bush, stretching over a 40 km front, with neither side able to establish a telling advantage. However, on the morning of 12 August, a German signal unit on the plateau noticed a huge cloud of dust heading southeast. The Herero were retreating into the Omaheke sandveld rather than surrendering to the enemy.

Over the next months thousands of Herero men, women and children, with their cattle, died of hunger and thirst on the trek into exile in Botswana. In the years immediately following the battle and the exodus of the Herero, the land around the Waterberg was sold off to European settlers. The small graveyard near the rest camp is testimony to some of those who fell during the battle.

Wildlife

The 40,549 ha area was proclaimed a park in 1972, originally as a sanctuary for rare and endangered species, initially buffalo and roan and sable antelopes were relocated from the Kavango and Caprivi regions. The aim was to breed these animals and then restock the areas from where they originated. Blue wildebeest from Daan Viljoen Park, near Windhoek, and white rhino from Natal, South Africa, followed. Black rhino were reintroduced to the area from Damaraland in 1989. Today, it is possible to see 25 species of game including, leopard, gemsbok, eland, giraffe, kudu, jackal, hyena and baboon, as well as those animals mentioned above. As an aside, while these programmes have been remarkably successful overall, we were told of one incident where a rhino died after pitching over a sheer cliff, in either a bold bid for freedom, or tragic display of blindness.

In addition to the game, the park has an estimated 200 species of birds, and in particular is home to the only breeding colony of Cape vultures in Namibia (although there are now thought to be only three pairs left). An intensive aware-ness campaign is underway, aiming both to educate farmers to limit the use of poisons, and seeking to reverse bush encroachment on the plateau to increase grazing land for species such as kudu and gemsbok, upon which the vultures feed. Other common species are birds of prey such as the black eagle, the booted eagle and the pale chanting goshawk, as well as smaller birds such as the red-billed francolin, whose distinctive call can be heard at sunrise, five different hornbills, and the attractive (and attractively named) rosy-faced lovebird.

Bernabé de la Bat Restcamp

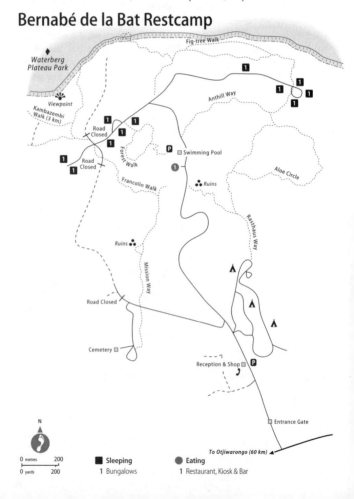

N

0 metres 200
0 yards 200

■ **Sleeping**
1 Bungalows

● **Eating**
1 Restaurant, Kiosk & Bar

Camp trails There are 10 demarcated walking trails around the camp and up onto the plateau. Photocopied maps should be available from reception, if not, get your bearings using the three-dimensional display at reception and strike out along the well marked trails. These gentle one to three hour walks are an excellent way of seeing the ruins of the Old Mission, as well as enjoying the flora and fauna without undertaking a major expedition.

Hiking
See map of Bernabé de la Bat Rest Camp, page 120

We recommend you make the effort to walk up to the plateau following the 'Mountain View' trail. The walk to the top takes 30-45 minutes, with plenty of rock hyrax (or 'dassies') to keep you company. This is an enjoyable hike and the view from the top is superb, particularly at dawn and dusk. You will need to be reasonably agile in parts, and not dawdle for too long after sunset.

Waterberg Wilderness Trail A four-day guided wilderness trail in the Okarakuvisa Mountains, starting on every second, third and fourth Thursday of the month (April to November only), overnighting at the rustic base camps in the wilderness area, with an (armed) expert on the region's flora and fauna to lead you. Recommended. Only one group (six to eight people) is permitted per week and reservations should be made well in advance at the NWR Windhoek reservations office, see page 36. ■ *N$200 per person, hikers must bring their own food and sleeping bag.*

Book ahead to enjoy these spectacular 4-day hikes

Waterberg Unguided Hiking Trail This unaccompanied trail, also recommended, starts at the Bernabé de la Bat rest camp office before taking hikers up onto the plateau for four days. It is aimed at reasonably fit, self-sufficient hikers and nature lovers who want to enjoy both the scenery and wildlife and have an adventure.

See map of Unguided Trail on page 122

Once up on the plateau itself, the trail winds around the sandstone kopjies on the southeastern edge of the plateau, through glades of weeping wattle, silver bushwillow and laurel fig trees. Everywhere there are signs of the close presence of game, the dung piles of the white and black rhino, and the spoor of kudu, giraffe, gemsbok and baboon. It is important to take care to walk relatively slowly so as not to surprise any rhino or buffalo, which might charge if frightened. If this happens your best bet is to climb the nearest tree, failing this, turn and face the onrushing beast and sidestep at the last moment. Then change your pants.

The trail is divided into four stages of 13, 7, 8, and 14 km respectively, each of which can be completed in a morning's walk. The first day's walk takes you along the edge of the plateau. There are several good viewpoints, notably Omatoko view close to Commiphora Kopjie. Your first night is spent in Otjozongombe shelter. For the second day the path skirts along the rim of Ongorowe Gorge. There is no need to push yourself along this stretch, the overnight shelter – Otjomapenda – is only seven km away. The third day can also be taken gently. The path follows an eight km loop bringing you back to the same shelter. The final day's walking follows a different path all the way back to Bernabé de la Bat restcamp. The trail is generally well marked, but in the odd place it is necessary to look for the footprints of previous trailists, and this adds to the adventure of the walk. Although the distances are not great, and the walk is not nearly as demanding as the Naukluft and Fish River Canyon Trails, it can get very warm during the daytime, especially carrying a pack with provisions, sleeping bag, water and camping stove. Nights can be cold with sub-zero temperatures not uncommon, so take warm clothes. Accommodation is in stone shelters with pit latrines; water is provided, hikers must take everything else.

As the early morning and early evening are the best times to see game, a good plan is to walk each stretch early in the day, drop your bags and rest up at camp during the midday heat, and then go for an exploration of your site before dark. After four days of the solitude and silence of the plateau it can be strange going back down the mountain into civilization again.

Hikes start every Wednesday (April-November). Only one group (3 to 10) people is permitted each week and reservations should be made well in advance at the Windhoek Reservations Office.   *N$90 per person, hikers must provide their own food and equipment and the trail is undertaken at the hiker's risk.*

Essentials

The park is open year round and reservations for all accommodation should be made at the Central Reservations Office in Windhoek. The resort has a shop, restaurant, bar, filling station (no diesel) and swimming pool with pleasant views.

Sleeping **D** *4 bed bungalows*, *3 bed bungalows*, *2 bed de luxe room*, fairly densely packed alongside each other but clean and recently refurbished (an improvement on the standard national park 'barracks') with hot showers; all fully equipped aside from crockery and cutlery. **F** *Caravan and campsites*, ablution blocks with cooking rings, braai pits. Entrance fee: N$20 adults, N$2 children under 16, N$20 cars.

Guestfarms in the area If you fancy staying in greater style, the new **A** *Waterberg Wilderness Lodge*, T306303, F306304, wwl@natron.net, well signposted 8 km past the entrance to the Waterberg Plateau Park on the D2512. Has 6 large en-suite doubles and a family unit, set beside a small river at the foot of the plateau, within the Waterberg Conservancy, with good shade and peaceful ambiance. They have some short guided walks and drives (although not on the plateau, as these are currently only available through the national park). Full board. Certainly the greatest luxury in the environs, but steeply priced. 'Premium' campsite planned. **A** *Hamakari Hunting Lodge*, T302214, located 64 km from the B1 on the D2476, roughly 40 km from the park, also takes non-hunters in their pleasant, large farm, a little further away, must be booked in advance, full board, including drinks and all activities (bar hunting); you are as well to stay in Otjiwarongo as here.

Waterberg Unguided Trail

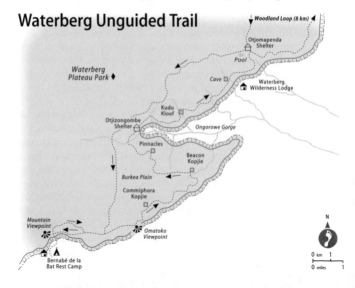

If you are travelling north from Windhoek towards Grootfontein or Namutoni Camp in Etosha National Park consider the following alternative route. After visiting the Waterberg, continue northeast along the D2512 (you'll need a map) taking in further views of the plateau, although don't expect decent views over the bush, as the surrounding acacia savannah is thick and the terrain extraordinary flat; to the south and east it stretches like this all the way to the Kalahari.

Moving on

Outjo

Outjo serves as a commercial centre for the large white-owned farms of the region and more recently has developed as a staging post for tourists on their way to Damaraland and the famous **Etosha National Park**. If you have been travelling in the south of the country, or have come up from the coast, you will notice a far greater number and variety of trees in the landscape. This is an area of woodland Savannahh supporting both cattle and abundant game. As you continue north towards Etosha, keep an eye out for antelope sheltering in the shade of the trees.

Phone code: 067
Colour map 1, grid B5
Altitude: 1,300 m

The North

Getting there You will almost certainly be en route to or from Etosha and travelling on the C38. Outjo is 73 km northwest of Otjiwarongo and 114 km south of Okaukuejo rest camp in Etosha National Park. Outjo is also a good jump-off point for Damaraland and Kaokaland, with both Kamanjab and Khorixas within easy striking distance on good tarred roads, the C40 and the C39, respectively. **Tourist offices** *SWA Gemstones*, Hage Geingob Ave, doubles as the curio shop. Very helpful on local information, also have a few maps for sale, you will find a decent spread of Etosha information and souvenir books available in the park itself.

Ins & outs

The name comes from a Herero word, *outjo*, meaning 'little hills', after the abundance of these surrounding the town. The first Europeans to settle here were big game hunters and traders. Tom Lambert is often cited as the founder of the settlement. In 1880 he arrived with his family and built a small garden on the river close to where the old **Water Tower** now stands. Before he could start cultivating the land he had to get permission from the Herero chief Manassa to build a home close to the water supply.

    In 1895, part of the German army was stationed here, during their period of residence they built several solid buildings, some of which still stand today. These included the **Water Tower** (see below), **Franke House** and a large fortress on the west bank of the river, the later no longer survives. One of the more important roles for the army when they were not at war, was to help to try and prevent the spread of Rinderpest from the Kaokoland and Angola. They also acted as early anti poaching units.

Background

Overnighters won't miss much if they head off first thing in the morning, but anyone with an interest in local history might enjoy a visit to the museum as well as admiring the old **Water Tower**. The **town museum** contains an account of the local history and a collection of gemstones, examples of which can still be picked off the ground if you know where to look. ■ *Mon-Fri, 1000-1230, 1430-1630, free.* The **museum** building is also known as **Franke House**. This was one of the first homes to be built in Outjo, and dates from around 1899, its first occupant was the commander of the German garrison, Major von Estorff. Major Victor Franke was one of the last local commanders who made a name for himself in leading a punitive raid against the Portuguese in Angola in 1914 (see below).

Sights

In 1900, the settlement ran into its first problems of water supply, the natural fountain could no longer provide for all the extra people and livestock. At the end of the year the German troops started to dig a well in the dry river bed, while concurrently beginning construction of the **Water Tower**. The role of the tower was to house a wooden pump powered by wind sails. In March 1902 the first water started to flow, it was lifted into a concrete dam and then carried over 600 m by pipes to the army barracks, a hospital and the stables. The 9.4 m high tower remains, being made from local stone and clay, but the sail mechanism has not survived. Today the tower stands on a stone platform between the *Etosha Garten Hotel* (who own the land it stands on, and have plans to tidy it up) and the dry river bed, it is protected as a national monument and is an important local landmark, rather like the Franke Tower in Omaruru.

A less well known monument from the past is the **Naulila memorial** standing in the old German cemetery. In October 1914 a group of German officials and accompanying soldiers were massacred by the Portuguese near Fort Naulila on the Angolan side of the Kunene River. More troops were killed a couple of months later, on 18 December 1914, when a force under the command of Major Victor Franke was sent to avenge the earlier loss of life! In 1933 the Naulila memorial was built in memory of both expeditions.

Sleeping   **In/near town**   **B/C** *Onduri*, Church St, T313405, F313408, onduri@iafrica.com.na is a large, characterless hotel with 45 plain, en-suite rooms with a/c and telephone, decent restaurant, off-street parking, overpriced. **C** *Etosha Garten*, Krupp St, T313130, F313419, www.etosha-garten-hotel.com has expanded to 21 spacious and colourful en-suite rooms, most set around the tranquil and shady garden with well established Jacaranda trees. A HAN award winner, the restaurant is excellent, for all meals, one of the best rural menus in the country, bar, swimming pool, they can advise on (indeed organise) excursions to Damaraland and Etosha and are a good base to explore from, returning to a grand evening feast. They also own the next door Water Tower, which they plan to revamp. Recommended. **C-F** *Ombinda Country Lodge*, T313181, F313478, signposted 1 km south of Outjo on the C38. 15 en-suite chalets, most thatched with reed walls, electric lighting and colourful fabrics, tasty a la carte menu served in a large thatched *lapa* by the swimming pool, 2 tennis courts and a 9-hole golf course (rackets and clubs can be hired). Basic campsite at N$30pp. **D-F** *Camp Setenghi*, T/F313447, 5 km south of Outjo, signposted off the C38. Five bungalows and 5 bush tents, B&B, swimming pool and bar with

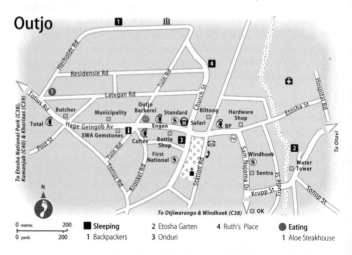

Outjo

0 metres 200
0 yards 200

■ **Sleeping**
1 Backpackers
2 Etosha Garten
3 Onduri
4 Ruth's Place

● **Eating**
1 Aloe Steakhouse

lovely views, set amongst the rock formations of the Ugab Terrace, N$30pp camping amongst the trees. Recommended, but may be about to change hands. **E** *Ruth's Place*, 313386, 3 simple rooms in centrally located house, fridge, secure parking. **E-F** *Backpackers*, T313470, simple rooms, a dorm and camping.

Guestfarms in the area **A/AL** *Ombundja*, T312123, ombundja@iafrica.com.na, 58 km from Outjo on the C40 for Kamanja. Has 6 thatched, en-suite rooms, game drives, large swimming pool, horse riding, full board, all inclusive, hunting possible, a little expensive. **A** *Namatubis*, T313061, F312203, namatubi@iway.na, 16 km north on the road to Etosha. Has 23 large but dull rooms, comfortable large beds, many with fridge, table and kettle, swimming pool in lovely garden, excellent and plentiful home-cooked buffet if booked ahead, a restful overnight spot, but with little charm. **B/C** *Saturn*, T312029, www.natron.net/tour/saturn, 69 km from Outjo on the C39 for Khorixas. A German hunting farm, with 5 en-suite rooms generously decorated with skins and trophies, large swimming pool and nice outdoor lapa/restaurant/bar. **B/C** *Okonguarri Wilderness Lodge*, T290302, F290333, signposted off the C39 to Khorixas. Billed as a psychotherapeutic centre with 5 s/c chalets, swimming pool, providing a restful spot for the exhausted traveller.
   Also *Bambatsi Holiday Ranch* and *Vingerklip Lodge* - See Northwest chapter, Khorixas for details.

Eating For excellent 'continental' cuisine (with local touches) food, go straight to the *Etosha Garten*, run by an Austrian couple; those preferring Afrikaans (meaty) dishes will do well at *Ombinda*. The *Outjo Bäckerei*, Hage Geingob Ave, is great for breakfasts and light lunches, cake and coffee, and doubles as the internet café. The *Aloe Steakhouse* is great for a beer and game of pool, but not recommended for food.

Shopping Well served with supermarkets, the last place to stock up (although you should really have done so in Otjiwaronga) before the wilds (and inflated prices) of Damaraland or Etosha. *Hardware Shop*, Hage Geingob Ave, camping equipment and fishing tackle for hire, and camera repair service.

Transport It is 318 km from Windhoek; 114 km to Okaukuejo (Etosha NP); 145 km to Kamanjab; 133 km to Khorixas; 73 km to Otjiwarongo; 688 km to Ruacana. **Train** Outjo is at the end of a disued branch line. The Windhoek-Tsumeb train stops at Otjiwarongo, from where passengers for Outjo have to travel by road. There are relatively frequent shared taxis available for the connection, but no regular bus service.

Directory **Banks** All three, and all except FNB with ATM. **Communications** Internet café at the Outjo Backerei, Hage Geingob Ave, with 2 computers, N$25 per half hour. Worth emailing home from here, if only for an excuse to tuck into the pastries; there is no public internet access north or west of Outjo.

Routes There are several very different routes one can follow from Outjo, whichever you choose make sure you have refuelled and have plenty of water, all of the routes lead into remote regions, where there is minimal traffic and supplies in small village centres cannot be relied upon. Take the C40 for Kamanjab, the C35 then continues north into the Kaokoland, Opuwo and Ruacana. To complete a circuit follow the C46 from Ruacana to Ondangwa where you rejoin the B1 which leads back to Tsumeb and Otavi. Due east from Outjo, the C39 takes you into the heart of Damaraland, to Khorixas and the tourist sights around the Brandberg. Follow the C38 north for Etosha National Park, this is the main route into the park; after 96 km the road reaches Andersson Gate, from here it is a further 18 km to Okaukuejo, the main rest camp.

The North

Etosha National Park

Phone code: 067
Colour map 1, grid B5

Etosha is one of Africa's great national parks, the game viewing here is on a par with Kruger, Hwange, the Masai Mara and Serengeti. Some 114 mammal species, 110 reptile species and more than 340 different bird species have been identified, and three well appointed rest camps cater for the hundreds of daily visitors. Each rest camp has a floodlit watering hole, which offers overnight visitors the chance to see good numbers of game in an unusual environment. A large proportion of the park is either closed to the public or inaccessible by road, which has enabled conservationists to carry out important studies of wildlife.

The central feature of the park is the Etosha Pan, a huge depression which in years of exceptional rainfall becomes a lake again, although even then the majority sits only a few centimetres deep. There are no roads across the pan, but along the southern fringe is a network of gravel roads which offer some exceptional views of this natural feature which can be clearly seen from space. A visit to Etosha is rightly one of the highlights of any visit to Namibia.

Ins and outs

Getting there

Road By Oct 2001, there will be 3 park entrances open to the public, **Andersson Gate** to the north of Outjo, **Von Lindequist Gate** at the eastern end of the park and the new **Nehale Iya Mpingana Gate** in the north-eastern section, named after the Owambo king of 1885-1908, offering access to and from the far north. All other gates are currently **closed** to the public. The shortest route from Windhoek, 447 km, is to follow the B1 north as far as Otjiwarongo, from here take the C38 for Outjo and continue north to Andersson Gate. For visitors approaching from the Caprivi, follow the B8 south as far as Grootfontein, from here take the C42 to Tsumeb where the road joins the B1, follow the signs for Etosha, Ondangwa and Oshakati. The turn-off for the Von Lindequist Gate and *Mokuti Lodge* is clearly signposted 74 km from Tsumeb. Namutoni camp is just inside the park. Nehale Iya Mpingana Gate opens Oct 2001; it is hoped visitors will consider continuing up to the Far North region of the country. Once completed, expect signposts on the B1, roughly 80 km south of Ondangwa.

Air Each of the 3 camps within the park (Okaukuejo, Halali and Namutoni) have their own airstrips which are used by tour operators and charter companies. There are also scheduled **Air Namibia** flights to *Mokuti Lodge* from where it is only a couple of kilometres to Von Lindequist Gate and on to Namutoni camp (see below). All of the smarter lodges can arrange fly-ins to the airstrip at any of the rest camps or at *Mokuti Lodge* by Von Lindequist Gate. They will collect and provide guided drives within the park.

Train While most people travel in their own vehicle, either self-drive or as part of a tour, it is possible to take the new luxury train service from Windhoek to the outskirts of the park, and enter for day visits. An interesting new option is offered by TransNamib, the national rail service, called the ***Northern Desert Express***. (This has developed out of the success of their ***Windhoek-Swakopmund Desert Express*** service, detailed on page 92). The train departs Windhoek each Mon at 0900, with a long afternoon stop (and wine-tasting tour) in Omaruru. Overnight is spent on the train travelling to Tsumeb, arrival is at 0900 the next day. From here, guests are transferred by bus to Mokuti

The North

Private Reserve for an afternoon game drive, overnight at *Mokuti Lodge*, a morning game drive and lunch, before being bussed back to Tsumeb for a 1400 departure on Wed. Arrival in Windhoek at 1500 on Thu. Price from N$2500-3200 per person, sharing, for the round trip, depending on season. Reservations Windhoek T061-2982600, Swakopmund T064-400372, www.transnamib.com.na/dx or through *Mokuti Lodge*.

Best time to visit

The park is open year round, but there are three distinct seasons which affect the game-viewing experience. Many regard the best time to visit the park as the cooler, drier winter months, Aug and Sep, as shortage of natural pools elsewhere in the park draws animals to the artificial waterpoints, many of which are visible from the rest camps or reachable by car. The other popular time of the year for visitors is during Dec and Jan (when it is very hot); this is more to do with local school holidays than any particular condition within the park. It may be difficult to book accommodation during the most popular periods, especially at weekends. If visiting from overseas, consider booking your accommodation prior to your arrival within Namibia (see page 36 for details). For bird enthusiasts the best time to visit the park is during and after the rains, Nov-Apr.

Background

The central feature of Etosha is the large pan which covers 23% of the park. The first Europeans to see the pan and write about it were Charles Andersson of Sweden and Francis Galton from Britain, who came here in 1851 en route to Owamboland. They were very disappointed to find it to be bone dry having been told it was a large lake. Galton estimated the pan to be nine miles (14 km) in breadth and at least 15 miles (24 km) wide, but as anyone standing on the southern fringe will appreciate the mirage effect had disguised its true size. Etosha Pan is 130 km long and 72 km wide, a fantastic and most unusual natural feature.

The name is usually translated as Great White Place or Place of Emptiness. There is a San legend of a group who strayed into Heiqum lands only to be surrounded by brutal hunters who killed all the men and children. One of the young women rested under a tree with her dead child in her arms, she wept so much that her tears formed a giant lake. After the sun had dried her tears the ground was left covered in salt – and so the Etosha Pan was formed. The pan is indeed very alkaline, sediment samples have a pH higher than 10, with a sodium content of more than 3%. This attracts the local wildlife, which requires salt in its diet.

The North

The Heiqum have lived around the pan for generations, surviving as hunter-gatherers. They are a group of people related to the Bushmen who live around Outjo, Tsumeb and Grootfontein, their language is a Nama dialect. Today many are employed as assistants in the park to watch over the animals and carry out repairs to pumps and fences.

The first European interference in the region came in the 1890s when the German administration was faced with the rinderpest outbreak. To try and control the spread a livestock-free buffer zone was established along the southern margins of the pan. In order to enforce the restrictions on the movement of cattle, two small military units were posted in tiny forts at Namutoni and Okaukuejo. The park (along with two other reserves) was created in 1907 by Governor Friedrich von Lindequist. Since its proclamation, the boundaries have been significantly changed on a number of occasions. In 1907, the reserves incorporated an area of 93,240 sq km, including all of the present day Kaokoland from the coast to Ruacana. In 1947, the Kaokoland was allocated to the Herero-speaking people. Less than 10 years later the Elephant Commission recommended the park also include land between the Ugab and Hoanib Rivers, the new park was larger than ever at 99,526 sq km. The current size came about after the Odendaal Commission recommended the creation of a Damaraland homeland in 1970 – the park currently covers an area of 22,912 sq km.

The German forts at Okaukuejo and Namutoni were converted into police posts to help establish control over the Owambo kingdoms to the north. The fort at Namutoni was made famous after it was attacked by several hundred Ndonga warriors serving King Nehale. On 28 January 1904, four German soldiers and three ex-servicemen managed to resist the attack during daylight hours. During the night they managed to escape from the fort before it was

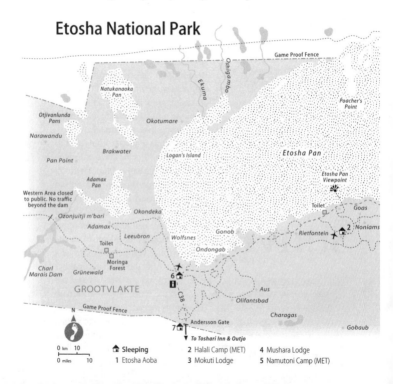

Etosha National Park

Game Proof Fence

Oshigambo

Ekuma

Natukanaoka Pan

Poacher's Point

Otjivanlunda Pans

Okotumare

Narawandu

Brakwater

Logan's Island

Etosha Pan

Pan Point

Adamax Pan

Etosha Pan Viewpoint

Western Area closed to public. No traffic beyond the dam

Ozonjuitji m'bari

Okondeka

Toilet

Goas

Adamax

Gonob

Rietfontein

2 Noniams

Leeubron

Wolfsnes

Toilet

Ondongab

Charl Marais Dam

Grünewald

Moringa Forest

6

GROOTVLAKTE

C38

Aus

Olifantsbad

Charagas

Game Proof Fence

Gobaub

N

Andersson Gate

7

▼ To Toshari Inn & Outjo

0 km 10
0 miles 10

🛏 Sleeping
1 Etosha Aoba

2 Halali Camp (MET)
3 Mokuti Lodge

4 Mushara Lodge
5 Namutoni Camp (MET)

The North

overwhelmed the next day and burnt to the ground. The present building at Namutoni dates from 1906 when a new and larger fort was completed. Once the new reserve had been created, the military significance of the post declined; the last troops stationed here surrendered to the South African forces under the command of General Coen Britz on 6 July 1915. In 1957 the fort was restored as a tourist camp.

Wildlife

There are countless drives and waterholes that you can visit for game-viewing purposes, they all have their different merits, but it is impossible to recommend any one point ahead of another. The wardens are the best source of advice as to where game is congregating and where the cats and large mammals have been spotted each day. As a tip, remember it always pays to be patient – once you have found a waterhole that appeals to you just turn the engine off, keep quiet and wait.

The most commonly occurring species are the animals which prefer open savannah country. You can expect to see large herds of blue wildebeest, gemsbok, Burchell's zebra, springbok and elephant. After the rains many of these animals migrate to pastures which are in areas closed to the public. A good reason for visiting Etosha is to see the endangered black rhinoceros. The resident population is reckoned to be one of the largest in Africa. While it is difficult to spot these animals in thick bush, they frequently visit the floodlit waterhole at Okaukuejo. During the heat of the day they tend to lie up and you are unlikely to spot them on a drive.

The park is home to three uncommon antelope species: the black-faced impala, Damara dik-dik and roan antelope. The roan antelope were introduced to the park in 1970. In one of the earliest cases of moving animals by aircraft, a small herd was transported by Hercules from Khaudum Game Reserve in Bushmanland. These are shy animals and tend to be only seen in the inaccessible western areas. The black-faced impala is easily recognized as an impala but with a distinctive black facial band. Originally from Kaokoland, a large herd was translocated and released within the park. The largest groups used to occur near Namutoni, but like all wild animals they will move to the water and pasture. The Damara dik-dik is the smallest antelope in Namibia, the adult only weighs 5 kg. They are shy animals favouring wooded areas; you may catch a glimpse of family groups, but such a small animal often quickly disappears.

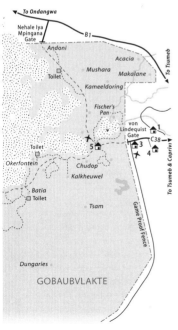

6 Okaukuejo Camp (MET)
7 Ongava Lodge

The North

Essentials

Rest camps

There are 3 rest camps in the park, each managed by Namibia Wildlife Resorts; bookings are handled by the head office in Windhoek (see page 36). The park headquarters are at **Okaukuejo**, the other two camps are **Halali** and **Namutoni**. The facilities at each rest camp are similar: there is a parks office which you will have to visit first to find which accommodation unit you have been allocated, a shop which sells a few curio items and food and drink for campers, a restaurant which serves 3 meals per day (and kiosk serving drinks and snacks open when the restaurant is shut), a bar, a filling station (you can cover a surprising distance while game viewing), a swimming pool and a post box (Okaukuejo has a proper office). The speed limit throughout the park is 60 kph.

Entrance fees (payable at the gates, or your rest camp if you are overnighting within the park): Adults: N\$30 per day. Children: N\$2 per day. Cars: N\$10 per day. Gates are open: sunrise to sunset. Camp offices are open: sunrise to 1300, 1400 to sunset, all visitors staying overnight must be in the camps by sunset when the camp gate will be locked. **Do not stay out in the park after sunset**, you may find yourself in serious trouble if you fail to time your return to the camp by sunset. In the event of a breakdown or a puncture **do not leave your car**, you may be attacked, stay in the vehicle until help arrives. For this reason, make sure you always have a supply of food and water when out game viewing.

The shops are open: Mon-Sat 0730-0900, 1100-1400 and 1730-1930; Sun 0800-0900, 1200-1400 and 1800-1900. Restaurant meal times: breakfast 0700-0830; lunch 1200-1330; dinner 1800-2030. During peak season the restaurants can get crowded in the evening; you may have to wait for the initial rush to eat their meal before you can get a table. Okaukuejo post office hrs: Mon-Fri 0830-1300, 1400-1630.

Sleeping

All accommodation must be vacated by 1000, rooms can be occupied from 1200. During local school holidays visits to Etosha are limited to a maximum of 3 nights per camp

Although you are encouraged to book accommodation in advance, it is possible to obtain a bungalow on the day if there is space. Check at the office at Namutoni or Okaukuejo for availability, either of these offices can advise you of the situation in all 3 camps. If camping, be aware that even in peak season, they rarely turn away last-minute campers, and there seems to be little control over what constitutes 'full'. While there can be frustratingly long queues at the ablutions, and you may find yourself sharing cooking facilities with your neighbours, a full camp has its own distinctive, excited atmosphere, which all adds to the fun.

All bungalows are en-suite with towels and bedding, some have hotplates but visitors must provide their own crockery and cutlery. The central booking office for park accommodation is in Windhoek at the Kaiserliche Landesvermessung building, corner J Meinert and Molte st, close to the Kudu statue; T061-236975-8, F224900, www.namibiawildliferesorts.com Open for information Mon-Fri: 0800-1700 and for reservations Mon-Fri: 0800-1500. All accommodation must be paid for in advance, credit cards are accepted. Bookings by telephone will be accepted 11 months in advance. Written bookings can be made up to 18 months in advance, and will be processed 12 months in advance. Written bookings should be addressed to: The Customer Care Manager, Reservations, Namibia Wildlife Resorts Ltd, Private Bag 13267, Windhoek. All applications should include details of accommodation required (see below for details), date of arrival and departure (give alternative dates for popular periods, see above), number of adults and children (with age), one passport number and full home address with contact telephone numbers. While the process is clearly designed for local residents there is no reason why one should not apply from abroad several months prior to your arrival in Namibia.

This is the largest of the 3 camps, the central feature of the camp is a circular limestone water tower close to the administration block. A few minutes at the top is recommended, both for the views of the plains and Etosha Pan in the distance, and to help orientate yourself within the camp. In addition to luxury bungalows and simple rooms, there is a camping and caravan site with (barely sufficient) communal facilities. There are 2 swimming pools next to the restaurant (with little shade), where in the midday heat, Europeans are to be found cooking themselves.

Okaukuejo

Colour map 1, grid B5

18 km from Andersson Gate, 70 km to Halali, 140 km to Namutoni

The restaurant is sensibly priced with a choice of dishes for each meal. The whole complex was rebuilt after a fire in 1997. Unfortunately the service, while polite, can be slow and disorganized. Away from the offices and shops is a floodlit waterhole which can get quite busy but is always rewarding for game viewing. Bench seats are arranged behind a protective wall and there is a thatched miniature grandstand. Please refrain from talking loudly when in the vicinity of the waterhole, it is very easy to startle a shy animal, especially at night, and you will not make yourself popular with other guests. There is a good chance of seeing black rhino and elephant with young at this waterhole and the 3 big cats also often drink here.

National parks accommodation Staying in the park is less comfortable than in some of the nearby lodges, but offers you the opportunity to visit the waterhole after sunset, as well as enjoy being surrounded by the full, rumbling and shrieking African night-time chorus. Adjacent to the waterhole (with thatched roof) are bungalows 3, 5, 7, 11, 13, 18, 19 and 20. Although they tend to offer less privacy, as the rest of the camp arrives at dawn and dusk, you may be rewarded with your own private views in the middle of the night. All rooms and bungalows have en-suite bathroom, fridge, kettle, bedding and towels.

B *Luxury Suite*, 4 beds, 2 rooms, stove, TV, cutlery and crockery provided. **C** *Luxury Bungalow*, 2 rooms, 4 beds, hotplate, cutlery and crockery provided. **C** *Bungalow*, 2 rooms, 4 beds, as for the luxury version but less spacious. **D** *Bungalow*, one room with 3 beds, hotplate. **D** *Bungalow*, one room with 2 beds, hotplate, the cheapest option for bungalows. **D** *Standard Room*, one room with 2 beds, no hotplate. **D** *Economy Room*, as above, marginally smaller and cheaper. **E** *Campsite*, dusty but shaded, electricity available, pricey at N$140 per site per day (max 2 people, one tent), plus N$15 per additional adult, communal facilities that can develop queues in busy periods, take your chance for a shower when you can; popular with overland buses; **day visitors** can hire out **picnic sites** for N$80, although it is on your conscience to pay as no one checks, day visitors have use of all facilities, including communal kitchens and ablution blocks.

Private lodges and camps On the C38 between Outjo and Andersson Gate are a number of lodges catering for visitors looking for more comfort and attention than you will find within the park. **L** *Ongava Lodge*, reservations T061-225178, F239455, www.ongavalodge.com Entrance by Andersson Gate, then 9 km to the lodge, 18 km to the tented camp. Has 10 beautifully crafted, en-suite, thatched doubles, furnished to an exceptional standard, with views across the mopane woodland from the swimming pool that are hard to tear yourself away from, excellent food; part of the highly regarded Wilderness Safaris operation, and usually fully booked. There is a separate canvas/thatch tented camp with 6 luxury tents run independently of the lodge,

The North

www.ongavatentedcamp.com, should you fail to find space or prefer to be closer to nature. Both offer morning excursions into Etosha, brunch, siesta, afternoon tea and drive within the reserve (30,000 ha, bordering Etosha) sealed with a sumptuous evening meal. They offer day and night guided walks (and rhino tracking), which can be a pleasure after being confined to your vehicle within the national park. There is talk of a further 'luxury bush camp' at the edge of a 10,000 ha restricted access area, with foot safaris, which would be an excellent bush-living experience, but with all creature comforts supplied. As they operate along strict conservation lines, they are also hoping to gain government agreement to remove the fence between themselves and the park, offering unrivalled access in comfort for the (well-heeled) visitor. Recommended. **A/AL** *Naua Naua*, T333418, F333447, www.nauanaua.com is a beautiful new camp 26 km south of Andersson Gate, then a further 15 stony km off the C38, with 13 very spacious, en-suite, thatched rooms, opened in 2000. Small swimming pool with lovely views over the plains, cosy restaurant and bar in large central building, cheetah-feeding and walking trails, game and sundowner drives, airstrip with air safaris available in vintage plane. Great care and attention to detail in the building of this new lodge, and limited numbers, means an intimate and close to nature experience. If Ongava is full, this is your best bet. **C** *Toshari Inn*, T/F333440, www.resafrica.net/toshari-inn, located 26 km south of Andersson Gate then signposted off the C38, has 16 large en-suite rooms (most can fit 4 people), some s/c, restaurant, swimming pool. Good value alternative to the accommodation in Etosha; campsite planned for 2002. **E-F** *Eldorado*, T333421, schroder@iway.na, located 7 km south of Andersson Gate on the C38. Has 10 fixed tents with twin beds, bedding, private ablutions, table, seating, crockery, and braai, homemade dinner and breakfast available on request, good farm stall with seasonal fresh produce, homemade foods and local crafts, cheap campsite. Your best 'budget' option in the area.

Halali
Colour map 1, grid B5

Located more or less midway, 74 km, between the two other camps. This was the third camp to be opened in the park. While it is less developed and visually less attractive than the other two, the camp has an excellent restaurant and a refreshingly large (20 m) swimming pool. The floodlit waterhole is beautiful located (although not particularly regularly frequented by game) at the base of a kopjie. There are walks all around the camp, including up and over the small kopjie; make sure you are quiet as you approach. One of the advantages of staying at this camp is that you are in the centre of the park, thus there are more waterholes within a short driving distance. It is also less popular with overland buses. If you are planning a visit to Etosha a recommended itinerary would be to spend your first night at either Okaukuejo or Namutoni, and then 2 nights at Halali, and exit the park at the opposite end to which you first entered. This way you will not only see all the camps, but you will avoid doubling back on your route too much. Alternatively, in peak season, you might enjoy exploring the routes to the west of the pan, where there are a number of man made water points and, usually, fewer tourists.

National parks accommodation All rooms and bungalows have en-suite bathroom, kettle, bedding and towels. Some of the accommodation blocks are a bit close together, when the camp is full you have limited privacy; at the back of each bungalow is a braai area. **B/C** *Luxury Suite* 2 rooms, 4 beds, stove, microwave, fridge, cutlery, crockery and TV. **C** *Luxury Bungalow* 2 rooms, 4 beds, hotplate, fridge, cutlery and crockery. **C/D** *Economy Bungalow*, hotplate. **D** *Standard Room*, Single room with 2 beds, stove, fridge. **E** *Campsite*, dusty but fairly well shaded, clean communal facilities with plenty of hot water, electricity; pricey at N$140 for 2 per day, N$15 per additional adult; day visitors can hire out picnic sites for N$80, although it is on your conscience to pay as no one checks, visitors have use of the communal kitchens and ablution blocks. Recommended restaurant, shop selling basic provisions, bar open 1800-2130.

Some 140 km from Okaukuejo, allow at least 3 hrs to drive between the two camps, you are always likely to stop for something, even if it is to allow an elephant to cross the road. For many visitors, this is their favourite camp, with its striking, whitewashed, converted fort, palm-fringed swimming area and picturesque, thatched game-viewing point. However, during the day there are frequently large tour groups stopping for lunch and a look at the museum in the fort. While the old German fort is an impressive centrepiece, the camp lacks established shade trees. The swimming pool is shaded by well established makalani palms, in a grassed garden close to the restaurant/bar complex. There is a floodlit waterhole surrounded by tall grasses and reeds, but the visitors book reported few sightings on our last visit. The camp was last refurbished in 1995, prior to hosting part of the Miss Universe contest.

Namutoni
Colour map 1, grid A5

National parks accommodation All rooms and bungalows have en-suite bathroom, fridge, kettle, bedding and towels. **B/C** *Luxury Suite*, 2 rooms, 4 beds, stove, cutlery and crockery. **C** *Luxury Flats* 2 rooms, 4 beds, stove. **C** *Standard Chalets* 2 rooms, 4 beds, stove. **D** *Standard Room* single room with 2 beds. **D** *Standard Flat* single large room with 4 beds, stove, frying pan. **E** *Economy Room* single room with 2 beds, some have shared bathroom. **E** *Room in Fort* basic 2-bed room, communal facilities. **E** *Campsite*, a greener site than at the other 2 camps but with less shade, electricity available; pricey at N$140 for two per day, N$15 per additional adult; communal kitchen and excellent ablution blocks, can get crowded, popular with overland buses.

The rooms in the fort are small and dark. The best room is the luxury flat, which consists of two good size rooms, a fully equipped kitchen and a private bathroom. Unfortunately, it is located by the museum, so you will have to endure a steady flow of visitors peering in. Tourist office and petrol station open sunrise to sunset, shop 0700-1830, kiosk 0830-1200 and 1330-1800, bar 1400-2130.

Many of the visitors to Etosha who enter via Andersson Gate leave via the Von Lindequist Gate in the east of the park. From here it is 35 km to the main Tsumeb-Ondangwa road, the B1. Just outside the park are a couple of luxury game lodges as well as the Mokuti airfield served by Air Namibia.

Outside the park

Private lodges and camps **A/AL** *Mushara Lodge*, T229106, F229107, www.musharalodge.com, 1 km from the main road then 7 km to Von Lindequist Gate, has 10 pristine, thatched en-suite bungalows with a/c, fridge/minibar, telephone and mosquito net. Highly rated restaurant, bar, decent sized swimming pool, guided game drives, walks around the property, airstrip. Unusually for this area, the lodge is privately owned by a young and energetic German couple, the lodge is immaculately tended, with not a blade of grass out of place, and yet still intimate, your best bet east of the park. **A** *Etosha Aoba*, T229100, F229101, www.etosha-aoba-lodge.de Turn off 10 km from Von Lindequist Gate, then 10 winding km further to lodge. Has 9 small, thatched en-suite bungalows with veranda, a much more 'natural' feel than most upmarket lodges, comfortable, without being pristine, hidden among indigenous Tamboti trees. Small swimming pool, large thatched bar/restaurant area and pleasant sundowner drives to nearby Fisher Pan. **A** *Mokuti Lodge*, T229084, F229091, www.resafrica.net/ mokuti-lodge is an enormous and impressive set-up located a couple of km from the main road just outside Von Lindequist Gate. The main complex is in a huge, thatched barn, beautifully rebuilt after a fire in 1997. 106 en-suite a/c thatched rooms of varying size, set in a small woodland area with neat gardens; restaurant has a very good reputation, bar, pool bar, 2 swimming pools, playground, 2 tennis courts, small museum of 1997 fire, large curio shop, game drives in double-decker bus and walks on the property available. An impressive place, it loses out to other establishments because of its size, but if you like to be anonymous in large, impersonal establishments, this could be for you. **C** *Sachsenheim Game Ranch*, T230011, F230072, on the B1, 3

The North

km north of the C38 for Etosha, 30 km from Von Lindequist Gate. Has 11 simple doubles with fan, shaded gardens, swimming pool, dining area, **F** basic campsite under improvement, this is the closest campsite outside the east end of the park. A hunting farm, not recommended in mid-summer, otherwise, a pleasant spot.

Transport *Air Namibia* flies to Mokuti Lodge from Windhoek's Eros airport.

Road to the Triangle

After a couple of days driving at slow speeds on the gravel in Etosha it feels quite strange as you drive along the C38 towards the main highway. What is most noticeable is the quiet. When you reach the B1, there is a choice of heading northwest to **Ondangwa** and **Oshakati**, or turning southeast towards **Tsumeb**. If you choose to travel north you will experience a Namibia that is totally different from the rest of the country, the most noticeable fact being the people: over 50% of the country's population live in this area. This region used to be known as **Owamboland**, but it has now been divided up into four new regions (see page 178 for details of the Far North).

As the road approaches Tsumeb, much of the land is given over to large commercial agriculture to feed the mining labour force and other local residents. Although this part of the country receives a reasonable amount of rainfall, it is still necessary to irrigate crops. Since the mines came into production, water has been drawn from two unusual lakes which are found in the bush close to the main road, **Lake Otjikoto** and **Lake Guinas**. A picturesque alternative route to Otavi, if you are not yet fed up of driving on gravel roads, takes you close to the southeast corner of Etosha. Following the D3028 and D3025, the route does not take significantly longer than the B1 via Tsumeb.

Routes Once in Tsumeb you are faced with another choice. If you are heading for the Caprivi region follow the C42 to Grootfontein and then the B8 to Rundu. Alternatively, follow the B1 south towards Otavi and the middle of the country. In Otjiwarongo the road divides yet again, the C33 via Omaruru is the road towards the coast at Swakopmund, stay on the B1 for the quickest route to Windhoek.

Otjikoto and Guinas Lakes

Colour map 1, grid B6 **Lake Otjikoto** is set back 100 m from the main road (B1), amongst the trees, but it is well signposted. When the sun shines the waters of the lake look very blue and clear. It is possible to climb down to the lake shore via a rock stairway; this is not encouraged and swimming is forbidden. **Lake Guinas** lies further from the road along the D3031. It is clearly signposted, but the site has not been developed. The lake was formed in the same manner, but there is no easy access to the lake shore the sides are precipitous. If you are able to visit this lake in May you will see it at its best, surrounded by flowering aloes on the rock faces. The rusty remains of a large steam pump lie nearby, a legacy of efforts in the 1920s to irrigate local citrus orchards. Both of the lakes lie on private farms and, as you can imagine, they are popular with scuba divers. This is a very complex form of **diving** and should not be attempted by inexperienced divers. Prior permission is required from the farmers.

Each of the lakes was formed by the collapse of a ceiling in a huge dolomite underground cavern. They are technically known as '*sink holes*'. The caverns were formed after water leaked into the dolomite rocks, following a minor earthquake which fractured the rocks. Once in contact with the limestone, the water slowly dissolved the rock. The cross-sectional view of the lake can be described as an upside-down mushroom. A popular myth is that Lake Otjikoto is bottomless, this is not so, but the flooded cave system extends for much further than was originally believed. Lake Guinas is considerably deeper; it has been measured to over 200 m. The levels in both lakes fluctuate as water is pumped for irrigation.

Lake Otjikoto is home to an interesting range of fish, most of which are 'alien' species. A sub-species of the common Tilapia was introduced to the lake in the 1930s, and the lake is home to a very unusual type of bream. The bream has a protective habit of carrying the eggs and when they are first born, the young fish, in its mouth. The dwarf bream, *Pseudocrenoolabrus philander disperses*, live in the dark depths of the lake Scientists have postulated that these fish moved to the depths after the shallower waters became overpopulated due to the absence of predators.

The name *Otjikoto* is said to come from the Herero and can be loosely translated as 'the place which is too deep for cattle to drink water'. The first Europeans to come across these lakes were Francis Galton and Charles Andersson, who camped beside Lake Otjikoto in May 1851. In 1915 the retreating German army took the decision to dump their weapons in Lake Otjikoto so the South Africans could not make use of them. There are mixed accounts about what actually was thrown in, but there is no doubt about the pieces which are on show in Tsumeb museum. A large ammunition wagon is also on display in the Alte Feste museum in Windhoek. In 1916, a team of divers under Sergeant G Crofton and J de Villiers of the Special Intelligence Unit of the Union forces was sent to try and recover some of the armaments. They managed to find a mix of small arms and ammunition, five cannons, 10 cannon chassis and three machine guns. In 1970, an ammunition wagon was found at a depth of 41 m, in surprisingly good condition. In the early 1980s, divers recovered some more pieces, including a Sandfontein cannon. All of the most recently discovered items have been carefully restored and are now on show in the Khorab room in the excellent Tsumeb museum.

■ *There are some interesting, well made curios for sale, toilets, a couple of caged warthogs rolling in the mud and a* **F** *small (noisy with traffic, but well serviced) campsite. An admission fee (N$7 per person) is charged, for which you can get close to the lip of the lake and take photographs into the depths, or of the breadth of the lake with a wide-angle lens.*

Transport Lake Otjikoto is 24 km north of Tsumeb, well signposted off the B1. Just before you reach the lake there is another turning on the right, the D3043. If you follow this for 19 km and then take a turn onto the D3031 you will find yourself beside Lake Guinas.

The Triangle

When you look at a map of northern Namibia, the roads which link the towns of Otavi, Tsumeb and Grootfontein quite clearly form a triangle. They are part of a prosperous region which produces a significant proportion of the country's maize crop and is also an important mining centre. Because of their proximity to Etosha and the Waterberg Plateau, and being en route to and from the Caprivi, a significant number of visitors pass through these small, simple towns. The museum in Tsumeb and the Hoba Meteorite are worth a detour, and there are some beautifully located guestfarms to accommodate you. This is the last outpost of German colonial influence – north of here the countryside and the atmosphere is totally different to that in the centre and the south of the country. All three towns are suitable (although Otavi only barely) for stocking up with supplies and cash, but none merit a stopover of any length.

Otavi

Otavi is the first of the three 'triangle' towns you reach when driving north from Windhoek on the B1. It is also the smallest and offers little of interest to the tourist. In the past it was an important mining centre and the scene of many feuds between the Ovambos, Hereros and Bushmen.

Background It was the **copper** that brought the boom period to the town. Work on a narrow-gauge railway began in November 1903 and was completed in August 1906, after being interrupted by the Herero-German war. The railway was built to carry copper ore to Swakopmund. The German colonial company which ran the mine and built the railway was the **Otavi Minen-und Eisenbahn-Gesellschaft (OMEG)**; there are some excellent photographs of the railway on show in the OMEG museum house in Swakopmund (see page 218 for further details). Major mining operations continue today, but they are based in and around Tsumeb, leaving Otavi with a run down feel. Other minerals found in the Otavi mountains are lead, vanadium, cadmium and zinc. Just outside of the town is an Amethyst mine; this is worth visiting to see samples in their natural state.

Sights The only local site is the **Khorib Memorial**, 2 km north of the town. Unlike some memorials in Namibia this one is particularly plain. There is a small stone plaque close to the railway. It was unveiled in 1920 to mark the end of German rule in South West Africa in July 1915, when local officials surrendered to the Commander of the Union Forces, General Louis Botha. The German officials were the Commander of the German forces in South West Africa, Colonel Victor Franke and the Governor of South West Africa, Dr Seitz.

Sleeping **D** *Palmenecke*, Hertzog Ave, T/F 234199, opened in 2000, a friendly and comfortable palm oasis (literally 'corner') with 5 large and bright en-suite doubles with a/c, TV and desk, price is B&B, all meals available, there are occasional braais in the welcoming and cosy thatched lapa surrounding the tiny swimming pool. Recommended. **D** *Otavi Gardens*, Unie St, T/F234334. Under new ownership, undergoing extensive change. While they do have a beautiful, central thatched bar/restaurant, which is worth a visit for a beer or meal, it is too early to tell how the place will feel once completed. They plan to have 10 en-suite doubles. **F** *Municipal Caravan Site*. A distinctly off-putting place, very down at heel place, with tiny, drab chalets and grubby, dusty camping spots with electricity, braai area, light, very basic ablutions; if you are looking for a campsite, then rather opt for the decent municipal campsites in Tsumeb or Grootfontein.

Guestfarms in the area B/C *Khorab Safari Lodge*, T234352, F234520, khorab@iafrica.com.na, 5 km south of Otavi on the B1, has 10 en-suite doubles in thatched bungalows, each with fan, fridge and desk; swimming pool with lapa, good restaurant, bar and lounge in large thatched barn popular with tourists and local farmers in the evenings. **C** *Ghaub*, T/F240188, www.namibsunhotels.com, 4 km west of the D2863/D3022 junction (NB not to be confused with the nearby hunting farm Gauss). Set in the lovely Otavi Mountains Conservancy, well worth a drive through even if you aren't planning to stay the night (plan your own loop along the D2863 and D3022). Opened in 2000 with 10 large en-suite doubles, each with veranda and great views over a huge lawn, the large swimming pool and across the valley. The main house is an old Rhenish Mission Station (est. 1895), and the impressive trees date from that time, giving the feel of an English country estate, but with African touches everywhere. Full board, including drives, guided walks in the hills (they have Bushman engravings), an excursion to the nearby bat caves (the third largest in Namibia) or large underground reservoir/cave for those interested. Campsite planned for 2002. Worth staying a couple of nights to enjoy the tranquillity of the spot as well as the activities on offer. Recommended. **D** *Zum Potjie*, T/F234300, F221964, www.resafrica.net/zumpot, 8 km north of Otavi, 2 km off the B1. Has 5 basic but clean en-suite bungalows. The attraction is the home-cooking, your resourceful Afrikaans hosts source most of their ingredients from the farm. **F** Campsite with simple ablutions and camp kitchen; upgrade planned for 2002.

If you don't need accommodation, a *Spar*, **First National Bank** with ATM, post office or telephone, then don't turn into town. The 24-hr Total on the main road also does take-aways. There is also a BP 30 km south of town. Limited **Tourist information** available from the municipal building next to the *Municipal Caravan Site* during office hrs. Otherwise, try the lodge owners. — **Directory**

If you are heading for Etosha National Park or Oshakati, follow the B1 to Tsumeb (63 km), where the B1 turns northwest. This road takes you past Otjikoto and Guinas Lakes, after 73 km there is a left turning, C38, to Etosha National Park (Von Lindequist Gate). An alternative, more scenic route to Etosha (and taking a similar time), is to head northwest on the D3028 for 44 km, turn left at the D3025, and rejoin the D3028 before meeting the tar road close to Namutoni. The road passes quite close to the southeast border of the national park, offering an appetizer of game viewing before you enter the park proper. — **Routes**

Follow the B8 out of town for Grootfontein (92 km), Rundu and the Caprivi Strip. Before you reach Grootfontein there is a sign to the left for the Hoba Meteorite (see page 144). Visitors travelling from the north have another 353 km to Windhoek on the B1 via Otjiwarongo and Okahandja.

Tsumeb

Tsumeb is the largest of the three triangle towns in northern Namibia and was developed as a major mining centre. The name Tsumeb derives from the Hain/Ohmbushman word Tsomsoub meaning 'to dig a hole in loose ground', and the Herero word Otjitsume meaning 'place of frogs'. The reference to frogs derives from the green, red-brown and grey streaks of copper and lead ores found in the ground in the local rock. These are supposed to resemble frog spawn scooped out of a waterhole and sprinkled around on the surrounding rocks! The town's coat of arms acknowledges both Tsumeb's mining and frog connections by depicting a pair of frogs squatting alongside mining tools.

Phone code: 067
Colour map 1, grid B6

Thanks to the wealth generated by the mines, Tsumeb is an attractive town boasting some fine old colonial buildings and a palm tree lined central park with wide lawns. It is also the last stop before passing north of the so-called 'Red Line', separating the enclosed commercial cattle farms to the south from the communally-owned lands to the north. Travelling north across the Red Line one moves away from 'European' Namibia and into the heart of Owamboland, where almost half of all Namibians live.

The first stop any visitor should make is **Travel North Namibia**, OMEG Allee, T220157, T081-1246722 (mob). Helpful and efficient, there is little you cannot organize from here, including good value car hire deals with *Imperial* to visit Etosha. Agents for *Air Namibia*, *Intercape Coaches* and *Western Union Money Transfer*. Cellphone available 24 hrs if you have problems. — **Ins & outs**

History

There is evidence of the smelting and mining of copper in the Tsumeb area as long ago as the Stone Age, and certainly both Damara and Owambo communities were known to be skilled smelters and workers of the metal. As the different Namibian tribes came into increased contact with each other during the second half of the 19th century, so disputes arose over the ownership of the land around Tsumeb. White traders, active in Namibia by this time, were also interested in the minerals in the area and a number succeeded in gaining land concessions around Tsumeb.

Serious European interest in the area was signalled in 1892 when the London-based South West Africa Company obtained a mining concession, and early the following year the geologist Matthew Rogers visited Tsumeb to carry out further investigations. In 1900, a new company, the Otavi Minen – und Eisenbahn – Gesellschaft (OMEG), was formed in order to raise more money to develop mines in the area.

Following the construction of a road between the settlement and the mines and the sinking of two new shafts, the first nine tonnes of copper left Tsumeb for Swakopmund at the very end of 1900. Although this first copper was carried by ox-wagon, by August 1906 the narrow-gauge railway to Swakopmund had been constructed. This improved export channel proved a massive boost to the efficiency of the whole operation, and by 1908 the company was already generating significant profits.

This was to signal the start of almost a century of mining at Tsumeb, interrupted only by the two World Wars and the more recent miners' strike. Ownership of the mines passed into the hands of the Tsumeb Corporation (TCL) following Germany's defeat in the Second World War, and they continued to develop mining capacity. Tsumeb's mines are today a major producer of copper, lead, zinc and precious minerals – silver and gold. The corporate tax paid by the mines contribute significantly to Namibia's overall tax revenue, and so place mining at the heart of the Namibian economy (see Background, page 355, for further details).

Sights

Tsumeb Museum Located in the old German Private School building dating back to 1915, the museum has a fine display of the town's mining history including a display of minerals. There are also exhibits of traditional costumes, artefacts and photographs, and a fascinating collection of German First World War weapons and ordnance retrieved from Lake Otjikoto, where they were dumped prior to the German surrender to South Africa in 1915. This is, in our view, one of the best museums in the country. Sadly with the closure of the mine, its future is uncertain. The building had been given to the community by TCL, but may now have to be paid for. Money that has been painstakingly collected for repairs and new items will probably disappear into the receiver's pockets. ■ *T220447. Mon-Fri 0900-1200 and 1500-1800, Sat 1500-1800, N$5 adults, N$2 students, N$1 children.*

St Barbara Catholic Church This church, on the corner of Main and 3rd streets, consecrated in 1914, was dedicated to the patron saint of mine workers, and for 13 years served as the town's only church. It dominates the centre of the town, and the unusual tower above the entrance is particularly eye-catching.

Trouble at TCL

In August 1996, miners working at three TCL owned mines downed tools, starting Namibia's largest ever industrial dispute. The strike, which was to last for 45 days, started because of a wage dispute, however over the course of the seven-week stoppage it became clear that the miners were fighting for much more than this. 'In view of the magnitude of the dire exploitation at TCL, I do not know what the outcome of this strike will be,' said Peter Nholo, Mineworkers Union Of Namibia (MUN) Secretary-General, one day before the start of the strike. 'But I can assure you that when the strike ends, TCL will never be the same again,' he concluded.

In effect the miners were claiming gross discrimination between white and black employees at the mines, and the payment of near slave wages to black miners. Some were taking home N$541 (œ75) a month after 30 years' service at the mine. In reply TCL claimed that with a 30-35% drop in world copper prices in Jun 1996, the company could not afford to pay its miners the 13.5% increase demanded by the MUN.

The dispute was eventually settled with the help of government mediation and a wage increase of 10.5% was agreed upon, however the MUN did have to agree to the retrenchment of some workers. On the other side, a commission of inquiry was appointed to investigate labour practices at the mines. 'There are no two ways about it ... Apartheid and Broederbond TCL must be destroyed and buried 20,000,000 km down the earth so that it never rises again,' vowed Labour Minister Moses Garoeb.

Overall the strike cost TCL an estimated N$70 mn and the company never really recovered. Mining activities limped on into 1998 when the company announced that it could no longer sustain losses being incurred.

As it turned out, the effects of the strike were far greater than anyone imagined. Suddenly on 16 April 1998, a provisional liquidation order was filed. For over a year there were rumours that a buyer had been found for the mine. Sadly though, the mine finally closed in April 1999 with the loss of 2,000 jobs. For the Tsumeb community it was a devastating blow, one that is still felt today as the town struggles to find jobs for the ex-miners and a new role for itself in the new millennium.

OMEG Mineneburo On 1st Street, this looks remarkably like a church, however it was designed in 1907 by Joseph Olbrich to symbolize the wealth and power of the MEG company at the time. The building is currently used as a gymnasium. In the early 1970s it served as the local kindergarten.

Tsumeb Cultural Village The village is on the southern outskirts of town, another (in this instance, Norwegian backed) project trying to harness tourism to benefit the local community. The aim is to have families from each of the eight Namibian tribes living here in traditional huts, wearing traditional dress, and each 'contributing' by either making crafts for sale or dancing, playing music, cooking and selling traditional food. The crafts are priced reasonably (no need to haggle); proceeds are split between the individuals and the project. Worth stopping by en passant. They are hoping to become part of tour groups' agendas, offering simple meals, as well as providing **F** accommodation, in 3 basic huts, for a sense of living like they do/did, with mats (or camp beds, for softies), sink and communal ablutions. Again, funds benefit the community, so do take a look. ■ T220787

The North

Essentials

Sleeping

There is a style choice to be made between the two excellent hotels in Tsumeb: the modern chic of the Makalani or the fading colonial grandeur of the Minen

C *Makalani Hotel*, T221051, F221575, www.makalanihotel.com has 18 clean en-suite rooms, TV, phone, a/c, secure parking, swimming pool, recently tastefully redecorated, restaurant and pub/bar. **C** *Minen Hotel*, T221071, F221750, www.minenhotel.com is a German-owned hotel with pleasant mature gardens, 49 en-suite rooms, a/c, telephone, TV, pub lunches served in the garden, restaurant with extensive menu, and attached bar, swimming pool. An atmospheric old-style hotel, full of character. **D** *Hotel Pension Kreuz des Sudens*, T221005. Small, friendly, German-run guesthouse with 3 en-suite doubles with fan, swimming pool and restaurant. **D** *Pension OMEG Allee*, OMEG Allee, T220631, F 220821, 6 clean en-suite doubles with a/c, TV, fridge, safe and kettle, weird and wonderful cacti in the front garden. **D/E** *Tsoutsomb Bungalows*, T220404, F220592. Choice of 4-bed or 6-bed bungalows, central, quiet location, good value. **D/E** *Pension Travel North*, T220157, mobT081-1246722 after hrs, F220916. Clean but very simple doubles with access to on-site facilities of laundry, car hire, email, snacks, beer garden, tours and transfer services. **F** *Municipal Caravan Park*, B1 southern edge of town, T221056, 21 green, shaded and spacious caravan/campsites, each with own braai area, table, seating, electricity and water, communal ablutions. Also the best spot for a picnic.

Tsumeb

■ Sleeping		**● Eating**
1 Makalani	4 Pension OMEG Allee	1 Etosha Café
2 Minen	5 Pension Travel North	2 Juwika
3 Pension Kreuz des Sudens	6 Tsoutsomb Bungalows	3 Steinbach Bakery

The North

Guestfarms in the area **AL** *La Rochelle*, T221326, F220760, www.la-rochelle.com.na, 40 km north of Tsumeb on the C83. Has 10 en-suite doubles with minibar and phone. Principally a hunting farm with plenty for the 'tourist' to do while the hunters are away: heated swimming pool, tennis, gym, jacuzzi, horse riding, hiking or sitting by the water-hole; book ahead to avoid clashes with hunters. **C/D-F** *Tamboti Lodge*, T222498, F222497, tsmapt@aiafrica.com.na, 11 km off the B1 on the D3067, junction 16km north of Tsumeb. Will have 14 en-suite doubles with fridge once work is completed in late 2001; 4 are thatched. Self-caterers welcome, although the restaurant does good, cheap food. Also 56 beds (bedding provided) in 2 converted railway sleeper carriages, with ablution blocks attached to one end; obviously cramped, simple and roasting hot in summer, but entertaining for children. **F** Campsite under improvement for end 2001. Small swimming pool, regular visits from game at nearby waterhole, including cheetah, eland and giraffe. **D** *Muramba Bushman Trails*, T220728, F220916. Take the C75 north from Tsumeb for 64 km, turn right onto the D3016, look out for signs after 6 km. 4 double huts with hotplates and communal ablutions. **F** Camping possible. A fascinating new venture which takes the visitor out into the country to learn about the ways of the Heikum bushmen. The main trail is only 2.5 km long, but you may be out all day with your guide. Cost approximately N$160pp, includes drinks and midday meal. Longer hikes also possible. Advance booking only.

Makalani Hotel and *Minen Hotel* both have restaurants serving lunch and dinner. **Eating** *Etosha Café*, Main St. Pinafored waitresses, excellent cakes and coffee, light meals plus tourist shop. Recommended. *Juwika Restaurant*, 3rd St, T221766. Excellent steaks. *Steinbach Bakery* , Main St. Light meals, coffee etc.

For those interested in buying unusual rocks and semi-precious stones, Tsumeb is a **Shopping** good place to do your shopping. Also self-caterers' final chance to stock up with fresh fruit and vegetables en route to Etosha.

Local **Car hire**: *Avis*, Jordan St, T220520. *Imperial*, T220728. **Long distance** **Air**: *Air* **Transport** *Namibia*, T067-220520, F220821. **Bus**: *Star Line*, T067-220358: **Oshakati** (4 hrs): Mon, *427 km to Windhoek* Thu, Fri, Sat, 1115. **Train**: See timetable, page 383. *107 km to Namutoni* *247 km to Ondangwa*

Banks *Bank Windhoek*, *First National Bank* and *Standard Bank*, all on Main St, with **Directory** ATMs and money changing facilities. **Communications** **Post Office**: Post St, Mon-Fri 0800-1630, Sat 0800-1130. **Internet**: On OMEG Allee, N$25 per hr, very slow connection: bring a book, 0900-1900, Fri 0900-2200, Sat 0900-1300, 1600-2100, Sun 11-1300, 1700-1900. **Teleshop**: OMEG Allee, close to the Municipality. **Medical services** *Jacobs Pharmacy*, Main St. *Private Hospital*, T221001. **Useful addresses** **Police**: 8th Rd, T10111.

Grootfontein

The northern market town of Grootfontein is one of the trio of towns, the others being Otavi and Tsumeb, located in the so-called maize triangle. Blessed in Namibian terms by high annual rainfall of 450-650 mm, the Grootfontein area supports a wide range of agriculture on its predominantly white-owned farms. Apart from the usual livestock farming of cattle, sheep and goats, the farms here produce most of Namibia's commercially grown maize, sorghum, cotton, peanuts and sunflower. In years of drought, the country remains a net importer of maize; Namibia required emergency aid in the worst years of the past decade.

Phone code: 067 *Colour map 1, grid B6*

The town itself is a pleasant enough place with its limestone buildings and tree-lined streets, and is particularly attractive in September and October when the purple jacaranda blossom and red flamboyants appear. With two reasonable, small hotels, a good municipal campsite, and the nearby Hoba Meteorite, Grootfontein is a good place to stop between Windhoek and the Kavango-Caprivi regions.

History With an abundant supply of water and good grazing, the area has been home to both game and humans for many thousand years. In pre-colonial times the town was known to the Herero as *Otjiwandatjongue*, meaning 'hill of the leopard'. The earlier Nama and Berg Damara inhabitants called the area *Gei-ous*, meaning 'big fountain', from which the Afrikaans name Grootfontein is derived. The fountain and the Tree Park, planted by the South West African Company, can both be seen today on the northern edge of town close to the municipal swimming pool and adjacent Olea Caravan Park.

In the 1860s, two elephant hunters, Green and Eriksson, used the fountain as a base from which to launch their hunting expeditions. However the first Europeans to settle in the area arrived around 1880, followed soon after by the so-called 'Dorsland Trekkers' who in the mid-1880s established their own Republic on land purchased from Owambo chief, Kambone. The Republic of Upingtonia, as it was called, survived for a mere two years before collapsing.

In 1893 the South West Africa Company established its headquarters at Grootfontein and in 1896 the settlement was enlarged by a group of settlers from the Transvaal. In the same year the *Schutztruppe* constructed a fort and administrative centre, and in 1904 a tower was constructed, providing the garrison with an excellent vantage point from which to survey the surrounding area. In 1922 the limestone extension was added.

Between 1923 and 1958 the fort served as a school hostel, after which it was abandoned. A public appeal in 1974 saved the building from demolition, and in 1975 it was declared a national monument, and also served as an assembly point for Angolan refugees. In 1977 it was renovated and in 1983 the **Alte Feste**, 'Old Fort', museum was opened, with a local history exhibition inside and a display of industrial items outside.

Grootfontein itself officially became a town in 1907, and the following year the narrow-gauge railway linked the town with Otavi and Tsumeb. The

Grootfontein

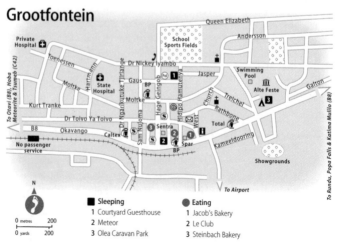

Sleeping		Eating
1 Courtyard Guesthouse		1 Jacob's Bakery
2 Meteor		2 Le Club
3 Olea Caravan Park		3 Steinbach Bakery

town has subsequently grown to become the centre of Namibia's maize industry, evidenced by large silos at the end of the railway line, with a significant cattle industry.

The **Alte Feste Museum**, just west of Olea Caravan Park (municipal campsite) is worth visiting for its history of the town and the local area. Exhibits include local minerals, restored carpenter's and blacksmith's shops with working machinery, and traditional crafts. ■ *Tue and Fri, 1600-1800, Wed 0900-1100, for access at other times, T242351, free.*

Straussen Ostrich Farm,located 6 km from Grootfontein off the Tsumeb road (just off the D2859 for Hoba), has a showroom with information 'from the egg to the bag' and shop selling meat and jewellery, restaurant in shaded garden, guided tours at N$10pp.

In town C *Courtyard Guesthouse*, T240027, F240073, platinum@iway.na has 6 plain but spacious en-suite rooms, a/c, satellite TV, fridge, swimming pool, secure parking, email for residents (although you'll get a better connection next door at the internet café), small gardens. Some tasteful touches to the fairly square rooms; not a place to write home about, but still your best bet in town. **D** *Meteor Hotel*, T242078, F243072, meteor@iway.na has 18 rooms, a/c, phone, bar/beer garden and restaurant are popular with locals, especially pizza night (Fri) and Sun buffet (1200-1400). **D-F** *Olea Caravan Park*, T243101, the municipal campsite, reception open 24 hrs. Four 4-bed bungalows and 9 pleasant, shaded camp/caravan sites with electricity, water, table and seating and braai area, shared ablution block; care should be taken with valuables as the campsite is close to town and, although guarded, not secure. Although not oppressive, traffic from Okavango Rd can be heard through the night.

Guestfarms in the area C-F *Guest Farm Koukuas*, T232033, 85 km north of Grootfontein, on the D3016, by the D2855 junction. An attractive fort-style building, with en-suite rooms, pleasant gardens, bar, restaurant and natural swimming pool among the rocks, walking trails, campsite. Recommended for families. **D** *Guest Farm Rietfontein*, T231512, F231511, www.namibsunhotels.com.na, 1 km south of the D2804/B8 junction, 28 km west of Grootfontein. Has 8 en-suite doubles, swimming pool, bar, restaurant, TV lounge, located on a working farm, tours available. **D-F** *Lala Panzi Guest Lodge*, T/F243648, 5 km south of Grootfontein, just off the B8. Adequate en-suite bungalows and basic campsite, quirky, large restaurant and bar, swimming pool. reasonably priced. **F** *Die Kraal*, T20300, 7 km northeast of town on the B1. 4 simple campsites with basic ablutions, excellent restaurant, bar.

Located in the middle of the triangle is your best bet in the region: *Ghaub*, see above under Otavi. For those travelling to Rundu, there are a number of options: *Kalkfontein*, *Dornhügel* and *Roy's Camp* (page 153).

Die Kraal, T20300, 7 km northeast of town on the B1, has excellent steaks (particularly local game) for lunch and dinner, sometimes overrun by an overlander busload since Lonely Planet 'discovered' them, call ahead to check availability. Simple campsite available, recommended as moving, let alone driving, afterwards, is not recommended. Be sure to pitch your tent before dinner. *Le Club*, Hidipo Hamutenya St, T242414, decent bar with large TV for sports; restaurant specializes in steaks and fish from the nearby lakes, beer garden. *Meteor Hotel*, quieter ambience, broad menu including fish, steaks, ribs and game dishes. *Backerei & Café Jacob*, Okavango Rd. On the way out of town towards Rundu, excellent coffee and pastries, and often a host of well fed locals tucking in at the tables. Recommended. *Backerei Steinbach & Café*, Hage Geingob Ave. Also serves light meals, coffee and pastries throughout the day.

Transport It is 460 km to Windhoek; 280 km to Tsumkwe; 807 km to Katima Mulilo. **Bus** See time-table, page 382.

Directory **Banks** *Bank Windhoek*, Sam Nujoma Dr; *First National Bank*, Dr Toivo Ya Toivo St and *Standard Bank*, Bismarck St, all have ATMs, and there is a further Bank Windhoek ATM next to the Spar. **Communications** **Post Office:** Bismarck St, Mon-Fri 0800-1630, Sat 0800-1130. **Internet** cafe; Hidipo Hamutenya St, with excellent 64kbps connection, open office hrs. **Medical services** *The State Hospital*, Hartmann St, T242041, *Private Hospital*, T240064, *Dentist*, T242125. Very helpful and well informed **Tourist office**, Municipality Bldg, T243102, beware early closure: open 0730-1600. **Useful addresses** Police: T10111.

Hoba Meteorite The Hoba Meteorite is an impressive lump of metal, the largest known single meteorite in the world, weighing in at around 60 tonnes and measuring 2.95 m by 2.84 m. It was discovered by Johannes Brits in 1920 whilst he was hunting in the area. After various people tried to get a souvenir piece of it, the meteorite was declared a national monument in 1955.

The meteorite is believed to be between 190 and 410 million years old, and fell to earth at least 80,000 years ago Made of 82% iron (which really shows when you see it up close), the meteorite also contains 16% nickel, which South West Africa Company manager, T Tonnessen, proposed mining in 1922 – fortunately he never got round to it. There are suggestions that the Hoba Meteorite is merely the largest fragment of an even larger meteorite which broke up during entry into the earth's atmosphere, in which case there may be other fragments lying around in the area waiting to be discovered.

There is a small charge to get to the meteorite, some panels with information, a basic nature trail, good braai/picnic facilities and a small shop selling information leaflets, souvenirs and drinks. It really is an unusual lump, worth the short detour to see this mysterious visitor from space. ■ *Getting there: Follow C42 towards Tsumeb for 3 km, then take D2859 for about 15 km, following sign to Meteorite.*

Dragon's Breath Cave In the hills around Grootfontein there are reputed to be a number of underground caves on private farms. One such cave is known as Dragon's Breath Cave, located on Haraseb farm, 41 km from Grootfontein, 61 km from Tsumeb. It is reputed to be the largest discovered underground lake in the world. While attracting caving teams from all over the world, the cave is closed to the general public. We decided to include this short piece in case access improves in future.

The entrance to the underground system is via a narrow crevice in some dolomite rocks. The first obstacle to negotiate is a 4 m drop, managed with the use of a cable ladder. At the bottom you find yourself in a sloping cavern, which you exit onto a narrow ledge, from where it is a further 18 m down to the point where you can first see the lake. This viewpoint is an opening in the cavern roof directly above the lake waters. A rope is used for the final 25 m to the water.

The surface area of the lake is almost 2 ha – the equivalent of four rugby pitches. The water in the lake is crystal clear and very deep. A small raft is required to cross the lake to a small stone beach. In late 2001 the cave remained closed to the public, with no plans to open the site.

Bushmanland

When you look at a road map of Namibia there is a large blank area in the northeast with very few roads or settlements. This is the region commonly known as Bushmanland. Like Kaokoland in Namibia's northwest, this is tough country to travel in – you should not even consider exploring here unless you are familiar with four-wheel driving in soft sand and off road. There are no facilities for the tourist and visitors must be completely self-sufficient; food, water, petrol, tents and so on must all be brought with you. On Namibia's border with Botswana is the remote and little visited **Khaudum Game Reserve**. *Visitors to Khaudum should have at least two vehicles travelling together. Elsewhere in the region it would always make sense to travel with another vehicle. This is a very remote area, even by Namibian standards. In a wilderness of over 7,000 square miles there is only one settlement of any note –* **Tsumkwe**, *275 km from Grootfontein, via the* **C44**.*

The countryside is flat and dry, the few roads that are marked are no more than tracks in places and there are few signposts. South of the C44 are a couple of pans, Kbebi Pan and Nama Pan, which tend to flood after rain and then attract wildlife from all over the Kalahari region. It is very difficult to travel in these areas after the rains, known as the Panveld, since the roads turn into impassably slippery mud. Dotted about this level landscape are the occasional baobab tree and patches of savannah forest, as well as remote San communities.

Tsumkwe may be the regional administrative centre, and the largest settlement in the region, but it is no more than a ramshackle collection of shops, trading stores and bottle shops. You may find Bushman art for sale in stalls or small shops; ostrich egg bracelets and necklaces and colourful beaded bags are the most common items. The Nyae Nyae Cooperative markets all art in the region, the revenue generated being vital to the survival of the individual craftsmen and women and the local craft 'industry'. If you plan to explore the area make sure you have sufficient fuel for your planned mileage. There is a police station and **Nature Conservation** office, which is useful for anyone traveling on to the reserve; the office will be able to advise on the condition of the roads and location of the wildlife. Look out for a large baobab tree, Nature Conservation is close by.

Tsumkwe
Colour map 2, grid B4
There is no petrol available here

Sleeping The only place to stay is **B** *Tsumkwe Lodge*, reservations T/F067-220060, 5 thatched, en-suite bungalows, restaurant, bar, accessible by 2WD, but you'll need to hire a Land Rover to explore any further (expect to pay N$800 per day, with a driver and guide). They offer walking trails and traditional crafts and rituals. They can arrange a visit to the nearby Ju/'hoan Bushman village, game drives and fly-in charters. It is 50 km from Tsumkwe to the southern entrance to Khaudum Game Reserve.

Khaudum Game Reserve

This is a desperately remote reserve, with a wide variety of animals and bird life. There are no facilities in the park, visitors have to be totally self sufficient, many of the roads are very sandy and it is easy to get stuck. Most visitors in this region are heading here.

Colour map 2, grid A5

Getting there Driving from Grootfontein on the gravel C44, take a left just before entering Tsumkwe, follow the road behind the village school and look out for the signs to the park and Klein Döbe. Before you reach the park entrance you will pass a Nature

Ins & outs

The North

Tourism and the San

The San once roamed an area several times the extent of the current 'Bushmanland' living as hunter-gatherers. Sadly this is no longer the case, more than any other ethnic group in the region they have suffered from coming into contact with the modern world. There is high unemployment and a serious problem of alcoholism in most communities. If you come into contact with the San communities be courteous at all times and respect their traditions. In most areas it is possible to pitch your camp anywhere, however if you are near a village make sure you seek their permission. Tourism has only just started to find its way into this region, the first people who pass through first must be careful to leave the right impressions.

Conservation field station. If you are north of the reserve on the B8, there is a road south off the B8 at a village called Katere, 120 km east of Rundu. The turning is well sign-posted. Once you are on the road driving south, check with people at regular intervals that you are on the right route; there are plenty of tracks, masses of sand and no sign-posts. **Best time to visit** The climate of the area has two distinct seasons: the rainy season extends from late Nov until Mar, which is also the hottest time of the year. The rest of the year, Apr to Nov, is a long dry season. It's best to avoid late summer, Dec to Mar, when rain renders the vegetation very dense and the roads impassable. This is, however, the best time for birds. During the winter, Jun-Oct, game numbers seem to improve in the park, particularly close to the artificial waterholes along the *omuramba*.

Background Khaudum was proclaimed in 1989, covering an area of 384,000 ha along the Botswana border on the edge of the Kalahari. The park was established to conserve one of the few true wilderness areas in Namibia. The vegetation is a dense mix of short and tall dry wood-land; in winter, most trees shed their leaves and game viewing is much eas-ier. The dominant trees are wild teak, wild seringa and copalwood. The shorter trees, those less than 5 m in height, include the Kalahari apple-leaf, silver cluster leaf and the shepherd's tree. All of these trees are able to grow on the thin sandy soils of the Kalahari. Running through the park are several fossil rivers known as *omuramba*. In the north of the park, close to the campsite, are the Khaudum and Cwiba *omuramba*. The soil along the margins of these *omuramba* have a high clay content and therefore support a differ-ent range of trees, a mix of thorns – camel, umbrella and candle as well as leadwood. After the first summer rains look out for the flowering knob thorn.

Khaudum Game Reserve

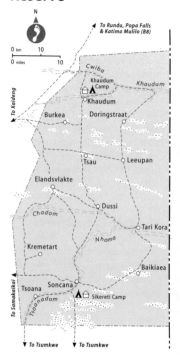

The *omuramba* no longer flow as rivers, but they fill up and store water which is gradually released during the dry season. They are made up of peat beds and are often identifiable due to abundant reed beds. The lush vegetation within them and along their margins make them a natural east-west migration route for game.

If you expect animals around each corner when on a game drive, then this is **Wildlife** not the game park for you. Here, game viewing is a real skill, you have to be patient and know something about the animals – what they eat, when they eat, where they prefer to be at different times of the day, and so on. Since very few people visit the park the animals are not used to the sound of engines and they are more likely to bolt than ignore you. There are no fences around the park so all the animals are free to move along traditional migration routes during the year, meaning that at certain times of the year there are quite a few animals in the park.

The park is an excellent place to see Roan antelope; wild dogs are regularly spotted. Other animals you can expect to see on a good day are kudu, eland, steenbok, gemsbok, blue wildebeest, giraffe, elephant, hartebeest, reedbuck, tsessebe, jackal, spotted hyaena, lion, leopard and perhaps cheetah. The mix of vegetation habitats provides a wide variety of birds: over 300 species have been recorded, with more than 70 migrant species after good rains.

There are two camps in the park, Khaudum in the north and Sikereti in the south, both **Sleeping** run by Namibia Wildlife Resorts. These are very simple camps and everything, bar water, needs to be brought with you. **E** *Khaudum Camp*, 3 4-bed huts and campsites, braai area, communal ablutions, a beautiful location beside the Khaudum *Omuramba*, overlooking the flood plain. **E** *Sikereti*, 3 4-bed huts, communal open-air kitchen, campsite, set in a pleasant woodland environment. Bookings through NWR in Windhoek. This is probably the least visited of the parks because of the logistics of getting here, but once here the true wilderness experience is highly rewarding.

The North

The Northeast

5

The Northeast

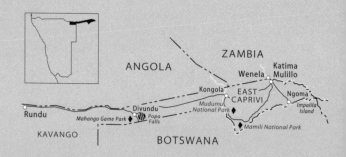

The Kavango and Caprivi regions provide the visitor with a welcome change from the relentlessly dry landscapes for which the country is famous. The northeast boasts a landscape dominated by rivers, green for most of the year, where local farmers can hoe their fields, anticipate rain with relative certainty and harvest their staple crop of grain each year. This is not to say that the people who live here are wealthy, but few will have suffered the hardships brought about by the heat and drought in the south.

For the overseas visitor, the region offers something of 'real' Africa, and presents a new range of vegetation and wildlife, albeit in a similarly beautiful and unspoilt environment. The political troubles of 1999 appear to have completely subsided, and the lodge owners will welcome you warmly after a barren period. Souvenir hunters will find some of Namibia's finest local crafts in the community run markets and roadside stalls. It certainly is a long drive from Windhoek, but for many, the northeast is their favourite corner of the country.

Kavango

Malaria is a risk in the northeast: you should take prophylactic drugs, especially during the wet season

*Between Grootfontein and Rundu there is a marked shift in both vegetation and human influence. Finally the arid lands are left behind, as you enter the wettest region of Namibia. The average annual rainfall in the Kavango region is more than twice that of the south, although, again, most of the rain falls between November and March. Even more striking is the contrast in the style of farming, from the commercial low intensity farming south of the **Red Line**, to the subsistence living of the small farmers and communities of the north. Almost all the tourist lodges and camps are located in strategic positions along the lush riverbanks, where the scenery is at its most beautiful and game and birdlife is at its most plentiful.*

Some 57 km north of Grootfontein there is a turning east (C44) for **Tsumkwe** (222 km) and **Khaudum Game Reserve**. This is a tough region to travel in and should not be explored by inexperienced off-road drivers, even if you have the right vehicle. See page 145 for details. After the Tsumkwe turning, there are no other junctions of note before the B8 reaches Rundu. You will encounter a checkpoint at the **Red Line**, the fence dividing the north and south of the country, built to prevent foot-and-mouth disease and rinderpest from migrating south into the large commercial ranches. At the checkpoint, 131 km south of Rundu, are a small shop, take-away and petrol station. The change in landscape and roadside activity north of this divide is striking, you are entering... Africa!

Depending on the season, between the Red Line and Rundu you will probably see by the roadside heaped piles of watermelons, contorted gourds or bowls of monkey oranges, as well as some local handicrafts. The number of stalls selling carvings appears to have reduced in recent years. Only a few remain and their range is limited but keep an eye out for bargains: after an extended period of reduced tourist traffic, the laws of economics are in your favour. Avoid driving this stretch after dark as goats and cattle regularly stray into the road; in daylight, enjoy the homesteads, perhaps purchase crafts or fresh produce from roadside stalls. While the road is tarred all the way, beware pot-holes and roadworks.

Kavango & Caprivi

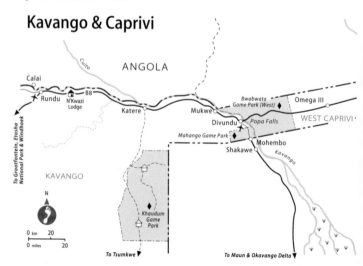

★

Things to do in the Northeast

- Enjoy a sundowner at the *Zambezi Hotel's* **floating bar**.
- Join the **mokoro fishermen** on any of the region's perennial rivers, either self-propelled in your own canoe or under escort from a talented oarsman.
- Enjoy a picnic breakfast by the large baobab in **Mahango Game Park**, counting the birds and watching the elephants drink.
- Browse the **Caprivi Arts Centre** in Katima Mulilo and pick up a souvenir.
- Relive the days of colonial splendour at one of the **luxurious riverbank lodges** – Lianshulu Lodge and Impalila Island are justifiably famous.

Sleeping

Travelling north If you prefer the hospitality of rural guest houses rather than town hotels, there are some good options north of Grootfontein off the B8. **A** *Dornhügel*, T067-240439, T081-1288820 (mob), www.natron.net/tour/dorn/huegel.htm 11 km north of Grootfontein take the D2844 (through Berg Aukas, where the tar ends), the farm is signposted 24 km from the B8. 3 doubles, 2 singles, all en-suite, small but decorated with African touches, large lapa with bar and restaurant by the swimming pool, tennis court, lounge with small library. A friendly and tranquil spot, if a little overpriced. **D**, T067-243731. 14 km north of Grootfontein, signposted, 1 km off the B8. 6 immaculate en-suite rooms set around a courtyard with clean swimming pool, large kitchen and dining room that guests can use to self-cater; book food in advance. A pretty working farm with green, shaded gardens, good value. Recommended. **D-F** *Roy's Camp*, T/F067-240302. At the Tsumkwe junction (C44), 57 km north of Grootfontein. 4 thatched en-suite huts intriguingly created with indigenous materials, green, shaded campsite with braai sites and communal ablutions. Nice bar by swimming pool, restaurant (book meals in advance), short hiking trail. Recommended. **F** *Die Kraal*, T240300. Simple camping with 4 small sites. It's worth pitching your tent before supper as you won't be able to move after the fantastic meaty fare. A popular stop with overlanders, so worth booking ahead.

The Northeast

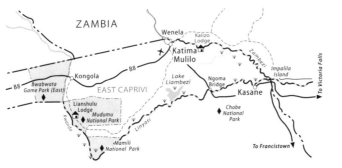

Rundu

Phone code: 066
Colour map 2, grid A1

After the long straight drive northeast from Grootfontein the sprawl of Rundu is a welcome sight. The town spreads inland along the banks of the Okavango River, the opposite bank is Angola. Since 1993, Rundu has been the provincial capital of the Kavango region and consequently is home to an impressive number of municipal offices, schools, hospitals and banks, as well as supermarkets and petrol stations. You will see far fewer white faces than in the south, and almost none after dark; at the weekends the town gets very lively around the gambling and drinking dens.

Remember to refuel in Rundu before continuing, supplies east of here are limited and far between

Ins and outs There are several options available for continuing your journey. It is possible to drive straight through to Katima Mulilo (518 km). If you have already driven from Grootfontein, this would make for a tough day's driving, and you should ensure there is sufficient time to arrive in daylight. At the small village of **Katere**, 120 km east of Rundu on the B8, is the well signposted turning south to Khaudum Game Reserve (4WD only). There is also a sign north to Kavango River View Restcamp here: ignore it, it no longer exists. Once at Khaudum, the intrepid might want to exit via the south and complete a circuit back to the main road just north of Grootfontein. Another popular option is to drive as far as **Popa Falls** and spend the night at the NWR campsite, Ngepi Camp, or one of the private lodges along the banks of the Okavango River. The next day you have the option of exploring the Mahango Game Park, entering Botswana, or continuing east through Caprivi towards Katima Mulilo. Of course, you could stay a while in Rundu - there are some excellent lodges and the sun setting over the Okavango River is a sight that's hard to beat.

Background Rundu was at one time a thriving border town, but the independence struggle brought most commercial activity to a halt. The character of the town is quite different from other Namibian towns, the Portuguese influence from across

Rundu

Sleeping
1 Kavango River Lodge
2 Ngandu Safari Lodge
3 Omashare River Lodge
4 Tambuti Lodge

Eating
1 Casa Mourisca
2 Hunter's Tavern & Supermarket

the border is strong, and there is no legacy of the German past. There are lovely views over the Okavango River, particularly from the Kavango River Lodge, and there are opportunities for fishing, watersports, quad-biking and four-wheel driving to entertain the active visitor. An annual river carnival, with colourful and noisy floats processing downstream, has established itself on the calendar. An annual trade fair has taken place since 1998, which is helping to promote the Kavango region for businesses and institutions. Rundu is certainly picking up as a commercial centre and looks set for further growth as peace and stability become ingrained on both sides of the border and tourists and businesses return. However, most tourists use Rundu as a staging post to the quieter and longer established destinations further east, where the abundant rivers and plentiful game offer a compelling package.

Rundu itself, either despite, or indeed because of, the continued instability in Angola, has burgeoned in the last few years. There has always been quite a collection of supermarkets, but two of these have been refurbished in recent years and sell a very broad range of products. Rundu's bottle stores have some of the most extensive ranges in the country, there are numerous clothes and 'From China' shops, and enough furniture shops to supply half of Namibia. There's also a useful Cymot to stock up on camping/fishing supplies. The two banks (*FNB* and *Bank Windhoek*) have four ATMs between them; the end of the month is not as desperate as in previous years.

The lodges are all fairly well signposted. Many of them advertise boat trips on the Okavango River, but be warned that these may well not be possible between May and November when water levels are too low. However, the energetic may enjoy a paddle in a canoe.

Sleeping
■ *on map*
Price codes:
see inside
front cover

In/near town A-C *Tambuti Lodge*, T255711, tambuti@namibnet.com A new place by the river at Rundu 'beach', confounding those who are closing down in the region, with 5 pretty, large bungalows, including one 'honeymoon', further construction expected. Grassed lawn with well-established trees, swimming pool, good, small restaurant/bar. The Swiss owner enjoys quad-biking and canoeing and will lead an excursion if booked. Still settling in, but looks a very good bet. **B-C** *Kavango River Lodge*, T255244, F255013, kavlodge@tsu.namib.com 14 en-suite rooms with a/c, TV and kitchens, decorated in African style, set high above the river looking west, with fabulous river views in the evening. Tennis court in good order, pool and campsite under construction. Discounted rates available at weekends when government/business reps are not in town. **C/D-F** *Ngandu Safari Lodge*, T256723, F256726, ngandu@mweb.com.na A large place with 22 pretty en-suite double huts, all with a/c and fridge, many with TV and small kitchen. Also 4 small houses, with 4 beds. Restaurant, bar, curio shop, laundry, small swimming pool, quad bikes and canoes for hire. Green, shaded campsite with lights, water, electricity, security guards and communal ablutions. Your best value bet in town, but lacking a good view of the river. **C-D** *Omashare River Lodge*, T256101, F256111. 20 spacious en-suite rooms with satellite TV, a la carte restaurant, long wooden verandah, 'ladies' bar, conference facilities, take-aways from adjacent coffee shop. Swimming pool set in large lawn, views of river in the distance. A modern hotel, owned by De Beers, better suited to the business traveller or government official than the tourist. **C** *Sarasungu River Lodge*, T255161, F256238. Follow signs past the *Ngandu Safari Lodge*, 4 km from town. 9 en-suite thatched reed cottages, one luxurious 'honeymoon' bungalow, restaurant, bar, small swimming pool. Excellent location by the river for birdwatching and canoeing. In good condition, but was still **closed** for business in Aug 2001, awaiting the return of tourists in greater numbers.

The Northeast

Guest farms in the area A/B *Hakusembe Lodge*, T257010, F257011, hakusembe@ mweb.com.na Stunning riverside location,16 km west of Rundu: take the B8 towards Grootfontein, after 2 km turn northwest on the C45 towards Nkurenkuru, turn right after 10 km at the signpost and follow signs for a further 4 difficult km. Road under improvement; call ahead for road conditions, after heavy rain the only access is by boat from Rundu. 6 beautiful en-suite thatched huts with river views, excellent restaurant, stylish wooden bar, swimming pool and sundowner pontoon on the river. Long activity list includes powerboat and canoe 'safaris', fishing, watersports, microlighting, horse riding and mule safaris. Price is half board, no activities. The Rundu Barge Carnival (first weekend in May) begins from here – participants build their own rafts and drift down to Rundu town. Completely and carefully revamped in 1999 by new English owner whose manager puts it well: 'What we do, we do *right*.' Recommended. **C** *Kaisosi River Lodge*, T255265, F256566, www.namibia.co.za 6 km east of Rundu, signposted, 2 km north of the B3402. 16 large, thatched, en-suite chalets, square and simply decorated, restaurant, bar, 2 swimming pools, green, shaded area by the river. Fairly well maintained over the 'quiet' period, but suffering from lack of being lived in and in need of a coat of paint everywhere. Camping available. **D** *N'Kwazi Lodge*, T081-2478776 (mob). 13 km east of Rundu off the D3402, well signposted, then 3 winding km towards the river. 14 spacious, thatched, en-suite bungalows tastefully decorated with African touches and wooden walls, restaurant, bar, swimming pool, good selection of river activities, good birding. The whole camp (and their campsite) is set in neat, well kept grounds with plenty of shade and lawns. Recommended. **D** *Okavango Adventure Lodge*. Ignore the signs, **closed** for business in Aug 2001.

Eating
● *on map page 154*

The supermarkets in town stock everything for self-caterers. Eating out is limited, only the lodges cater regularly for tourists. Of these, *Hakusembe* (although a challenge to get back from in the evening), *Tambuti Lodge* (small and intimate) or *Omashere*, in order, are your best bets. *Casa Mourisca*, T255487, is open 7 days a week, from 0800 until late. It has a restaurant, steakhouse, 2 bars and a disco. New owner, probably your best of a poor choice in town. If passing on to East Caprivi, food is available at **Hunter's Tavern**, bar and restaurant open late, located next to the Shell garage on the B8. The adventurous might enjoy the street food available through the day behind the main market (near *Casa Mourisca*).

Shopping

While officially it is only the military who may, a large number of Angolans cross the border to do their shopping (for food) in Rundu. For the tourist, there is a long history of wood carving in the Kavango region, but with the tail-off in visitors a number of stalls and cooperative outlets have disappeared or now make larger items for local lodges and South Africans. You will find the community crafts centres at Kongola and Katima Mulilo a better bet.

Transport
257 km to Grootfontein;
518 km to Katima Mulilo;
438 km to Mudumu NP (for Lianshulu Lodge);
186 km to Popa Falls

Across the Okavango River is the Angolan town of **Calai**, which you may be able to enter for the day without a visa. Check carefully with the police on both sides of the border or else you could find yourself facing a large US$ 'fine'. Rundu – Calai border open daily: 0700-1700. **Air** Air Namibia, T255854. **Road** For *Intercape* coaches from Windhoek on their way to Victoria Falls, see timetable on page 382. There are plenty of shared **taxis** arriving and leaving from the Shell garage on the B8, roughly 2 km south of the town centre.

Directory

Banks *First National*, with ATMs. **Tourist information** Your best bet for local information and activities is to ask the lodge owners, especially *Ngandu Safari Lodge*.

Caprivi

The Caprivi region is a land of fertile, flat floodplains surrounded by perennial rivers, a far cry from the arid lands of the Kalahari or the Namib-Naukluft. The regional centre is Katima Mulilo, a busy commercial centre on the banks of the Zambezi. Don't dwell in town, the attractions of the region are the tranquil lodges, plentiful game and birdlife and beautiful river scenery, centred in the rarely visited game parks. All four parks (Mahango, Mudumu, Mamili and the new Bwabwata) offer a similar experience, with few tourist facilities, made up for by pristine woodland and riverine floodplain with abundant local and migrant wildlife. The national park along the narrowest part of the Caprivi Strip (the one-time Caprivi Game Reserve) has recently been deproclaimed to make way for the communities that live there to develop their subsistence farming existence. Activities include watersports, fishing, four-wheel driving and game viewing, before carrying on into Botswana and Zimbabwe for the magnificent Chobe Game Park and famous Victoria Falls. It is only a three hour drive from Katima to Victoria Falls.

Background

The Caprivi Strip is a classic example of how the former colonial powers shaped the boundaries of modern Africa. The strip is 500 km long, at its narrowest only 32 km wide, while at the eastern end it bulges to almost 100 km wide before narrowing to a point at the confluence of the Zambezi and Chobe rivers where the boundaries of Zimbabwe, Namibia, Zambia and Botswana meet.

During the struggle for independence, the Caprivi region was home to the South African Army and police and, as a consequence, no one really knows what went on up here. There were secret army camps, the airfield at Mpacha (now Katima Mulilo) was used for air strikes into Angola and Zambia, and the region was closed to anyone who didn't live here or have a reason for visiting. From the early 1960s until 1990 the region was in a constant state of war. There was a brief resurgence of 'trouble' in late 1999 (see box on page 167) but today the area is regarded as being safe for tourists (the embassies eased their discouragement from visiting in June 2001), although the local communities remain poorly off, economically, as a result.

As you drive along the B8 towards Katima Mulilo you are striking directly through the anomaly that is the Caprivi Strip and it is hard to avoid the sensation that you are entering the heart of the African continent. It is a region blessed with some fabulous forests and rivers and a wide variety of wildlife. Visits to any of the game parks will always be remembered for their remote beauty, great variety of flora and range (if not head count) and game. The lodges make the most of their riverbank settings and are well worth settling into for a few days to enjoy the scenery and activities they offer. At the eastern end of Caprivi is the isolated town of Katima Mulilo. Remember where you are on the map when you pass through. You will have earned your cold beer by the time you reach the Zambezi.

Mahango and West Caprivi

Just before the B8 'Golden Highway' crosses the Okavango River into the Caprivi Strip turn south (the D3403) following numerous signposts for lodges on the way to **Mahango Game Reserve** and the border with **Botswana**. The area is served by a relatively busy (and rutted) gravel road and, as well as being a destination in itself, this is the shortest route from northern

Berlin Conference – carving up the strip

The Caprivi Strip owes its origins to the Berlin conference when the European colonial powers decided how to carve up Africa between themselves. On 1 July 1890, Britain traded Heliogoland and the Caprivi region for Zanzibar and parts of Bechuanaland, present day Botswana. Germany planned to use the strip as a trade route into central Africa, but even before the outbreak of the First World War this plan was thwarted by the activities of Cecil Rhodes in modern day Zimbabwe.

The strip was named after the German Chancellor, General Count Georg Leo von Caprivi di Caprara di Montecuccoli. Unlike the rest of Namibia the region has little to show from the German period of rule. The strip returned to British control at the outbreak of the First World War, less than 25 years after the Germans had assumed control of the region. The return to British control came about in a most unusual fashion. The story goes that the German governor was having afternoon tea with a senior British official from Rhodesia, when a message arrived saying that war had just been declared between the two countries. The German governor was placed under arrest and the territory under his control annexed.

In 1918 the land was incorporated into Bechuanaland and thus ruled by the British. In 1929 it was handed over to the South African ruled South West Africa – at independence it remained part of Namibia.

Namibia to **Maun** and the **Okavango Delta**. The NWR camp at **Popa Falls** has long been a popular overnight destination, dating from the days when the road between Rundu and Katima Mulilo was all gravel and an overnight limb-restoring rest was a necessity.

Divundu
Colour map 2, grid A5

The town is signposted both east and west every 10 km for nearly 200 km; when you arrive all you find is an *Engen* petrol station (0600-2100) and fairly well stocked supermarket. From here, it is 35 km south on the D3403 to the border, passing through the Mahango Game Reserve (no motorbikes permitted). Along this road is a good range of accommodation, all of which survived the downturn, partly through sheer resilience and partly reflecting the continued popularity of this route into Botswana and the Okavango Delta.

Sleeping and eating E *Divundu Guest House*, T259031. In the 'village', behind the Engen. 6 simple, thatched, en-suite rooms, a bar with pool tables and restaurant. It lacks river views and is not as atmospheric as Popa Falls, but offers good value, simple rooms.

Popa Falls

Colour map 2, grid A2

Don't swim in the river (except perhaps in the 'falls' themselves, and only after taking local advice) as, in addition to crocodiles, there is bilharzia in the water

Be warned, Popa Falls are not falls at all, rather a series of rapids, waterways and islands on the Okavango River. When the river is low the highest visible drop is about 3 m. There is a walkway into the middle of the river, after this you are free to scramble over the rocks in the middle of the river. At this point the channel is about 1 km wide with the river split into a series of channels making their way through the rocks. The adjacent accommodation is among the finest under NWR control in Namibia: comfortable, in good working order, cheap and very much in tune with the natural environment. The campsite suffers from the inflated park charges, but is set among lovely grassed lawns, by the water's edge. This is a popular spot for travellers on the way to Botswana and a convenient stopping place when travelling between Kavango and East Caprivi. The area is protected as a national park but is very small and apart

from birdlife, a few hippo and some crocodile there is little wildlife to be seen.
■ *Entrance charge: N$20 pp, N$20 per car. Fishing permits N$2.*

D/E *Standard Huts*, thatched and clean, with 4 beds, bedding, communal kitchen and **Sleeping**
ablutions. Good value, even fairly stylish in a 'natural' way. **F** *Campsite*, green and picturesque, decent ablutions and bush kitchen, with the sound of the rapids to soothe
weary drivers to sleep. Expensive for solo/couple campers, better value available at
Ngepi downstream.

AL *Ndhovu Lodge*, T064-403141, F403142, lvincent@iafrica.com.na 17 km from the *Along the D3403*
B8, well signposted, about 2 km down track towards the river. Luxury tented camp at a *between Popa Falls*
beautiful spot by the Okavango River. 7 en-suite, fairly basic, thatched/canvas tents *and Mahango Game*
with twin beds and veranda, restaurant, bar, pool, shaded lawn. The main attraction is *Reserve is the*
following riverside
Roy Vincent's knowledge and love of the area and the bush, he guides game walks and *accommodation.*
drives into the park and excursions along the river in his boat. Pricey, but recom- *Light aircraft for any*
mended. **B** *Suclabo Lodge*, T/F259005, F259026, www.suclabo.iway.na Well sign- *of these lodges use*
posted, 6 km from the B8, 1 km off the D3503. 11 thatched, en-suite bungalows with *Bagani airstrip, close*
electricity, fan, veranda and river view. Swimming pool in nice shaded lawns, attractive *to the entrance to*
central restaurant and bar, sundowner deck 10m above the water for safe views of the *Popa Falls*
hippos and crocs, fishing trips. Aimed at German tour groups, named after the owner,
Suzzie, and her children Clara and Boris. **D-F** *Mahangu*, T259037,
www.iwwn.com.na/mahangu Next door to *Ndhovu* (see above). 6 thatched huts in a
shaded, green spot by the river, very tidy, swimming pool, camping available. Good
value, but without the personal care of the pricier lodges. **F** *Ngepi Camp Site*,
T/F259005 (bookings through *Suclabo Lodge*, above) or T259126,
www.ngepi-experienceafrica.com Well signposted 12 km from the B8, 5 km from the
D3403. Basic (no lights or electricity) campsite beautifully set by the Okavango River,
grassed and well shaded, with hot showers, a central dining/braai area and lively bar.
Traditional dances some evenings. Daytime activities include canoeing, fishing, boating or trips in a *mokoro*. Well informed, friendly, young host, popular with overlanders,
but large enough to combine the occasional party with privacy for the independent
traveller. Recommended.

Mahango Game Park

This is a pleasant, small reserve which borders the perennial Okavango River. *Colour map 2, grid A5*
It boasts probably the best birding in the country, as well as a good chance of
seeing rare antelope (roan and sable). Visitors travelling through the region
should allow a day by the river; even if you do not see the large herds of elephant, the mixed forest and bush country is beautifully scenic and full of life.
Drive carefully, the road (suitable for standard cars) regularly has game on it.

Getting there If approaching from Botswana through the Mohembo border post, **Ins & outs**
you will be in the thick of the park immediately. The northern gate of the park is 12 km
from Popa Falls, 232 km from Rundu and 310 km from Katima Mulilo.

Getting around There are few roads for game-viewing purposes. In addition to the
main road running through the park, there are two side tracks, one for ordinary cars
and the other only suitable for four-wheel drive vehicles. The ordinary track to the east
follows the river. When in full flood it can be impassable, but the gate attendants will
let you know. This track is about 15 km; there is a large baobab and a picnic spot overlooking the river at Kwetche. The western trail is 31 km and follows the course of the
two omurambas in the park. These roads are very sandy in the dry season, and slippery

The Northeast

after the rains. Nevertheless, this is a special drive through unspoilt bush country, a glimpse of just what national parks are trying to preserve.

Information Entry permits (N$20 per person, N$20 per car) are issued at the northern park gate. If you are just passing through en route to/from the Botswana border a permit is not required. Fishing permits are N$2. If you have limited four-wheel driving experience it is best to stick to the ordinary road which offers game (and driving challenge) enough. There is **no accommodation** in the park, but there's a NWR restcamp at Popa Falls, plus the lodges and camps off the D3403, detailed above.

Best time to visit There are two distinct seasons. Between 500 and 600 mm of rain is expected in the **rainy season** (Dec-Mar) when it gets hot, with the average daily maximum over 30°C. The **dry season** extends from Apr-Nov with no rain expected and evening temperatures falling to around 7°C. The best time to visit during the winter months is Jun-Oct, when game will be found close to the river and waterholes. Birdlife is prolific Nov-Mar; after the rains, when insects are abundant and many of the trees flower and carry fruit.

Background Mahango has a lot in common with Khaudum Game Reserve. Both are remote with a common boundary with Botswana, neither have been developed beyond the cutting of a few tracks suitable for four-wheel drive vehicles, and both were created in 1989 just before Namibian independence.

At only 28,000 ha (20 x 14 km); Mahango is a relatively small park. Its southern boundary is the border with Botswana, its eastern boundary the Okavango River. Year-round water ensures regular game in the park, and there are large seasonal influxes, particularly of migrant elephant. There are no fences, but the presence of man at the perimeter acts as a barrier. The

Popa Falls, Mahango & Bwabwata (West) Game Parks

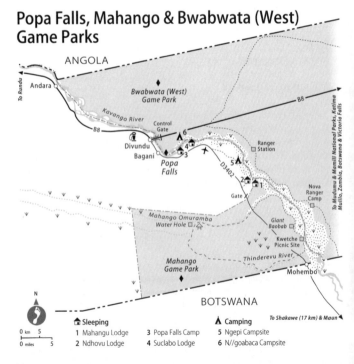

ANGOLA

BOTSWANA

⌂ Sleeping		Λ Camping
1 Mahangu Lodge	3 Popa Falls Camp	5 Ngepi Campsite
2 Ndhovu Lodge	4 Suclabo Lodge	6 N//goabaca Campsite

0 km 5
0 miles 5

The Northeast

Motorbikes and animals do not go together

Both Namibia and Botswana have a policy which does not permit motorbikes in national parks and game reserves. This is understandable when one considers the potential dangers posed by a herd of elephant or buffalo. The down side of this policy is that it makes it quite difficult for anyone on a motorbike to exit from the Caprivi Strip region of Namibia into Botswana. It is not possible to cross the border between Namibia and Botswana at Mohembo since the road passes through Mahango Game Reserve.

At the eastern end of Caprivi it is not possible to enter Botswana via Ngoma Bridge because the road runs through Chobe National Park until you reach Kasane. Mark Easterbrook writes that you have to drive to Katima Mulilo and then go via Zambia (Wenela border) – the road on the Zambia side is as bad as all reports, in fact you will be lucky to drive at much more than 15 kph. Unless you really wish to see the Caprivi region it would probably be easier to exit Namibia via the B6 from Windhoek to Gobabis and Buitepos. You are then faced with a long road via Ghanzi to Maun.

migrant herds move between Angola and the Okavango Delta. They tend to cause some damage to crops, trees and structures in passing, an ongoing cause of conflict with local communities.

It is worth noting that some people believe the parks were created for the wrong reasons (for example, the relocation of Caprivi secessionists), but like Mudumu and Mamili national parks to the east, if these parks had not been declared they would have quickly fallen prey to woodcutters, hunters and poachers and Namibia would have lost a unique and valuable resource. All of the game parks are set in beautiful countryside, with the key attraction being the plentiful wildlife made possible by the perennial (and picturesque) Okavango River. You only have to compare the appearance of the land on either side of the boundary lines to appreciate the importance and value of the parks. The park and the lodges further upstream benefit from the existence of the newly proclaimed Bwabwata Park on the opposite bank. Herds of elephant regularly come to the far bank to drink in early winter evenings, a stunning site.

Vegetation One of the attractions of Mahango is the variety of vegetation in such a small area. There are three distinct habitats, and with each comes different birdlife and conditions for the game. The river provides a mix of trees, reeds and grasses along its banks and on the floodplains. The dominant tree species are Kalahari apple-leaf, water pear and jackal-berry; along the floodplain margins you will see the wild date palm. If you visit one of the private camps or Popa Falls Restcamp you will find many of the riverine trees have been helpfully labelled. A tree which every visitor quickly learns to recognize is the baobab. There are several groups within the park, including a distinctive clump just before the Kwetche picnic site, marked on the map.

Away from the river, the vegetation is predominantly open dry woodland, aside from a couple of omurambas, or fossil rivers (see Khaudum Game Reserve, page 145), which run west-east towards the Okavango River. The omurambas are covered with open grassland with tall acacia and bushwillow along their margins. For a few months after the rains, pools of water collect in the omurambas, offering good game viewing. Between Mahango omuramba in the north and Thinderevu omuramba in the south the vegetation is dry woodland with some dense patches of Zambezi teak, wild seringa and wild teak. This is beautiful country to walk in, but there are dangers (buffalo and

The Northeast

elephant); those unfamiliar with the region and with bush walking are advised to employ the good value and informative services of a local guide, particularly Roy Vincent.

Wildlife If you are fortunate you will encounter a wide variety of animals in this small park. It is home to some rare (certainly in Namibia) antelope: sable, roan (both shy but readily indentified by their magnificent curved horns), reedbuck, tsessebe and sitatunga. The sitatunga is very difficult to spot since it is small and lives in thick swamp areas; if you manage to see one, consider yourself very lucky. They are only found in large numbers in the Okavango Delta. Reedbuck are also quite difficult to spot, they tend to inhabit the floodplains. Keep an eye out here for red lechwe. Along the riverbank are good numbers of kudu and Chobe bushbuck, and rather fewer duiker and steenbok.

Apart from antelope, you can expect to see elephant, hippo, crocodile, warthog, baboon and vervet monkey, and you may spot lion and leopard. Remember, the large herds of elephant are migrants: outside the dry season sightings will be fewer.

Finally, it is important not to forget the birdlife in the park. Over 300 species have been recorded throughout the year and twitchers can expect to spot over 50 different species in a couple of hours' sitting by the river at Kwetche. The different habitats in the park help attract the wide variety of species; it is interesting to compare the birds you will see along the river-banks with those that you come across in the woodlands – even amateurs can quickly start to recognize how the species vary between different areas of the park. Along the open river area, look for the rare African skimmer, whitefronted and whitecrowned plovers, and white-fronted and little bee-eaters. On the riverine fringe, you may see the rare western banded snake eagle, Meyer's and Cape parrots, swamp boubou and African golden oriole. The omuramba environment attracts the rare wattled crane, slaty egret, herons, copperytailed and Burchell's coucals, openbilled stork and longtoed plover. In the woodland areas, look for raptors including Dickson's kestrel, Steppe, lesser spotted and booted eagles, as well as arrowmarked and blackfaced babblers and sharptailed starling.

Crossing into Botswana If you plan on driving straight through Mahango Game Park to the border, you do not need a permit or to pay any park fees. The **Mohembo border post** with Botswana is **open** 0600-1800. The quality of the road on the Botswana side used to have a bad reputation but is now surfaced. The first settlement you reach is Shakawe, 17 km from the border. The road continues south with the 'panhandle' of the Okavango Delta to the east. The first accommodation is *Shakawe Fishing Camp*, 15 km further south. Welcome to Botswana, Namibia never seemed so cheap!

Bwabwata Game Park

Colour map 2, grid A6
Namibia's newest park

This park is in the process of being established from the remnants of the old Caprivi Game Park that covered the entire 204 km stretch from Divundu in the west to Kongola in the east. Bwabwata is to be two separate parcels of land, both roughly 30 km wide and occupying the full 35 km depth of the Strip, bordering the rivers at the far eastern and far western ends. The rest of the former park has been deproclaimed and land is to be given over to the isolated rural communities that live along the B8, centred on the old military posts. From February 2000 until 'further notice', this section of the B8 was navigable only by twice-daily escorted convoy, although the road is expected to be opened up to regular traffic soon. While there are no stopping places or viewpoints along the way, keep an eye out for game, particularly elephant, in the morning and evening.

Assuming the convoy is 'lifted', passengers (and even drivers) will have better distraction than reading a book. Roadside stalls may open and community projects (see below) may have a chance to take off. There is no fuel available along the Strip; Divundu is a fairly safe bet, but be sure to fill up in Rundu and Kongola to be sure.

During the independence struggle, this area was the South African Army Buffalo Base, the training grounds for the infamous 32nd Battalion and Third Force. Sadly, the army hunted out much of the game, as well as the 'baddies'. It is said that Western Caprivi was kept as the private hunting ground for John Vorster who used to come up here and go hunting from helicopters. With a bit of care the animals will return.

A short distance east of the police checkpoint at Bagani Bridge, near Divundu, is a turn-off south to a community based project, **N//goabaca Community Campsite** – pronounced 'N (click) goabaca' and meaning 'boiling water', the Kxoe name for Popa Falls. The site suffered from lack of access while the convoy was in operation but looks set to be revitalized. The initiative was started by the local Barakwena community living near Popa Falls, the campsite being in line with the MET's policy to involve communities in conservation and ensure that the people who live in wilderness areas directly benefit from tourism, to compensate for the negative impact of wild animals destroying crops and livestock. Campsites such as this generate important employment for each community, although most schemes have only recently started and have yet to generate much revenue, let alone repay loans or contribute towards future community self-help projects; funds are channelled through the Integrated Rural Development and Nature Conservation (IRDNC) and Namibian Community Based Tourism Association (NACOBTA).

Sleeping & eating

F *N//goabaca Campsite* offers basic but picturesque sites in a prime position on the eastern bank of the Okavango River, overlooking Popa Falls. 4 large sites, lush and shaded by large riverine trees, grassed areas, flush toilets, hot showers, fireplace and reed chalet kitchens. Water and firewood available. The nearest shops are at Divundu. Boat trips can be organized through the lodges on the western bank. Guided walks used to operate from here, and may again; for a small fee, locals introduce you to traditional knowledge of plants and their uses. Another local attraction is the Mushangara Rock Pools. If you are not keen on walking, there is good fishing (buy your tackle in Rundu) or birdwatching.

East Caprivi

The region is verdant and lush, with very little development. The exception is the regional capital, Katima Mulilo, which is well served by banks and shops and has a good range of accommodation. Elsewhere, basic homesteads are dotted infrequently along the roadsides and the parks have no tourist facilities whatsoever. Regular rainfall and floods support a riverine and omuramba ecosystem, sometimes as much as 80% underwater, with plentiful game and birdlife but accessible only by boat and four-wheel drive for much of the year. Beware when driving off the B8; sand, mud or water can slow progress and fray nerves. Many roads are best travelled by four-wheel drive or on foot.

The Northeast

Region of rivers

A closer look at a map of Eastern Caprivi reveals the unusual feature that, except for a 90 km strip of land along the northern border, between the Kwando River and the Zambezi River, the region is completely surrounded by rivers. The Kwando-Linyanti-Chobe forms the border to the west, south and southeast, with the Zambezi, the border with Zambia, to the northeast. Enclosed by these rivers is a landscape which is largely flat, with numerous floodplains, ox-bow lakes, swamps and seasonal channels.

The hydrography of the area is particularly interesting because in years of good rain the flow of water in stretches of the rivers can be reversed and water actually spill into the Okavango Delta system, a completely different (internally draining) watershed. Before 2000, these were all thought to be drying up, but the Kwando, Zambezi and Okavango came back in force in 2000 and 2001. With a map in hand, consider the complexities of the river system, starting in Angola, where the **Cuando** River rises in the Luchazes mountains. As this river flows southeast it forms the border between Angola and Zambia before it cuts across the eastern end of the narrowest part of the Caprivi Strip (the eastern border of the Bwabwata Game Park). Where the river cuts through Namibia (past Kongola) it is known as the **Kwando**. Having cut across the Caprivi Strip, the river once again becomes an international boundary, this time between Botswana and Namibia. At Nkasa island, the southwest corner of Mamili National Park, the river channel turns sharply to the northeast and becomes known as the **Linyati** River until it reaches just south of **Lake Liambezi** (at one time 100 sq km and an important source of food and water for the surrounding villages, since May 1985, dry and prone to fire); from here it becomes the **Chobe**, which flows into the **Zambezi** at Impalila Island. Confused? It's even worse 'on the ground'.

These are all shallow gradient, slow flowing rivers. While it is highly unusual, when the Zambezi is exceptionally high the flow of water in the Chobe and Linyanti can be reversed. Water flows back up the Chobe and into Lake Liambezi, in the past, water from the Zambezi has been known to flood right across the plains between Katima Mulilo and Ngoma Bridge and drain into the northern shores of Lake Liambezi via a depression known as the **Bukalo Channel**.

Similarly, water from the Kwando River can enter the Okavango system via a channel known as the **Selinda Spillway** or **Magwegqana Channel**. Because of the difference in elevation the waters usually only flow a few kilometres to the west, however this channel drains into the **Mababe Depression** via the **Savuti Channel** and, in very wet years, water from the Kwando has been known to drain into the Savuti Marsh in Botswana.

Community projects

East Caprivi is seeing a rapid growth in communal area conservancy formation, giving communities more rights and responsibilities to manage the natural resources with which they co-exist. In order to develop respect for the national parks, the communities need to see that the park and tourism directly benefits them. Some initial opposition to game conservation came from farmers suffering crop damage (elephant and hippo) and loss of livestock (lion, leopard and crocodile), but it seems that poaching has been reduced as the problem animals become worth more to the community than the damage they cause. The principal income earners for communities are NACOBTA projects promoting arts and crafts and developing basic but well positioned campsites. Model villages, with displays of traditional crafts and rituals, have also proved popular, **Lizauli village** being one that has gained recognition. Additionally, funds are transferred to the community from a tourist bed levy; for example, every visitor to *Lianshulu Lodge* pays an additional N$20 per night, with monies jointly administered by local leaders and community-based conservation programmes.

Around Kongola

At the eastern end of **Bwabwata Game Park** the B8 crosses the Kwando River. *Colour map 2, inset*
This area was heavily manned during the fight for independence but game is
gradually returning, particularly elephant, for which it is an important migration route for water. Unfortunately, in summer 2001 a new hunting concession was granted, virtually overlooking *Namushasha Lodge* on the western
side of the river; protest may yet put this situation right. Namushasha Lodge
provides the best access into this underdeveloped region, with a boat from the
lodge to an open four-wheel drive for game drives.

Kongola is little more than a petrol station, a few buildings and a series of signs
advertising camps and lodges along the road to **Mudumu National Park** and
Mamili National Park, two of Namibia's least developed parks. Both of these are
set in beautiful countryside, and as with Bwabwata, both are just starting to see the
return of wildlife which was displaced and killed during the war for independence
and South African occupation. At the B8/D3511 junction, by the Shell petrol station, is the *Mashi Craft Market*, T252518 or NACOBTA, T061-250558,
www.nacobta.com.na, open Mon, Wed, Fri from 0900-1600. Opened in 1997 as
a community project, it sells a range of traditional handicrafts from over 125 makers in 15 different parts of the Caprivi region. As well as baskets and mats made
from the makalani palm, there are interesting bracelets, earrings and other pieces
of traditional jewellery. Quality is improving, although it started from a low base.
Mud Hut Trading, based in Windhoek's Namibian Craft Centre, sustained the
project when tourists were scarce through 1999 and 2000 and has put considerable effort into training the craftsmen and women. There are now also annual
competitions, with displays of the finest crafts at the Omba Gallery in Windhoek.
By spending your money here you can be sure the benefits are going directly to the
community. In 1999, the craftsmen and women earned N$50,000 (N$28,000 in
2000, due to the political trouble), mostly from visiting tourists.

Lizauli Village, a short distance from *Lianshulu Lodge*, is a traditional village
in appearance and layout, but one that has been constructed for the benefit of
tourists. During the day a group of local people pass their time here waiting to
show visitors around and explain a variety of traditional activities. One of the
most comforting aspects of a visit here is that you do not feel like an intruder
walking around private homes, neither does it have that theme park feel.

The complete tour lasts at least an hour, after which you have ample opportunity to ask questions about all aspects of rural life. On a typical visit you will
be shown a collection of household objects and how they are used, including a
crude but effective mousetrap, the girls will perform a couple of dances and
the village blacksmith will demonstrate how the farm implements are forged.
The tour finishes with the whole group acting out a village dispute with the
elders being called upon to resolve the matter. This is an enjoyable introduction to a way of life far removed from that of the tourist from overseas.
■ *Daily, 0800-1700, N$20pp, must be pre-booked either through Lianshulu
Lodge or Tutwa Tourism in Katima Mulilo.*

Mudumu National Park

Mudumu National Park's charm lies in its simplicity, with no residents, few *Colour map 2, inset*
visitors and increasing numbers of game. Apart from some very simple bush
camps, the only place to stay is the upmarket Lianshulu Lodge, which is a special place, the first upmarket lodge in the area and a pioneer for tourism,

The Northeast

conservation and community projects. The original owners have gone, but the charm of the bush, sensitively coupled with luxury, very much remains.

Ins & outs
See also map on page 168

Getting there Just east of the Kwando River, turn south off the B8 by the Engen garage at Kongola, onto the D3511. After 35 km you will see a sign indicating the entrance to the park, marked also by the lack of subsistence farmers and land cleared for millet fields. It is 40 km from the B8 to the turning for *Lianshulu Lodge*. **Getting around** There is a MET office at Nakatwa camp, but you needn't report here if you are staying at *Lianshulu Lodge*. Report to Nakatwa if you are venturing into the more remote corners, or planning to spend the night at either of the simple campsites, particularly regarding the state of the roads, which can become impassable, even to 4WD drivers, when the water is high.

Background Mudumu National Park was proclaimed in 1990, just before independence, and measures over 100,000 ha. In the early 1960s, the Eastern Caprivi had the greatest concentration of wildlife in Namibia. Between 1974 and the early 1980s the region was managed as a private hunting concession and much of the game was shot out. Part of the independence process agreed that no pre-independence proclamations would be changed. While this might appear to be good news for the protection of wildlife in Mudumu and Mamili, it is worth noting that the creation of these two parks was against the will of the local people as there was no proper consultation with the villagers. Since independence there has been a conscious effort to establish community-based conservation projects in the region, aiming to generate revenue for the local communities (see above). At present the park remains a backwater as far as the MET is concerned: there are no gates at the entrance to the park, and you are unlikely to meet anyone from the wildlife department (or indeed any human) as you drive along the few tracks in the park.

Before the park was proclaimed, *Lianshulu* obtained a concession to establish a lodge by the Kwando River. Today the lodge is very much associated with the park, although not for day-to-day management. *Lianshulu* continues to play an active role in getting the local community to benefit from tourism.

Vegetation A large part of Mudumu is dominated by mopane woodland, interspersed with camel thorn, Natal mahogany, mangosteen and mixed acacia. Within the woods are depressions which become flooded after the rains. The western boundary of the park is marked by plentiful reeds along the Kwando River, and remnants of riverine forest (with woodland waterberry trees) and grassed flood plains. Soil is primarily kalahari sandveld with belts of clay and alluvium where the forest occurs.

Wildlife The best game viewing is in winter, June-October, before the heat and, more importantly, rain comes. After the rains, numerous ponds of water form away from the perennial Kwando and sightings become more rare. The animals you are most likely to see are hippo, crocodile, elephant, buffalo, kudu, impala, steenbok, warthog, Burchell's zebra, southern reedbuck, red lechwe, oribi and baboon. If you are lucky you may catch a glimpse of tsessebe, roan, sable, sitatunga, duiker, spotted hyena and lion. Leopard, cheetah and even wild dog have been seen in the area, but are extremely rare. Hunted out were giraffe, eland, wildebeest and waterbuck. There remain occasional poachers (for food), but game numbers are on the increase, regardless. Birders should be on the lookout by the water for slaty egret, rufousbellied heron, wattled crane, wattled and longtoed plovers, redwinged pratincole, copperytailed

Treason in the Caprivi

In early November 1998, the Namibian government claimed to have unearthed a plot, led by former DTA opposition leader Mishake Muyongo and others, to launch an armed rebellion aiming to secede the Caprivi Region from the rest of Namibia. Details emerged of a secret bush training camp where secessionists were being trained by former members of SWATF and Koevoet, organizations which had fought against SWAPO during the independence struggle. Branded as 'terrorists' by the government, the secessionists fled to Botswana, with whom Namibia has a long-standing territorial dispute, claiming political asylum. Over the following days and weeks more Namibians, including the former Governor of Caprivi, John Mabuku, and Chief Boniface Mamili, went into self-imposed exile. By April 1999 over 2,400 Namibians had fled the Caprivi region claiming that they had been persecuted by the authorities in Namibia.

While the Namibian government accused Muyongo and other leaders of committing treason, ordinary villagers, including members of the marginalized San community, were invited to return to their homes. On 2 August 1999, armed invaders crossed from Zambia into Katima Mulilo and in a series of skirmishes over several days killed policemen, occupied the police headquarters and took control of the NBC (radio) building. It quickly became clear that they did not have the resources for a sustained campaign, and as quickly as the invaders appeared, they were suppressed. In late 2001, 120 people still await trial on counts of treason; they are unable to get legal representation and have not been granted bail.

In a series of separate incidents, tourists were regularly being mugged while driving along the Kongola to Divundu strip. An increasing number of cars were flagged down by people posing as military before having their contents liberated. This came to a peak in December with a tragic incident in which three French tourists were not just robbed but brutally murdered. No one claimed responsibility and no one was caught and brought to trial. The government's claim that it was the work of UNITA rebels from Angola (however unlikely, given the proximity to Namibia's main military base on the Strip, Omega III) underlined the sense of lawlessness in the area and caused all Western governments to declare a no-go zone. Virtually overnight, the number of tourists visiting the area fell to zero.

In response, since February 2000, a convoy with military escort has been running twice a day and there have been no further incidents. Intercape Mainliner services were resumed in September 2000 and in June 2001 the Prime Minister, Hage Geingob, and a delegation visited the area to officially proclaim it 'safe' for tourists again. The embassies have all relaxed their warnings regarding the area, although they recommend staying on the main road (there is only one) and not travelling at night (never a good idea in Africa).

This combination of events firmly scared tourists away from this beautiful corner, and they are only trickling back slowly. The local community (black and white) has been hit very hard and eagerly await the return of tourists. While the case against the secessionists continues, there is a feeling of calm in the area once again, and we have no hesitation in recommending that you include the area in your itinerary.

The Northeast

coucal and the occasional coppery, and purplebanded sunbird. Woodland areas are home to Bradfield's hornbill, mosque swallow, Anrot's chat, longtailed and lesser blue-eared starlings, broadbilled roller and yellowbilled and redbilled oxpeckers.

Sleeping **L** *Lianshulu Lodge*, reservations, T061-254317, F254980, www.namibiaweb.com/lianshulu Well signposted off the D3511, 40 km south of the B8, then a further 4 km to main lodge, 8 km to bush lodge. Main lodge has 11 thatched en-suite chalets, including one 'honeymoon suite', all comfortable, tastefully decorated, with river views. Bush lodge has a further 9 chalets of similar style. Large, beautiful, central dining area, lounge and bar, swimming pool, attractive gardens by the river, protected from roaming elephants by electric fence. The excursions, with informative guides, are the main attraction; they offer walks, boat trips and game drives. Full board. Opened in the early 1990s and still regarded as one of the best lodges in the country, now managed by a Southern Africa luxury lodge management team. The bush lodge is similarly lavish and large, although since 1999 this has only been used as overflow accommodation due to the reduction in visitor numbers; you are unlikely to stay here. Recommended.

A *Namushasha*, reservations T061-240375, F256598. Well signposted 20 km south of the B8 on the D3511, 4 km from turning, past their airstrip and a few large baobabs.16 en-suite doubles, nicely built of thatch and reed, set in shaded gardens by river, swimming pool, bar, restaurant, power boat and open-top 4WD excursions in the Golden Triangle, short marked walking trail. Campsite (with bush bar) planned for 2002. Mixed feedback from visitors (although the Golden Triangle excursions are recommended); generally caters for German tour groups.

Mudumu, Mamili & Bwabwata (East) National Parks

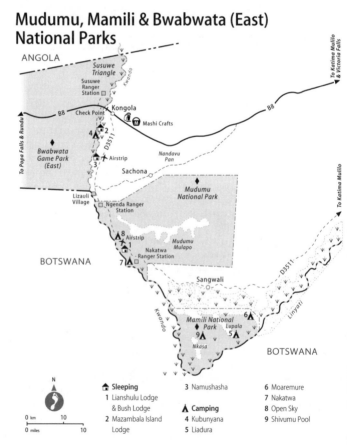

Sleeping
1 Lianshulu Lodge & Bush Lodge
2 Mazambala Island Lodge
3 Namushasha

Camping
4 Kubunyana
5 Liadura
6 Moaremure
7 Nakatwa
8 Open Sky
9 Shivumu Pool

E-F *Open Sky*, T253048, F252238, tutwa@mweb.com.na Well signposted off the D3511 south of *Namushasha*, 4 km to the camp off the road. A simple campsite on the river, with 3 permanent en-suite reed/thatch tents, solar power for electricity, bar, nice lounge with small library, no food at present, large, shaded, but somewhat unkempt campsite, adequate ablutions. They offer mokoro, boat and game excursions (although *Namushasha* have a 4WD parked on the far bank, for an altogether more interesting drive). Bookings through *Tutwa Tourism* in Katima Mulilo.
F *Mazambala Island Lodge*, T229075. Signposted off the B8 2 km east of Kongola Bridge, 4 km to lodge, a 4WD may be necessary, if indeed you can get there at all; call ahead, or travel carefully, particularly through floodwater. A simple bush camp with 4 permanent tents and campsite, bar, lounge, food if ordered in advance, canoe trips.
F *Kubunyana*. Turn off the D3511 7 km south of the B8, the camp is 4 km further on. The final few hundred metres to the site may be underwater, hoot your horn for help, access is possible by canoe (and a place above high water to park your car exists). A community campsite with 4 permanent double tents, decent communal ablutions, plus 4 campsites with simple field kitchen.

Mamili National Park

A seldom visited park tucked in the southwestern corner of Eastern Caprivi, across the Kwando River from Botswana. It is the only area of conserved swampland in the country, roughly 32,000 ha, of which 8% is underwater after good rains. It resembles the Okavango Delta in Botswana, but with none of the development. The principal attraction is the birdlife (an amazing 430 recorded species), but there is plenty for the game viewer. However, there are no facilities and, for the majority of the roads, a four-wheel drive is essential (thick sand or mud, year round) – or travel on foot. Whenever you visit, you are likely to be the only people in the park. With the right vehicles and experience (ie guides!) it can be most rewarding.

Colour map 2, inset

Getting there From the B8, travel south along the D3511 through Mudumu until you see signposts for Mamili. There is no entrance gate, you are now in the park. As at Mudumu, the MET has a very limited presence here, there should be a ranger at the Shisinze Station, signposted off the D3511. You can continue via Linyandi (petrol sometimes available) to Katima Mulilo. Ask before attempting the drive, the road is not well or regularly maintained.

Ins & outs

Getting around Remember, the water is in charge here. Ask the ranger before attempting to reach the informal campsites (there are no facilities whatsoever) at Shivumu Pool or along the Linyati River, at Liadura or Moaremure. The park is usually flooded between May and Aug, but this depends in part on how much rain has fallen upstream and what the level of water is in the local rivers (as mentioned above, the area has unusual hydrography); in years of good rains the two large islands, **Nkasa** and **Lupala**, are cut off from the main road for months. During the dry season these 'islands' become part of the picturesque undulating landscape. Henk Coetsee's 1998 Tourist Map of the Caprivi Region is recommended for its many maps and good descriptions of parks, roads, flora and fauna.

Visitors must report at the Ranger station at the entrance to the park, 8 km south of the Sangwali tuning off the D3511. As noted, the park is only accessible by 4WD, whether dry or wet you will require experience to drive in such conditions. **Do not take risks**, if you get stuck it might be a long wait before help arrives. Rangers do patrol the park on the look-out for poachers and squatters, but if you have failed to report to the station it could be several days before you are found.

The Northeast

Best time to visit Most rain falls between Dec and Mar, which is a good time for viewing birds, but the roads can be very slippery. After the rains there tends to be more wildlife in the park, but that's when most of the tracks are likely to be impassable.

Background Mamili was created at the same time as Mudumu. These are the only two protected areas in Eastern Caprivi, an area which 35 years ago had the richest concentration of wildlife in Namibia. While considerably smaller than Mudumu, it possesses a unique environment with plenty to reward the tourist. After good rains the park resembles the Okavango Delta in Botswana.

Wildlife The variety of animals you can expect to see is more or less the same as for Mudumu. The large area of swampland means that you are more likely to see the antelope which favour this environment – red lechwe, sitatunga and waterbuck. If you are lucky you may also see puku, another swamp antelope which is only found along the Chobe River and is quite rare. Unlike Mudumu, you may also come across giraffe in the woodlands. Overall, the game viewing in this park is unpredictable as a large proportion of the animals still migrate between Angola and Botswana. Poaching and hunting have also left their mark. During the dry season the park has a reputation for large herds of buffalo and migrant elephant. Lion and leopard also live in the park, but you are likely, at best, to see only their spoor.

Sleeping There are 3 campsites, as basic as they come, 2 on the Linyanti River, at **F** *Liadura* and **F** *Moaremure*, and the other at the northern end of the Nkasa pool at **F** *Sishika*. You will have to be completely self-sufficient, including water (unless you have a purifying kit).

Katima Mulilo

Phone code: 066
Colour map 2, inset

Katima Mulilo is the regional capital of Caprivi, an ugly town whose position on the banks of the Zambezi River is easy to forget once you're in town. Mimic a lodge owner and use it to replenish and refuel, and enjoy the picturesque accommodation and plentiful water and land activities in the Eastern Caprivi, before moving on to the fabulous Chobe National Park in Botswana and Victoria Falls in Zimbabwe. After you have reprovisioned and made plans for your evening's accommodation, make for the pontoon bar at the Zambezi Hotel, sadly only open 1600-1900, for that beer you promised yourself way back in Rundu.

Ins & outs **Getting there** Between Kongola and Katima Mulilo the tarred B8 is in fairly poor condition. About 20 km west of Katima Mulilo is Katima Mulilo airport, served by Air Namibia flights; the Namibian Army's 2nd Battalion has a base and road checkpoint on the way. This was an important military base during the occupation by the South African army (the site is now used by the Namibian army), you can still see the remains of the mortar-proof parking shelters for the South African Air Force beside the runway. If you are arriving by air make sure you have arranged in advance to be collected by your hotel as there are no taxis or buses. There is a card telephone outside the terminal building and a kiosk selling cool drinks. The B8 splits at Katima Mulilo; the Zambezi River is straight ahead; a left turn takes you to Zambia (4 km), right goes through town, then on 57 km to the border with Botswana at Ngoma Bridge.

Background Your first stop as a tourist should be at *Tutwa Tourism and Travel*, just before you reach the T-junction at the Zambezi where the B8 splits. They have numerous maps and are well informed about excursions and lodges, and will happily answer your Caprivi questions, geographical or political, as best they can, and sell you the odd curio. The MET have nothing, bar an outdated, unreadable, photocopied map.

The town has reasonable facilities including 24-hour garages, a post office, pharmacies, a Bank Windhoek, Air Namibia office, hardware stores, bottle stores and supermarkets, most of which are situated around a central square which is the centre of all activity. A trip to the Caprivi Arts Centre is recommended – take a look at the locally woven and carved crafts and do the community a favour by picking up a bargain or two. Watch out for closing times, however, as the town is on Central African Time in winter (put simply, your watch will say 1600 when they close the doors at what for them is 1700).

There is a good selection of lodges in the Katima Mulilo area. While they were all hard hit **Sleeping** by the 'downturn', the ones mentioned below survived (some better than others). Note that while the fishing is excellent, boat trips for game viewing are better in Kasane or Victoria Falls, assuming you are travelling in this direction, or Lianshulu or Namushasha lodges on the Kwando River – there is little wildlife on this wide stretch of the Zambezi.

In town C *Zambezi Hotel*, T253203, F253149, katima@iafrica.com.na is a fairly square 1970s style hotel but with pleasant gardens and an excellent riverside location, including a floating moored pontoon bar, open every evening from 1600-1900. 25 en-suite rooms with a/c, floodlit pool, restaurant with good evening set menu (Mon-Sat) at N$60pp, bar, TV lounge. The adjacent golf course is pleasant for a morning or evening stroll (or jog). Note the small cemetery just outside the hotel gate, with its large headstone for the previous magistrate of the Caprivi, LEF Trollope. F Grassed campsite on the riverbank upstream from the main complex, adequate ablutions, some lights, security guards. **D/E** *Mukusi Cabins*, T253255, F253359. By the Engen garage on the B8, 1 km west of town. 18 small wooden cabins, the 'de-luxe' rooms have TV and en-suite, the 'standard' have shared ablutions. Next door is the nicest restaurant/coffee shop in town. **D/E** *Guinea Fowl Inn*, T253349 (if it works). Not significantly cheaper than others in the area, and definitely the worst, despite a beautiful setting by the Zambezi. All rooms off a single shabby corridor, separated by thin walls. Bar, restaurant, F camping on the overgrown lawns permitted.

Lodges in the area B *Kalizo Lodge*, T252802. Far from town, on sweep of the Zambezi: take the B8 for Ngoma Bridge for 18 km, then the D3508 signposted for Kalambesa, next signpost after 20 km, 5 km to the lodge (4WD needed after rain). En-suite rooms in A-frame, wood, reed and thatch chalets overlooking the river, restaurant with excellent food, bar, swimming pool, plenty of river and riverbank activities, lovely riverside location. Rooms perhaps a bit simple for the price. F campsite with ablutions. . D *Caprivi Cabins*,

Katima Mulilo

ZAMBIA

Zambezi River

To Wenela Border Post

To Botswana (Ngoma Border Post),
Caprivi Cabins & Hippo Lodge

Tutwa
Tourism
Shell

Caltex

Caprivi Arts
Centre

Central
Square

Bakery

Engen

To Rundu

N

0 metres 500
0 yards 500

■ **Sleeping**
1 Guinea Fowl Inn
2 Mukusi Cabins
3 Zambezi

● **Eating**
1 Mad Dog McGee's

The Northeast

T252288, F253158, crtechZA@mweb.com.na Signposted off the B8 for Ngoma, 6 km from town. Has 8 thatched double chalets, en-suite, with fridge, under improvement, but already cosy and pretty. Shaded lawns, small pool, bar and dining area overlooking the river, lounge with TV and library. Excellent for activities: the new owner is a keen kayaker and owns an enormous, ex-military 4WD truck. They offer interesting game drives to remote locations, particularly by the Chobe River. **F** Camping permitted, plus they have car hire. Recommended. **D/E** *Hippo Lodge*, T/F253684, colourgem@ iafrica.com   Left turn off the B8 for Ngoma, 5 km from town (their signpost may still be stuck in red tape, in which case it is the turning immediately after Caprivi Cabins), the lodge is 2 km from the road, keep going until you reach the river. Has 19 en-suite rooms in thatched chalets, simple but with natural feel, green and shaded, bar and deck over the river, good for birds and . . . hippo. Restaurant haphazard, prebooking vital, new kitchens being built. Relaxed feel, not the heights of luxury, but good value, boat and fishing trips possible; having survived the downturn, investment is needed to achieve the potential it clearly has. Campsite to reopen once ablutions rebuilt (after the kitchens – 'these things take time!').

Eating   In town, your best bet for dinner is *Mad Dog Mcgee's* , which can get quite colourful once the beer has been flowing. For lunch or coffee, head for *Mukusi Cabins*, open until 1600 Mon-Sat. The *Golf Club* throws a party on Fri night, but is a shadow of its former self (as is the course). Plenty of take-aways available, as always.

Activities   The Zambezi is popular for **fishing** – bring all your tackle with you (Rundu is the nearest town with a decent range of gear). The rivers support good populations of tiger fish, bream, nembwe, and barbel. Boats can be organized at any of the lodges, or through *Tutwa*.

The *Zambezi Hotel* and *Hippo* and *Kalizo* lodges all have **boats** available for hire for excursions to view hippo, crocodile and birdlife, available to non-residents; excursions further from the 'big city' are more likely to provide game. *Caprivi Cabins'* new management looks set to offer a range of waterborne activities, particularly canoeing.

The 9 hole **golf course** next to the *Zambezi Hotel* was unplayable in mid-2001, but with new road and bridge building activity expected, there may be a pick-up in fortunes. It wouldn't need too much work to make a nice course. Clubs used to be available for hire. Enquire at the hotel.

Shopping   Most shops are around the central square. The **Caprivi Arts Centre** is next to the open market, which stocks the fairly broad range of carvings, decorated earthenware, weaving and simple jewellery made in the region. In the last few years, training has been provided, and quality is now reliably good. The arts centre is responsible for the marketing and sale of crafts, with revenue going straight to the craftsman or woman; it is certainly worth a browse for souvenirs. You'll smell the next door **market** which has limited stock, but you might find seasonal fruit and veg, or, in the clothing section, perhaps a colourful *shitenge* (wrap-around skirt).

Transport
1361 km to Windhoek
660 km to Rundu
1485 km to Swakopmund
3340 km to Johannesburg

Katima Mulilo is an ideal stopping place on the way to or from Zambia, Botswana and the rest of Namibia with good accommodation and places to eat. Lifts for hitch-hikers can be arranged near the Shell fuel station. **Air** *Air Namibia*, office in the main square, airport 20 km southwest of town off the B8. Passengers travelling from Victoria Falls have to disembark and clear customs so the plane is usually on the ground for about 75 minutes. There is nothing to see or do at the airport except to sit on incredibly uncomfortable wood and brick seats. **Road** For *Intercape Mainliner* coaches bound for Windhoek or Victoria Falls, see timetable on page 382; picks up by the Engen station.

Banks *Bank Windhoek*, open Mon-Fri 0900-1530, Sat 0800-1000, with efficient a/c, two ATMs (often busy). Buy your ZAR, Botswanan Pula (for use at the border) and USD for use in Vic Falls/Zimbabwe here. If you are heading for Botswana then it is a good idea to buy some Pula here since the officials at the Ngoma Bridge border will not accept Namibian Dollars (ZAR, USD are fine), otherwise the nearest bank in Botswana is 54 km away in Kasane. If you have just entered Namibia the next banking facilities are in Rundu and then Grootfontein. **Useful addresses** Police station at the *boma*, an area of government offices on the B8 towards Ngoma Bridge. Foreign registered vehicles entering Namibia must purchase a Cross Border Certificate (CBC) which checkpoints and immigration will want to see, currently N$70 for a car, available from opposite the police station (signposted).

Impalila Island

At the eastern tip of Caprivi, by the confluence of the Chobe and Zambezi Rivers, is the easternmost outpost of Namibia – Impalila Island. The island sits in the Kasai channel between the Zambezi and Chobe. At its eastern end is another small island, Kakumba, which lies opposite the Botswana town of Kazangula where Zimbabwe, Zambia, Botswana and Namibia all meet (officially in the middle of the great Zambezi).

Impalila Island and the banks of Botswana at Kasane are home to a number of upmarket lodges, which offer excellent boat excursions, and all have game drives into the remote riverbank area of Chobe National Park and the abundant game that drinks there. It's strange to think of these lodges as part of Namibia, but that's what their tax bill (if not their phone number) says. They are accessed by boat from Kasane in Botswana, which is 57 km from Ngoma via the tarred road through Chobe National Park, or by plane to the small airfields at Kasane and on the island. There are customs and immigration facilities on the island. In dry periods, with an exceptionally good four-wheel drive and GPS, it is possible to reach Impalila Island overland, remaining within Namibia; an experienced guide is needed for this route. The aquatic attractions include superb **fishing** and **rapids** (Mombova and Chobe), as well as excursions up the Indibi River (western end) for game viewing in the papyrus fringed flood plain. There are several fine walking trails on Impalila Island which will take you past the local villages (picturesque but with associated cattle and rubbish). The stunning location of this island, with its abundant wildlife, tranquil rivers and beautiful lodges makes getting here well worth the effort. En route, if you have come by four-wheel drive, it is certainly worth spending some time along the river in Chobe National Park; central reservations in Maun is T26-661265.

Sleeping

L *Chobe Savanna Lodge*, T+267-71310098, F650280 is a new addition in 2001 with 12 thatched, en-suite safari tents with private balcony over the river, a/c and minibar, swimming pool, restaurant, panoramic bar and sun deck, fishing, game viewing by boat and 4WD, as well as from your bedroom. **L** *Ichingo Chobe River Lodge*, exchange in Botswana T+267-650143, F650223, www.natron.net/ichingo has 8 luxury tents with open-air bathrooms and balcony, overlooking the Chobe and tastefully decorated. Attractive dining room, lounge and bar, boat trips for river fishing or cruising, whitewater canoeing or mokoro trips for drifters into the Caprivi flood plain recommended. Every visitor will leave feeling most privileged, a beautiful spot. **L** *Impalila Island Lodge*, reservations in South Africa T/F+2711-7067207, www.impalila.co.za Has 8 en-suite chalets overlooking the Mombova rapids, swimming pool, curio shop,

The Northeast

lounge, small library. The centrepiece of the dining area is a large baobab tree. Elevated bar above the river, with the roar of the rapids in the background. An excellent lodge in a most exclusive location. Closed Feb. **L** *Susuwe Lodge*, T+2711-7067207, F-4638251, www.susuwe.co.za with 6 beautiful, spacious en-suite doubles with plunge pool and balcony overlooking the river, central lounge and dining area, library, curio shop, rates include full board, 4WD and boat excursions and guided walks. **L** *Zambezi Queen & King's Den Lodge*, T353203, F253631, katima@iafrica.co.na has 10 wooden en-suite chalets with balcony right on the river and individually carved African motifs on much of the furniture, restaurant, bar, shaded lawns, price is full board, river activities included. The huge riverboat, the *Zambezi Queen* (which is sadly too big to navigate the river in anything but highest flood season) is moored at the lodge and offers alternative, luxurious (but fairly small) cabins as overflow accommodation.

Ngoma Border Post (Botswana)
Colour map 2, inset

The border with Botswana (open 0600-1800) is 62 km from Katima Mulilo on a new tarred road. About 14 km before the border is the well signposted turn-off for an excellent community-run campsite. **F** *Salambala*, T252875, has 4 separate sites with room for 4 tents on each, each with its own wash block with hot water and flush toilet, braai area and simple camp kitchen. A short walk takes visitors to **Salambala Pan** and a hide (well, the frame of a hide, the rest is expected shortly) for viewing the regular elephant and small game that come to drink and bathe here. Water is pumped in when it gets low, but it looks as though the local farmers are bringing their cattle to drink here, so they may be putting the game off. Take care on the 4 km track to the site from the B8, there are sandy stretches which ordinary vehicles should not attempt. An alternative is available, but you'll need to use your wits to find it – hopefully, the community will have heeded complaints and directed traffic (and cattle) better by the time you visit.

From Ngoma it is 57km to Kasane (for Impalila Island) and a further 90 km via Kazangula border (and ZAR100 for a Zimbabwean vehicle insurance levy for hire cars) to Victoria Falls with it's majestic scenery and plentiful money changers and petty thieves. As one Caprivi resident put it, 'You would be committing a *serious* crime, to get this far and not see Vic Falls.' Travel from Katima Mulilo to Vic Falls (217 km) takes you through Chobe National Park: including border crossings, it should take no more than 3 hours. There is a campsite, the *Buffalo Ridge* (Pula 22pp), at the Botswana side of the Ngoma crossing. A cross border certificate (CBC), available from opposite the police station in Katima Mulilo, is required to take a vehicle **not** registered in Namibia out of the country. You will need a small amount of Botswanan Pula (Pula 10 in 2001) to buy the road levy to drive in Botswana, valid for a year. Make sure you have some currency (ZAR, USD or Pula) as it is an irritating 100 km round trip to the bank in Kasane and back to the border post. Border open: 0600 to 1800, but beware of time changes due to Central African Time.

The Botswana post is at the far end of the bridge after crossing the broad Chobe river valley, after a disinfectant dip. There are a number of upmarket lodges, fuel and some shops in Kasane.

Wenela Border Post (Zambia)
Colour map 2, inset

The border with Zambia is 4 km from town on a new tar road. A bridge over the Zambezi is planned, meanwhile you get to enjoy the car ferry to Sesheke. The border post is open 0600-1800. There are reputed to be some nice lodges on the far side, but I'm afraid they are outside the scope of this book. **NB** The road on the Zambian side is notoriously bad, only take this route if you have to. As with the Botswana border post, a CBC is required to take a vehicle **not** registered in Namibia out of the country.

The Far North

6

The Far North

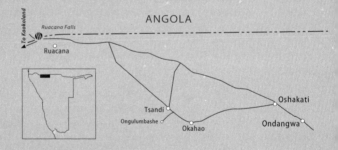

The Far North, or Owamboland, is a dusty, overgrazed, overpopulated area with few attractions for the tourist. A great deal of money is flowing into the region from government and overseas aid expenditure on education, health care, the civil service, police and military and there are significant visible infrastructure investments. The area is evidently booming, but the visitor will quickly appreciate that tourism is not the engine for this growth.

However, for those with the time and energy, there is plenty to discover: this is how the majority of the country lives. The towns are an interesting mix of urban and traditional tempered by a vibrant Portuguese/Angolan influence, there are plentiful small bars, big businesses and municipal workers spending their money. Out of town, the landscape is dominated by the fascinating geography and agronomy of the oshanas, *on which so many rely.*

Things to do in the Far North

- Be amazed by the efforts of the 19th-century missionaries and explore the numerous **churches and churchyards** in villages dotted across the region.
- Smell a new flavour of Africa with a **day trip to Angola** from Oshikango.
- After heavy rain, witness the raging torrent of the Kunene River at **Ruacana** as floodwater is released from the Caleque Dam just a few hundred metres upstream.
- In the drying *oshanas*, try your hand at **basket fishing** with the patient proponents of the art.

Background

Formerly known as Owamboland, the far north of Namibia is now divided into four political regions (Oshikoto, Ohangwena, Omusati and Oshana). This area is home to over half of the country's population (over 800,000 people), with much the greatest population density (over 10 per sq km on average, against a national average of just over 2). This part of Namibia is typified by a different relationship between man, animal and land; you will notice a significant increase in traffic (cars, bicycles and donkeys). Herds of goats and cattle criss-cross the roads, and all along the way wooden, fenced homesteads are visible, strings of children make their way to and from school and the tireless collectors of water go about their daily grind. After the vast, uninhabited expanses of the south, it is a striking reminder of how much of Africa lives.

The unnatural division in the structure of life in the country is the **Red Line**, located 120 km south of Ondangwa on the B1, a fence which separates the animals of Etosha and the large commercial farms of the south from those of the communal small farmers of the north. The movement of livestock, meat and animal products from north to south is forbidden, ostensibly to prevent foot-and-mouth disease and rinderpest from infecting the commercial herds of the south. For the tourist, this means any skins, horns, trophies or other animal products either need not to be brought north in the first place, or require a veterinary note specifying the health of your souvenir before being allowed to return south.

Climate Although they seem to be increasingly unreliable, the rains are expected to arrive at the beginning of the year, making March-May the most colourful, verdant months to visit. The yearly average (about 500 mm) usually falls in heavy thunderstorms, with resulting damage to crops and flooding; the surface water flows to the *oshanas*, on which the local agronomy relies. Crops are planted, grown and reaped before July/August, when most of the *oshanas* have dried up. This is the time to witness the bizarre spectacle of groups of women with handmade fishing baskets wading in shrinking muddy pools, doing their best to catch an addition to the supper pot. For the remainder of the year, expect dust, heat and breath-sapping hot winds. The dust can be like a mist, requiring headlights for driving, and the landscape becomes surreal and moon-like. For your comfort this period is best avoided.

The *Oshana* While few overseas visitors visit the region, those who do are rewarded with an
environment insight into a unique and highly fertile ecosystem.

The *oshanas* are a system of shallow watercourses and *vleis* which first appear in south-central Angola and reach as far south as the Etosha Pan. Most of these 'rivers' are several hundred kilometres long, but they only flow for a few months each year after the rains. In years of exceptionally heavy rainfall there can be widespread flooding. These floods are known as the *Efundja*. The last major *efundja* was recorded in 1954. Recent (2000 and 2001) plentiful rain has meant that the *oshanas* have not dried out until September, extending the productive season for a few more valuable weeks. But the high water levels also highlighted that many homesteads are now vulnerable to floods, should there be exceptionally heavy downpours in coming years.

Aerial photography reveals a pattern of watercourses akin to a river delta emptying into the ocean, but in this case they drain internally into pans, the largest of which is at Etosha. The watercourses are mostly empty, left over from earlier fluvial periods, with alluvium deposits and high salt concentrations. An optimal season sees the rains start in November and fall regularly from December to March. There is water in the *oshanas* from January until July. Farmers prepare their fields and cattle are herded back from distant grazing to benefit from the new pasture near home, enriching the farmers' diet (mostly dairy, but occasionally beef). Crops are reaped before the water evaporates, and this is the peak fishing season as the fish have reached a reasonable size and the ponds are small enough to catch them. Then it's back to mealie pap for the remainder of the year.

Given the large number of people subsisting directly off the land in this region, the *oshanas* play an important role in the well-being of the population. The government is struggling with population increases and erratic rainfall to protect the environment and manage it sensibly. Water is pumped from the Calueque Dam in Angola, but this is for drinking, and there are very few irrigation schemes (Ongwediva being an exception) that can compensate for poor rains. Without rain, the basic crops such as *omahangu* (millet) fail and there are no fish. Additionally, the groundwater level drops and boreholes run dry, pastures remain barren and cattle have nothing to eat. Quickly, a land of plenty becomes a desolate, desperate, disaster zone, an embarrassment for the government in what is its home territory. The visible overgrazing, erosion and deforestation, added to increasing soil salinity and frequent water shortages, put in question the continued balance of the ecosystem. Its successful management is one of the government's greatest challenges. They cannot afford to get it wrong as relocation of such a number of people (even ignoring

The Far North

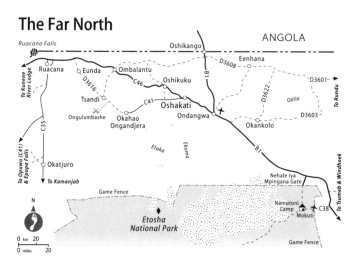

the social issues) is virtually impossible in a country as dry and poorly suited to subsistence agriculture as Namibia. Put simply, everyone prays for rain.

Driving through the region, one can't help wondering where the money comes from. While many grow and rear a good deal of their consumption needs, as very few produce an excess to sell for income. Principally, money comes from the government (pensions, official jobs and infrastructure investment) and migrant labour, with traders benefiting from a good number of Angolans heading south for supplies.

Ondangwa

Phone code: 065
Colour map 1, grid A5
686 km from
Windhoek
256 km from Tsumeb
35 km from Oshakati

*Driving north from the **Red Line** (where there is a 24-hour Engen garage, bottle store and takeaway), the first significant concentration reached is Ondangwa. In addition to small roadside shops and bottle stores, there are a couple of smart new malls with banks and supermarkets. The landscape is dominated by lonely makalani palms, the mopane having long since been cut down for firewood or used to build homesteads. This is the second largest town in this populous region and fairly well provisioned. The only tourist attraction is the informative and well presented Nakambale Museum at Olokonda, signposted off the B1 before you reach town.*

Background Overgrazing, deforestation and lack of regular rain has reduced the surrounding area to a desolate, sandy rubbish tip, with forlorn cattle wandering and wondering where their grazing has gone. This is communal land buckling under population pressure. The **makalani palm** trees have survived in the harsh landscape, perhaps because of their inefficiency as firewood, and offer attractive silhouettes at sunset. For a few weeks after heavy rains, the *oshanas* fill with water and pale pink and white lilies miraculously appear; you may also see the cone-shaped fishing baskets in use. The open markets in July and August are evidence that the fish grow to an impressive size in their shrinking *oshanas* – often little more than big puddles.

While there is nothing for the tourist in town, there is a sense of having 'arrived'. Activity of people and traffic flow increases dramatically, there are more roadside stalls, and developments extend further away from the road. There is more litter, more abandoned, gutted cars and less vegetation. In town, modern shopping centres – housing banks and insurance companies,

Ondangwa

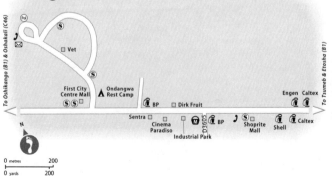

supermarkets and furniture stores – have been developed. A four-star hotel has appeared in the northern edge of town. Throughout the area, the colourful *cuca* shops (rechristened bottle stores) enliven the roadside with their artistry and imaginative banners; look out for 'Water is Life', 'Lipstick Entertainment', 'Club – The System' and 'Friendship Only', among others. The travel-weary might be interested in the small *Cinema Paradiso*, showing fairly recent American blockbusters in a 50-seater auditorium.

The Nakambale Museum is the tourist highlight of the area. Housed in the original (1893) mission house, much of the collection is devoted to the lives and impressive work of the Finnish missionaries in northern Namibia since the 1870s; in particular, to Martti Rautunen, who translated many (particularly religious) works into local languages and was given the Owambo name, 'Nakambale'. There are some excellent and informative displays of traditional musical instruments, household utensils, clothing, tools, snares and clothing. Surrounding the house are a large church, a cemetery with beautifully maintained marble graves for the Rautunen family, and a traditional Ndonga homestead. Guides are available to bring the place to life and, with pre-booking, visitors can enjoy demonstrations of Ovambo life and culture, eating, singing, dancing and even sleeping in the traditional way. ■ *Mon, Tue, Thu, Fri 0800-1300, 1400-1700, Sat 0800-1300, Sun 1200-1700. Small entrance charge. T245668, olukonda.museum@elcin.org.na Look for signposts for the Olukonda National Monument 4 km southeast of the B1, travel 5 km along the D3629.*

Nakambale Museum

During the week, accommodation may be booked with government officials, trade fair visitors, businessmen and NGO staff. **In town C** *Cresta Lodge*, T241900, F241919, www.cresta-hospitality.com Located just off the B1, at the northern end of town, by the Oshikango turning. 90 en-suite rooms with a/c, TV, radio, telephone and modem connection, desk and kettle, restaurant, bar, coffee shop with good cakes and savouries, large conference facilities, a very clean, international standard hotel, fairly square and impersonal but with some interesting African carvings and wall hangings. **E-F** *Ondangwa Rest Camp*, T/F240351, www.oshana.namib/restcamp 3 simple canvas permanent tents with beds and bedding and a small area (being expanded) for camping, with water, light, braai and electricity point and communal ablutions. This is as pleasant a town centre restcamp as you could expect, set around a small pond with noisy geese, popular outdoor bar with TV (and rugby fans), small, good restaurant. Internet cafe planned. The owner, Frik Coutsee, offers overnight tours down to the little visited northern border of Etosha and is a fount of information on the area and Kaokaland. Recommended.

Sleeping

In the area D *Punyu International*, T240556, F240660. Well signposted off the B1, 4 km southeast of town on the B1, turn for Eenhana (D3622), 1 km from the junction. Simple urban hotel with little intimacy, 85 en-suite rooms with a/c, TV, phone and desk. Restaurant with pleasant outdoor seating, 2 bars. Punyu (Owambo for 'generosity') has a finger in many pies, you'll see his sign everywhere, including a bakery (with no bread!) opposite the hotel and car hire (T240313) including 4WD vehicles. **E-F** *Elcin Guest House*, T248189. 2 km past the *Punyu International* on the D3622. 10 very basic rooms, including a dorm. **F** *Nakambale Museum Camp*, T245668, olukonda.museum@elcin.org.na At the museum, see directions above. Space for a few tents, plus a traditional mud hut with reed mats on the floor and thatched roof. Very basic ablutions, water, electricity, braai put, small curio shop. **F** *Limbandingula*, on the B1, 53 km southeast of Ondangwa. A simple, reasonable truckers halt for the weary traveller, with 6 en-suite rooms, basic bar and food.

The Far North

Shopping **Crafts** Approaching Ondangwa from the south, as well as the bottle stores aplenty, you should see roadside stalls selling traditional baskets woven from the makalani palm leaves, bowls and calabashes. The revenue derived from these items is important to the individual craftsmen and women who produce them. The stalls may look unattended, but stop your car and someone will be there in a flash. The markets in Ondangwa and Oshakati, also worth browsing, may have carved cups, bowls, snuff containers, knives and colourful material. None of these are produced for tourists, they are the preferred implements and materials of the homesteads.

Transport **Air** *Air Namibia*, T40655, F40656, the airport (and Air Namibia office) turn-off is 5 km northwest of Ondangwa on the B1; 3 flights a week to **Windhoek – Eros** airport. There are numerous **taxis** plying south to Windhoek and destinations en route.

Directory Ondangwa has a post office, all three banks (with ATMs), numerous petrol stations, a vet (for clearance to cross the Red Line with any animal skins, horns, etc that you may have), and police station. There is also a small cinema (*Paradiso*) that takes up to 50 people and shows relatively recent films. The hospital is by the *Elcin Guest House*, 7 km south of town on the D3622 for Eenhana.

Ondangwa to Angola

Colour map 1, grid A4

For 6 months of the year there is a time difference between Namibia and Angola, and although there are no signs to warn you, vehicles drive on the right

While civil war continues in Angola, there has been no recent 'trouble' near the Namibian border for years. Economic links with the north of Namibia are improving; many Angolan traders head south for supplies, and wealthier Angolans come to spend their US$ in this land of relative plenty. With Angolan businesses taking an ever higher profile, you may hear Portuguese being spoken. Some Namibians venture north, mainly for cheaper petrol, cattle and goats. For the visitor in search of a different flavour, try an afternoon in the Angolan village of **Santa Clara (Oshikango)**.

The road from Ondangwa to the border is busy with Angolan trucks and for the last kilometre the road is lined with traders. The customs and immigration offices on the Namibian side are a bricks-and-mortar statement of national pride. The buildings on the Angolan side of the border show all the evidence of war damage. It is possible, with a minimum of red tape, to go over to Santa Clara for a few hours. It is advisable to walk the short distance, you may invite unnecessary problems by taking your car. There do not appear to be formal immigration checkpoints so respond helpfully to officials who may approach you – they are most likely to be Angolan police dressed in Namibian uniforms with the insignia removed. The border is open 0800-1800.

In the centre of **Santa Clara**, about 400 m from the border, are several bars on the right which are worth a try; Namibian dollars can be used.

Sleeping **D** *Namib Contract Haulage Investment Centre Motel*, T061-234164/65. 5 km from the border on the road to Engela and Okalongo. 8 en-suite rooms with a/c and TV. **E** *Peter's*, T06751-61545. 500 m before the border. 12 rooms with fan.

West to Ruacana At **Ongwediva**, 10 km southeast of Oshakati, there is a small concentration of shops, a *Standard Bank* with ATM, *Spar* and *Engen* garage. Many education and environment ministry offices are located here, and the annual Trade Fair (end August) takes place in a huge, new conference facility. There are a few shops, including the **Traditional Shop**, set back from the road, for Owambo and Himba jewellery, traditional dresses and skins. On the B1 is the **D** *Hotel Seven Valleys*, T230149, Expert@mweb.com.na with 8 simple and pleasant en-suite rooms with satellite TV, fridge and kettle, pretty garden. No bar/restaurant facilities.

Oshakati

Oshakati has many faces. There is the 'town', the former South African military base, where government employees, expatriates and the successful live in detached houses set in leafy gardens close to the video shops, private schools and public library. There are the various 'locations' where shanty-type dwellings of corrugated iron and scrap metal are dotted with NGO and municipally built public lavatories and stand pipes. In between these extremes are those with housing and services of a basic standard, mostly lowly government workers of some kind.

Phone code: 065
Colour map 1, grid A4
721 km from Windhoek;
35 km to Ondangwa;
152 km from Ruacana

The commercial centre of Oshakati and the north happens where the high street banks and the open market, *Omatala*, face each other across the dusty main road. The University of Namibia has its Northern Campus in town, and you will notice a major influence of municipal buildings and services. But, while there is certainly money in the area, the impression remains that life for the majority in Oshakati is hard.

B/C *Oshakati Country Lodge*, T222380, F222384, countrylodge@mweb.com.na has 46 large, en-suite rooms with a/c, TV, desk and kettle. Nicely built with African touches to good standard, central reception and bar in huge thatched barn, restaurant serving good food around swimming pool in pleasant lawned garden. Opened in 1999, easily the nicest place in town. **C** *Santorini Inn*, T220506, santorini@osh.nam.com has 29 en-suite rooms and chalets each with a/c, satellite TV, telephone and kettle, set around a swimming pool and garden courtyard, bar, restaurant (with good pizza), squash court. **C/D** *Oshandira Lodge*, T220443. Follow signs, located at the edge of town by the airstrip. 19 a/c rooms with TV and phone. Set in well watered green gardens with a few caged parrots. Popular restaurant and bar, with seating either indoors or around the swimming pool. **D-E** *Rocha's*, T221800, F224282, 25 en-suite rooms, including 'luxury' ones with a/c, TV and phone, square and basic in an exceptionally ugly concrete building. The only attraction is the location beside the nice restaurant/bar of the

Sleeping

The Far North

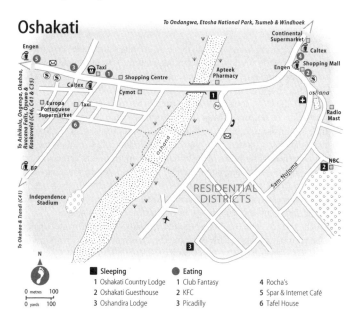

Oshakati

To Ondangwa, Etosha National Park, Tsumeb & Windhoek

Continental Supermarket

Engen

Caltex

Shopping Mall

Engen

Taxi

Shopping Centre

Apteek Pharmacy

Caltex

Cymot

oshana

Europa Portuguese Supermarket

Taxi

Radio Mast

To Ashikulu, Ongenga, Okahao, Ruacana Falls, Opuwo & Kaokoveld (C46, C41 & C35)

BP

oshana

NBC

RESIDENTIAL DISTRICTS

Sam Nujoma

Independence Stadium

To Okahao & Tsandi (C41)

N

0 metres 100
0 yards 100

■ **Sleeping**
1 Oshakati Country Lodge
2 Oshakati Guesthouse
3 Oshandira Lodge

● **Eating**
1 Club Fantasy
2 KFC
3 Picadilly

4 Rocha's
5 Spar & Internet Café
6 Tafel House

same name. **E/F** *Oshakati Self-Catering Guest House*, T221027, 7 rooms in a simple house, communal facilities, basic and good value, with a bar next door that can get busy. **E/F** *Bicho Lodge*, T22122. On the B1, 9 km southeast of Oshakati. 9 simple en-suite rooms with desk, colourful and clean, small restaurant and bar.

Eating   In addition to the more formal places listed below is a KFC and many takeaways/bars and market stalls where you can get a taste of what the locals eat. Of the bars, try *Piccadilly*, *fairly comfortable, or, later at night*, *Club Fantasy*, arranged around a collection of armchairs and low tables, frequented by businessmen, and good for mixing and finding out what is going on in town; expect South African disco hits, a good dose of *soukous* – the infectious Zairean dance – and the Angolan *kazomba,* open Wed, Fri and Sat.

The *Oshakati Country Lodge* is your best bet for food, serving good and not over-priced food at tables by the swimming pool; or have a snack at the airy indoor bar with TV, pool table and draught beer. *Rocha's* serves simple, tasty Portuguese chicken, steak and cod in a friendly atmosphere. The table settings and decor are pleasant but not fussy and as the evening progresses it is easy to forget you are sitting beside the roadside in Oshakati. The *Tafel House* has a beer garden with seating under thatched roof, draught beer, good simple meals at a reasonable price; at weekends there is a disco which is cheaper and more intimate than *Club Fantasy*.

Shopping   Local magnate and powerful Namibian figure Frans (Oupa) Indongo has his **Continental Supermarket** in Oshakati, selling everything you need for rural survival – cast iron cooking pots, car stereo systems, saddles, water drums, nylon leopard-skin underwear, curtain hooks and plenty more. It also has a cheap and amazingly well stocked bottle store. The range of spirits and special liqueurs is final evidence, if necessary, of Namibians' love of drinking. There cannot be many places in Africa which offer five different brands of Tequila! There is a Continental No 2 in Ongwediva and No 3 is the new *Spar* in the centre of Oshakati, which has a good coffee bar inside. Try the **Europa Portuguese Supermarket** for camping supplies.

Directory   **Car hire** *Ovambo Car Hire*, T222952, F222955, bdewet@iafrica.co.na **Internet** café by the *Spar*, excellent connection speed, open Mon-Fri 0900-1900, Sat 0900-1300.

Oshakati to   Continuing north from Oshakati, the sense of being somewhere becomes elu-
Ruacana   sive as the ribbon development peters out. Only the scattered homesteads and schools are a reminder that this is still one of the most densely populated parts of Namibia. The direct route from Oshakati to Ruacana follows 160 km of good tar road, the C46, along the Ogongo canal. This route will take you through Oshikuku, 28 km, and Uutapi (Ombalantu), 100 km. Depending upon the time of year you will either pass through flood plains (usually March-May), or dry sandy pans, dotted with clusters of makalani palms, homesteads and *mahangu* fields. The most striking feature of the landscape is its flatness. Instead of passing straight through the region for Kaokoland, consider making a short detour to explore some of the villages of the Oshana and Omusati regions. Remember as you pass through that this is where the majority of Namibians call home. President Sam Nujoma was born in a village close to Okahao.

The C41 to Okahao is 73 km of good tar, clearly signposted from Oshakati. The tar is replaced by a fairly poor gravel road heading west to Tsandi, a further 30 km on the D3612. From Tsandi either continue northeast 30 km to the C46 at Ombalantu or take the D3616 to Onesi and then join the C46 near Ruacana. Take care if travelling in a saloon car. As with all such roads don't let the needle go above 80 kph: there are many fatal accidents involving visitors each year on such roads.

Heroes Day

On Heroes Day (26 August) the site becomes the focus of national interest. Given Namibia's tiny population, national events are normally characterized by empty stadiums and skilful camera work making small huddles of people look like throngs. At Ongulumbashe on Heroes Day, Namibia can honestly boast a crowd of several thousand. Over the past few years this annual event has developed into a symbol of both national pride and reconciliation. Lasting one full day, with visitors camping out before and after the event, the events of 1966 are commemorated and those who fought during the struggle are honoured. Performance and cultural presentations are made by representatives of the 13 regions – traditional praise songs and colourful dances in traditional costumes. The most popular of these is a dramatic re-enactment of the battle of Ongulumbashe complete with carved wooden AK 47s. The victorious combatants

end by raising the Namibian flag as did the real fighters after each victory in the bush. The flag was flown then lowered and carried with the unit wherever they went. As far as is known, at no point during the bush war did the SAD succeed in capturing the Namibian flag.

Along with the performances speeches are made and prayers said before the people – civilians, heroes, heroines and politicians alike sit down and eat together. Away from the pompousness of Windhoek, the bush is a great leveller and you are likely to find yourself filling your plate shoulder to shoulder with some of the most powerful men in the country.

Namibia's recent history is still painfully fresh and the culture of commemoration is only just developing. If Ongulumbashe is anything to go by then there is a good chance that in spite of the past Namibia may yet develop a national, historic identity which is both meaningful and dignified.

The Far North

Okahao & Ongandjera

Ongandjera is the birthplace of **President Sam Nujoma**, while Okahao is *Colour map 1, grid A4* the largest village in the region, just a kilometre from the president's traditional homestead where his elderly mother still lives and where the president still makes frequent visits. Okahao is dominated by a large ELCIN church, cemetery and hospital, while Ongandjera appears to be one large school and nothing else. The whereabaouts of the Nujoma homestead is not at all obvious; if you do not find it, take comfort in the fact that, being virtually identical, the great man was raised in one of these homesteads. About 2 km before reaching Okahoe is the new **D/E** *Ongozi Guest Lodge*, T252025, F252026, with 16 simple, clean, en-suite rooms, restaurant, bar, conference room, devoid of decoration, although an impressive baobab tree sits out at the back, and they have planted rows of trees that, if you are reading this in 2010, might afford some shade.

The road to Tsandi takes you deep into the Oshana region; mopane trees and **To Tsandi &** makalani palms dominate, interspersed with wonderful baobabs. Just before **further north** the road turns into Tsandi there is a signpost for Ongulumbashe (see below), scene of an important event in the struggle for independence.

Tsandi is a more attractive village than Okahao and, if time permits, you might like to pause here to savour a different pace of life. There are several well-stocked, reasonable bars, often full of drunken characters.

While there are many around, keep an eye out for the huge baobab tree as you head north for **Ombalantu**. This is not as well known as the **baobab at**

Uutapi, which has served as a prison and is now a church. **Uutapi** is the main town of Ombalantu and is developing rapidly. As you approach from the south you will notice the large number of newly constructed government buildings and shops. To visit the baobab, obtain permission first at the police station; it is something of a national monument. The *Super Foods* restaurant opposite the hospital and the *Onawa Supermarket* on the C46 are the best options for eating and provisions.

Ongulum-bashe
Colour map 1, grid A4

Soon to be declared a national monument, this is the historic site where the first shots of the liberation struggle were fired in 1966. Deep in the bush, southwest of President Nujoma's birth place, a group of PLAN (Peoples Liberation Army of Namibia) combatants were ambushed by South African soldiers having been betrayed by a high ranking soldier who, it later emerged, had been trained in espionage by the South Africans in the 1950s. When visiting the site it is hard to believe that the PLAN combatants were not totally taken aback by the South Africans' precise knowledge of their whereabouts. It really is the middle of nowhere; far from any main routes or settlements and not a hint of landscape, the countryside is flat, scrubby mopane woodland. Before setting their ambush, the South Africans apparently harassed the civilian population in their search for the 'terrorists'. It is hard to imagine who they found to harass. In spite of their opponents' surprise, the PLAN fighters won the battle of Ongulumbashe and the struggle for Namibian independence was born.

Today the site is marked with a monument to the heroes and heroines of the liberation struggle (see Heroes Day box on page 185) and there is talk of setting up a permanent exhibition. There is little to see or do here, although the original bunkers dug by the combatants in 1966 are still intact in the vicinity. Interestingly, the replica bunkers constructed in 1990 as a commemoration have collapsed.

Ruacana and Ruacana Falls

Phone code: 065
Colour map 1, grid A3
873 km from Windhoek
152 km from Oshakati

Ruacana Falls are not the destination they once were. The Calueque Dam in Angola has stopped any flooding and the steady stream that does come through is deviated through the hidden turbines of the hydroelectric power station. However, this corner of the country is certainly worth a visit; the Kunene River continues to flow, there is a range of watersports including excellent whitewater rafting and canoeing, beautiful riverside accommodation and the chance to see the photogenic Himba and their villages.

Ruacana itself is a useful supply stop for those planning to explore northern **Kaokoland**. The town only came into being as a camp for workers involved with the construction of the Ruacana Hydroelectric Project. The Kunene River provides both an important source of power for Namibia and water for irrigation in Owamboland, the water being carried by the **Ogongo canal** alongside the C46 to lands beyond Oshakati.

Ins & outs
There are no banks here or in Opuwo

Ruacana is well signposted, 5 km south of the C46; the airport is 3 km east along the C46. A legacy of the armed conflict in the area is that there is only one entrance into the settlement. This was an important South African military base; the barbed wire and bomb shelters are hard to see, but there is the feel of a military camp. Do not wander too far off the roads, there are still **landmines**. There is a BP garage, the only fuel in the area, with well-stocked shop (open 0800-1800), a small supermarket 200 m further along the same road, hospital and post office. The BP is also the place to ask about accommodation, there is a small (*Osheja*, T270092) guest house and campsite, neither of which can be recommended, rather press on to the attractive sites/lodges on the banks of the Kunene.

The Falls

Ruacana Falls are 15 km from Ruacana, well signposted from the C46. The falls can be spectacular, but this requires consistent heavy rains (ie summer). The flow of the Kunene River is controlled by the Calueque Dam, a short distance upstream in Angola. For views of the Falls, March-April are your best bets to see water crashing over the rocks. The heavy rains in early 2000 caused the authorities to open the floodgates, allowing the falls to flood in their full splendour. Year-round, the flow of the river is increased with demand for electricity (weekdays in the morning and evening) and it takes roughly 4 and 8 hours for the flow to reach *Kunene River Lodge* (for rafting) and Epupa Falls respectively.

Below the falls is a gorge which ends at **Hippo Pools** where there are a couple of small islands in the middle of the channel. There was a campsite here, but with the lack of water, the attraction of the area has disappeared. It used to be possible to climb the 500 steps to the bottom of the gorge, check in Ruacana at the police station. The frontier runs down the middle of the river below the main falls.

Sleeping

The lodges and campsites are all wonderfully positioned on the banks of the Kunene, reached by taking the C46 as far as Ruacana Falls, where the tar runs out and the gravel D3700 winds its way along the southern bank of the river, past small Himba homesteads. Outside the rainy season, this route is navigable (with care) by ordinary saloon cars. **D-F** *Kunene River Lodge*, T065-274300, kunenerl@osh.namib.com, 56 km west of the C46 junction for Ruacana. Bungalows, permanent tents and campsite, swimming pool, bar, restaurant; year-round activities include excellent guided rafting and canoeing, fishing, quad-biking, mountain biking and birdwatching. Recommended. **E-F** *Omunjandi Rest Camp*, T221815, 12 km west of the C46 junction for Ruacana. Permanent tents and campsite, bar and food (if booked), good ablutions. **F** *Okapupa Rest Camp*, T065-231071, T067-221624, T081-1291624 (mob), 39 km west of the C46

The Far North

Ruacana Falls

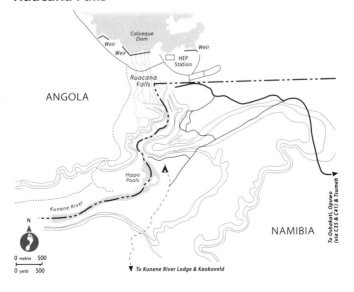

junction for Ruacana. A stunning spot with good communal facilities and a large, open, thatched central bar/dining area. Excellent meals and watersports (with guides) during school holidays and most weekends but book ahead, particularly if you are in a group and/or want to enjoy guided rafting or canoeing. Nicer 'bush' ambiance than the *Kunene River Lodge*, very quiet outside peak periods. **F** *Omumborongbonga Camp Site*, T222200, 21 km west of the C46 junction for Ruacana. Quite a mouthful to say, pleasant, simple riverside site with basic ablutions and water only.

Exploring Kaokoland

162 km to Epupa Falls
150 km to Opuwo
272 km to Kamanjab
302 km to Sesfontein

From the Ruacana Falls to the Atlantic Ocean the Kunene River constitutes the border between Namibia and Angola. It is a pleasant and welcome sight as it weaves its way through the Ehomba Mountains, and then the Zebra Mountains, before plunging over the smaller (but still impressive from ground level) **Epupa Falls**, 175 km west of Ruacana. There are also two sets of rapids at **Enyandi** and **Ondorusu**. The river enters the Atlantic Ocean along the northern extremity of the Skeleton Coast Park, this also marks the northern limits of the giant sand dunes which first appeared 1,700 km south, along the banks of the Orange River. The name Kunene was given to the river by the Hereros. In their language it means, 'right-hand side'; the name refers to the land north of the river. The lands to the south are known as the **Kaokoland**, 'land on the left-hand side'. In Angola the local name for the river is *Omulongo*, 'the stream'. Most visitors to Kaokoland approach it from the south via Kamanjab and Sesfontein, or they fly in on excellent, but expensive, organized safaris (see Windhoek tour companies, page 90).

Getting around The roads in northern Kaokaland have a tough job, with the undulating terrain and sporadic downpours. In the dry season, most are navigable in an ordinary car, but always ask before you attempt any of these roads. The local camp and lodge owners are your best source of information, and the Shell road map of Kaokaland your best companion for the journey. A four-wheel drive vehicle is required (plus experience and plenty of time) for a few of the routes. If you have approached through Oshakati you can avoid back-tracking by returning south via the C35 past the western end of Etosha National Park to Kamanjab. For Epupa, four-wheel drivers can take the D3700 westward along the banks of the Kunene the entire 162 km of the journey, which is very challenging west of the *Kunene River Lodge*. Ordinary cars must head south on the D3701 via Epembe and Otjijanjasemo, follow signs for Epupa Camp. Epupa is one of the most isolated tourist sites in Namibia. While it is certainly possible and worth it, few overseas visitors drive up, most join organized tours.

The Northwest

7

The Northwest

One of the last true wilderness areas in southern Africa, Kaokoland lies in the extreme northwest of Namibia. It is an area with stunning landscapes. From the Kunene River to the north, down the Skeleton Coast Park to Damaraland in the south, the area is a rugged, mountainous wilderness. Both the Damara, with their clicking tongue, and the photogenic Himba, with their ochre-skinned beauty, live in simple villages, mostly subsisting as goat and cattle herders. Namibia's best known rock art is located in the hills of Damaraland, which also offer some excellent hiking.

In the very north, the Kunene River flows sedately to the sea from the Ruacana Falls hydroelectric power station. For 300 km, this forms the peaceful border with Angola, and offers watersport enthusiasts one to five day whitewater canoeing and rafting excursions. The 32-m Epupa Falls are roughly half way to the Atlantic, a beautiful rift in the rock, adorned with villagers washing and bathing in the pools, precariously perched giant baobab trees and glorious palm-fringed sunsets. While the game was mostly shot out before independence, there is plenty to entice birders and fishermen. The area is often inaccessible to saloon cars, preserving Kaokoland as a world unto itself. It offers a glimpse into the past, while at the same time being on the verge of massive and fundamental change.

Damaraland

This sparsely populated region is a highland desert wilderness, home to uniquely adapted animal species such as the desert elephant and the last free roaming black rhinos in the world. Damaraland covers the southern half of the Kaokoveld, the area of northwest Namibia, and together with Kaokoland forms what is now deemed the Kunene political region. A huge area stretching almost 600 km north to south and 200 km east to west, Damaraland is bordered by the Hoanib River to the north, the tar road to Swakopmund to the south and Etosha and the Skeleton Coast to the east and west.

The Northwest

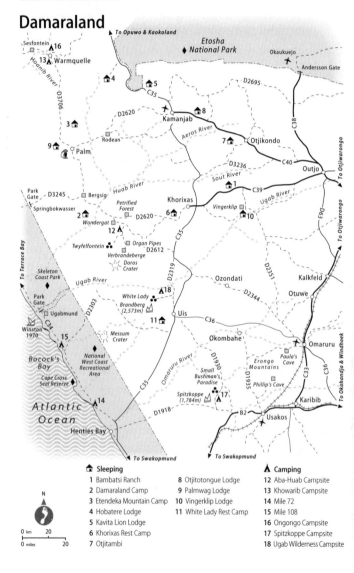

Damaraland

N

0 km   20
0 miles   20

🏠 Sleeping		
1 Bambatsi Ranch	8 Otjitotongue Lodge	
2 Damaraland Camp	9 Palmwag Lodge	
3 Etendeka Mountain Camp	10 Vingerklip Lodge	
4 Hobatere Lodge	11 White Lady Rest Camp	
5 Kavita Lion Lodge		
6 Khorixas Rest Camp		
7 Otjitambi		

🏕 Camping	
12 Aba-Huab Campsite	
13 Khowarib Campsite	
14 Mile 72	
15 Mile 108	
16 Ongongo Campsite	
17 Spitzkoppe Campsite	
18 Ugab Wilderness Campsite	

Things to do in the Northwest

- Dip into the mysterious and little known world of **Rock Art** – the Northwest houses some of the world's oldest and best preserved examples of our ancestors' work, in some magical locations, particularly Twyfelfontein, Brandberg, Spitzkoppe and the Erongo Mountains.
- Experience two worlds colliding in an Opuwo bar by sharing a local brew with a traditionally dressed **Himba** tribesman.
- Run the **Kunene River rapids**, either in canoe or by raft. You never knew sitting down could be this much fun.
- Take a walk along the riverbank below **Epupa Falls**, escape the madding crowds and clock the stunning views only a few hundred metres from the crowded entrance.
- Boy racers and rock chicks, equip yourself well, put aside your trepidation and make the **expedition** across van Zyl's Pass to the remote Marienfluss and Hartmann's valleys.

Getting there Damaraland can be approached from a number of directions. If you headed north from Windhoek and made Etosha National Park your first stop you would be likely to enter via Kamanjab. Another option is to visit a guest farm in the Omaruru region and then head west into the heart of Damaraland. The following text follows one of the more popular routes, which is to head north out of Swakopmund to Henties Bay and then head inland to either Spitzkoppe (D1918), or via the C35 to Uis. **Getting around** Because of the remoteness and lack of traffic, travellers should carry spare fuel, water and food when travelling in Damaraland. Since virtually all the roads in the region are gravel, it is preferable to drive with a pick-up truck ('bakkie') or four-wheel drive. There are a number of tour companies offering guided hiking and driving trips in the region.

Ins & outs

The Northwest

The region encompasses some of Namibia's most dramatic natural features such as the **Spitzkoppe** and **Brandberg** mountain ranges, the **Petrified Forest** west of Khorixas and **Burnt Mountain** and **Organ Pipes** near **Twyfelfontein**, site of Namibia's largest collection of Bushman rock art. All of these are well prepared for exploration on foot with local guides, while other less accessible places of interest are the Bushman paintings at **Numas Ravine** and the ancient volcanic **Messum Crater**.

Background

Inhabited for centuries by the Damara people, the area around Okombahe (between Omaruru and Uis) was first proclaimed a 'reserve' for the Damara by the German colonial administration in 1906. Following the Odendaal Commission report in 1964, which led to the creation of Bantustans in Namibia, a separate Damara tribal homeland was proclaimed in this region. Further acts in 1968 and 1969 cemented this arrangement and, in 1971, a Damara Advisory Council was formed. This was part of an overall strategy on the part of the South African government to incorporate Namibia as the country's fifth province and mirrored similar policies in South Africa itself. At independence in 1990, Damaraland was incorporated into the newly proclaimed Kunene Region.

The majority of Damaras are engaged in subsistence livestock farming. There are no sizeable towns in the region, however a network of lodges and campsites, some community-run, provide comfortable and scenic accommodation for visitors to this beautiful region.

Tour companies *Damaraland Trails and Tours*, T061-234610, F239616, offer 2 and 3 week guided tours which include a number of days hiking, good for those looking for a 'bush experience'; *Desert Adventure Safaris*, T064-404459, F404664, www.das.com.na have fly-in and 4WD safaris, using *Palmwag Camp* as a base (see below); *Nawa Safaris*, T/F061-227893, have guided driving safaris with the flexibility to design your own trip.

Southern Damaraland

Southern Damaraland is dominated by two of Namibia's best known mountains, Brandberg and Spitzkoppe. These are particularly impressive because they rise out of the flat gravel plains, and both have given rise to community campsites bringing in very welcome income to the inhabitants of the drought affected region. Heading north, the plains give way to rolling hills, dissected by numerous seasonal rivers. Most places of interest can easily be visited in a saloon car. If you wish to stay at the communal campsites, which tend to be located close to the principal attractions, you will need to have a degree of self-sufficiency and carry some basic supplies, crockery and a sleeping bag.

Uis

Uis was once an important tin mining town, but since the principal mine closed in 1990, the town has dwindled to a forlorn shadow of its former self. Tourism is replacing tin as the mainstay of the economy; there are a couple of new places in town, and a fabulous new campsite in the Ugab riverbed just off the road to the White Lady.

Background
Phone code: 064
Colour map 1,
grid C4
128 km from
Henties Bay;
121 km from
Omaruru

Although small scale tin mining has taken place in the area since the first half of this century, it was not until 1951 that a full scale mining operation started. In 1958 the South African mining giant ISCOR took over the mining rights and built the town, which flourished until the mine's closure shortly after independence. Evidence of this are the many gravel mounds dotted around the perimeter of town. Today local miners, with overseas donor assistance, are once again mining tin, tantalite and tourmaline on a small scale.

Sleeping All are in town, well signposted. **D** *White Lady*, T/F504102, a long, thatched bungalow with 6 spacious en-suite doubles (B&B). There is a large braai area (where the neighbour will cook local specialities if there is sufficient demand), lapa and swimming pool. New in 2001, the best rooms in town. **F** Campers welcome (N$30pp) with adequate ablutions and braai facilities. **D** *Brandberg Rest Camp*, T/F505038, F505037, brandbrg@iafrica.com.na has one large guesthouse (14 max), 4-bed flats and doubles, all en-suite but with an institutional feel, restaurant, bar, swimming pool, **F** camping with electricity also available. Can arrange tours of the nearby mines and mineral-rich areas, notice required. They offer internet access, and are your best bet for getting to Spitzkoppe or Brandberg if you have no transportation of your own. **D-E** *Haus Lizenstein*, T504052, F504005, lizen@iway.na has recently opened for trade, with three doubles in a detached bungalow, which are clean and tastefully decorated, B&B, TV lounge, braai area, improved camping planned for 2002.

Shopping Small Duareb craft shop and craft factory making picture frames, candles and colourful prints, also offer local 'guided township tours'. Opposite the *Brandberg Rest Camp* are a post office, payphone, basic shop, butcher and a petrol station (0500-2100). It is advisable to fill up here given the scarcity of petrol stations in the region.

White Lady

The White Lady is the best known of a number of Bushmen paintings situated in a 1.5 km radius of each other in the Tsisab Ravine. The first paintings in the area were 'discovered' in 1909 by a German soldier, Hugo Jochmann, however the White Lady itself was only found in 1918 following a successful ascent of the Königstein peak by three friends, Reinard Mack, A Griess and George Schultz.

Initially the paintings were believed to have been influenced by early Mediterranean art, mainly due to their superficial resemblance to early Cretan art, but also as a result of contemporary European belief that nothing original could possibly have originated from southern Africa. (This same line of thinking also attributed Mediterranean origins to the Great Zimbabwe Ruins in neighbouring Zimbabwe.)

The main authority on rock art at the time, Abb, Henri Breuil, was shown a watercolour of the White Lady at a science congress in Johannesburg in 1929, and concluded that the main figure in the painting was a woman of European origin. This theory came to be widely accepted however more recently, after detailed further research, it has been concluded that the painting is indeed of local origin, most likely the work of Bushmen. The White Lady is no longer believed to be a woman at all, rather it is thought that the figure is actually a man, probably a **shaman** or medicine man daubed with white body paint.

Transport From Swakopmund either head up the coast via Henties Bay and take the C35 or take the B2 towards Usakos and branch north on the D1918 and D1930. Both are well sign-posted. From the north or east, take the C35 either to or from Omaruru and Khorixas. The gravel roads are all a little windy in places but in good condition.

Spitzkoppe

One of Namibia's most recognizable landmarks, the 1,784 m Spitzkoppe or 'pointed hill', rises some 700 m above the surrounding plain. The mountain's distinctive shape has given rise to its nickname as the Matterhorn of Africa. The main peak, or **Gross Spitzkoppe**, is one of three mountains in the area, the others being the **Klein Spitzkoppe** at 1,572 m and the dome-shaped **Pondok Mountain**.

Background Geologically, these three mountains are grouped with the Brandberg range to *Colour map 1, grid C4* the north; all are ancient volcanoes. The violent break up of Gondwanaland 500-750 million years ago caused explosive activity through these volcanoes; their granite cores have been exposed by millions of years of erosion, creating the **inselbergs** or 'island mountains' that we see today.

The northwest face of Spitzkoppe was first climbed in 1946, the west face in 1960, and today the mountain still attracts climbers. Tourists and students are drawn by a number of Bushman paintings – the best known found at **Bushman's Paradise**. The area is also a great place to hike, camp and enjoy the clear desert air and fine views.

Rock art After checking in at the gate and gathering a map (and possibly a guide), make the short but steep hike from Pondok to Bushman's Paradise; the smooth, precipitous slopes are rendered easily accessible by a well positioned chain. At the top is a richly vegetated natural amphitheatre and large overhang which protects the paintings from the elements, but unfortunately not the vandals. There are still interesting paintings and the views of the surrounding countryside make the climb worthwhile. Local guides will be able to take visitors to the sites of Bushman paintings, in particular the **Golden Snake** and **Small Bushman's Paradise**.

Sleeping Originally established in 1993, a small campsite is run by the local community, supported by a German NGO and Women's Action for Development (T061-227630). Visitors are charged N$10 for entering the area and encouraged to buy souvenirs from the small crafts shop, which also provides information, maps and can arrange guides, donkey trips. Meals can be also be provided, book ahead. **F** *Spitzkoppe Community Tourist Camp*, T064-530879, basic bungalows and campsites, in stunning location among the rocks, with braai facilities and pit latrines. Bring water and firewood, these are scarce but can usually be bought on arrival if you are without.

Transport Turn off the B2 onto the D1918 23 km west of Usakos. Turn right almost immediately onto the D1930 for 19 km, and left onto the D3716 for 13km. Well signposted. Actually in the Erongo Region politically, Spitzkoppe is geologically linked to the mountains further north in Damaraland.

Brandberg –
the White Lady
Colour map 1, grid B3

From Uis take the
C35 north for
14 km then turn
west onto D2359
for a further 22 km

The immense Brandberg Massif lies south of the Ugab River about 40 km northwest of Uis. It has Namibia's highest peak, Konigstein, at 2,573 m and is the site of one of Namibia's most intriguing pieces of Bushman art – the so-called White Lady. Like the Burnt Mountain further north, the Brandberg owes its name to its striking colouring, particularly vivid at sunset. Getting to the paintings involves an energetic hike up a well-marked track from the car park at the end of the D2359. You must be accompanied by a guide (N$10) and depending on your level of fitness the walk to the White Lady will take 30-60 minutes. Wear a hat and decent walking shoes and take water with you. The relative cool of early morning and late afternoon is the best time to make this walk.

Enjoy the walk up the Tsisab Ravine: the Damara guides are well informed about local fauna and flora, and will happily answer questions and show off their clicking prowess should you be interested in learning a few simple greetings in their language. There is plenty of birdlife, but the chance of seeing klipspringer, mountain zebra and the other indigenous smaller mammals is small due to the number of visitors to the valley. The site of the White Lady is protected by some rather unsightly iron railings, made necessary by previous visitors throwing water on the paintings to make them stand out more clearly – at the same time eroding them. Again, the guides are well briefed on what is known of the paintings, although you should not expect a masterful thesis on rock art. While most people are content to turn back, the guides will happily lead the adventurous over boulders to the other more remote and less famous paintings.

Camping E-F *Ugab Wilderness Camping*, T504110, F504004, venture@iway.com opened in summer 2001. Turn off at signpost 7 km before Brandberg, then 10 km along winding road to the riverbed. A fabulous new, NACOBTA backed campsite, with beautiful sites in the riverbed with panoramic views of the Brandberg and regular visits from the famous desert elephants. Luxury tents can be rented, B&B. Sites share excellent ablutions (bucket showers, to conserve water), and there are firewood, cold drinks and beer for sale. A tranquil and beautiful riverbed site, with large trees shading the summer heat, and little wind in the winter. You are a 17 km drive from the White Lady here; guided hikes to other parts of the Brandberg are possible from here, also 4WD trips to the local mine (via the Mountain of the Moon) and scenic drives, all worthwhile; there is more to the area than 'Her Whiteness'. Recommended.

The Northwest

Located on the southern side of the Brandberg, Numas Ravine is the site of **Numas Ravine**
numerous rock paintings believed to be the work of Stone Age inhabitants.
Visiting the art is best done as part of a multiple day hike, carrying all your
provisions and with a local guide. Ask at either the White Lady car park, Ugab
River Campsite or Brandberg Rest Camp for information on best current
routes and guides.

Both these sites are accessible only by four-wheel drive, with a guide. A NWR **Messum &**
permit is necessary for Doros Crater and you should contact the office in **Doros Craters**
Windhoek for details. Messum Crater is easily missed by a first-time visitor; it
is more of a shallow depression almost 25 km across. Although interesting for
those with a background in geology, neither really merit a detour if your vaca-
tion time is limited.

Khorixas

There are no tourist attractions in Khorixas. It is the administrative centre of *Phone code: 067*
the Kunene region and capital of Damaraland, but in truth, it is hard to see *Colour map 1, grid B4*
much evidence of this. There is a reasonable rest camp, the only bank in the *441 km to Windhoek*
whole of the Kunene region (*Standard*, with ATM), 24-hour garage, bakery, *133 km to Outjo*
butchery, supermarket, small craft market and post office. Curio hawkers and
beggars regularly pester tourists as they fill up with fuel; ignore them and buy
your curios at the craft market, or at the Petrified Forest further west.

The *Khorixas Rest Camp* is the only place to stay in town and, if you are happy to pay **Sleeping**
the price of the bungalows, is a pleasant enough place. For those on their way to
Twyfelfontein, the *Twyfelfontein Country Lodge*, *Mowani Mountain Camp* or
Aba-Huab Campsite are much better options. So too is the luxurious *Huab Lodge*, situated between Khorixas and Kamanjab; details under Kamanjab. **B-C** *Khorixas Rest
Camp*, T331196, F331388, www.iwwn.com.na/khorixas has 38 en-suite bungalows set
in green gardens with large swimming pool, restaurant and bar, small food/curio shop,
plus a dusty **F** campsite with communal facilities. Well signposted on your way west, 1
km north of town; sadly, while the food is reasonable and the swimming pool wonderful on a hot day, the bungalows are dull and overpriced.

Khorixas Rest Camp is your best bet; the bakery in town sells coffee and cake and is an **Eating**
interesting place to people watch.

The town lies just west of the junction between the C39 from Outjo and the C35 **Transport**
between Kamanjab and Uis. The intrepid can reach here from Palmwag in Kaokaland
via the D2620, or from Torra Bay on the coast via the D3245 and D2620. There is no
public transport. The best bet for hitching a ride is to have a chat with tourists filling up
at the petrol station en route to sites in remote Damaraland.

West of Khorixas

West of Khorixas the D2620 winds its way through the mountains, following
the Aba-Huab valley into the picturesque heart of Damaraland. If you are
lucky, you might catch a glimpse of the desert elephants along the dry river
course (and there is usually spoor to be seen on the road). During the heat of
the day the beasts tend to remain in the shade of the large trees.

Most tourists are heading for the stunning rock formation and plentiful
rock engravings at **Twyfelfontein**. There are also unusual geological

The Northwest

formations of the **Petrified Forest**, the **Organ Pipes** and **Burnt Mountain**. The **Wondergat** is a little more difficult to find and most organized tours will not bother to stop here. While Twyfelfontein, Organ Pipes, Burnt Mountain and Wondergato are often grouped together (they lie within a few kilometres of each other), it is the paintings, the walk and the geology of Twyfelfontein that are far and away the most interesting attractions in the area. If pushed for time, ignore the other sites and focus your attention on just Twyfelfontein. Better light and cooler temperatures mean that early morning and late afternoon are probably the best times to visit, if you are able to stay in the area.

Ins & outs From Khorixas, take the D2620; the Petrified Forest is well signposted after about 60 km, with a large thatched information hut, plenty of locals and a kiosk selling cold drinks. Continue for a further 15 km and turn left on to the D2612 for Twyfelfontein, clearly signposted. From Brandberg, head noth on the C35 for 58 km, turn left on the D2612, again Twyfelfontein is clearly marked. From either direction you will turn south onto the D3254, and before you reach any of the attractions pass the community camp site by the Aba-Huab river (see below for details). If you are not planning to spend the night at Twyfelfontein, or in Damaraland at least, make sure you start early, as the road needs careful, slow driving, and the distance is considerable.

For 'inner' Damaraland, return to the D2620 and continue west. You will pass a sign for the exclusive and highly regarded Damaraland Camp, before either continuing north towards Palm or west on the D3245 for 92 km to Torra Bay, via the Spingbokwasser checkpoint. At Palm you have the choice of heading north to Sesfontein and Kaokoland, or remaining on the D2620 as it loops east to Kamanjab.

Petrified forest
Colour map 1, grid B3

Declared a national monument in 1950, the Petrified Forest lies on a sandstone rise in the Aba-Huab Valley, affording a fine view of the surrounding countryside. Around 50 fossilized trees reckoned to be 260 million years old lie scattered over an area roughly 800 by 300 m, some of them so perfectly preserved that it is hard to believe that they aren't still alive. The absence of roots and branches suggests that the trees in the Petrified Forest do not originate from this area, rather that they were carried here by floodwaters resulting from retreating glaciers. After being deposited here the logs were saturated with silica-rich water which penetrated into the cells of the trees, gradually causing petrification.

The largest trees here measure more than 30 m in length with a circumference of 6 m and belong to a type of cone-bearing plant which flourished between 300 and 200 million years ago. Still alive, scattered among the fallen trees, are some fine examples of *welwitschia mirabilis*, ancient-looking, desert-dwelling plants, some of which are over 1,000 years old. ■ *Getting there: 58 km west of Khorixas on D2620. Beware the many 'false' forests set up by entrepreneurial locals. At the entrance are a great piles of interesting rocks that might interest the geologist or souvenir hunter, and a few locally made, low quality curios. There is no entrance fee, instead visitors are obliged to engage the services of a local guide (N$20, tips welcomed), some better than others, to show them around.*

Twyfelfontein
Colour map 1, grid B3
100 km from Khorixas

Early inhabitants of the area must have been attracted to the valley by the small freshwater spring on the hillside and by the game grazing in the valley below. There is evidence of habitation over 5000 years ago. The Damara who lived here named the valley **Uri-Ais** or 'jumping fountain' after this source of freshwater. However it was renamed Twyfelfontein or 'doubtful fountain' in 1947 by the first white farmer to acquire the land; he considered the fountain too weak to support much life.

The site was declared a national monument in 1952, but sadly this did not prevent many of the engravings being defaced or stolen, and local Damaras are now employed as guides to protect the rocks and inform the visitors.

A total of over 2,500 engravings cut into the rock-face of the huge boulders strewn around have been identified. These engravings have been categorized into six phases ranging in age from around 300 BC to as recent as the 19th century. The majority of the engravings depict a wide range of different species of game, including elephant, rhino, lion and various antelopes. There are, interestingly, far fewer depictions of human figures.

Although experts believe that rock paintings and engravings featured in ceremonies intended to imbue the hunters with the power to catch game, the picture of a seal on one of the rocks is particularly interesting considering that this site is over 100 km from the sea. This suggests that some engravings may literally have been items in a gallery of game the Bushmen were familiar with.

There is a long loop trail which visitors can follow, again a guide must be employed. The trail takes a leisurely two hours to complete; it is advisable to wear a hat, stout shoes and to carry water with you. Before embarking on the trail, it is worth spending a moment looking at the display by the car park. This outlines the geological and archaeological history of the area. There is also a plan of the trail showing where the principal engravings are to be found. Even if you are not especially interested in rock art, Twyfelfontein is a fantastic place to come and watch the sunset, whilst imagining what life must have been like for earliest inhabitants of the area. ■ *N$10 per person, plus N$25 for your guide. There are a couple of shaded parking places, toilets (fed by water from the original spring), some local curios and a small kiosk selling cool drinks. Any money spent here will be going back into the local community.*

Organ Pipes
Colour map 1, grid B3

For many visitors the Organ Pipes and Burnt Mountain are of only passing interest, however for anyone interested in the early history of the earth and its geology they are fascinating glimpses into the past. The Organ Pipes are a series of perpendicular dolerite columns set at the bottom of a shallow gorge 3 km after the turn-off onto the D3254. These elegant rocks, some up to 5 m long, were formed 120 million years ago when the cooling dolerite split into distinct columns which form the pipes we see today. The easiest way to approach the site is to drive past the small (unsignposted) car park and turn left up a sandy riverbed a little further on. From here you can walk along the riverbed to the pipes without having to scramble down from above.

Burnt Mountain
Colour map 1, grid B3

The Burnt Mountain or Verbrandeberge is at the end of the D3214, a section of a 12 km long mountain rising some 100 m above the plain. During the daytime the mountain is bleak and uninviting, however the distinctive colouring of the rocks appears at sunrise and sunset when the imaginative might contest that mountain is 'on fire'. The rocks are dolerite and are believed to have been formed over 130 million years ago as a result of volcanic activity.

Wondergat
Colour map 1, grid B3

The Wondergat, set down a short track off the D3254, 3 km before reaching Aba-Huab campsite, offers an interesting view into the bowels of the earth. The hole is believed to have been created when a subterranean river washed away a chunk of earth. Its depth is still unknown – a team of divers turned back due to lack of oxygen at 100 m, without reaching the bottom.

The Northwest

Sleeping
& eating

Beware: elephants
occasionally pass
near or even through
the camp; they are
not dangerous if
you remain indoors
or inside your tent

AL *Mowani Mountain Camp*, reservations T061-232009, F259430, www.namibianet.com/visions, signposted off the D2612, just southeast of the turning (D3254) for Twyfelfontein. A new (Feb 2001), exclusive, intimate camp with thatched en-suite chalets, imaginatively constructed on stilts among huge boulders, each with balcony and lovely views, full board, swimming pool, hot air balloon rides, trips in search of desert elephants. **A/AL** *Twyfelfontein Country Lodge*, reservations T061-240375, F256598, www.namibialodges.com, well signposted off the D3214 just before entrance to Twyfelfontein rock art. Opened by Prime Minister Hage Geingob in Jul 2000 with great fanfare, this is a large budget, luxury spot, that has been built with natural materials to blend in with the landscape (which it does, by and large). Very popular with upmarket tour groups, with 56 tidy but fairly simple en-suite doubles, large restaurant and bar with excellent views and hefty prices, swimming pool for residents, airstrip (charter flights available) and good curio shop. Not an intimate place, but certainly smart, and with a fabulous location.

F *Aba-Huab Community Campsite*, located by the Aba-Huab River, 5 km before Twyfelfontein, on the D3254. Small, thatched, A-frame shelters with braai facilities, plentiful campsite space and hot water, but insufficient communal wash and toilet facilities. A new bar and restaurant has recently been built along with a small 'exclusive' campsite (with adequate ablutions) over the road. The camp is busy, and very popular with overlanders; there is evidence of new building works, so hopefully the ablutions/services will increase to match demand. The camp has a fantastic location on the banks of a tributary of the Huab River and is (usually) a peaceful spot for recovering from the rigours of the awful road to get there. Walks in the surrounding valley may provide a sight of the desert elephants.

East of Khorixas

Vingerklip

Colour map 1,
grid B4
This is a picturesque,
comfortable base
from which to
explore the whole
Damaraland region

Also known as the **Kalk Kegel** or 'limestone skittle', the Vingerklip is a 35 m high limestone rock sitting on a 44 m circumference base. This unusual landmark was formed by erosion of the Ugab River floodplain over a period of 30 million years. There is no fee to explore the site, and there are numerous walks that offer different angles of view of the unusual skittle. Perhaps the best is to be had from the Vingerklip Lodge itself, which will sell the heat-sapped day visitor a meal or snack, and even provide a swim in one of their pools. The Ugab Terrace is visible all along the valley, and offers good hiking opportunities. Ask at the Lodge for route information. ■ *Getting there: take the C39 east for 54 km from Khorixas, turn south on D2743 for 22 km.*

Sleeping A *Vingerklip Lodge*, T290318, F290319, www.vingerklip.com.na, located adjacent to the entrance to the Vingerklip, has 24 en-suite thatched rooms, tastefully decorated, with verandah and views, 2 swimming pools, walking trails to the striking Vingerklip (2 km away) and for the adventurous on the nearby Ugab Terrace. Bar, restaurant and separate sundowner hut all have lovely views. Recommended. **B/C** *Bambatsi Holiday Ranch*, T313897, F313331, bambatsi@natron.net, signposted on the C39, 70 km from Outjo. Has 7 simple but pleasant en-suite doubles, swimming pool, tennis court, game drives, range of hiking and mountain biking trails in nearby hills, superb location with magnificent views. A good example of the well run family guestfarm, with day trips to local rock art and tourist sites in the region. Recommended. They also run the neighbouring *Gasenairob* guestfarm, with 3 doubles in an older farm house.

The Northwest

Wildlife of East and
Southern Africa

"Well, make up your mind", said the Ethiopian, "because I'd hate to go hunting without you, but I must if you insist on looking like a sunflower against a tarred fence."

"I'll take spots, then," said the Leopard; "but don't make 'em too vulgar-big. I wouldn't look like Giraffe – not for ever so."

"I'll make 'em with the tips of my fingers," said the Ethiopian. "There's plenty of black left on my skin still. Stand over!"

Then the Ethiopian put his five fingers close together (there was plenty of black left on his new skin still) and pressed them all over the Leopard, and wherever the five fingers touched they left five little black marks, all close together. You can see them on any leopard's skin you like, Best Beloved. Sometimes the fingers slipped and the marks got a little blurred; but if you look closely at any Leopard now you will see that there are always five spots—off five fat black finger-tips.

"Now you are a beauty!" said the Ethiopian. "You can lie out on the bare ground and look like a heap of pebbles. You can lie on the naked rocks and look like a piece of pudding-stone. You can lie out on a leafy branch and look like sunshine sifting through the leaves; and you can lie right across the centre of a path and look like nothing in particular. Think of that and purr!"

How the Leopard got his spots
Just So Stories, Rudyard Kipling

Wildlife of East and Southern Africa
Text: adapted from original version by Margaret Carswell with additional material from Sebastian Ballard. Photographs: BBC Natural History Unit Picture Library, Bruce Coleman Collection, gettyone Stone Images, Gus Malcolm.

Contents

The big nine

It is fortunate that many of the large and spectacular animals of Africa are also, on the whole, fairly common. They are often known as the "Big Five". This term was originally coined by hunters who wanted to take home trophies of their safari. Thus it was, that, in hunting parlance, the Big Five were Elephant, Black Rhino, Buffalo, Lion and Leopard. Nowadays the Hippopotamus is usually considered one of the Big Five for those who shoot with their cameras, whereas the Buffalo is far less of a 'trophy'. Also equally photogenic and worthy of being included are the Zebra, Giraffe and Cheetah. But whether they are the Big Five or the Big Nine, these are the animals that most people come to Africa to see and with the possible exception of the Leopard and the Black Rhino, you have an excellent chance of seeing them all.

■ **Common/Masai Giraffe** *Giraffa camelopardis* (top). Yellowish-buff with patchwork of brownish marks and jagged edges, usually two horns, sometimes three. Found throughout Africa in several differing subspecies. ■ **Reticulated Giraffe** *Giraffa reticulata* (right). Reddish brown coat and a network of distinct, pale, narrow lines. Found from the Tana River, Kenya, north and east into Somalia and Ethiopia. Giraffes found in East Africa have darker coloured legs and their spots are dark and of an irregular shape with a jagged outline. In southern Africa the patches tend to be much larger and have well defined outlines, although giraffes found in the desert margins of Namibia are very pale in colour and less tall – probably due to a poor diet lacking in minerals. ■ **Buffalo** *Syncerus caffer* (above). Were considered by hunters to be the most dangerous of the big game and the most difficult to track and, therefore, the biggest 'trophy'. Generally found on open plains but also at home in dense forest, they occur in most African national parks, but like the elephant, they need a large area to roam in, so they are not usually found in the smaller parks.

■ **Cheetah** *Acinonyx jubatus* (left). Often seen in family groups walking across plains or resting in the shade. The black 'tear' mark is usually obvious through binoculars. Can reach speeds of 90km per hour over short distances. Found in open, semi-arid savannah, never in forested country. Endangered in some parts of Africa but in Namibia there is believed to be the largest free-roaming population left in Africa. More commonly seen than the leopard, they are not as widespread as the lion. ■ **Lion** *Panthera leo* (below). Nearly always seen in a group and found in parks all over East and Southern Africa. ■ **Leopard** *Panthera pardus* (bottom). Found in varied habitats ranging from forest to open savannah. They are generally nocturnal, hunting at night or before the sun comes up to avoid the heat. You may see them resting during the day in the lower branches of trees.

Wildlife of East and Southern Africa

■ **Black Rhinoceros** *Syncerus caffer* (right). Long, hooked upper lip distinguishes it from White Rhino. Prefers dry bush and thorn scrub habitat and in the past they were found in mountain uplands such as the slopes of Mount Kenya. Males usually solitary. Females seen in small groups with their calves (very rarely more than four), sometimes with two generations. Mother always walks in front of offspring, unlike the White Rhino, where the mother walks behind, guiding calf with her horn. The distribution of this animal has been massively reduced by poaching and work continues to save both the Black and the White Rhino from extinction. You might be lucky and see the Black Rhino in: Etosha NP, Namibia; Ngorongoro crater, Tanzania; Masai Mara, Kenya; Kruger, Shamwari and Pilansberg NPs and private reserves like Mala Mala and Londolozi, South Africa.

■ **White Rhinoceros** *Diceros simus* (right). Square muzzle and bulkier than the Black Rhino, they are grazers rather than browsers, hence the different lip. Found in open grassland, they are more sociable and can be seen in groups of five or more. More common in Southern Africa due to a successful breeding programme in Hluhluwe/Umfolozi NP, South Africa. The park now stocks other parks in the region. ■ **Elephant** *Loxodonta africana* (above). Commonly seen, even on short safaris, throughout East and Southern Africa, though they have suffered from the activities of war and from ivory poachers. It is no longer possible to see herds of 500 or more animals but in Southern Africa there are problems of over population and culling programmes have been introduced.

Wildlife of East and Southern Africa

■ **Hippopotamus** *Hippopotamus amphibius* (top). Prefer shallow water, graze at night and have a strong sense of territory, which they protect aggressively. Live in large family groups known as "schools". ■ **Mountain zebra** *Equus zebra zebra* (above). Smallest of the three zebras shown here, with a short mane and broad stripes, it is only found in the western cape region of South Africa on hills and stony mountains. ■ **Common Zebra (Burchell's)** *Equus burchelli* (left). Generally, broad stripes (some with lighter shadow stripes next to the dark ones), which cross the top of the hind leg in unbroken lines. The true species is probably extinct but there are many varying subspecies found in different locations across Africa, including: **Grants** (found in East Africa) **Selous** (Malawi, Zimbabwe and Mozambique) and **Chapman's** (Etosha NP, Namibia, east across Southern Africa to Kruger NP). ■ **Grevy's Zebra** *Equus grevyi*, (bottom left) larger than the Burchell's Zebra, with narrower stripes that meet in star above hind leg, generally found north of the equator. Lives in small herds.

Larger antelopes

On safari the first animals that will be seen are almost certainly antelope, on the plains. Although there are many different species, it is not difficult to distinguish between them. For identification purposes they can be divided into the larger ones which stand about 120 cm or more at the shoulder, and the smaller ones about 90 cm or less.

■ **Common** *Kobus ellipsiprymnus* and **Defassa** *Kobus defassa* **Waterbuck** 122-137cm (right). Very similar with shaggy coats and white marking on buttocks. On the Common variety, this is a clear half ring on rump and round tails; on Defassa, the ring is a filled in solid white area. Both species occur in small herds in grassy areas, often near water. Common found in East and Southern Africa, Defassa only in East.

■ **Nyala** *Tragelaphus angasi* 110cm (above). Slender frame, shaggy, dark brown coat with mauve tinge (males). Horns (male only) single open curve. As the picture shows, the female is a very different chestnut colour. Like dense bush and found close to water. Gather in herds of up to 30 but smaller groups more likely. Found across Zimbabwe and Malawi.
■ **Eland** *Taurotragus oryx* 175-183cm (right). Noticeable dewlap and shortish spiral horns (both sexes). Greyish to fawn, sometimes with rufous tinge and narrow white stripes down side of body. Occurs in groups of up to 30 in both East and Southern Africa in grassy habitats.

■ **Sable antelope** *Hippotragus niger* 140-145cm (left) and **Roan antelope** *Hippotragus equinus* 127-137cm (bottom left). Both similar shape, with ringed horns curving backwards (both sexes), longer in the Sable. Female Sables are reddish brown and can be mistaken for the Roan. Males are very dark with a white underbelly. The Roan has distinct tufts of hair at the tips of its long ears. Found in East and southern Africa (although the Sable is not found naturally in East Africa, there is a small herd in the Shimba Hills game reserve). Sable prefers wooded areas and the Roan is generally only seen near water. Both species live in herds. ■ **Gemsbok** *Oryx gazella* 122cm (below). Unmistakable, with black line down spine and black stripe between coloured body and white underparts. Horns (both sexes) straight, long and look v-shaped (seen face-on). Only found in Southern Africa, in arid, semi-desert country. Beisa Oryx occurs in East Africa.

■ **Greater Kudu** *Tragelaphus strepsiceros* 140-153cm (above). Colour varies from greyish to fawn with several white stripes on sides of the body. Horns long and spreading, with two or three twists (male only). Distinctive thick fringe of hair running from the chin down the neck. Found in fairly thick bush, sometimes in quite dry areas. Usually live in family groups of up to six, but occasionally larger herds of up to about 30. ■ **The Lesser Kudu** *Tragelaphus imberis* 99-102cm is considerably smaller, looks similar but lacks the throat fringe of the bigger animal. Has two conspicuous white patches on underside of neck. Not seen south of Tanzania.

■ Brindled or Blue Wildebeest or Gnu *Connochaetes tauri- nus* (right) 132cm. Often seen grazing with Zebra. Found only in Southern Africa. ■ **The White bearded Wildebeest** *Connochaetes taurinus albojubatus* is generally found between central Tanzania and central Kenya and is distinguished by its white 'beard'.

■ Hartebeest, 3 sub-species, (right) and **Topi** (above). In the Hartebeest the horns arise from boney protuberance on the top of head and curve outwards and backwards. **Coke's Hartebeest** *Alcephalus buselaphus* 122cm, also called the **Kongoni** in Kenya, is a drab pale brown with a paler rump. **Lichtenstein's Hartebeest** *Alcephalus lichtensteinii* 127-132cm, is also fawn in general colouration, with a rufous wash over the back, dark marks on the front of the legs and often a dark patch near shoulder. The **Red Hartebeest** *Alcephalus caama* is another subspecies that occurs throughout Southern Africa, although not in Kruger NP. **Topi** *Damaliscus korrigum* 122-127cm. Very rich dark rufous, with dark patches on the tops of the legs and more ordinary looking, lyre-shaped horns.

Smaller antelopes

■ **Impala** *Aepyceros melampus* 92-107cm (left). Bright rufous in colour with a white abdomen. From behind, white rump with black lines on each side is characteristic. Long lyre-shaped horns (male only). Above the heels of the hind legs is a tuft of thick black bristles (unique to Impala), easy to see as the animal runs. Black mark on the side of abdomen, just in front of the back leg. Found in herds of 15 to 20 in both East and Southern Africa.

Wildlife of East and Southern Africa

■ **Thomson's Gazelle** *Gazella thomsonii*, 64-69cm (left) and **Grant's Gazelle** *Gazella granti* 81-99cm (above). Superficially similar Grant's, the larger of the two, has slightly longer horns (carried by both sexes in both species). Colour of both varies from bright to sandy rufous. Thomson's Gazelle can usually be distinguished by the broad black band along the side between the upperparts and abdomen, but some forms of Grant's also have this dark lateral stripe. Look for the white area on the buttocks which extends above the tail on to the rump in Grant's, but does not extend above the tail in Thomson's. Thomson's occur commonly on plains of Kenya and Tanzania in large herds. Grant's Gazelle occur on rather dry grass plains, in various forms, from Ethiopia and Somalia to Tanzania.

■ **Vaal Rhebuck** *Pelea capreolus* 75cm (right). Sometimes confused with the Mountain Reedbuck where the two species coexist. The Rhebuck has a long, slender neck and a woolly coat and narrow, pointed ears. Brownish grey in colour, its underparts and the tip of its short bushy tail are slightly paler. The horns (male only) are quite distinctive: they are vertical, straight and almost parallel to each other. It lives in family groups of up to 30. They are usually found in mountainous or hilly regions where there are patches of open grasslands. ■ **Springbuck** *Antidorcas marsupialis* or Springbok, 76-84cm (below). The upper part of the body is fawn, and is separated from the white underparts by a dark brown lateral stripe. A distinguishing feature is a reddish brown stripe which runs between the base of the horns and the mouth, passing through the eye. The only gazelle found south of the Zambezi River. You no longer see giant herds, but you will see Springbuck along the roadside as you drive between Cape Town and Bloemfontein in South Africa.

■ **Steenbok** *Raphicerus campestris* 58cm (right). An even, rufous brown colour with clean white underside and white ring around eye. Small dark patch at the tip of the nose and long broad ears. The horns (male only) are slightly longer than the ears: they are sharp, have a smooth surface and curve slightly forward. Generally seen alone, prefers open plains, often found in more arid regions. A slight creature which usually runs off very quickly on being spotted. Common resident throughout Southern Africa, Tanzania and parts of Southern Kenya. ■ **Sharpe's Grysbok** *Raphicerus sharpei* 52cm (bottom). Similar in appearance to the Steenbok, but with a white speckled rufous coat. Nose dark brown, white belly. Horns (male only) are very short and sharp, rising vertically from the forehead. Prefers stony and hilly country, often seen amongst kopjies, could be confused with the klipspringer. Lives alone except during the breeding season. Often seen under low bushes, which they browse upon, looking for new shoots and any small fruits. Limited distribution in East Africa, but common along the mountainous areas of the rift valley. In South Africa you are likely to see the **Cape Grysbok**.

■ **Oribi** *Ourebia ourebi* 61cm (left). Slender and delicate looking with a longish neck, sandy to brownish fawn coat. Oval-shaped ears, short, straight horns with a few rings at their base (male only). Like the Reedbuck it has a patch of bare skin just below each ear. Live in small groups or as a pair. Never far from water. Found in East and Southern Africa. ■ **Kirk's Dikdik**, *Rhynchotragus kirkii* 36-41cm (below). So small it cannot be mistaken, it is greyish brown, often washed with rufous. Legs are thin and stick-like. Slightly elongated snout and a conspicuous tuft of hair on the top of the head. Straight, small horns (male only). Found in bush country, singly or in pairs, East Africa only.

■ **Bohor Reedbuck** *Redunca redunca* 71-76cm (above). Horns (males only) sharply hooked forwards at the tip, distinguishing them from the Oribi (top). Reddish fawn with white underparts and short bushy tail. Live in pairs or small family groups, in East and Southern Africa. Often seen with Oribi, in bushed grassland and always near water. ■ **Suni** *Nesotragus moschatus* 37cm (left). Dark chestnut to grey fawn in colour with slight speckles along the back. Head and neck slightly paler with a white throat. Distinct bushy tail with a white tip. Longish horns (male only), thick, ribbed and sloping back. One of the smallest antelope, they live alone and prefer dense bush cover and reed beds in East and Southern Africa.

Wildlife of East and Southern Africa

Wildlife of East and Southern Africa

■ **Gerenuk** *Litocranius walleri* 90-105cm (right). Disinct long neck, often stands on hind legs to browse from thorn bushes. Likes arid, semi-desert conditions. Only found in Kenya and possibly Uganda.
■ **Bushbuck** *Tragelaphus scriptus* 76-92cm (below). Shaggy coat with variable pattern of white spots and stripes on the side and back and 2 white, crescent-shaped marks on front of neck. Short horns (male only) slightly spiral. High rump gives characteristic crouch. White underside of tail is noticeable when running. Occurs in thick bush, especially near water. Either seen in pairs or singly in East and Southern Africa.
■ **Klipspringer** *Oreotragus oreotragus* 56cm (bottom right). Brownish-yellow with grey speckles. White chin and underparts, short tail. Distinctive, blunt hoof tips. Short horns (male only). Likes dry, stony hills and mountains. Found only in Southern Africa.

■ **Common (Grimm's) Duiker** *Sylvicapra grimmia* 58cm (above). Grey fawn colour with darker rump and pale colour on the underside. Dark muzzle. Prominent ears divided by straight, upright, narrow pointed horns. This particular species is the only duiker found in open grasslands. The duiker is more commonly associated with a forested environment. Common throughout Southern and East Africa, but difficult to see – it is shy and will quickly disappear into the bush.

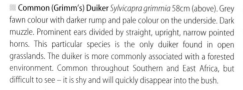

Other mammals

Although the antelopes are undoubtedly the most numerous animals to be seen on the plains, there are many other fascinating mammals worth keeing an eye out for. The following are some of the more common mammals that you may see in East and Southern Africa.

■ **Warthog** *Phacochoerus aethiopicus* (left). Almost hairless and grey with a very large head, tusks and wart-like growths on face. Frequently occurs in family parties and when startled will run at speed with their tails held straight up in the air. Often seen near water caking themselves in the thick mud which helps to keep them both cool and free of ticks and flies. Found in both East and southern Africa.

Wildlife of East and Southern Africa

■ **African Wild Dog** or **Hunting Dog** *Lycaon pictus* (above). Easy to identify since they have all the features of a large mongrel dog: a large head and slender body. Their coat is a mixed pattern of dark shapes and white and yellow patches, no two dogs are quite alike. Very rarely seen, they are seriously threatened with extinction. Found on the open plains around dead animals, but not a scavenger. They are in fact very effective hunters, frequently working in packs. ■ **Dassie** (left, above Rock hyrax, left below Tree hyrax) *Dendrohyrax arboreus*. There are three main groups of this small, guinea-pig-like rodent: the rock hyrax, the yellow spotted hyrax and the tree hyrax. Tree hyraxes are nocturnal and feed in trees at night. They have longer fur than the rock hyrax. The rock hyrax, also nocturnal, lives in colonies amongst boulders and on rocky hillsides, protecting themselves from predators like eagle, caracal and leopard by darting into the rock crevices if alarmed. Found only in Southern Africa.

Wildlife of East and Southern Africa

■ **Bat-eared fox** *Otocyon megalotis* (right). Distinctive large ears (used for listening for prey underneath the surface of the ground) and very short snout are unmistakeable. Greyish-brown coat with black markings on legs, ears and face. They are mainly nocturnal, but can be seen lying in the sun near their burrows during the day. Found in East and southern Africa.

■ **Civet** *Viverra civetta* (right). Yellowish-grey coarse coat with black and white markings and black rings around eyes. Nocturnal animal rarely seen and quite shy. Found in woody areas or thick bush. ■ **Black-backed Jackal** *Canis mesomelas* 45cm (bottom). Foxy reddish fawn in colour with a noticeable black area on its back. This black part is sprinkled with a silvery white which can make the back look silver in some lights. Often seen near a lion kill, they are timid creatures which can be seen by day or night.

■ **Serval** *Felis serval* 50cm (left). Narrow frame and long legs, with a small head and disproportionately large ears. Similar colouring to a cheetah, but the spots are more spread out. Generally nocturnal, they are sometimes seen in bushy areas, near rivers or marshes. Found in both East and Southern Africa. ■ **Spotted Hyena** *Crocuta crocuta* 69-91cm (below). ■ **Brown Hyena** *Hyaena brunnea* (opposite page, centre). High shoulders and low back give characteristic appearance. Spotted variety is larger, brownish with dark spots, a large head and rounded ears. The brown hyena, slightly smaller, has pointed ears and a shaggy coat, more noctural. Found in both East and Southern Africa.

Wildlife of East and Southern Africa

■ **Caracal** *Felis caracal* (left). Also known as the African lynx, it is twice the weight of a domestic cat, with reddish sandy colour fur and paler underparts. Distinctive black stripe from eye to nose and tufts on ears. Generally nocturnal and with similar habits to the leopard. They are not commonly seen, but are found in hilly country, sometimes in trees, in both East and Southern Africa.

Apes

Baboons

■ **Chacma** *Papio ursinus* (top). Adult male slender and can weigh 40kg. General colour is a brownish grey, with lighter undersides. Usually seen in trees, but rocks can provide sufficient protection from predators. Occur in large family troops, have a reputation for being aggressive where they have become used to man's presence. Found in East and Southern Africa. ■ **Hamadryas** *Papio hamadryas* (right). Very different from the other two species, the male being mainly ashy grey with a massive cape-like mane. The face and buttocks are bright pink, and the tail does not appear broken. Females lack the mane and are brownish in colour. ■ **Olive Baboon** *Papio anubis* (top, opposite page). A large, heavily built animal, olive brown or greyish in colour. Adult males have a well-developed mane. In the eastern part of Kenya and Tanzania, including the coast, the Olive Baboon is replaced by the Yellow Baboon *Papio cynocephalus*, smaller and lighter, with longer legs and almost no mane in adult males. The tail in both species looks as if it is broken and hangs down in a loop.

■ **Vervet** or **Green Monkey** *Cercopithicus mitis* (above). Appearance varies, most commonly has a black face framed with white across the forehead and cheeks. General colour is greyish tinged with a varying amount of yellow. Feet, hands and tip of tail are black. They live in savannah and woodlands but have proved to be highly adaptable. You might think the Vervet Monkey cute: it is not, it is vermin and in many places treated as such. They can do widespread damage to orchards and other crops. On no account encourage these creatures, they can make off with your whole picnic, including the beers, in a matter of seconds. Found in East and Southern Africa. ■ **Chimpanzee** *Pan troglodytes* (left) and the **Gorilla** *Gorilla gorilla* (centre, page 18) are not animals you will see casually in passing, you have to go and look for them. They occur only in the forests in the west of the region in Uganda, Rwanda and Zaire. In addition there are some Chimpanzee in western Tanzania.

Reptiles

■ **Blue-headed Agama** *Agama atricollis* (opposite page, top) and **Orange-headed Agama** *Agama agama* (right) up to 20cms long. Only the males have the brightly coloured head and tail. They run along walls and rocks and are frequently seen doing 'press-ups'. You will notice them around your lodge or camp site. They make lovely photos, but are not easy to approach. The Blue-headed is the most common and more widespread of the two.

■ **Monitor lizard** *Varanus niloticus* (centre and right) up to 200cm long, about half this being tail. Greyish brown in colour, with lighter markings. It stands fairly high on its legs and constantly flickers its tongue. It is fairly common and you have a good chance of seeing one, especially near water. Found in both East and Southern Africa.
■ **Crocodile** *Crocodilus niloticus* (above, hatchling). Particularly common on the Nile in Uganda, but also occurs elsewhere in East and Southern Africa. Though you might expect to find it in Lakes Edward and George, it does not occur here, but is plentiful in the other large nearby lake – Lake Albert.

■ **Green Chameleon** *Chamaeleo gracilis* (below). Well-known and colourful reptiles, there are several species of Chameleon, but this is the most common and is fairly widespread. ■ **Tree Frogs** *Hylidae*, (bottom). There are many different sorts of tree frog. They are all small amphibians which are not often seen, but occasionally one can be found half way up a door post or window frame which it has mistaken for a tree. They are usually bright green or yellow, often with pretty markings.

Wildlife of East and Southern Africa

Water and waterside birds

Wildlife of East and Southern Africa

Africa is one of the richest bird areas in the world and you could spot over 100 species in a single day. The birds shown here are the common ones and with a little careful observation can all be identified, even though they may appear totally strange and exotic. To make identification easier, they have been grouped by habitat. Unless otherwise stated, they occur both in East and Southern Africa.

■ **Greater Flamingo** (96) *Phoenicopterus ruber* 142cms (right). The larger and paler bird of the two species found in Africa has a pink bill with a black tip. ■ **Lesser Flamingo** (97) *Phoenicopterus minor* 101cms, deeper pink all over and has a deep carmine bill with a black tip. Both occur in large numbers in the soda lakes of western Kenya.

■ **Hammerkop** (81) *Scopus umbretta* 58cms (top left). Dull brown in colour with a stout, moderately long bill. Distinctive large crest which projects straight backwards and is said to look like a hammer. A solitary bird usually seen on the ground near water – even roadside puddles. Builds an enormous nest in trees, large and strong enough to support the weight of a man. ■ **Pied Kingisher** (428) *Ceryle rudis* 25cms (above). The only black and white kingfisher. Common all round the large lakes and also turns up at quite small bodies of water. Hovers over the water before plunging in to capture its prey. ■ **Blacksmith Plover** (258) *Vanellus armatus* 30 cms (right). Strongly contrasting black, white and grey plumage. White crown, red eye, black legs. Common resident found around the margins of lakes, both freshwater and alkaline, also close to rivers and cultivated lands. Distinct, high-pitched call which it utters when it that feels its nest or young are threatened.

■ **NB** The number in brackets after the birds' names refers to the species' 'Roberts' number, which is used for identification purposes in Southern Africa. This code is not used in East Africa, but it can still help in cases where the same species has a different local name.

Wildlife of East and Southern Africa

■ **Fish Eagle** (148) *Haliaeetus vocifer* 76cms (left). This magnificent bird has a very distinctive colour pattern. It often perches on the tops of trees, where its dazzling white head and chest are easily seen. In flight this white and the white tail contrast with the black wings. It has a wild yelping call which is usually uttered in flight. Watch the bird throwing back its head as it calls. ■ **Goliath Heron** (64) *Ardea goliath* 144cms (below). Usually seen singly on mud banks and shores, both inland and on the coast. Its very large size is enough to distinguish it, but the smaller **Purple Heron** (65) *Ardea purpurea* 80cms, which frequents similar habitat and is also widespread, may be mistaken for it at a distance. If in doubt, the colour on the top of the head (rufous in the Goliath and black in the Purple) will clinch it.

■ **African Jacana** (240) *Actophilornis africana* 25cms (left). This is a mainly chestnut bird, almost invariably seen walking on floating leaves. Its toes are greatly elongated to allow it to do this. Its legs dangle down distinctively when in flight. Found in quiet backwaters with lily pads and other floating vegetation.

Wildlife of East and Southern Africa

■ **Paradise Flycatcher** *Terpsiphone viridis* male 33cm, female 20cm (right). Easily identified by its very long tail and bright chestnut plumage. The head is black and bears a crest. The tail of the female is much shorter, but otherwise the sexes are similar. It is seen in wooded areas, including gardens and is usually in pairs. In certain parts, notably eastern Kenya, its plumage is often white, but it still has the black head. Sometimes birds are seen with partly white and partly chestnut plumage. ■ **Egyptian goose** (102) *Alopochen aegyptiaca* (below) 65cm. Brown to grey-brown plumage. Distinct chestnut patch around the eye and on the centre of the breast; wings appear white in flight. Red/pink legs and feet. This is a common resident found throughout the region except in arid areas. Occurs in small flocks and pairs. Most likely to be seen around the margins of inland waters, lakes, rivers, marshes, pans and cultivated fields.

■ **Crowned Crane** (209) *Balearica pavonina* 100cms (right). It cannot really be mistaken for anything else when seen on the ground. In flight the legs trail behind and the neck is extended, but the head droops down from the vertical. Overhead flocks fly in loose V-shaped formation. Not a water bird, but quite common near Lake Victoria, it also occurs in much of the rest of East Africa as well.

Birds of the open plains

■ **Ground Hornbill** (463) *Bucorvus cafer* 107cm (left). Looks very like a turkey from a distance, but close up it is very distinctive and cannot really be mistaken for anything else. They are very often seen in pairs and the male has bare red skin around the eye and on the throat. In the female this skin is red and blue. Found in open grassland.

■ **Bateleur** (146) *Terathopius ecaudatus* 61cm (above). A magnificent and strange looking eagle. It is rarely seen perched, but is quite commonly seen soaring very high overhead. Its tail is so short that it sometimes appears tailless. This, its buoyant flight and the black and white pattern of its underparts make it easy to identify. ■ **Secretary Bird** (118) *Sagittarius serpentarius* 101cm (left). So called because the long plumes of its crest are supposed to resemble the old time secretaries who carried their quill pens tucked behind their ears. Often seen in pairs hunting for snakes, its main source of food.

Wildlife of East and Southern Africa

Wildlife of East and Southern Africa

■ **Ostrich** (1) *Struthio camelus* 2m (right). Male birds are predominantly black, while the females are usually a dusty dark brown. Found both in national parks and on open farm land. The original wild variety has been interbred with subspecies in order to improve feather quality. In South Africa the region known as the Little Karoo was once the centre of a boom during which millions of birds were kept in captivity. The Ostrich is sometimes seen singly, but also in family groups.

■ **Kori Bustard** (230) *Otis kori* 80cm (top left). Like the Secretary Bird, it quarters the plains looking for snakes. Quite a different shape, however, and can be distinguished by the thick looking grey neck, caused by the loose feathers on its neck. Particularly common in Serengeti National Park and in the Mara. ■ **Red-billed Oxpecker** (772) *Buphagus erythrorhynchus* 18cm (above). Members of the starling family, they associate with game animals and cattle, spending their time clinging to the animals while they hunt for ticks. ■ **Cattle Egret, Forktailed** (71) *Bubulcus ibis* 51cm (right). Follows herds and feeds on the grasshoppers and other insects disturbed by the passing of the animals. Occasionally too, the Cattle Egret will perch on the back of a large animal, but this is quite different from the behaviour of Oxpeckers. Cattle Egrets are long legged and long billed white birds which are most often seen in small flocks. In the breeding season they develop long buff feathers on the head, chest and back.

Woodland birds

■ **Superb Starling** *Spreo superbus* 18cm (left) and **Golden-breasted Starling** *Cosmopsarus regius* 32cms (below). Both are common, but the Superb Starling is the more widespread and is seen near habitation as well as in thorn bush country. Tsavo East is probably the best place to see the Golden-breasted Starling. Look out for the long tail of the Golden-breasted Starling, and the white under tail and white breast band of the Superb Starling. Both are usually seen hopping about on the ground.

■ **Little bee-eater** (444) *Merops pusillus* 16cm (above). Bright green with a yellow throat, conspicuous black eye stripe and black tip to a square tail, lacks the elongated tail feathers found in many other species of bee-eater. Solitary by day, but at night often seen bunched in a row. Favours open woodlands, streams and areas where there are scattered bushes which can act as perches. Look out for Carmine bee-eater colonies in sandbanks along rivers. This beautiful bird is an intra-African migrant. ■ **Drongo** (541) *Dicrurus adsimilis* 24cm (left). An all black bird. It is easily identified by its forked tail, which is 'fish-tailed' at the end. Often seen sitting on bare branches, it is usually solitary.

Wildlife of East and Southern Africa

■ **Red Bishop** (824) *Euplectes orix* 13cm (right). Brown wings and tail and noticeable scarlet feathers on its rump. Seen in long grass and cultivated areas, and often, but not invariably, near water. Almost equally brilliant is the **Blackwinged Bishop** *Euplectes hordeaceus* 14cm. Distinguished by black wings and tail and obvious red rump.

■ **Red-cheeked Cordon-bleu** *Uraeginthus benegalus* 13cm (below). Brown back and bright red cheek patches. They are seen in pairs or family parties and the females and young are somewhat duller in colour than the males. They are quite tame and you often see them round the game lodges, particularly in Kenya and parts of Uganda and Tanzania but not in Southern Africa.

■ **Red-billed Hornbill** (458) *Tockus erythrorhynchus* 45cm (above). Blackish-brown back, with a white stripe down between the wings. The wings themselves are spotted with white. The underparts are white and the bill is long, curved and mainly red. Use the tops of thorn trees as observation perches. ■ **White-crowned Shrike** (756) *Eurocephalus rueppelli* 23cm (right). Black wings, tail and eye stripe, brown back. Throat and breast white, with a distinct white crown. Always seen in small parties, making short direct flights from one vantage point to the next. Walks confidently on the ground amongst debris in the dry bush country they tend to favour. Look out for them in 'feeding parties' in acacia woodlands. Similar in appearance to the White-headed Buffalo Weaver *Dinemellia dinemelli* 23cm, though not related.

■ **Helmeted Guinea Fowl** (203) *Numida meleagris* 55cm (left). Slaty grey with white speckles throughout, bare around the head which is blue and red with a distinct horny 'casque' – the helmet. A common resident in most countries, found close to cultivated lands and open grasslands. Highly gregarious, during the day the flocks tend to forage on the ground for food; rarely do they take to flying and even then it is usually only for a short distance. At night the birds roost communally, making a tremendous din when they come together at dusk. Look out for them near water, they tend to approach the source in single file.

■ **Red-billed Francolin** (194) *Francolinus adspersu* 35cm (below). Medium sized brown bird, finely barred all over. Legs and feet red to orange, yellow eye with bare skin around it. This particular species is found throughout central and northern Namibia, Botswana and western Zimbabwe. Other similar species with only minor variations are found throughout East and Southern Africa. An annoying bird which makes itself known at dawn around campsites with a harsh cry that speeds up and then suddenly stops.

■ **D'Arnaud's Barbet** *Trachyphonus darnaudii* 15cm (above). Quite common in the dry bush country. A very spotted bird, dark with pale spots above, and pale with dark spots below. It has rather a long dark tail which is also heavily spotted. Its call and behaviour is very distinctive. A pair will sit facing each other with their tails raised over their backs and wagging from side to side and bob at each other in a duet. All the while they utter a four note call over and over again. "Do-do dee-dok". They look just like a pair of clockwork toys.

■ **Lilac-breasted Roller** (447) *Coracias caudata* 41cm (left). The brilliant blue on its wings, head and underparts is very eye-catching. Its throat and breast are a deep lilac and its tail has two elongated streamers. It is quite common in open bush country and easy to see as it perches on telegraph poles or wires, or on bare branches.

Wildlife of East and Southern Africa

Urban birds

The first birds you will see on arrival in any big city will almost certainly be the large numbers soaring overhead. Early in the morning there are few, but as the temperature rises, more and more can be seen circling high above the buildings. The following (with the possible exception of the Quelea) are often seen in either in towns or near human habitation, although you may see them elsewhere, such as arable farmland, as well.

◼ **Black-headed Weaver** *Ploceus cucullatus* 18cm (right). Male has a mainly black head and throat, but the back of the head is chestnut. The underparts are bright yellow and the back and wings mottled black and greenish yellow. When the bird is perched, and seen from behind, the markings on the back form a V-shape. Often builds its colonies in bamboo clumps.

◼ **Marabou Stork** (89) *Leptoptilos crumeniferus* 152cm (above, with fish eagle devouring a flamingo). Overhead, its large size, long and noticeable bill and trailing legs make it easy to identify. Although this bird is a stork it behaves like a vulture, in that it lives by scavenging.
◼ **Hooded Vulture** (212) *Neophron monachus* 66cm (right). Medium size vulture, dark brown, pink head. This is one of the smallest of the vultures and is unable to compete with other vultures at a carcass. Often solitary, feeding on small scraps of carrion as well as insects and offal.

■ **Red-billed quelea** (821) *Quelea quelea* 13cm (left and below). Similar colour and markings to a common sparrow, black face and a distinct thick red bill. Widespread throughout tropical Africa, a quiet bird when alone or in pairs. Best known for their destructive abilities around harvest time. They gather into flocks of several hundreds of thousands and can wipe out a seed crop in a single day. When they reach plague proportions they are treated as such and destroyed.

Wildlife of East and Southern Africa

■ **Scarlet-chested Sunbird** *Nectarinia senegalensis* 15cm (above). Male is a dark velvety brown colour with scarlet chest. Top of the head and the throat are iridescent green. The tail is short. One member of a large family of birds which are confusingly similar (particularly the females), rather like the weavers. Often perches on overhead wires and in parks and gardens, especially among flowers, allowing you to get a good look at it.
■ **African Pied Wagtail** (711) *Motacilla aguimp* 20cm (left). Black and white with a white band over the eye, black legs. Common where resident throughout the region. Associated with human habitation, sports fields, city parks and drains, also seen on sand bars along river beds. A very tame bird which you may be able to approach in some hotel gardens.

Northern Damaraland

Loosely defined as the lands to the north of the Huab River, the landscape of northern Damaraland rolls beautifully, with small settlements dotted throughout the flat-topped mountains and valleys. There are plentiful, freely roaming springbok and isolated herds of goats and their goatherds. The authorities have tried to embrace eco-tourism and get maximum return for minimum damage by granting concessions to a few private lodges. Each of these lodges has a unique character; to fully appreciate the expertise and knowledge of their guides, aim to spend at least two nights at any one of them.

Sleeping

L *Damaraland Camp*, reservations T061-225178, F239455, www.damaraland.com Signposted at the C39/D2620 junction, 110 km west of Khorixas; guests leave their vehicles in a car park by the road and are transferred 12 km to the camp by 4WD. Has 8 en-suite twin tents with shady verandas overlooking the valley, central bar and dining area, rock swimming pool and curio shop. Price is full board and includes 'activities': stargazing, 4WD excursions to rock art and guided walks (recommended) with the hosts/experts who bring the desert landscape to life. If you are very lucky you might just see the elusive desert elephants. Often full, book in advance.

AL *Etendeka Mountain Camp*, T061-226979, F226999, 8 double tents with basic shared ablutions, located by the Grootberg Mountain, providing a genuine bush-tracking experience, following the trail of the last free-roaming black rhino in the world. The camp collects a voluntary bed-levy from visitors for local nature conservation and development projects, directed towards promotion of non-consumptive tourism, with local community involvement. The rhino tracking experience is offered by *Bircornis Safaris*, T064-404459, F404664, in conjunction with **Save The Rhino Trust**, T064-403829, srtrhino@iafrica.com.na **A** *Palmwag Lodge*, reservations T064-404459, F404664, dassaf@iafrica.com.na (or palmwag@iafrica.com.na direct) has 12 simple en-suite bungalows among makalani palm trees, restaurant, 2 pleasant swimming pools and poolside bar which will also serve snack meals for guests staying at the campsite. Exposed **F** campsite with privacy but few grassy pitches, peg carefully against the wind. Game drives and hiking trails, a good base to explore the area. Accommodation and tours are usually fully booked, book ahead. **Getting there**: *Etendeka Mountain Camp* and *Palmwag Lodge* are each located off the D3706, a short distance north of the veterinary control gate. Both are clearly signposted, 140 rutted km from Khorixas (150 km from Kamanjab). By the veterinary control gate is a petrol station (daylight hours) and puncture repair shop.

B *Ermo Game Farm*, T330220, www.namibiaweb.com/ermo 55 km from Kamanjab; take the C35 north, after 8 km turn east, follow signs from junction with D2763. Has thatched bungalows, farm cuisine with game a speciality of the house, swimming pool, game walks and drives and floodlit waterhole with viewing platforms. **B** *Rustig Toko Lodge*, T330250, F330037, www.mweb.com.na/rustig Take C35 north for 8 km, turn right on to D2763, after 13 km take D2695 signposted to farm. HAN award winner with 6 thatched en-suite bungalows, swimming pool, garden, meals in the farm house, hiking trails. **F** Camping available at shaded site with communal ablutions.

Transport

From Palmwag, the D3706 continues north towards Sesfontein and into Kaokoland. Ask ahead about road conditions before heading north in a saloon car. This is the border between Damaraland and Kaokoland and travel north of here is preferably in a 4WD, with 2 vehicles (see page 205). Assuming road conditions allow, continue to Sesfontein and call in at the spring at Warmquelle. Otherwise, take the D2620 towards Kamanjab. From Kamanjab there is a good tarred road all the way to Etosha National Park.

The Northwest

Kamanjab

Phone code: 067

Colour map 1, grid B4

There is 24-hour petrol, a bakery, supermarket, post office and police station at Kamanjab; if heading north, fill up with fuel and provisions since this is the last source before reaching Opuwo or Ruacana. The only place to stay in town is the small but pleasant *Oase Guest House*, also your best bet for food.

Sleeping In town: **B** *Oase Guest House*, T/F330032, 6 en-suite doubles and a family unit, excellent lunches for those en-route and larger evening meals for overnighters, friendly hosts, bar, tiny plunge pool, curio shop selling locally made wares.

In the area: There's a huge selection of places to stay in the area, many making use of their proximity to Etosha and interesting natural geographical features to create a beautiful experience for the visitor. **L** *Huab Lodge*, T697016, F697017, www.classicsafaricamps.com   46 km north of Khorixas on the C35 look for a left turning to Monte Carlo (D2670), then a further 35 km. Has 8 large thatched en-suite bungalows with tasteful décor, private balcony with views across the Huab River, delicious farm cooking and good wine list, swimming pool plus a hot spring to enjoy in the cool evenings, game drives, guided hiking and horse riding to rock paintings. Recommended, a luxurious lodge set in a private nature reserve, regular HAN award winner. **A** *Otjitambi*, T312138. Located 7 km down the D3246, off the C39, 47 km southeast of Kamanjab. Has expensive simple doubles in the main house and **E** 4 good value simple en-suite bungalows nestled among palm trees 300 m away. Large swimming pool, table tennis, jacuzzi baths fed by nearby hot spring, nice views and walks, horse riding (call ahead), small **F** campsite with basic ablutions. A little frayed at the edges – if they are out of space, try the *Ngaango Safari Camp* on the way back to the main road. **B** *Otjitotongwe Lodge*, T/F330201, www.emcglobal.com/cheetah, 24 km east of Kamanjab, signposted from the C40. Has 6 en-suite thatched bungalows lit by gas lamps, thatched bar/restaurant and small swimming pool. 4 tame and 14 wild cheetahs live nearby and organized feeding sessions afford good photo opportunities, hiking trails through interesting fossil rocks and trees, half board, game drives all inclusive. Large, well serviced **F** campsite with separate 'bush bar'. Recommended. **B** *Ondundu Wilderness Lodge*, T/F312152, reservations T+2721-4199596, ondundu@ capetranshospitality.com, 48 km east of Kamanjab off the C40. Has 3 large en-suite bungalows and a central building with high thatched roof, all built into the rocks, swimming pools, hikes, horse riding. **B** *Hobatere Lodge*, T330261, www.resafrica.net/ hobatere-lodge   Take C35 north from Kamanjab for 80 km then follow the signs for 16 km. Has 12 en suite thatched bungalows, central lounge, bar and restaurant, swimming pool, waterhole. A relaxing lodge overlooking the Otjivasondu River, trips into the western part of Etosha can be organized from here, as well as hiking and game drives on the ranch itself. Recommended. **C/D** *Franken*, T330245, www.namibsunhotels.com 6 km down the D2620, 7 sandy km west of Kamanjab (avoid getting stuck by keeping a steady speed). Has 4 nice, thatched bungalows and 3 simple doubles in the old farmhouse, pretty garden, waterhole, dinner available if booked ahead. **C** *Kavita Lion Lodge*, T330269, www.kavitalion.com Take the C35 north for Ruacana, well signed after 35 km. Has 5 comfortable en-suite double bungalows, restaurant, swimming pool, nature trail and trips into the west of Etosha, **F** campsite also available with braai sites and shared ablution facilities. Recommended. The lodge is home to the new **Afri-Leo Foundation**, which raises funds for lion protection and territory conservation. **D** *Klein Lichtenstein*, T330270, F330037, 25 km west of Kamanjab off the D2620, 5 en-suite doubles in a rather bleak bungalow, barren garden, but they have tried to liven the place up with paint and imaginative room structure.

Kaokoland

Kaokaland is often described as one of the last truly wild areas in southern Africa. The attractions of the area are the simple beauty of the mountain landscape, the ruggedness of the access routes and the tranquility enjoyed by those reaching the northern and western corners. En route, as well as four-wheel driving challenges, is the opportunity to see the unique and photogenic Himba villages and people. And the Kunene River rewards the weary traveller with the beautiful Epupa Falls, watersport possibilities and numerous riverside lodges and camps.

The region is bounded by the Skeleton Coast Park on the west, the perennial Kunene River to the north, the C35 gravel road to the east and Damaraland to the south. There are no tarred roads in the region, no banks, and supplies of food and basic supplies are only available in the main centres. Visitors to the area need to have a degree of self-sufficiency, but allowing time in your schedule to visit the region will be amply rewarded.

Kaokoland measures roughly 40,000 sparsely populated sq km, with just **Background** under 30,000 mainly **Herero** and **Himba** inhabitants. The much photographed Himba people are descendants of the earliest Hereros, who migrated into this area early in the 16th century. Around the middle of the 18th century the pressure of too many people and cattle in this dry, fragile environment led to the migration of the main body of the Herero to the rich pasturelands further south, leaving behind the Himba.

The Himba are a semi-nomadic, pastoral people who follow their cattle and goats in search of good grazing. Many of them maintain traditional dress, language and behavioural codes, which has made them an attraction both to anthropologists wishing to study their customs and culture and tourists with a 'romantic' notion of Africa. Today the Himba way of life is threatened by the intrusion of traders, tourists and the proposed Epupa Dam Scheme (see box). More Himba are starting to live in permanent settlements, such as the regional 'capital' Opuwo, and many are adapting their customs and lifestyles as they come into contact with the rest of the world and attempt to meet the demands of living in the late 20th century.

Just as the Nama and Herero peoples were exploited by European traders who introduced strong, mass-produced alcohol during the 19th century, today Himba communities are vulnerable. As well as the food staples, metal beads (for jewellery), fat and ochre (for skin colouring) and basic medicine, Angolan and Owambo traders bring liquor, often bartered for goats or cattle. As alcohol tolerance is so low, unscrupulous traders threaten to damage the structure of village life.

Tourists, too, pose a threat as they come into contact with a culture they *The Himba will* know little or nothing about; by encouraging the Himba to sell their images *happily pose for your* for the tourist camera in exchange for cigarettes, sweets and tobacco, a proud *photographs but they* and highly successful people are turned into a cliché of the 'noble savage'. *do expect payment* Whilst there is undoubtedly a place for tourism in the Kaokoland and for contact with the Himba, caution and sensitivity should be exercised at all times. If possible, a local guide should liaise between tourists and the Himba to ensure that local customs and people are respected. A number of community projects (see Purros Conservation Project, page 209, and box on NACOBTA, page 35) have developed in response to this need for controlled and non-exploitative form of tourism. Visitors to Kaokoland may well want to support these local initiatives.

The Northwest

Wildlife The range of wildlife in Kaokoland is more limited than you may have come to expect in Namibia. The efforts of hunters and poachers, and the inevitable slaughter for food during the struggle for independence rendered many areas devoid of game. However, the legendary **desert elephant**, still roams the remote western river valleys. They have extra long legs that can carry them 70 km in a day in search of food and water and can last four or five days between drinks. The **black rhino** also survives here, the last place in the world where it roams uninhibited.

There are small herds of gemsbok, zebra, giraffe and springbok, as well as lion, leopard and cheetah. Despite the inhospitable conditions, game survives. These animals are not accustomed to human presence; if you have come from Etosha, the place will appear barren and the game you do see very skittish. Plans have been afoot for a number of years to declare the western part of Kaokoland (to the Skeleton Coast park) a conservation area and allow game

Kaokoland

⌂ Sleeping	⋏ Camping	
1 Epupa Camp Lodge	5 Camp Syncro & Public Campsite	9 Ongongo Campsite
2 Fort Sesfontein Lodge	6 Epupa , Omarunga &	10 Purros Community Campsite
3 Kunene River Lodge	Hot Springs Campsites	11 Serra Cafema Camp & Public
4 Ohakene Lodge	7 Khowarib Campsite	Campsite
	8 Kunene Village Rest Camp	

Do's and don'ts of travelling in Kaokoland

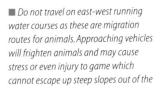

■ Do not travel on east-west running water courses as these are migration routes for animals. Approaching vehicles will frighten animals and may cause stress or even injury to game which cannot escape up steep slopes out of the river course.

■ Do not camp in river courses, both to avoid night-time encounters with large game and the risk of flash floods in summer during the rainy season.

■ Ensure that all rubbish is taken out of the area. Do not bury or leave anything for scavengers to get at.

■ Do not camp at waterholes or springs. Animals have to travel long distances to reach water and if you are camped there game will be too scared too drink. Likewise never wash anything in the springs or waterholes as they provide local inhabitants, both people and animals, with drinking water.

■ Respect the customs of the Himba and never enter seemingly deserted settlements. As a semi-nomadic people, the Himba move around with their animals to return later to villages which may appear abandoned but in reality are not.

■ Do not enter a kraal uninvited and when inside never walk between the sacred fire and the main hut. Never take photographs without first having obtained permission and negotiate payment beforehand if you must take photos.

---

numbers to improve; if successful, at least one part of this great wilderness area will be preserved for the future.

Tour companies If you are unable or unwilling to make an independent trip to Kaokoland, consider an organized tour. These are not cheap, but having a guide familiar with the terrain and practicalities can enhance your enjoyment of the holiday, particularly if you are an inexperienced driver or 'unlucky'. And it may not be so much more costly, given the expense of hiring 2 4WD vehicles. *Desert Adventure Safaris*, T064-404459, F404664, www.das.com.na, run tours to and from *Serra Cafema Private Camp* in Hartmann's Valley on the banks of the Kunene River; they also organize fly-in tours with 4WD trips to Epupa Falls and other parts of the region. *Ermo Safaris*, T/F061-257123, www.namibiaweb.com/ermo, run *Omarunga Camp* at Epupa Falls and offer fly-in safaris in the region. *Kaokohimba Safaris*, T/F061-222378, kaohim@nam.lia.net, run the private, thatched *Camp Syncro* in the Marienfluss Valley by the Kunene River, book in advance, the company organizes fly-in, hiking and 4WD cultural tours using local guides. Recommended. Also try *Mopani Safaris*, based in Outjo, T067-313138, www.mopani.com.na, and *Ohakane Safaris*, based in Opuwo, T065-273031, ohakane@iafrica.com.na

Transport **Self-drive tourism** This is becoming increasingly popular. With it is the risk that the under-prepared may venture into the area and expose themselves unwittingly to danger. Maps of the area give the misleading impression that there is a well established system of roads allowing free access to many parts of Kaokoland. Nothing could be further from the truth. Roads are often little more than dirt tracks, which become impassable bogs during the rainy season. The rocky, mountainous terrain of much of the region makes all travel extremely slow and hazardous. Outside Opuwo and Ruacana, the region is devoid of amenities, with no fuel, very few shops with limited supplies and almost no telephones. And this is a large part of the attraction; a vast wilderness and small isolated communities living a subsistence existence off the land.

While many roads, in the dry season, are passable by careful driving in a 2WD car, it is advisable to travel by 4WD, and ideally in convoy. All vehicles should carry 2 spare tyres and puncture repair kits, basic spares such as oil and fuel filters, fuel, water and food and a decent medical kit. Wherever you are, stick to existing tracks, as

The Northwest

The Dorsland Trekkers of Kaokoland

In the remote northwestern corner of Namibia there are several monuments to one of the most unusual and hardy group of trekkers to leave South Africa during the 19th century. The origins of this trek date back to 1872 when the Rev Thomas Burgers was elected president of the Transvaal. On hearing of the election results a highly religious group known as the 'doppers' decided to leave the Transvaal because they opposed the teachings of their new president.

The term doppers, meaning dampers, was used because the group had a reputation for opposing all forms of social-progress. One of their arguments that is frequently quoted was their claim that the construction of railway lines was the work of Satan. So in 1874 a group suddenly abandoned their homes, packed the wagons and set off into the Kalahari desert with absolutely no idea of the climatic and physical perils that lay ahead. They were driven by the belief that the trek was necessary to bring them to the land of Beulah (after the biblical land of rest). As they journeyed further into the Kalahari many of the women, children and livestock died from fever, heat exhaustion and dysentery. They came to be known as the 'Dorsland Trekkers' – or the thirstland trekkers. By 1876 part of the group had reached the grasslands that are now part of Etosha National Park.

Close to the perennial spring, which they renamed Rietfontein (reed fountain), is a lone mopane tree providing the shade for the grave of a trekker woman, Johanna Alberts (1841-1876).

Eventually a group of trekkers reached Humpata in Angola, having passed through Kaokoland. Within Kaokoland there are a couple of monuments to the trek, one at Otjitunduwa, 90 km north of Hobatere Lodge; and a second at Swartbooisdrift where they crossed the Kunene into Angola. In between the two monuments are the ruins of a small church at Kaoko Otavi in the Joubert mountains. Within a couple of years the trekkers were quarrelling amongst themselves and the group started to fragment. Some of the party decided to return to the Transvaal, others returned as far as Grootfontein where they set up the capital of the Republic of Upingtonia, after buying some land from a local Owambo chief. The republic was abandoned in 1893 when the South West Africa Company started to prospect for minerals in the area. The Dorsland Trekkers never fulfilled their dreams of Beulah but they are a tremendous example of the toughness and the will power required of people if they wished to travel in Namibia before the arrival of the Germans at the end of the 19th century.

pre-Second World War tyre tracks are still visible in some coastal valleys. There are a few lodges and campsites in the area (see below); bush camping is forbidden in the Hartmann and Marienfluss valleys.

Before you drive yourself in the area, be sure at least to read a four-wheel driving guide, and preferably take a course. Jan Joubert's *Practical Guide to Off-Road Adventures in Southern Africa* is a recommended introduction to the challenges faced, and there are many similar books. Read up also on the flora and fauna of the area, to more fully appreciate your environment. Buy the *Shell Kaokoland Kunene Region Tourist Map*; while some of the roads marked no longer exist, it is the best of the region and provides information, both practical and regarding the wildlife and vegetation in the area. Most importantly, stock up well, allow plenty of time and get advice from lodge owners and fellow travellers as to the conditions ahead before embarking on each stretch of your journey.

Planning your route in Kaokoland

The routes outlined below assume visitors arrive via Damaraland from Swakopmund. However, self-drive visitors who entered Namibia via the Caprivi Strip are likely to follow all the routes in reverse – entering Kaokoland in the north from Oshakati and Ruacana, and then working their way south into Damaraland.

One of the most important considerations when visiting Kaokoland is to carefully plan your route in advance, and carefully to calculate distances, fuel consumption and the number of nights camping. Always make sure you have at least an additional two jerry cans of fuel above your estimated needs, especially if you are heading for Hartmann's Valley.

While distances may look small from the map, on the ground you will average no more than 50 kph. It takes on average two hours to cover the 73 km between Okongwati and Epupa Falls. You need to allow at least three hours just to cross **Van Zyl's Pass. NB: This can only be driven east-west**. Only very experienced four-wheel drivers should even contemplate the route. If heading for Hartmann's Valley, you will have to camp one night in the wild when travelling in each direction, whether you start from Opuwo or Purros. Finally, if you find yourself exploring the area during the rainy season be prepared to wait several hours, even days, before being able to cross certain riverbeds (there are no bridges in the region); do not attempt to drive up river courses if they have recently flowed. Allow at least four days after rain before driving along riverbeds.

Do not be put off from visiting this region, but do come prepared and take heed of all local advice. One of the most important points to remember is the degree of isolation and lack of services. It may not be the end of the world if you suffer a broken axle or run out of fuel, but it may take a week or more to get going again. During this period you are going to need to be self-sufficient, particularly in food, water, fuel and medicine.

Khowarib
Colour map 1, grid B3

This small village and Warmquelle, below, are of little interest in themselves to the passing tourist, however they have each started a community campsite in recent years. These are worth patronizing since it is one of the few ways in which these marginal communities benefit directly from tourism.

Driving north, the first village you will reach is Khowarib, about 77 km from Palm. The village is spread out along the banks of the perennial Khowarib River, which irrigates local agriculture and attracts tourists to the riverside campsite, signposted by the crossing. A visit to the Anmire (meaning 'Form your own opinion'), a traditional Damara Village, shows old and new style dwellings; food, singing, dancing and ritual displays can be enjoyed, if booked in advance. ■ *Apr-Dec, Mon-Fri 0900-1600, weekends 0900-1300.*

With the help of a local guide it is possible to drive up the gorge and explore upstream. However, if you choose to drive up the riverbed remember to observe all the rules concerning minimizing your impact on the local environment, and only do so in convoy.

Sleeping F *Khowarib Rest Camp*, very basic campsite plus traditional Damara huts with braai pit and water, but the setting more than makes up for it. There is one 'exclusive' camping spot by the river, with no facilities (4WD only). There is always a small flow of water over the high weir and one can carefully climb down and enjoy a natural shower or bathe in one of the small pools. Next to the campsite is a small camel ride operation run from the *Save the Rhino* camp. These camels were given to the

The Northwest

community after they had been used for an adventure along the Namibian Coast through the Namib Desert.

Warmquelle Unfortunately for Khowarib the campsite at Warmquelle, 11 km further on up the road, has an even more enticing water feature – a year-round natural pool which is large enough to swim in. Like Khowarib, the village of Warmquelle has little to offer the visitor, beyond refreshing patches of green in this dusty environment. Worth a quick look, however, are the remains of a **Shutztruppe Fort**: there is a stone entrance with tower, stables with stone cribs and the prison with two cells, dating from 1895. There are plans to restore the buildings and install a tourist information centre. Warmbad is also the place where Bondelswarts leader, Jan Christiaan Abrahams was shot, which led to their uprising in 1903. This event is re-enacted every year around 25 October. Skirmishes continued until peace was agreed in December 1906; the local cemetary houses numerous interesting gravestones. ■ *For further information on the area, or perhaps to engage a guide to take you to the sites, contact Ronnie Mathewis, T0638, ask for 11.*

Water from the spring, which feeds the Warmquelle pool, is piped for domestic needs and to irrigate a few small fields growing maize and vegetables, following the efforts made by a Greek farmer who, long before tourists started visiting the area, built a series of irrigation channels to nearby fields. A few sections of this aqueduct still remain hidden in the scrub bush.

Sleeping **F** *Ongongo Campsite*, 6 km from Warmquelle up a narrow track, if you fail to see the signs just keep following the water pipe. This is navigable, with careful driving, in a saloon car. 6 shaded campsites with braai pit, basic communal toilets and showers, set in picturesque limestone valley. Firewood and cool drinks for sale, walking trails, swimming in natural pool. At one end there is a waterfall which flows during the rainy season (Nov-Apr). Look out for the turtles which live in the pool. A couple were released in here a few years ago and started a family. This is a wonderful stop, particularly if travelling during summer.

Sesfontein The name originates from six springs which surface in the area. In 1896, fol-
Colour map 1, grid B2 lowing the devastating rinderpest epidemic which killed off huge numbers of both livestock and game, the German colonial authorities established a number of control checkpoints across the country; these now form the so-called **Red Line** which demarcate the boundary between commercial and subsistence livestock farming in the country. Sesfontein formed the most westerly in a string of such checkpoints.

Following the construction of a road between Outjo and Sesfontein in 1901, the German authorities transported materials to build a military outpost. This was designed to assist in the prevention of poaching and gun running in the area and although a fort (complete with vegetable garden) was built, by 1909 Sesfontein had been relegated to the status of police outpost before being finally abandoned in 1914. The fort fell into disrepair but was given a reprieve in 1987 when the former Damara administration renovated it. Today the fort has found a new role as home to the *Fort Sesfontein Lodge*.

Sleeping **C** *Fort Sesfontein Lodge*, T275534, F275533, reservations T061-252508, www.natron.net/tour/sesfontein/lodged.htm, has 14 en-suite rooms, cool spacious restaurant, bar, large swimming pool, pleasant shaded gardens with palms and bougainvilia; simple **F** campsite with communal facilities outside the fort. Book ahead for tours and hikes in Damaraland and Kaokoland. **F** *Para Campsite*, T273125, shaded sites with communal ablutions, soft drinks for sale, walks possible. Located 3 km west of Sesfontein Gate.

Transport Sesfontein lies 31 km north of the Hoanib River on the D3706 and is the northernmost point in Damaraland. There is an Engen garage just before the lodge gate, with small shop.

If you are in a saloon car, ask about the road conditions before continuing north. In a four-wheel drive, head 10 km southeast to Anabeb and take the D3704 north to Opuwo. This is the best route to Epupa Falls. Alternatively, continue north on the D3707 towards Purros and Orupembe. This is the shortest route to Hartmann's Valley; ensure you have sufficient supplies and fuel before leaving Sesfontein.

Heading north

Follow the D3707 to Purros along the Hoanib River. This is one of the best places to view the desert elephant as well as other wildlife in the area. However it can be dangerously difficult to find your way without a guide, so we have elected not to provide sufficient detail to navigate through this corner of the region without one. If you are sufficiently well prepared and guided, allow yourself most of the day to reach Purros. With reference to the Kaokoland Shell Map, **Dubis** is a narrow gorge which one can drive through, **Amspoort** is the furthest point to which you can drive. At this point the river passes through another narrow rocky gorge, you are only about 40 km from the Atlantic Ocean. However this is part of the Skeleton Coast, which is closed to the public.

Sesfontein to Purros

This is a joint project between the local community at Purros Village and Integrated Rural Development and Nature Conservation (IRDNC) based in Swakopmund. The project's aim is to develop sustainable tourism in the area to benefit tourists and the local community and to preserve the environment and the wildlife. Community game guards, funded by the World Wide Fund for Nature (WWF) through IRDNC, help to protect the game from poachers.

The area supports populations of desert elephant, black rhino, giraffe, gemsbok, ostrich and small numbers of predators such as leopard, cheetah and lion. Local guides offer game drives or hikes into the surrounding area and there is a plant trail intended to educate visitors about plants used in traditional medicines.

During guided visits to local Himba or Herero villages the emphasis is on tourists behaving as guests, spending some time talking with local people, rather than treating them as if they were attractions in a zoo. For further details contact the manager at the *Purros Community Campsite*.

Purros conservation & eco-tourism project
Colour map 1, grid A2

The Northwest

Sleeping F *Purros Community Campsite*, 4 shaded, private sites each with flush toilet, shower, braai, water and room for 4 tents. Bar, walking trails, firewood for sale. Note the desert elephants pass through the camp if in the area. Exercise caution if you are visited, campers have been forced out of their camp in the past. A percentage of the fee goes to the Purros Development Committee Fund used for development projects in the area. If you have time it is worth spending a couple of nights here in order to fully appreciate the beauty and appeal of the region. This is one of our favourite camps in Kaokoland.

North of Purros is the part of Kaokoland where all the advice and warnings about travel come into play. Driving sensibly you can expect to get just beyond Red Drum before having to pitch camp in the wild. **Red Drum** is literally a painted drum full of stones and bullet holes. Take a left for Hartmann's

North of Purros

Valley and a right for Marienfluss Valley. Remember it will not be possible to return from Marienfluss Valley via Van Zyl's Pass. However there is an alternative route to Opuwo and Epupa Falls (be very careful about carrying sufficient fuel). From Red Drum, drive back towards Orupembe and take the road marked to Otjihaa on the Shell Map. Although not shown, this joins the D3703 south of Otjitanda. There is no campsite at Orupembe.

Most visitors drive back as far as Orupembe and then take the D3707 and D3705 to Opuwo. This is a very long day's drive and you should make an early start from your camp near Red Drum if you expect to reach Opuwo before dark. This is the most sensible route to take since one can refuel and purchase fresh food before continuing north to Epupa Falls – an easy day's drive from the Kunene River Campsite just outside Opuwo.

Opuwo

Phone code: 065
Colour map 1, grid A3

Surrounded by low-lying hills, Opuwo, which means 'the end' in Herero, is a small and uninspiring town in the middle of the bush. The town grew into a permanent settlement and administrative centre for the region during the bush war prior to independence, when the South Africa Defence Force used it as a base from which to launch expeditions into the surrounding area. A smart lodge and decent community campsite provide lodgings for tourists passing through to the more isolated, attractive spots in the region.

Opuwo's name is indeed appropriate as it is both the first and last place offering supplies, fuel, accommodation and telecommunications in the region, although there are at present no bank facilities (*Standard Bank* expected in early 2002). Along or just off the main street are the two petrol stations, the few shops, post office, a helpful garage (*S&T Motors*, T081-2481262) for emergency repairs, an information centre and the town's bars. The residential areas are a few streets of bungalows, built during the bush war for army and government personnel; these now house government officials and the few business people in the area. Not far away are the Himba and Herero settlements.

If you fancy a walk around a nearby Himba settlement/township, you can ask at the garage for a guide. These will usually be unemployed school leavers who will speak English and therefore be able to translate for you. It is also a way of putting a little money into the local economy as crafts and other souvenirs can be bought directly from the people themselves. Do not take photos without negotiating first.

Sleeping
Options are limited
as most tourists
are en route in or
out of the region

C *Ohakene Lodge*, T273031, F273025, ohakane@iafrica.com.na is located behind the Shell garage, offering en-suite rooms, a lovely bar and good restaurant around a flood-lit swimming pool. They arrange trips to Epupa Falls and the Himba villages and are accustomed to tour groups, and are the best place to ask for information or help. They also have a tented camp in a nice location 5 km from town with 7 double tents with field kitchen and basic shared ablutions. **E-F** *Kunene Village Rest Camp*, T273043, is an excellent community campsite set in a sheltered valley, well signposted down a bad road 2 km from Opuwo, the other side of a hill. There are 4 simple rooms with en-suite showers, plus 6 grassed sites, each with a braai, table and seating under thatched shelter. The central wash block is very basic but clean and fitted with solar lamps (the hot water soon runs out). The reception area has a pleasant bar with a seating area overlooking the camp. The camp is surrounded by a fence to keep goats out, but is still vulnerable to theft, keep your belongings with you in the tent or locked in your car.

Ohakene Lodge generally only provides food to guests but it is worth asking – smart **Eating**
clothes may help. Your best bet otherwise is the ***Bakery*** which offers takeaway hamburgers and tasty meat pies, or you'll have to resort to the supermarkets and takeaways specializing in goat and chips.

Don't be put off by the rather seedy-looking bars. People in town are generally friendly **Bars**
and interested in visitors and chatting over a beer or two. At the T-junction for the C41, next to the information centre, is a decent bar and ***Verona Bar*** and ***Cuvelai No 1*** have pool tables where strangers are welcome to take on the locals.

The local crafts shop, set up by missionaries, is located on the one main street and sells **Shopping**
locally made and used baskets, jewellery, dolls, carvings, clothing and ornaments. These, thankfully, are no longer the family heirlooms of the vendors, but are now produced for sale, with designs sometimes adapted to be more appealing to tourists. If you intend buying these kinds of souvenirs this is the place to do so, as the money goes directly to the craftsmen and women, at a fraction of the price in Windhoek. There is a small, relatively helpful tourist office at the junction with the C41, with a few curios.

There is little point in coming here by public transport unless you plan on hiring a vehi- **Transport**
cle from the *Ohakene Lodge* and then continue into Kaokoland to visit the popular *235 km Khorixas*
sights. There is, however, an occasional local taxi service to Epupa, and a fair amount of *290 km Oshakati*
tourist traffic (usually fairly well loaded) should you be looking to hitch a lift.

Driving out of Opuwo can be a bit confusing. For Epupa Falls take a left out of the Shell garage and follow the pot-holed, tarred road north past the Himba settlement on the right side. The C41 will take you the 60 km to the C35 Ruacana–Kamanjab road; well signposted, turn right out of the Shell garage and immediately left past the BP garage, sports stadium and airfield. Right out of the Shell and straight on will take you eventually to the *Kunene Village Rest Camp*.

The C41 to the C35 junction for Ruacana or Kamanjab is a good quality gravel road. The **Routes**
D3700 to Okongwati is also a good gravel road, after this the Epupa Falls road needs to be driven with care. The shortest route to Hartmann's Valley is via the D3703 through the Steilrand Mountains, but this involves negotiating Van Zyl's Pass, very much 4WD only.

This small settlement marks the end of the reasonable D3700 from Opuwo. **Okongwati**
There is a police station, basic store and a scattered collection of houses. There *Colour map 1, grid A2*
is a small sign for *Epupa Camp* (for Epupa Falls), which takes you across a wide sandy riverbed shortly after leaving the village.

By the time you reach Okongwati you need to have already decided which route you are going to follow. The reason for this is simply the availability of fuel and the distances you plan on covering. Opuwo is the most northeasterly source of fuel. There are three possible routes you can follow, each will take you through beautiful country, each demands advance planning.

The most straightforward route is to continue 71 km north to Epupa Falls, spend **Okongwati to**
a couple of nights here and then return by the same road. However if you have **Epupa Falls &**
sufficient fuel (and experience and clearance, it is a rocky road) you can follow the **Ruacana**
Kunene River upstream from Epupa Falls to Ruacana. Note this road does not follow the river as closely as some people expect. It is a narrow track and very hard going in places. If you wish to visit Ruacana and drive along the river we would recommend you drive back to Otjiveze and take the D3701 signposted *Kunene River Lodge*. The adventurous and well equipped will take the D3703 towards Van Zyl's Pass and the Hartmann Mountains. See below for further details.

North of Okongwati the road passes through some pleasant woodland and a sign for the Traditional Himba Demonstration Kraal at Omuhunga, where tourists can view a traditional **Himba homestead** and take photographs if so inclined. The locals are well accustomed to the invasion, and will happily strike a series of poses for you. Don't be alarmed by their insistence on payment, by the mock wailing and forced tears of the children, or the beration of the eldest if you fail to meet their expectations. If you don't like it, don't take photographs, there are plenty of postcards for sale. Alternatively, wait until you get to Epupa where, if you stay for a couple of days, you may get to know the locals a little and enjoy less 'posed' photographs. About 10 km before the Falls are a couple of colourful Himba graves, with impressive piles of cattle horns.

While this road is not smooth or easy, outside the rainy season it is usually navigable by saloon car. Check both your rental agreement and lodge owners' advice before you travel this route. It is essential to take sufficient fuel as there is none at Epupa. There are, however, a couple of small shops selling fresh bread (the clay oven is outside) and whatever stocks have been brought in from Opuwo. Cold drinks and beer are available to refresh those without an onboard fridge.

Epupa Falls

Colour map 1, grid A3 The falls are a beautiful series of cascades where the Kunene River drops a total of 60 m over a distance of about 1.5 km. The main drop is roughly 32 m. As the river drops, it divides into a multitude of channels creating hundreds of small vegetated islands. While most people content themselves with a quick peek at the falls by the road, there is a track along the rocks high above the river, downstream of the falls, affording fine views back towards the falls. From here you can appreciate the extent and beauty of them, and see the range of vegetation (particularly the precariously placed baobabs). Beware of snakes on land and crocodiles in the water. Just before sunset drive a short way back towards the airfield and take the only track to the right. This leads up to the top of the hill where you are presented with a magnificent view of the falls and all the islands. An ideal spot for your sundowner.

Over the past few years, Epupa has welcomed a considerable amount of tourist activity. A thatched structure by the approach to the falls is under construction and will house collections of local crafts. You will encounter a few (mostly South African) self-drive visitors and the occasional tour group being ferried from airstrip to Himba village to Falls to lodge; but this is a truly beautiful spot and one can only hope that too much tourism doesn't spoil it. Part of its charm lies in the effort required to get here, and the feeling of remoteness once here.

The *Epupa Camp* and *Hot Springs Camp* are community sites maintained by locals, managed by *Kaokohimba Safaris* who also contribute 20% of the income into a fund administered by the Namibia Nature Foundation. This money is made available to local development projects. Don't be put off by the Himba who will approach soon after your arrival. These people are not thieves, but friendly and poor. They rely on tourists, and are happy to earn by selling you a curio item, showing you around or collecting firewood for you.

Sleeping L *Epupa Camp*, T695102, epupa@mweb.com.na, reservations, T061-232740, located about 1 km from the falls, follow the track upstream past the village. Has 9 canvas tents with en-suite shower and toilet, a lapa with eating area and bar, price is full board, and includes a trip to a Himba village and sundowner drive. The smartest accommodation

Epupa Dam project

The proposed Epupa Dam and hydroelectric power plant project has been the subject of controversy in Namibia since 1996, and has rallied politicians, civil servants, anthropologists, civil engineers, community leaders and conservationists against each other.

The Epupa scheme is intended to meet Namibia's energy needs for the next 25 years, reducing her dependency on importing energy from South Africa. Power generated by the hydro-electric plant will also be used to pump water through the proposed pipeline from the Okavango rover to Windhoek, which cannot grow further without solving its water problems.

Much of the Himba community opposes the scheme, fearing that the dam will destroy their way of life as pastures and ancestral graves will be flooded and an influx of thousands of construction workers will overwhelm this semi-nomadic community. Despite these fears, senior government officials have repeatedly come out firmly in favour of the scheme, claiming that the project will bring much needed development in the form of schools, clinics, roads and businesses to this underdeveloped region.

Consultations between the Himba community and the government have been bedevilled from the start as the Himbas felt that the government was never really interested in their views. The increasing politicization of the project saw the Himbas employ the services of the Legal Assistance Centre and a tour of European capitals by Himba leaders seeking support from overseas.

The whole project has been further complicated by the findings of the feasibility study which has considered two alternative sites for the dam. The Baynes site is less environmentally damaging but not economically feasible without the reconstruction of a war-damaged dam further up-river in Angola. The Epupa site would displace 1,100 people, affect 5,000 occasional users of the site, and drown 95 archaeological sites and 160 Himba graves. In addition, the Namibian and Angolan governments have also yet to reach agreement as to which site to move ahead with.

Yet another uncertainty is the financing of the project will come from. At a cost of around US$550 mn, it is clear that Namibian government will need to raise funds from overseas. At the same time, an alternative source of energy is under consideration off the southwest coast of the country. The Kudu gas field – a vast reserve of natural gas situated under the sea-bed – has also been the subject of a feasibility study. If the cost of building a 1,000 km pipeline from the gas field to South Africa's Cape Province is deemed affordable, the Epupa scheme would not be necessary on energy grounds.

Perhaps more than anything else, the Epupa debate highlights the conflict between those who see grand projects to fuel industrial development as the way to survive in an ever-changing world, and those who seek to preserve the last remnants of the old Africa.

in the area, a HAN 2000 Best Rest Camp award winner, expensive, but with informative and friendly hosts. Originally built for the experts involved in the feasibility study (see box) for the Epupa Dam project. Despite being very much a going concern, the agreement with the Himba (who own the land) permits no fixed structures, which is perhaps just as well given the considerable flooding in 2000.

B *Omarunga Camp*, managed and owned by *Ermo Safaris*, T061-257123, www.namibiaweb.com/ermo (see tour companies above), has 10 comfortable, en-suite canvas tent with twin beds, open dining area next to the river, bar and restaurant (also open to outside guests, book food 5 hours in advance). Good**F** campsite with hot showers and plenty of shade, also located by the river. The whole complex is fenced. Recommended, book in advance for the main camp. **F** *Epupa Community Campsite* and *Hot Springs Campsite*, large campsites with braai pit and running water, many (cold) showers and flush toilets. Both have lovely locations on the river, close to the falls.

Okongwati to Marienfluss & Hartmann's Valleys

As noted, the crossing of Van Zyl's Pass is not to be treated lightly. If you reach here with less than three hours of daylight remaining, camp by the road and cross the pass in the morning. As you negotiate the precipitous road keep an eye out for large rocks – either remove or replace them. The road gets very little maintenance from the authorities. The pass was built by Van Zyl with the help of a few Himba and an ox cart and is a tremendous feat of engineering. Many of the tracks in the area still follow the routes taken by Van Zyl and his team. A word of warning, don't expect all the routes on the Shell map to actually exist, some are just the old trails left by Van Zyl. If you started your day's journey in Opuwo you will not manage to cross the pass before nightfall.

Marienfluss and Hartmann's Valleys – The Kunene River

Colour map 1, grid A1 Having got this far, both valleys are worth visiting. The **Marienfluss Valley** is very scenic and relatively greener than Hartmann's Valley. As the Shell Kaokoland map notes, the valley is known for its 'fairy circles'. If you are interested in seeing such circles but can't get here then a couple of days spent at the *NamibRand Nature Reserve* near Sossusvlei will teach you all that is currently known about their origins. No camping is permitted in either valley. Keep to existing tracks.

Hartmann's Valley is closer to the Atlantic and yet much more arid. It has a strange atmosphere when the sea mists drift inland, rather like at Swakopmund. The drive is a tiring one and you should allow three hours to complete the 70 km to the campsite.

As you drive up each of these valleys it is difficult not to feel a certain sense of achievement and good fortune to be able to visit such a beautiful and fragile environment. Somehow nothing else in Namibia has quite the same impact as a week or more discovering the beauty of Kaokoland. One final comment from us: please observe all the advice on how to behave in these areas otherwise they could well end up like much of the Skeleton Coast – a private concession area which only the wealthy can afford to visit.

Sleeping

Marienfluss Valley *Camp Syncro*, run by *Kaokohimba Safaris*, not open to the public, arrangements may be made in advance by contacting the company in Windhoek, T061-222378, kaohim@nam.lia.net **F** *Okarohombo Campsite* by the Kunene River, 5 simple campsites with communal flush toilets, showers, taps and shade provided by a few camel thorn trees, a scenic camp which helps make the long and tiring journey worthwhile, the more provisions you have the more you will be able to relax and enjoy this unique spot. Bring firewood/charcoal, and be sure to ask the locals the safest spot for swimming in the river – there are crocodiles.

Hartmann's Valley *Serra Cafema*, run by *Desert Adventure Safaris*, T064-404459, F404664, www.das.com.na, in Swakopmund. A private campsite used only for clients of fly-in safaris, luxurious tented camp with 5 double tents, swimming pool in shaded, grassed riverside site. Excellent for birding, good fishing, walking and 4WD trails. Himba villages nearby. **F** *Public Campsite*, very basic campsite looked after by the local Himba people. Very little English spoken, you might find someone who understands Afrikaans. Visitors need to be totally self-sufficient, including firewood and water.

The Coast

8

The Coast

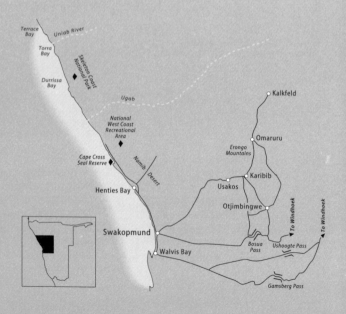

For many visitors to Namibia the coast could easily be passed over as they go in search of wildlife and the romance of the African bush portrayed in so many brochures and television programmes. But for Namibians, and many South Africans from the Johannesburg and Pretoria areas, the coast provides a relaxing and cool contrast to the heat and dust of the interior. Each year thousands descend on the resorts for a few weeks of fishing, boating, swimming and, increasingly these days, adventure sports. The coast provides a series of striking contrasts between the dunes of the desert and the wild South Atlantic Ocean, epitomized by the rusting hulks of sunken ships lying along the Skeleton Coast. For those on a smaller budget, one can take a boat trip and go whale and seal spotting just off the coast, with the orange sand dunes of the desert providing a dramatic backdrop. The Namibian coast must rank as one of the most evocative wilderness regions in the world and, as with so many of the great wildernesses in the world, you will probably end your day with more questions than answers.

The Coast

Swakopmund

Phone code: 064
Colour map 1, grid C3

Surrounded on three sides by the arid Namib desert and on the west side by the cold waters of the South Atlantic, Swakopmund is surely one of the most unusual and fascinating colonial towns in the whole of Africa. In a period of a little more than 25 years the German Imperial Government built a succession of extravagant buildings which today represent one of the best preserved collections of German colonial architecture still standing. Today, Swakopmund is Namibia's premier holiday resort, with a steady flow of visitors all year round, culminating in December and January when thousands of people descend from the hot interior to enjoy the temperate climate of the coast.

History

'The municipality since 1909 has made every effort to create an up-to-date township. The water supply is the best in the whole Protectorate and shortage is never felt in the town. There is an Electric Power Station, Ice and Mineral Waters Factories, a first class Hospital and Nursing Home, Public Library, German, Dutch and English Churches, High-class Schools and

The Coast

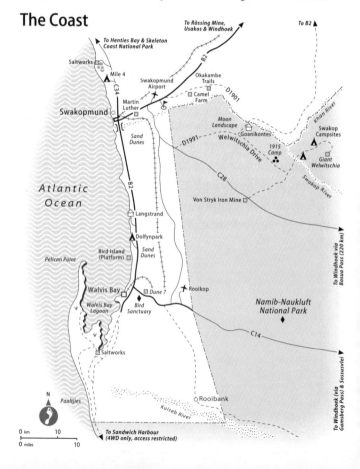

Thing to do on the Coast

- Go birdwatching at the **oyster farm** and snack on fresh oysters and champagne.
- Take a cruise in **Walvis Bay lagoon** and check out the dolphins, seals, flamingos and pelicans.
- Get an adrenalin rush **quad-biking over the dunes** of the Namib Desert.
- Check out the vast **seal colony** – and the smells – at Cape Cross.
- Explore the abandoned whaling settlement at **Sandwich Harbour** where the towering dunes meet the sea.

Hostels and a lot of Corporations and Clubs.' – Swakopmund Publicity Association, 1924-25.

This is how the town proudly promoted itself during the inter-war years, yet less than 30 years earlier no more than 30 Europeans lived in the newly established town. As a visitor to this modern town it is always worth pausing and questioning why and how the town came to be here. If ever there was a town in Africa that owed its origins to colonialism it was Swakopmund.

The first Europeans to encounter the barren Namibian coastline did not stop here; the Portuguese sailors left monuments to mark the points where they had ventured ashore, but there was no attempt made to settle anywhere along this section of the Atlantic coast. But when the German protectorate was proclaimed in 1884 the British had already claimed possession of Walvis Bay, forcing the Germans to look elsewhere for a suitable coastal port. The choice of Swakopmund had a lot to do with the immediate availability of fresh water. While there were other more suitable sites along the coast, the Germans selected Swakopmund as the point to develop a future harbour and settlement because, first, the immediate hinterland was not a mass of sand dunes which inhibited the inland development of transport routes, and second, a short distance up the Swakop River valley there was a fresh water supply.

In August 1892 the German gunboat, *Hyena*, landed just north of the Swakop River and two beacons were raised by the crew to mark their position. At the time this was one of many possible locations for a port along the coast that the Germans were looking for. Today history recounts that the landing in 1892 marked the origins of Swakopmund, however it was a combination of chance and a tough spirit that saw the establishment and growth of a town at this point on the coast. The first 40 settlers were landed in 1893 by four boats, but thereafter they had to fend for themselves. There was no accommodation, there was nothing; many of these early settlers ended up living in what have been described as 'caves', on the beaches. Today the town can be a grim place on a misty day, imagine how it was for the first settlers at the turn of the century. Gradually a town developed and people were able to move inland and establish trading posts and mission stations, but it was the resilience of the earliest settlers that set the pattern. After the First World War the town fell into decline as the nearby port of Walvis Bay assumed the role as the premier town on the coast. Many businesses and government offices also moved.

Until the 1970s Swakopmund may have been a forgotten town, but many of the citizens made their mark – today this is one of the most unusual and vibrant communities along the western coast of Africa; and what's more it has a special place in German history. The modern town is experiencing a building boom that is taking many people by surprise. Tourism is now an integral part of the local economy, and many people in the area depend upon the thousands of visitors each year. During the month of December the

The Coast

population on the coast is said to double, hotels are full, restaurants require a booking and to the frustration of local residents there are no parking places in the town centre.

Roads, railways
& the desert
Much of Swakopmund's early history was a battle to establish a port that could effectively supply the settlements inland. Like all colonial regimes of the period, the colonies were regarded as an important source of raw materials and new territories for trade. If they were to effectively exploit the interior the Germans had to somehow overcome the inhospitable Namib desert, which in age before railways and motorcars represented a tremendous natural barrier.

The first road to be built between the coast and the interior was known as the '**Baaiweg**'. It was built by the local leader Jan Jonker in 1844. Most of the early traffic consisted of ox wagons carrying copper from Matchless Mine to Walvis Bay, but the 350 km journey proved to be uneconomic and the route was then seldom used. All this changed when a harbour was built at Swakopmund, and in 1896 records show that 880 ox wagons used this road. But this heavy traffic quickly exposed the local weaknesses; each year more than 12,000 oxen had to be fed and watered across the Namib desert, there were no waterholes and no suitable pastures, losses were very high. In 1897 the government was forced to turn to the railways to try and overcome the problems posed by the desert.

Work on the first railway started in September 1897, and like the mole construction project the work greatly contributed to the growth of the town as workshops, supplies and storage sheds were provided. This first railway was a narrow gauge (60 cm), a great achievement for the times considering the obstacles and the remoteness of the colony. The first stage went as far as Jakalsswater, 100 km inland; by July 1900 the railway had reached Karibib, and on 19 June 1902 the first train from Swakopmund arrived in Windhoek, a journey of 382 km. This part of the state railway remained open until March 1910.

In 1903 work had begun on a second narrow-gauge railway, known as the Otavi railway line. In 1900 the Otavi Mine and Railway Company (OMEG: Otavi Minen-und Eisenbahngesellschaft) had started to mine copper ore in Tsumeb, but because of the unreliable state service they opted to build their own railway line. Their chosen route into the interior proved to be a more sensible one than that followed by the state railway, and the quality of engineering was much higher. When the full line opened on 12 November 1906 it was the longest narrow-gauge line in the world at 567 km. The running of the line was taken over by the government when the state railway was closed in 1910. The stretch between Tsumeb and Usakos was only widened in 1960.

Up until 1914 all the German efforts had been concentrated on connecting the port of Swakopmund with the rest of the country. But once the colony had been taken over by the British, Swakopmund quickly fell into disuse since the far more favourable site of Walvis Bay could be exploited. During the First World War the troops from the Union of South Africa built a railway line between Walvis Bay and the Swakop River in just over two months, but unlike the German-built railways this was a broad-gauge track, measuring 106.7 cm. The problem proved to be crossing the Swakop River; the first railway bridge was washed away in 1917. As the German army retreated inland they destroyed the existing narrow-gauge railway, but this merely paved the way for the South African engineers to replace the tracks with a broad-gauge railway. Following the Treaty of Versailles the railway network was taken over by the South African Railways and Harbour Administration. While the network was improved and extended in the interior the problem of crossing the

Swakop River remained unaddressed. A railway bridge was built between 1925-26, but in January 1931 the structure was washed away by the river in flood. It was not until 1935 that a secure bridge was built across the river, a short distance inland from the current road bridge. Today's visitor to Swakopmund may well wonder what all the fuss was about, but during the early years of Swakopmund the river caused great damage as well as loss of life. The dry riverbed may well look innocuous today, but with sufficient rainfall inland the flood waters can drastically alter the current landscape.

As you drive along the surfaced road between Swakopmund and Walvis Bay it is worth remembering that this stretch of road was first opened in August 1959, and only surfaced in 1970. The railway that ran between the two towns had to be re-routed in 1980 when the sand dunes finally reclaimed another transport route. You will feel very safe driving between the two towns today, but a hundred years ago the Namib was a real threat.

Climate

Although the town lies in a true arid desert, the cold Benguela current which flows from south to north along the coast acts as a moderating influence. The climate on the coast is temperate, temperatures range between 15-25°C. The sea temperature ranges between 14-18°C, too cold for swimming for any period without a wet suit. Swakopmund receives less than 15 mm of rain per year as the rain clouds have to travel all the way over Africa from the Indian Ocean. As you walk about the town note how most buildings have no gutters or drain pipes. The only moisture comes in the form of a sea mist that can reach up to 3 km inland. It is because of this mist that the coastal strip of the Namib desert has a unique living environment. There is sufficient moisture to support over 50 different lichen species and many other larger plants. These plants in turn provide food and water for hardy animals such as the gemsbok and springbok that also live in the desert.

Sights

For Namibian residents, Swakopmund is popular as a beach resort which provides a comfortable contrast to the hot interior. International visitors come here for the sea, the desert and the fine collection of German colonial buildings. Although most of these old buildings are closed to the public, much of their elegance lies is in their exteriors and can be enjoyed whilst strolling around town. The buildings are listed in a sequence that could be followed in a walk starting from the *Strand Hotel*. If you choose to follow the route allow a couple of hours and avoid the hottest part of the day. There are plenty of cafés and bars to call in on along the route.

Beach area

The *Strand Hotel* was built close to the point where **The Mole** joined the mainland. As noted in the history section Swakopmund was never the ideal place for a harbour or port, there was no natural bay or sheltered spot as at Walvis Bay and Lüderitz. In 1898 the government decided that a mole should be built in order to create an artificial harbour basin. The whole project acted as a great stimulus for the fledgling settlement, such a giant engineering project required a lot of preparation and additional facilities; these took more than 10 months to put in place and included a piped water supply for making cement, a small railway line, the opening up of a quarry and the provision of housing for the labour force. The foundation stone was laid on 2 September 1899, and the mole officially opened on 12 February 1903. It had proved to be a far greater job than imagined, the 375 m construction had cost 2.5 million marks.

The Coast

Along the mole were three steam-powered cranes that could transfer the freight from ships to barges. Unfortunately the planners were totally ignorant to the ocean currents and within two years of completion large amounts of silt started to build up on the south side of the mole. By July 1904 the tugs could only enter the artificial basin at high tide. By 1906 the whole basin had silted up and in the process created Palm Beach that is so enjoyed by today's tourist. After the Herero War the government looked for an alternative solution and plans were drawn up for the construction of a jetty. A wooden jetty was quickly built, which in turn was replaced by the iron jetty which can still be seen today (see below). These days the mole is used as a launch point for pleasure boats and the original harbour basin is a pleasant sheltered swimming area. If you are lucky you may see a dolphin or two swimming around in the bay as you walk out to the end of the mole.

Tucked away in the gardens behind the museum is the port **Lighthouse**. The first version, built in 1903, stood at only 11 m; in 1910 a further 10 m was added. The lighthouse marked the harbour as well as warning ships off the treacherous Skeleton Coast – the light can be seen more than 30 km out to sea. Next to the lighthouse is the **Kaiserliches Bezirksgericht** that serves as the Presidential holiday home. The presence of heavily armed soldiers will alert you to his presence and it is advisable to keep well clear during such visits. It

Historic Swakopmund

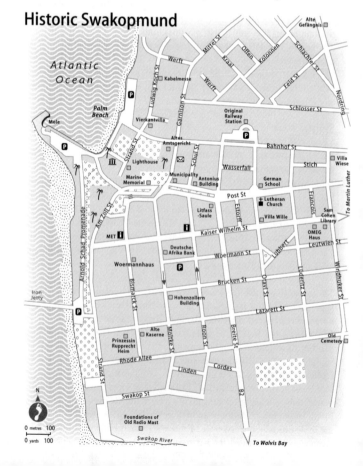

seems there is no such thing as an 'innocent' tourist to the young soldiers. The building was originally the first magistrates court in Swakopmund.

Close to the lighthouse is the **Marine Memorial**, a monument to members of the First Marine Expedition Corps who died during the Herero War, 1904-05. The statue was designed and cast in Berlin, and presented to the town by the crew of the German gunboat, *Panther*, in July 1908. The figure represents a marine standing by his wounded colleague, ready for action.

As you walk north along the beach look out for Ludwig Koch Street just beyond the municipal swimming pool. There are a couple of contrasting colonial buildings along the seafront. At number 5 is **Vierkantvilla**, the last house assembled by the 'Hafenbauamt' for the construction of the harbour mole. The interesting thing about this building is that it was prefabricated by Fa. Zadek in Germany for the Kaiser government. It was shipped out to Africa and erected on a stone foundation in 1899. Further along the street is a solid double storey building built in 1901 for the Eastern and South Africa Telegraph company. **Kabelmesse** was the principal office for the employees who installed the undersea cable from Europe to Cape Town. A branch from this cable surfaced a few kilometres north of Kuisebmond. When the railway was first built between Walvis Bay and Swakopmund it ran right along the beach; there was a siding at the spot where the cable ran ashore, named 'Cables'. This area of beach is still known as Cables and appears as so on many maps. At the outbreak of the First World War the cable was severed, and then removed when the wireless telegraph was installed.

Away from the centre of the town in Nordring Street, is the **Alte Gefängnis** (Old Prison). When the prison was completed in 1909 it stood right out of the town. The building has such a fine façade that it has frequently been mistaken as a hotel or private mansion. There is a tale which recounts the first visit of an official in the South West Africa administration who on seeing the solitary building for the first time exclaimed: 'I wouldn't mind staying there.' Local dignitaries politely replied, 'That, your honour, is the prison.' Currently undergoing a face-lift, the building is still used as a prison today so be very discreet when trying to take a photograph!

Alte Gefängnis

Close to the police station on the corner of Bahnhof and Garnison streets is a lemon yellow building in a well kept garden full of succulents and palm trees. This is the **Altes Amtsgericht**, built in 1906 as a school but then used as the magistrates office after the state had to complete the building when the private source of funds ran out. After falling into disrepair the building was restored in 1976. During office hours you may be able to get a glimpse of the interior. The building was designed by Otto Ertl who was also responsible for designing the prison and the Lutheran church; notice how features such as the gables and turrets are similar between these buildings.

Bahnof Street

A short walk along Bahnhof Street will bring you to *Swakopmund Hotel and Entertainment Centre*, one of the newest and most comfortable hotels in town. Until the early 1990s this was the **Railway Station**, and passengers from Windhoek would alight here into this fine colonial building. While all the building work has destroyed any trace of the railway line there are plenty of old photographs on display in the hotel restaurant and reception area which capture the scene perfectly. Before the conversion took place there was only one structure here, the building which is now the hotel reception and evening bar. The original platform is the terrace which overlooks the swimming pool. The building was designed by the architect C Schmidt, and built in 1901,

The Coast

whilst the central tower was added at a later date by W Sander. In 1910 the main railway line was closed, but the station continued to act as a terminus for the narrow-gauge railway, the Otavi Railway Company. After the First World War the broad-gauge railway was once again opened and continued to terminate here until a new station was built a short distance inland on the other side of Nordring. In October 1972 the building was declared a national monument, so guaranteeing its future.

Post Street It may not be the most interesting sight but the **Litfass-Saule** on the corner of Post and Breite streets has an unusual background. This rather tatty looking pillar is an original advertising post dating from the days before radio and television. There were similar posts all over the town to which people used to stick their promotional posters. This is the only post still standing. Litfass was a printer in Berlin who first thought of the pillars in 1855. Post Street is a pleasant wide road with some palm trees on the centre island, as you can see there are a variety of old buildings to admire all along this street.

The **Municipality** dates from 1907 when it started life as a post office, telephone exchange and living quarters for the personnel. Perhaps one of the reasons this and many other buildings are still standing is due to the high standard of craftsmanship and attention to detail that was typical of the period. The architect, Redecker, included the following clause in the contract with the builders: 'the building must be built as stipulated in the contract and associated plans; all wood must be seasoned and dry; qualified artisans must be engaged for each task; the roof nails must be 4 cm apart and countersunk.'

A short distance along Post Street is the **Antonius Building**. Over the years there have been many additions to this building, but between March 1908 and 1987 it was Swakopmund's only hospital. In the early days it was staffed by sisters of the Franciscan order, later on it was run by the Roman Catholic church.

The neo-Baroque **German Evangelical Lutheran Church** was designed by the government builder, Otto Ertl, in 1909, and built by FH Schmidt. The parsonage was completed in 1911 and as with several other important buildings and homes of the wealthy the church roof was covered with copper. On 7 January 1912 the inaugural dedication service was held in this grand building. At the time the white population of Swakopmund was about 1,400.

Across the road from the Lutheran Church is the **Old German School** building. Still in use as a school, its new extension to the right has none of the Baroque style of the original building which was opened in 1913 and was designed to fit in with the church.

Central Swakopmund **Villa Wille**, Otavi Street, now enjoying a renaissance as a Victorian period piece hotel (see below), is a fine example of a comfortable private residence of the colonial period. This was the home of Hermann Wille who was responsible for building some of the most elegant buildings in Swakopmund. Originally he designed it as a bungalow but then decided to add a second floor and today it is one of the most noteworthy buildings in Swakopmund with a fine balcony and a turret (a popular feature of the time) with a copper roof. Unfortunately, Wille only enjoyed a short life in Swakopmund, he was killed in action in 1915.

If you walk along Kaiser Wilhelm Street for a couple of blocks you will have reached the **OMEG Haus** and museum next to a small botanical garden and snake park. Around the corner in Windhuker Street is the excellent Sam Cohen library (see below).

One of the finest colonial buildings in Swakopmund is the **Hohenzollern Building**, on the corner of Brucken and Moltke streets. The most obvious feature, on the roof above the front door, is the statue of a kneeling Atlas holding up a globe of the world. In 1988 the original cement figure had to be replaced with the present plaster-of-Paris version. The building dates from 1909 when it started life as a hotel but in 1912 the building was taken over by the municipality after the hotel licence had been revoked by the local magistrate. The hotel had become a well known gambling den. When the municipality moved out the building was converted into private flats.

The **Alte Kaserne (Old Schützenhaus)**, was built in 1906 as a fort for the Second Railway Company who were involved with the construction of a wooden jetty. The style of the fort was considerably different from other forts of the period, notably Fort Namutoni. The front of the building measured 55 m with a tower in the centre facing out to sea, the other sides measured 45.5 m. A turret was built at each corner; the turret loopholes were included more for decoration than practical purposes. Today the most interesting feature is to be found in the entrance hall directly below the main tower. Now used as a reception for the youth hostel, the walls are covered with original paintings which represent the 26 emblems of the German Alliance States which were united in 1871 to form a unified German nation state. There is also a plaque with the names of the soldiers who died during the Herero War. Even if you are not staying here they are well worth closer examination.

On the opposite corner of Bismarck and Lazarett streets is another original colonial building, now a pension for visitors. The **Prinzessin Rupprecht Heim** is a fine single-storey building dating from 1902. It was first used as a military hospital, but in 1914 it was taken over by the Bavarian Women's Red Cross who renamed the building after their patron, Princess Rupprecht, the wife of the crown prince of Bavaria. For many years the building served as a peaceful nursing home until it was converted, and some out buildings added, into a private guest house.

Heading back along Bismarck Street, the **Woermannhaus** is easily recognized as the building on the high ground with a decorated tower. Housing the reservation office of the Ministry of Environment and Tourism, visitors can still climb the tower and visit an art gallery on the first floor and the local library. The Woermannhaus dates from 1905 and was designed by Friedrich Höft as an office for the Damara and Namaqua Trading Company. In 1909 the building was bought by another trading company, Woermann, Brock and Co. The Damara Tower was used as a lookout position to see when ships arrived at sea, and when ox wagons arrived from the desert. Between 1924 and 1972 the building served as a school hostel. When it was closed in 1972 it was in such a poor state of repair that the municipality planned to demolish the building. Fortunately a successful campaign saved the building; restoration was completed in 1975 and the public library moved into part of the building. ■ *1000-1200, 1500-1700.*

Bismarck Street

At the lower end of Brücken Street you can view the town from a different angle by walking to the end of the jetty. In 1910 the German government decided that it was time to build a permanent **Iron Jetty**. A contract was entered with the bridge builders, Flender, Grund and Bilfinger to complete the jetty in 3½ years for a cost of 3½ million marks. Before work on the jetty could start workshops and storage rooms had to be built on the shore, these were only finished in November 1911. The original plans were to build a bridge reaching 640 m out to sea, carrying two parallel railway lines of 490 m. These lines would carry a loading platform with two cranes; a third crane was planned for the shipping of marble from the Karibib region. Each of the iron

The Coast

posts supporting the jetty were filled with cement. Progress was slower than planned and by September 1912 only 100 m had been completed.

At this stage the contractors ran into the first problems with shifting sand banks. When work stopped at the outbreak of the First World War a third of the jetty had been completed for a cost of 2½ million marks. In 1919 one side of the jetty was covered with planks so that it could be used by visitors and fishermen. In 1931 and 1934 the Swakop River flowed for more than four months after exceptionally good rains in the interior. In 1934 parts of the town were destroyed by the floodwaters and silt from the Swakop River pushed the sea 3 km back from the present coastline. The jetty stood high and dry with a set of steps added at the end to help people get to the ocean. Slowly the sea washed away the silt and the present coastline was restored.

In 1985 the jetty had to be closed for safety reasons. The following year an appeal raised money for the necessary repairs but unfortunately it would seem the work done was inadequate. At present the jetty is closed and the town is again faced with the problem of raising funds to make it safe again.

If you have been following the recommended walk this marks the end of the tour. The *Tug* by the jetty is as pleasant a place as any for a sundowner and a good fish meal. Alternatively you could walk along the cool **Arnold Schad Promenade** back to the *Strand Hotel*.

Radio mast At the southern end of Strand Street behind the new Fisheries and Marine Centre are three small buildings which were once the anchor points for the radio mast used by the Germans until 1914. In December 1911 the Germans erected a strong transmitter which could communicate with Windhoek, ships along the coast as well as a similar transmitter in Duala, in the German Cameroon. This 85 m high steel tower became of great strategic importance at the outbreak of the First World War since it enabled the German navy to operate in the South Atlantic and threaten all the allies' shipping. When the British government asked the Union of South Africa to invade German South West Africa it was to both silence this radio and gain control of it for themselves. On 14 September 1914 the British auxiliary cruiser – *Armadale Castle* – started to bombard the radio mast, but failed to score a hit. At the time they did not know that the Germans had already dismantled the equipment and moved the radio inland on 13 August. To try and stop the bombardment the remaining personnel cut two of the cables causing the tower to collapse, no more shots were fired at the town that day. Ten days later the British cruiser *Kinfauns Castle* bombarded the town hitting the customs shed by the lighthouse with a lucky shot. Forty years later these ruins were converted into Swakopmund Museum.

Museums & libraries Close to the *Strand Hotel*, by the Mole, is the **Swakopmund Museum**, founded in 1951 by Dr Alfons Weber and transferred to its present site in 1960. The collection is very strong on local German history and the geography of the Namib desert. A small museum shop stocks a wide selection of historical leaflets (mostly in German) plus the usual choice of postcards, slides and books on Namibia. Visitors interested in rocks and minerals will find an impressive collection to the right of the entrance. Next door to the uranium mine show cases are a series of shops and rooms recreating the days of German occupation, and this is one of the most interesting displays in the museum. Overall this is a worthwhile museum which both educates and entertains; given that there are not that many museums worth visiting in Namibia, an hour spent here should be of interest to most visitors. ■ *Mon-Fri, 1000-1300, 1400-1700; adults N$7, children N$3.*

Martin Luther – the steam ox

Just out of town beside a clump of palm trees on the Windhoek road stands one of Swakopmund's most famous historical monuments, a rusty old steam engine known as 'Martin Luther'. In 1896 a First Lieutenant Edmund Troost of the Imperial Schutztruppe on a trip back to Germany came across a mobile steam engine at the engineering works in Halberstadt. Aware of the heavy losses suffered by the ox wagons he saw this new machine as the answer to Swakopmund's problems. He was so sure of the idea that he paid for the steam engine out of his own pocket and arranged for its transportation from Hamburg to Swakopmund. But when the ship arrived in Swakopmund the offloading equipment could not cope with the 280 cwt iron machine, so the boat proceeded to Walvis Bay where the engine was successfully landed. Troost was forced to leave the machine at the harbour for four months because of his military obligations elsewhere. When he finally returned to Walvis Bay he found that the engineer he had retained to drive the steam engine had left and returned home when his initial five-month contract had expired.

The first attempt to drive the steam engine to Swakopmund was undertaken by an American who it quickly became

apparent knew little about such machines. The going was very tough, the machine continually got stuck in the sand, and by the time a Boer completed the journey for Troost a further three months had elapsed. The whole venture was never that successful – apart from the problems of weight the machine also consumed vast amounts of water and there was no one able to carry out regular maintenance and repairs. In all, about 13 tonnes of freight were transported inland; two trips were made to Heigamchab and several journeys to Nonidas, the first source of water inland. In 1897 the engine broke down where it stands today and Troost was forced to give up his venture. Fortunately by now the government in Germany had released funds for the construction of a railway.

One of the most frequent stories you will come across in Swakopmund is how the steam engine got its name. The tale goes that shortly after it had ground to a halt a Dr Max Rhode is reputed to have said during a meeting at the Bismarck Hotel: 'Did you know that the steam ox is called "Martin Luther" now because it can also say – "Here I stand; I cannot do otherwise"?' The original statement was made by the German reformer, Martin Luther, in 1521 in front of the German parliament in Worms.

The interesting small museum in the **OMEG Haus**, Kaiser Wilhelm Street, is devoted to transport and photography in and around Swakopmund during the German occupation. Note the diving helmets that were used during the construction of the jetty, each weighing 15 kg. Outside in the courtyard are a couple of restored items from the Otavi railway. This was the site of the first station for the railway line. At a later date the railway was moved to the state railway station, the present day *Swakopmund Hotel*. The OMEG house was the goods shed. ■ *1000-1300, 1400-1700, no charge.*

Anyone with a keen interest in Namibian history should visit the excellent **Sam Cohen Library**, next to the OMEG Haus. Here you will find most of the material that has ever been published on Swakopmund; of particular interest is the collection of historical photographs and old newspapers. Anyone able to read German will find plenty of fascinating reading here. The town reading library is housed in the Woermannhaus, Bismarck Street. ■ *0900-1300, 1500-1700.*

National Marine Aquarium Fish are fed daily at 1500; on Tuesday, Saturday and Sunday they are hand-fed by divers. The new centre has a large central tank with a walk-through tunnel – the tank contains some sharks and sting rays plus a mix of smaller fish. There are smaller tanks with lobster, crabs and prawns. A fascinating glimpse at marine life, allow about 30 minutes unless you are there during feeding time. ■ *Strand St, T405744. Tue-Sat, 1000-1600, Sun, 1100-1700, closed Mon; adults N$6.*

Excursions

The Saltworks Located 6 km to the north of town off the Henties Bay road, C34, the Saltworks are a must for any keen birder. Follow the dirt track around the salt lakes, on the coastal side is the Seabird Guano House, drivers in a saloon car will have to stop by the fence. The terrain is a mix of ponds and canals surrounded by a gravel plain, off the sandy beach is a guano platform. It is advisable to arrive here in the early morning before human activity at the works and on the beach disturb the birds. In addition to the resident population of waders, many migrants can be seen between September and April. A comprehensive bird list has been put together by Dr G Friede whose small booklet can be bought at the museum. Species recorded at the Saltworks include: (resident) avocets, chestnut banded plover, oyster catcher, Cape teal, Cape shoveller, grey heron, black winged stilts, the pelicans and cormorants breed on the guano platform; (migrants) whimbrel, turnstones, little stint, knot, ringed plover, sanderling and bartailed godwit. Salt no longer naturally occurs in the area, however water is pumped from the ocean into the shallow pans and during the following 15 months evaporation results in the formation of salt crystals which are then collected. The whole area is a private nature reserve.

Other birdwatching sites The **Swakop estuary**, just beyond the *Hotel Garni Adler*, can easily be visited by foot from the centre of town. Here there is a mix of reed beds and the sandy beach, find a sheltered spot and you should be rewarded with a variety of waders and land birds. The **Sewage Works** are another site for birds, visitors must obtain a permit at the Altes Amtsgericht, Garniston Street. ■ *Access is limited to working hours, 0800-1700.* The final recommended location for birding is 10 km to the east of town. Follow the road towards the airport and Windhoek, take a right turning for the camel farm and look out for a castle-like building on a small hill. This is **Nonidas Castle**, now a hotel (see accommodation section), and behind the castle in the river bed are a couple of vleis surrounded by reed beds and shrubs. Amongst the species of birds you might spot here are moorhen, red billed teal, dabchick, marsh warblers, black-winged stilts, African black oyster catchers, swallows and martins. A visit here can be easily combined with a tour of the camel farm or horse riding with *Okakambe Trails*, (see below).

Other excursions Assuming you have your own vehicle there are several other popular day trips. For most visitors a drive up to Henties Bay and **Cape Cross Seal Reserve** will be all they see of the infamous Skeleton Coast. This bleak-looking coastline continues all the way up to Angola and after several hours of driving most visitors will get the picture. See page 246 for information on the coast north of Swakopmund. Another popular excursion is to follow the **Welwitschia Plains** drive in the Namib section of the Namib-Naukluft National Park. The full route is about 135 km long and can be covered in four-five hours, however if you take a picnic this can be turned into a pleasant leisurely day trip. Follow the B2 out of town for the airport and Windhoek, take a right turn on to the C28 sign-posted for Windhoek via the Bosua Pass. **NB** Permits for the Namib Desert and Welwitschia Plains must be purchased in advance from the Ministry of Environment and Tourism, Bismarck Street, see below for full details.

One of the more interesting ways of enjoying the desert landscape is to ride on a camel. About 12 km from the town centre, off the B2, is a **Camel Farm**, T400363. ■ *Rides can be organized every afternoon between 1400-1700, advance notice advised.* As you drive out to the farm there is a large pipeline visible to the right of the main road, this is the water supply for Swakopmund; the pipe supplies over 11.5 million cubic metres a year, most of the water comes from the Omaruru and Kuiseb Rivers.

Once a fortnight, a tour to **Rössing Uranium Mine** departs from the *Schweizerhaus Hotel*. While this is undoubtedly a fascinating glimpse into a major mining operation and one that provides much needed employment in this part of the country, like everything associated with the nuclear industry there is a sense of 'look how good and safe we are'. Even if this is the case, the giant scar on the landscape could never be passed off as environmentally sound. Recommended. Note that tours are conducted in English only. ■ *Every first and third Fri of the month, 0800-1200. Bookings must be made in advance at the museum, T402046, N$17.50 adults, N$8.50 children.*

Tours

There are plenty of tour companies to choose from in Swakopmund and Walvis Bay and in the past couple of years the variety of trips on offer has increased. Below is a brief summary of the most popular sights – details for many of the locations are described elsewhere in the text, particularly those in Damaraland, the Namib desert and the Skeleton Coast National Park. The value of joining a tour depends upon the quality of your guide and which off-road locations you are taken to. If you have already hired a car then trips to Cape Cross, Walvis Bay and Spitzkoppe can easily be done under your own steam. However, for more specialized trips into the Erongo Mountains, the Kuiseb Delta, down to Sandwich Harbour or into the Namib Desert a guided tour can be thoroughly rewarding. The prices shown here are only intended as a guide; small groups may be asked to pay a little more.

Town tours are only worth going on if you don't have your own vehicle or find it too hot to walk around. Most of the interesting buildings are centrally located

The **Namib desert tour** is one of the most worthwhile trips on offer. While many of the companies no longer go into the national park, you will still get to see all of the desert sights. Most tours criss-cross the country to the north of the Swakop River, where you will drive through the amazing moon landscape, be introduced to many of the unusual plants which manage to survive in this arid environment, and see some spectacular rock formations. Some desert tours include a visit to Goanikontes spring. ■ *N$200pp.*

Tours to **Cape Cross Seal Reserve** involve a lot of driving and limited sightseeing. The landscape is typical of much of the Skeleton Coast, but after a while it becomes very repetitive. The outing should include a stop at the Saltworks, a good location for birds (see above), and the fishing resort, **Henties Bay**. ■ *Total distance 250 km, N$200pp.* A variation on the full desert tour will combine a visit to **Walvis Bay** (there is little of interest here) with a visit to the impressive dunes which line the road between Swakopmund and Walvis Bay. ■*N$160pp.* If you have no plans to travel in Damaraland then a tour to **Spitzkoppe** should be considered. This is a long day trip and you can expect to spend a lot of time in the vehicle. The tour will start by driving up the coast as far as Henties Bay before turning inland towards the mountains. Around the Spitzkoppe are a number of interesting rock paintings. Some

The Coast

companies will include a visit to a small mineral mine where you can buy semi-precious stones. ■ *Over 400 km driven, N$250pp.* This and the desert tour are probably the two most interesting outings on offer.

Dolphin tours from Walvis Bay are offered by a number of companies (see Walvis Bay section). These are usually half-day tours of the harbour and lagoon areas and one can expect excellent sightings of seals, dolphins, flamingos and pelicans. For those contemplating a trip up to Cape Cross Colony to see the seal reserve, these tours offer an excellent alternative that avoids both the long drive and the pungent smell! A further possibility – if you are lucky – is the chance of spotting whales as they make their way up and down their migratory routes to and from the Antarctic. At around N$300 per person these tours are good value for money and recommended with or without whales!

Sandwich Harbour tours are, at the time of writing, enjoying new found popularity as the word has spread that there is abundant birdlife there. Many of the tour companies listed below and in the Walvis Bay section offer these day-long trips. However, the drive down is long and tough and without a knowledgeable guide to explain the history of the settlement and the geography of the lagoon area, you may find yourself disappointed. However, a trip with *Turnstone Tours* (see below) who are the Sandwich Harbour specialists is definitely worthwhile and for many visitors is the highlight of their visit to the coastal area.

Fly-in safaris   For those visitors short on time but long on cash a number of companies (details below) offer flying safaris both along the coastal and the Namib desert and also to places as far afield as Lüderitz in the south and Etosha and Kaokoveld in the north. Shorter half-day trips offer visitors superb aerial views of Sossusvlei and the Kuiseb Canyon, while a full day tour to Kaokoveld, for example, includes a visit to Himba villages, lunch and then a flight back down the Skeleton Coast. ■ *Trips start at around N$800pp and go up to more than N$2000 – expensive, but recommended for those able and prepared to meet the cost.*

Essentials

Sleeping
■ *on maps, page 232*
Price codes:
see inside front cover

Swakopmund has a wide choice of rooms covering all budgets and the number of establishments seems to increase each year as the economy comes to depend more and more heavily on tourism. Whilst some of the older establishments still cater for predominantly German-speaking tourists, the majority now cater for the needs of visitors from Europe, North America and from countries further afield such as Taiwan and Japan. There are a number of hotels and guest houses in Hotel Garni category with breakfast as the only meal on offer, but with a wide choice of restaurants and cafés in the town this not need be a problem. In addition to the hotels and guesthouses, Swakopmund also offers the possibility of fully equipped self-catering apartments – many of them on or close to the beach. For those independently-minded visitors, or those people interested in staying for a week or longer at the coast these can offer an excellent alternative. Apartments can be booked through a number of agents acting on behalf of the owners (see contact details below).

Note that all categories of accommodation in Swakopmund are likely to be fully booked around the peak Christmas period. Even at other times of the year occupancy rates may be very high. You are therefore strongly advised to book your accommodation in advance or at the very least to check on availability before arriving. Given that more and more establishments have email facilities it should be little trouble to contact them in advance.

Lappiesdorp – Tent City on the Beach

In 1947 the municipality set aside an area, close to the present day Municipal Bungalow Park, as a temporary campsite with 10 tents to cope with the large number of holidaymakers. This proved to be a great success and the following year 50 tents were erected on the site which became known as 'Lappiesdorp'. In 1949 the site had swollen to 400 tents occupied by an estimated 2,000 people. Each year the council was faced with the same problem of providing enough accommodation for the Christmas influx of holidaymakers.

In 1952 the council built the first small bungalows (which are still in use today); by 1972 more than 200 bungalows had been built, ranging from luxury self-catering units to the most basic of shelters. The camp continues to be very popular, particularly since most hotels in Swakopmund are too expensive for the average Namibian. Just below the camp is the sandy bed of the Swakop River, where the original concrete pillars from the first railway bridge can still be seen leaning in all directions after being washed away by the great flood in 1932.

AL *Swakopmund Hotel and Entertainment Centre*, (known as the Entertainment Centre), PO Box 616, Bahnhof St, T400800, F400801, www.namibweb.net/shec 90 a/c rooms, light and airy rooms with MTV. The *Platform One* restaurant has a limited à la carte menu but the buffets are of the highest standard, – booking advised at weekends. Heated swimming pool, shops, hair salon and car hire. The casino and amusement arcade tend to appeal more to the Swakopmund residents than any of the guests at the hotel. The front building is the original railway station built in 1901, look at the old photographs to see where the trains used to pull up. An excellent hotel that caters primarily for international visitors. The service here is of a higher standard than most Windhoek hotels. By far the best of the three principal hotels in town. Recommended. **A** *Hansa Hotel*, PO Box 44, 3 Roon St, T400311, F402732, www.hansahotel.com.na Until the old railway station was converted this was for many years the top hotel in town. 55 rooms arranged around a garden courtyard with palm trees. The restaurant has a good selection of Namibian and continental dishes, bar, spacious and comfortable guest lounge. A smoothly run hotel in the centre of town which many still regard as the best in town. Recommended.

B *Hotel Eberwein*, PO Box 2594, Kaiser Wilhelm St, T463355 F463354, www.eberwein.com.na Located on the main street coming into town, this splendid colonial era home has been tastefully converted into a Victorian style hotel. The 17 rooms, including 4 luxury doubles, are comfortably furnished and equipped with all mod cons. Breakfast included, dinner upon request, nice bar with a good range of South African wines, recommended for those who want the colonial experience. **B** *Sam's Giardino Hotel Pension*, PO Box 1401 89 Lazarett St, Krammersdorf, T403210, F403500, samsart@iafrica.com.na Located on the edge of town facing the desert, this Swiss-owned hotel has been built in the style of Swiss mountain chalet. With 10 simple but clean and pleasant rooms facing the garden, breakfast is included with a four-course dinner also offered. An excellent bar well stocked with fine South African wines and regular wine-tasting evenings, mini-library/reading room with plenty of information on Namibia, a selection of fine cigars and friendly relaxed atmosphere, this hotel is recommended for those wishing to avoid the formality of the bigger hotels but still enjoy the same level of service. 3 times winner of the HAN hotel garni category award. **B** *Sea Breeze Guesthouse*, PO Box 2601, Swakopmund, 48 Turmalin St, T463348, F463349, www.seebreeze.com.na Italian-run establishment offering four self-catering flats and a selection of en-suite single and double rooms. Great location about 3 km from the town centre, reports welcome. **B** *Strand Hotel* PO Box 20, on the

The Coast

beach front close to the lighthouse, T400315, F404942, strandhotel@namibnet.com 45 rooms, restaurant, a shady terrace bar serves light lunches. Popular family holiday hotel with comfortable rooms. The only hotel right on the beach with ocean views.

C *Beach Lodge,* PO Box 79, T400933, F400934,1 Stint St, Vogel Strand, 5 km from the town centre, beachl@iafrica.com.na, www.natron.net/tour/belo/main.html   Excellent location on the sea front, all rooms en-suite with fireplace and sea view. If you are

The Coast

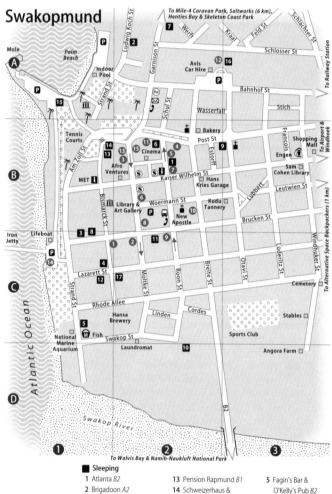

Swakopmund

N

0 metres   200
0 yards   200

looking to be out of the town centre and enjoy some serious sea breezes, then try this one. **Deutsche Haus,** PO Box 13, T404896, F404861, 13 Lüderitz St, deuhause@mweb.com.na, close to the town centre. Family-owned and run establishment with 18 rather plain double and 2 single rooms. Rooms include breakfast with lunch available every day except Sat and dinner to be introduced shortly. Recently extended and renovated there is a sauna and small indoor swimming pool, bar and TV lounge. Despite the name the hotel also caters for non-German speakers too. Popular with tour groups, good value for money. **C** Europa Hof , PO Box 1333, 39 Bismarck St, T405898, F402391. 35 rooms, cool but gloomy restaurant with a menu anyone from Germany will feel at home with. Secure off-street parking, popular with organized tour groups. The whole building looks totally out of place in Swakopmund – the timber frame and flower boxes would not seem out of place in the Alps. **C** *Garni Adler*, PO Box 1497, 3 Strand St, T405045, F404206. 14 rooms, TV, breakfast room, but no evening meals, residents' bar, indoor heated swimming pool and sauna, private and sheltered sun deck on the roof. A very clean and neat hotel. Secure off-street parking. The new fisheries building has partly spoilt the location but this remains a pleasant and peaceful location. Popular with German tour groups, but recommended outside busy periods. **C** *Schweizerhaus*, PO Box 445, 1 Bismarck St, T400331, F405850. 24 rooms on the first floor, some with ocean views, short beds, clean and spacious rooms, bath and shower, TV. Rooms on the inside overlook a courtyard which is also an aviary for parrots: unfortunately this means the balconies are not very clean. Restaurant, private residents' bar in the back garden. While this is a fully fledged hotel the reception area doubles up as the popular *Café Anton*. It is a bit awkward checking in with all your baggage when everyone is enjoying coffee and cakes. A good value hotel still under family management, helpful and friendly young staff. Recommended. **C** *Seagull*, PO Box 1162, 60 Strand St, T/F405287, bed and breakfast, 3 double rooms with en suite bathroom and TV, lounge, self-catering facilities also available. Short walk from the shops and beach.

D *Atlanta*, PO Box 456, Roon St, T402360, F405649. 10 rooms, en suite bathroom and TV, good restaurant. *Fagin's Bar* is a lively local drinking haunt, secure parking. **D** *Brigadoon*, PO Box 1930, 16 Ludwig Koch St, T406064, F464195. 3 comfortable self contained cottages with small garden overlooking Palm Beach. Ideal for a family or visitors wishing to avoid hotels. Secure parking, a short walk from the museum and post office. Run by the friendly Bruce and Bubble from Scotland providing a pleasant change. Recommended. **D** *Hotel Burg Nonidas*, PO Box 1423. 10 km outside town on the B2, T 400384, F400384, performancemotors@namibianet.com 12 simple but comfortable rooms offering b&b and bar lunches. Located in this historic colonial era building, the hotel overlooks the Swakop river and for those looking for a peaceful retreat away from town this is eminently suitable. **D** *Digby's Dig-By-See*, PO Box 1530, 4 Brücken St, T404130, F404170. 12 rooms. Chintzy breakfast room, evening meals available. Popular well established set-up, run by Stella and Manfred. Becoming expensive. **D** *El Jada Bungalows* , T/F400348, seagull@iafrica.com.na, 12 km outside town just off the B2 next to the camel farm. 5 fully equipped bungalows with braai places and a small communal kitchen. Situated next to the Swakop river, the site has a pleasant garden with small swimming pool and is a good place to relax and watch birds for those so inclined. If it's peace and quiet at a sensible price you are looking for, this place is recommended. **D** *Pension D'Avignon*, PO Box 1222, 25 Brücken St, T405821, F405542. 10 rooms, clean but a little cramped. No restaurant, TV lounge, sheltered swimming pool. Visitors from Germany will feel most welcome, for the rest of you look elsewhere. **D** *Pension Prinzessin-Rupprecht-Heim*, PO Box 124, 15 Lazarett St, T402231, F402019. 20 rooms some with shared bathroom. A quiet and somewhat staid pension, good value for anyone on a medium budget, off-street parking and a sheltered garden at the back. **D** *Pension Rapmund*, PO Box 425, 6 Bismarck St, T402035, F404524. 25 rooms, breakfast available but no restaurant. One of the most welcoming and friendly pensions and therefore often full. Call in advance. Recommended. **D** *Strauss Holiday and overnight Flats*, PO Box 2542, 10 Feld St, T081-1244937 F463699, www.natron.net/tour/ggh/main.htlm 7 fully-equipped apartments with two double beds one with en-suite facilities, TV, telephone, braai facilities. A bit of a walk from town and rather chintzy décor but good value for money. **D-E** *Swakopmund Municipal Restcamp*, Swakop St, T402807, F402076. Advance reservations through the Municipality. A mix of bungalows which can sleep 2-6 people: the most basic are known as 'Fisherman', these have bunk beds, shower, a small seating area plus a hot plate, thin walls. At the other end of the scale are luxury bungalows with 2 bedrooms, bathroom, lounge/dining area, kitchen with crockery (no glasses or towels provided). In between are 4-bed bungalows and flats which are good value, and A-frames with a lot of character. Out of season the camp is frequently recommended as a good value self-catering set-up. During peak periods it is unlikely that a visitor from overseas will get in since the bookings open months in advance, and for many Namibians this is the only comfortable accommodation they can afford in Swakopmund. The camp is to the left of the main road after crossing the bridge coming into town from Walvis Bay.

E *Haus Garnison*, 4 Garnison St, T404456, F405246, garni@iafrica.com.na Holiday apartments suitable for anyone considering a longer stay, secure parking, will be fully booked during peak periods, but competitive rates might be negotiated during the slack season. **E** *Jay Jay's*, PO Box 835, Brücken St, T402909. Restaurant, bar with pool table. Well established cheapo hotel, the bar can get a bit rough and rowdy. A mix of 12 small rooms and dorm in an old rundown building. Short walk from the town centre. **E-F** *Restcamp Sophia Dale*, Street 1901 (12 km outside town on the B2), T/F403264, www.sophiadale.com Bungalow, caravan and camping sites with braai places, wash block. An alternative to staying in town, with great views of the desert and the Erongo Mountains on a clear day. **F** *Alternative Space*, PO Box 1388, 46 Dr Alfons Weber St, T/F402713. Small dorms, kitchen, laundry, free pickup. A welcome peaceful location right on the outskirts of town, out towards the airport. A long walk from the centre but a good unofficial establishment. **F** *Karen's Attic*, Corner Otavi and Post Streets, T403057. A relatively new backpackers', secure and comfortable. 6-bed dorm plus 5 double rooms and kitchen with microwave and freezer. Secure off-street parking. Lacks a garden to relax in, but perfect central location, everything in walking distance. Recommended. **F** *Youth Hostel*, Lazarett St, in the converted Alte Kaserne (old barracks). Dorms, double rooms, camping, communal washing facilities. Off-street parking in a sheltered courtyard with a small patch of lawn and some shade. Only open for young people, 15-30 years.

Agents for self-catering apartments *Namibia Holiday Services*, PO Box 277, 23 Kaiser Wilhelm St, T 405442 F 404826, www.henric-estates.com *Nel's Estates*, PO Box 3626, Vineta, Swakopmund, T081-1270290, seaside@iafrica.com.na

Eating
• *on map page 232*

Most of the major hotels have attached restaurants but after several meals their menus can seem a little limited. However, Swakopmund has the best choice of restaurants in Namibia outside of Windhoek including a number of restaurants offering high quality affordable seafood. Check opening times as quite a few will be closed Sun or Mon evenings.

Bayern Stübchen, 13 Garnison St, T404793. Popular amongst those looking for the traditional German meal, excellent food, but not everyone's cup of tea. *De Kelder*, 11 Moltke St, T402433, closed Sun. Good for steaks, seafood with a couple of vegetarian choices, set back from the road in an arcade, uninspiring interior. *Erich's*, 21 Post St, T405141. A dull tiled interior, but a vibrant seafood restaurant during the season, a bit pricey. Closed Sun. *Frontiers*, 18 Moltke St, T404171. A medium priced set-up which tends to cater for groups. Interior vaguely similar to a Hard Rock Cafe, choice of steaks, salad and a couple of traditional Namibian dishes. *Hansa Hotel*, 3 Roon St, T400311. Quality food and service as befits this excellent hotel. Visitors from overseas will find the choice of food and wine of the highest standard. Recommended. *Kücki's Pub*, 22 Moltke St, T402407. A long-time favourite with all visitors to Swakopmund. Recently re-bought and renovated by the original owner, this popular local haunt is a great place for eating seafood. Traditional restaurant arrangements downstairs and pub type seating upstairs. It is advisable to make a reservation if you are planning to eat here in the evening. *Lighthouse Pub and Restaurant*, Pool Terrace, Main Beach, next to the Museum, T400894. Outdoor terrace overlooking the sea and inside bar and dining. Offers a wide range of dishes from excellent fresh seafood to steaks, burgers, and pizzas. Good atmosphere, sensible prices and great views. Recommended, booking advised. *Mandarin Gardens*, 27 Brücken St, T402081. Owned and run by a mainland Chinese from the north-east, this restaurant offers as close to authentic Chinese cuisine as you will find in Namibia. A pleasant change to the range of dishes on offer elsewhere with a takeaway service. Try the dumplings! *Napolitana*, 32 Breite St, T402773. Real pizzas prepared in a wood oven and a range of pastas and meat dishes. Popular with locals and tourists from the Mediterranean, prices are very reasonable and the atmosphere friendly and relaxed. Recommended. *Platform One*, Bahnhof St. This is the *Swakopmund Hotel* restaurant, a smart room which has been decorated with railway memorabilia. The Sun evening buffet is to be recommended, plenty of fresh seafood and a wide selection of meat dishes, limited à la carte choice. Booking is necessary during busy periods, attentive service. *Swakopmund Brauhaus*, The Arcade 22 Kaiser Wilhelm St T402214. New restaurant offering traditional German dishes, Namibian game and fish and great cooked breakfast. A good place to stop and relax during a walk about town. *The Tug*, Strand St, by the iron jetty. Cool beers, a great sunset with an ocean view, what more do you want? Come here, relax and enjoy the break, good seafood, sister restaurant to *The Raft* in Walvis Bay. Bookings required. Recommended. *Western Saloon*, 8 Moltke St, the name sums up the interior. The seafood is good and so are the steaks, easy-going medium priced restaurant.

All of the restaurants are licensed and some have a small bar area where you enjoy a beer before going to your table. For anyone looking for a more lively set-up there are several bars to choose from. These cater for an odd mix of overlanders, the young hip Swakop crowd who look too young to drink, and an older crowd who just like bars. **Bars & cafés**

In recent years several new street cafés have opened, providing Swakopmund with a pleasant alternative to the quiet, enclosed a/c cafés of old. These all serve light snacks and some excellent coffee – a rare item in Namibia. Included in the list is the local *Internet Café*, which not surprisingly is very popular with overseas visitors, particularly groups from the overland trucks. **NB** Most of the places have opened during the last three years and with Swakopmund's rapid development and booming tourist industry there are bound to be new places emerging. Please let us know if you discover a new favourite hangout.

African Café, corner of Brucken and Bismarck streets. A colourful alternative to the staid atmosphere found in some of Swakop's older cafés. Good value snacks, decent sounds, bar, pool table. Designed to appeal to the backpackers. Erratic opening times, may not be doing as well as hoped, but this is just a feeling. *Baungart Deli*, Brucken St. A welcome but an unusual sight in southern Africa, a health food shop. If you have suffered a diet of meat with meat for several weeks this shop will seem like paradise, let's hope it survives, recommended for all things fresh and green. *Café Anton*, Bismarck St. A very popular bakery in the lobby of the *Schweizerhaus Hotel*. A good range of cakes and pastries to

The Coast

takeaway. Recommended. *Fagin's Bar*, Roon St, close to the *Atlanta Hotel*. Swakop's version of an Irish pub, but without the draught Murphy's. The T-shirts overhead tell their own story. A popular bar where most are welcome and at weekends you can enjoy a late lively evening. Recommended for any fan of bars. *Internet Café*, Moltke St. Coffee counter at the back, good sounds, helpful staff and excellent links to the outside world. Keen and ambitious management, should become an important port of call for most overseas visitors. *O'Kelly's Pub*, Roon St. A basement bar-cum-night-club. Fun when the place is busy, hot and dull at other times. Difficult to judge the mood when you first have to get past the doorman. *Out of Africa*, Post St. A very popular café which spills out onto the palm-shaded street. Excellent coffee and cappuccino. The ideal place to write a few postcards. Recommended. *Pandora's Box*, Ankerplatz, Bismarck St, doubles as a café and curio shop. A great place to catch the sun in the morning whilst enjoying a traditional Namibian fry-up breakfast! *Putensen Café Treffpunkt*, Kaiser Wilhelm St, coffee, cakes, bit of a time warp. *Swakopmund Bistro*, Moltke St. Casual bar serving tasty snacks and excellent draught beer plus a choice of imported beers (check sell by date). Small outside seating area with steady trade. Recommended.

Shopping   As Namibia's principal domestic resort Swakopmund has a particularly good selection of shops selling tourist items, not all of these are as tacky as you might imagine; there are some excellent cloth shops and some interesting art studios. It may seem a strange item to buy on holiday but the locally made kudu shoes from the *Swakopmund Tannery*, 7 Leutwein St, are highly regarded and will last for many years; the factory shop also stocks handbags and smaller leather goods. *Desert Gems*, Roon St, opposite the *Hansa Hotel* for anyone interested in buying gem stones, polished or in their natural state. *Karakulia*, The Arcade, good selection of karakul rugs and wall hangings, some of the finest Namibian products to take back home, all of a high standard. Alternatively go to the factory on Knobloch St and take a tour around and see how the carpets are made. *Kristall Gallerie*, , corner of Garnison and Bahnhof Streets, has a display of crystals and other semi-precious stones and replica of the original Otjua Tourmaline Mine as the hook to get you to come in to the jewellery boutique. Worth it if this sort of thing appeal to you. *Peter's Antiques*, 24 Moltke St, a must for anyone interested in German colonial history, excellent collection of Africana books, as well as some genuine tribal antiques. Not cheap but the quality is excellent and the knowledgeable owner also worth talking to. *Safariland*, Kaiser Wilhelm St, large selection of smart safari clothes and T-shirts, not cheap, but the quality is excellent.

Sports   **Fishing**   The coastline either side of Swakopmund is famous for its superb fishing. Many of the local cars seem to have a set of rods permanently attached to the roof. Check at the MET office for details of the strict regulations which control angling. Fishing trips are run by several operators, see below for details.

Golf   *Rossmund Golf Course* has 18 holes with grass greens, palm trees and shrubs add to the character. There is a restaurant in the club house, golf clubs can be hired, T405644. Avoid trying to play a round in the heat of the day.

Horse riding   *Okakambe Trails*, 11 km from town centre, follow the B2 towards the airport, take a right turn, D1901, the stables are close to the camel farm, T404747, 405258. A variety of day, half-day or longer rides are possible. If you are an experienced rider this is one of the most pleasant ways to explore the amazing desert landscape – good fun, recommended, overnight rooms available.

Quad-biking   *Desert Explorers*, on the main road to Walvis Bay just before Long Beach, T 406096, bookings necessary through any agent in town. Offers a 35 km round trip of thrills (and hopefully no spills) through the desert with some great views and photo opportunities. Instruction and safety equipment provided – recommended for adrenaline junkies!

Skydiving The local club meet at the airport at weekends, lessons are available, ask for a contact number at the tourist office. **NB** There have been some fatal accidents in recent years (but not in Swakopmund); if you are experienced check all the equipment closely.

Swimming There is an indoor heated pool next to the museum, Strand St, closed during the middle of the day. Within the complex is the *Swakop Hydro*, T402866, a fully equipped health centre with a sauna, steam bath, aromatherapy and a range of beauty treatments.

All of the companies in Swakopmund, Walvis Bay and Henties Bay offer a selection of similar tours. It always pays to shop around and ask fellow guests at your hotel whether they might recommend anyone. Prices do vary, but then so too does the quality of the guide, the maximum group size, the comfort of the vehicle and the quality of any food and drink that might be included in the tour price. Prices range from N$250-400pp for day tours. Before you make your choice find out how many people will be in the group and if possible what their nationalities are as a mixed-language group will get far less out of their guide. As it can also get very hot in the middle of the day, this is not the time to find oneself squashed in the back of a Land Rover with an awkward view. If the tour you wish to go on is not running on the day that suits your timetable don't be persuaded into joining another tour; check first with another company, there is plenty of choice. Finally if you are not happy with the tour inform the local tourist offices as some companies are not yet accustomed to providing the level of service and value that international visitors expect.

Tour operators

Afro Ventures, PO Box 1772, Hertzog Berlin Bldg, 14a Kaiser Wilhelm St, T463812, F400216, one the most professional operators on the coast, friendly and helpful, recommended. *Atlantic Aviation*, PO Box 465, 5 Roon St, T404749, F405832. An experienced charter company which can fly guests to most popular destinations in Namibia. All types of excursions catered for, short flights across the surrounding area through to day trips to Lüderitz or Epupa Falls. *Compion Aviation* , Kaiser Wilhelm St, T403575, specializing in desert elephant and black rhino spotting tours in conjunction with *Palmwag Lodge* in Damaraland, tours start at N$1400 per person based on a maximum group size of 5 persons. *Desert Adventure Safaris*, PO Box 1428, Roon St, T/F404072. Slightly cheaper than other companies, longer tours for small groups can be put together to suit your needs. *Inshore Safaris*, an excellent local company with plenty of experience – see page 245 under Walvis Bay. *Namibia Safari Trails*, PO Box 1946, T404158, F406098. Local day tours (6 hrs), longer trips to Brandberg or Kuiseb Canyon. *Namib Tours*, PO Box 1428, Roon St, T/F404072. Another option for the full selection of day tours in the Swakop region. *Okakambe Trails*, T402799. Guided tours from horseback. Advance booking necessary for rides lasting more than a single day. An excellent way to enjoy the remote hinterland. Experience helps. *Pleasure Flights and Safaris*, PO Box 537, T/F404500. Strongly recommended if you wish to appreciate the Namibian landscape from the air, flights up to the Kaokoveld and as far south as Lüderitz are possible. *Sunrise Tours and Safaris*, PO Box 442, 8 Roon St, T/F404561. Fishing trips as well as sightseeing. *Swakopmund Adventure Centre*, PO Box 456, Roon St, T406096, F405649, located in the *Atlanta Hotel* building. This is for the young, local tours with a difference, agents for *Desert Explorers'* 'Quad bikes', helmets and goggles provided, good fun. *Turnstone Tours*, PO Box 307, T/F403123, www.swk.namib.com/turn Run by Bruno and Kate Nebe, Turnstone is the Sandwich Harbour specialist working closely with MET, as well as offering excellent overnight camping trips into the Namib Desert, Damaraland and the Erongo Mountains. Whether your interests are geological, ornithological, botanical or just general you will get individually tailored, in-depth, expertly guided trips. All tours (max 7 people) are conducted by Bruno or his assistant Michael and include pick-up from hotel or guesthouse and all snacks or meals including soft drinks. Strongly recommended.

The Coast

Tourist information *Ministry of Environment and Tourism*, Woermannhaus Ankerplatz, Bismarck St. Open Mon-Fri, 0800-1700, bookings can only be made 0800-1500. A helpful office where you can now make bookings for any *Namibia Wildlife Resorts* accommodation and also where permits are issued for visits to the Skeleton Coast National Park (Torra and Terrace Bay), the Namib-Naukluft desert. The office can provide a little local information, but the *Namib-i* office is the best source for specific tourist information. When this office is closed permits can be issued from *Hans Kries* garage, Kaiser Wilhelm St, or *CWV Service Station* and *Sud-West Service Station* in Walvis Bay. There is no excuse for not having a permit if stopped. The desert is well patrolled by MET staff, make sure you observe all the regulations and respect the fragility of the local environment. Do not litter, and that includes cigarette butts. *Swakop Info Bureau*, PO Box 829, T/F404827, corner of Roon and Kaiser Wilhelm Streets. A well run office, Almuth and Elizabeth are helpful and enjoy their work. In addition to local tourist information covering accommodation and tour operators you will find *Air Namibia*, T405123, have a desk here where you can reconfirm and purchase tickets.

Transport

30 km to Walvis Bay
395 km to Windhoek
76 km Henties Bay
120 km to Cape Cross

Local Car hire All the major companies have an office in Swakopmund, staff will meet flights at the airport where you will be able to pick up your car. *Avis*, Bahnhof St, in the Entertainment Centre, T405792, F405881. *Budget*, T404118, F404117. *Into Namibia*, 1 Moltke St, T464157, F464158, 4WD and organized tours. *Nonidas Car Hire*, T400352, F404956. **Cycle hire** *Cycle Clinic*, 10 Roon St, T402530. **Taxi** There are a couple of local services, this is the safest and easiest way to get to Walvis Bay for a look around. *Raiwin Call Car*, T081-1281289 (mob) (0700-2100), expect to pay about N$180 for a lift to Walvis Bay.

Long distance Air: *Air Namibia*, Bismarck St next to Ankerplatz at Woerman Tower, T405123, have regular flights between Swakopmund and other regional centres in Namibia. The airport is a small room with some seats and toilets, there is a public telephone and boxes to deposit hired car keys at the end of your trip. These flights are rarely fully booked, but if the plane has a lot of baggage it will take fewer passengers to keep to a safe weight. As noted elsewhere, the *Air Namibia* schedules are continually changing so if you are planning your holiday on a tight schedule check in advance their current schedules before arranging car hire and hotel accommodation.

If you have not arranged to collect a hire car on your arrival make sure you arrange with your hotel to collect you from the airport. The local taxis do not make a habit of going to the airport to meet each flight. The local *Avis* representatives may give you a lift into town, assuming they are meeting the flight. If it looks as if you are stranded, it is a short, hot walk to the main road; you should not have to wait long for a lift into town. The walk into town is too far in the heat, even without luggage.

Lüderitz, 75 mins. **Windhoek – Eros**, 45 mins.

Road: *Intercape* coaches drop passengers off by *The Talk*, Roon St, a café with a small information service which is also a convenient place to make telephone calls from. For Windhoek (4 hrs) via Karibib and Okahandja, see timetable on page 382. **NB** Namibia daylight saving – service departs 1 hr earlier between the first Sun in Apr and the first Sun in Sep.

Train: The railway station is on the desert side of Nordring St; reservations, T643538. If time is not an issue then the service between Windhoek and Swakopmund/Walvis Bay is a comfortable alternative to the long distance coach. But note, Namibian railways must rate as one of the slowest services in Africa. For timetables for services to Windhoek, Tsumeb (via Omaruru and Otavi), Walvis Bay and Windhoek, see page 383.

In April 1997 a new luxury service was introduced, *The Desert Express*. The train and whole service has been modelled around existing luxury services in South Africa. Windhoek (10 hrs): check-in 1300, Mon, Wed and Sat. The service arrives in Windhoek at 1000 the next morning. (see page 92 for further details).

Banks All the main banks have an office in the centre of town, all with 24-hr ATMs.
Avoid pay-day at the end of each month, it can be chaos in small branches.
Commercial Bank of Namibia, Kaiser Wilhelm St, has a bureau de change which is the
quickest and easiest place to change money or cash travellers' cheques. *First National
Bank*, Moltke St. *Standard Bank* and*Windhoek Bank*,both on Kaiser Wilhelm St.

Directory

Communications The main **Post Office** is in Garnison St next to the police station.
Open Mon-Fri 0830-1300, 1400-1630; Sat 0900-1200. Outside the post office are some
public telephones and a booth selling phone cards, this is the cheapest place to make
international calls from. Faxes can be sent from 55 Kaiser Wilhelm St, but this service is
only available Mon-Fri, 0830-1300. **Internet** *Internet Café*, Moltke St, in the Woerman
and Brock centre. Plenty of computers with quick links and a coffee and cake counter.
Open 6 days a week from 0800-1800. *Internet Café*, Roon St, next to Pleasure Flights
Office, popular with the overlander crowd, friendly service, coffee available.
Swakopmund Adventure Centre, internet café and convenient place to book your
quad-biking or sandboarding adventure.

South of Swakopmund

The southern boundary of Swakopmund town is marked by the estuary of the
Swakop river. Drive over the bridge and you are on the tar road leading down
the coast to Walvis Bay. Prior to Walvis Bay being returned to Namibia in
1994, there was a border and immigration control point on the far side of the
river. The 30-odd km drive down the coast snakes between the rolling sand
dunes inland and the Atlantic Ocean to the west, making this one of the pretti-
est drives in Namibia. On your way, you will pass the holiday resorts of Long
Beach or Langstrand and Dolphin Beach, opposite which adrenaline seekers
can try out quad-biking over the dunes. Finally, the two townships of
Narraville and Kuisebmond appear on either side of the road just before a
roundabout which signals the start of Walvis Bay proper

Just before you reach the outskirts of Walvis Bay look out for a large
wooden platform in the sea. This is known as **Bird Island** and was built to
provide a nesting site for seabirds from which man could collect guano. Still in
use today, the platform can yield close on 1,000 tonnes in a single year. There
are always plenty of seabirds to watch in the vicinity. Beyond the platform you
may occasionally see one of the drilling platforms which are being used to
look for off-shore gas fields.

Walvis Bay

*Had it not been for two colonial powers seeking to gain a foothold on this remote
coastline, it is unlikely that both Swakopmund and Walvis Bay would have
thrived. Nevertheless, today, Walvis (as it is affectionately known) represents a
pleasant alternative to the relative bustle of Swakopmund. Moreover, if the somewhat Disneyesque charms of Swakopmund leave you cold, then Walvis Bay is the
town for you, particularly if you enjoy birdwatching or just want a convenient
base from which to explore the Namib-Naukluft Park.*

*Phone code: 064
Colour map 1, grid C3*

Compared with Swakopmund, the port town of Walvis Bay has far fewer historical buildings and monuments to enjoy. In truth, much of the town is a grid
of characterless modern buildings, however the town is currently enjoying a

The Coast

The amazing Benguela Current

The Benguela Current plays a very important role in contributing to the well being of Namibia. The fishing sector provides about 22% of all exports and remains a large source of employment in the private sector. In addition to providing the ideal conditions for fish to breed in, the cold waters of the current cool the air over the ocean, which when it comes into contact with the hot dry desert air produces a mist. As this mist drifts inland it brings moisture to a desert which otherwise would be almost completely devoid of life.

The fish equation is quite simple: the ocean current is rich in nitrogen which supports an excess of plankton, the plankton is the favourite diet of whales and pelagic fish such as pilchards and anchovies, which live in giant shoals. The abundance of fish attracts seabirds, seals and people.

renaissance after the quiet years following its return to Namibia. Anyone who visited five years ago would be surprised at the developments that have taken place, in particular the increased number of options on the accommodation front as well as restaurants and tour operators. Visitors from South Africa can fly direct to Walvis Bay, but to get to Swakopmund they either have to change flights and airports in Windhoek, or endure a 40-minute drive from the airport which serves Walvis Bay.

History

The first known European to visit Walvis Bay was **Bartholomeu Dias** who entered the bay on 8 December 1487 in his flagship, the *Sao Christovao*, while searching for the tip of Africa and a possible sea route to Asia. He named the sheltered lagoon the 'Golfo de Santa Maria de Conceicao'. The bay was one of the finest natural harbours along a barren coast, having been formed by the floodwaters of the Kuiseb River, before the natural silt load blocked the delta.

The modern town of Walvis Bay is located on the edge of this deepwater bay and tidal lagoon. An 18 km long sandspit forms a natural breakwater against the Atlantic Ocean, and the tip of the spit is marked by an automatic lighthouse, Pelican Point – which doubles as a small seal colony. The spit joins the mainland to the south of Walvis Bay forming a shallow lagoon famous for its superb variety of birdlife an important wetland providing many species with important feeding and breeding grounds. In all, a total of 45,000 ha are now protected as a nature reserve.

Back in 1487 it was not the birdlife that was of interest to the Portuguese sailors, it was the shelter from the ocean, but when they landed they found there to be no surface fresh water. Accordingly Dias named the area the Sands of Hell. For the sailors this was not the wealthy country they were seeking to trade with and so they quickly pushed on further towards the Cape.

The name Walvis Bay, or bay of whales, originates from the 16th-century Portuguese maps which showed the bay as 'Bahia das Bahleas', due to the large numbers of migratory whales passing this way. In 1487 Dias and his crew had taken note of the abundance of fish in the coastal waters and when the first chart of the area was drawn up he had called the area around the bay 'Praia dos Sardinha', the coast of sardines. During the 17th century, British and American ships frequented the area in search of whale meat and seals, from time to time using the natural harbours at Walvis Bay and Sandwich Harbour, but there were no attempts made to explore the interior. Eventually the Dutch in

Cape Town decided to investigate the hinterland, prompted by the rumours of great cattle and copper wealth. On 26 February 1793 Captain F Duminy, in the ship *Meermin,* landed and annexed the Bahia das Bahleas, renaming it Walvis Bay. But the land remained in Dutch hands for only a few years; in 1795 the British occupied the Cape and Captain Alexander travelled up the coast to Walvis Bay, where he hoisted the British flag.

The growth of the settlement was very slow; a few traders made the epic journey from Cape Town and some missionaries passed through for the Rhenish Missionary Society. Up until the time that the Germans started to develop Swakopmund the small community at Walvis Bay prospered on the cattle trade, and copper from the Matchless Mine in the Khomas Hochland close to Windhoek. As noted in the Swakopmund section, the coast at this time was linked with the interior by a road known as the **Baaiweg**, built by Jan Jonker in 1844. Most of the early traffic consisted of ox wagons.

During the 1870s unrest in the interior led to the British government in the Cape being asked to intervene to protect missionaries and traders. However, the British concluded that the lands were too poor to make it worthwhile to add the territory to the British Empire. Instead it was decided to consolidate their position at Walvis Bay: by controlling the movement of goods and people to the interior they hoped to be able to influence or even control the events inland. On 12 March 1878 Commander RC Dyer formally annexed the area, the boundaries being described as follows: 'on the south by a line from a point on the coast 15 miles south of Pelican Point to Scheppmansdorf; on the east by a line from Scheppmansdorf to the Rooibank, including the Plateau, and thence to 10 miles inland from the mouth of the Swakop River; on the north by the last 10 miles of the course of the said Swakop River'. Rooibank had been included since it was the closest place with fresh water and greenery. The rest of the 750 sq km enclave was desert.

For the next 50 years the fortunes of Walvis Bay were influenced by the development of the German colony of South West Africa; as Swakopmund grew and prospered so the amount of traffic using Walvis Bay declined. The outbreak of the First World War was to change everything for good. Once the South African troops had built the broad-gauge railway the port was quick to develop, and in 1927 a newly dredged harbour was opened by the Earl of Athlone, Governor-General of South Africa. At the same time a new source of fresh water was discovered in the bed of the Kuiseb River, which helped guarantee the future of the town.

At the end of the First World War Walvis Bay was given to South Africa to govern as part of the mandated territory of South West Africa. This remained the case until 1977 when South Africa declared Walvis Bay to be part of the Cape Province. Despite pressure from the United Nations, South Africa refused to give up the small enclave as it served both as an important commercial port and as location of a South African military base. In 1992 South Africa relented and agreed to a joint administration without any border controls; on 28 February 1994 South Africa returned Walvis Bay to Namibia.

The port represents a great asset for Namibia which, if properly developed and well managed, can challenge ports such as Durban and Maputo for trade destined for countries such as Zimbabwe, Botswana, Zambia and even Malawi. In 1996 a private company, the **Walvis Bay Export Processing Zone Management Company**, was established to help attract more businesses to Walvis Bay and to take advantage of the port and its improved access to the hinterland. Both the Trans-Kalahari and Trans-Caprivi highways have been completed, thus reducing the transport time of commodities to and from

The Coast

Zambia, Zimbabwe, Botswana and South Africa by up to 14 days. Slowly the town is starting to benefit from the improved economic climate, and this and the increased volume of tourists choosing to visit the town and surrounding area are providing the local population with grounds for optimism.

Sights

Despite its long history the town has surprisingly few old buildings. For most visitors the attractions here are in the sea, not on the land. The earliest building in Walvis Bay is the **Rhenish Mission Church**, 5th Rd, a small structure surrounded by modern private homes. It was made in Hamburg as a prefabricated kit in 1879 and in 1880 the wooden building was erected on the waterfront. As the harbour grew in importance it was decided to move the church to its present site. Once reassembled, the wooden walls were plastered to help prevent wood rot. The last service was held here in 1966.

On the inland side of the town is a small **Bird Sanctuary** built around several freshwater ponds. If you follow 13th road inland, take a left by the signpost close to the dairy farm. The track climbs over a couple of dunes before you reach a hide on stilts overlooking two pools. There are often flamingos and pelicans to be seen here. If you follow the road past another pool you will join the main surfaced road to the airport.

Other minor attractions include **Dune 7**, on the outskirts of town, on the C14, the highest dune in the area. A small picnic site has been set up amongst some palm trees. The best time of the day to visit the dune is close to sunset, when the views are spectacular but the sand is not so hot for walking on.

Essentials

Sleeping
■ *on map opposite*
Price codes:
see inside front cover

The choice of accommodation in Walvis Bay has improved in recent years, reflecting the mini-boom the town now enjoys. There are now a number couple of comfortable options for both the tourist and business traveller, as well as several good value guesthouses and small hotels and a choice of self-catering accommodation. There is even a good backpackers for anyone who finds Swakopmund too busy!

A-B *Burning Shore Beach Lodge*, PO Box 3357 Walvis Bay, 152 4th St, Longbeach, T207568, F209836, burningshore@namibnet.com, a recent addition to the accommodation available at this resort and owned by the same group as the *Intu Afrika Lodge* in the Kalahari. Offers 4 suites and 3 luxury rooms and great views over the ocean and the desert. Report welcomed. **B** *Lagoon Lodgec*, PO Box 3964, 2 Nangolo Mbumba Drive, T200850, F200851, www.namibweb.net/lagoonlodge Established and run by French couple Wilfred and Helene Meiller, this is the only guesthouse located right on the lagoon. 6 comfortable, individually styled rooms all with excellent views, and warm hospitality make this the most pleasant place to stay in town. Recommended. **C** *ALtlantic*, PO Box 46, 7th St. T202811, F205063. 18 rooms, the restaurant had a good reputation but has failed to respond to changing times in Walvis Bay, bar. **C** *Courtyard Hotel* , PO Box 3493, 6, 3rd Rd, courtyrd@iafrica.com.na Situated close to the lagoon this new and comfortable addition to Walvis' guesthouses has 13 en suite double rooms with TV, phone and an indoor swimming pool and a pleasant garden. **C** *Langholm Hotel*, PO Box 2631, 2nd St West, T209230, F209430, www.langholm.com.na A clean new building with 11 rooms, en suite bathrooms, lounge and bar, no restaurant. Ideal if you are looking for somewhere more quiet. **C** *Levo Guest House*, PO Box 1860, 3rd St, Langstrand, T/F207555. Guest house with 3 double rooms plus self-catering chalets, suitable for 4 people, with sea views. A well

The Coast

run small establishment. A full range of fishing trips and cruises can be organized from here. Out of town location. **C** *Ngandu Lodge* , PO Box 3192 Walvis Bay, corner of 1st Rd and 9th St West close to the lagoon, T207327/8, F207350, theart@mweb.com.na 7 rooms, 5 en-suite, breakfast room, bar, pool room, laundry and conference facilities, popular with local visitors. **C** *Walvis Bay Protea Lodge*, PO Box 30, corner of 10th Rd and 7th St, T209560, F209565. Part of a large South African chain. 26 a/c rooms, M-Net TV, no restaurant. A functional clean hotel located in the centre of town, more suited to the business traveller than tourist.

D *Asgard House*, PO Box 1300, 17th Rd, T209595, F209596. An old fashion private home with 5 double rooms with en suite bathrooms. Recommended. **D** *The Courtyard*, PO Box 2416, 16 3rd Rd, T206252, F207271. 17 rooms, all well appointed with en-suite bathrooms, fridge, microwave and TV. The rooms are arranged around a neat green courtyard with a little shade. Facilities include a sauna and a small indoor heated swimming pool. There is no restaurant but the excellent *Raft* restaurant is only a short walk away. One of the better places to stay at in Walvis Bay. **D** *Lagoon Chalets*, PO Box 2318, 8th St West, Meersig, T207151, F207469. Basic self-catering chalets which can sleep up to 6 people. Limited privacy. Restaurant and bar close by. Nothing special. **D** *Park Guest House*, 105, 8th St, T207224. A new safe block with off-street parking. Clean rooms with en-suite bathrooms. **D-E** *Seagull's Inn Guest House*, 215 Sam Nujoma Drive, T202775, F202455. Self-catering or set menu meals available. Recently refurbished, good value for the budget minded.

Walvis Bay

E *Dolphin Park Recreation Resort*, Private Bag 5017, T204343 F204528, gkruger@ walvisbaycc.org.na, midway between Walvis Bay and Swakopmund, 20 one-bedroom en-suite chalets, swimming pool, hydroslide and recreation area. Popular with families. **E** *Esplanade Park*, Private Bag 5017, T206145. 26 self-catering bungalows set amongst shaded lawns overlooking the lagoon. Suitable for 5-7 people, simple but clean. Each unit has a fully equipped kitchen, bathroom TV, garage and braai area. They represent good value holiday accommodation provided by the municipality, advance booking essential during school holidays. **E** *Langstraat (Long Beach) Coastal Resort*, Pvt Bag 5017, T203134, F204528 gkruger@ walvisbaycc.org.na A choice of 2 or 4-bed flats, plus camping with electric points and shade. Within the complex are 2 restaurants, a jetty bar, shop and laundry. This is a very popular holiday centre during local school holidays, it is close to the beach with plenty of watersport facilities for children. **F** *Esplanade Campsite*, PO Box 86, T205981. Somewhat bleak campsite located close to the lagoon. 35 pitches, protected from the winds by some sad low hedges. Close to the swimming pool and sports facilities. Office hours 0800-1300, 1400-1700. Quiet in the low season, better options available up the coast. **F** *The Spawning Ground*, 55, 6th St, T205121/0811295121. The only true backpackers' in Walvis Bay. 4 dorms, each with 4 unusual bunk beds, communal TV lounge and a well equipped kitchen. Camping possible in a simple bare garden. Good source of local info for the budget traveller. Given that there is less to do in the town itself many visitors tend to stay here for some R&R. Eugene is the owner. Recommended if you find yourself in Walvis on a tight budget.

Eating
• on map page 243

Blue Café and Probst Bakery, corner of 9th St and 12th Rd, T202744. A popular German bakery, recommended for light lunches and snacks. *Chi Lin*, Seagull Mall, 8th St, T209046. Closed Thu. The local Chinese option. A pleasant change from standard Namibian fare, but you may find some dishes are not quite what you expected. *Crazy Mama's*, 7th St, T207364. Good value steaks, seafood as well as excellent pizzas and pasta dishes. Popular amongst budget travellers. *Hickory Creek*, 140, 9th St, T207990, part of the Spur chain. Solid South African fare, always good value, filling and friendly service, children well catered for, salad bar, similar menu throughout the region. *Lalainya's*, 7th St, T202574. Once one of the smarter places to eat in town, like similar well established outlets it has failed to move with the times. Nevertheless it can still be recommended if you are looking to eat good seafood with a wide choice of wines. *The Raft*, Esplanade, T204877. A light and spacious dining area built on stilts in the lagoon. A wide selection of dishes, seafood, pasta, fresh salads and the usual choice of steaks. Popular with the local business community. Always worth a visit to watch the sunset from the bar and the pelicans flying into the lagoon. Sister restaurant to *The Tug* in Swakopmund, unfortunately the current manager appears indifferent to the clientele. *The Waldorf*, 10th Rd, T205744. An alternative for lunches and daytime snacks. Typical Namibian fare. Closed evenings.

Tour operators

If you find yourself in Walvis Bay don't feel that you have to contact a company in Swakopmund to organize one of the many outdoor activities that are widely promoted in all the tourist literature. There are several excellent operators in town who you can meet face to face and will plan any trip you might wish, thus saving you a drive up to Swakopmund. The most popular trips centre around visits to the Namib desert, inland from Walvis Bay and Swakopmund. However there are countless other options. The following is a list of what is on offer: contact any of the operators listed below and they will be able to provide further details and up-to-date prices. As a guide expect to pay between N$250 and N$400 per person. **Tours** Oysters and Flamingo; Sandwich Harbour; Kuiseb Delta; Welwitschia Desert; Cape Cross and Spitzkoppe Tour. **Activities** Kayaking, sandboarding, parasailing, windsurfing (outstanding conditions in Walvis Bay Lagoon), quad-biking, skydiving, donkey cart rides, horseback safaris, fishing trips and peaceful birding cruises.

The Coast

African Heritage, PO Box 1185, Walvis Bay, T207401, F204850, afrherit@ iafrica.com.na Nangolo Mbumba Drive 3. Offers mini jeep tours in the desert including champagne breakfast or customized tours into the Namib Naukluft park. *Eco Marine Kayak Tours*, PO Box 225, Walvis Bay, T/F203144, jeannem@iafrica.com.na Kayak tours for both the experienced and the beginner. Choose between leisurely tours of the coastal wetlands and longer trips to Pelican Point for the more fit. Guides carry GPS and VHF comms. Contact Jeanne for further details. At N$220 per head this is good value for money and is recommended. *Inshore Safaris*, PO Box 2444, 12th Rd, opposite **Walvis Bay Tourism Information Bureau**, T202609, F202198, T081-1285223 (mob), www.inshore.com.na An excellent local company with plenty of experience. If visiting from overseas contact in advance to organize regional tours to suit your timetable and budget. Tours from 7-17 days can be planned, covering both popular and less frequently visited sights. Their Kaokoland and Damaraland tour can be strongly recommended. The company is also only one of two local operators offering day trips to the spectacular Sandwich Harbour. The company also has the only concession to go into the Walvis Bay saltworks and oyster farm for half-day birdwatching tours featuring a cast of flamingos and pelicans amongst the 40-plus species that can be observed. Ask for Chris and enjoy Namibia in another light. *Kuiseb Delta Adventures*, T/F200191, kdelta@iway.na Offers quad-bike tours of the Kuiseb Delta including a visit to a nara plantation and a Topnaar graveyard. You may want to check whether the owner has okayed this with the Topnaars themselves before taking such a tour. *Levo Fishing and Pleasure Tours*, PO Box 1860, T207555, levo@namibnet.com, at the Walvis Bay Yacht Club on the lagoon. Seal and dolphin cruises and/or quality fishing tours with local fishermen who have years of experience. Clients have the choice to fish from boats or remote beach locations, always remember to protect yourself from the sun. The principal angling season is between Nov and Mar; sharks can be caught all year round. The largest are usually caught between Nov and May. Deep sea trips also available with sufficient advance notice. *Mola Mola Safaris*, PO Box 980, T205511, F207593. Daily dolphin and seal tours around the harbour and fishing trips for the enthusiast. Ask for Neels or Megan. *Westair Wings Charters*, PO Box 741 Walvis Bay, T200094, charter@ wb.westwing.com.na, Windhoek-based charter outfit who have recently opened a local office. Working with *Inshore Safaris* (see above) now offering scenic flights over the desert, the coast and into Damaraland. Any feedback welcomed.

The *Tourist Information Centre*, PO Pvt Bag 5017, T205981, F204528, is located just inside the civic centre, a large complex set back from 10th St, opposite 2nd Rd. The office is well run by the ever-helpful Renate. Make this your first stop in Walvis Bay and you will get a lot more out of the town and its surrounds. *Walvis Bay Tourism* PO Box 926, T209170, F209171, walvisinfo@iml.com.na, a privately run Information Bureau at 12th Rd opposite the Probst Bakery, is supported by tourist companies in the town and is also a source of up-to-date and useful information. **Tourist information**

Local Car hire *Avis*, T207520, 405544, Rooikop airport. *Budget*, T204624, F202931, 081-1286900 (mob), Rooikop airport. *Imperial*, T207391, 081-1278110 (mob), Nangolo Mbumba Drive. **Transport**

Long distance Air: Airport at Rooikop, 10 km east of town off the C14. There are direct flights to Windhoek, Johannesburg and Cape Town. *Air Namibia*, T203102, 202938. *SA Express*, T2012222, fly from South Africa. Airport Shuttle Service, T207224.

Road: 30 km to Swakopmund, 389 km to Windhoek. For *Intercape* luxury coach service to Windhoek (5 hrs) via Swakopmund, see timetable on page 382. Coaches arrive and depart from outside the Omega Service Station, corner Sam Nujoma and

The Coast

15th Rd. **NB** Namibia daylight saving – service departs 1 hr earlier between the first Sun in Apr and the first Sun in Sep.

Train: T208504. If you are not in a hurry there is an overnight train service to Windhoek. This train is a useful way of returning to Swakopmund if you have been visiting Walvis Bay on a day trip without your own vehicle. For trains to Tsumeb via Usakos and Otjiwarongo, and Windhoek, see timetable on page 383 . Both services stop at Swakopmund (90 mins).

Directory **Useful addresses** *Club Internet*, 13th Rd, T206627. *Hospital*, T203441. **Police**, T202055. *Private Clinic*, T207063. *Pharmacy*, T202271, 205051. *MRI Medrescue*, T200200, 24-hr response.

North of Swakopmund – the Skeleton Coast

Henties Bay

Phone code: 064
Colour map 1, grid C3

Named after Major Hentie van der Merwe who started fishing here in 1929, this is the most northerly settlement of any note on the Namibian Atlantic seaboard. For much of the year it is just a quiet collection of bungalows on a windswept, sand blasted coast, coming to life during the summer season with around 10,000 visitors. Traditionally, most of these visitors have been Afrikaans-speakers, either from the interior or from the Jo'burg/Pretoria areas, intent on some serious fishing. Apart from the splendid coastline and fine sandy beach, there is little else to do here, and the majority of international visitors are unlikely to find much of interest here, unless it's solitude you want!

The first main road to the left after the tourist office, Duineweg, leads to the best hotel in town. As you turn left look out for Benguela Street on the left, where all the shops are. Opposite the *Hotel de Duine* is a dramatic 9-hole **golf course** set in a valley leading down to the beach. A round here will test your ability to cope with windy conditions.

Sleeping
Most of the accommodation consists of holiday flats and apartments which get booked months in advance over the peak Christmas period. For the remainder of the year there should be no difficulty in finding somewhere to stay unless you happen to coincide with a fishing tournament or festival. **D** *Hotel de Duine*, PO Box 1, Duine Rd, T500001, F500724. 20 rooms with TV and en suite bathroom and a restaurant known for its good seafood. Attached bar with slot machines and odd shape pool tables, and outside a swimming pool, squash court, recently refurbished. Clear views across Atlantic from its high perch, close to the beach and golf course, the last comfortable hotel north of Swakopmund on the coast. Useful source for local information. **E** *Die Oord Restcamp*, PO Box 82, Elf St, T/F500239. Clean, simple self-catering holiday flats. 8 four-bed, 4 five-bed and 3 six-bed chalets. Peaceful location just to the north of town. As with much of the accommodation in the region these will only be fully booked during local school holidays. For much of the rest of the year you may well be the only guests. **E** *Eagle Holiday Flats*, PO Box 20, 175 Jakkelsputz Rd, T500032, F500299. Whitewashed self-catering flats, clean with tiled floors, TV, a bit stark, part of the Eagle Centre complex where there is a supermarket, restaurant, bottle store and Total petrol.

Eating
Eagle Steak Ranch, Jakkelsputz Rd, T500543. Generous helpings of solid Namibian fare, strong emphasis on steaks, but still a pleasant place to eat. *Hotel de Duine*,

T500001. Well known for its seafood, a good place to try crayfish, but order in advance to guarantee freshness. *Spitzkoppe*, Duine Rd, T500394. Restaurant with a lively bar and gambling parlour. A busy spot in season, but quiet for the rest of the year.

There are also a number of early morning/late night snack bars, takeaways and the *Which Way* coffee shop.

Directory

As you approach from Swakopmund look out for a petrol station on the left just before a right turn to Usakos. Beyond the petrol station is the **Post Office** on the corner of Pelican St. A left here will take you to the seafront. Just beyond the Usakos turning, on the right, is the *Namib-i*, T500880, tourism office, housed in a new brick building. The **police station**, T500201, is just behind the building. There is a branch of *Bank Windhoek* just past the information office with a 24-hr ATM. This is the last bank for some distance if you are travelling away from Swakopmund. The next banks are located in Omaruru or Khorixas.

Transport

Driving out of Henties Bay there are 3 different routes to explore, assuming that you have approached from Swakopmund. The easiest route to follow is the **D1918** inland, passing close to the Klein Spitzkoppe (1,572 m) and Gross Spitzkoppe (1,784 m) before joining the **B2** near Usakos. The other two routes will take you into some of Namibia's finest wilderness areas. Just north of the village the **C35** turns east into the heart of Damaraland; this is the road to Uis and the Brandberg (2,573 m). Finally you can follow the **C34** along the coast, this road will take you as far as you are allowed to self drive in the Skeleton Coast National Park – the government-run camp at Terrace Bay, which is 273 km from Henties Bay. En route you will pass the camps at Mile 108 and Torra Bay.

Henties Bay

N

Not to scale

2 Die Oord Restcamp
3 Eagle Holiday Flats

● Eating
1 Eagle Steak Ranch
2 Spitzoppe

■ Sleeping
1 De Duine

The coast road

Unless you are just visiting **Cape Cross** for the day it is advisable to be self-sufficient if you continue to drive north along the coast. Make sure you fill up with petrol in Henties Bay as well as with drinking water and food. As noted above it is possible to drive as far north as Terrace Bay; once you have crossed the **Ugab River** you are in the **Skeleton Coast National Park** (southern section). To travel beyond the Ugab River requires a MET permit from the office in Swakopmund or any other MET office. It is possible to stay at **Torra Bay** and **Terrace Bay**, approximately 273 km from Henties Bay where petrol is available. There are two roads leading inland from the coast, but remember that this is a sparsely populated region and care should be taken when driving on these gravel and sand roads. If you have an accident or a breakdown you may have a long wait before the next vehicle comes along. Once you have driven as far as Cape Cross you should be well aware of the possible dangers.

The Coast

National West Coast Recreational Area

Colour map 1, grid C3   The National West Coast Tourist Recreational Area extends from the northern boundary of the Namib-Naukluft National Park to the Ugab River. The Ugab forms the southern boundary of the Skeleton Coast Park. Although part of the protected Skeleton Coast, this area is not subject to quite the same stringent controls as those that apply to areas of the Skeleton Coast National Park. The area is open all year round and there are no restrictions on when you can travel through here. For most visitors the only area of interest is the **seal colony** at Cape Cross; the rest of the coastline is flat and monotonous, and most visitors come for the fishing. If you are not visiting the Skeleton Coast National Park there is no point travelling beyond Cape Cross – shipwrecks such as the *Winston* are very disappointing and the Messum Crater can only be visited with a guide and a four-wheel drive vehicle.

Sleeping   Between Swakopmund and the Skeleton Coast National Park there are 4 campsites, all managed by *Namibia Wildlife Resorts*: **Mile 14**, **Jakkalspütz**, **Mile 72** and **Mile 108**. They are very basic sites designed to serve the needs of the angler more than the holidaymaker. Each site has communal washing facilities and sheltered eating areas. You must bring all your own food, fuel and camping equipment. A simple shop appears at some of the sites during the local school holidays during Dec-Jan. Water has to be paid for at Mile 72 and Mile 108. During the Christmas school holidays it is usually possible to purchase fuel at these 2 campsites. Anyone looking for more comfort should consider *Hotel de Duine* in Henties Bay or try the new *Cape Cross Lodge* (see below) next to the seal colony.

Cape Cross Seal Reserve   Pick up any tour brochure in Swakopmund and you will see trips to Cape Cross being advertised. There are 23 breeding colonies of **Cape fur seals**, *Arctocephalus pusillus*, along the coast of South Africa and Namibia and this is reputed to be one of the largest and best known. Apart from being the location of an important seal colony the reserve has had an interesting history.

Colour map 1, grid C3

In 1485 the Portuguese navigator, Diego Cão landed at Cape Cross. This was the furthest any European had so far reached down the coast of Africa, and to mark the event he erected a stone cross on the isolated stony headland, inscribing it thus: "Since the creation of the world 6,684 years have passed and since the birth of Christ, 1,484 years and so the Illustrious Don John has ordered this pillar to be erected here by Diego Cão, his knight." Diego Cão died at Cape Cross and was buried in some high ground close by. His original cross was later removed and taken to Berlin by the Oceanographical Museum. In 1974 the whole area was landscaped and a couple of replica crosses now stand amongst the rocks.

As you walk to the shoreline from the office you pass a small graveyard which dates from the turn of the century. Between 1899 and 1903 there was a small thriving community at Cape Cross which was involved in the collection of guano from nearby islands in a salt pan. The records show that 124 people died and were buried here. Around 1900 this was a busy little port which was even served by a railway. The guano industry was so prosperous that a 16-km railway track was laid across the salt pan to facilitate the collection of guano. In its heyday there were steam locomotives working here.

Estimates as to the number of seals here vary between 80,000 and as many as 250,000 during the breeding season (November/December). The bulls start to arrive here in October to claim the land for their cows. The whole scene during the birth of the young pups can be quite disturbing as many of the newly born seals get crushed by adults, others drown, and then there is always the threat posed by jackals and hyenas. The colony is located just beyond the crosses, a short drive from the entrance. This has to be one of the smelliest places in Namibia and it really is a relief to get away again after having taken in the sight of tens of thousands of seals basking on the rocks or surfing amongst the waves.

■ *Daily 1000-1700. A short distance into the reserve is an office. N$10 adults, N$10 car. The only facilities here are some toilets, fresh drinking water and a couple of small kiosks. Getting there: 55 km north of Henties Bay just off the C34. Entrance gate 3 km from the junction.*

Sleeping A *Cape Cross Lodge*, PO Box 259 Henties Bay, T0812538998/061240616, maripet@iafrica.com.na Not yet open to business in Sep 2001, this new hotel in Cape Dutch style is situated on the beach just north of the seal colony – but out of the 'smell zone' – and has 8 en-suite rooms each with private balcony with sea views. Offers tours into the desert and to the Tsiseb Conservancy comprising the Messum Crater, the Brandberg and Ugab River West. The rate includes dinner, bed, breakfast and afternoon tea. Reports very welcome.

About 33 km north of Cape Cross the salt road divides in two. The salt road, **C34**, continues to follow the coastline towards the campsite at **Mile 108**, while the side road, **D2303**, turns inland and heads towards the Brandberg West Copper Mine. This road is heavily corrugated and best driven in a four-wheel drive. As you approach the entrance gate to the Skeleton Coast National Park there is a signpost for the wrecked fishing boat, *Winston*. Do not drive on the salt pans, despite their dry appearance, it is easy to get stuck here. Visitors with the correct permit can drive on into the national park.

A pleasant alternative to visiting the Skeleton Coast is to join the Ugab River Hike which starts from Ugabmund and follows the river inland before looping through some hills where there are some caves and natural springs. If you have the time this is a walk worth joining, a very interesting way of learning about the environment and life on the Skeleton Coast. The full hike is 50 km long and usually takes three days to complete. Hikers must bring and carry all their own food and bedding for the duration. As with the Fish River Canyon hike a medical certificate must be handed over to the trails officer. ■ *Second and fourth Tue each month, Apr-Oct, limited to 8 people, N$200pp.*

Ugab River hike

Sleeping F *Save the Rhino Trust Ugab River Base Camp*, a community camp run in conjunction with Save The Rhino Trust. Simple campsites with basic showers and toilets, and craft shop. Visitors will need to be completely self-sufficient as there are no supplies for sale here. The camp serves as a base for patrols monitoring the desert rhino and elephant populations, and local community members are also available to provide visitors with assistance or to act as guides on game drives or walks. Bookings not necessary – payment in cash N$ or South African rand. To get there, drive north from Henties Bay on the coast road as far as Mile 100 and immediately after the campsite turn right onto the D2303. The road ends 75 km later at the campsite. The last 6 km are a bit rocky but should be OK even for saloon cars, providing sufficient care is taken. For further details contact the *Save the Rhino* office on Knobloch St, Swakopmund, opposite the Karakulia factory.

The Coast

Skeleton Coast National Park

Colour map 1, grid C3

The Skeleton Coast is one of the finest and most unusual coastal wildernesses in the world. It stretches between Swakopmund in the south to the mouth of the Kunene River, marking the border with Angola. The strong currents and swirling fogs of this Atlantic coastline had long been a hazard to shipping and when the term Skeleton Coast was first applied to it in 1933 by newspaperman, Sam Davis, the term stuck. Davis had been reporting on the search for a Swiss airman, Carl Nauer, whose plane had disappeared along the coast while trying to break the Cape Town to London solo air record. No trace was ever found. Today it is the elements that were responsible for so much loss of life – the desert, wide-open space, isolation and solitude – that attract the majority of visitors to the coast.

Ins & outs

Getting there The park can be entered in the south, from the West Coast Recreational Area, or in the east from Damaraland. Whichever gate you enter by you must make sure there are sufficient hours of daylight to either travel through the park or reach your camp. The southern gate, by the Ugab River, is known as **Ugabmund** and is about 207 km from Swakopmund; it is a further 162 km to the camp at Terrace Bay. The eastern gate, **Springbokwasser**, is 178 km from Khorixas. The quality of the road heading inland from the gate is not as good as the coast road. Torra Bay is 50 km from the gate, Terrace Bay 98 km. Permits are required to travel in the park, and all accommodation must be booked and paid for in advance. **Best time to visit** The park is open all the year round, but the camp at Torra Bay is only open Dec-Jan. During the Christmas period both Torra Bay and Terrace Bay get quickly booked up, mostly by local fishermen. As in Swakopmund it never gets too hot thanks to the cooling influence of the ocean, but during the winter months it can get cold at night.

Background

In order to get the maximum out of the park it is worth making the arduous journey as far north as Terrace Bay, assuming there is accommodation available. Driving between Swakopmund and Henties Bay will quickly make you realize how repetitive and dull much of this coastline is,

The Skeleton Coast

Möwe Bay — Lighthouse
Hoanib
Skeleton Coast Park -North (Limited access)
0 km 20
0 miles 20
Hunkab
Control Gate — Seal Beach — Dunes
Terrace Bay
Atlantic 1977 — Uniab Delta
Torra Bay — Uniab
Henrietta 1968 — Torra Bay (Open Dec & Jan only)
Koichab — Springbokwasser
Montrose II 1973 — National Park Gate
Luanda 1969 — Salt Pans
Bergsig
Atlantic Pride — Toscanini Diamond Mine — Huab
Oil Rig — Sand Dunes
Ambrose Bay — Gravel Plains
South West Sea - 1976 — Skeleton Coast Park -South
Durissa Bay — Park Boundary
NP Gate — Hike — Ugab
Winston 1970 — Salt Pans — Brandberg West
Mile 108
Messum — D2303
Bocock's Bay — Messum Crater
Horing Bay — National West Coast Recreational Area
Seal Reserve
Cape Cross — Cape Cross
Mile 72 — C35
Omaruru
Henties Bay
Cape Farilhao — D1918
Jakkalspütz
Lichen Fields
Rock Bay
Mile 14
Swakopmund
Pelican Point — Rössing Mine — Khan — To Windhoek
Walvis Bay

To Palmwag & Sesfontein
D2620
D3245
To Twyfelfontein & Khorixas
To Khorixas
To Spitzkoppe

- - - - 4WD only

but once you get out of the vehicle and start to explore the dry rivers and the occasional salt pans on foot, the park can be enjoyed at a different level. The peace and solitude is amazing, the air is clean and fresh and at night the stars are like you've never seen them before. If this does not sound like fun then proceed no further north than Henties Bay, where you can take the C35 and head inland for a different area of Namibia.

For many people the Skeleton Coast is synonymous with shipwrecks – just **Shipwrecks** about every photograph promoting the wild coastline will include a rusting, beached hull. The Portuguese used to call the area the Sands of Hell and before the days of modern communications and transport this 1,600 km long coastline represented a real threat to shipping. Sailors knew that if they did survive a wrecked ship then their problems had only just begun. The land behind them was a dry desert, and there were very few known natural sources of drinking water. The few places that did occasionally have drinking water (the riverbeds) were home to wild animals such as lion, leopard and elephant, which in turn represented another threat to the sailors' lives. A third factor that added to the dangers for survivors was the remoteness. Before 1893, when the first people were landed at Swakopmund, there was no settlement of note along more than 1,000 km of coastline. Which way would you head off if you had survived? Unfortunately the most spectacular wrecks are all found in the areas which are closed to the public in the far north. A little background to some of the wrecks has been included in the route description below.

Between Ugabmund and Terrace Bay the coastal road crosses four westward **Wildlife** flowing rivers: the Ugab, Huab, Koichab and Uniab. These ephemeral rivers only flow when sufficient rain has fallen in the interior, and even then they will only flow for a short period each year. For the rest of the year they represent long narrow oases that are home to migratory birds, animals and the few plants that can flourish under drought conditions.

The animals which may be seen in the park have all adapted in different ways to overcome some of the problems the desert creates. The smaller species such as genet, caracal, baboon, springbok, jackal and brown hyena live in the desert all year round; the larger animals, such as black rhino, elephant and lion, tend to migrate along the channels in search of food and water. The lion may well no longer occur along the coast, but when they were roaming the beaches they were known to have fed upon Cape cormorants, seals and the occasional stranded whale. Gemsbok, kudu and zebra are occasionally seen inland in the mountainous regions, while at the coast the Uniab Delta is a good location for viewing gemsbok. During low tide black-backed jackals can be seen on the beach scavenging on dead birds, fish and seals. There is stiff competition for scraps among the hyena, ghost crabs, crows and gulls.

While the sighting of an elephant or some kudu would normally be a great thrill, most visitors to the coast are on the lookout for the diverse birdlife. More than 200 bird species have been recorded within the park including vagrants which have been blown off course during the winter. Most of the birds live along the coast since there are few areas of wetlands with fresh water inland. At the seashore look out for sanderling, turnstone, several species of plover as well as cormorants and Arctic terns. Further inland along the riverbeds you will come across birds which favour gravel plains and cliff faces. Along the Ugab River hiking trail the augur buzzard, peregrine falcon, black eagle and rock kestrel have all been seen; after a little rain the reed beds are home to a few weavers and warblers.

The Coast

Vegetation   Like much of the wildlife, most of the plants growing in the park occur in the four major riverbeds which dissect the park. Two of the most common shrubs are the **dollar bush**, *Zygophyllum stapfii*, and **brakspekbos** *Zygophyllum simplex*, both of which can be found in the riverbeds. The former is a semi-deciduous shrub with small leaves shaped like a 'dollar' coin. It will only grow where there is some groundwater as it has not adapted to make use of the sea mist. Brakspekbos, a food source for the black rhino, can be recognized by looking for an off-green carpet in a shallow depression where rainwater would drain.

The only other vegetation you are likely to come across are the amazing variety of lichens. The bright orange lichens, which cling to rock outcrops facing the ocean, add a welcome splash of colour to the grey landscape. Over a hundred different species have been recorded in the Skeleton Coast National Park, all depending upon the coastal fog for moisture, in the moist air the plants become soft and many change colour.

Essentials   To travel north of the Ugab River you must have a permit, available from the MET office in Bismarck St, Swakopmund. No motorcycles are allowed into the park. You will not be allowed to cross the Ugab River after 1500 or to pass the gate at Springbokwasser after 1700 if heading for Terrace Bay. Each gate can issue a day permit to drive directly through the park but you must enter the park before 1500 to allow sufficient time for the journey. *Entrance charge* adults N$20 per day, car N$10. Petrol is available at Terrace Bay all year round and Torra Bay when it is open during Dec-Jan. There is also a basic grocery store at Terrace Bay. All camps have plenty of freezer space for anglers. If you are planning on spending a night in the park you will be required to produce your reservation form from Windhoek.

Sleeping   All campsites and rooms have to be booked in advance through NWR in Windhoek. There are only two sites within the national park, **Terrace Bay** and **Torra Bay**, see below for details. Torra Bay is **only open** during **Dec-Jan**. Accommodation at Terrace Bay is all-inclusive; Torra Bay is a basic campsite – you will need to bring everything with you, even the water for the showers has to be trucked in.

Durissa Bay to Terrace Bay

Colour map 1, grid C2   The boundary between the National West Coast Recreational Area and the Skeleton Coast National Park is marked by the **Ugab River** which flows into Durissa Bay. The Ugab is one of Namibia's major rivers, rising over 500 km inland, east of Outjo; after good rains it is an important source of water in Damaraland. A giant skull and crossbones adorns the gate by the Ugabmund park office. If you are staying in the park you must produce your booking permit at the office. **NB** This gate closes at 1500 each day for traffic going as far as Terrace Bay or Springbokwasser. If you are staying at *Mile 108* you can go into the park at a later time so long as you return to Ugabmund by sunset.

As you cross the wide river notice the variety of trees and shrubs growing in the sandy bed. Some of the well-established plants are stunted since they have had to survive in windswept conditions with long periods of moisture stress. Whenever you approach these riverbeds try to be as quiet as possible since there is always a chance of seeing a small herd of springbok resting in the shade or a shy family of kudu browsing the acacia trees.

Once across the river the salt road stays close to shore. One of the first shipwrecks you see is the *South West Sea*, wrecked in 1976. Just after you have crossed the **Huab River** there is a signpost indicating an **old oil rig**. While you will see the remains of various mining ventures along the coast, this is the only case of oil exploration. In the 1960s Ben du Preez went ahead and erected the rig

Twitching for a Tern

If you are not fishing on the Skeleton Coast there is a high chance you will be looking at the birds which at times seem to be everywhere. It has been estimated that over 300,000 wading birds seasonally visit the Namib coast. Some of the most popular birds are also those that are the easiest to identify: plovers, cormorants, sandpipers, flamingos and white pelicans. But this stretch of coast is also home to one of the rarest and smallest terns found in the world, the Damara tern (Sterna balaenarum).

It has been estimated that of the 2,000 breeding pairs left in the world, 1,800 inhabit Namibia; the rest are found close by along the coast in South Africa and

Angola, where they favour the open coastline and its sandy bays. The Damara tern is only 23 cm long, with a white breast and a black head. In flight it is similar to a swallow. Such a small bird is not able to carry much food for the young so to limit the amount of flying they have to do they tend to nest close to the food supply. Their size also influences the more precise location of their nests. They are unable to defend their nests against jackals and hyenas, so to try and avoid predators they nest on the salt pans and the gravel plains up to 5 km inland. This is another reason for observing the park off-road regulations, for once disturbed a breeding pair will abandon the chick.

despite numerous warnings that the scheme was unlikely to succeed. Today the rusty rig lies on its side providing the perfect nesting area for a breeding colony of Cape cormorants. Between September and March visitors are asked to stay in the car park so as not to disturb the birds during the breeding season. On the beach you can visit the wreck of the fishing schooner, *Atlantic Pride*.

About 50 km from the park entrance you reach the point marked Toscanini on most maps. This is the site of a derelict **diamond-mine** – only a few small diamonds were ever found. Today the legacy of the operations are a few cement slabs which acted as foundations for the buildings and the ruins of the sorting plant. There are a couple more wrecks in the ocean here, but there is little to see.

Soon after crossing the Koichab River, which has more sand than vegetation, there is a junction in the road. This is the only other access road for the Skeleton Coast Park, the D3245. A right here leads to **Springbokwasser** gate, 40 km inland. There are some fine sand dunes along this stretch of road as well as some *welwitschia* plants growing in the dry riverbeds.

Continuing north on the salt road you reach the seasonal fishing resort, **Torra Bay**. In the 16th century, Portuguese sailors named it Dark Hill after the dark capped hills which they could see while they were looking for fresh water. These days there is a very simple, **F** *Camp Site* at Torra Bay, managed by NWR. This site is only open for December and January. Anyone planning on staying here must be totally self-sufficient, though during the holiday season petrol and a few basic groceries are also available. Aside from the solitude the great attraction for this site is the excellent fishing. During the few months the camp is open it is necessary to book a pitch if you plan on spending a night here. Despite restrictions on where to fish and drive there has been extensive damage caused by vehicles on the beaches.

Torra Bay

Between the temporary camp at Torra Bay and the permanent camp at Terrace Bay is one of the most interesting attractions in the southern part of the Skeleton Coast National Park, the **Uniab River Delta**. The river has split into five main channels plus a number of reed ringed pools which are formed by

Uniab River Delta

The Coast

seepage from the riverbed. After good rains this is the perfect spot for birders. There are a number of walks in the delta, including a trail to a waterfall and a small canyon, which lie between the road and the beach. Check with the parks authorities what the situation is here from year to year since the amount of rainfall and the size of the flood can change the lie of the land between seasons. But if you hear there is water here then it is well worth the drive. Within the delta are several hides and parking spaces, each with a different view of the system. Look out for the shipwreck, *Atlantic*, at the river mouth.

Terrace Bay Having enjoyed the delta it is a short drive to the final destination, **Terrace Bay**. The camp and all the outbuildings were once part of the mining operation owned by Ben du Preez. When the company was declared bankrupt the state inherited all the facilities at the camp. **Sleeping** Bookings can only be made through the Central Reservations Office in Windhoek. **B** *Bungalows* with en-suite facilities, the price includes all three meals plus freezer space for anglers. There is a grocery shop with basic supplies and petrol is also available. The camp is built next to an old mine dump. There is an airfield to the north of the complex. Visitors to the park are allowed to drive a further 14 km along the coast to Seal Beach, this being the absolute northern limit for private visitors. At this point you are over 380 km from Swakopmund in the heart of the Skeleton Coast National Park.

Skeleton Coast Wilderness

When reading about Namibia's desert from Oranjemund to the Angolan border, a recurrent theme is the emphasis placed upon how fragile the desert environment is and the need to control people's access to the most sensitive areas. When the Skeleton Coast National Park was proclaimed in 1967 the park was divided into two zones, each one about 800,000 ha in extent. The southern zone is the 210-km long coastal strip between the Ugab River in the south and the Hoanib River to the north. The boundary of the park extends no more than 40 km inland. Access to the northern zone is tightly controlled and, for the tourist, limited to those who join the exclusive fly-in safaris organized by the sole concessionaire in Windhoek.

The northern section of the park extends from the Hoanib River (although tourists are only permitted to travel 14 km north from Terrace Bay camp, as far as Seal Beach) to the Kunene River, which forms the border with Angola – a distance of about 290 km. This section of the national park is managed as a wilderness area and is sometimes referred to as the **Skeleton Coast Wilderness**. While the government has chosen to allow a private operator access to this area, there are still tight controls in place on how the operation must be run in order to guarantee a minimum of environmental impact from each tour group. In addition to these regulations, most of the area is also off-limits to the concession holder. Access to the northern section is limited to the area between the Hoarusib and Nadas Rivers, a strip of coastline measuring about 90 km long by 30 km wide.

Official tours There is only one company which holds the rights to organize fly-in safaris to the wilderness areas of the Skeleton Coast, *Wilderness Safaris*, PO Box 6850 Windhoek, Namibia T061-274500, F239455, www.wilderness-safaris.com The concession is technically held by the company *Olympia Reisen* and considerable controversy has surrounded their operations on the Skeleton Coast. However, they have now sub-leased the concession to *Wilderness Safaris* – a well-known and entirely reputable operator in southern Africa. The company recommends that all tours should be booked through a specialist Africa travel agency in your own country.

Tours depart twice a week on Wed and Fri and cost US$2645 per person sharing for the 4-day safari and US$2930 per person sharing for the 5-day trip. For these bargain prices you can expect unique access to close on 240,000 ha of the Skeleton Coast National Park with its vast sand dunes, towering canyons, seal colonies and shipwrecks. With luck you will see a wide range of desert-dwelling wildlife such as springbok, gemsbok, desert elephants, brown hyena, jackal, ostrich and, if you are extremely lucky, cheetah. The day starts with breakfast in camp and then a day out in the park taking in the scenery, the flora and fauna before returning to camp for sundowner and dinner. This is the Namibia frequently used to promote the country as a tourist destination, yet ironically only a few hundred people get to enjoy it each year.

Unofficial tours   A typical 'alternative' safari might fly you into a private camp in the Huab Valley, visit Terrace Bay for the morning and then fly on to a camp in Kaokoland near the Kunene River before returning to Windhoek. On such a trip you will certainly get to see plenty of the Skeleton Coast as well as the remote north-east, but you will not have set foot in the wilderness areas. The cost of such a 4-day trip would be in the region of US$1,850 per person.

The Hinterland

*There are several routes from Windhoek to the coast. The most straightforward is to take the main B2 via Okahandja, Karibib and Usakos, which will take between three and four hours. More interesting though is to explore the hinterland and to travel via one of the three passes – the Bosua, Ushoogte or Gamsberg – and stop along the way to enjoy the spectacular views. Of the three, the Bosua is the quickest and provides the opportunity to stop and see the ruins of **Liebig Haus** and **Von François Fort**, while the Gamsberg is certainly the most dramatic.*

The Coast

All three routes are gravel roads without any petrol stations or shops along the way. Furthermore, they each include some extremely steep sections. If there has been heavy rain you may have difficulty negotiating certain sections in a heavily loaded, low-slung saloon car.

The Khomas Hochland is the rugged, upland area, lying between 1,750 m and 2,000 m, which joins the central highland plateau with the escarpment, where the land falls dramatically away to the gravel plains of the central Namib. The surface of the Hochland was laid down in Karoo times some 180-300 million years ago; subsequent erosion has carved out the sharp ridges and rolling hills characteristic of the area.

Following the C28 out of Windhoek past Daan Viljoen Game Park, the tar road turns to gravel near the first landmark, the **Matchless Mine**. Archaeological evidence suggests that copper mining and smelting was taking place in the Khomas Hochland area some 200-300 years ago, although commercial exploitation of the copper reserves only started in 1856. The first manager of the mine, run by the Walvis Bay Mining Company, was Charles John Andersson (see page 262). The mine was closed down for the first time in 1860, reopened briefly but without success in 1902 by the Deutsche Kolonialgesellschaft, and then reopened for the third time between 1970 and 1983 by the Tsumeb Corporation Limited (TCL). The collapse of world copper prices during the 1980s once more forced the closure of the mine, which is now abandoned and closed to the public.

Bosua Pass
Colour map 1, grid C5

A further 16 km down the road is the abandoned **Liebig House**, built in 1912 for Dr R Hartig, director of the Deutsche Farmgesellschaft. This double-storey house must once have been a splendid place to live, with its fountain in the main downstairs room and fine views over the surrounding rolling highlands. A little further on lie the ruins of **Von François Fort** named after the 'founder' of Windhoek. The fort was one of a number of military outposts built after Von François established his headquarters in Windhoek, and was designed to protect the route between Windhoek and Swakopmund. It was, however, later turned into a **Trockenposten**, or 'drying-out post', for alcoholic German soldiers!

The pass itself has a 1:5 descent down to the gravel plains of the Namib and is not suitable for trailers or caravans. West of here, the road heads straight as an arrow through the Namib to Swakopmund.

Ushoogte Pass
Colour map 1, grid C5

In Windhoek, take the main road towards the University of Namibia (UNAM) and ignore the turn-off south towards Rehoboth. Continue past the university out of town on the C26 for 32 km until the road branches right onto the D1982. This road continues past *Hohenhorst Guest Farm* towards the 1:10 Ushoogte Pass, on past *Niedersachsen Guest Farm* before eventually joining the main C14 highway to Walvis Bay.

Gamsberg Pass
Colour map 3, grid A2

Probably the most popular of the three passes, the Gamsberg is sometimes called Namibia's Garden Route. It certainly offers spectacular scenery, and is

The Hinterland

Sleeping		
1 Albrechtshöhe Game Farm	7 Okahandja Lodge	13 Swartfontein Guest Farm
2 Hakos Guest Farm	8 Okomitundu Guestfarm	14 Tsaobis Leopard Nature Park
3 Khan River Lodge	9 Prospect Hunting Lodge	15 Weissenfels Guest Farm
4 Melrose Game Farm	10 Rooisand Desert Ranch	16 Wilhelmstal Nord
5 Namibgrens	11 Rostock Ritz	
6 Namib-Naukluft Lodge	12 Solitaire Guest Farm	

well provided with accommodation and activities en route. The name is a mixture of the Nama word *gan* meaning 'closed' or 'shut' and the German *berg* meaning 'mountain', and refers to the flat-topped Gamsberg mountain (2,347 m) which dominates the view. This 1,000 million year old granite mountain rises 500 m above the surrounding highlands and has survived further erosion, thanks to a sandstone cap formed about 200 million years ago when most of this area was covered by an inland sea. It is worth stopping at the top of the pass to enjoy the views of the surrounding hills and to contemplate the snaking descent towards the desert floor. Before reaching the Namib, however, the road must still make its way through the Kuiseb Pass (see Kuiseb Canyon, page 273) after which it joins the C14 for the final 110 km stretch to Walvis Bay.

The Gamsberg region boasts some challenging terrain, and proximity to Windhoek attracts hikers, horse riders and four-wheel drive enthusiasts. Hikers will find a chat with *Gamsberg Trails*, T061-231603, gamsbergtrails@packsafari.com helpful. There are trails from most farms: the *Namibgrens Rest Camp* has one of the more popular, the Dassie Trail. Excellent multiple-day horse trails originate from *Farm Hilton*, T061-217940, F256300, www.reitsafari.com who have developed a challenging and well regarded nine-day trans-desert route to the sea, covering some 400km. The **Isabis** and **Weener** four-wheel drive trails are signposted off the D1265 and C26 respectively, both within 15 km of that junction.

Additionally, astronomically minded visitors will probably already be heading for *Hakos* guestfarm, a star-gazer's paradise, while hunters should book well ahead to enjoy *Prospect Hunting Farm*.

A *Rooisand Desert Ranch*, T062-572119, reservations T234342, F248338, bhuber@   **Sleeping**
mweb.com.na, about 30 km east of the C14/C26 junction at the base of the Gamsberg pass. Has 5 a/c rooms, TV, restaurant, bar, good size swimming pool. A good base from which to explore the Gamsberg Mountains on foot. Trips to Bushman paintings and the Kuiseb Canyon. **A** *Swartfontein Guest Farm*, T572004, reservations T061-226979, logufa@lianam.lia.net, on the D1261, 15 km south of the D1275 junction. Has 5 tastefully furnished rooms; Italian hosts; superb food. Recommended.
A *Prospect Hunting Lodge*, T/F061-234441, prospect@mweb.com.na, on the C26 just east of the Gamsberg Pass. Caters for small groups of hunters (or those not opposed to it, at least). They can accommodate a max of 4 hunters and up to 5 others. Guests typically stay 3-7 nights at a stretch. Rates are all-inclusive, game is on the menu; meals and booze are included, rooms are in a lovely old building, adorned with trophies and skins. Swimming pool, game and bird viewing at nearby dams. Your host, Ben Steenkamp, is your interesting, opinionated, outspoken hunting guide. Book in advance.

A/B *Game Farm Melrose*, T061-234298, F234606, 43 km southwest of Windhoek on the C26. A full activity set-up, with tame cheetah to feed, a swimming pool, game drives and walking trails, hunting, horseriding and horse/donkey carting, pool and billiards, table tennis, badminton/volleyball, etc. Almost all activities cost extra. 9 en-suite doubles, 1 luxury suite, bar, lounge restaurant. Also **F** well provided campsite at N$40pp, with ablutions, electricity and braai pits. **B** *Hohenhorst Guest Farm*, T061-234328, damuller@mweb.com.na, off the D1982, 24 km southwest of the junction with the C26, 56 km from Windhoek. Has 9 en-suite doubles, large swimming pool, pool table, excellent restaurant, hiking, riding and 4WD trails. **F** Camping also available. **B** *Farm Niedersachsen*, T062-572200, F572201, niedersa@natron.net, off the D1982, midway between Windhoek and Walvis Bay. Has 5 en-suite doubles set in rolling hills near the Kuiseb River. The farm is mentioned in *The Sheltering Desert*'and 4WD tours of surrounding landscape are available to enthusiasts. Good, clear night sky for stargazers.

The Coast

B/C *Hakos*, T/F062-572111, www.natron.net/tour/hakos, signposted 7 km north off the C26, 130 km from Windhoek. A star-gazer's paradise. Hakos is Nama for 'the place where no-one will disturb you'. The owner was manager of the neighbouring Max Planck Institute for Astronomy observatory for 25 years, which can be accessed. Hakos offers 'star tours' for beginners, and they often have enthusiasts (mostly German) with their own observation and photographic equipment, particularly in winter, when the skies can be relied on to be clear – and cold, they are 1,830 m above sea level. Take a look at www.ias.webwide.de for the Internationale Amateur Sternwarte's information, who operate here. 10 en-suite doubles, full board, heated indoor swimming pool. Guided mountain walks and challenging 4WD trails available. **F** camping at N$40pp. Recommended, for an introduction to the southern hemisphere's night sky. **C** *Weissenfels Guest Farm*, T062-572112. Follow C26 towards Gamsberg Pass from D1265 junction, follow signs. 5 basic, en-suite rooms, small swimming pool, hiking, horse riding and mountain biking trails, game viewing, bird watching in Gamsberg Mountains, good South African cuisine. They will accommodate campers, if asked.

D *Corona Guest Farm*, T/F572127, corona@natron.net, signposted off the C26 by the *Rooisand Desert Ranch*. 10 en-suite doubles on large farm at the foot of the Gamsberg Pass.

Usakos

Phone code: 064
Colour map 1, grid C4
211 km to Windhoek
147 km to Swakopmund

The first town east of the Namib desert on the main B2 road from Swakopmund, Usakos lies on the southern bank of the Khan River, nestled in the last hills before the Namib, at the edge of a vast expanse of nothingness. The town originally developed around the railway workshops which were built to service the narrow-gauge Otavi line, completed in 1906. Until 1960, the town prospered but when the old steam locomotives were replaced by diesel engines it lapsed into its present sleepy state.

Nowadays the town's main role is one of service centre to vehicles plying their way to and from Swakopmund /Walvis Bay and Windhoek. Although there is a decent small hotel in town, there doesn't seem any reason to stay here. As a reminder of the town's heyday, **Locomotive no 40** stands in front of the railway station, one of three Henschel steam trains built in Germany for her colony's narrow-gauge railway

Sleeping **D** *Bahnhof Hotel*, T530444, F530765, www.hop.to/namibia has been extensively rebuilt and reopened in summer 2001, with 10 large en-suite doubles with TV, a/c and telephone, bar with TV for rugby matches, beer garden, restaurant, conference room, secure parking. Young, friendly and informative hosts, the best bet in town. Recommended. **D** *Usakos Hotel*, T/F530259 has 10 en-suite doubles some with a/c, off-street parking, restaurant, ageing owners; rumoure dto have been subjected to arson in 2001 and while they are still open for business, this retains a faded feel. **E/F** *Die Bahnmeister*, T/F530554, is in an old railway building, with a locomotive out front, backing onto the tracks (and occasionally noisy, with trains infrequently passing through the night); 4 doubles, aiming for the backpacker market. **E-F** *Namib Würste Farm Shop and Camping*, T530283, on the B2 on the western outskirts of town is a good place for a lunch / coffee stop (open until 2000, and later for those staying the night), they have excellent biltong and rusks for sale, and whatever local produce is in season. They have 3 doubles (B&B), 24 beds in a train sleeper carriage (clean and fun, but a little warm in summer), a simple, good menu and grassy campsite, with ablutions and braai pits, no electricity.

Transport **Train** For trains to Swakopmund, Tsumeb via Otjiwarongo, and Windhoek via Okahandja, see timetable on page 383.

Eating is either at one of the hotels or from the takeaway at the Shell Ultra at the eastern edge, or Engen at the western edge, of town. Both are open 24 hrs. There is a supermarket, bottle store, butcher, post and telecoms office and *First National* (they have an ATM) at the Shell Ultra. Directory

Erongo Mountains

The Erongo Massif of towering granite mountains is easily visible about 40 km north of Usakos and Karibib. Like the **Brandberg** and **Spitzkoppe** inselberg, it is the remnant of an ancient volcano. A further attraction is the **Phillip's Cave** national monument, containing a number of Bushmen paintings, first made famous by the prehistorian Abbé Breuil (see page 195). Although most of the range is only accessible by four-wheel drive, it is possible to visit the *Ameib Ranch*, and take tours to the following sights and rock formations from there.

Guestfarms C/D-F *Ameib Ranch*, T530803, F530904, www.natron.net/tour/ameib/ main.html At Usakos turn onto D1935 towards Okombahe, after 12 km turn right onto D1937 to the farmhouse. Has 8 en suite double rooms, 2 cottages, 3 chalets, pleasant gardens, small plunge pool, restaurant and bar; plus a rest camp with 4 bungalows and camping facilities, communal ablution block, braai facilities, waterhole close to main house, good scenic and game walks and birdwatching. **Sleeping**

A short drive from Ameib Ranch, plus a 20-30 minute walk over a series of low hills, takes hikers up to the cave. This is in fact an overhang on one of the highest hills in the area and offers excellent views over surrounding countryside, making it easy to see why Bushmen used this place. There are numerous paintings of the Bushmen themselves, as well as buffalo and the famous white elephant. **Phillip's Cave**

Bull's Party and **Stone Elephant Head** Both sites have interesting rock formations, in particular the 'balancing' rocks at the Bull's Head.

Karibib

This tiny bustling town lies almost exactly half-way between Windhoek and Swakopmund on the main B2 highway. Although most people zip through on their way to and from the coast, there is more to the town than first meets the eye. There are a number of fine old colonial buildings on the main street, the **Navachab Gold Mine** just south of town and the internationally reputed **Marmorwerke**, or marble works, lying to the north of the town. *Phone code: 064*
Colour map 1, grid C5
175 km to Swakopmund
181 km to Windhoek

In the early years of the 20th century, the train between Windhoek and Swakopmund only travelled during the daytime, so passengers needed hotels for the overnight stop in Karibib. The present day **bakery**, on the left hand side coming from Okahandja, was one of these hotels and survived until 1950 when it was converted into a bakery. The **Rösemann Building**, a little further down the road, was built in 1900 and the façade has remained virtually unchanged since. Originally the headquarters of the trading firm Rösemann and Kronewitter, it was later converted into a hotel. The **granite building** further down the street, resembling a church, was in fact used by a local merchant, George Woll, as both his shop and living quarters. The **Christuskirche**, made partially of marble from the nearby marble works, dates back to 1910. **Sights**

Out of town, the **Marmorwerke** was started in 1904 and produces high quality marble, considered to be the hardest in the world. About 100 tonnes of marble is quarried each month. This is first cut up into smaller blocks and then processed into floor and bathroom tiles, ornaments and tombstones. It is hard to believe, but marble from Karibib is exported to Italy. The **Navachab Gold Mine**, lying southwest of town, was started in 1987, two years after gold was discovered on Navachab Farm. The gold is actually of quite low quality; 750,000 tonnes of rock are processed each year.

Sleeping   **In town D/E** *Hotel Erongoblick*, T550009. 15 doubles, 11 en-suite, swimming pool, squash court, restaurant, off-street parking in this former boarding school, which still retains the institutional feel. Clean and good value.
   Guestfarms in the area A *Etusis Lodge*, T064-550826, F550961, www.etusis.com, 36 km from Karibib, follow the signs from town. A HAN award winner with 7 en-suite thatched bungalows and 6 bush tents, restaurant, bar, swimming pool, waterhole, game drives, 4 well mapped hiking trails, mountain biking and horse riding. **B** *Okondura Nord Guest Farm*, T503983, F503968, www.natron.net/tour/okondura-nord, 19 km from Wilhemstal, look for signs from B2. Has 5 en-suite doubles, farm drives, walking trails.

Eating   Your best bet in the evenings is the *Western Bar and Restaurant*, lively with good food; alternatively the *Springbok Steakhouse* located in the old railway station. By day, the *Karibib Bakery & Café*, or a snack from the coffee shop at *Henckert's* (see below).

Sports   The *Klippenberg Country Club* is 2 km south of town (well signposted) and welcomes visitors to its 9-hole golf course, swimming pool, squash and tennis facilities. Non-players can enjoy good views from the bar/restaurant. Fairly empty except at weekends.

Transport   **Bus**   For *Intercape* buses to Swakopmund and Walvis Bay, and Windhoek, see timetable on page 382. **Train**   For trains to Swakopmund, and Windhoek via Okahandja, see timetable on page 383.

Directory   **Banks** *First National Bank* with ATM. **Services** 24-hr Total (as you head west) and Engen (east), small supermarket, butchery, bakery and post office. **Tourist office**   There is a small tourist office, a token but functional weavery, a few curios and an enormous range of (gem) stones, both local and imported, at the *Henckert Centre*, T550028, who also do coffee and simple meals and can arrange tours to the goldmine and marble quarry. Located on the main road, opposite the *Western Bar*.

Otjimbingwe

Colour map 1, grid C5
55 km south of
Karibib on the D1953

Once the administrative centre of German South West Africa, now a forgotten, dusty village in the bush, Otjimbingwe is situated south of Karibib at the junction of the Swakop and Omusema rivers. Opinions on the origins of the name of the town differ, the most common meaning given being 'place of refreshment', referring to the spring in the Omusema River.

History   The town rose to prominence due to its position on an established ox-wagon route half-way between Windhoek and Walvis Bay. A mission station was established here in 1849 by the Rhenish missionary, Johannes Rath, although it was not until 1867 that the first church was built. However, it was Otjimbingwe's role as a trading post that made it an important centre.
   In 1854, the Walvisch Bay Mining Company had made the settlement its headquarters after the discovery of copper in the area. A trading post was set up and soon a roaring trade, typical of the time, was going on in arms,

ammunition, alcohol and livestock. In 1860, the hunter, explorer and trader Charles John Andersson (see page 262) established his headquarters here, the first permanent trading post in the area. His subsequent involvement in the Herero-Nama wars to defend his trade routes was significant in drawing the small European population into Namibian tribal conflict, and further focused attention on Otjimbingwe.

After Curt von François moved his small garrison to Windhoek in 1890, the town started to decline and, following the construction of the narrow-gauge railway between Windhoek and Swakopmund in 1902 which bypassed the town, Otjimbingwe became increasingly irrelevant. A few historical monuments do still make the town of interest to students of 19th-century Namibian history.

Sights

The **church**, completed in 1867, is the oldest to have been built to serve the Herero community. Although Herero leader Zeraua was not himself a Christian, he arranged for 10,000 bricks to be made for the church. As with other early mission stations, the church doubled as place of worship and mini-fort during the on-off Herero-Nama wars of the time. The tower was only added later in 1899.

The **old powder magazine**, an 8-m tower, was originally built by the *Missionhandelgesellschaft*, or mission station trading company, to protect its goods during attacks by the Nama. Following the collapse of the company in 1882, the tower passed into the hands of the Hälbich trading firm.

The **wind motor** was put up in 1896 by the Hälbich family in order to generate power for their machinery in the wagon factory next door. The motor also pumped water to the settlement from a nearby fountain.

Sleeping

Guestfarms D *Tsaobis Leopard Nature Park*, T064-550881, F550954, tsaobis@ iafrica.com.na, 52 km south of Karibib, signposted 11 km off the C32, follow the signs from town. Has 10 2-bed self-catering bungalows, swimming pool, game viewing. Established as a leopard sanctuary in 1969, offers good hiking in rugged bush country with the chance of seeing the elusive leopard in its natural habitat. Book ahead.

Omaruru

The C33 tar road heads due north from just outside Karibib and 48 km later arrives at the small historical town of Omaruru. Set in the heart of game-farm country, the town is surrounded by an impressive array of mountains, the most prominent being the Oruwe or Omaruru kopjie southeast of town. Omaruru is renowned in Namibia these days for having the country's only vineyard, the Kristall Kellerei, and is a centre of mineral production and trading.

Phone code: 064
Colour map 1, grid C5
242 km to Windhoek
236 km to Swakopmund

History

The area around the town has been home both to humans and game for thousands of years, evident from the numerous sites of Bushmen art found here. Following in the footsteps of the Bushmen were the Damara and then the Herero who were probably grazing their cattle here from early in the 19th century. In fact, the name Omaruru is derived from the Herero *omaere omaruru* meaning 'bitter curd' which is apparently how the cattle's milk tasted after eating one particular local bush.

The first European to reach the area was the missionary Hugo Hahn on a visit to Omburo, east of Omaruru, in 1851. In 1867 the evangelist Daniel Cloete arrived with a group of Damara; however, due to drought, they left the following year. In 1868 Herero Chief Zeraua settled down here but it was only

The Coast

after another missionary, Gottlieb Viehe, arrived in 1870 that the town was 'officially' founded.

In 1858, Charles Andersson, attracted by the area's plentiful game, established a hunting camp on the banks of the Omaruru River. In 1870, the hunter Axel Eriksson and brewer Anders Ohissen formed a partnership to exploit the game and by 1880 they had succeeded in wiping out all the elephant, rhino, lion and giraffe that had once lived in the area.

Throughout the 1880s, Omaruru was a focal point for Herero-Nama battles, and was attacked repeatedly before peace was finally secured in 1889. As part of the consolidation of German rule in Namibia, a garrison was stationed here at the end of 1894, and following this the town started to grow. The first postal agency was opened in 1895 and in 1896 the garrison moved into a new fort – today serving as the magistrate's court. By the end of 1896 Omaruru had the largest population of European settlers in Namibia. However, the great rinderpest epidemic of 1897 wiped out the last remaining game in the area as well as taking a heavy toll on the settlers' cattle; many were forced to leave the area. Nevertheless, the military garrison continued to grow and a new barracks and sick bay were completed by 1901.

In 1904 the Herero rose up against the German occupiers and the town was besieged. At the time the military commander, Captain Franke, was away in the south helping to put down the Bondelswart uprising. Nevertheless, he marched 900 km in 20 days and broke the siege by leading a cavalry charge, thereby defeating the Herero. In 1907, to commemorate Franke's victory, work began on the **Franke Tower**, which was officially opened the following year.

In 1909 the town received full municipal status and over the course of this century continued to steadily grow. Today, Omaruru is a sleepy little town in the heart of guestfarm country.

Sights **Franke Tower** is on the southern bank of the Omaruru River. The tower was declared a national monument in 1963 and offers a good view over the town from the top. Usually kept locked, the key is available at either the *Central Hotel* or *Hotel Staebe*. Check the staircase inside: it looks a bit fragile.

The **Mission House**, the oldest building in Omaruru, now serves as the town museum, focusing on the early history of the area. Made from clay bricks, the house was built by missionary Gottleib Viehe and completed in 1872, and was where he completed the first translation of the gospel into Oshiherero. Later the house also served as a temporary military post and a meeting place between Herero and German leaders. Collect the key from the tourist office at the Municipality building on Wilhelm Zeraua Street.

The **Kristall Kellerei**, T570083, F570593, is the only vineyard operating in Namibia, and certainly worth a tour and/or meal before you leave town. Helmut Kluge planted 4 ha of Colombard and Ruby Cabernet vines in 1990 and since 1996 has been perfecting his Colombard white (to which he adds oak chips) and Ruby Cabernet red wine. Samples are sent each year to Stellenbosch for quality control, and he hopes to achieve 'export quality' wines in 2002. He produces between 4,000 and 6,000 litres per year, split equally between white and red, distribution of which he carefully controls so that he has a supply available for those coming to enjoy his meals and wine tours. From 2002, only he and a few chosen local guest houses will sell his wine. Bottling (into 500 ml bottles) takes place every August. He and his wife conduct wine tours personally throughout the year at a modest $10 per person, each one ending in a tasting in his restaurant. The food is recommended, either on its own or accompanied. Also worth a taste are his various schnapps

(schnapps, lemon, prickly pear and wine yeast). Before you ask, he will not be able to expand production due to the scarcity of water in the area.

Omaruru Game Park is only 800 ha in size, but home to a wide variety of animals and rare birds. It is a well vegetated park with plenty of old large trees and water points. You can expect to see giraffe, zebra, kudu, gemsbok, eland and klipspringer. For the keen birder there are eight species of birds to be seen which only occur in the Erongo region. Day trips to the park are organized by the *Omaruru Caravan Park*, for four to seven people per trip; tours depart at 1000 and return by 1700. Bring your own packed lunch and drinks. If you have an extra day this is a most enjoyable outing. Recommended.

In town D *Central Hotel*, T570030, F571100, central@africaonline.com.na has 10 double rooms and 2 rondavels, recently partly redecorated, colonial building with a classic shaded veranda, cool rooms, spacious, welcoming bar with TV, beer garden, swimming pool. **D/E** *Hotel Staebe*, T570035, F570450, staebe@iafrica.com.na is south of the river, with 24 stark en-suite doubles with phones and kettle, good German cooking, small bar with draught beer, swimming pool, off-street parking. A good value, clean hotel, recommended by locals. **D/E** *Naomi's Palm Garden*, T570142, F570165 is one small flat (3 bed) nicely decorated with African touches, fridge, coffee, breakfast available whenever you want it, secure parking, good value if you can get it, more personal than the others. **E** *Eva's B&B* has 3 en-suite doubles, breakfast served in the pleasant cacti/succulent garden; major improvements planned.

Camping **D-F** *Omaruru Caravan Park*, T570516, 6 simple chalets plus campsites with own braai facilities and bathrooms, tables, electricity and light, outdoor kitchens, green and clean, with cheap meals. **F** *Kashana Landhaus*, T570204, is a better bet, with 3 shaded sites with all amenities, restaurant and bar planned for 2002. No road noise and secure parking.

In the area Omaruru has an excellent selection, but each is quite pricey for what is offered. **A/AL** *Epako Lodge*, T064-570551/2, F570553, www.etosha.com/epako-game-lodge, 22 km northeast of Omaruru on C33, is a large lodge with 11,000 well-stocked ha, 21 en-suite rooms with a/c, telephone and mini-bar, excellent French cuisine, bar, swimming pool, tennis, TV lounge, guided walks on request, game drives to Bushman paintings, chance to see elephant, rhino, cheetah, leopard and wide range

Sleeping

The Coast

Omaruru

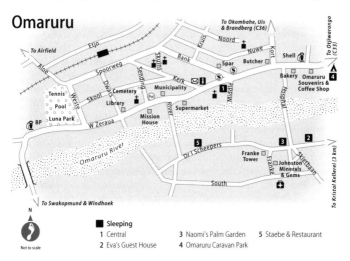

Sleeping
1 Central
2 Eva's Guest House
3 Naomi's Palm Garden
4 Omaruru Caravan Park
5 Staebe & Restaurant

of antelope (a bit like visiting the zoo, actually). Somewhat impersonal, and lacking in 'African' feel, but worth the trip for the food. **A** *Erongo Wilderness Lodge*, T064-570537, F570536, www.orusovo.com/erongo Located 11 km southwest of Omaruru on D2315. Just off the road is a (secure) car park that you must use unless you have a high-clearance 4WD – you will be transported the short distance to the lodge (walk if you arrive unannounced!). Has 10 en-suite, stilted cabins with thatched covers, straddling enormous granite rocks. Central lapa with restaurant, bar and lounge, lovely evening views of the enormous ruddy granite blocks; small swimming pool built among the rocks, scenic drives to rock art and plentiful game. New young South African couple are in charge. Part of the recently established Conservancy (200,000 ha), reintroduction of black-faced impala and black rhino planned, and involvement in leopard surveys. Pricey for fairly simple accommodation, but with masses of character and good range of activities. Book ahead. Recommended. **A/AL** *Omburo Health Resort*, T081-1291140, jstaby@mweb.com.na, 30 km east of Omaruru on D2328. Has 5 en-suite doubles with an adjoining lounge, jacuzzi in each room, small swimming pool, sauna and massages, small gym, healthy menu, TV lounge; excursions to nearby thermal spring. Nothing special, overpriced. **A/AL** *Roidina Safari Lodge*, T064-71188, T081-1259060 (mob), roidina@iafrica.com.na, 21 km north of Omaruru on C33 then 7 rough km along farm track. A newly completed (summer 2001), Swiss-owned lodge with 5 luxurious, thatched en-suite rondavels with large (mostly 4-poster) beds, fan and safe, plus one family suite on the first floor of the stunning, large thatched restaurant/bar overlooking waterhole. Swimming pool, game drives, landing strip. The owner was still looking for capable 'hands-on' management to create an enterprise around the excellent facilities. Self-catering units, mountain retreat and museum (old karakul and catte farming implements) planned. Call for progress report (possible hunting). Recommended, if it develops as planned. **A** *Erongo Lodge*, T570852, reservations T061-253992, F221919, www.discover-afrika.com, 45 km southeast of Omaruru, follow D2315, then D2316, follow signs. Has 5 en-suite doubles, bungalows, swimming pool, mainly a hunting farm, also has rock art in impressive Erongo Massif. **A** *Otjandaue*, T570821, 21 km east of Omaruru on D2328, a hunting lodge with nice bungalow for 3 doubles with fridge, lounge and piano, emblazoned with huge trophies and skins. Swimming pool; meals taken in pleasant outdoor thatched braai area. Rumours of imminent closure, call ahead.

B *Erindi-Onganga*, T290112, F232624, fjeske@mweb.com.na has 4 en-suite doubles, good home cooking, swimming pool, hiking, game drives, donkey-cart rides – a tranquil, remote, low-key guestfarm. To get there take C36 towards Uis and after 6 km turn right onto D2344. After a further 35 km turn onto D2351 and drive for 27 km, following signs to guestfarm. **B** *Immenhof*, T/F067-290177, www.colourgem.co.za is a businesslike tourist and hunting lodge catering mainly for Germans, with 9 large en-suite doubles, swimming pool, interesting farm tours (with rock art) and hiking trails. The owner is a multi-lingual (9 languages, including Herero and Ovahimbo) pilot, whose flights to isolated corners of the country (where he can translate) are recommended. **B** *Okosongoro Safari Ranch* , T/F290170, 38 km north of Omaruru on the C33. 'Place of the Zebras' (in Herero) with 5 en-suite rooms, good home cooking, game drives, walking trails, principally a hunting farm. **B** *Omaruru Game Lodge*, T064-570044, F570134, www.omaruru-game-lodge.com, 15 km east of Omaruru on D2329. Has 20 en-suite doubles in pretty thatched bungalows (5 s/c), set in shaded gardens with cactus-lined, lit paths, restaurant and bar overlooking dam, swimming pool and braai area. Game drives view all major antelopes, elephant, zebra, giraffe and maybe leopard. Caters for tour groups, but maintains an intimate atmosphere. **B** *RL Farm*, T081-1273040, www.rl-farm.de, 22 km southeast of Omaruru, signposted off the C33. A HAN 2000 award winner with 9 en-suite doubles in thatched bungalows, with fan and TV, swimming pool, half-board, attractively built, but principally a hunting farm, so book ahead. **B** *Schönfeld*, T/F067-290190, www.schoenfeld-namibia.de 40 km north of Omaruru, take the D2337 southwest for 13 km (and through 4 gates). Has fort ramparts that come into view from a distance, towering above the lovely old farmhouse with 7 en-suite doubles and 2 family rooms, great food, swimming pool, horse riding and game drives. Call ahead, they also do hunting.

D *Onduruquea Lodge*, T/F064-570832, onduru@iafrica.com.na, 28 km southeast of Omaruru, signposted off the C33. Has en-suite doubles in thatched bungalows with a/c, large swimming pool, game drives, bush walks, horse riding. **D-F** *Ondombo-West B&B*, T067-290117, signposted off the C33 1 km from the D2338 junction, is a working farm with 3 simple doubles in a bungalow adjoining the farmhouse; plus a new, clean campsite with electricity, lights, water and braai pit at each site, communal ablutions.

Eating Apart from the 2 hotel restaurants, the *Omaruru Souvenir Shop & Coffe Shop* serves excellent breakfast, lunchtime snacks and takeaways. It has a good curio shop and swimming pool at the back for patrons. Recommended.

Festivals Every year on the last weekend before **10 Oct**, the Herero hold a march to and from the cemetery where former leader Wilhelm Zeraua is buried. Worth a visit if you are in the area.

Shopping *Johnston Minerals and Gems*, Franke St, open 7 days, is owned by an American miner/geologist couple who have a good (legitimate) supply of local stones which they work on the premises; fairly priced and beautifully presented. He is a gemstone polisher and she has worked with gold for over 20 years. Worth a visit, they will take their time explaining the trade/stones to you.

Sport **Golf** *Club House*, T570516, still signposted from town, in total disrepair in summer 2001, this may change. **Swimming** The pool next to the tennis club is Olympic size. **Adventure sports** *Action Safaris*, T570185, F570451, actionsa@iafrica.com.na advertise quad-biking and microlighting for thrills, ostensibly to get you to/above the local flora and fauna of the game park.

Transport **Train** For trains to Swakopmund, Tsumeb via Otjiwarongo, and Windhoek via Okahandja, see timetable on page 383.

Directory **Banks** *First National Bank* and *Standard Bank*, on corner of Bank and W Zeraua streets, both with ATM. **Communications** Post Office, corner of Church and W Zeraua St, Mon-Fri 0800-1630, Sat 0800-1130. **Hospitals** Doctor, T570033. Hospital The State Hospital, T570037, follow Hospital St south over the river. **Tourist offices** *Namib-i*, W Zeraua St, T570261, next to the Post Office. Good information on the many excellent guestfarms in the area, with directions and up-to-date prices. **Useful addresses** Police, near corner of Sending St and W Zeraua St, T570010.

Rock Art **Anibib Farm**, located 52 km west of Omaruru on the D2315 (follow signs), is said to have one of the largest collections of rock paintings in Namibia. Over an area of 2,000 ha are a host of rock paintings depicting both humans and animals, as well as a range of Stone Age tools and jewellery which have been left in their original spots. There are two guided trips per day intended to give visitors a real insight into the paintings and tools and to ensure the preservation of the sites. Bookings should be made beforehand on T06622320 (farmline) 1711.

Kalkfeld

Phone code: 067
Colour map 1, grid B5
Kalkfeld is simply a staging post on the C33 between Omaruru and Otjiwarongo for those looking for the Dinosaur Footprints. The village has petrol (not 24 hour), a small general and bottle store, a post office and police station.

Dinosaur Tracks
About 150-200 million years ago, the 25 m tracks of a two-legged, three-toed dinosaur were embedded in the (at the time) soft, red Etjo sandstone. The dinosaur was probably one of the forerunners of modern birds and, much like an ostrich, had powerful hind legs. Declared a national monument in 1951, the site at *Otjihaenamaperero Farm*, located 29 km east of Kalkfeld on D2414, is well worth a visit. Be careful not to turn north to *Mt Etjo Safari Lodge* accidentally. Stop at the farmhouse and ask permission first.

Sleeping
Guestfarms A *Mount Etjo Safari Lodge*, T290173, F290172. Located 37 km from Kalkfeld, take the D2414, then D2483 (well signed after 22 km). Named after the 2000 m, 18 km long flat mountain that dominates the view. Has 26 spacious en-suite rooms (and one 'presidential suite'), with varying positions and degrees of luxury; castle-style ramparts and flamingos welcome you, gardens and comfortable lounges overlook the birds and game (including hippo) that come to drink, game drives, escorted game walk. Plentiful buffet dinners served in a sheltered outdoor 'boma'. There are 2 further, more intimate lodges, away from the main rather crowded complex – one for tourists (Rhino Lodge), the other for hunters, both with 8 doubles. The surrounding land is well stocked with white and black rhino, lion, leopard, cheetah, elephant and a host of antelope. The lodge has been in the tourist business since the 1970s, and was the site of the historic Mount Etjo Declaration supervised by the UN, which effectively ended the bush war and gave birth to independent Namibia. Rates are half board; an impressive lodge and interesting curio shop with details of animal spoor to improve your skills, perhaps too popular with large tour buses. Also **E** *Dinosaur Campsite*, along the way to their own private prints (about 4 km from the main road, one on foot, but you'll need a guide to find them), 6 fully equipped sites amongst the trees overlooking a dam, 3 km from the main lodge; pricey unless you split the site cost between 4.

F *African Tented Camp*, T/F067-306275 on *Farm Ehameno*, 12 km from the B1 on the D2483. Has 3 green canvas double tents in a military style camp with water, bucket showers, firewood, camp kitchen and large braai area. You must bring everything with you, but it has character and is good value at N$30pp.

The Namib-Naukluft

9

The Namib-Naukluft

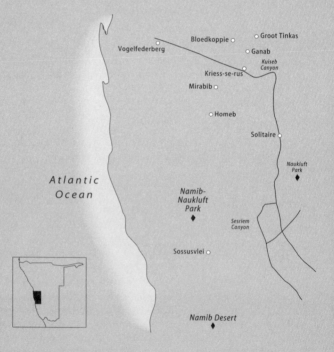

First proclaimed in 1907 and progressively enlarged over the years until it reached its present size in 1986, the Namib-Naukluft Park is the largest nature reserve in Africa, covering an area more than twice the size of Wales. Geographically, the park is divided into four distinct areas of which three are covered here: the gravel plains of the central Namib between the Swakop and Kuiseb Rivers, known as the Namib Desert Park; the mountainous knuckle of land stretching inland south of Solitaire to just west of Büllsport, known as the Naukluft Park; and the towering sand dunes south of the Kuiseb River, which we label here simply as Sossusvlei. The fourth area, the seemingly endless sand sea south towards Lüderitz, has been declared out of bounds to tourists due to the presence of diamonds and the fragility of the ecosystem.

The area attracts geographers, ecologists, hikers and tourists alike, for it is truly remarkable. On the larger scale, flights and balloon trips over the mountains and dunes in light aircraft provide visitors with a breathtaking view of the magnificent natural formations. At the opposite extreme, researchers analyse and hikers enjoy a glimpse of the fascinating variety of life that survives in the inhospitable sand and heat. And more than anything, the region typifies what Namibia has in abundance: majestic, uninhabited, seemingly unending space.

Things to do in the Namib-Naukluft

- Enjoy a sundowner from the top of **Dune 45**, before rolling all the way down.
- Splash out on a **flight over the dunes** – the shifting sea, dune and mountain landscapes will take your breath away, even if the air turbulence doesn't.
- Load up with water and **explore the desert floor** where you'll be astonished by all the creeping, crawling activity.
- Survey the plains from atop the **Spreetshoogte Pass**.
- Walk the **Dassie Trail,** spending the night in a remote mountain shelter.
- Relive the dream/nightmare of wartime survival by exploring the **Kuiseb Valley** with a copy of *The Sheltering Desert* under your arm.

The Namib Desert

The Namib Desert is a narrow strip of land stretching for 2,000 km north to south and never extending more than 200 km from west to east. Bounded by the cold waters of the South Atlantic Ocean on its west and an escarpment to the east, the Namib passes through three countries, South Africa, Namibia and Angola. In this chapter, our coverage is limited to the central Namibian areas that are accessible to tourists, namely the portion between the Swakop River in the north and the dune fields of Sossusvlei to the south. The majority of the desert further south is out of bounds to tourists, while the other accessible portion, within Namibia, encompassing the National West Coast Tourist Recreation Area and Skeleton Coast Park, is covered in the previous chapter.

The Namib Desert is generally believed to be the 'oldest' desert in the world, having enjoyed or endured arid and semi-arid conditions for around 80 million years. This does not mean that the climate has remained static during that period, nor that the dunes are old. On the contrary, the desert itself has been changing as a result of climatic shifts, one of the most significant being the development of the cold Benguela Current, about five million years ago, which plays an important part in maintaining the Namib's extremely arid conditions.

The great sand dune fields visible at Sossusvlei are also 'recent' occurrences, probably having developed after the Benguela Current was formed; they are migrating north and west in a constant cycle thanks to the prevailing wind.

Although the common perception of a desert is a hot, dry barren wilderness, the Namib actually has distinct climate zones. At an altitude of 300-600 m, the desert is watered each morning by a rolling fog caused by the cool off-shore air meeting the hot dry air from inland. This fog allows a host of life forms, such as lichens, succulents and small bushes and the insects and animals that feed off them, to exist in an otherwise inhospitable environment.

Closer to the escarpment, beyond the reach of the daily fog, the desert is hot and dry, sustaining only the hardiest forms of life. The gemsbok, for example, is specially adapted to these conditions and has an in-built cooling system to keep the blood flowing to its brain cool enough to survive in these otherwise intolerable temperatures. Ground squirrels position themselves so that their upturned tails serve as sunshades, and a number of species of beetle have extra long legs which afford them 'stilts'. Raising their bodies above the surface of the desert allows them to benefit from cooler air just above ground level.

The Dune Sea

The sand dunes of the Namibia south of the Kuiseb River are sometimes referred to as a **dune sea**. This is because the dunes are not stationary – on the contrary they are ever-moving and ever-changing as the wind blows the sand in different directions.

All the dunes in the Namib are composed of grains of quartz with a few heavy minerals, such as ilmenite, also present. The dunes rest on a base of sand where the so-called 'mega-ripples' are found; these can be as large as 50 cm high and are shaped by the wind. Above this base is the 'dune slope' and then the 'slipface', the area at the top of the dune where the sand is constantly cascading. Try walking up to the top of a dune and you will feel the effects of the slipface as you seem to endlessly climb without ever reaching the top!

Sand dunes come in many shapes and forms and of the most common types are found in the Namib. South of Walvis Bay and close to the coast are the transverse dunes, so-called because the axis of the dune lies perpendicular to the strong winds blowing mainly from the south. Around Sossusvlei are found parabolic or multi-cycle dunes, formed by winds of more or less equal strength blowing from every direction. The third kind, the parallel linear dunes, are most commonly found in the Homeb area. It is believed that this series of 100 m high north-south dunes, which generally lie about 1 km apart, are caused by strong south and east winds which blow at different times of the year. The most mobile dunes, the barchans, are most visible in the Lüderitz area, especially at the deserted town of Kolmanskop, where the dunes have invaded the abandoned houses.

The distinct, different types of sand found in the Sossusvlei area are the result of wind and water acting together. The yellow sand originates in the Namib itself, but the deep red sand usually found in the Kalahari desert has reached the Namib by being washed down into the Orange River far to the south before being blown by the wind northwards again into the Namib. Standing on top of a dune at Sossusvlei one can see the rippling dune sea extending far into the distance.

The mobility of dunes varies. The largest move perhaps no more than a metre each year. Barchans can, especially if of low altitude, travel more quickly – at up to 50 m per year. Mobile dunes create a hazard for transport since roads can be covered quickly in high wind conditions. Elsewhere, cultivated lands can slowly be inundated with sand.

Stabilizing sand dunes is a difficult matter. The large dune systems are unstoppable and man's attempts to halt their advance have rarely succeeded for long. Smaller dunes can be stabilized by planting them with a close graticule of drought resistant grass or other plants, which once established can be inter-planted with desert bushes and shrubs. This process is slow and expensive though generally very effective even in very dry conditions. More cheap and dramatic is to build sand fences to catch moving sand, tar-spraying dunes or layering dunes with a plastic net. The results are less aesthetically pleasing than using the traditional vegetation cover system and are less long-lasting unless combined with planting, though in the driest areas of the Sahara these are the only possible methods of fixing mobile dunes.

Multicycle dunes

Barchans

Transverse dunes

The Namib-Naukluft

Other insects and animals have developed different strategies to allow them to survive in this environment, some simply retreat below the surface of the desert, either into the dunes themselves or by burrowing into the desert floor.

The desert is also an archaeological storehouse, abounding in a whole range of stone tools, pieces of pottery or paintings left by the earliest inhabitants of this region. As such they play an important role in informing us how early humans made use of the natural resources of the desert in order to survive. They also beg the question as to *why* did humans spend periods of time in the desert when there was an abundance of better-watered land further inland?

The desert is a fragile environment and both plant and animal species struggle to survive here. Visitors to the desert should therefore be extra-sensitive to this environment and abide by the following rules:

■ When driving, stick to existing roads and tracks, as tyre marks can scar the desert floor for decades. Similarly lichens and other fragile plants which play an important role in the ecology of the desert can be easily destroyed.

■ Do not collect any samples of plant or vegetable life from the desert. Take photos or make sketches to keep as souvenirs.

■ When camping in the desert take firewood with you, never collect wood. Many dead-looking trees or bushes come alive again after rain.

■ Any fossils or archaeological objects should either be left where they are or sent to the Desert Ecology Research Unit (DERU), PO Box 1592, Swakopmund. Unfortunately the research unit is not open to the public. Alternatively, contact the Desert Research Foundation of Namibia in Windhoek, T061-229855, www.drfn.org

The Namib Desert Park

Ins & outs   **Access and information** Permits are not necessary for visitors travelling on the public roads through the park (the C14, C26, D1982 and D1998). However, those planning to travel on any of the signposted tourist roads, or stay at any of the campsites here, must obtain a permit beforehand. These can be obtained from Central Reservations in Windhoek, Hardap, Sesriem, Lüderitz and the tourist office in Swakopmund (Bismarck St). More locally, these permits can also be obtained from Hans Kries Service Station and the My Lounge in Swakopmund, and from the Omega, Suidwes, CWB and E-Tour Service Stations and the Anglers Kiosk in Walvis Bay.

Accommodation within the park is at the basic campsites detailed below. Visitors to the region unwilling to camp should stay either at the coast (Walvis Bay or Swakopmund) or consider the lodges on the inland fringe of the desert and neighbouring mountains (for suggested route and available accommodation, see Hinterland section, page 255). All eight small campsites within the Namib Desert Park can be booked in advance through Namibia Wildlife Resorts Central Reservations in Windhoek (see page 36). Visitors to these campsites need to be entirely self-sufficient, taking water and firewood with them. The only amenities are drop toilets, braai areas and picnic sites.

Background 'We stared down in fascination. It was an impressive and intimidating sight, landscape inconceivable under a more temperate sky and in milder latitudes. Barren cliffs fell away steeply into deep ravines all around the main canyon like a wild and gigantic maze. They had a name, the "gramadoelas", and as someone had aptly said, they looked as though the Devil had created them in an idle hour.' So wrote Henno Martin, a German geologist, who during the Second World War spent 2½ years with his friend Hermann Korn living in the desert in order to avoid internment. His book *The Sheltering Desert* describes their experiences as they struggled to survive in the harsh and unforgiving Namib environment and is well worth reading before visiting the region.

The campsite is located by the Kuiseb River bridge in the river course. The river may flood during the rainy season and visitors should check when booking the site.

Named after an early European resident of Swakopmund who was interested in the game in the Namib area, this site is located in a dry watercourse surrounded by camel thorn trees. Short walks around the area give visitors access to three typical central Namib habitats: the watercourse, calcrete plain and the schist or crystalline rock.

Kuiseb Canyon
Colour map 3, grid A2
On the C14 at the base of Kuiseb Pass

Kriess-se-Rus
Colour map 3, grid A2
107 km east of Walvis Bay on the C14

Namib Desert Park

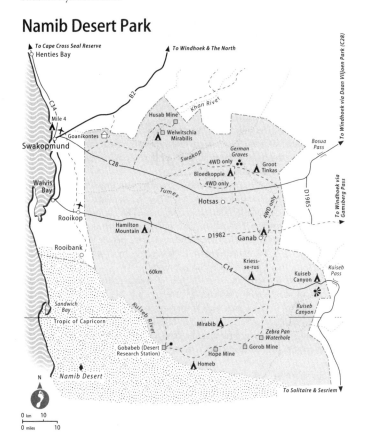

The Namib-Naukluft

Nara melons

The Nara melon is endemic to the Namib desert, in particular the Kuiseb River area. A member of the cucumber family, the nara grows in sandy places where its roots are able to burrow deep down into the earth as far as the water table. In order to reduce water loss, the stems of the plant are almost leafless, thereby also preventing animals from eating it. The nara is dioecious, meaning it has separate male and female plants. The male plant, which flowers for most of the year, provides a ready source of food for one particular species of dune beetle. One crop of the melons, which grow to about 15 cm in diameter, is produced each year in late summer providing food for desert dwellers such as jackals, gerbils, crickets and beetles.

Traditionally the nara has also been a source of food for the Topnaar Namas, who have lived around the lower reaches of the Kuiseb River for several centuries. At harvest time the fruit is collected on donkey carts and carried back to camp, where the flesh and seeds are separated from the rind and roasted over a fire. The seeds are then separated from the pulp which can be eaten as it is or dried and eaten at a later date. Archaeological sites in the Namib provide evidence in the form of seeds that the nara melon was an important source of desert food to prehistoric humans.

Mirabib
Colour map 3, grid A2
Off the C14 in the direction of Gobabeb

This is a granite inselberg rising above the desert floor accommodating two groups at a time. Rocky overhangs offer protection from the sun and carbon dating has revealed that early humans took advantage of this site some 8,500 years ago. There is also evidence of more recent visits by pastoralists about 1,600 years ago. A small waterhole, **Zebra Pan**, located 35 km southeast of here is visited by mountain zebra, ostrich and gemsbok.

Homeb
Colour map 3, grid A2
Turn off C14 towards Zebra Pan and continue on this track as far as the Kuiseb River

Located on the banks of the Kuiseb River, this campsite – capable of accommodating several parties – offers excellent views of the nearby sand dunes. Although the river only flows when good rains are received in the highland areas west of Windhoek, this site demonstrates the role of the Kuiseb River in preventing the huge dune field south of here from encroaching onto the gravel plains to the north.

Seasonal water from the river and occasional rain means that there is a sufficient supply of underground water to support substantial riverine vegetation and to provide water for animals and humans. The Topnaar Namas, one of the groups of original Khoi living in Namibia, have their home at a village at Homeb. Sometimes called the Naranin or Nara people due to their close dependence on the nara melon which grows here, most of the Topnaars now look for work in Walvis Bay or Swakopmund.

There is a good chance at Homeb of seeing game such as steenbok, gemsbok and baboons, as well as a fairly large number of birds. In particular look out for birds of prey such as the lappet-faced vulture, black eagle and booted eagles, as well as the noisy red-billed francolin, the well-camouflaged Namaqualand sandgrouse and the attractive swallowtailed bee-eater. **NB** Coverage of the Gamsberg area is found in the previous chapter.

Ganab
Turn off the C14 onto the D1982 in the direction of Windhoek

This site near a dry watercourse is named after the Nama word for the camelthorn trees which are found here. Although rather a dusty site it gives the visitor a good idea of the expanse of the Namib desert, and the nearby bore-hole and windmill are an attraction for game. A host of mammals have been spotted here, including gemsbok, springbok and zebra, as well as predators such as spotted hyena, aardwolf, bat-eared fox and caracal.

The Namib-Naukluft

Only accessible by four-wheel drive, this is an ideal place to camp in the Namib. The surrounding area is an interesting place for hikes, although the heat means that early morning and late afternoon are the best times to do this. After good summer rains the nearby dam, an unusual site in the middle of the desert, is full of water and attracts both game and birdlife.

Groot Tinkas
Turn north off the C28 from Swakopmund to Windhoek, or north on the small track leading from Ganab

Close to Groot Tinkas stands the 'blood hill' granite inselberg, a popular campsite in this part of the Namib. The sites on the western side of the hill are very sandy, requiring four-wheel drive to get there. It is well worth exploring the immediate area, not least for the fascinating rock formations found here. About 5 km east of the campsite lie the ruins of a German colonial police station and the graves of two policemen which date back to 1895.

Bloedkoppie
55 km northeast of the C28 from Swakopmund

A smaller inselberg than Bloedkoppie, nevertheless an interesting place to visit, especially after summer rains. Water collects in a number of rock pools which, for a short while, become home to a host of small invertebrates, such as the crab-like *triops*. The development of all these creatures has to be rapid as the water only remains in the pools for a few weeks. During this brief period, the eggs which have been lying waiting for the rain must hatch, the creatures must mature, mate and lay eggs for the next generation to emerge when the rain returns.

Vogelfedeberg
Colour map 3, grid A1 From Walvis Bay take the C14 east for 51 km and then turn off at the sign

South of Vogelfedeberg lie the **Hamilton Mountains**, not officially on the tourist route, but nevertheless an interesting place for those with the energy to go for a hike. This limestone range climbs between 300 m and 600 m above the Namib plain and benefits from enough fog-water to allow a fascinating range of plants to grow here. In particular look out for blooming succulents following summer rains and the occasional lily.

The Naukluft Park

The park was proclaimed in 1964 as a sanctuary for the Hartmann's mountain zebra before being joined with the Namib Desert Park in 1979 to form the Namib-Naukluft Park. The name Naukluft derives from the narrow kloof or gorge on the eastern side of the mountain range. This rugged, mountainous area hides deep ravines, plunging gorges, crystal clear rock pools and a variety of game totally at odds with the desolate surrounding desert. Accessible only on foot or on horseback the Naukluft Park is an ideal place for hiking and has a number of superb trails, ranging from the 10 km Olive Trail to the 120 km eight-day Naukluft Hiking Trail.

Colour map 3, grid A1

Getting there The entrance to the park is 10 km south of Büllsport on the D854 and can be approached from a number of directions. From Windhoek take the B1 south to Rehoboth and then immediately south of the town turn west onto the gravel road C24. This passes the small settlements of Klein Aub and Rietoog (petrol during daylight hrs) before gradually descending from the central highlands into the semi-desert around Büllsport. From the coast the C14 passes through the central Namib climbing steeply and tortuously through the Kuiseb and Gaub passes past Solitaire to Büllsport. From the south the most direct route is on the **C14** from Maltahöhe.

Ins & outs

The geological history of the area starts 1,000-2,000 million years ago when the base of the mountains was formed by volcanic rocks, granites, and gneisses. Between 750 and 650 million years ago the whole of this part of Namibia was

Geology

flooded by a shallow tropical sea which formed the next layer of rock – mainly black limestone. The actual mountains themselves were formed between 550 and 500 million years ago during a period of crustal movement when large sheets of sedimentary rock formed and were set in place. These rock sheets give the tops of the Naukluft mountains their characteristic nappes or folds. Porous limestone deposits caused by evaporating limestone-rich water are also common all over the range and suggest a much wetter past.

Vegetation For such a harsh environment the mountains are home to a surprisingly large number of plants and trees. These range from common gravel plain species such as corkwood trees and wild raisin bushes to mountain species such as shepherd's tree, quiver tree and mountain thorn bushes. The deep gorges with their perennial streams are home to a wide range of different species such as sweet thorn and cluster figs which attract large numbers of birds.

Game The park is home to a host of small mammals, many of them nocturnal and therefore easily missed. These include Cape hare, ground squirrel, badger, and yellow mongoose, as well as the common and easily spotted rock dassies, which make up the bulk of the black eagle's diet. Of the larger mammals, the Naukluft Park is home to the unique Hartmann's mountain zebra which live only in Southern Angola and Namibia. A zebra sub-species, the Hartmann's differ from plains zebras by being about 14 cm taller and also by virtue of a slightly different pattern of stripes on the lower back. Antelopes such as klipspringers are common and easily spotted as they bounce from rock to rock, as are duiker and steenbok. The mountains with their rocky overhangs, gorges and caves are an ideal home to leopards, shy animals not easily spotted, but nevertheless the most significant predators in the area. Smaller predators like black-backed jackal, bat-eared fox, African wild cats and aardwolfs are also common in the park, although like many of the smaller animals, most of these are nocturnal and therefore difficult to spot.

Birds Due to its position between the desert to the west and the highlands to the east, the park lies at the limits of the distribution of a large number of endemic Namibian species. Furthermore the perennial streams in the deep kloofs attracts birds that otherwise would not be found in this environment. Late summer (February-March) is an excellent time for bird-spotting in the park when species such as the Herero chat, Rüppell's korhan, Monteiro's hornbill, cinnamon-breasted warblers and African black ducks can be seen.

Hiking Without a doubt some of the most exciting hiking country in Namibia is found here in the Naukluft mountains, both within the national park and from the neighbouring guestfarms. There are hikes to suit just about anyone, but conditions can be hard and all hikers should make sure they come properly equipped with decent boots and a hat as well as ensuring they take enough water with them (minimum 2 litres per person per day). For those people planning longer hikes involving overnight stops in the mountains it is absolutely essential to take warm clothing as the temperature at night, even in summer, can drop close to freezing, and windproof clothing is recommended.

Olive Trail A 10 km, four to five hour hike, ideal as a starter for those unaccustomed to the conditions. The walk gets its name from the preponderance of wild olive trees encountered en route. The trail starts from the car park close to the campsite with a steep climb to the top of a plateau giving great views of the main Naukluft gorge. From here the path continues northwest as far as a

War in the Naukluft Mountains

In 1894 the Naukluft Mountains were the setting for a series of skirmishes and battles between the Nama leader Hendrik Witbooi, and the German forces led by Theodor Leutwein. The outcome of these battles played an important role in the consolidation of German control over Namibia.

In April 1893 the Germans, led by Captain Curt von Fran‡ois, had attacked Witbooi's stronghold at Hoornkrans west of Rehoboth, forcing Witbooi and his followers to flee. Signed affidavits by survivors of the attack (Hendrik Witbooi Papers Appendix 3) give a vivid picture of this bloody raid. 'A little before sunrise the German soldiers opened fire on us and stormed the place. ... When we heard the firing we ran out of our houses; we had no opportunity of making resistance but fled. ... Houses were set on fire and burned over the bodies of dead women and children.'

Following this attack Witbooi pursued a guerrilla war against the Germans, using his superior knowledge of the countryside to harass and outwit the German forces. Finally however, Witbooi was forced to retreat and chose the inaccessible Naukluft Mountains as the last refuge for his followers, including women, children and livestock. The decisive battles of the war took place in the Naukluft between 27 August and 5 September 1894.

An account of the fighting by German commander Major Leutwein gives an idea of how tough it must have been for both sides to have waged a war in these mountains. 'The troops followed the tracks left by the Hottentots' livestock; more often than not, however, it was extremely difficult to discern these tracks on the rocky ground. For this reason, the enemy could be pursued only during the day ... the sun burned down from a cloudless sky, while the temperature dropped to several degrees below zero during the night ... no fires could be lit. ... The troops were exhausted, clothing and shoes in tatters; casualties had reduced their already thin ranks....'

Despite superiority in arms and ammunition these deprivations prevented the German forces from defeating Witbooi, on the other hand Witbooi was not able to successfully break out of the siege. Eventually, the two sides fought each other to a standstill and on 15 September Witbooi signed a conditional surrender which required him and his supporters to return to Gibeon, to accept the paramountcy of the German Empire and the stationing of a German garrison at Gibeon. In return Witbooi retained jurisdiction over his land and people, and the right to keep guns and ammunition.

Concluding his account of the battle in the Naukluft, Leutwein wrote, 'The enemy had suffered only minor losses. ... It proved that the Hottentot was far superior to us when it came to marching, enduring deprivation and knowledge of and ability to use the terrain ... it was only in weaponry, courage, perseverance and discipline that the troops surpassed the enemy.'

huge social weaver nest, and then turns east into a river valley. This valley gradually deepens until a narrow gorge has to be crossed with the assistance of chains anchored into the rocks. Don't be alarmed, this is easily achieved by even the most timid, with some application. From here onwards the trail more or less follows a jeep track back to the starting point.

Waterkloof Trail A 17 km, seven hour trail, considerably more demanding than the Olive Trail, although well worth it. This hike starts from the campsite and is an anti-clockwise circular route which first leads past a weir up to a series of beautifully clear rock pools which, although cold, make for wonderful swimming. From here the trail climbs steadily up to a high point of 1,910 m

The Namib-Naukluft

just over halfway round from where there are stunning views over the whole mountain range. As the path descends it follows part of an old German cannon road used in the campaign against Hendrik Witbooi in 1894. The last 6 km of the walk follow the Naukluft River back to the campsite.

Naukluft Hiking Trail Reputed to be one of the toughest hiking trails in southern Africa, the full distance of 120 km is normally completed in eight days, although it is possible to shorten this to a four-day 58 km trail. Accommodation on the trail consists of a farmhouse on the first, third and last nights and simple stone shelters on the other nights. Water is provided at the overnight stops but fires are not permitted, making a camping stove essential. It goes without saying that this trail is only for the fit and experienced hiker! A good map of the trail is available from tourist information on Independence Avenue in Windhoek. Due to extreme summer temperatures the trail is only open from 1 March to the third Friday in October to groups of between 3 and 12 people who must book in advance. ■ *Bookings can only be made through the Central Reservations Office in Windhoek. N$95pp, regardless of hike duration, including accommodation at either end of the trail.*

Naukluft Hiking Trail

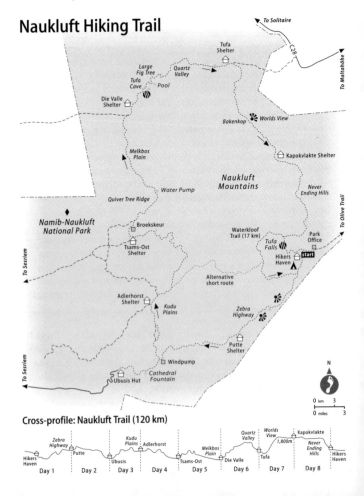

Cross-profile: Naukluft Trail (120 km)

Naukluft 4WD trail There is also a self-guided trail for four-wheel drive enthusiasts. The trail is 73 km long and has to be driven within two days. Groups must have all their own equipment and fuel, maximum four vehicles. ■ *N$200 per vehicle. This includes overnight accommodation which consists of simple shelters with basic ablutions (including shower).*

Open to day visitors, admission: N$20 adults, N$2 children, N$20 cars. Campers should **Essentials** book in advance. **F** *Koedoesrus Campsite*. 8 campsites with braai facilities, shared ablution block with hot showers, no shop, but drinking water and firewood are available. A small information centre next to the office provides information on the flora and fauna in the park.

Solitaire

Once featured in a Toyota advertisement, and the subject (in fact, title) of a *Phone code: 063* Dutch novel, Solitaire is actually just a dusty, desolate farm between the gravel *Colour map 3, grid A2* plains of the Namib Desert Park and the dunes of the southern Namib. The name Solitaire is derived from the lone dead tree standing next to the service station, a motif frequently seen on publicity posters for tourism in Namibia. The mountains to the east are an extension of the Naukluft Mountains, to the north is the flat-topped Gamsberg Mountain and to the west lie the massive red dunes of the heart of the Namibia

Solitaire is usefully placed with fuel, toilets, soft drinks, beer, ice, home-made bread and cake, meat and basic supplies. It also has **F** dormstyle beds in a tin bungalow and a simple campsite (T293387). Just north of town is a new and comfortable guest farm bearing the town's name.

There are numerous places to stay in the area north and east of the Naukluft Park, centred around Solitaire and Büllsport. Take a good look at the road map before choosing your accommodation; make sure your overnight stops correspond to your daytime activities to minimize unnecessary gravel road driving. While there are many activities in the region, we make the (rather bold!) assumption that you will be either coming from or travelling to Sossusvlei, and so provide distances to the entry point to the dunes at Sesriem.

Guestfarms A *Ababis*, T293362, F293364, ababis@natron.net, at the D1261/C14 **Sleeping** junction, 100 km from Sesriem. Under new management (the daughter of the German owner) from Aug 2001. 4 en-suite doubles and 3 rooms in the main farmhouse, communal lounge, payphone and pretty shaded veranda for summertime relaxation, game drives and hiking trails in the surrounding Naukluft Mountains, all inclusive, but still pricey, even for this part of the country. **A** *Namib Naukluft Lodge*, T061-263082/3/6/7, F215356, www.natron.net/nnl, 18 km south of Solitaire off the C36, 70 km from Sesriem. Has 16 double rooms each with a private veranda, restaurant, swimming pool with adjacent thatched bar overlooking desert. On many luxury tour itineraries, this was at one time the luxury choice in the area, but the design disappoints and the place feels tired, next to the newer competition. Offers a good value morning excursion to the dunes, with picnic breakfast and park entry, N$300 pp. Serviced by a daily shuttle from Windhoek.

A/B *Büllsport*, T693371, F693372, www.natron.net/tour/buellsport, at the C14/D854 junction, 124 km from Sesriem. Has 8 en-suite double rooms with facilities for the disabled, swimming pool, petrol station (available sunrise to sunset), small store, payphone, horse riding and hiking trails in the surrounding Naukluft Mountains. Full board. Not as charming or pretty as others nearby, fairly pricey. **A/B** *Zebra River Lodge*,

The Namib-Naukluft

Sesriem & Solitaire

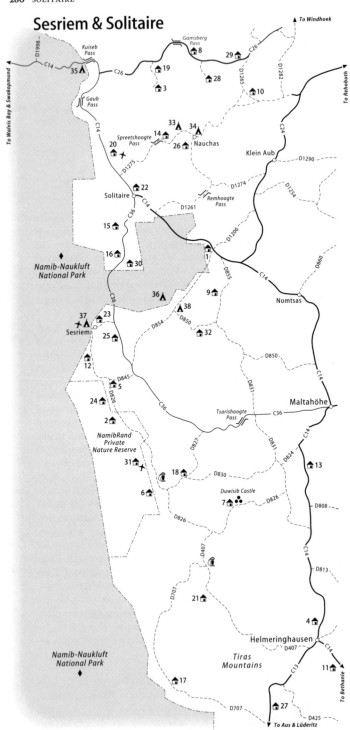

N

0 km 10
0 miles 10

T693265, F693266, www.zebrariver.com Take the C14 to Büllsport, turn onto D854, after 42 km turn onto D850, farm is signposted 19 km down this road; 91 windy km to Sesriem. Set deep in a canyon in the Tsaris Mountains, a superb lodge consisting of 6 en-suite double rooms, a sheltered verandah surrounds an imaginatively designed plunge pool, full board with plentiful, excellent food, and knowledgeable, friendly hosts. Rob is a fount of information on the geology of the region and his farm (on which the oldest known shell fossil, 550 million years, was discovered in 2000), the moon and stars (explored through his telescope), flora and fauna, local history, and more. Hiking to perennial springs, 4WD drives. Recommended, particularly if you've been racing around the country and need a couple (or more) days to relax and spoil yourself.

B *Desert Homestead*, T293243, sosses@ iafrica.com.na, on the C14/D854 junction, 38 km from Sesriem. An excellent mid-range option opened in May 2001, very tastefully created by young South African owners, in (and with) the style of the *Wilderness Lodge* which they used to manage, but more affordable. 16 large bungalows with en-suite bathrooms and fabulous views. Small swimming pool, shop, restaurant for guests (and lunch for drive-by visitors). Good value for the region. Well located for the dunes, morning and evening horse riding in nearby hills. Recommended. **B** *Haruchas*, T293399, F061-251682, haruchas@natron.net, on the D855, 19 km south of the C14 junction, 119 km from Sesriem. Has 4 en-suite double rooms and one 4-bed, 2-room family chalet, swimming pool, hiking, 4WD and game drives, dinner, B&B all inclusive, homemade curios. **B** *Rostock Ritz*, reservations T064-403622, F403623, kuecki@mweb.com.na, www.rostock-ritz.homepage.com, signposted off the C14, just south of the Gaub Pass, 30 km northeast of Solitaire. Has 22 en-suite rooms with a unusual 'traditional' adobe design, which cope very well with the heat. A HAN 2000 award winner.

The Namib-Naukluft

Restaurant overlooks the plains below, good food, certainly worth a lunch stop. Swimming pool with shaded terrace. Good, long hikes to the nearby canyon, water and day packs provided, all routes clearly marked. Horse trails, Bushman paintings. A tasteful, peaceful lodge. Recommended. **B** *Namib Rest Camp*, T293211, namibrestcamp@mweb.com.na, 27 km south of Solitaire on the C36 then 6 km along farm track, 62 km from Sesriem. A simple restcamp with 12 bungalows and 4 family units, all en-suite, available self-catering or full board. Swimming pool with a shaded bar and braai area (restaurant under construction), quad-biking, evening trips to the Diep River offer an interesting chance to view petrified dunes, fuel station. Overpriced, unimaginative design and a little run down, but with **F** 5 good campsites with light, water, no electricity, shared ablutions. **B** *Solitaire Guest Farm*, T572024, F/email via *Weltevrede Guest Farm*, details below. Follow signs from 'downtown' Solitaire, 6 km north along a farm track, off the C14, 90 km from Sesriem. This is a new venture owned by *Weltevrede*, notable in NOT being a working farm but dedicated entirely to tourists. 5 carefully crafted en-suite doubles, full board, with a small swimming pool, comfortable lounge and peaceful garden. Recommended, a good mid-range option in this pricey region.

C *Camp Gecko Safari Lodge*, T572017, geckonam@iafrica.com.na On the D1275, north east from the C14 junction; keep your eyes peeled, it is hard to spot. Has 4 luxury en-suite tents in shaded, large lapa/restaurant, three hiking trails, guides, game drives, horse riding. The Ongwe Animal Training School is located here, where different kinds of animals are trained for filming purposes. Book ahead. **C** *Namibgrens Rest Camp*, T572021, F061-222893, rabie@namibnet.com Take D1275 from the C14 to the Spreetshoogte Pass and follow the signs. It is 130 km from Sesriem, 47 challenging km from the C14.has 9 double rooms, self-catering or full board, around an old farmhouse (in the family for over 60 years) with huge trees (shade in summer) and a lovely conservatory (warmth in winter). Located at 1,760 m on the Spreetshoogte Pass, with superb views of the desert below – be warned, it gets cold at night. There are beautiful hiking trails in the mountains (with Bushman art – the Dassie Trail is the most popular) with overnight stops in basic huts (with hot water), and 4WD trails. Maps are provided. Also offers **F** camping (N$35pp) in pretty area with old farming memorabilia, large communal braai area, water, decent ablutions, no electricity. **C** *Camp Nauchas*, T062-572009, F061-257870, on the D1261, northeast of the D1275 junction. Has 6 simple double bungalows with shared bathrooms and kitchen (no cutlery), also small campsite at N$35pp, food available on request, shop, pool table, small police station next door. **C** *Nomtsas*, T293521, nomtsas@iafrica.com.na, 50 km north of Maltahöhe on C14. Has comfortable en-suite rooms, full board and a good range of activities, including swimming, hiking, game drives, and can arrange excursions to local sights. **C-E** *Weltevrede*, T293374, F293375, aswarts@mweb.com.na, 35 km south of Solitaire on the C36, 49 km from Sesriem. Offers 10 en-suite rooms, swimming pool, bar, guests can either self-cater or eat on the farm. A simple but relaxing operation on a working farm. **F** Campsite with communal cooking and ablutions. **F** *Guisis Bush Camp*, T062-572001, can provide tents, basic provisions, firewood and petrol – report to petrol station, camp is 1 km off the D1261, between the D1275 and D1274 junctions. **F** *Camp Alberta*, T572020, F061-222893, E as above, 4 km east of *Namibgrens*, 134 km from Sesriem. 4 large campsites at N$50pp, provide meals on request, mainly cater for 4WD enthusiasts with good drives in nearby hills. Try here if *Namibgrens* is full. They offer hunting.

Sossusvlei

The C36 gravel road winds south out of Solitaire into the Namib desert, through a 20 km section of the Namib-Naukluft Park where there is a good chance of seeing wild ostriches, springbok and gemsbok. It continues south through the red earth before turning east to the Tsarishoogte pass in the **Tsaris Mountains** with stunning mountain scapes either side, and eventually reaching the small town of **Maltahöhe**. The D826 is the turn-off for Sesriem, approximately 80 km of fairly tricky, undulating, loose gravel from Solitaire, and is well indicated.

Ins & outs
Phone code: 063
Colour map 3, grid A2

Background

One of most visitors' highlights of Namibia is a trip to the massive sand dunes surrounding Sossusvlei (actually the pan or valley floor that you will park on). This is one of the world's most striking, well preserved and easily accessible desert landcapes, and is well worth the effort of getting there.

Sossusvlei is actually a huge pan surrounded by towering sand dunes, reputed to be the highest in the world. While you will quickly realize this is an exaggeration when you arrive (there are towering dunes as far as the eye can see), it is a spectacular region of the Namib Desert. In years of extraordinary rains, such as 1997 and 2000, the Tsauchab River breaks through the sand and flows all the way to Sossusvlei, filling the pan with water and presenting the surreal site of ducks and even flamingos wading amid the dunes. The water gradually seeps into the ground, where it is tapped by the long roots of the camel thorn trees and nara plants living here.

Access to the *vlei* itself is either by four-wheel drive or or on foot. There is a car park for 'ordinary' vehicles 5 km short of the *vlei* (65 km from the gates). The gates are open from before sunrise to after sunset (and campers within Sesriem get a 15 minutes headstart on 'outsiders') to allow visitors to enjoy the more photogenic and comfortable early morning and late afternoon. There is a sporadic shuttle from the ordinary car park throughout the day (N$50pp) that will transport you the final 5 km. Instead of following the herd straight up the

Sossusvlei & Sesriem Canyon

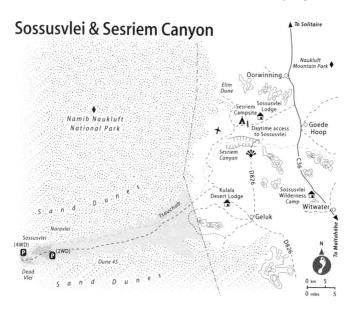

To Solitaire

Naukluft
Mountain Park

Oorwinning

Elim
Dune

Sesriem   Sossusvlei
Campsite   Lodge

Daytime access
to Sossusvlei

Goede
Hoop

Namib Naukluft
National Park

Sesriem
Canyon

D826

Kulala
Desert Lodge

Sossusvlei
Wilderness
Camp

Witwater

C36

Geluk

S a n d   D u n e s

Tsauchab

Naravlei

Sossusvlei
(4WD)

P   P (2WD)

Dune 45

Dead
Vlei

S a n d   D u n e s

D826

N

To Maltahöhe

0 km   5
0 miles   5

The Namib-Naukluft

Balloon trips

Balloon trips over the Namib desert are organized by Namib Sky Adventure Safaris and start either from Sesriem or from Camp Mishwo (see below). The trips start at sunrise when the pilot and assistants unfold the balloon with the aid of a petrol driven fan before attaching the basket in which the pilot and passengers will ride. The pilot then lights the propane gas lines and gradually inflates the balloon with blasts of hot air until it is vertical and the basket is resting on the ground below it. Take-off is barely noticeable and within a few minutes the balloon is high above the desert floor.

Depending on the direction and intensity of the wind, the balloon heads off into the desert and passengers get a spectacular bird's eye view of the dunes and the desert itself, where the innumerable tracks of ostrich, springbok, gemsbok and other desert dwellers are clearly visible in the sand. The flight itself is incredibly gentle, only punctuated by blasts of burning gas from the propane tanks, and lasts for about an hour. Landing offers the greatest sensation of the trip as the balloon steadily loses altitude before bumping along the ground and scrapping against the sand before eventually lurching to a halt.

After landing, a back-up car arrives carrying everything necessary for a champagne breakfast in the desert, after which passengers are driven back to Sesriem.

nearest dune, we suggest that you walk a few hundred metres beyond the final car park to the Dead or Hidden Vlei to enjoy the tranquillity and scenery of the area, before climbing one of the less crowded surrounding dunes. Being even one ridge away from the crowds transports you into your own silent and awesome desert wilderness; on clear days your view over the dune sea extends to around 100 km in all directions. There are no restrictions to walkers: orientate yourself from the top of a dune and explore at will. Remember, it very quickly gets warm, but if you set off before the sun gets too high you can quite easily cut straight across the dunes for the 3 km (as the crow flies) to the ordinary car park.

It is extremely important to respect Nature Conservation's request that, while in the park, vehicles must remain on the road in order not to damage the fragile desert environment. Walking is permitted anywhere and good walking shoes with woollen socks (going barefoot in summer will blister your soles), snacks and plenty of water are strongly recommended. ■ *Entry for the day is N$30 per person and N$20 per car.*

Getting there The tarred road to **Sossusvlei** lies beyond a gate inside the rest camp where a permit must be obtained before driving into the park. It is 65 km to the pan itself, and it's worth stopping at the photogenic Dune 45 (coincidentally, 45 km from the gate) and (if you've got the energy) climbing to the top for the view of the surrounding dune sea. This is a lovely spot to watch the sun setting over the dunes to the west before scurrying back to the gate before it closes (and you get fined…).

Activities **Desert flights** This is a fantastic way to appreciate the majesty and enormity of the dunes, marvel at their abrupt stop at the coast, see the geological shift at the mountains to the east and be back on the ground in time for breakfast. Can easily be combined in a day with a trip to Sossusvlei itself and a guided desert walk with an expert. Any of the more expensive lodges will be happy to arrange the excursion for you, all you have to do is get up early, swallow your travel sickness pills, and gather your camera films together. A charismatic enthusiast and long time guide to the region is Herr Breiting, T293403, who runs reasonably priced (and flexible as to duration and scope) flights in his 4-seater plane (ie 3 passengers). Flights are rarely cancelled due to inclement weather or wind (unlike balloon trips) and can be arranged at the last minute (even the night before) for early morning starts – he will collect you from your local airstrip. Obviously, you should book in advance to ensure availability. Budget US$80-100 per person per hr in the air.

Ballooning Another fantastic way to view the region from the air. The technological limitations of balloons (ask Mr Branson) make this a hit-and-miss way of getting views of the dunes (let alone the sea – panic if you do). Always cancellable on days of inclement weather or wind direction, this is recommended if you would like to experience ballooning, rather than as the best way to see the dunes from the air. In fact, as the support vehicle may not enter the dunes, any risk of sailing over them results in the balloon being immediately grounded. The trip is elegantly concluded with a champagne breakfast while the silk is stowed away. A very memorable start to any day, and, as above, can easily be combined in a day with a trip to Sossusvlei itself and a guided desert walk with an expert. Contact *Namib Sky Adventure Safaris*, T293233, F293241, namibsky@mweb.com.na Expect to pay N$1,800 per person.

Desert hikes Far from being a desolate, lifeless landscape, the desert is full of scurrying, clinging life, adapted to survival against the heat and aridity. The desert floor is brought to life with the aid of an informed guide, although, as before, you are advised to carry snacks, water, and dress appropriately. The company *Sossus-on-Foot*, T293217, sossusft@mweb.com.na, offers morning or evening walks of 2-3 hrs, of varying difficulty, for roughly N$250pp. Alternatively, *Tok Tokkie Trails*, T0668 ask for 5230 or reservations T061-235454, offer guided desert walks and arrange overnight accommodation under the stars; rates roughly N$700 pp per night, all inclusive.

Sesriem Canyon

Located near the campsite and entrance to Sossusvlei is another interesting geological feature, the sharp schism in the earth known as Sesriem Canyon. The name Sesriem is derived from the *ses riems* or six lengths of rope that were needed to haul water out of the gorge from the top. This narrow gorge is a deep slash in the earth 1 km long and up to 30 m deep running west before eventually flattening out as it approaches Sossusvlei. Needless to say, it is not recommended after heavy rain; however, it very infrequently acts as a channel these days.

The Tsauchab River, which today only runs after good rains fall in the Naukluft mountains, cut the gorge some 15-18 million years ago during a significantly wetter period in the Namib's history. The canyon itself was created by continental upheaval somewhere between two to four million years ago which resulted in the creation of most of the westward flowing rivers in the Namib desert region.

The canyon is located 4 km from the campsite; ask at the office and follow signs, it is a poor gravel road and the cars parked in the dust indicate your destination. It is an interesting place to walk and appreciate the multiple rock layers exposed there. After good rains pools of water form at the bottom of the gorge; take along your swimming gear and enjoy a quick dip.

Sleeping

Be sure to look at the distances from Sesriem before committing yourself to a particular lodge as you should avoid driving before sunrise and after sunset as much as possible. There are an additional 5 upmarket lodges in the NamibRand Nature Reserve, detailed separately at the end of this chapter, due to their slightly different offering and environment.

At Sesriem E *Sesriem Rest Camp*, T063-693247, F693249 (advance reservations with Namibia Wildlife Resorts in Windhoek) has room for 26 groups of campers (and an overflow). The campsite is inside the gates to Sossusvlei, providing campers with a 15 min headstart on 'outsiders' in the morning for those uninterrputed dawn views and photos. Beware the overflow area where you may be alone, or grouped in with overland buses. Communal ablutions, fairly well stocked shop with postcards, films, phonecards, wood, beer, meat and tinned food. Book in advance, this site is, unsurprisingly, popular. ■ *Gates open sunrise to sunset only, there is **no entry after sunset**. Camping is more expensive than other NWR sites, at N$140 per site.*

Guest lodges in the area L *Sossusvlei Wilderness Camp*, reservations T061-225178, www.sossusvleicamp.com, is one of the best lodges in the country, built in the style of a wilderness camp with raised wooden walkways linking 9 thatched en-suite units; each unit has a private plunge pool, veranda and stunning uninterrupted view. Rooms are built into the rock with plenty of character. Recommended, if money is no object, although you can get similar views, and 'experience' at other nearby, less expensive camps. From Jul to Oct, they also operate the **L** *Sossusvlei Wilderness Tented Camp*, www.sossusvleitentedcamp.com, with 6 tents set up in a remote corner of the farm, providing a closer to nature experience while still laying on the style, full board. **AL** *Kulala Desert Lodge*, T293234, F293235, www.kulalalodge.com, 17 km south of Sesriem on D826, has 12 thatched 'kulalas' (en-suite double bungalows, with a roof you can sleep on or stargaze from) with veranda, half board, swimming pool, horse riding. On a large farm (21,000 ha) with private entrance to Sossusvlei, making this the closest accommodation to Sossusvlei, with phenomenal views. **AL** *Sossusvlei Lodge*, T693223, F693231, sossusvl@iafrica.com.na, www.movenpick-hotels.com, adjacent to *Sesriem Campsite*. Has 45 tent-cum-bungalow structures designed to blend into the desert, comfortable, en-suite doubles, restaurant, bar with lovely views, nature videos in the evening, swimming pool, full board. Expensive, but very well located, the closest non-campers can stay to Sesriem camp, the main entrance to Sossusvlei, making it handy for dawn and dusk views and photography. 4WD excursions to the dunes offered. **A/B** *Hammerstein Rest Camp*, T693111, F693112, 60 km from Sesriem on C36. Has 10 en-suite double rooms, 5 bungalows, dinner, B&B provided, swimming pool, caged leopard and tame zebra, scenic drives. Once award-winning, now overpriced and tired from underinvestment, catering largely for German tour groups. Although they don't advertise it, they also offer **F** camping with very basic facilities at $25pp.

B-E *NamibRand Family Hideout*, T061-223926, F232890, www.members. mweb.com/nrfhideout, accomodates up to 10, self-catering, numerous activities available, N$500-1200 per night for the hideout, dependent on length of stay. Ask about discounts. **C** *Nubib Nature Camp*, T385713, reservations 061-234342, eden@ mweb.com.na, off the D827, 20 km southwest of the C36, 104 km from Sesriem. 'Numib' means 'peace', named after an agreement was signed between the Nama and German troops nearby; an excellent addition to the region's accommodation, with 10 imaginatively constructed en-suite concrete/canvas structures and a central bar and restaurant. Hikes to perennial springs in the mountains, scenic drives, overnight hikes in the desertscape, good game viewing, giraffe to be introduced in near future. Full board, good value. Recommended. **C/D-F** *Betesda Rest Camp*, T693253, F693252, betesda@iway.na, 40 km from Sesriem on C36, en-suite rooms and self-catering chalets built from local materials, swimming pool, horse riding, hiking, farm trips, food available if booked. The owner has an interesting collection of racing trophies; small curio shop, lovely mountain views, handily placed for Sossusvlei. Stony campsite by riverbed; cheap, but poor ablutions and no electricity. **E-F** *Tsauchab River Camping*, T293416, F061-227011, tsauchab@triponline.net, follow signs 1 km from the D854/D850 junction, 72 km from Sesriem. Run by a young South African couple with a huge amount of energy; they offer a broad range of sites in imaginative locations along a 3 km stretch of the river, farm shop, bar, will cook if warned in advance, excellent new ablutions, firewood and candles, no electricity. Also 'exclusive' sites in a beautiful part of the farm available at a premium, well worth paying. Tree houses in the lower branches of huge wild fig trees under construction. A few N$ more pricey than some, but worth it, particularly if you stay more than dusk til dawn. There are donkey cart trips, lovely walks and 4WD trails in the area. Recommended.

NamibRand Nature Reserve

NamibRand extends over 200,000 ha, incorporating some of the most beautiful and spectacular scenery of the Namib Desert

A short distance south of the dunes at Sossusvlei lies the largest private nature reserve in the country. As a private reserve the development has been carefully controlled and guests can enjoy an exclusive insight into the ecology of this fascinating region with expert and enthusiastic guides.

There are five private camps to choose from, each situated in their own area of the reserve, each offering slightly different activities and types of accommodation. For anyone fearing the crowds of Sossusvlei, or the limited offering of some of the other lodges in the region, a stay at NamibRand is recommended. In order to fully appreciate the area it is recommended you spend up to three nights in the reserve.

Background

It will quickly become apparent to guests that the NamibRand Nature Reserve is an ambitious and worthy enterprise, closely linked to man's changing ideas about his environment. The Reserve is an amalgamation of several private farms which were either bought or agreed to join the project.

In the 1950s, the area was allocated to individual farmers who introduced sheep to the area, cut roads and put up fences and water points. After 30 years of marginal farming it became apparent that the local environment was just not suited to commercial farming. A series of drought years in the early 1980s forced several farmers to sell their land. It was at this point that the idea of NamibRand started to emerge.

In 1984, Albi Brückner bought *Farm Gorrasis* because of the sheer beauty of the landscape. Several years later he bought two neighbouring farms, *Die Duine* and *Stellarine*. It quickly became apparent that throughout the drought years the game had survived and flourished. The Reserve today is made up of a series of farms which have had their fences removed in order to allow the wildlife to roam freely; over 200 km of fencing and 120 km of roads have been removed, and pipelines serving waterpoints installed. In order to support and develop the project a series of different operators have taken out 'concessions' on the farms and now offer a range of activities designed to introduce and educate visitors about the wonders of the

Namib Desert. In the future, there are hopes to establish an information and training centre, and also to reintroduce black rhino into the area.

Essentials There are currently 5 camps/lodges in the area. Each offers hiking or late afternoon drives during which you have a good chance of viewing oryx, springbok, hartebeest, ostrich, zebra and, occasionally, leopard. The birdlife is particularly varied for this region, with over 120 species recorded. Each lodge will happily arrange a breathtaking light aircraft or balloon ride over the dunes (see Sossusvlei Activities above), if this is not already included in your agenda. Likewise, for desert walks.

If your time is short, it is possible to organize fly-in safaris, each including a low-level flight over the dunes at Sossusvlei; again, your hosts or travel agent will be used to organizing this sort of transportation. Independent travellers wanting to splash out should make their own arrangements with private charter flight companies (see page 38).

There is a petrol station on the D826, just north of the D827 junction, which is useful, in that it allows you to continue along this beautiful route, rather than heading away from the dunes towards Maltahöhe.

Sleeping **L** *Sossusvlei Mountain Lodge*, T063-293329, sml@iafrica.com.na, reservations
See map page 280 T+2711-8073720, www.afroventures.co.za, in Johannesburg. On the D826, 9 km south of the D845 junction, 26 km from Sesriem. Competes with the *Sossusvlei Wilderness Lodge* as the smartest place in the area, opened in 2001, with 10 luxurious doubles, stunning views, excellent food and extensive wine list. Satellite TV, internet access for guests, all game and scenic arrangements possible. Star-gazing skylight over beds, plus observatory. Recommended, if money is no object. **L/AL** *Wolwedans Dunes Lodge*, reservations T061-230616, F220102, www.wolwedans.com, on the D826, 40 km south of Sesriem. A stunning set-up, located on the edge of the dunes, superb view over the valley and ancient mountains; 8 beautifully decorated, luxurious, en-suite chalets on stilts, with private veranda. The central dining area has a separate bar and a comfortable lounge to which you can retreat, should the wind start to howl. Exquisite food and service. **AL** *Wolwedans Dune Camp*, reservations T061-230616, F220102, www.wolwedans.com A short distance from the *Dunes Lodge*, this was the first camp to be built in the dunes. 6 en suite tents all on raised wooden platforms. Wooden walkways link the tents with the central dining and lounge block where guests gather for their sundowner before enjoying an alfresco dinner. This is an unforgettable camp in the perfect location. Aside from the superb views the principal attraction here is the limited number of guests. Recommended. **AL-A** *Die Duine Guest House*, T/F06638-5230 or T061-235454. Signposted off the D826, just north of the D827 junction, a further 11 km west of the road, 95 km from farmhouse to Sesriem. This friendly guesthouse provides guests with the opportunity to explore and enjoy NamibRand by foot. Visitors are accommodated in the old farmhouse in 3 large en-suite doubles. Marc and Elinor take guests on walks through the mountains, typically with a night camping under the stars. Everything is done for you, all you carry is your water. At the end of the day, you will arrive at a camp with a welcoming fire and good food waiting for you. Strongly recommended for a desert experience.

B *Camp Mwisho*, T293233, F293241, namibsky@mweb.com.na, On the D826, 20 km south of the D845 junction, 37 km from Sesriem. An intimate camp, one of the first operators to run balloon trips over the desert, and still the best known and regarded offering 4 double tents with en-suite facilities, with meals taken in the renovated farmhouse. Afternoon and sundowner game drives, balloon rides first thing in the morning, weather permitting (see Sossusvlei Activities above).

Finally, there is a budget option in the area, the **F** *Sossusvlei River Campsite*, just off the D826, 2 km north of the D845 junction, 15 km from Sesriem. Well located, with adequate communal ablutions, but requires 4WD for access.

The South

10

The South

The south of Namibia is an arid, sparsely populated region with isolated farmhouses and communities scratching a living from the rocky ground. While seemingly inhospitable, there is widespread cattle farming and plentiful game, two perennial rivers (the Fish and Orange), the awesome Fish River Canyon and the frankly unusual, isolated ex5istence that is Lüderitz. The distances are vast, but there is plenty to catch the eye, with mountain ranges, red Kalahari sand and quiver trees, herds of kudu and circling birds of prey, pleasant dams for watersports and the sand-enveloped diamond boom town of Kolmanskop.

Geographically, the south encompasses all the land from Rehoboth to the South Africa border and from the borders with Botswana and South Africa in the Kalahari Desert to the ancient Namib and cold waters of the South Atlantic Ocean. The central highland plateau runs like a spine down the middle of the region and it is along this narrow strip of land that the majority of the population lives.

The South

Background

Physically, the south is a semi-arid region of vast plains stretching as far as the eye can see. To the west lie a series of mountain ranges demarcating the edge of the plateau and the pro-Namib desert region. Just north of Keetmanshoop stands the ancient volcano Brukkaros, towering 650 m above the surrounding plain, and in the moonscape of the far south lies the Fish River Canyon, an artery through which the Fish River flows down to its confluence with the Orange River.

Politically, the south is divided into the Hardap and Karas Regions, with their administrative centres at Mariental and Keetmanshoop respectively. The only other towns of significant size are Rehoboth and the old German coastal town of Lüderitz. However, all over the south there are a scattering of

The South

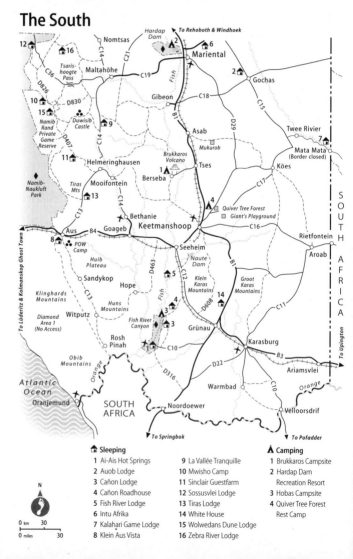

🏠 Sleeping

1 Ai-Ais Hot Springs
2 Auob Lodge
3 Cañon Lodge
4 Cañon Roadhouse
5 Fish River Lodge
6 Intu Afrika
7 Kalahari Game Lodge
8 Klein Aus Vista
9 La Vallée Tranquille
10 Mwisho Camp
11 Sinclair Guestfarm
12 Sossusvlei Lodge
13 Tiras Lodge
14 White House
15 Wolwedans Dune Lodge
16 Zebra River Lodge

▲ Camping

1 Brukkaros Campsite
2 Hardap Dam Recreation Resort
3 Hobas Campsite
4 Quiver Tree Forest Rest Camp

0 km   30
0 miles   30

The South

★

Things to do in the South

- Go hike, bike and ride the **Fish River Canyon** by staying upstream of the national park at the Fish River Lodge.
- Enjoy the *Cañon Roadhouse*'s **award-winning menu**, extensive wine list and entertaining Wild West decor.
- Devour some of the freshest **seafood and shellfish** you will ever come across, washed down with superb chilled wine, at *Ritzy's* in Lüderitz.
- Keep your promise of returning to Kolmanskop in the early or late hours of the day and watch the shadows play with this **ghost town**.
- Soothe and restore your overheated self with a swim and a beer by **Oanob Lake Dam**.
- Tackle a remote corner of the world by joining the **4WD** concession across the dunes and to the coast from Saddle Hill, just north of Lüderitz.
- Hike, bike or ride from *Klein Aus Vista* – you may catch glimpses of the **wild horses** or gemsbok – and return to the isolated luxury of their *Eagle's Nest* chalets.

smaller towns and settlements, many of them dating back to the days of the first European missionaries.

The economy of the south has always been based around livestock farming. In pre-colonial times the Nama people grazed their animals on the vast plains, watering them at the springs of Rehoboth, Hoachanas, Gibeon, Berseba, and Bethanie, now all small settlements. Following the arrival of European missionaries, traders and settlers, the majority of the land was turned into vast white-owned ranches, many of over 10,000 ha, and for much of this century the wealth of these farmers was built on the back of trade of the wool of the karakul sheep (see box page 349). Although the Basters in Rehoboth managed to hold on to their land, following the Odendaal Commission Report in 1962, the Nama people were forced into a Namaland Bantustan located west of the main road between Mariental and Keetmanshoop.

Attractions in the region include the **Oanob Lake Resort** and **Reho Spa Hot Springs** in Rehoboth and the **Hardap Dam Resort and Game Park** near Mariental. On the edge of the Namib Desert is the delicate **Duwisib Castle**, an outpost of European elegance in the middle of the veld, and further south lie **Brukkaros volcano**, the **Quiver Tree Forest**, the vast **Fish River Canyon** and **Ai-Ais Hot Springs Resort**.

For hiking enthusiasts there are two tough trails and one moderate one. The 120-km **Naukluft Trail** passes through the rugged, spectacular Naukluft Mountains where Nama leader Hendrik Witbooi made a stand against the German forces in 1894. The 84-km **Fish River Canyon Hiking Trail** is a four-day hike into the canyon and along the Fish River as it snakes its way south from the observation point at Hobas to the hot springs at Ai-Ais. Or you may prefer a relatively easy hike up and into the crater of the Brukkaros volcano, with its own ecosystem and fine views of the surrounding plains.

The South

This region is the size of Germany and, with towns and settlements far apart, it is difficult to explore properly without your own vehicle. The rail network runs through Mariental and Keetmanshoop as far as Karasburg and the border at Ariamsvlei, and there are some bus services to the major towns. Beyond that, there is a network of relatively frequent shared taxis, mostly to the smaller settlements. However, to get to the sites of interest – in particular the Fish River Canyon – the only alternative to driving yourself is hitch-hiking, which may involve long waits in the hot sun, with lifts few and far between. **Essentials**

South from Windhoek

The B1 is a good, tarred road leading all the way to the two southern border crossings at Noordoewer and Ariamsvlei, 800 km and 855 km from Windhoek, respectively. In places, the road becomes quite narrow and great care should be exercised when overtaking the large trucks which ply their way up and down the highway between South Africa and Windhoek, particularly at night. The B1 has acquired the unfortunate nickname of 'the road of death' due to the high number of fatal accidents that take place on it. **Avoid driving this road at night.** Similarly, during morning and afternoon rush hours, large numbers of Rehobothers commute in cars, pick-up trucks and mini-buses to and from their jobs in Windhoek. At such times this stretch of the road is uncharacteristically crowded, by Namibian standards.

Despite its rather sinister nickname, the road between Windhoek and Rehoboth is a beautiful route, winding through the picturesque ranchland of the Auas Mountains. Approximately 30 km south of Windhoek is the *Aris Hotel*, a pleasant place to stop for coffee or a meal. On this stretch of the road troops of baboons rooting around in the bush for food are a common sight; also keep an eye open for warthogs, mongoose, guinea fowl and yellow-billed hornbills.

Just south of Rehoboth the C24 branches west off the main B1 and leads to the Reemhoogte Pass, one of three spectacular routes which descend to the Namib desert floor. From here you can head west into the Naukluft Mountains or southwest towards Sossusvlei.

Rehoboth

Phone code: 062
Colour map 3, grid A3

Situated 87 km south of Windhoek at the foot of the Auas Mountains, Rehoboth is home to the Basters (literally, 'Bastards'), a fiercely proud and independent people who are the descendants of a group of farmers of mixed European and Khoisan blood. The town has very little to recommend it; some say this is part of a deliberate policy to marginalize the Basters' hometown. A plunge in the Reho-Spa resort pool to cool off (or the hot spring to warm up) is recommended, but the resort looks like it hasn't had a penny spent on it since opening in 1985. Nearby Oanob Lake, by contrast, is stunning, with new lakeside thatched chalets, well tended camping sites and a range of watersports and entertainment for families.

History   The hot springs had been known for centuries by the Swartbooi Namas who called the place *Anhes*, meaning 'smoke', which referred to the steam rising from the hot water. A more permanent settlement was established in 1844 by Rhenish Missionary, Heinrich Kleinschmidt. This original mission station lasted for 20 years before being abandoned in 1864 following an attack by the Oorlam Afrikaners under Jonker Afrikaner. Kleinschmidt's congregation dispersed following their defeat and Kleinschmidt and his family walked through the bush for four days before reaching the safety of the mission station at Otjimbinwge, where Kleinschmidt laid down and died.

The Basters migrated to the area from the Cape in 1870 and under the leadership of Hemanus van Wyk established a settlement at the site of the now abandoned Rhenish mission station. The name of the town comes from the Bible: 'He moved on from there and dug another well, and no one quarrelled over it. He named it Rehoboth, saying, "Now the Lord has given us room and we will flourish in the land." ' (Genesis Ch26, v22).

In the years following the arrival of van Wyk and his people in 1870, the mission station was rebuilt. One of the earliest buildings to be completed was the Lutheran Church in Church Street; with its distinctive brickwork it is reminiscent of the Putz architechtural style of the Ombudsman's Office in Windhoek.

The Baster community has traditionally been a farming community, living a more or less self-sufficient farming existence, similar to that of the white Afrikaner settlers. Fiercely independent, Christian and western-oriented in their culture, the Basters have managed to hold on to their land despite attempts by the German and South African colonial governments to take it away from them.

From the 1920s up until independence, the Rehoboth community was governed by a *kaptein* (traditional leader) and his *raad* (council) who had jurisdiction over all aspects of community life except for the law. A white magistrate appointed by the colonial government held these powers. Matters concerning agriculture, education, local government and health were all managed by the *raad* assisted by seven *volksraad* or 'people's councils' from around the region. In effect the Rehoboth district existed as a semi-autonomous region within Namibia.

After independence, a section of the Baster community, under the leadership of the former kaptein, Hans Diergaardt, fought a court battle with the central government to keep control over the traditional communal land of the town itself and the land in a radius of 10 km around it. The most recent Supreme Court ruling in 1996 handed control of the land to the government, to be administered by the town council, thus depriving the traditional leadership of the right to administer the land. Just before his death in 1998, Diergaardt made peace with PM Hage Geingob, and Rehoboth finally appears to have put aside its dispute with the new Namibian state.

Located in the former residence of the town's first postmaster, built in 1903, the museum houses an interesting record of the community's history and culture revealing the fascinating twists and turns in the history of this unusual 'Lost White Tribe'. There is also information on local flora and fauna, and in the garden a display of traditional huts of the different ethnic groups. The museum will also arrange visits to an iron-age site out of town, by prior arrangement. ■ *0900-1200, 1400-1600 Mon-Fri and 0900-1200 Sat, T522954, www.natmus.cul.na/nam_mus/rehoboth* **Rehoboth Museum**

The best option for accommodation in Rehoboth itself is the *Reho Spa Recreation Resort* (hot springs), but much better are the lakeside chalets and camping facilities of the *Oanob Lake Resort*. See relevant sections below. If desperate, there is the *Akasia* B&B by the turn off in town to the *Oanob Lake Resort*. There are no restaurants to recommend in town. There are takeaways (including a fish & chip shop) and simple fare from the various garages; for a beer you could try *The Pink Palace*, which doubles as the town's casino. **Sleeping & eating**

Road For *Intercape* coaches to Cape Town, Keetmanshoop, Windhoek and Upington, see timetable on page 382. Coaches pick up and drop off at the main service station on the B1, as do local shared **taxis** (frequent service to Windhoek, and south down the B1). **Train** For trains to Keetmanshoop via Mariental, and Windhoek, see timetable on page 383. The station is **10 km** from town. Not recommended. There is a small store and decrepit *Bahnhof Hotel*. **Transport** *87 km to Windhoek*

The town is well equipped with petrol stations (24 hour), supermarkets and bottle stores. **Banks** *First National Bank*, with ATM. **Communications** The Post Office is **Directory**

The South

next to the museum, and the Police station and Namibia Telecoms (for international calls) are next door. There is a 'computer centre', which advertises email but can't be relied on for a connection. **Health** Hospital, follow signs for Reho-Spa. Dentist, again, near the museum, T524122, F523930.

Reho Spa Recreation Resort
Colour map 3, grid C3

Known to the indigenous Nama people for centuries, the hot springs here have been developed into a spa resort run by Namibia Wildlife Resorts, now suffering the signs of neglect. The camp has the look and feel of a military barracks, but there is a fine 20 x 20 m indoor thermal bath with huge ceiling in 1960s style structure, grassy picnic areas and a 25 m outdoor swimming pool.

The resort is open year round and, amazing as it may seem, the bungalows often get booked up: reservations T522774, or centrally in Windhoek through NWR. Picnic/braai sites are available for day visitors. **D-E** *Bungalows,* six bed two-room, or five and four bed one-room, with bathrooms and kitchen. Also 'VIP' suites, as above but with crockery and cutlery. **F** Camping and caravan sites, maximum 8 persons per site, communal ablution and cooking facilities.

■ *N$10 for adults, N$1 for children, plus a further N$10 for adults and N$5 for children to enter the thermal baths. Getting there: Follow the signs off the B1 onto the gravel road, turn right immediately after the Catholic Church. The road curves to the left before reaching a crossroads. Turn right here (you will be able to see the military barracks style buildings on your right) and the entrance to the resort is a further 400 m on the right.*

Oanob Lake Resort
Well signposted west off the B1 in and just north of Rehoboth (on either the D1280 or D1237)

The dam was completed in 1990 and supplies Rehoboth's water. Originally there were plans to set up some irrigated crop cultivation by the dam, but so far this has not materialised. Unusually, this resort is not in the hands of Namibia Wildlife Resorts, and as such is able to respond to growth in demand by providing new facilities and accommodation. This is just what they have done, with two good restaurants/bars, excellent chalets and campsite and a range of facilities for the visitor to enjoy. The blue water of the lake is a welcome sight amidst the arid thorn veld of the surrounding countryside; this is justifiably a popular summer weekend and holiday spot for locals. Tourist numbers have risen recently, and attractive, comfortable accommodation overlooking the lake has just been built.

Birdwatching There are a few ostriches, as well as colonies of cormorants, pelicans, darters and other water birds living on and alongside the lake, plus some noisy, inquisitive turkeys, hens and a peacock roaming the campsite.

Hiking and watersports There are a few marked walks laid out around the lake, along which it is possible to spot springbok, baboons and other smaller mammals. A speedboat ride and tour of the lake costs N$10 per person; visitors can also hire pedalos or canoes for N$10 per person. For the more hands-on visitor, there is a jet ski available for N$40. Windsurfers with their own boards can also make use of the lake, however there are no boards at present available for hire.

The resort is open all year round, pre-booking is recommended but by no means essential. There are shaded, grassy braai sites for day visitors at N$80-100 per site (depending on location), as well as two picturesque and reasonable thatched bar/restaurants, one overlooking the children's pool. **C-F** *Lake Oanob Resort,* T522370, F524112, oanob@iafrica.com.na, has three-six bedroom luxurious, chalets and rooms, beautifully positioned by the lake. The only possible complaint might be of over-exuberance from day visitors during the summer. Immaculate grassed, shaded campsites, adequate ablutions. Recommended.

The South

Guestfarms in the area L-A *Intu Afrika Game Lodge*, reservations T061-248741, F226535, www.intuafrica@iafrica.com.na From the north, turn east off the B1 at Kalkrand onto the C21, then right on the B1268, follow signs. From the south, take the C20, left after 12 km on the D1268 and follow the signs is a beautiful collection of lodges set amidst the red sand dunes of the Kalahari. Price depends on the season and degree of elegance of your room; all guests share the swimming pool, restaurant, game drives and birdwatching. They bought 3 lions in Dec 1999, which they are carefully preparing to return to the wild, and will happily talk interested visitors through the process. A !Kung Bushman village is a particular attraction of this lodge, with the opportunity to go on nature hikes with Bushman guides. Book in advance. On the same farm is the cheaper option of a new **D** tented camp (B&B) or **E** campsite, separate from the main lodges. Recommended.

B/C *Bitterwasser Flying Centre and Lodge*, T063-265300, F265355, bitterwa@ mweb.com.na 10 km north of the C20/D1219 junction, roughly 75 km from Mariental, or by air taxi from Windhoek. Has been a gliding centre for afficionados for 40 years; a group of German and Swiss enthusiasts (there are currently 28 partner owners) bought the land in 1994 and after initial construction of some basic rondavels for themselves, the lodge has been extended with some wonderful accommodation for tourists. There are 26 a/c chalets, a swimming pool, and a fabulous thatched central lapa containing the bar and restaurant. The principal attraction is the gliding; a number of world records have flown from here. The expanding agenda for landlubbers, grounded partners and children includes excursions into the Kalahari, mountain biking, and ballooning. Call for details, and book as far ahead as possible if in the 'season' (Oct-Jan).

E-F *Gravenstein/Panorama Game Farm*, T062-581408 or reservations T061-231164. Take the C25 past Rehoboth Station, look for the sign after 32 km. A somewhat dilapidated working farm, with numerous en-suite rooms dotted around in the farm buildings. Satellite TV, swimming pool, recreation room, gym, aviary, game drives, horse riding, walks, hunting in season, restaurant and bar or self-catering. Also has a camping and caravan site. One of the cheapest options for staying on a working farm around, but neither luxurious, nor easily reached.

The B1 south from Rehoboth passes through the ranching land of the Baster community, before reaching the village of Kalkrand with its garage, bottle store and takeaway stand. About 20 km north of Kalkrand, at the Duineveld Crossroads, there are a number of roadside stalls where springbok skin rugs are sold by locals from Duineveld. The skins themselves are bought from commercial farmers and then stitched together and lined with karakul fur before being sold. The sale of these rugs plays an important role in the economy of the village.

South from Rehoboth

The South

Mariental

Phone code: 063
Colour map 3, grid A4

Mariental is a small, quietly flourishing market town in the heart of southern Namibia and is the administrative centre of the Hardap Region. The nearby Hardap Dam is the largest reservoir in Namibia and provides water for irrigation, making it possible to cultivate animal fodder, as well as some fruit and vegetables. A local ostrich abattoir caters for this increasingly important industry, and what survives of the karakul trade in the south is centred around Mariental. Sitting astride the main routes into the Kalahari and Namib deserts, Mariental also services the needs of farmers in these areas.

Despite Mariental's quiet success, it is not the most exciting place in Namibia and is windswept and dusty in spring and autumn, ferociously hot in summer and bitterly cold in winter. Mariental is home to a large number of Nama-speaking people, descendants of the early Khoi inhabitants of Namibia.

History Mariental was officially founded in 1920 following the construction of Namibia's first Dutch Reform Church, however it was well known to the early Nama inhabitants who referred to the place as *Zaragaeiba* meaning 'dusty'. The present name is derived from 'Marie's Valley', bestowed upon the settlement by the first white settler, Herman Brandt, in honour of his wife.

Mariental

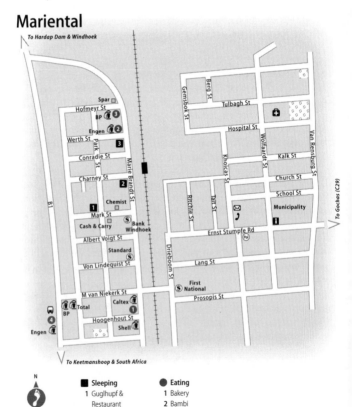

To Hardap Dam & Windhoek

To Gochas (C29)

To Keetmanshoop & South Africa

N

0 metres 100
0 yards 100

■ **Sleeping**
1 Guglhupf &
  Restaurant
2 Mariental
3 Sandberg

● **Eating**
1 Bakery
2 Bambi
3 Ice Cream Parlour
4 Wimpy

The South

Following some rather turbulent early years during the anti-German war of 1904-07 and the arrival of the railway in 1912, Mariental settled down to life as a quiet *dorp* in the middle of the veld.

Sleeping

C/D *Mariental Hotel*, T242466, F242493, hoofmot@mar.namib.com is the most comfortable place to stay in town. The hotel has 18 en-suite rooms with a/c and phone, there is a small swimming pool with thatched braai lapa, gym and secure off-street parking. The restaurant is light and airy, if a little more expensive than average. 2 bars (lively at weekends) to choose from, pool table, fruit machines. **C/D** *Sandberg Hotel*, T242291, F240738, a reasonable, if rather rundown, option with en-suite rooms with a/c and phone. There is an unremarkable restaurant and bar, as well as occasionally lively Basement Disco. **C/D** *River Chalets B&B*, T240515, F242418, ejumtl@iafrica.com.na, offers en-suite self-catering chalets with a/c and TV, by the Engen garage on the B1, walking distance from town. **D** *Guglhupf* , Park St, T240718, F242525, modest, en-suite rooms, with phone, some with a/c. The bar and restaurant are popular with the local crowd.

Eating

Mariental Hotel and *Guglhupf Café & Restaurant*, popular with locals, with tasty, filling, steaks, schnitzel and ribs washed down by local draught beer, reasonably priced, your best bet. *Mariental Hotel* offers standard fare in decent dining room. *Bambi Restaurant* at the Engen Garage on Marie Brandt St offers fry-ups and steaks, reputedly fairly terrible. Fast food junkies could head for the *Wimpy* at the large Engen garage on the B1 just south of town (telephone, toilets and shop available), while picnickers should pop into Spar, just off the B1 north of town, for provisions.

Transport
264 km to Windhoek
228 km to Keetmanshoop

Bus For *Intercape* coaches to Cape Town, Keetmanshoop, Upington, and Windhoek, see timetable on page 382. Also served by *Bailey's Transport*. **Train** For trains to Keetmanshoop and Windhoek, see timetable on page 383. The station is in the middle of town.

Directory

Banks *Bank Windhoek*, T242381 and *Standard Bank*, T242371 are both found on Marie Brandt St. *First National Bank*, T242351, is on Drieboom St. All 3 have ATMs and money changing facilities. **Communications Post Office**, Khoicas St, Mon-Fri 0800-1630, Sat 0800-1130. Telephone (international) next door. **Medical services** *The State Hospital*, T242333. **Police** T10111, Ernest Stumpfe St.

The South

Hardap Dam Recreation Resort and Game Park

The **Hardap Dam** was first proposed in 1897 by German geologist Dr Theodor Rehbock but it took a number of surveys and a further 63 years before construction began on what is now Namibia's largest dam. The name Hardap derives from the Nama word meaning 'nipple' or 'wart', which is how the surrounding area of low conical-shaped hills appeared to the early inhabitants.

Colour map 3, grid A4
Off the B1, 15 km
north of Mariental.
Follow the road 6 km
to the resort entrance

   The dam has a surface area of 25 sq km and has a number of functions. It provides water to irrigate 2,500 ha of wheat, maize, lucerne, cotton, grapes and vegetables, all cultivated on small holdings. It also provides Mariental with its water and acts as a flood-prevention mechanism, needed in 1997 and 2000, the first years of very heavy rainfall since construction.

   As a bonus, the dam is an angler's paradise, being well-stocked with such fish as yellowfish, carp, mullet and catfish, and the resort is a popular weekend getaway for people living in the area. There are commanding 180-degree views from the glass-walled restaurant which has been built on the cliffs by the northern edge of the dam.

The **Hardap Game Park** is operated by Namibia Wildlife Resorts, and the facilities show the standard lack of attention and general tiredness typifying all the government's properties. Geographically, the park is divided into two sections, both of which can be accessed for game drives. A small section of 1,848 ha is located near the resort along the northern edge of the dam, and this is where the resident population of **black rhino** lives. These are Namibia's southern-most black rhinos, having been introduced from Damaraland in 1990. The larger section of the park measures 23,000 ha and includes a 15-km game drive. This lies to the south of the dam, with an abundance of game. Upon proclamation as a game park, the area was restocked with antelopes, such as kudu, gemsbok, eland, red hartebeest, springbok and mountain zebra. Leopards too have been spotted in the area of the Great Komatsas River.

Angling　There are fishing spots at various points along the northern shore of the lake. Permits, and a map of permitted fishing spots, are available from the resort office or from the magistrate's office in Mariental. Anglers are advised to watch out for the park's black rhinos, particularly when emerging from your vehicle.

There is a private concession for a ferry service on the lake. *Hardap Ferries* T063-240805, T081-2494200 (mob) encourages anglers to 'come and catch the big one' from the boat. Follow the signs near the park entrance.

Birdwatching　A large number of birds can be observed around the dam, thanks to the diverse habitats on offer. Water birds, such as pelican, cormorant, darter and spoonbill, can be seen on the lake itself, as well as fish eagle and a small number of osprey. The reed beds below the dam wall support large numbers of herons and between April and October are home to white dwarf bitterns. Following the roads through the park, there is a good chance of seeing ostrich, kori bustard and the ubiquitous Namaqua sandgrouse.

Hiking　There is a newly marked 5-km hiking trail in the northwestern corner of the park, which takes roughly two hours to complete. Vegetation along the route consists of dwarf shrub savannah such as shepherd's tree, stink-bush, wool bush and brittle thorn, with camel thorn and buffalo thorn found growing in the dry river-courses. As the trail passes by the banks of the Great Komatsas River, the ruins of the country's first school for whites can be seen. Shortly

The South

Hardap Dam

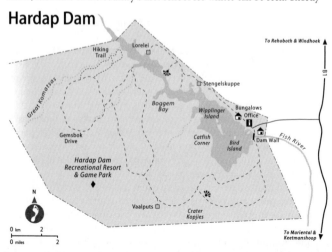

after there is a spring surrounded by shady trees, making a good place to sit down, have a picnic and a break. As with all hiking in Namibia, it is important to take along a minimum of 2 litres of water per person.

Hikers should **watch out for black rhino** along the route, especially when passing through patches of dense vegetation. Should the need arise, standard advice is not to panic and to try to get up a tree or large boulder. Failing that, face any charge and step aside at the last moment. Being virtually blind, the rhino should sail on past!

The resort is open year round, but experiences very high (35°C+) daytime temperatures in summer (Dec-Mar) and very cold (0°C) night-time temperatures in winter (Jun-Jul), so these may not be the best times to visit. Accommodation can be booked through Central Reservations in Windhoek. Gates are open from 0600-2300. The resort has a good, reasonably priced restaurant with panoramic views of the lake, filling station and shop (closes 1800), conference centre, 4 tennis courts and 25-m swimming pool. Day visitors permitted sunrise-1800, later if dining, entrance fee N$20 adults, N$2 children, N$20 car. **Sleeping D** *5-bed bungalow*, fully equipped, 'luxury' bungalows also provide crockery and cutlery. **E** *2-bed bungalow*, field-kitchen cooking facilities. **F** *Dormitory, camping & caravan sites*, shared ablution blocks and cooking facilities.

Essentials

East of Mariental

Some 10 km north of Mariental, the C20 heads east into the Kalahari Desert towards the small cattle town of Aranos. En route it passes **Stampriet,** a small settlement where thanks to artesian water flowing in from the Kalahari, fruit and vegetables are cultivated. At Stampriet, the C15 heads south along the Auob River towards Gochas. Along this route lie a number of battle sites and memorials dating back to the 1904-07 war of resistance against the Germans.

Stampriet & Gochas
Colour map 3, grid A4

South of Stampriet, 20 km along the C15, is the farm **Gross Nabas**, the sight of one of the bloodiest battles of the war. A small monument on the main road commemorates the battle of 2-4 January 1905, during which the Witbooi Nama inflicted heavy losses on the German forces. Another monument, a further 24 km on, indicates where a German patrol was ambushed and killed in March of that year.

Gochas is a desolate place and lives in hope of a reopening of the Mata Mata border gate into South Africa's Kalahari Gemsbok National Park (or Kagaligadi Transfrontier Park, as it has been renamed, as it spans the Botswana/South Africa frontier) for an upturn in its fortunes. There is a 24-hour petrol station, general store, grubby hotel and cemetery with numerous German graves from the early 1900s.

Guestfarms A *Anib Lodge*, T240529, F240516, www.natron.net/tour/anib/lodgee.htm Turn off B1 10 km north of Mariental onto C20. Follow for 24 km, well signposted. Has 6 luxurious en-suite rooms next to the farmhouse, swimming pool set in a small lush garden, friendly service and wholesome German home-cooking, curio shop, game drives and birdwatching although not a stocked game farm, all inclusive.

If you've travelled to Gochas it is almost certainly to visit the attractive **B/C** *Auob Lodge*, T063-250101, F250102, afrideca@iwwn.com.na, 6 km north of Gochas on the C15 (NB Drive carefully on the C15, it undulates and oncoming traffic can give you a surprise). Has 16 en-suite rooms, swimming pool with outdoor courtyard, squash court, bar, restaurant, horse riding and game drives (to view antelope, giraffe and zebra). They offer excellent deals in the low season – be sure to book ahead, you really don't want to stay in the *Gochas Hotel*. **B** *Kalahari Game Lodge*,

The South

reservations T061-259262. 8 en-suite A-frame chalets, self-catering available, plus a **F** campsite, restaurant, bar, shop, swimming pool, petrol. Offers good game viewing, birdwatching, horse riding and hiking trails. Situated on the 27,000 ha *Sandheuwel Game Ranch* neighbouring the park. The gate at Mata Mata remains closed by red tape, but the game is fairly plentiful on the farm in any case, and, should you be so inclined, the local community have hunting concessions (and provide guides). Ask for details at the lodge. If they are full, nearby is the **B-F** *Donkerhoek Guest Farm*, T0668. You'll need a full tank of petrol to get there as, it 's 300 km from Mariental. Follow the C15 past Gochas to the (closed) Mata Mata gate, and 250 km from Keetmanshoop along the C17 past Koes, turn right on the C15 to South African border and follow signs. Because of the distances involved the lodge is not as popular as it might be, but this is undoubtedly yet another fascinating region of Namibia. Worth visiting if time is no matter.

Between Mariental and Keetmanshoop

Gibeon
Phone code: 063
Colour map 3, grid B4

Gibeon is a medium sized village lying some 70 km southwest of Mariental off the B1 and is perhaps best known nowadays as the source of the Gibeon meteorites displayed in the Post Street Mall sculpture in Windhoek. Although the present name refers to the biblical character, the early Nama settlers called the area *Gorego-re-Abes* or 'drinking place of the zebras'.

Founded in 1863 by Kido Witbooi and the Rhenish Missionary Knauer, Gibeon is home of the Witbooi clan, which in the second half of the 19th century developed into a closely-knit, politically active community of Nama clans. Under the leadership of Hendrik Witbooi, Gibeon was a focal point of anti-German resistance in the south, which led to the establishment of a military post here in 1894. In the same year Gibeon was officially named a district and construction of a fort began.

In the 1890s, after the discovery of kimberlite pipes, there were various unsuccessful attempts to mine diamonds in the area, however these were abandoned in 1910. In 1915, Gibeon was the site of a bloody battle between invading South African and German troops, during which 41 soldiers from both sides died and 96 were wounded. A graveyard where those who died are buried is found close to the station.

Although Gibeon has a long and interesting past, unfortunately none of the colonial buildings remain and it is not really worth the 9 km detour from the B1 to visit. There is no petrol station, just a bakery/shop, bottle store and payphone. However, the area is developing as a regional arts centre; women in the settlements nearby have grouped together to produce, market and sell colourful embroidery of birds, animals and African designs on dark cotton backgrounds. The *Gibeon Folk Art* project (T251098) is backed by the Rossing Foundation and sells through Windhoek. Their model is the ANIN project in Hoachanas, longer established and now providing regular income to over 250 local women.

Mukurob
Phone code: 063
Colour map 3, grid B4

Close to the settlement of Asab, 100 km south of Mariental, lies one of Namibia's former best-known landmarks. A 34 m pinnacle of rock used to balance precariously on a narrow neck and base of shale was known in English as the 'finger of God' and in Afrikaans as the *Vingerklip*. The part sandstone, part conglomerate rock survived the erosion of the Weissrand Plateau to the east, but tumbled from its perch in 1988 as a result of seismic tremors experienced after the Armenian earthquake of 7 December.

Legend has it that the Nama and Herero speaking peoples were constantly boasting that each had the best pastures. The Nama reputedly told the Herero that they could boast to their heart's content for they (the Nama) had a rock on their land that was unsurpassable. In response the Herero are supposed to have slaughtered 10 oxen and with the hides made ropes which were attached to the neck of the rock. The Nama jeered as the struggling Herero failed to pull down the rock saying *Mu-Kuro*, 'now you see', thereby giving the rock and place its Nama name. Perhaps the Herero had the final say, after all. ■ *Getting there: At Asab on the B1, turn onto the D1066 and follow for 12 km. Turn right onto D620 and continue for a further 10 km.*

Alternative route to Keetmanshoop

Just south of Mariental on the B1, the tarred C19 crosses the Fish River, and heads west towards the small town of Maltahöhe, on the edge of the Namib Desert, 110 km away. From Maltahöhe there is a choice of roads; west through the spectacular Tsarishoogte Pass before descending into the Namib Desert and on to Sesriem and Sossusvlei; or south past Duwisib Castle and the Schwartzberge, through the hamlet of Helmeringhausen to Bethanie, Keetmanshoop and Lüderitz. The clear desert air and the absolute emptiness of the landscape make this part of southern Namibia well worth the effort of driving through for those with the time and inclination to prolong their journey. Once you have spotted a nice view, stop and turn off the car engine and drink it all in; this is surely one of the reasons you came.

The small town of Maltahöhe, situated on the edge of the Namib desert, was founded in 1900 and owes its name to Malta von Burgdorff, wife of the German commander of the Gibeon garrison. The town was once an important agricultural centre, the nearby farm Nomtsas was established as a sheep farm of some 100,000 ha by the turn of the century. Later, Maltahöhe became the centre of the karakul trade, but years of drought and the collapse of karakul prices brought hard times to the town. Many of the white commercial farmers were forced to sell up and leave, and the resulting loss of revenue killed off many of the businesses in town. While Maltahöhe does have a decent hotel, the town is now a run-down and faded reminder of its former self. The area around the town is spectacular, encompassing the Tsaris, Namgorab and Nubub mountain ranges that border the central highland plateau.

Maltahöhe
Phone code: 063
Colour map 3, grid A3

The South

Sleeping In town: **C/D** *Maltahöhe Hotel*, T293013, F293133, is the main place to stay in town, a regular HAN award winner, well-run if a little smug, with 27 simple en-suite rooms with fans and phone, swimming pool, shaded garden. The restaurant serves good value, tasty, home-cooked food and the bar is the only place in town to sit and relax in the evening. Nice enough, but you are better off in one of the many fabulous guest farms in the region. **C** *Atelier du Désert*, T/F293304, T081-1248204 (mob), bgenevincent@hotmail.com, www.natron.net/genevieve, offers 5 en-suite doubles, a tastefully decorated, more intimate addition to the town's limited offering. Book meals in advance. **D** *Pappot Rest Camp*, T293091, with 3 simple bungalows and a **F** campsite, also serves as the town's bakery and tourist information office.

Guestfarms in the area: **B** *La Vallée Tranquille*, T/F293508, valleet@iway.na, 60 km south of Maltahöhe on the C14. Run by pleasant French owner with 9 en-suite doubles, more under construction. Good food and tasteful décor, swimming pool, price is for half board. Actively promoting the local community's interest in tourism with a 'genuine' Nama camp, where descendants of the original hut-dwellers will return to a reconstructed camp and live in the traditional style. Revenue will go direct to the locals. Stay

2 days to see everything; worth a detour, it sounds promising. **B** *Burgsdorf*, T293013, F293200, 16 km south of Maltahöhe on the C14, then a further 10 km along their bumpy farm track. 7 en-suite rooms, pretty courtyard with succulents and orange trees, large swimming pool, game drives and walks to animal viewing hide, sundowner drive. Hang-gliding and paragliding available for those who fancy it. **B/C** *Daweb*, T/F293088, www.natron.net/tour/daweb, 2 km south of town on the C14. Has 6 comfortable en-suite rooms, a working farm since 1896, they offer farm tours, where blesbok, kudu, oryx and springbok share the 18,000 ha grazing with the cattle, and good birdwatching. Available full board or self-catering, nice communal braai area. Also offer **F** camping with clean ablutions and water.

Tour operators The recommended *TokTokkie Trails*, T0668, ask for 5230, is based here, offering guided tours into the NamibRand Nature Reserve. **Directory** There are 2 24-hr garages, payphones, a post office, police station, excellent butcher, bottle stores, takeaways and a *Standard Bank*, T293011, with no ATM – all are located on or just off the main street. You may have to use your wits, as every sign appears to point in the wrong direction.

Duwisib Castle

Phone code: 063
Colour map 3, grid A2

Duwisib Castle is a unique reminder of Namibia's colonial past and is situated in an improbable location in the rugged, dry veld on the edge of the Namib desert southwest of Maltahöhe. Designed by the architect Willi Sander who was also responsible for Windhoek's three hill-top castles, Duwisib was commissioned in 1907 by Hansheinrich von Wolf and his wife Jayta, an American heiress. Von Wolf had arrived in Namibia in 1904 to serve in the Schutztruppe as a captain in command of a regiment. It was during this time that he became interested in the area around Maltahöhe. In 1906 he resigned his commission and returned to Germany where he met Jayta. The two were married in April 1907 after which they arrived to settle in Namibia, buying Farm Duwisib from the Treasury.

The castle took two years to build, a remarkably short time considering that many of the building materials were imported from Europe via Lüderitz, from where they were hauled by ox wagon across the Namib desert. Herero workers were employed to quarry stone from a nearby site, Italian stonemasons were brought from Italy to finish off the stone and actually build the castle, and carpenters from Germany, Sweden and Belgium were responsible for the woodwork.

Von Wolf and his wife soon became known as the Baron and Baroness by the local German and Afrikaner farmers in recognition of the lavish lifestyle they enjoyed. The von Wolfs employed seven Europeans to assist in managing the castle and the business. 'Baron' von Wolf bred horses from imported Australian and British stock and some people believe that the wild horses of the Namib seen today in the Aus area are survivors of his original stud. He also imported Hereford bulls from England and wool sheep from the Cape.

In 1914, just before the outbreak of the First World War, the von Wolfs left for England to buy further stock for their stud. During the voyage war broke out and the boat they were travelling on was forced to seek shelter in Argentina where they were interned. Released a few months later, von Wolf was determined to join the German forces, which he succeeded in doing, only to fall at the Battle of the Somme in September 1916. Jayta never returned to Namibia to reclaim her property or to sell the farm, and died in New Jersey in 1946 at the age of 64. The farm itself was bought and sold twice before eventually, in 1979, the then colonial administration of South West Africa bought the castle with the intention of preserving it as a heritage site.

The castle is designed in neo-romantic style, with elements of both Gothic and Renaissance architecture present. In addition there is a collection of antique European furniture on display, as well as old armour, paintings, photographs and copperplate engravings. The courtyard at the rear of the castle has an ornamental fountain and a pair of large jacaranda trees, which provide shade during the heat of the day and, when in flower (September-October), fill the courtyard with their scent.

■ *Open year round 0800-1700, with cafeteria and small curio shop. N$20 adults, N$5 children. Getting there: Coming from either Maltahöhe or Helmeringhausen, take the C14, then the D831 before turning onto the D826. The roads are rough, but manageable in an ordinary car. Well signposted from the rutted main roads (drive with extra care), but then poorly, take the turning away from the campsite once in the grounds.*

Sleeping **By the Castle**: Accommodation is in the hands of Namibia Wildlife Resorts, **D/E** *Farm Duwisib Rest Camp*, nfy-elke@mweb.com.na, with 2-bed, 4-bed and 6-bed bungalows with self-catering facilities, swimming pool and landing strip. Full board can be arranged, located beside the castle. **F** *Duwisib Castle Camping* is by the entrance to the grounds of the castle, with 10 large and pleasant pitches under huge camelthorn trees with braai pit, water, no electricity and dingy ablution facilities with haphazard hot water.

Guestfarms in the area: **A-D** *Namseb Rest Camp*, T293166, F293157. Take D36 northeast out of Maltahöhe and follow the signs. 5 fully equipped en-suite chalets on this working ostrich farm, 16 en-suite double rooms, swimming pool, a la carte restaurant or self-catering, game drives. **B** *Spitzkoppe Castle Guestfarm*, T293206, F293208, 55 km south of Maltahöhe on the C14, and a further 11 km along farm track. 6 en-suite doubles in an old German farm, TV lounge, swimming pool, walking and 4WD trails and game drives. **C** *Daweb Guestfarm*, T293088, 2 km outside Maltahöhe on C14. 6 en-suite double rooms, restaurant, game drives, birdwatching, walking trails, camping also possible.

This small settlement lies 120 km south of Maltahöhe on the gravel C14, en route for Bethanie, Aus and Lüderitz. There is a petrol station open 0800-1800 Monday-Saturday, a general store, bottle store and small hotel. It is worth visiting the **Agricultural Museum** to look at the old farming implements, an old fire engine used at Lüderitz and one of the ox-wagons used to transfer building materials and furniture from the coast to Castle Duwisib. The key is available from the hotel next door.

Helmering-hausen
Phone code: 063
Colour map 3, grid C3

Farm Mooifontein, 19 km south of Helmeringhausen on the C14, was the site of a German military station during the colonial period. The bodies of German soldiers who died while fighting the Nama lie in the graveyard, which contains a memorial in the form of a chapel. The iron gates were forged from the rims of ox-wagon wheels.

Sleeping **In town**: **D** *Helmeringhausen Hotel*, T283083, F283132, hhotel@natron.net. Small, friendly country hotel with newly refurbished en-suite rooms, dining room, bar and braai area, B&B. Hotel owner arranges tours to local places of interest.

Guestfarms in the area: **A/B** *Dabis Guestfarm*, reservations T061-232300, F249937, farm direct 0638, ask for 6820, photographer@mweb.com.na, 10 km north of Helmeringhausen on C14. 7 en-suite rooms, fresh farm food on this working farm, hiking, game viewing, all inclusive, but still quite expensive. **B** *Konkiep Lapa*, T621121, 60

The South

km southeast towards Bethanie along the D425 from the C13. Smart lodge with watering holes for viewing game, interesting engravings at Zuurberg Rock and challenging 'Ekora' 4x4 trail. **C** *Sinclair Guestfarm*, T06362 ask for 6503, reservations T061-226979, www.natron.net/tour/sinclair/sinclair.htm, take D407 northwest out of Helmeringhausen for 50 km and follow the signs to the farm. One of the oldest guestfarms in Namibia, 5 en-suite doubles, restaurant, game drives, hiking, landing strip. A nearby abandoned copper mine makes for an interesting excursion for the geologically inclined, all inclusive, caters mostly to German guests. **D** *Lovedale Self Catering Cottage*, T0638 ask for 6130, 19 km from Helmeringhausen on the D407. Fully equipped 3 bedroom house on working farm, swimming pool, horse riding, hiking. **D** *Schwarzkuppe Guest Farm*, T293304, T081-1248204 (mob), by the D808/C14 junction. Opened in 2001, with 4 en-suite doubles (B&B), a self-catering flat and **F** campsite (at $35pp). A reasonable roadside place to stop off, with good value traditional Boer (ie meaty) meals. **E-F** *Saraus Rest Camp*, T064-500701, 081-1244915 (mob), 35 km north of Helmeringhausen, signposted off the C14. Simple doubles (B&B) and well equipped campsite, especially for larger groups, communal facilities, electricity, indoor eating area. Also have a caravan for hire.

Tiras Mountains Conservancy The area around the C13/D707 junction is the newly declared Tiras Mountains Conservancy, a collection of farms that offer a range of 'back to nature' experiences, principally walking in their remote and under-appreciated (in their view) region. Hikes from their farms take the visitor into dune and mountain scapes that are unimaginable from the dusty roadside, with walks to and through rock art, succulents, quiver trees, plus bird and game viewing. Worth a couple of days in your agenda, as an introduction to Namibia's outback.

Sleeping These working farms have decided to operate interdependently for tourism, so you can either knock on a specific door, or contact T0638 ask for 6522, F061-242535, eco@iafrica.com.na for the range of guest rooms, chalets and camp sites available. On the C13, just north of the D707 junction, is **C/D-F** *Tiras Haus*, T0638 ask for 6930, with 2 pretty self-catering bungalows (or full board if requested), guided nature walks and 2 campsites (N$55pp) at a remote, mountainside site a few km from the farm house, with new pristine facilities and wonderful views. **D** *Namtib Desert Lodge*, T0638 ask for 6640, reservations T061-233597, namtib@iafrica.com.na, signposted off the D707, northwest of the C13 junction. Has 5 en-suite chalets, very welcoming owners, game drives, hiking trails, horse riding.

Keetmanshoop

Keetmanshoop lies at the crossroads of southern Namibia and is principally a transit stop to and from South Africa, with a wide range of relatively pricey accommodation. However, it is also a convenient base from which to explore the 'deep' south, in particular the Fish River Canyon, the nearby Quiver Tree Forest and the Brukkaros volcano close to the old Nama settlement at Berseba.

Ins & outs
Phone code: 063
Colour map 3, grid B4

Getting there The B1 from Mariental and Windhoek is a fairly dull straight run. You will see Brukkaros volcano to the west and a long low ridge to the east, atop which is the Commonwealth War Graves (on the C18, signposted, quite far out of your way if you have no specific interest). Heading south you pass the village of Asab (24-hr Shell garage, bottle store, shop and truckers hotel), a signposted turn off for Iganigobes Hot Springs, Quiver Tree Forest and camping (all very basic and fairly run down) and the village of Tses (Caltex garage open 0700-2000, turn here for Berseba and Brukkaros). The

B1 continues for a further 160 km to Grünau where it branches into the B3 heading east through Karasburg to the South African border at Ariamsvlei. The B1 itself reaches the South African border at Noordoewer after 142 km. From Keetmanshoop, the B4 heads west towards the Aus Mountains before descending to the desert floor, eventually arriving at the old German seaside town of Lüderitz 350 km away. **Tourist offices** *Southern Tourist Forum*, 5th Ave, T221166, F223818, munkhoop@iafrica.com.na, open Mon-Fri 0800-1200, 1330-1600, has a miniature replica of the toppled Vingerklip in the office; very helpful for information and arrangements for travel and accommodation in the south.

Keetmanshoop is effectively the capital of the south and one of the oldest **History** established towns in Namibia. The original settlement, dating back to the late 18th century, was originally known as *Modderfontein* due to the presence of a strong freshwater spring. Nama herders trekking north from the Cape settled here, calling the place *Swartmodder*, after the muddy river which ran through the settlement after good rains.

During the middle part of the 19th century, the Barmen Society gradually established a series of mission stations in the south of Namibia at places such as Bethanie, Warmbad and Berseba. In 1866, following a request by converted Namas living at Swartmodder, Johan Schröder was sent by Reverend Krönlein, the pastor at Berseba, to establish a mission station at Swartmodder. After struggling to build a church and home for himself and his family, Schröder appealed to the Barmen Society for funds to develop the station. Johan Keetman, a rich industrialist and Chairman of the Barmen Society, personally donated 2,000 marks to pay for the building of a church, and in appreciation Schröder renamed the settlement Keetmanshoop (Keetman's Hope).

Like many other settlements in Namibia at the time, Keetmanshoop functioned both as a mission station and as a trading post. A successor to Schröder, Reverend Thomas Fenchel, came into conflict with the European traders who bartered liquor, usually brandy, with the Nama herders in exchange for livestock which was then sold in the Cape. Once the liquor was drunk the only source of food for the herders was the mission station.

In 1890, a freak flooding of the Swartmodder River washed away the original church, but Fenchel and his congregation had rebuilt it by 1895 from when it served a multiracial congregation until 1930. Abandoned for many years, the church was restored and declared a National Monument in 1978 and today houses the Keetmanshoop Museum.

The year 1890 also saw a wave of German immigrants to the new colony and particularly to this area, and in 1894 a fort was established in the town. In the following years as soldiers were discharged from the army, many bought farms or settled in the town which grew to support the surrounding farms. The growth of the town convinced the authorities of the necessity of improving communications and the railway to Lüderitz was completed in 1908. In the following year the military handed over the town to a civil authority and Keetmanshoop became the administrative centre for the south of the country.

Economically, the town's prosperity was built upon the karakul sheep industry which reached its peak in the early 1970s; since the decline of the industry (see box) Keetmanshoop has earned its keep more mundanely as a transit point for goods and people travelling between Namibia and South Africa. There are glimmers of hope that new businesses will be established to help alleviate unemployment in the community. An ostrich meat processing plant was built in 1997, which 'processes' 100,000 birds a year, and has a hatchery and tannery alongside; 300 tons of meat are exported per

The South

year. An international pilot training centre for pilots from throughout the SADC region was established at the town's airport at the end of 1999, thanks to the efforts of Works, Transport and Communications Minister, Hampie Plichta, a native of Keetmanshoop.

Sights The old Rhenish Mission Church on Kaiser Street now houses **Keetmanshoop Museum**. The displays focus on the history of the town, information on the surrounding area and a small art exhibition. Outside, by the rock garden of aloes, succulents and cacti, a traditional Nama hut stands cheek to jowl with early trekkers' wagons. The stone church itself is a fine example of early colonial architecture, with its original corrugated iron roof and bell-tower with weather-vane, and inside there is an elegant pulpit and wooden balcony. The church looks particularly attractive at night when it is floodlit. ■ *T223316, open Mon-Thu 0700-1230 and 1330-1630, Fri 0700-1230 and 1330-1630.*

The former post and telegraph office, the **Kaiserliches Poststamp**, designed by government architect, Gottlieb Redecker, and built in 1910, is another of Keetmanshoop's fine early buildings. The building now houses the useful **Southern Tourist Forum** and Air Namibia offices and is located on 5th Avenue by Central Park.

Sleeping While the town has a good selection of accommodation, Keetmanshoop is not the place to dawdle and you may find it pricier than other parts of the country. All the establishments listed below are in/near town. Visitors heading east via Koes to the Kalahari will pass the *Panorama* campsite after about 40 km, and should refer to the Mariental section (see *Kalahari Game Lodge*, page 301). Those heading west/southwest towards Fish River Canyon and the coast should refer to those sections for the accommodation in the area.

Keetmanshoop

■ **Sleeping**	6 Home Sweet Home	3 Bird's Mansions &
1 Bird's Mansions	7 La Rochelle	Internet Café
2 Bird's Nest		4 JT's Bar & Grill
3 Canyon	● **Eating**	5 Lara's
4 Central Lodge	1 Andre's	6 Schutzen Haus
5 Chapel Inn	2 Balaton	7 Trans-Namib Club

0 metres 200
0 yards 200

B-C *Canyon Hotel*, 5th Ave, T223361, F223714, http://resafrica.net/canyon-hotel is a well-managed, friendly hotel with comfortable en-suite rooms with a/c, TV and phone. Built 25 years ago, the hotel has a new wing, a total of 70 spacious rooms, gym, restaurant, coffee shop and bar by the swimming pool – a good place to escape from the intense summer heat of the south, and passers-by are welcome to use the facilities free of charge. Recommended. **C/D** *Bird's Mansions Hotel*, 6th Ave, T221711, F221730, www.birdnest.com has 23 en-suite rooms with a/c and TV, very central, secure parking and laundry. Internet cafe and good restaurant on site. **D** *Bird's Nest B&B*, 16 Pastorie St, T222906, F222261, birdnest@iafrica.com.na has 5 en-suite a/c rooms with TV, phone and secure parking, communal braai area, plentiful breakfasts, dinner if booked ahead. **D** *Central Lodge*, 5th Ave, T225850, F223532, opened Jul 2001, comfortable lodge with 12 en-suite rooms with a/c and TV, swimming pool, bar and conference facilities. **D** *Chapel Inn*, 31a Kaiser St, T223762, pleasant, central B&B. **D** *Gessert's B&B*, 138 13th St, Westdene, T/F223892, T081-2490106 mob. A small, friendly, family-run guesthouse with en-suite rooms and swimming pool, slightly out of town, follow signs. **D** *Home Sweet Home*, 19 Luchtenstein St, T081-11275397, central, self-catering flats. **D** *La Rochelle*, 21 6th Ave, T223845. A smart new guest house on the side of the hill overlooking the town. **E-F** *Lafenis Rest Camp*, T224316, F224309, on the B1, 5 km south of town, 19 simple but adequate 4-bed en-suite bungalows with TV and a/c, restaurant, and campsite with adequate facilities and wild west decor.

Camping **F** *Municipal Campsite & Caravan Park*, T223316, F223818, in the centre of town, with pleasant, good value campsites, electricity, adequate ablution blocks (they charge extra if you take a shower) and laundry facilities, as in any town centre campsite, beware of thieves. **C-F** *Quivertree Forest Restcamp*, T/F222835, quiver@iafrica.com.na is well placed for morning or evening photography, 16 km from Keetmanshoop on the D29. Accommodation is in en-suite rooms with full board or B&B in the farmhouse, 8 fully equipped self-catering 'diving bells' with 2-4 beds, or camping with electricity, lights and basic ablutions by the Quivertree Forest itself, 1 km from the farmhouse. **F** *Garas Quivertree Park & Restcamp*, T223217, morkel@namibnet.com is 22 km north of Keetmanshoop on the B1, very basic campsite with ablutions. **F** *Panorama*, 40 km from Keetmanshoop on the C17 to Koes.

Busy by day, Keetmanshoop becomes a dark and unwelcoming town once the sun goes down; you are best picking a dinner spot and settling in for the evening. The two smartest places in town, whose kitchens stay open until 2200, are the *Canyon Hotel*, offering Namibian game dishes as well as fish, pasta and other European dishes, with a decent selection of wines to go with the food and the *Bird's Mansions Restaurant*, within the hotel, serving a good range of meat and fish with tasty sauces. *Lara's Restaurant*, 5th Ave and Schmiede St, is cheaper and reasonable and has a well attended bar in the evenings. *JT's Bar & Grill* is where the lads go for a pint, by the Engen on 5th Ave. *Andrés*, Fenschel St, not licensed, has excellent pizzas and cheap burgers. *Balaton Restaurant*, Mittel St, closes at 1700, serves tasty Hungarian goulash, chicken paprika, etc, as well as the usual light meals and takeaways. *Schutzen Haus*, 8th Ave, is a German club offering pub food, draught beer and right-wing jollity. *Trans-Namib Club*, Schmiede St, charges N$5 admission and is much the same, but for the Afrikaaner.

Eating
Kitchens typically shut at 2100

The South

Swimming pool Excellent 50-m municipal swimming pool, just off 8th Ave, open Sep-Apr.

Sport

Transport

500 km Windhoek
340 km Lüderitz
300 km Noordoewer
(South Africa border)

Road For *Intercape Mainliner* coaches to Cape Town via Upington, and Windhoek via Mariental and Rehoboth, see timetable on page 382. Coach picks up and drops off in front of *Andrés Restaurant*. It is also possible to catch a minibus to Cape Town or Johannesburg. Also *Baileys Transport*, T061-262522. **Train** Station on the edge of town. For trains to Windhoek via Marienthal, Ariamsvlei and Upington, see timetable on page 383.

Directory

Banks *Bank Windhoek*, *First National Bank* and *Standard Bank* are all situated on Fenschel St, and all change money and ATMs. **Communications** Post Office 5th Ave, Mon-Fri 0800-1630, Sat 0800-1200. **Internet** access available from the *Horse & Bell Café*, open to midnight, with good connection speeds – N$20 per hour. **Medical services** *The State Hospital*, T23388, signposted just off B1, 1 km north of town. There is a very well stocked new pharmacy on the corner of Mittel/7th Ave. **Useful addresses** Police 5th Ave, T10111.

Naute Dam

Colour map 3, grid B4
Drive 30 km west on the B4, then south on D545 for 20 km until you see the sign for the dam

Located on the Lowen River, surrounded by a series of small conical hills, Naute Dam is Namibia's third largest dam and a lovely spot to escape the heat of the surrounding sandy hills. The dam provides Keetmanshoop with all its water, in addition to providing water for some small scale irrigation. At one time there was talk of a recreation area and nature park, but the plan never came to fruition and nowadays visitors are few and far between.

Birdwatching and hiking Twitchers will find colonies of pelicans, cormorants, darters, Egyptian geese and other water birds on the reservoir. There are no specific trails laid out, but it is quite possible to walk around the dam. There is a variety of game in the vicinity of the dam, as the animal spores on the sand dunes testify, and kudu, springbok, ostrich and other small animals may be spotted. There is a 10 km 'nature drive' that can be followed.

Camping There is a demarcated camping area close to the boat launch site by the dam with no toilets, taps or washing facilities, so all but the self-sufficient would be better just to stop by for a swim and picnic. Access appears to be unrestricted and free of charge. In case of problems (the dam is sometimes locked), carry on past the entrance; the keys can be obtained from the staff at the water purification plant, 1 km before reaching the dam.

Quiver Tree Forest and Giant's Playground

The **Quiver Tree Forest** is one of the main attractions of southern Namibia. The 'trees' are in fact aloe plants or *aloe dichotoma* which usually only grow singly, but which in a few places grow in large groups, and are ambitiously called forests. The plant's name derives from the former practice of some of the San and Nama peoples of hollowing out the light, tough-skinned branches of the plant to use as quivers for their arrows. The forest was declared a National Monument in 1955 and the quiver trees themselves are a protected species in Namibia. It is forbidden to carry off any parts of the trees.

A good time to visit the forest is either early in the morning for sunrise, or late afternoon for sunset, when the clear light offers good photo opportunities. The view south over the veld to the Karas Mountains is especially beautiful at these times.

The **Giant's Playground** is 5 km further northeast on the D29. Let yourself in via the farmgate and drive up to a car park. From here there is a short trail through the most striking formations. This is an area covered in huge, black, basalt rocks balanced precariously on top of each other. These strange formations were caused by the erosion of sedimentary overlying rocks 170 million years ago. The playground is a pleasantly eerie place to go for a gentle late afternoon walk before catching sunset at the Quiver Tree Forest. **NB** Do not climb on the rocks, they may be well balanced but they are not that secure. There is a lodge and a campsite close to the entrance to the Quiver Tree Forest, see Keetmanshoop section above for further details.

■ *Both attractions are on private land – the local farmer has a lucrative trade in charging a N$15 pp entrance fee. Getting there: Follow signs from the B1 north from town, turn onto the D29 after 3 km.*

Brukkaros volcano

This mountain dominates the skyline to the west of the main road between Mariental and Keetmanshoop. A climb to the top is well rewarded with superb views of the surrounding plains. The name Brukkaros is the German equivalent of the Nama name *Geitsigubeb*, referring to the mountain's supposed resemblance to the large leather apron traditionally worn by Nama women around their waist.

Getting there Turn off the B1 at Tses, 80 km north of Keetmanshoop, follow the C98 for 40 km towards Berseba, then take the D3904 north for 18 km to Brukkaros. The D3904 reaches a gate at the foot of the volcano, where a N$15 pp and $10 per car entry charge is levied. There is a payphone here. Visitors with 4WD vehicles (with good clearance) will be able to drive a further 3 km up to the simple campsite (see below). **Best time to visit** For those based in Keetmanshoop, set off early in the morning; avoid hiking in the heat of the day in summer. If you plan on looking in on en route between Windhoek and Keetmanshoop be prepared for an early start and a long day.

Ins & outs
Colour map 3, grid B4

Brukkaros, whose evolution began 80 million years ago, was formed when molten lava intruded into rocks about 1 km below the earth's surface. The lava must have encountered underground water, creating steam which caused huge pressure, raising the overlying rocks into a dome 400 m high and 10 km across. The process was then repeated, but the cover of overlying rock was thin enough to be blown out in a vast explosion. Sedimentation and erosion over several hundred thousand years created the crater floor; simply put, rain washed the finely-shattered rock fragments into the crater, which is roughly 2 km across.

Background

In 1930, the American Smithsonian Institute declared the mountain the perfect site to establish a research station to study the surface of the sun, thanks to the incredibly clear desert air. While the observatory has not functioned for years, this point on the north-western rim of the crater is an ideal place to take in the view over the surrounding plains. The Germans established a heliograph on the eastern rim around 1900. There is a functional VHF radio mast on the rim.

Hikers have a moderate 4 km hike from the parking area to the crater lip. From here the path, such as it is, leads down into the crater and across a dried riverbed, past a number of ancient quiver trees before starting the climb to the radio mast on the northern rim of the crater. There are still signs of the scientists' stay at the volcano – ancient rusting tins, a few old bottles and some graffiti etched into the trunks of the quiver trees. It's all fairly awesome and eerie. At any moment one expects a hungry creature from a Hollywood B-movie to come crawling over the lip of the volcano and gobble you up. The walk itself is not very tough, but there is no water and no shade on the mountain, so it is absolutely essential to take at least 2 litres of water per person.

Hiking

The South

Karakul sheep

The use of Karakul sheep pelts to make high quality leather and fur clothes, formed the backbone of the farming industry in southern Namibia from the early 1920s to the mid-1970s. Often called Namibia's 'black gold' the karakul sheep originated in Bokhara in central Asia, from where they were imported to Germany in the early 1900s.

Experimental breeding started in Germany in 1903 and Paul Thorer, a prominent fur trader, started promoting the idea of exporting the sheep to German colonies. The then Governor of German South West Africa, Von Lindequist, supported the idea, and the first dozen sheep were brought into the country in 1907. In 1909 a further consignment of 22 rams and 252 ewes arrived, followed by smaller numbers of the animals in the years leading up to the First World War. After the end of the war an experimental government karakul farm was set up at Neudam near Windhoek, in order to develop and improve the quality of the pelts. Breeders succeeded in developing pure white pelts in addition to the more normal black and grey ones, and although the former Soviet Union and Afghanistan produced larger numbers of the pelts, Namibian karakul fur was internationally recognized as being of the finest quality.

In 1919 the Karakul Breeders Association was founded to consolidate this new industry, and by 1923 thousands of the pelts were being exported to Germany. Over the next 50 years the numbers of pelts exported each year mushroomed to a peak of 3.2 million in 1973, earning millions of dollars for the farmers of the south. However, a combination of severe drought and changing views in Europe during the 1970s about the ethics of slaughtering millions of lambs only 24 hours old for their pelts, sent the karakul fur industry into decline.

In response to this most farmers in the south switched to breeding dorbber sheep for their meat which guarantees a more reliable source of income, not affected by swings in the fashion industry. However, the recent extreme drought in Namibia has forced many farmers to sell all their livestock, creating a severe economic crisis in the farming industry of the south. Ironically however there has been a revival in the price of karakul pelts and demand for karakul wool in order to make carpets at present outstrips availability. Perhaps the hardy karakul sheep, well adapted to conditions of drought, will make a comeback to supply this new demand.

Camping Established in July 2001 with the help of NACOBTA, the simple but beautifully located community campsite is 3 km from the entrance gate. Campers are charged N$25 pp for the most basic of facilities (pit latrines, call ahead to check if there will be water available). The hardy will be rewarded with fantastic views of the night sky, particularly around the new moon.

Berseba The small Nama village of **Berseba**, 18 km away, is one of the oldest established settlements in southern Namibia, and dates back to 1850. As with other early 19th century settlements in Namibia, its establishment as a separate polity was directly linked to the acquisition of a missionary by the community. In 1851, Berseba was said to number 700 inhabitants and was lead by Paul Goliath, who had been the *onder-kaptein* or deputy chief at Bethanie during missionary Schmelen's stay at the settlement.

Today the village numbers about 2,000 people and is rather a depressed community with little or no work for the adult population, who are dependent on their goats and sheep for survival. There is one public phone but no evident shop.

West from Keetmanshoop

The B4 heads west from Keetmanshoop over the high veld past Seeheim and Goageb towards the small mountain town of Aus 230 km away. After leaving Aus, the road descends rapidly from the edge of the central highlands plateau to the desert floor, where it cuts a swathe through the sand dunes for a further 120 km until it reaches Lüderitz. The last stretch through the Namib desert is one of the most stunning drives in Namibia, allow yourself a minute to stop and to enjoy the calming silence, and stop off at the watering hole for the desert horses.

Seeheim
Phone code: 063
Colour map 3, grid B4

Nothing to see, merely two places to stop for lunch or overnight. **C/D** *Seeheim Hotel*, T063-250503, signposted off the C12, just south of the B4, has cultivated a wild west hotel feel (which has led to it appearing in three feature films), has comfortable en-suite rooms, swimming pool, satellite TV lounge, a decent bar and restaurant, petrol, hiking trails, horse riding and hunting safaris. A picturesque spot, but baking hot in summer and with a fairly brusque welcome. **F** *Klippen Terrace*, T063-250514. This is just west of Seeheim on the B4 and a great place to stop for a drink/light lunch or fresh coffee with tasty homemade fare on the way to/from Lüderitz. They have a small, clean camping site. Very simple bungalows on the surrounding hillocks, with communal bathrooms, are planned.

Heading 8 km further west is the **E-F** *Kuibis Castle Guest House*, T063-258371, with 4 doubles, where you can choose to eat with the family in their dining room or self-cater. Their shop sells excellent home-made jam and cookies, biltong and basic provisions.

Goageb
Phone code: 063
Colour map 3, grid B3

This dusty village is only noteworthy as the turn-off to Bethanie (not much of an honour), but if you are desperate, try the reasonably cheap, **E** Konkiep Motel, T283566, F283107, which also houses the village bar, restaurant and petrol pump (not 24 hour).

Bethanie
Phone code: 063
Colour map 3, grid B3

The C14 is tarred for the 15 km to Bethanie, another forgotten town that now serves the local community with a garage, takeaway, well stocked shops, and a hotel dating back to 1880, the **D/E** *Bethanie Hotel*, T283013, with 4 rooms, bar, restaurant, pool table. A further 35 km towards Helmeringhausen is the smarter **C** *Konkiep Lapa*, described above under Helmeringhausen.

Aus

Phone code: 063
Colour map 3, grid B2

This small settlement perched high up in the Aus Mountains is famous in Namibia for receiving occasional snowfalls during cold winters. After summer rains, the area is also renowned for the beauty of its wild flowers and hiking trails, particularly around *Klein Aus Vista*, west of town. The village consists of a small hotel (doubling as the bottle store), guest house, railway halt, police station, well-stocked shop and garage, and a line of old cottages.

History

Aus was established as a prisoner-of-war camp in 1915 following the surrender of the German colonial troops to the South African forces. The site was chosen for its strategic significance, situated as it is on the railway line between Keetmanshoop and the harbour at Lüderitz. This made it possible to ship food and equipment from Cape Town via Lüderitz to the camp.

By 15 August 1915, 22 POWs and 600 guards were stationed here, initially living in tents. At one stage the camp held more than 1,500 prisoners, many of these people were German nationals who had never been in the army but had been making their living as farmers and traders. The hot summer days and cold winter nights made life virtually unbearable, and in the face of South African apathy to improve the situation, the inmates themselves set about making bricks which they used to build their own houses. By the end of 1916 none of the prisoners were living in tents and they were even selling their surplus to their South African guards at 10 shillings per 1,000 bricks.

By 1916 the prisoners had built their own wood stoves on which to cook and the authorities had provided water for washing and laundry purposes. It seems as if the South African garrison was not so enterprising and continued living in tents until 1918 when barracks were finally constructed.

Following the signing of the Treaty of Versailles at the end of the First World War, the prisoners were gradually released, the last group leaving on 13 May 1919 after which the camp was closed. Unfortunately little remains of the camp beyond a few weather beaten walls and foundations and a commemorative plaque.

Sights   The site of the old **POW Camp** can be visited and is indicated by a National Monuments plaque on a rock. It really is a desolate place, and as you walk around, images of the place in its heyday are not hard to conjure. Unfortunately, the only literature available is printed in Afrikaans. ■ *Turn off B4 into the village. Drive up the hill past the hotel and petrol station and continue for a further 3 km to the turn-off for Rosh Pinah. Ignore this, take the left fork, after 500 m the remains of the camp are to the right, drive slowly, the turning by the small trees can easily be missed.*

Garub Pan   If you fail to catch a glimpse of the famous desert horses from the main road it is always worth making a short detour to the Garub Pan. Here you will find an artificial water point and a viewing shelter with information board and visitors book. The site is 1 km north of the B4, 22 km west of Aus. The horses are usually here in the winter, when there is little standing water elsewhere in the area. The herd numbers between 60 and 150 horses; there were more before 104 were caught and auctioned to farmers in 1987 and 1992, after drought had reduced grazing to unsustainable levels. This process of capture and sale was not repeated in the late 1990s, resulting in 60 horses dead. They are now overseen by the Namib Feral Horse Trust, a collaboration between the Lüderitz four-wheel drive club and the Lüderitz MET.

Sleeping   **C-F** *Klein Aus Vista*, T/F258021, ausvista@ldz.namib.com, well signposted 2 km west of turning off the B4 for Aus. A wonderful spot, worth spending an extra day on your holiday. In addition to a lovely campsite in the hills (12 sites, some with wind shelters, with water, but no electricity or light), a dorm cabin and large en-suite 'luxury' rooms (half-board) in the main house, there are a couple of isolated cottages 7 km from the farmhouse, built into the rocks, and blessed with superb views across the desert. There are mapped trails in the hills which can be followed on foot, horse or mountain bike, taking from a few hours to 3 days. Recommended. They offer 4WD and horse-back excursions to see wild horses (check www.namibhorses.com) and can provide information on the Namib Feral Horse Hiking Trail, an easy 3-4 day trail with well-provisioned overnight huts. Recommended. **D/E** *Bahnhof Hotel*, T258044. This rather quaint village centre hotel has adequate rooms with and without en-suite facilities, a restaurant and acts as the local bar, which can get very lively. **E-F** *Namib Garage One-Stop B&B*, T258029, F258017, reception at the Caltex garage/shop. This was the garage owners' house and feels like they only left yesterday, 4 en-suite rooms, campsite (N$20pp). The well stocked shop sells meat and fresh produce.

Wild horses of the Namib

The legendary wild horses of the Namib are probably the only wild desert-dwelling horses in the world, and their origins are a source of much speculation. Romantics suggest that they are the descendants of the stud kept by 'Baron' von Wolf at Duwisib Castle 160 km away. Other less fanciful suggestions are that they escaped from surrounding farms or that they originate from horses left behind by the German troops when they fled Aus in 1915.

These horses are uniquely adapted to survive in their desert environment. They move slowly, sweat less and drink as infrequently as once every 5 days, their only source of water coming from a bore-hole at Garub sunk especially for them. A blind here allows visitors to observe the horses from close up on the rare occasions when they do come to drink.

The numbers of horses are constantly fluctuating in response to the grazing conditions – only the toughest can survive the frequent droughts. However, during good rainy seasons grass grows on the dunes and the horses are able to fatten themselves in preparation for the lean years ahead. At one time a proposal was made to tame some of the horses and use them for patrols in the Etosha National Park, but nothing came of it.

Lüderitz

The small coastal town of Lüderitz is one of Namibia's oddities, a faded, picturesque German colonial town lying between the inhospitable dunes of the Namib desert on the one side, and the vast iciness of the South Atlantic on the other. Ironically, both desert and ocean provide the resources necessary for Lüderitz's survival; diamonds from the desert and fish, rock lobster, seaweed and more diamonds from the ocean.

Phone code: 063
Colour map 3, grid B2

Twenty years ago, the town was as good as dead, but thanks to the reopening of the diamond mine at Elizabeth Bay and an improvement in tourist numbers and fishing catches, Lüderitz is currently enjoying a mini-boom. The harbour has been expanded and a smart Waterfront Development is underway, which will boast accommodation, shops, kiosks, offices and restaurants when complete. Proposals to redevelop around the headland to the excellent Nest Hotel are under consideration. And the town remembers to enjoy itself – in 1996 it staged the first traditional German carnival since 1960.

Stone implements and skeletons found around Lüderitz area testify that **History** Khoisan people were visiting the area long before the first Europeans arrived. The Portuguese explorer Bartholomeu Diaz was the first European to set eyes on Lüderitz Bay when he sought refuge from a South Atlantic storm on Christmas Day, 1487. Upon his return from the Cape of Good Hope in July 1488 he erected a stone cross, following Portuguese seafaring traditions of the time.

The next European to show up was Cornelius Wobma, an employee of the Dutch East India Company, who was sent to investigate the possibility of establishing trading links with the local Nama communities. He failed and although the Dutch authorities at the Cape annexed the bay and surrounding islands in 1593, it was to be a further 200 years before further European influence arrived.

From 1842 onwards, European ships exploited the rich guano resources on the islands around the bay, with up to 450 ships anchored in the bay simultaneously. The cold seas of the South Atlantic also proved to be rich whaling grounds. Between 1842 and 1861, the British-ruled Cape Colony annexed all the islands along the coast.

The South

In 1883, Heinrich Vogelsang negotiated a treaty with Nama chief Joseph Fredericks of Bethanie on behalf of the merchant Adolf Lüderitz. This treaty entitled Lüderitz to acquire all the land within a five mile radius of the harbour and cost £100 and 200 rifles. The following year Lüderitz persuaded Chancellor Bismarck to offer German protection to the area, and this event signalled the beginning of the development of the town itself. Unfortunately, Lüderitz himself did not live long enough to see the growth and development of his settlement, as he died in a boat accident whilst exploring the Orange River. The town was named in memory of him.

The main development of the town took place in the early 1900s during the period of German colonisation, first as a base and supply point for the Shutztruppe during the 1904-1907 German-Nama war, and then as a wild

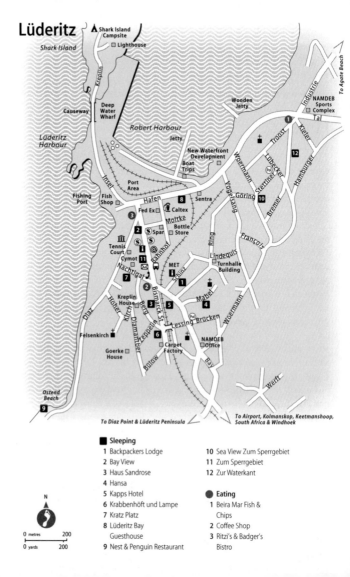

Lüderitz

N

0 metres 200
0 yards 200

To Diaz Point & Lüderitz Peninsula
To Airport, Kolmanskop, Keetmanshoop, South Africa & Windhoek

■ Sleeping
1 Backpackers Lodge
2 Bay View
3 Haus Sandrose
4 Hansa
5 Kapps Hotel
6 Krabbenhöft und Lampe
7 Kratz Platz
8 Lüderitz Bay Guesthouse
9 Nest & Penguin Restaurant
10 Sea View Zum Sperrgebiet
11 Zum Sperrgebiet
12 Zur Waterkant

● Eating
1 Beira Mar Fish & Chips
2 Coffee Shop
3 Ritzi's & Badger's Bistro

west type boom town following the discovery of diamonds in the nearby desert in 1908. Lüderitz was officially declared a town in 1909 and enjoyed a prosperous growth up to and during the inter-war years.

Lüderitz went into decline following the relocation of the Consolidated Diamond Mining Headquarters (CDM) to Oranjemund in 1938. Ironically, the stagnation of the economy prevented the development of the town and thus ensured the preservation of the original buildings, which gives the town its quaint turn-of-the-century feel. During the 1970s interest in Lüderitz as a tourist destination grew and rock lobster, fishing and seaweed industries were developed.

The renaissance of the town is now in full swing with the harbour once again busy, hotels full and migrant workers arriving from the north of Namibia looking for work. Like many tourist centres in Namibia, Lüderitz can get busy during the school holidays; book accommodation in advance if possible. The peak tourist season lasts from June through to September, the winter months. However, because of its relative inaccessibility, the town never gets as overrun as Swakopmund. A word of warning – Lüderitz is a very windy town. Despite what the residents may claim (they are clearly oblivious to the average gale!), the wind blows most days. The worst time is between the end of December and mid-February. During this period the winds can be strong enough to knock you off your feet and enforce a 60 kph speed limit along the approach road for safety. The last 20 km of the main road pass through shifting sand dunes, if you hit a ridge of sand at speed it is like running into cement and can easily cause one to lose control – beware and observe local advice. Camping on Shark Island can be quite an experience. If you choose to visit the beach when the wind is blowing wear long trousers and don't carry anything lose. When we last visited Agate Beach the strong winds managed to tease open a buttoned-down shirt pocket and make off with a few dollar notes!

While the wind may take some getting used to, don't be put off visiting the area. One significant aspect of the local climate is the absence of the thick fog that plagues Walvis Bay and Swakopmund. This is thanks to the town's position in a bay, thereby protecting it from this phenomena. Quite often you can see the bank of fog off Diaz Point, but that is as close as it gets to town. In fact, many of the long time residents who moved to Swakopmund during Lüderitz's decline have returned, unwilling to contend with the terrible fog further up the coast.

Sights

Lüderitz has a number of fine old colonial buildings and a small museum which can easily be explored in a couple of hours walking around the town.

A walk up Bismarck Street, the main thoroughfare, will take you past the **Deutsche-Afrika Bank** building, built in 1907 on the corner of Diaz Street. Further up the street is the **Station Building**, commissioned in 1912 and finished two years later. The railway line from Lüderitz to Aus was completed in 1906 and became important as a means of transporting troops into the interior during the 1904-1907 German-Nama war. Following the discovery of diamonds in 1908 and the subsequent extension of the railway line to Keetmanshoop, the existing station became too small and the German Colonial Administration authorized the building of a new station.

The **Old Post Office**, found on Shintz Street, was completed in 1908, and originally had a clock in its tower, but this was removed in 1912 and transferred to the church. The building now functions as the local MET offices. The

Turnhalle Building on Lindequist Street dates from 1912-13 and was originally a gymnasium, but now doubles as the town library and mini-theatre.

Two of the town's most impressive buildings, the **German Lutheran Church**, or Felsenkirche (Church on the Rocks), and **Goerke House** are situated on neighbouring hillock tops in the old part of town. Each has an excellent view of the town centre and harbour area. The foundation stone for the Church was laid in 1911 and the building was consecrated the following year. The building is notable for its fine stained glass windows and as with the Christuskirche in Windhoek, the altar window was donated by Kaiser Wilhelm II and the altar bible by his wife. ■ *Open daily for an hour from 1700 in winter and from 1800 in summer. Payment by donation.* Just below the church in Berg Street is an interesting collection of original town houses. Unfortunately these can only be viewed from the outside. To get a better idea of what they would have looked like inside, visit Goerke House.

Goerke House The house was named after its original owner Hans Goerke who had been a store inspector in the Shutztruppe and then became a successful local businessman. CDM acquired the house in 1920, sold it to the government in 1944 when it became the town magistrate's official residence, and then repurchased the building in 1983. The house lay empty between 1980-83 after the magistrate was recalled to Keetmanshoop (there not being enough crime in Lüderitz to warrant his presence).

From the outside, the house is an array of different architectural styles incorporating Roman and Egyptian, amongst others, and inside it is possible to imagine what many of the crumbling houses at nearby Kolmanskop must have looked like in their heyday. There is a fine stained-glass window above the staircase depicting a flock of flamingos on the beach, as well as an excellent view over the town and harbour from the balcony of the main bedroom. The house operates as an occasional guesthouse for NAMDEB's VIP guests, so it may be shut during your visit. ■ *Diamantberg St, Mon-Fri 1400-1500 and Sat/Sun 1600-1700. Informative introduction provided, N\$5.*

Lüderitz Museum The museum was founded by Friederich Eberlanz who arrived in Lüderitz in 1914. Fascinated by the local flora, he started a private collection which grew to incorporate ancient stone tools, rocks and other items he discovered. This private collection attracted a wide interest and the existing museum was established in 1961. Today the museum also has displays of local history, the mining industry and an interesting collection of photos and artefacts of the indigenous peoples of the country. Look for the photo of the group of Bushmen after a big feed, as Laurens van der Post puts it in *The Lost World of the Kalahari*, "made him look like a pregnant woman...in this way nature enabled him to store a reserve against dry and hungry moments." ■ *Diaz St. Mon-Fri, 0830-1100, Sat, 0900-1100. N\$5. The Lüderitz Foundation Tourist Office is also located in the museum, although you'll get more out of Lüderitzbücht Safaris and Tours on Bismarck St.*

Lüderitz Peninsula excursion

Assuming you have your own vehicle and that the winds are not too strong, an interesting excursion can be made around the peninsula south of town. Follow the Keetmanshoop road out of town and look out for a signpost for Diaz Point just after the buildings end. From here a twisting gravel road heads south round the coast through a moonscape of rocky bays, mud flats, beaches and small islands.

Shortly after passing the water tower, the Second Lagoon comes in to view. When the tide is out it is possible to cut the corner and cross the mud flats here, but you are better sticking to the road in a saloon car.

A few km beyond the lagoon you have the choice of heading straight to the southernmost point of the peninsula, **Grosse Bücht** (6 km) via the D733, or continuing on the D701 to **Griffith Bay, Sturmvogel Bücht** and **Diaz Point**. Either way, the road loops round; the following text describes the route in an anti-clockwise direction.

Most visitors head straight for **Diaz Point** and the viewpoint for Halifax Island, however if it is late in the afternoon it is worth following the D734 as far as **Griffith Bay** where you can enjoy a distant view of Lüderitz bathed in the evening sunlight. Continuing along D701, look out for a turning to the right after about a further 5 km. This road leads to **Sturmvogel Bücht**, one of the best bathing beaches in the area. Also of interest are the rusty remains of a Norwegian Whaling Station. It doesn't take much imagination to picture what used to occur here.

Just past the turning for **Shearwater Bay**, the road goes over a small ridge and presents a good view of Diaz Point. Take the next right to visit **Diaz Point**, 22 km from town. A large marble cross stands here, a replica of the original erected by Portuguese explorer Bartholomeu Diaz in 1487 on his way back to Portugal after sailing around the Cape of Good Hope. Access to the cross is via a wooden bridge and some steps up to an exposed position on a rocky headland. When the wind blows make sure everything is securely attached, it is easy to lose a hat or a pair of sunglasses. There is a simple toilet block in the car park. The nearby foghorn tower and lighthouse were built 1911-12, these can be visited by first making arrangements at the town tourist office.

All along this section of coast there is a profusion of wildlife; just off-shore from the Cross itself is a large seal colony and further down the coast on **Halifax Island** there are large numbers of jackass penguins and cormorants. Pink flamingos flock in the bays and also in small onshore lakes. The presence of so much wildlife is due to the cold, clean and abundantly fertile Benguela current, which provides ideal conditions for catching their prey of fish, rock lobster and oyster. The drawback for the tourist is the accompanying persistently strong, cold, southwest wind which makes warm clothes essential.

As you follow the D702 towards Grosse Bücht there are plenty of tracks off to the right which lead up to a variety of vantage points along the coast. Not all are clearly marked and it is easy to find oneself further down the road than your map might have you believe. At **Knocken Bay** and **Essy Bay** there are braai sites and basic toilets. Unfortunately these sites and all the other picnic spots along the route are spoilt by the trash left behind from previous revelry; mind your tyres as you negotiate broken brandy bottles and discarded soft drinks cans. If you can find the right road and then the right path there is a small cave cut into the rock face at **Eberlanz Höhle**. A little further on there is a sign for **Kleiner Fjord**, which is nice for a walk, but offers little at the destination.

Finally the broad south-facing **Grosse Bücht** comes into view. This is the furthest south one can travel along this part of the coast. When you reach a junction take a right and this will lead you to the western end of the bay and a decrepit braai site. The beach here is safe for swimming and popular with windsurfers. Just on the tide line are the rusty remains of a small boat which has an interesting local history. The boat was called the *Irmgard* and was used for cray fishing. When launched it was the first flat bottom steel boat to be built in Lüderitz. The builder and first owner was the father of the current manager of the *Nest Hotel*. The shortest route back to town is via the D733, about 40 minutes' drive.

Agate Beach   A similarly rocky drive north out of Lüderitz leads to Agate Beach (follow the signs from Hafen Street), a fine, sandy stretch of coast suitable for surfing and swimming, for those willing to brave the cold sea. Small piles of stones and mini-trenches dot the beach, remnants from past diamond and agate diggings. In the late afternoon there is a good chance of seeing wild gemsbok and springbok. **NB**   Most of the land on the inland side of the road is part of the NAMDEB concession area and thus closed to the public. It is not advisable to venture into these areas at any time. As you drive through Nautilus you are likely to be confronted with the depressing site of thousands of plastic bags blown from the municipal tips into various boundary fences. If ever there was a need for a clean-up campaign it is here in Lüderitz, especially given the striking beauty of the surrounding country.

Lüderitz Peninsula

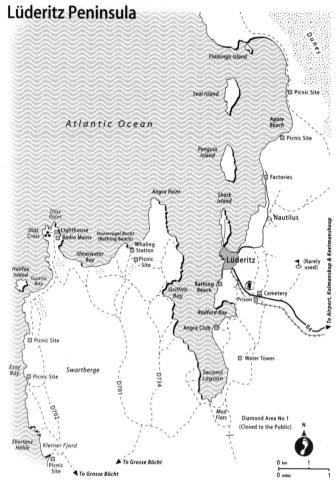

Flamingo Island

Seal Island

Atlantic Ocean

Penguin Island

Agate Beach

Picnic Site

Picnic Site

Factories

Angra Point

Shark Island

Diaz Point

Diaz Cross

Lighthouse
Radio Masts

Sturmvogel Bucht
(Bathing Beach)

Whaling Station

Nautilus

Shearwater Bay

Picnic Site

Lüderitz

Halifax Island

Guano Bay

Griffith Bay

Bathing Beach

Cemetery

Prison

(Rarely used)

Radford Bay

Angra Club

Picnic Site

Water Tower

Essy Bay

Picnic Site

Swartberge

Second Lagoon

D701

D734

Mud Flats

Diamond Area No 1
(Closed to the Public)

D702

Eberlanz Höhle

Kleiner Fjord

Picnic Site

To Grosse Bücht

To Grosse Bücht

To Airport, Kolmanskop & Keetmanshoop

B4

Dunes

N

0 km   1

0 miles   1

Related map
Lüderitz, page 316

The South

Tours

Most of the tours listed below are booked through *Lüderitzbücht Safaris and Tours*, lower end of Bismarck Street, T202719, F202863, ludsaf@ldz.namib.com or the *Kolmanskop Tour Company*, T202445, which runs most outings. Tours into diamond areas require four days pre-booking due to NAMDEB restrictions.

Bogenfels – 'Rock Arch' Tour

This is one of the most interesting tours one can enjoy in the Lüderitz region, but like the Elizabeth Bay tour described below it requires a certain degree of forward planning. Because most of the tour is within the *Sperrgebiet*, permits have to be processed in advance. The tour lasts a full day, the 55 m high rock arch lies 110 km south of Lüderitz. Most of the drive is across flat gravel plains, but to break the monotony there are also visits to another abandoned mining town, **Pomona**, and the **Idatel valley** which famously yielded surface diamonds, gathered by crawling prospectors in the moonlight. This is an enjoyable trip and made that little bit special as it allows one to enter an area of the desert that has been closed to the public for most of this century. ■ *N$400 pp, minimum of 4 people. Visitors need to provide the Kolmanskop Tour Company, T202380, with their names and passport numbers 4 working days in advance.*

Diaz Point & Halifax Island

This is a boat trip run by *West Coast Experience*, T204030, sedina@ldz.namib.com which has a small office in Bismarck Street. The schooner *Sedina* departs from Robert Harbour every morning at 0800, weather permitting. The full trip lasts for about two and a half hours. The route takes you between Shark Island and Penguin Island, past Angra Point and on to Diaz Point. Under ideal conditions you will land on Halifax Island and visit a colony of Jackass Penguins. You can also expect to see Heaviside Dolphins and a colony of Cape Fur Seals. ■ *N$100 adults, N$50 children; minimum of 6 people, maximum of 20, dress warm, with windproofs.*

Diamond Barge

The *Lady Luck* is moored in the harbour and now acts as a floating diamond museum. Tours depart from the wooden jetty at 1100 and 1500 daily and last for two hours. Guests are transferred in a ski-boat. On the boat you have the opportunity to sort diamond gravel and learn about the local history. There is a small coffee shop on board. ■ *N$50 adults, N$20 children; minimum of 4 people, maximum of 20. Bookings, T204030.*

Elizabeth Bay

This is a half day tour to a small bay which was mined for diamonds between 1911 and 1950. NAMDEB operates a small mine slightly inland of here, opened in 1991. The tour includes visits to the operations of the old and the new mines. A good insight into diamond production then and now. ■ *N$150 pp, minimum of 4 people, maximum of 10. Visitors need to provide the Kolmanskop Tour Company, T202380, with their names and passport numbers four working days in advance.*

4WD tours

Coastways Tours have been granted the tourism concession for the spectacular dune and surf area north of Lüderitz. Participants drive their own vehicles and cater for themselves, using the old mining camp at Saddle Hill as a base camp. Excursions total 450 km of beaches with Cape Fur seals, shipwrecks and spectacular coastal land and seascapes. ■ *N$660 pp, minimum of 8 people, contact Volker Jahncke on T202362, F203220, daggicw@iafrica.com.na*

The South

Essentials

Sleeping
■ *on map page 316*
Price codes:
see inside front cover

Lüderitz boasts an excellent selection of hospitable hotels and guest houses. **B** *Nest Hotel*, Ostend Beach, T204000, F204001, www.etosha.com/nest-hotel is the smartest option in town, built in 1997, HAN 2000 award winner, 70 en-suite doubles and 3 suites, with a/c, TV, phone and radio, small balcony and sea views. Good restaurant, bar with open terrace plus a Sunset bar at the top of the hotel (residents only). Swimming pool, conference facilities. Recommended. **B-C** *Sea View Hotel Zum Sperrgebiet*, Stettiner St, T203411, F203414, michaels@ldz.namib.com is the other HAN winner in town, on a hill in a quiet residential area, with balconies overlooking the harbour. 22 en-suite rooms, TV, phone, sauna, sheltered swimming pool, good restaurant and secure parking. Good value mid-range hotel.

C *Bay View*, Diaz St, T202288, F202402. 29 en-suite rooms, phone, fan, some with TV. Built around two small courtyards, one with swimming pool. Bar and snack bar downstairs, restaurant upstairs. Friendly and clean. **C** *Diamond Reef City*, Diaz St, T203850, F203853, fotofun@iafrica.com.na with 11 en-suite doubles with satellite TV. Bar, restaurant. Doubles as the local gambling den. **C** *Zum Sperrgebiet*, Bismarck St, T202856, F202976. Both 'Sperrgebiet' hotels are under the same ownership. 10 rooms, 5 en-suite, restaurant, a comfortable small option in the middle of town. **D** *Kapps Hotel*, Bay Road, T202345, F202977, dates back to the diamond boom days, now completely renovated. 21 en-suite rooms with TV, restaurant, secure parking. A bit stark, and noisy when Rumours gets going. **D** *Lüderitz Bay Guesthouse*, Hafen St, T/F203019. Friendly German style B&B in a grand old colonial building, currently overlooking dilapidated harbour buildings, which should improve as the Waterfront Development progresses. Communal TV lounge, secure parking. Self-catering flat also available. Recommended by readers. **D** *Zur Waterkant*, Bremer St, T/F203145. Choice of B&B or self-catering, a clean modern house in the suburbs, with balconies overlooking the harbour. Also recommended by readers.

Self catering **C** *NWR Lighthouse*, Shark Island, reservations through Windhoek central reservations (NWR) or in person at their offices on Schinz St, a fabulous self-catering option. The lighthouse has been converted, with 2 bedrooms, 2 bathrooms, fully equipped kitchen, satellite TV, lounge area, secure parking. It is the view from the top that makes this such a pleasure. Access is a little awkward via a ladder and a trap door, but then one is rewarded with a panoramic view of the harbour and the town laid out on the side of the two hills. From here one can watch the sun rise and set in a peaceful setting, so long as the wind doesn't blow. **D/E** *Hansa*, Mabel St, T/F203581, mcloud@africaonline.com.na is a pretty blue house with harbour views, 4 doubles, communal lounge, TV, bathroom and fully equipped kitchen. **D/E** *Krabbenhöft und Lampe*, Bismarck St, T202466, T081-1292025 (mob), taurus@ldz.namib.com is great for comfortable self catering, with a large family flat and smaller luxury flat on the first floor, and simpler rooms with shared facilities on the top floor. Located above the carpet factory (enquire here) in a fine old building, if the factory is closed, make a noise and someone will come and help you. **E** *Kratz Platz*, Nachtigal St, T/F202458. 5 rooms, those in the main house share 1 bathroom, central location, braai, laundry facilities. **D/E** *Haus Sandrose*, Bismarck St, T202630, F202365, sandrose@ldz.namib.com has lovely, fully equipped flats set back from the St in private courtyard, braai area, friendly owner, good quality curios out front. **F** *Backpackers Lodge*, 7 Schinz St, T/F202742 reservations, T203632 lodge. Dorms and double rooms, kitchen, spacious communal room, washing facilities, braai area. Central location, a welcome alternative for budget travellers to the exposed Shark Island campsite.

The South

F *Shark Island Campsite*, take a left at the end of Bismarck St and follow the road round **Camping** the harbour and across the causeway onto Shark Island. A rocky campsite overlooking the harbour and the ocean, clean communal facilities, great views at sunset but very exposed – make sure you securely peg your tent down, a couple of pitches have a small patch of grass and a degree of shelter.

There is a reasonable choice of restaurants in Lüderitz: most serve fresh seafood and **Eating** shellfish in season, in addition to the customary Namibian fare. As elsewhere, kitch- • *on map page 316* ens close fairly early. The hotels can be relied on for reasonable fare, but the best bet in town, by a distance, is *Ritzi's Restaurant*, hidden away within the *Badger's Bistro*. The chef is a young South African ex-diamond diver, now settled here with a young family. Excellent value, both the food and wine – aim for the specials, they will have just been landed.

Badger's Bistro, Diaz St, closed Sun, a lively bar serving pub grub to all comers, with pool table and TV. *Rumours*, Bay Road, restaurant and sports bar, popular with tourists and locals, probably your best bet for 'action' at the weekends. *Coffee Shop and Diaz Souvenirs*, T202856, corner of Bismarck St, open 7 days, excellent coffee and lunchtime snacks, light and airy central venue. *The Penguin*, T204000, located in the *Nest Hotel*. Good value N$80 buffets at the weekend plus an imaginative, reasonable value à la carte menu. Ocean view and outside seating area when the wind stops blowing. Worth a visit. *Beira Mar*, Hafen St, simple but good value fish and chips (and after-hours bottle store), out towards Agate Beach.

A waterfront development is under construction, in the style of the hugely successful **Shopping** V&A Waterfront in Cape Town. It aims to be the town's principal tourist attraction, with hotels, shops, restaurants and 'entertainment'. The first stage is expected to be finished by early 2002, and further development may build all the way around the headland to the *Nest Hotel*. **Lüderitz Carpet Factory**, T202605, top of Bismarck St, Mon-Fri 0800-1230, 1430-1700, Sat 0900-1200, produces high quality handwoven karakul rugs with interesting geometric patterns, visitors are welcome to watch the carpets being made and can place specific orders, excellent value.

If you are self-catering there is a *Sentra* on Hafen St and *Spar* on Moltke St, both have a bakery and a butchers' counter and are open until 1800 Mon-Fri and 1300 on Sat. The **Portuguese Supermarket** in Bismarck St is also open Sat afternoons 1600-2000. The bottle store is just up from Haus Sandrose on Bismarck St, try the *Beira Mar Fish & Chips* for after-hours booze. The fishmonger is just outside the gate into the harbour and the bakery is in Nachtigal St opposite *Kratz Platz*. A new camping equipment store (*Cymot*) is opening on Nachtigal St, or try the supermarkets or the small shop next to the bottle store.

The town has a 9-hole **golf** course, conditions unplayable in 2001 but may be **Sport** improved, ask at *Lüderitzbücht Safaris and Tours*. Elsewhere in Lüderitz you can try your hand at **fishing** or **windsurfing**. For the latter you will need to have your own equipment, including a wetsuit, and you should be proficient.

Air *Air Namibia*, T202850, F202845. Flights from Windhoek-Eros via Swakopmund **Transport** and on to Oranjemund and Cape Town. **NB** There can be delays if the wind is too *350 km to* strong, always allow yourself an extra day if connecting with an international flight. *Keetmanshoop*

Bus *Star Line*, T202875, service has replaced the passenger train between Lüderitz *650 km to* and Keetmanshoop. Mon-Fri departures at 1230 and Sun at 1130. The journey takes *Noordoewer* between 4 and 5 hours. Buses arrive and depart from outside the Old Railway Station *(South Africa border)* on the corner of Bahnhof and Bismarck Sts. *845 km to Windhoek*

The South

Directory **Banks** *Commercial Bank*, T202577, *First National Bank*, T202077 and *Standard Bank*, T202251 all have their premises on Bismarck St and all have money-changing facilities and ATMs. Beware the large queues on Sat mornings after payday. **Communications** Post Office: Bismarck St, Mon-Fri 0800-1630, Sat 0800-1100. NAMPost courier services T202351. FedEx, Banhof St, T203077, T081-1280235 (mob). **Internet**, Bismarck St, Mon-Fri, 0900-1300, 1400-1800; Sat, 0900-1200. T204084. Limited opening hours, but helpful, reasonable access speeds, 6 terminals. **Medical services** *State Hospital*, T202446. There is a surgery next door to the town museum. **Car Hire** Both Budget and Avis have offices in town. **Tourist offices** *Lüderitzbücht Safaris and Tours*, Bismarck St, T202719, F202863, ludsaf@ldz.namib.com is open daily, Sat until 1230 and Sun until 1000. An extremely helpful office that acts as the principal information office in town and booking agent for all the local tours. A short time spent here will help you plan a perfect stay in Lüderitz. Bookings for trips run by the *Kolmanskop Tour Company* can all be made here. See above under Tours for details.

Kolmanskop Ghost Town

Drive 10 km inland on B4, turn right and then follow signs

The former diamond boom town of Kolmanskop, finally deserted in 1956, is now a ghost town and lies crumbling in the desert 15 km inland of Lüderitz, gradually being weathered by the wind and buried by the sand. It is a fascinating place to visit, offering as it does a glimpse into an exciting part of Namibia's history.

In April 1908, Zacharias Lewala, a worker on the Lüderitz-Aus railway line, presented a shiny stone to his supervisor August Stauch, who was intelligent enough to obtain a prospecting licence before having it officially verified and thereby starting the diamond rush around the site of Kolmanskop. In the early days, in the nearby Itadel valley, stones were so accessible that prospectors with no mining equipment would crawl on their hands and knees in full moonlight collecting the glittering stones.

In September 1908, the Colonial Government declared a Sperrgebiet or 'forbidden zone' extending 360 km northwards from the Orange River and 100 km inland from the coast in order to control the mining of the diamonds, and in February 1909, a central diamond market was established.

The First World War effectively stopped diamond production, by which time more than 5.4 million carats of very high quality stones had been extracted from the region. The recession which followed the war hit the diamond industry badly. However, Sir Ernest Oppenheimer, the chairman of the Anglo-American Company, saw this as an opportunity to buy up all the small diamond companies operating in the Sperrgebiet, and combine them to form Consolidated Diamond Mines. CDM, as it became known, was to control all diamond mining in the area until entering into partnership with the Namibian government in 1995 under the new name of NAMDEB.

Kolmanskop enjoyed its heyday in the 1920s when it grew rapidly to service the diamond miners and eventually the families which followed. A hospital, gymnasium and concert hall, school, butchery, bakery and a number of fine houses were built in the middle of the desert, and at its peak there were as many as 300 German and 800 Oshiwambo adults living in the town. The hospital was ultra-modern and was equipped with the first X-ray machine in southern Africa (used principally for detecting secreted gemstones, rather than broken bones!).

The sheer wealth generated at Kolmanskop (peak production was over 30,000 carats per day) is demonstrated by the way in which water was supplied to the town. Every month a ship left Cape Town carrying 1,000 tonnes of water, and each resident was supplied with 20 litres per day for free. Those requiring additional water paid for it, at half the price of beer! The lack of fresh

The South

water to power steam engines also forced the building of a power station which supplied electricity, very advanced technology at the time, to power the mining machinery.

However, the boom years in Kolmanskop ended in 1928 when diamond reserves six times the size of those at Kolmanskop (although of lesser quality) were discovered at the mouth of the Orange River. The town of Oranjemund was built in 1936 to exploit these reserves and in 1938 most of the workers and equipment relocated from Kolmanskop to this new headquarters. Following this the town went into steady decline, although the last people (including the 100 full-time labourers employed to remove the encroaching sand) only left Kolmanskop in 1956, leaving this once flourishing town to time and the forces of nature.

Kolmanskop was rescued from the desert in 1979 following a CDM commissioned report to assess the tourist potential of this ghost town. In 1980, simple restoration began and the town was opened to tourism. At present the most carefully preserved/restored buildings are the **Recreation Hall** and those adjacent to the **Museum**. Sadly, following an expensive restoration of the Skittle Alley in the basement of the Recreation Hall, visitors are no longer permitted to play. In July 2001, NAMDEB was applying the finishing touches

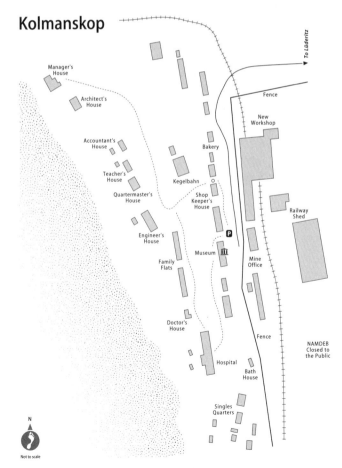

The South

to a restoration of the lavish **Manager's House**, complete with marble bath, grand piano and sun room.

Although it is not obligatory to join a tour it is worth following one to hear some of the historic detail and stories about Kolmanskop. After about 45 minutes you are left to your own devices to explore all buildings at your leisure. ■ *Guided tours in English and German, Mon-Sat 0930 and 1045, Sun 1000, starting at Kolmanskop Museum. N$25 per person, purchase tickets beforehand from Lüderitzbücht Safaris and Tours, on Bismarck St they can also arrange transport). Curio shop and cafe open during tour hrs.*

National Diamond Area

Colour map 3, grid B2 Following the discovery of diamonds at Kolmanskop in 1908 and the ensuing diamond rush the German colonial authorities declared a Sperrgebiet or 'forbidden zone' along the coast. This area extended from the Orange River in the south for 360 km northward to latitude 26S and inland for 100 km, and is known today as Diamond Area No. 1.

Exclusive mining rights for this area are held by NAMDEB, owned jointly by the Namibian Government and De Beers, and it is forbidden to enter the area without permission. Even where the Sperrgebiet becomes part of the Namib-Naukluft Park, access is strictly controlled and visitors are required to remain on the road at all times.

In 1994 a British-Canadian company NAMCO obtained off-shore diamond mining concessions at Lüderitz, potentially breaking the current NAMDEB monopoly. Diamond divers, many from South Africa, Australia and New Zealand, suck up the sea bed with powerful vacuum pumps, after which the gravel is sorted for diamonds. It is difficult, unpleasant work, which the divers can only carry out when sea conditions permit. The rewards, however, are potentially huge and consequently a small diver community lives in Lüderitz hoping to strike it rich. Their boats are visible in the harbour.

The Far South

Phone code: 063 Leaving Keetmanshoop, the B1 heads south through the Karas Mountains towards the crossroads settlement of Grünau. From here the B1 itself continues a further 147 km to the border at Noordoewer, while the B3 heads towards Karasburg, 51 km away, and continues to the border at Ariamsvlei, a further 108 km. Those travelling down the B1 have two choices for accommodation en route. **E** *Travelodge Narubis*, T/F250700, 60 km south of Keetmanshoop, has 10 simple doubles. **E** *Florida B&B*, T/F262069, 130 km south of Keetmanshoop, 30km before Grünau, has 3 s/c bungalows, with dinner available by booking ahead.

The route through the **Groot Karas Mountains** is particularly beautiful, especially after rain, when the bright light reflecting off the green veld contrasts the deep shadows cast by the rocky kopjes. The D26 (left turn, 70 km out of Keetmanshoop) winds its way through these mountains and provides an interesting detour for those on their way to Karasburg. The **E-F** *Mount Karas Game Lodge*, T225158, follow signs, turn right on the D259, is a tranquil spot nestled among the hills, but the owners have fallen on hard times (with their other business interests), and look to be closing down or selling. Call ahead to see if you are welcome.

An equally lovely route, travels south through the **Klein Karas Mountains**, west of the B1. This gravel road twists and turns, climbs and falls like a rollercoaster and must be approached with caution, however it takes you through breathtaking, pristine mountain scenery. Turn right onto the D608 6 km after leaving Keetmanshoop and continue for 125 km before turning left onto the C12 and into Grünau.

Grünau serves as a useful staging post for lorries and Capetonians on long-distance journeys. There are a few pleasant places to stay in the vicinity, a 24-hour breakdown service with telephone and a 24-hour Shell garage just out of town by the B1/B3 junction.

Grünau
Phone code: 063
Colour map 3, grid C4

Sleeping In Grünau: The only option in the village itself is the **E-F** *Grünau Hotel*, T/F262001, grunau99@iafrica.com.na, with 8 basic en-suite doubles, a bar, restaurant and small swimming pool, camping facilities and inadequate ablutions. Ownership is changing hands, and great investment is planned for late 2001, so quality and prices can be expected to rise.
In the area: **E** *Savanna Guest Farm*, T/F262070, zeldavs@iafrica.com.na, off the B1, 40 km north of Grünau, has ensuite doubles in an historical building (the busy German Shutztruppe again). **E** *Vastrap Guest Farm*, T/F262063, vastrap@iway.na, 5 km down the B3 towards the border, has 4 pleasant rooms with self-catering. **E** *White House*, T/F2622061, 11 km north of Grünau on the B1, has 6 simple self-catering rooms in a lovely old white house and 2 more in the farmhouse where the welcoming and informative owners will look after you, cook if you book ahead and even call around their neighbours to find alternative accommodation if they are full. Recommended. **E-F** *Grünau Motors Chalet and Caravan Park*, T262026, F262017, behind the Shell garage at the B1/B3 junction, reception is in the garage. 4 small s/c chalets and 4 rock-hard camping pitches, new and clean, each with new private ablutions, light, braai pit and electricity. Good value.

The drive from Grünau to Noordoewer climbs steadily to a plateau, beyond which it is all downhill to the Orange River, where summer temperatures can reach 50°C. It feels almost as if one is entering hell's kitchen, but the sight of the green irrigated riverbanks soon dispels that notion. For those into canoeing this is the place to start an Orange River Canoe Safari.

Fish River Canyon

This huge gash in the earth, Africa's second largest canyon, is one of Namibia's most popular destinations. Drive to the observation point at Hobas to witness the spectacular view and then head down into the depths of the canyon to enjoy the hot spring at Ai-Ais. Alternatively, for the fit and the adventurous, there is a four-day, 85 km hike through the canyon

There are two NWR resorts in the Fish River Canyon, Hobas (10 km from the canyon rim, with an observation point and campsite) and Ai-Ais Hot Springs Resort (by the riverbed, at the southern end). From Grünau, take the B1 south for 31 km, then turn onto the C10 which leads to Ai-Ais and the turn-off for Hobas. From Keetmanshoop take the B4 until the turn for the C12. Follow this for 77 km before the turn-off for the D601. This leads to Hobas and the D324 for Ai-Ais.
    The route south from Keetmanshoop is arguably the most desolate yet most impressive journey in Namibia. If you ever have wondered what the surface of the moon looks like, albeit in blinding sunlight, this is the place to find out. In defiance of the bareness of the arid, rocky landscape, a host of desert plants, cacti, succulents and quiver trees survive and even prosper.

Ins & outs
Colour map 3, grid C3

The South

Background The history of the Fish River Canyon begins roughly 1,800 million years ago when sandstones, shales and lava were deposited along what are now the slopes of the canyon. Between 1,300 and 1,000 million years ago, extreme heat caused these deposits to become folded and change into gneiss and granites. About 800 million years ago, dolerite dykes intruded into these rocks and these are now visible inside the canyon.

Between 750 and 650 million years ago, the surface of these rocks was eroded to form the floor of a shallow sea which washed over southern Namibia. The two final pieces in the jigsaw took place about 500 million years ago when tectonic movement caused a series of fractures which led to the formation of the Fish River Canyon. This early version of the canyon was deepened by the retreat southwards of glaciers during the Gondwana Ice Age some 300 million years ago.

However, this was not the end of the process. Within the main canyon a second or lower canyon was created by further movements of the earth's crust as it cooled. Initially a trough, this second canyon became the water-course which is now the Fish River. The Fish is the longest river in Namibia and plays an important role in both watering and draining southern Namibia. In particular, it feeds Hardap Dam, Namibia's largest artificial lake.

Early Bushman legends suggest an alternative origin to the canyon. Hunters were chasing a serpent called *Kouteign Kooru* across the veld; in order to escape the snake slithered off into this deserted place and in so doing caused the massive gash that is the canyon. Archaeological evidence suggests that the Bushmen, or their ancestors, were here 50,000 years ago, so perhaps they witnessed something….

With a supply of water even during the dry winter months and food in the form of fish and game birds, the canyon has attracted human beings for thousands of years. So far, six Early and three Middle Stone Age sites have been identified in the canyon as well as the remains of a number of pre-colonial herders' camps.

Although all the tourist literature boasts that the Fish River Canyon is second in size only to the Grand Canyon in Arizona, this is not actually the case. Although it remains unclear as to what criteria are used to measure the size of a canyon, it is actually only Africa's second largest after the Blue Nile Gorge in Ethiopia.

Sleeping Your sleeping arrangements, if you are not staying at *Hobas Campsite*, will probably be in the hands of **Gondwana Cañon Park**, a private operation that owns the 102,000 ha east of the national park. They have started developing the tourist potential of their stunning location, catering for organized tour groups and casual visitors and have become regular HAN award winners. **A** *Cañon Lodge* T266029, reservations T061-230066, F251863, www.namibiaweb.com/canyon has 26 en-suite rock chalets built into the huge boulders, each tastefully furnished and with wooden door and thatched roof. To get there from Keetmanshoop take the B4 for Lüderitz, after 32 km turn left onto the D545, signposted Naute Dam, follow this road past the dam wall until it joins the C12 after 33 km. Follow the C12 for 50 km towards Grünau, turn right onto the D601, signposted Fish River Canyon. After 20 km you will see the *Cañon Roadhouse* on your right, carry on to the D324, turn left, signposted Ai-Ais and follow the sign for the lodge (well, the lodge restaurant, for some reason), 8 km down this road. The best chalets are 11, 13, 23 and 25. Meals are served in the cool converted 1910 farmhouse, with a shaded terrace with views over the rocks and old farm implements and vehicles dotted around. Evening drives and horse trails on the farm. Day visitors welcome for coffee, beer, buffet lunch or a refreshing swim. Before leaving it is worth climbing one of the small hills to view the surrounds. An excellent lodge in a beautiful setting; expensive, but recommended.

Simpler accommodation is available at the **B/C-F** *Cañon Roadhouse* T063-266031, reservations as above, which has 8 double en-suite rooms around a pretty, shaded courtyard, swimming pool, excellent restaurant (under award-winning head chef Erno Bertolini) and petrol pump (not 24 hrs). The campsite has braai pits and good ablutions but no light or electricity. See above for directions. The *Cañon Guest House* is no longer open to the public. **C-F** *Fish River Lodge*, T/F063-223762, frlodge@iafrica.com.na, www.resafrica.net/fish-river-lodge is located north of the national park, in a 43,000 ha concession. Signposted off the C12, 18 km north of the turning for the Fish River Canyon (Hobas), 22 km along this track is the lodge. There is a range of interesting accommodation: B&B in double and family rooms with shared ablutions in 'The Farmhouse', with bar and restaurant; dorm rooms in 'The Stable'; the 'Koelkrans' self-catering wooden huts, as well as camping (4WD required for access) by the river. Numerous worthwhile guided 4WD and hiking trails (1-4 days) into their portion of the canyon, viewing rock engravings and wildlife and staying in remote shelters; they encourage you to 'enjoy the Canyon without worrying about the logistics'. A 5-day, 4-night hike is N$320pp. Book ahead, they can collect from Keetmanshoop. Recommended.

Hobas Campsite & Observation Point

About halfway along the canyon at Hell's Bend are a series of tortuous curves in the river (and canyon!). Along this stretch, about 80 km north of Ai-Ais, are a number of observation points perched on the edge of the canyon where its awe-inspiring splendour can be fully appreciated. Driving out from *Hobas Campsite* the first viewpoint you reach is known as Main Viewpoint. The view from here is the one that appears in most publicity brochures. There are several shaded picnic tables and braai sites. Set back from the road are a couple of basic toilets. As the viewpoint is westward facing, early morning rather than late afternoon is probably the best time to come here.

If you continue along the track from the car park, you reach Hiker's Viewpoint, the starting point for the 85 km Hiking Trail. The view from here is equally rewarding and it is well worth visiting both sites if you have time. Returning to *Hobas Campsite* look out for a turning to the right. This is a track which follows the edge of the canyon southwards for about 15 km. The road to the Sulphur Springs viewpoint is pretty good; beyond this it is only passable in a four-wheel drive vehicle. There is a path into the canyon at Sulphur Springs, being one of the escape routes for hikers unwilling to continue the full four days to Ai-Ais; you are not permitted to enter here.

Sleeping

F *Hobas Campsite*, one of the better NWR sites, located 10 km from the starting point of the Fish River Canyon Hiking Trail. Has 10 shaded pitches with braai pit and light, communal ablutions, swimming pool, small kiosk with frozen meat, beer and basic provisions, information centre (read the article on the wall of the 2 ultra-marathon runners who completed the Fish River Canyon hike in less than 12 hours!), cool drinks and T-shirts. This is a welcome oasis after the hot drive from either of the main roads. Being smaller than most, you are advised to book in advance through Central Reservations in Windhoek.

Fish River Canyon Hiking Trail

This 85 km four-day trail is reputed to be one of the toughest hiking trails in southern Africa, and is not for beginners or the unfit. Although the trail is more or less flat, loose sand and large boulders are tiring factors, which, added to the fact that hikers have to carry all provisions with them, cause some to take the option of an early emergency 'escape' route from the Canyon. For those who are fit enough and determined enough to complete the

The South

trail the four days are a magical wilderness experience, offering opportunities for game and birdwatching as well as wonderment at the scale and power of nature.

Trail information Due to extreme temperatures and the risk of flash flooding in summer, the trail is only open from 15 Apr to 15 Sep. Groups must consist of 3 persons minimum, 40 maximum. Medical certificates of physical fitness issued within the previous 40 days need to be shown to the ranger at Hobas before starting. No casual walkers permitted (one died in January 2001). Bookings must be made at Central Reservations in Windhoek (or at Mariental or Keetmanshoop MET offices); book well in advance. Transport from Ai-Ais can be arranged for N$50pp, and from *Cañon Lodge/Roadhouse* (for guests, and collection from Ai-Ais), for US$85 per vehicle. A final point to stress is to remove all your rubbish. In 1991 the Dorsland Hiking Club removed over 360 kg of rubbish from along the trail. Each year they conduct a similar clean-up walk and remove approximately 35 kg each year, most of this material is paper, all of it has been left by hikers.

The route The route starts from **Hiker's Viewpoint**, 10 km from Hobas campsite; transport can be arranged through lodges or from Ai-Ais or Hobas. From the rim, the path descends sharply to the canyon floor, losing 500 m in altitude on the way. Parts of the descent are very steep and it is advisable to make use of the chains. The route at the bottom follows the left hand side of the river over boulders and soft, loose sand – one of the worst stretches of the walk. The first overnight stop is 15 km downstream at the wonderfully soothing waters of Sulphur Springs, also known as **Palm Springs**.

According to legend, during the First World War two German soldiers sought refuge from internment in the canyon. One of them was suffering from skin cancer and the other from asthma, however after bathing in the hot springs these ailments were miraculously cured. Whether true or not these springs, bubbling up from a depth of 2,000 m at a rate of 30 litres per second, offer much needed relief for sore feet and muscles after the long first day's trek.

The South

Fish River Canyon

Heading south of Palm Springs the shortest route criss-crosses the river as far as the **Table Mountain** landmark some 15 km on. This section of the trail is extremely tiring as it involves struggling one's way through deep sand and gravel – not much fun. Further on, the canyon widens and the trail becomes firmer with more river crossings, more or less wet depending on the state of the river. If the rains have been good earlier in the year, trailists can expect to find a fair amount of water in the pools. Check with the rangers at Hobas regarding the availability of water.

Close to the 30-km point is Table Mountain, one of the more easily recogniszable natural landmarks along the trail. After a further 18 km, you will reach the first of four possible short cuts. At this point the alternative path avoids an area of scrub vegetation known as **Bushy Corner**. Around the next corner of the canyon is the second short cut. Here the path climbs up to the **Kooigoedhoote Pass**. If you choose to take this short cut you will miss seeing the **Three Sisters Rock** and the point where the Kanbis River joins the Fish River. However from the pass you will enjoy an excellent view of **Four Fingers Rock**. Along the third short cut you will pass the grave of Lieutenant von Trotha, a German soldier killed in 1905 during the German-Nama war and buried where he fell. A couple of km beyond the grave, back in the main canyon, is the second 'emergency' exit path. From here it is a further 20 km to Ai-Ais, a cold drink, soft bed and no more walking for a few days.

Equipment Hikers must take all their food with them – a camping stove is also needed as wood for fires is scarce during the first couple of days of the hike. Maps can be bought at Ai-Ais and Hobas. Water is almost always available en route (from the river), but for safety should be purified or boiled. A fishing line is worth taking, provided the river/pools are deep enough; freshly grilled fish is a great luxury after a hot day's hike.

A tent is not necessary but a sleeping mat and sleeping bag is, as the temperature can fall dramatically at night. Tough walking boots, a hat, a comprehensive first aid kit and plasters for blisters are all an absolute must.

Bird & game viewing Small mammals such as rock dassies and ground squirrels are a common sight in the canyon and with luck larger mammals such as klipspringer, steenbok and springbok may also be spotted. Kudu, gemsbok and mountain zebra live in and around the canyon but are harder to spot and leopards the hardest of all. The rock pools and reeds attract a large number of water birds, including the African Fish Eagle, grey herons and hammerkops and other birds such as bee-eaters, wagtails and rock pigeons are all common.

Ai-Ais Hot Springs Resort

Colour map 3, grid C3 The resort is very popular with families from Namibia and South Africa as a place to come and relax and lounge around in the thermal baths and outdoor heated swimming pool. As with all thermal springs the water is supposed to have natural curative properties and is especially beneficial for sufferers of rheumatism. The resort was refurbished after flooding in March 2000, but much of the accommodation remains adequate, rather than luxurious.

For those feeling energetic there are some enjoyable walks into the Canyon, especially pleasant in the late afternoon when the shadows are long and the heat off the rocks contrasts with the cool sand. It is also possible to hire a horse and ride into the Canyon. Outside the school holidays, the tranquillity of the resort may lull you into a state of complete relaxation.

Ai-Ais is a Nama name meaning 'fire-water', indicating the extreme heat of the hot springs here. Modern knowledge of the springs dates back to 1850 when a Nama herder discovered the springs whilst searching for lost sheep, however it is certain that Stone Age people inhabited the area thousands of years ago.

During the 1904-1907 German-Nama war, the springs were used as a base camp by German forces. Following the First World War the site was partially developed but it was not until 1969 that the site was declared a conservation area. The present resort was first opened in 1971, but almost immediately destroyed by the Fish River coming down in flood. Since then flooding has occurred three more times, in 1974 and 1988, and again in 2000, on each occasion forcing the closure of the resort for repairs.

Essentials   Open year round as of 2001, the resort offers indoor and outdoor thermal pools (for a cold swim, try the river), tennis courts, good restaurant (0700-0900, 1200-1400, 1800-2200), bar, shop (0800-1800) with basic provisions, firewood and cooking utensils, petrol (0600-1800), horse riding, hiking trails and bird watching in a beautiful and peaceful setting. Note, there are no banking facilities. T063-262045/6, F262047/8.

Sleeping   C *Luxury flat*, modern 2 bed flat, fridge, hot plate, bedding and towels. **D** *Flat*, fully equipped 4 bed en-suite flats, fridge, hot plate, bedding and towels, rather cramped for 4. **E** *Backpackers' bungalow*, simple 4 bed accommodation with own cooking but shared ablution facilities. **F** *Camping*, attractive, grassy camp and caravan sites, shared cooking and ablution facilities. The resort is often fully booked (apart from the campsite); reserve in advance and get confirmation by fax to avoid receiving a surprise at the end of a long drive. Entrance: N$20 adults N$2 children, N$20 per car, indoor thermal pool N$10 adults, N$5 children per session.

Karasburg   From the visitor's point of view, Karasburg is no more than a small settle-
Phone code: 063   ment en route for other places. It has a number of 24 hour garages, one rea-
Colour map 3, grid B4   sonable hotel and three smaller B&Bs, but otherwise is devoid of attractions for the visitor.

Sleeping and eating   D *Kalkfontein Hotel*, Kalkfontein St, T270023 or T270172, F270457. Offers 17 rooms, 11 with en-suite facilities, telephone and a/c. The hotel has a restaurant serving plain but acceptable meaty fare, a bar and lounge with TV, breakfast included, off-street parking but not secure. There are three simple B&Bs, all signposted from the main road: **E** *Hoons B&B*, T270200, **F** *Pela Pela Backpackers*, T270483, *Jeannie's B&B*, T270349. Simple and cheap eats available from the *Hanzell Restaurant*, next to the Engen Garage, plus there are takeaways and a Spar.

Transport   It is 712 km to Windhoek, 110 km to the border at Ariamsvlei. **Bus** *Intercape*, T061-227847, coach to Windhoek picks up and drops off in front of SP Motors. See timetable on page 382. **Train** For trains see timetable on page 383.

Directory   **Banks** *Bank Windhoek*, T270136 *First National Bank*, T270012, both offer money-changing facilities and ATMs. **Communications   Post Office**: Park St, Mon-Fri 0800-1630, Sat 0800-1130. Telephones outside. **Medical services** The *State Hospital*, T270167 is signposted on the southern outskirts of town. **Useful addresses**   Police: T10111.

South African border dispute

A bizarre and impassioned dispute appears to be developing between Namibia and South Africa. The dispute stems from the fact that Namibia claims its 400 km southern border runs to the middle of the Orange River, while South Africa has traditionally regarded its territory as extending to the north bank. The dispute is intensifying as there are newly discovered gas and diamond deposits on and below the riverbed, whose ownership would be altered by a shift of the boundary, with a large potential impact on tax revenues.

The last time South Africa's borders with Namibia were redrawn was when Walvis Bay was returned to Namibia in 1994, and Nelson Mandela commented at the time that the Orange River border would be reconsidered. Since then, the SA

government has produced a detailed survey of the area, with the border distinctly marked on the northern bank. Far from looking to appease her neighbours, the SA government is appealing to the Organisation of African Unity's policy against redrawing colonial borders to support its case. However, if it is not redrawn, the Namibians may be able to claim compensation.

Another contentious issue is that to mine the riverbed, companies would have to divert its course. This could compound the dispute with tensions over access to water, as the land bordering the river requires intensive irrigation for new farming ventures and there are heavy demands from new mining ventures inside the Namibian border, such as the Skorpion and Rosh Pinah mines.

Located 43 km south of Karasburg, Warmbad is the site of the oldest mission station in Namibia. In 1805 the Albrecht brothers Abraham and Christian started working with the semi-nomadic Nama people living in this area. Although Abraham died in 1810, Christian carried on to establish the mission station at Warmbad.

Warmbad
Phone code: 063
Colour map 3, grid C4

The village is also the site of a series of hot springs which give the place its name. The spring is surrounded by the ruins of the Old Fort and Mission Station and as with a number of such historical sites in Namibia, there are plans to establish a resort here. Until that happens Warmbad remains another tiny settlement stuck in the middle of the veld.

Border with South Africa

The border at Ariamsvlei is open 24 hours and consists of no more than a petrol station and the immigration offices. Apart from over-busy holiday periods it should not take too long to complete formalities here. Border post: T280020. The border at Velloorsdrif is open 0600-2200.

Ariamsvlei
Phone code: 063
Colour map 3, grid C5

Noordoewer is a small settlement on the banks of the Orange River, known for being one of the hottest places in Namibia. Fortunately, there is an abundance of water, used to irrigate fruit, in particular grapes. The village consists of the border post, a post office, Bank Windhoek T297144, a couple of garages and minimarkets and one hotel, the **C** *Camel Lodge*, T297171, F297143 with 24 a/c rooms with en-suite facilities, TV, restaurant, bar. It is also possible to camp here.

**Noordoewer &
Orange River**
Phone code: 063
Colour map 3, grid C4

A few kilometres northwest of town along the banks of the Orange River are the base camps for a number of canoeing and rafting companies (see page 48, Introduction on canoeing in Namibia). Spending a few days floating

Canoeing on the Orange River

The canoe safaris start first thing in the morning so everyone pitches up the night beforehand and makes camp on the green lawns by the river bank. It's a good taste of what is to come as during the four-day trip every night is spent sleeping under the stars by the banks of the river.

After some basic instructions in how the trip is going to be managed and a short environmental lecture, it's into the two-person kayaks. Clothes and sleeping bags are squashed into water-proof plastic drums which fit neatly into the boats and then the trip starts.

The size of the group depends on pot luck and given that you spend four days in each other's company it is important to get on with the other people in the group. The guides take care of everything – navigating the river, choosing campsites and preparing all meals, as well as pointing out the different species of birds and animals living on and along the river.

The canoeing itself is not difficult and although the first day can be tiring if you are unused to this kind of exercise, by the fourth day it feels as if you could carry on for another four days. For the first two days the river is quite narrow and passes through a ravine. This is where the best rapids are – fun without being frightening – the highlight being the sjambok or 'whip' rapids which involve a fast descent through the rock-strewn river with an eddy at the bottom for added entertainment.

Later in the trip the river widens, the current slows and there's time to take in the lush vegetation on the banks, watch the monkeys swinging in the trees, or take a swim in the river. This is when one has a chance to appreciate the unspoiled beauty of this river wilderness. The trip ends with a minibus ride from the exit point back to Noordoewer.

down the river either in (winter) or submerged alongside (summer) your canoe is a fabulous way to unwind from the rigours of the road – book ahead, most of these companies are based in Cape Town, but you can meet them here and park safely ahead of your trip. The standard trip is four days, starting first thing in the morning after a night in the main camp by the river, a hearty breakfast and safety talk. The groups are pot luck, with a range of ages and backgrounds on each trip, but the same experienced, entertaining guides. Throw yourself in (literally) and you'll have a wonderful time. Highly recommended.

Just over the border, with the Orange River as its northern boundary to the Atlantic, is South Africa's Richtersveld National Park, with its beautiful, unspoilt landscape, challenging 4WD routes and beautiful camping areas. If you can't make it to Kaokoland, this area is certainly worth exploring. For safety, a four-wheel drive vehicle is recommended, but there are numerous routes passable in an ordinary car. For more details of this, Namaqualand and further south … you'll need a new guidebook!

The South

Background

11

Background

History

Pre-colonial Namibia

Archaeological finds from southern Namibia suggest that humans have been wandering the vast plains, dense bush and harsh deserts of the country for around 45,000 years. Ancient cave paintings at the Apollo 11 shelter in the southern Huns Mountains have been estimated to be 27,000 years old and similar rock art of the same period has also been found at a number of sites around Damaraland in northwest Namibia. These are believed to have been the work of the **San**, or **Bushmen** as they are most commonly known, descendants of pre-historic people who had migrated from southern Africa into East and North Africa before subsequently returning to the tip of the continent.

The San were traditionally hunter-gatherers, extraordinarily successful at surviving in the bush and desert despite their limited technology and weapons. They lived in small bands of up to 50 people roaming across the veld in a continuous search for food and water, rarely coming into contact with other San groups. Rock art all around Namibia, clearly seen at sites such as Twyfelfontein and Brandberg, provides vivid evidence of the widespread distribution of San communities all over the country.

Around 2,000 years ago the San were joined by groups of **Khoi-khoi (Nama)** who had migrated from Botswana to the middle stretches of the Orange River. From here, it is believed that the group split into two, one group heading north and west into present day Namibia, the other group moving south into the Cape Province area of South Africa. Unlike the San, the Khoi-khoi were both hunter-gatherers and livestock herders, living a semi-nomadic existence moving around the country with their herds of animals. Despite the differences in lifestyle, it appears as if Khoi and San people co-existed peacefully with each other.

By the ninth century AD a third group were settled in Namibia living alongside the Khoisan (Nama and San); these were the **Damara** people. Sharing common cultural and linguistic ties with the Nama people, rather than the Owambo, Herero or other Bantu-speaking tribes in Namibia, the exact origin and migration route of the Damara into Namibia remains a mystery. Some anthropologists argue that the Damara must have originated in West Africa whilst others maintain that they developed alongside the Khoi-khoin in Botswana and merely migrated later to Namibia.

By the early 19th century the Damara were living all over Namibia both alongside Nama and Herero communities as well as in their own settlements which were reported to be more permanent than those of the Nama. They had also evolved a number of distinct characteristics; they practised communal hunting techniques, the cultivation of tobacco and *dagga* (marijuana), mined and smelted copper and manufactured soapstone pipes.

Bantu-speaking tribes started arriving in Namibia during the 16th and 17th centuries, having migrated south and west from the Great Lakes area of east and central Africa. These tribes settled in the northern parts of the country alongside or close to the perennial Kunene, Kavango and Zambezi rivers which more or less correspond to their distribution in present-day Namibia.

These peoples brought with them a variety of skills such as pottery and metalworking, and lived by a mixture of farming, fishing and hunting. This influx of people looking for land to establish semi-permanent settlements inevitably put pressure on existing groups, and the San and Damara in particular were forced to move further south or into less hospitable parts of the country on the fringes of the Namib and Kalahari deserts.

Background

The **Herero** people had arrived in Namibia from east and central Africa during the 16th century and had originally settled in the Kaokoland area in the extreme northwest of the country. As cattle herders they required increasingly large areas of land to feed their growing herds and by the middle of the 18th century the marginal veld of the Kaokoland had become overgrazed, and suffering severe drought, was no longer able to support the Herero.

Gradually the majority of the Herero migrated southwards, and by around 1750 the first groups of Herero came into contact with groups of Khoi-khoi in the Swakop River area. Pressure from the Herero pushing southward more or less coincided with the northwards migration of **Oorlam** groups from the Cape Province. These two opposing movements created enormous pressure which was to erupt into almost a century of upheaval and at times open warfare in central Namibia. It was against this backdrop that the first European missionaries and traders came into the country, and their presence contributed significantly to the eventual establishment of the German colony of Southwest Africa.

Namibia - historical

Oorlam migration

The emergence of industrial capitalism in England during the second half of the 18th century drastically changed the economy of the satellite Cape Colony. Urban centres grew and **Boer** farmers moved progressively inland, claiming land and resources further and further away from the reach of the English authorities in the Cape Colony. The Boer farmers' freedoms were won largely at the expense of the local Khoisan population who lost their land, their hunting grounds and livestock, and even their liberty, as many became servants or even slaves of these European farmers.

In the wake of these developments a new group of frontiers people emerged. These were the Oorlams, a mixed bunch of Khoi-khoin, runaway slaves, and people of mixed race descent who worked for the Boer farmers and traders as hunters and guides. They were baptized, had access to guns and horses and had shed the traditional lifestyles of other Nama groups. Some of these formed themselves into commandos, autonomous groups living separate from the European farmers and traders, surviving by hunting, trading and raiding the cattle of the Nama tribes living over the Orange River into southern Namibia.

Early missionary reports at the time described the Nama tribes of southern Namibia to be living in highly organized communities numbering in some cases over 1,000 individuals. They had large herds of cattle, sheep and goats, and were completely self-sufficient, producing all their own food and manufacturing the reed mats for their huts, as well as growing tobacco and *dagga*. The different Nama tribes co-existed peacefully, sharing and respecting each other's water and grazing rights.

Initial contact between the first Oorlam groups to cross the Orange River and the local Nama tribes was relatively peaceful, but as more and more Oorlams poured over the river, demanding watering and grazing rights, the level of conflict increased to open warfare. Although the Nama were superior in numbers to the Oorlams, they had far fewer guns and horses and with their large herds of livestock were less mobile than the Oorlams. Consequently the Oorlams were soon able to establish footholds in the region from where they continued to harry and raid the Nama tribes.

Over a 40 year period up until the 1840s, southern Namibia – or Namaland as it became to be known – was in a virtually constant state of turmoil. Traditional patterns of living were disrupted, a new economy emerged and previously pastoral people started to settle in more permanent settlements.

In the 1840s **Chief Oaseb**, a paramount Nama chief, and **Jonker Afrikaner**, the foremost Oorlam leader, struck a deal that allowed Nama and Oorlam groups to live in peace. This deal was struck against the increasing realization that there was now little difference between the Oorlam and the Nama. The intense struggle for land and water had brought the two groups close together and intermarriage had become commonplace, so that making distinctions between the two groups was increasingly difficult. Furthermore, Herero-speaking groups who had been migrating southwards for almost 100 years were threatening the common interests of both Oorlam and Nama.

Oaseb and Afrikaner divided the land south of Windhoek amongst themselves and Afrikaner was declared overlord of the Herero lands north of the Swakop River up as far as the Waterberg Plateau. By force of arms, Afrikaner was able to maintain his hegemony over these Herero groups with their large herds of cattle, and in so doing was able to control loosely most of central and southern Namibia. Until his death in 1861, Jonker Afrikaner was probably the single most influential leader in this part of Namibia.

Background

Jonker Afrikaner

One of the key figures in Namibia during the first half of the 19th century was Jonker Afrikaner, an Oorlam from the Cape Province who established his authority over the central and southern part of Namibia, and who established the settlement at Windhoek which was to eventually become Namibia's capital.

Jonker Afrikaner belonged to an Oorlam group who, around the turn of the century, crossed the Orange River and established a fortified village in the Karasburg District. The leader of the clan at the time was Jager Afrikaner, Jonker's father, who had killed his white employer, a farmer named Pienaar, in a dispute over wages and had subsequently fled over the Orange River beyond the reach of the Cape Province authorities. After his father's death in 1823, Jonker Afrikaner trekked north with a group of his followers, and by the 1830s had established himself as leader of central and southern Namibia.

Due to the lack of accurate historical records during this period, there are differing accounts of how Jonker established himself as the senior Nama/Oorlam leader. One explanation is that by force of arms and constant cattle raids upon neighbouring Nama tribes, Jonker was able to establish his predominance. Other theories suggest that Nama leaders, fearing the steady encroachment of the Herero on their grazing lands, called in Jonker to force the Herero back. The English explorer Sir James Alexander met Jonker in 1836 in the Rehoboth area and reported that the Afrikaners had defeated the Hereros in three decisive battles in 1835, allowing the Afrikaners to steal the Herero cattle and establish themselves as the dominant power in the area.

By the 1840s an informal but definite alliance between Jonker Afrikaner and other Nama chiefs, such as Oaseb and Swartbooi existed. The basis of the alliance recognized Jonker Afrikaner as an equal of the Nama leaders, gave the Afrikaners sovereignty of the land between the Swakop and Kuiseb rivers and made Jonker Afrikaner overlord of the Herero lands north of the Swakop River. In this way the Afrikaners effectively acted as a buffer between the Hereros to the north and the Nama tribes of the south, ensuring greater security for the Nama lands to the south. This informal alliance was officially confirmed in 1858 in an agreement between Chief Oaseb and Jonker Afrikaner.

During the 1840s and 1850s, Jonker established relations with various Herero leaders, in particular Chief Tjamuaha and his son Kamaherero and Chief Kahitjene. The basis of these relations obliged the Herero to look after Afrikaner cattle and to pay regular tributes in the form of cattle, and in return the Herero leaders were generally spared cattle raids and were able to enrich themselves at the expense of their fellow Herero.

In 1840, Jonker had established the settlement of Windhoek in the Klein Windhoek valley. In 1842, invited by Jonker, the first two missionaries Hahn and Kleinschmidt arrived to find a flourishing community, boasting a whitewashed stone church capable of seating up to 500 people. There were also well established gardens where corn, tobacco and dagga (marijuana) were being cultivated in irrigated fields. For the next 20 years Windhoek was to flourish as a centre of commerce between the Hereros and the Oorlam/Namas.

Jonker Afrikaner died in 1861 and the years immediately following his death were to see the gradual erosion of Afrikaner hegemony over central and southern Namibia, and the abandonment of the settlement at Windhoek.

Missionaries and traders

The first Europeans had appeared off the coast of Africa in the 15th century. In 1486, the Portuguese explorer **Diego Cao** erected a cross at Cape Cross and **Bartholomew Diaz** planted another at Angra Pequena near Lüderitz in 1486. However, the coast was barren and inhospitable, and the interior of the country at this time would have only been accessible to these explorers by crossing the Namib Desert. No other Europeans are believed to have visited Namibia until the late 18th century when a small number of Dutch settlers trekked north from the Cape Colony and established themselves as farmers. Following them a small number of traders also came to Namibia but without initially having any significant impact.

The earliest missionaries, from the **London Mission Society**, began to operate in southern Namibia at the beginning of the 19th century and were soon joined later by the German **Rhenish** and Finnish **Lutheran Mission Societies**. The appearance of the earliest missionaries coincided with increasing numbers of Oorlams crossing the Orange River, and the presence of these missionaries was crucial to the success of the Oorlam commando groups in establishing themselves in Namibia.

Missionaries were important in 19th-century Namibia as they fulfilled a number of different roles, in addition to their primary aim of preaching the gospel. Indeed one early missionary, Ebner, regretting that he was unable to provide the Nama leader Titus Afrikaner with a supply of gunpowder as earlier preachers had done, was driven to write that 'it seems to me that he is more interested in powder, lead and tobacco than in the teachings of the gospel'.

Until the arrival of the missionaries, the Nama communities in the south of Namibia were semi-nomadic, however, the building of churches and the development of agriculture saw the establishment of the first stable settlements. The stone-walled churches fulfilled the role of mini-fortresses, and the brass bells that the missionaries provided were an effective warning system during raids. Many missionaries also introduced agriculture to the communities in which they lived, and the more stable food supply that followed allowed larger numbers of people to settle in an area. In turn, these larger settlements allowed for improved defence against raids through better organization.

Second, the missionaries acted as focal points for traders from the Cape, who were able to supply the missionaries and their families with the goods they needed. In this way the trade routes to the Cape were established and kept open, thus guaranteeing the Oorlam leaders continued supplies of the guns and ammunition upon which they depended for their supremacy. In the early years of the 19th century it seems as if some missionaries even supplied the guns themselves. Schmelen, who established a mission at Bethanie in southern Namibia, found it necessary to 'furnish some of my people with arms'. Even in later years when the export of guns and gunpowder from the Cape was prohibited, Kleinschmidt, who operated the mission at Rehoboth, provided Chief Swartbooi with gunpowder.

The almost constant conflict brought about the breaking down of social structures, however, the missionaries armed with their Christian rules proved effective control mechanisms for tribal leaders. In 1815, referring to the Afrikaner clan, Ebner noted that 'it is only the baptised who are allowed ... to use the gun.' Blameless Christian behaviour was also a prerequisite to political positions in communities such as Bethanie, Rehoboth, and Warmbad, behaviour defined, of course, by the missionaries. Missionaries also performed the roles of social worker and doctor, and Jonker Afrikaner once explained to Schonberg why he wanted a missionary at Otjimbingwe '... traders come and go, but the missionary stays, and consequently we know where to get our medicines from.'

By the 1860s an extensive network of trading posts existed in Namibia, the most important being Otjimbingwe northwest of present-day Windhoek. Set up by the

Charles John Andersson

Charles Andersson was born in Sweden in 1827 of a Swedish mother and English father. After a short spell at the University of Lund in 1847 he abandoned his studies in order to hunt and trade with his father. In 1849 he left for England with the intention of pursuing a career of hunting and exploration in Iceland; he sailed for South Africa instead upon the invitation of an Englishman named Galton.

During the 1850s Andersson travelled and hunted for ivory all over southwestern Africa, visiting King Nangolo in Ondongo, exploring Lake Ngami and reaching the Okavango River. By 1860 he was in a position to buy up the assets of the defunct Walvis Bay Trading Company in Otjimbingwe and set up a trading company there. Andersson was interested in ivory and cattle for the Cape trade and was able to set up other hunters and traders to work for him. The fact that Andersson's trading post was permanent made it the first of its kind in Namibia. He could set up the best possible deals and, if required, travel to the Cape himself, leaving his trading partners to look after the business in Otjimbingwe.

The opening of the trading post at Otjimbingwe coincided with the outbreak of lung sickness in cattle in the region. This posed a serious threat to all the groups raising cattle – Nama, Herero and European alike. Determined to protect their herds and pastures from the deadly disease, Jonker Afrikaner and his allies were extremely reluctant to let Andersson drive his cattle south through their lands. Furthermore, by opening up Hereroland to trade, Andersson posed a threat to the hegemony of the Afrikaner clan.

In 1861, while Jonker Afrikaner was in Owamboland, Andersson set off with 1,400 head of infected cattle for the Cape. Between Otjimbingwe and Rehoboth he was attacked by Hendrik Zes, a close ally of Jonker Afrikaner, who made off with 500 of the animals. Although Andersson and his traders were able to force Zes to return the cattle, the incident served as a serious warning to him. Thereafter, Andersson started to recruit and train mercenaries, mainly from the Cape, to protect his trading interests.

By January 1862, five months after Jonker Afrikaner's death, Andersson was

Anglo-Swede **Charles John Andersson**, Otjimbingwe was also a key mission station for the Herero-speaking peoples. Under Andersson's influence the European community of missionaries, traders and hunters were gradually sucked into the escalating Herero-Nama conflict (see box).

Following the death of Jonker Afrikaner in 1861 and the defeat of the Afrikaners and their allies at Otjonguere south of Windhoek in 1864, the years leading up to 1870 saw a virtual constant jockeying for position amongst the various Nama and Oorlam leaders. Once again the southern and central parts of Namibia were the scene of skirmishes and cattle raids. This infighting amongst the Oorlam/Namas effectively allowed the Herero-speaking people under the leadership of Kamaherero to break free of Afrikaner dominance.

The 1870 Peace Accord

In 1870 Jan Jonker Afrikaner arrived at Okahandja with a large group of armed men with the intention of renewing the old alliance between Kamaherero and the Afrikaners. However, missionary Hahn intervened and when the treaty was concluded in September of that year the Afrikaners had lost their old rights over the Herero-speaking peoples. Furthermore, Hahn obtained permission for the Cape **Basters** to settle at Rehoboth. The Basters were a farming community of mixed Khoi-European descent who, having been forced from their lands in the Cape Province, had been looking for a *established as a successful trader, organizing expeditions north into Hereroland, gradually changing the focus of his interest towards ivory and ostrich feathers. However, his position was not secure, as he noted in his diary on 26 January 1862. 'The Hottentots [Namas] are fearfully jealous of me: they got a notion that I am the only person who benefits by my presence. I am not afraid of any Hottentot individually or collectively, but I may have to leave the country unless I resort to bloodshed.'*

The scene was then set for an escalation of the conflict between Andersson and his traders on the one hand and the Afrikaners and their allies on the other. A series of cattle raids and skirmishes took place during 1863, culinating in an attack on Otjimbingwe by the Afrikaners in June of that year. Andersson, his traders and mercenaries – the 'Otjimbingwe volunteers' as they had come to be known – routed the attackers, killing about a third of them including their commander Christian Afrikaner. However, the power of the Afrikaners was not broken, and guerrilla attacks on Andersson's cattle trains continued.

In 1864 Andersson decided to seek an alliance with the Herero chiefs in an attempt to muster a big enough army to settle the conflict in one decisive battle. The Hereros had a long series of grievances going back many years against the Afrikaners, and after a series of negotiations and the election of Kamaherero as chief of all Herero speakers, a joint army of about 2,500 men was put together. On 22 June 1864 the two armies met near Rehoboth in a battle that proved to be anything but conclusive. The Afrikaners retreated after a day's battle, neither having been defeated nor emerging victorious. Andersson's shin was shattered by a bullet, a wound he never fully recovered from. He sold his business interests to the Rhenish Mission and retired to the Cape to put together his bird book on Namibia.

He returned to Namibia in 1865 leaving his wife and two young children in Cape Town. However, he was never to return, and died in Owamboland in 1867 of a combination of diphtheria, dysentery and exhaustion.

place to settle. The Baster settlement at Rehoboth acted as an effective buffer between the Herero-speaking peoples and the Oorlam-Namas.

Peace was preserved between the Nama and Herero-speaking peoples throughout the 1870s, and it was not until the beginning of the 1880s that conflict broke out once more. However, this period of relative peace amongst indigenous Namibians also saw the consolidation of the position of the missionaries and traders – particularly the latter. As the Nama leaders developed a taste for manufactured goods and alcohol, the economy of Namaland – virtually all the land south of Windhoek as far as the Orange River – became inextricably linked with that of the Cape. As a result the numbers of hunters, traders and explorers entering Namibia grew uncontrollably, and this in turn saw the over-exploitation of animal and natural resources in the central-southern part of Namibia.

The hunters and traders were chiefly interested in obtaining ivory and ostrich feathers to export to the Cape. At the same time they were selling guns, coffee, sugar, soap, gin and brandy to the Namibians. The only way the Nama chiefs could support their habit for western manufactured goods and alcohol was by granting licenses to the hunters and traders, leading one explorer, A Anderson, to complain to the Cape government that 'every petty kaptein claims a license fee' for hunting, passing through and trading.

However, while the Oorlam/Namas of southern Namibia became caught up in this trading network, the Herero-speaking peoples living north of Windhoek remained

Background

Hendrik Witbooi

Hendrik Witbooi was born in 1830 and died in 1905 and was unique both as a Namibian and African leader. He was the first to realize that conflict between Namibians was of far less consequence than German attempts to colonize the country. Furthermore, he kept detailed written records of his thoughts and of contemporary events, including detailed minutes of meetings with other Namibian leaders and German officers.

Witbooi came from an Oorlam group brought over the Orange River by his grandfather Kido Witbooi sometime in the late 1820s. The group eventually settled in present-day Gibeon in 1863 and with missionary Knauer established their church and community. By 1871 missionary Olpp calculated that the Witboois numbered around 3,000 people living in about 30 villages around the Gibeon area. By 1893, Olpp reckoned that this number had doubled and were settled over an area stretching as far away as Gobabis in the east. In effect the Witboois became a nation of affiliated Oorlam commando groups and Nama tribes which Hendrik Witbooi came to be leader of in 1884.

Up until 1880, Witbooi and his wife and children lived in Gibeon . Missionary Olpp noted that Witbooi was a 'quiet' man, living more by hard work than by raiding. Baptized in 1868, Witbooi and his eldest son made the church the centre of their lives. In 1875 he became an elder of the church and from 1880 onwards, by his own record, his public actions were guided

by divine revelation. However, in early January 1883 Witbooi resigned from his position as elder of the mission church, apparently to devote his time to his growing political responsibilities and also in recognition of his role as leader-to-be of the Witbooi community.

In June 1884, Witbooi had negotiated the right to trek through Herero lands in order to settle further north. It seems that this proposed move was quite in line with Witbooi tradition, as Witbooi's grandfather, Kido, had declared Gibeon to be merely a temporary home. In his papers, Witbooi himself informed the missionaries and his father that the move was the will of God. The following year, however, when Witbooi attempted to make the move, despite two written assurances from Maherero that the previous year's treaty still applied, his followers were attacked and routed, cattle, horses and wagons stolen, and two of his sons killed. This event sewed the seeds of future conflict between Witbooi and Maherero.

The rest of the 1880s saw a series of battles between the different Namaland leaders that catapulted Hendrik Witbooi and his followers into the forefront of Namaland politics. At the same time, Witbooi was administering to the needs of his own community as well as dealing with both the Herero and Germans who were moving towards an alliance intended to control Witbooi. It was the energy and vision of Witbooi that allowed him by 1891

largely aloof from this burgeoning trade. True, they were the main purchasers of guns, for they had learned during the middle part of the century of the importance of modern weapons, but for the rest, trade with Hereroland was tightly controlled.

Given the vast numbers of cattle which the Herero were breeding, it seems strange that the European traders were not more active in their contact with the Herero. The main reason for this it seems, was a lack of interest on the part of the Herero in exchanging their cattle for western goods.

Unlike the inhabitants of Namaland who were experiencing a spiralling circle of dependency on imported manufactured goods together with the virtual invasion of their territory by Europeans of one description or another, the Herero-speaking peoples retained their traditional kinship-oriented pastoral way of life. In other words the Herero valued their cattle far more highly than any manufactured goods, and rather to have established his authority over the other Namaland chiefs, and to have established a fortified stronghold at Hoornkrans in the Gamsberg Mountains west of Rehoboth.

In 1890 the German Commissioner to Namibia, Heinrich Göring, wrote to Witbooi ordering him to return to Gibeon and to desist from any plans to attack the Herero, as they were now under German protection. In an extraordinary letter to Maherero at the end of May of that year, Witbooi warned Maherero that he would bitterly regret making a treaty with the Germans for 'I doubt that you and your Herero nation will understand the rules and laws and methods of that government … for he (Göring) will not act according to your will, or traditional law or customs.' Witbooi understood what the Herero had so far clearly failed to grasp, namely that the Germans intended taking absolute control over Namibia as part of their imperial designs.

Witbooi's warnings fell on deaf ears and between 1890 and 1892 he waged a campaign of cattle raids on the Herero, succeeding in carrying off thousands of animals. At the same time, anticipating war with the Germans, he secured a steady supply of weapons and ammunition from the Cape, using European traders and even a lawyer to assist him secure these supply lines.

In 1890, the Germans had established their headquarters in Windhoek, and had gradually been increasing their military strength. In April 1893, the German forces,

led by Captain Curt von François, attacked Witbooi's stronghold at Hoornkrans, forcing Witbooi to abandon his stronghold. Thereafter a guerrilla war ensued, with the Germans constantly attempting to locate and subdue the Witboois, who with their superior knowledge of the country, were able to harass and evade the Germans. The decisive battles took place between 27 August and 5 September 1894 in the Naukluft Mountains, to where Witbooi had retreated. Although superior in numbers, arms and ammunition, the Germans were not able to defeat Witbooi, on the other hand Witbooi was not able to successfully break out of this siege, and the two sides eventually fought each other to a standstill. A visit and hike in the Naukluft Park gives a vivid idea of how impossible it must have been for both sides to have fought under such conditions (see page 277).

On 15 September Witbooi signed a conditional surrender which required him and his supporters to return to Gibeon, to accept the paramountcy of the German empire and the stationing of a German garrison at Gibeon. In return Witbooi retained jurisdiction over his land and people, and the right to keep guns and ammunition. This treaty was largely respected by both sides until 1904, when the Herero declared war on the Germans. Witbooi also took up arms against the colonizers, but died in the saddle in 1905 from a bullet wound. Thereafter the Witboois largely withdrew from the war.

than exchanging cattle for goods, they actually increased the size of their herds.

Despite renewed cattle raids during the early part of the 1880s by Oorlam/Namas who succeeded in stealing thousands of head of cattle, ex-missionary Hahn – now a full-time trader – remarked that the Herero 'will in a few years make up for these losses. There is, perhaps, no people in the world who equals the Damaras (Hereros) as cattle breeders …'.

Namibia becomes a colonial possession

In 1880, after 10 years of relative peace, fierce fighting broke out once more in central Namibia. Once again the disputes were over cattle and grazing rights and they involved all the key players in central Namibia at the time. There were the Herero –

led by **(Ka)Maherero** as he came to be known – the Nama Swartboois, the Afrikaners under Jan Jonker, and the Rehoboth Basters (relative newcomers to the scene). All through 1880 and 1881 the fighting continued with a number of important leaders falling in battle, in particular Maherero's eldest son Willem in the fight for Okahandja in December 1880. Up until 1884 and the rise of **Hendrik Witbooi**, a bewildering series of shifting alliances, cattle raids and skirmishes characterized the scene in south and central Namibia.

However, it was the arrival of German representatives in 1884, the subsequent treaties with the Herero and the effective subduing of Hendrik Witbooi 10 years later that fundamentally changed the way in which Namibia was governed. Power steadily shifted away from traditional leaders, such as Witbooi and Maherero, into the hands of the German colonial administrators. Furthermore, over the next 25 years vast tracts of Namaland and Hereroland passed into the hands of the colonial government and individual settlers. This fundamental change culminated with the 1904-07 German-Namibian war which saw the final consolidation of colonial authority over the country, and the subjugation of the Namibian peoples by Europeans.

Between 1883 and 1885, the German trader and businessman **Adolf Lüderitz** negotiated a series of agreements which saw him buy practically the entire coastal strip of Namibia between the Orange and Kunene rivers, extending as far as 150 km inland. A settlement was established at **Angra Pequena**, soon renamed as **Lüderitzbucht**, which helped to open the country up to German political and economic interests. German policy in Namibia was that private initiative and capital would 'develop' the country, secured by German government protection.

In order to bring 'order' to Namibia, the German authorities pursued a policy of persuading local leaders to sign so-called protection treaties (Shuzverträge) with them. This they achieved by exploiting local conflicts to serve their own ends, and in the face of continuing conflict between Maherero and Hendrik Witbooi, were able to persuade Maherero to sign a protection treaty with the German authorities in 1885. In the same year Commissioner Göring wrote to Hendrik Witbooi ordering him to desist from continuing with his cattle raids against the Herero and threatening him with unspecified consequences.

However, these threats were empty gestures. During the period 1884-89 the official German presence in Namibia consisted of three officials based in a classroom at the mission school in Otjimbingwe, plus a small number of business representatives who effected the protection treaties. It was not until 1889 that the first force of 21 soldiers (Schutztruppe) landed in Namibia, to be followed by another 40 the following year, and only after 1894, following the subduing of Hendrik Witbooi, that significant numbers of settlers were able to enter the country.

Between 1894 and 1904 the Witboois sold a third of their land to European settlers, and the treaties that Samuel Herero signed with the German colonial government in 1894 and 1895 ceded Herero land to them. Meanwhile, following the death of old Maherero in 1890, the German administration established its headquarters in Windhoek and during the confusion over the succession of the Herero leader was able to consolidate its position there. However, the greatest sale of Herero land took place in the years after 1896 – the result of the trade on credit systems in operation at the time, the rinderpest epidemic of 1897 and the fever epidemic of 1898.

With the further opening of Hereroland to trade following the treaties signed with the German colonial administration, there was a dramatic increase in the number of traders operating in the country. For Europeans without their own capital but prepared to put up with the hardships of living in the veld, this was a perfect opportunity to make money and acquire cattle and land. Large firms employed these traders to go out to Herero settlements in the veld and sell their goods there. Due to the risks involved, all parties attempted to maximize profit, often adding 70 to 100%

onto the value of goods to achieve this. They were also quite happy to give the Hereros credit in order to encourage them to buy more and more, until the situation arrived whereby an individual or community's debt was greater than their assets.

In addition, following the rinderpest epidemic of 1897 in which up to 97% of unvaccinated cattle died, the only way in which the Hereros could pay for the goods they wanted or settle their debts was to sell land. An addiction to alcohol amongst many Hereros, not least their leader Samuel Maherero, also caused large debts which had to be settled through land sales. Although the colonial government attempted to put all business dealings between Europeans and Namibians on a cash basis, the protests of the traders brought about a suspension of this regulation almost immediately after its introduction.

Inevitably tension grew among the Herero as they saw their traditional lands gradually disappearing. The Rhenish Missionary Society petitioned the colonial government to consider creating reserves for the Herero where the land could not be sold, and despite initial resistance both within Namibia and from Germany, so-called paper reserves (because initially they only existed on paper) were created around Otjimbingwe at the end of 1902 and around Okahandja and Waterberg in 1903. However, there were many Herero leaders who were deeply dissatisfied with the land issue, and pressure was growing on Herero leader Samuel Maherero to take some action to recover lost lands – although he himself had been responsible for the sale of much of it.

The 1904-07 German-Namibian War

The three years of fighting between the German colonial forces and various Namibian tribes ended with victory for the Germans and the consolidation of their colonial rule over Namibia. Thousands of Namibians died either as a result of the fighting or in the aftermath and the effect that this had was to put a stop to organized resistance to outside rule. The trauma of defeat and dislocation meant that 50 odd years were to pass before the emergence of the independence movements in the late 1950s.

The war began following a revolt of the Bondelswarts Namas in the extreme south of the country at the end of 1903. The majority of German soldiers were sent to the south to quell the uprising and in January 1904 Samuel Maherero, under intense pressure from other Herero leaders and fearing for his own position as paramount Herero leader, gave the order to the Herero nation to rise up against the German presence in Namibia. At the same time he also appealed to Hendrik Witbooi and other Namibian leaders to follow suite.

During the first months of the uprising the Herero were successful in capturing or isolating German fortified positions, however, following the appointment of **Lothar von Trotha** as German military commander, the Herero were gradually forced to retreat from around Okahandja and other strongholds in central Namibia. They made a final stand at the waterholes at Hamakari by the Waterberg Plateau south of Otjiwarongo in August of 1904. The German plan was to encircle the assembled Herero, defeat them, capture their leaders and pursue any splinter groups which might have escaped. The Herero objective was to hold onto the waterholes, for without these they and their cattle would either die or be obliged to surrender.

The German troops attacked the Herero forces on 11 August with the battle continuing on a number of fronts all day. By nightfall no clear picture had yet emerged, however, the following day it became apparent that although the Herero had not been defeated, their resistance was broken and Samuel Maherero and the entire Herero nation fled into the Omaheke sandveld in eastern Namibia en route for

Botswana. Stories from those who eventually arrived in Betchuanaland (Botswana) tell horrific stories of men, women and children struggling through the desert, gradually dying of thirst.

A section of the German forces initially gave chase but by 14 August they had returned to the original battle site, both soldiers and horses suffering from exhaustion, hunger and thirst. The chase was once again taken up on 16 August but finally abandoned at the end of September as it was impossible to provision both troops and horses in the inhospitable sandveld.

On 2 October Von Trotha issued a proclamation ordering all Herero-speaking people to leave German Southwest Africa or face extermination, and then turned his attention to subduing uprisings in the south of the country. Just over a month later, Von Trotha received orders from Berlin to spare all Herero except the leaders and those 'guilty'. Following the retreat of the Herero, three more years of sporadic resistance to German rule took place in the centre and south of Namibia as the Nama-speaking people continued the revolt.

Much has been written on the German-Namibian War, specifically of the deliberate intention of the German colonial administration to 'exterminate' the Herero nation. Until recently it was widely accepted that the Herero nation was reduced from a population of 60,000-80,000 people before the war, to between 16,000-18,000 people after the war. Similarly, the generally accepted view is that the population of the Nama-speaking peoples was also reduced by 35-50% to around 10,000 people.

It is impossible to obtain accurate figures to either confirm or refute the allegations of genocide, however, some recent research, especially by the late Brigitte Lau, former head of the National Archives, challenges a number of popular conceptions of the war. In particular questions have now been raised on how the numbers were calculated and on the capacity of the German forces to actually set about the deliberate process of genocide.

The only figures available were based on missionary reports in the 1870s, but the missionaries only worked in a relatively small area of Hereroland. Furthermore, any accurate estimate of the numbers of Herero would have been near impossible, as the Herero were scattered across the veld. In addition, the effects of the rinderpest epidemic of 1897 and the fever epidemic of 1898 were also not taken into account. The suggestion is therefore that there were far fewer Herero than was originally believed.

As far as the capacity of German military to wipe out the Herero is concerned, medical records of the time show that the average military presence during the war was 11,000 men. Of these an average of 57% per year were sick from the effects of lack of water and sanitation, typhoid fever, malaria, jaundice, suicide and chronic dysentery. This information suggests that the German military presence was simply not capable of a concerted attempt to commit genocide – even if that had been the intention.

There is no question, however, that following the war both Herero and Nama prisoners of war died in concentration camps; there were executions of captured leaders and many survivors were forced into labour – working on the railroads and in the mines. By the end of the war, the German colonial administration was firmly in control of Namibia from the Tsumeb-Grootfontein area in the north down to the Orange River in the south.

Economic development

With the consolidation of German control of central and southern Namibia came rapid economic growth and infrastructural development. Land in the most productive areas in the country was parcelled up and given to settler families, forming the basis of much of the existing white agricultural wealth in the country today. The railway network, already in place between Lüderitz and Aus in the south and Swakopmund, Okahandja and Windhoek in the centre of the country, was expanded to reach the central-northern towns of Tsumeb and Otavi and Grootfontein, Gobabis in the east and Keetmanshoop in the south.

The discovery of diamonds at Kolmanskop near Lüderitz in the south in 1908 financed the economic boom in that part of the country – between 1908 and 1914, German mining companies cut a total of 5,145,000 carats of diamonds. The introduction of the **karakul** sheep to the south saw the start of the highly successful karakul wool and leather industry, which brought tremendous prosperity to white farmers in the ranchlands south of Windhoek. Finally, the development of the Tsumeb mines producing copper, zinc and lead brought wealth and development to the Tsumeb-Grootfontein-Otavi triangle in the central-northern areas.

While the wealth that accrued from this flurry of economic activity was concentrated in the hands of white settlers, the labour which built the railroads and worked the farms and mines was predominantly black. A vivid example of this was the estimated 10,000 Oshiwambo-speaking workers who came down from Owamboland in the far north (an area still outside German colonial control, although technically part of German Southwest Africa) to work on the railroads and in the mines. This was the start of migratory work patterns upon which the apartheid era contract labour system was built.

Self-government for the white population was granted by Germany in January 1909 and the following month the main towns including Windhoek, Swakopmund, Keetmanshoop, Lüderitz, Okahandja and Tsumeb were granted the status of municipalities. In Windhoek this period up to the beginning of the First World War in 1914 saw the building of many landmarks – in particular the **Christuskirche** (German Lutheran Church) and the **Tintenpalast** – now the seat of the Namibian Parliament. Self-government in German Southwest Africa lasted until the peaceful surrender of the territory to South African troops fighting on the side of the British in July 1915. This brought to an end the brief period of German colonial rule and ushered in the beginning of 75 years of South African rule.

League of Nations mandate

Following the end of the First World War and the signing of the Treaty of Versailles in 1919, the newly formed League of Nations gave the mandate for governing Namibia to Britain. The mandate, which was to be managed by South Africa on behalf of Britain, came into effect in 1921 and was the beginning of South African control of Namibia, which was to end only with independence in 1990.

The pattern of South African rule over Namibia was established from the start with the relentless expropriation of good farm land for white farmers and the removal of the black population, first to native reserves and later to the so-called homelands. When South Africa took over control of Namibia about 12,000,000 ha of land were in the hands of white (mainly German) farmers, however by 1925 a further 11,800,000 ha had been given to white settlers.

A great number of these new settlers were poor, illiterate Afrikaners who the Union government in South Africa did not want within their own borders. In this way Namibia effectively became a dumping ground for these unwanted farmers, who were given the most generous of terms. New farmers were not only given land for free, but also received credit in the form of cash, wire fences and government-built bore holes to help them get started.

In contrast, in 1923 the Native Reserves Commission proclaimed a mere 2,000,000 ha for the black population of the country who made up 90% of the total population. At the same time a series of laws and regulations governed where the black population was entitled to live and work, severely restricting their freedom of movement in the white-controlled areas. The most obvious consequences of these laws was the creation of a pool of readily available, cheap labour – the nascence of the contract labour system.

The bulk of the population of Namibia was forced to live in a narrow strip of land north of Etosha and south of the Angolan border, marked by the Kunene and Okavango rivers. The Red Line, a veterinary fence established by the Germans to prevent the spread of rinderpest and foot-and-mouth disease, effectively separated the communal grazing lands of the north from the commercial white-owned land of the centre and south of the country. This strip of land was far too small to support the number of people living there, obliging many to put themselves into the hands of the contract labour system by seeking work further south.

In 1925 two recruitment agencies were established to find workers for the mines in the centre and south of the country, and in 1943 these two original agencies were amalgamated into the South West Africa Native Labour Association (SWANLA). Potential workers were sorted into three categories – those fit and able to work underground, those suitable for work above ground at the mines, and the rest only suitable for farm work. Workers themselves had no choice in this and a document of the time stated that 'Only the servant is required to render to the master his service at all fit and reasonable times.'

The period following the Second World War saw further land give-aways, mainly as rewards to Union soldiers who had served in the war. By the mid-1950s a further 7,000,000 ha of farmland had been put into white hands and the number of whites in Namibia had increased by 50% to around 75,000. The last viable farmland was given away in the 1960s to white conservatives who supported the South African regime's hard-line apartheid policies.

At the same time the Odendaal Commission of Inquiry formulated a plan for the creation of **bantustans** or black homelands around the country, involving the forced removal of the black population from all areas designated for whites. The commission also called for the even closer integration of Namibia into South Africa and stated explicitly that 'the government of South Africa no longer regards the original (League of Nations) mandate as still existing as such'.

Road to independence

Following the end of the Second World War, the newly formed United Nations Organization assumed responsibility for the administration of the former German colonies, such as the Cameroons, Togo and Namibia. The UN set up a trusteeship system intended to lead to independence for these territories and in response the South African government sought to incorporate Namibia into South Africa. A series of 'consultations' with Namibian leaders during 1946 were intended to convince the UN that Namibians themselves sought to become part of South Africa. Although these efforts were unsuccessful, it was not until 1971 that the South African presence was deemed to be 'illegal'.

Organized resistance to South African rule took off in the 1950s and was initially led by Herero Chief **Hosea Kutako**, who initiated a long series of petitions to the UN. In 1957 the Owamboland's People's Congress was founded in Cape Town by Namibian contract workers lead by **Andimba Toivo Ja Toivo**, its prime objective being to achieve the abolition of the hated contract labour system. In 1958 Toivo succeeded in smuggling a tape to the UN giving oral evidence of South African suppression and for his pains was immediately deported to Namibia. The same year the name of the organization was changed to the Owamboland People's Organization (OPO) and in 1959 Sam Nujoma and Jacob Kuhangu launched the organization in Windhoek.

1959 also saw the founding of Southwest Africa National Union (SWANU), initially an alliance between urban youth, intellectuals and the Herero Chief's Council. In September of that year the executive of the organization was broadened to include members of the OPO and other organizations, thereby widening its base and making it more representative of the Namibian population as a whole.

These new organizations were soon in conflict with the South African authorities and the December 1959 shootings at the **Old Location** (see box, page 352) effectively marked the start of concerted resistance to South African rule. 1n 1960 the OPO was reconstituted into the **South West Africa People's Organization (SWAPO)**, with the central objective of liberating the Namibian people from colonial oppression and exploitation. SWAPO leader Sam Nujoma had managed to leave Namibia and was to lead the organization in exile until his return in 1989.

In 1966, SWAPO appealed to the International Court of Justice to declare South Africa's control of Namibia illegal. The court failed to deliver, even though the UN General Assembly voted to terminate South Africa's mandate. SWAPO's response was to launch the guerrilla war at Ongulumbashe in Owamboland on 26 August, with the declaration that the court's ruling 'would relieve Namibians once and for all from any illusions which they might have harboured about the United Nations as some kind of saviour in their plight'.

In the early stages, the bush war was by necessity a small-scale affair. SWAPO's bases were in Zambia, close only to the Eastern Caprivi region, and it was only after the Portuguese withdrawal from Angola in 1975 that it became possible to wage a larger scale campaign. In response to the launching of the guerrilla war, the South African government established military bases all across Namibia's northern borders, and as the scale of the fighting escalated during the 1980s, life became increasingly intolerable for the inhabitants of these areas.

On the political scene, SWAPO activists in Namibia were arrested, tried and sentenced to long prison terms. Among the first group to be sentenced in 1968 was Toivo Ja Toivo, at that time regional secretary for Owamboland. He was sentenced to 20 years imprisonment on Robben Island where he was to remain until 1984. Following the International Court of Justice ruling in 1971 that 'the continued presence of South Africa in Namibia [was] illegal', a wave of strikes led by contract workers broke out around the country, precipitating a further round of arrests of strike leaders.

Although the South African government succeeded in quelling the strikes of late 1971 and early 1972, the rest of the decade saw growing resistance to South African rule of Namibia. Ordinary Namibians everywhere, but especially in the densely populated north, buoyed by the International Court of Justice ruling, became politicized, resisting South African attempts to push forward apartheid policies to create separate bantustans around the country.

In response to pressure from Western countries South Africa struggled to find an 'internal solution' to the deadlock in Namibia which would both satisfy the outside world and at the same time defend white minority interests in the country. In 1977 the **Turnhalle Conference** (see page 79, Windhoek section) produced a draft constitution for an independent Namibia based on a three-tier system of government which would change little. Needless to say, no one was fooled and the war continued.

During the 1980s South Africa's position in Namibia became increasingly untenable. The bush war was expensive and never-ending and was seriously affecting the South African economy; at the same time attempts to find a political solution within Namibia which excluded SWAPO were proving impossible. Furthermore, opinion amongst the influential Western nations was swinging away from South Africa, making it inevitable that sooner or later Namibia would have to be granted independence with black majority rule.

Background

Shooting at the Old Location

In order to comply with apartheid policy regulations that a 5 km buffer zone should exist between white and black residential areas, Windhoek municipality formulated plans to remove the black and coloured communities from the so-called Old Location close to the city centre. It was intended that two new townships – Khomasdal and Katutura – would be the new homes for these communities, however the residents of the Old Location were not inclined to move. Their homes, businesses and lives were based in and around the Old Location, furthermore the proposed new townships were far out of town, had none of the necessary amenities, and the rents on the municipality-built houses were expensive.

Resistance to removal started as early as 1956 and was well established by the time matters came to a head in the second half of 1959 when the community of the

Old Location took a decision to boycott all municipal services, including the buses and the beer hall, an important source of municipal profit. On 9 December a procession of women succeeded in leading a demonstration from the Old Location to demonstrate in front of the house of the South African administrator. The following evening South African police and military units with armoured cars were sent into the Location, only to be met by gathering crowds and stone road blocks.

At around 2230 on the night of 10 December tear gas cannisters were fired into the crowd followed by gunshots, killing 13 protestors and wounding dozens more. The repercussions of the shootings were to be felt for many years, as the resistance of the inhabitants of the Old Location became a symbol of the wider Namibian resistance to apartheid policies and South African rule itself.

The key to the solution was the withdrawal of Cuban troops from Angola in return for the withdrawal of South African soldiers from Namibia. At the same time a United National Transitional Government (UNTAG) was to oversee the transition to independence, with elections taking place in November 1989. The final months leading up to the elections saw the return of SWAPO President **Sam Nujoma** from 30 years in exile along with thousands of ordinary Namibians who had also fled into exile during the long years of the bush war.

The main political parties were SWAPO and the DTA, formed in the wake of the unsuccessful Turnhalle Conference. Support for SWAPO was almost universal in Owamboland where the majority of the population lived, while the DTA looked to the south and much of the white community for its support. Although SWAPO won the elections it did not gain the two-thirds majority required to draw up a new constitution for the country.

Following the successful elections a new constitution was drafted by the various political parties, with the help of international advisers from a number of countries including the USA, France, Germany and the former Soviet Union. Widely viewed as a model of its kind, the new constitution guaranteed wide-ranging human rights and freedom of speech, as well as establishing a multi-party democracy governed by the rule of law. The final date for independence was set for 21 March 1990.

Background

Modern Namibia

Since independence the SWAPO government led by Sam Nujoma has pursued a policy of national reconciliation designed to heal the wounds of 25 years of civil war and over a century of colonial rule. Strongly supported by the various UN agencies and major donors, the Namibian government has set about to redress the injustices of the past and rebuild the economy, so badly damaged by the war. The mining sector, which is by far the largest sector of the economy, has been further developed and significant growth has also occurred in both the fishing and tourist industries. However, Namibia is still largely dependent on South Africa for foodstuffs and manufactured products, and this is one of the weak links in the economy.

The provision of educational and health care facilities to previously neglected sections of the community has also been a priority for the government, however this has placed a heavy burden on the country's finances. Education alone has been consuming around 30% of the national budget since independence, while the combined effects of rapid population growth (around 3.5%) and an inflation rate hovering around the 10% mark have made it difficult for the country to address the problem of massive unemployment.

Elections in 1994 saw SWAPO win with a massive 68% of the vote, which effectively gave the party the right to change the constitution if it had wished to do so. Throughout 1998 a debate raged debate whether or not the constitution should be changed to allow the president to stand for a third term raged. On the one hand, it was argued that allowing the generally popular Sam Nujoma to stand for a third term would contribute to stability and continuity in this young nation. On the other hand, some Namibians and external observers believe that changing the constitution would set a dangerous precedent and set Namibia on the path to becoming a one-party state.

The debate effectively ended in November 1998 when the Namibian Constitution Amendment Bill, allowing President Nujoma a third term in office, passed through the final parliamentary stage. General and presidential elections held at the end of 1999 saw another convincing SWAPO victory, and Sam Nujoma duly commenced his third term in office as president. Despite numerous rumours that 'Sam' is about to stand down in favour of one or another of his senior ministers, there is no solid evidence that he is ready to pass on the reins of power to a younger generation.

Around this time, the bizarre events in the Caprivi (see box on page 167) which saw the Governor of the region, prominent leaders and ordinary citizens flee to Botswana and apply for political asylum were the first indications of serious unrest since independence in 1990. In addition, renewed fighting in the Angolan civil war and Namibian government support for the MPLA government saw incursions by both UNITA and MPLA soldiers from Angola. At the same time well-publicized attacks on foreign tourists in 2000 damaged tourist confidence in the country.

An additional and unnecessary distraction from the serious business of creating economic growth was the country's involvement in the conflict in the Democratic Republic of Congo to prop up the now assassinated Laurent Kabila. Despite the Prime Minister's explanations that Namibia was 'fighting for peace' and 'going every inch' for negotiations to end the conflict, the real reasons behind Namibia's involvement remain somewhat murky.

Nevertheless, not all is doom and gloom. During the late 1990s and first part of the new century, the Namibian economy continued to grow, albeit slowly, and the further development of the Walvis Bay port and the completion of the Trans-Kalahari and Trans-Caprivi highways demonstrates the government's commitment to international commerce and trade. The tourism sector has been a bright beacon as the country has emerged as one of Africa's best-known secrets. Namibia is also an active member of the Southern African Development Community (SADC). Above all else, human rights and freedom of speech continue to be respected in Namibia and the rule of law prevails.

The biggest challenges facing Namibia as she moves into her second decade of independence and the new millennium are to address poverty and unemployment, find a fair solution to the land debate and get to grips with the **AIDS** epidemic. With education and training high on the government's list of priorities and the all-round will to see the country prosper, Namibia's future is potentially bright.

Economy

Since independence Namibia has enjoyed steady but unspectacular economic growth, but this has been checked by periods of drought and low world commodity prices. Per capita income in 2000 was estimate at US$3,884, ranking the country 87th in the world, higher than neighbouring Botswana and Zimbabwe. However, this figure disguises the great inequality in income distribution: according to the World Bank's *Gini* coefficient – an indicator of economic inequality – Namibia enjoys the most unequal income distribution in the world. Most of the productive ranch land still lies in the hands of a minority of white farmers, as it did until very recently in neighbouring Zimbabwe. Similarly, most commerce and industry is controlled by a minority of whites and a small black middle class, while the mass of the population earns a meagre living from subsistence farming, from the service industry and from the informal sector.

In February 2001, President Sam Nujoma announced a plan to resettle around 250,000 people on 9,500,000 ha to be purchased from the minority 4,000 white farmers who collectively own over 30,000,000 ha of land. At an estimated cost of around US$125 mn it is unclear how the government will purchase this land without substantial foreign aid. If this is not forthcoming, the government will have to find ways of appeasing this mass of landless people whose expectations have been raised.

Between 1990 and 1995 the economy grew at an average rate of 4.5%, but a 3.2% population growth has eroded many of the economic gains. Continued population growth and an average annual growth rate of less than 3% between 1996 and 2000, plus average inflation of 4.5% over this period, means that a majority of Namibians are actually getting poorer. In 1982 mining contributed to 26.9% of GDP, by 1995 this figure had fallen to 11%. Tourism and the fisheries sector have made significant contributions to recent growth and agricultural output remains more or less constant. However, these sectors have been unable to absorb the increase in the number of Namibians looking for work.

In 1995, 66% of the adult population were literate, primary school enrolment was 83% (1993), while secondary school enrolment was 42% (1991). Namibia has placed a high priority on education – since independence the system has been rationalized and the quality and relevance of the education for all Namibian children has been improved. Over 10% of GDP is devoted to education, a proportion exceeded by few countries in the world. In the long run the government is hoping to reap the dividends, assuming sufficient jobs can be created.

The Namibian health care system is one of the government's four priority sectors. Before independence the system concentrated on curative care for the urban elite, while neglecting the majority of the poor. The system was racially based with inequitable quality and access to care. The government has embarked upon a programme to redistribute resources from curative to primary care. Investment in health care has been 14% of government spending, a high proportion by regional and international standards. Improvements have been made but many of the remote rural areas are still without access to clinics and community health workers.

However, the major health issue facing Namibia is the desperately serious AIDS epidemic that will have profound social, demographic and economic impact consequences for the country. According to the Ministry of Health, the rate of HIV infection has grown 8% in 1998 to 17% in 1999 and 26% in 2000. This is despite widespread public education campaigns in the media, and a much healthier and open debate than was previously the case about how to tackle this serious problem.

Economic performance Mining

In simple statistical terms Namibia is mineral rich. The country has the world's largest **uranium** mine at Arandis near Swakopmund, and Namibia is Africa's second largest producer of zinc, its third largest producer of lead and fourth largest supplier of copper. The diamond mines around Lüderitz are the leading producers of gem-quality diamonds in the world; and then there are significant reserves of silver, gold, tin, cadmium, zinc, vanadium, tungsten and germanium. There are over 40 different operating mines and quarries in the sector, producing a wide range of precious metals and minerals.

Overall the sector is the largest private sector employer and the largest source of corporate tax. But since 1989 the industry has had to undergo major structural readjustments and retrenchment, during which period the contribution to GDP has fallen from 28% to 11% (1995), while the absolute value has not varied a great deal in constant prices since 1988. Mining is always vulnerable to demand and world-wide price fluctuations, and during the 1996 industrial dispute at TCL it was claimed that the company had had to cope with a 30-35% drop in world copper prices (see box page 139). While the sector may be an important source of employment it does not employ that many people. In 1983 the sector employed 16,600 people, by 1992 this figure had fallen to 11,400. This was mainly due to job losses at Rössing Uranium and Namdeb Diamond Corporation and the closure of the Namib Lead Mine. The April 1994 Minerals Act was promulgated to govern all future prospecting and the government has been working hard to diversify the sector and promote small-scale mining. It will take some time before the sector is not dominated by large-scale foreign owned companies, which employ a limited number of Namibians, and repatriate a large proportion of their profits overseas. At present many of the locally owned small mines suffer from a lack of financial assistance, technical expertise and administrative skills.

Diamonds

In recent years the **diamond** industry in Namibia has undergone some major changes, both in means of production and ownership. At the end of 1994 a new operating company, Namdeb Diamond Corporation, acquired the diamond assets of the Consolidated Diamond Mine based in Oranjemund. The new company is equally owned by the Namibian government and De Beers Centenary AG. While the importance of income from diamonds has declined they remain an important source of income for the government. In 1980 diamonds contributed to 40% of the state revenue, but this figure quickly fell to just 9% in 1983. More recently trade in diamonds has accounted for N$818 mn in 1992, 22.7% of Namibia's total exports. A recovery in prices has led to several operations being reopened but overall the trend around Lüderitz and Oranjemund is to increase the exploitation of offshore diamond fields. The Namibian Minerals Corporation, NAMCO, holds the concession rights to over 1,000 sq km offshore, an area estimated to contain 73,000,000 carats of gem diamonds. In 2000 total production of diamonds was 2,100,000 carats.

Uranium

Some 50 km inland from Swakopmund is the **Rössing** uranium mine, the world's largest single producer of a low-grade uranium. The mine has been developed by the Rio Tinto-Zinc group. The first oxide was extracted in 1976, since when the mine's fortunes have fluctuated along with world prices. Most of the uranium is sold to Europe, Japan and Taiwan on long-term contracts. In 1994 a deal was struck with Electricité de France which ensured survival through to 2001, and the recent change of management saw promises made to keep the mine open for another seven years. Once the reserves are eventually exhausted the mine is committed to a major environmental clean-up project: while it will not be difficult to dismantle machinery and housing, how best to deal with the giant hole in the ground is another matter.

Oil & gas Prior to independence there was no investment in the exploration for hydrocarbon potential because of political uncertainty. Since 1990 offshore geological investigations have revealed conditions to be similar to the north, off the coast of Angola, where oil has already been discovered. A World Bank study has indicated that there may be up to 14 years' worth of natural gas reserves in the **Kudu** fields offshore from Lüderitz. In 1993 the exploration rights were awarded to a consortium of Shell and Engen. While exploration continues no plans have yet been announced as to whether or when the proven reserves may be extracted.

Agriculture Agriculture is a very important sector in terms of the employment it provides. Despite the fragile environment and constant threat of drought, the sector contributes 38.5% to the economy, the second largest portion after the service sector. The most important component is livestock, beef and mutton production accounting for almost 75% of the gross agricultural income. The sector directly or indirectly supports over 70% of the total population. Of all the economic sectors agriculture is the most emotive: under successive colonial governments much of the land was expropriated from the black majority to a few white settlers. This led to a dualistic agricultural sector with just over 4,000 white farmers owning 43% of agricultural land under freehold title, while approximately 150,000 households own 42% of the land.

Since independence the government has been very cautious in its approach to the land question. In 1991 a national conference on land reform was held. The conference rejected radical land expropriation, but recommended that the government place a ban on foreign ownership of agricultural land and called for redistribution of commercial land within the provisions of the constitution. In 1995 the government drafted the **Commercial Land Reform Act** which prescribed the procedure for land acquisition and distribution. Small-scale farmers have been helped with low-interest loans but the issue of tenure remains unresolved. While the government remains undecided on how to deal with the issue of land redistribution a new worrying trend has emerged where the wealthy new black élite are enclosing communal land for private use. This has been made possible by the gradual breakdown of traditional forms of land administration, and once again it is the smallest and most poor farmers who suffer.

Namibia's low and erratic rainfall pattern places severe limits on potential rain-fed agriculture. It is only possible to grow a single rain-fed crop each year, and this has to be in areas where the annual summer rainfall is more than 450 mm. The yields for rain-fed crops are affected by the uneven distribution of rains during the wet season and by poor soils. Many of the soils in the north suffer from deficiencies of zinc, phosphorus and organic matter. In order to obtain high yields the government is forced to use expensive imported fertiliszers and other chemicals. Namibia remains a net importer of basic food crops and drought has forced the country to appeal for emergency food aid on several occasions in recent years. In 1994 Namibia produced 76,000 tonnes of cereals, in 1995 this figure was only 41,000 tonnes and in 1999 this figure had dropped further to 28,600 tonnes. Faced with this decline in productivity, the only option for the government is further dependence upon imports.

The centre of the beef industry is the eastern central part of the country where a variety of breeds freely roam the nutritious grasslands. White farmers have developed Bonsmara and Afrikaner breeds as well as Brahman and Simmentaler to suit local conditions. Most beef products are chilled and vacuum packed before being exported frozen to South Africa and the EU. The export market demands lean beef from cattle of between 20 and 36 months old. When Namibia signed the Lomé convention it agreed to supply the EEC with 10,500 tonnes of beef in 1991 and 1992 and this had risen to over 38,000 tons in 1999. With every beef scare in Europe, Namibia has benefited with increased demands for its free-range beef. Although the last few years have been kind to cattle farmers, the arable sector livestock ranching remains vulnerable to drought.

Namibia ranks amongst the top 10 in the world in terms of the value of its catch. The **Fishing** fishing industry is in the same league as Norway and Canada and bigger than the UK or Australia. The cold waters of the **Benguela** current produce a nutrient-rich system which is very productive and typified by a low number of species being present but with large numbers of individuals per species. While these waters are ideal for industrial scale exploitation the careful management of the resources is vital (see below).

The recently revived Namibian industry is subdivided into two sectors, white fish and pelagic. The **white fish** species – kingklip, hake, sole, monk and snoek – occur along the continental shelf which stretches from the Kunene River in the north to the Orange River in the south. The total exploitable area is some 60,000 nautical square miles. The **pelagic** species – pilchard and horse mackerel – are found in more shallow waters which stretch from just south of Walvis Bay to Cape Frio in the north. The industry has yet to start exploiting the waters beyond the edge of the continental shelf.

The fishing industry is an excellent example of how conditions have changed to the benefit of Namibia since independence. Prior to independence Namibia had no control over the illegal fishing which took place within the internationally recognized fishing zone of 200 nautical miles (370 km), the exclusive economic zone (EEZ). As Namibia did not exist as an independent nation no foreign fishing fleet was obliged to pay any of the taxes or licence fees that would normally be due when fishing within another nation's EEZ. Without any controls in place this nearly resulted in the total destruction of some of the richest fishing waters in the world. Over-fishing during the 1980s resulted in the closure of five out of nine processing factories and the loss of jobs for four-fifths of the work force. It was estimated that foreign fleets were catching over 80% of the fish within Namibian waters, and that this catch was worth at least 1,500 mn rand.

Immediately after independence the new government proclaimed the existence of Namibia's EEZ and instructed foreign vessels to respect the zone and cease fishing within it. The government has been quick to introduce legislation which promotes the conservation of the marine environment and the managed exploitation of marine resources. The National Fisheries Act was passed at the end of 1992. By introducing new quotas and awarding long-term concessions the government has managed to facilitate the recovery of stocks while at the same time seeing its revenue grow each year. In 1992 a government-owned National Fishing Corporation was set up.

The fisheries sector contributed to 70% of the growth in real GDP in the two-year period from 1990 to 1992. In 1990 fishing contributed 1.5% to GDP, by 1994 this figure had risen to 3%. In 1992 the value of the landings was N\$800 mn, in 1994 the combination of higher prices for hake and pilchards meant the value of the landings had increased to N\$1,200 mn. A further examination of the figures shows that the fishing sector accounted for close to 22% of all exports in 1994 (Bank of Namibia). This tremendous growth has only been made possible by a considerable amount of investment both by local and foreign private sector firms. Over N\$400 mn has been invested in upgrading the Namibian fishing fleet and the construction of new onshore processing plants. A new factory has been built in Lüderitz and a processing plant in Walvis Bay. The number of people employed by the sector has increased from 6,000 to over 9,000, making the fishing sector the second largest source of private-sector employment behind mining.

It is estimated that fish stocks have more than doubled since independence, but the government has been wary not to increase the catch limits too quickly, despite

Background

pressure from within the industry, as it is very easy to over-judge the extent of any recovery. A good example of how effective the recovery has been is to look at figures for hake, one of the most important species. Before the Namibian government was able to introduce controls hake was being heavily over-fished. As much as 600,000 tonnes had been caught in a single year. In 1991 the catch was limited to 60,000 tonnes, for 1992 the limit was set at 90,000 tonnes and in 1993 the permitted catch was raised to 120,000 tonnes. Throughout this period research showed that the stocks were continuing to recover. In 1994 a joint report published by the FAO and the Namibian Sea Fisheries Research Institute in Swakopmund noted that it could take at least a decade for all the severely depleted fish stocks to recover to former levels. A worrying trend was the considerable year-to-year variation in some stocks, the government must plan carefully for the future, despite the unexpected level of recovery for some fish species.

As long as Namibia is careful in its management of its marine resources the sector will continue to be a valuable source of income. Further investment is required but this will lead to a more efficient industry and greater profits in the long term. But while stocks of white fish, anchovies and pilchards have all shown signs of growing, the tale of the rock lobster is not so good, the 1995 allowable catch was set at 230 tonnes, in 1990 the figure had been 1,800 tonnes. A reminder that not all the components in a damaged ecosystem can recover at the same rate. A final positive point that will help ensure the future success of the industry is that all the fish come from one of the least polluted coastal seas in the world. There are no perennial rivers polluted by industry, and virtually no sewage, either raw or treated flows into the ocean. With expert quality control the industry should be able to expect premium prices for most of its products.

Other sectors The **tourist** sector is rightly regarded as having a tremendous potential for growth. Namibia has a wild and varied landscape ideal for up-market, high-value, low-volume tourism. Since independence the country has enjoyed a peaceful existence, an important factor for the tourist industry. Many tourists from overseas are attracted to remote areas which are essentially 'unspoilt', and Namibia has an abundance of such areas. These are also the areas where the local community have no employment opportunities and have suffered the most during periods of drought. If the right training can be provided for these people they will be able to directly benefit from tourism. Since independence there has been a 50% growth in the hotel and restaurant sector. New hotels and guest farms have opened across the country, this has meant that room occupancy rates have remained around 50%. In 1993 an independent study reported 255,000 visitors with 60% from South Africa. Since 1990 tourism receipts have increased from N$300 mn to over N$1 bn, the sector now contributing 6% to GDP and being the third largest foreign exchange earner. For future developments the government is looking closely at community-based tourism. Rural communities must enjoy the benefits of conservation policies, especially if such tourist projects are based in communal areas. Once people start to derive significant benefits from wildlife and conservation policies they are more likely to work with the government and private sector to preserve the environment. Rural households must enjoy a cash income as well as job opportunities.

The **manufacturing** sector provides less than 8% of annual GDP and it remains a small sector based around processing meat, fish and minerals for export. The sector has a high cost structure and operates with a low competitiveness. Many of the businesses were established under an apartheid government where wages were not linked to productivity. Most goods have in the past been produced in South Africa thus the sector remains underdeveloped within Namibia. Small-scale and informal sector industries have limited access to credit and markets, poor management skills and outdated technologies. Future success and growth will depend in part upon these issues being fully addressed in the long term.

Background

Culture

Namibia is a blend of many different peoples and cultures, similar in some respects to the 'rainbow' nation next door. Home to the **Bushmen**, the oldest inhabitants of southern Africa as well as to the more recently arrived Europeans, Namibia's culture has absorbed both African and European elements and fused them into a blend of the two. The choral tradition brought from Germany has been adopted and modified and is one of Namibia's most vibrant art forms, while cooking in a *potjie*, a traditional three-legged iron pot over an open fire, is a favourite pastime of many Namibians.

Namibia's population of approximately 1,800,000 has doubled in the past 30 years and is currently growing at an exponential 3.5% per year. While most Namibians still live in the rural areas, practising subsistence farming of one form or another, increasing mobility and a lack of employment opportunities in the rural areas are causing a rapid migration to the towns. As people lose touch with their homes and traditional ways of life and adopt a more urban, western lifestyle, the levels of crime and unemployment experienced in many western cities are unfortunately also becoming a fact of life in Namibia.

In a predominantly rural country where many aspects of culture are closely linked with land ownership, unresolved land issues dating back to pre-colonial, colonial and apartheid days are still live issues for many communities. One recent example saw the blockade of the **Etosha Game Park** entrance by groups of Bushmen calling for the return of their traditional lands. Other communities, such as the Rehoboth Basters, have been involved in a series of court cases with the government over the issue of ownership of traditional lands.

As in South Africa, and until recently in neighbouring Zimbabwe, the majority of quality commercial farmland is still in the hands of white farmers. The problem of how to satisfy the demands of landless peasants whilst not alienating an important revenue-generating section of the community is yet another unresolved issue facing the government. The events of the last year or so in Zimbabwe have caused rumblings in Namibia, and while few (at least openly) support a similar appropriation of land in Namibia, this issue will not go away.

People

Namibia's people consist of 11 major ethnic groups scattered around the country. From semi-nomadic cattle herders and hunters to the sophisticated black and white urban elite, ethnicity is an important unifying force in this sparsely inhabited country. Since independence in 1990 there has been a resurgence of support for traditional leaders who the government has banned from becoming political leaders. At the same time there are tensions between different ethnic groups, in part for historical reasons and in part due to the overwhelming numerical superiority of the Oshiwambo-speaking peoples and their strong support for and involvement with SWAPO – the governing party.

Nevertheless, for the time being, unlike some other African countries, Namibia is largely free of tribal conflict. The government's stance on the issue was summarized by Prime Minister Hage Geingob at a 1993 conference on tribalism. 'For too long we have thought of ourselves as Hereros, Namas, Afrikaners, Germans, Owambos. We must now start to think of ourselves as Namibians.'

Background

Owambo Made up of 12 tribes in all, of whom eight live in Namibia and four in Angola, the Owambo are the single largest ethnic group in Namibia with an estimated population in 1994 of 670,000. Traditionally the Owambo live in round, pallisaded homesteads built on raised ground between the *oshanas*, seasonal lakes which flood during the rainy season.

The few hectares of land surrounding each homestead is farmed with livestock such as cattle, goats and sheep for which the men are traditionally responsible. Crops are also grown, in particular finger millet, *omuhango*, which is used to make porridge and brew beer; other crops grown are sorghum, maize, beans and pumpkins, and this is traditionally the work of the women.

During the apartheid era tens of thousands of Owambos migrated to the central and southern parts of the country in search of work. In recent years the lack of availability of land and water have forced many more people to abandon subsistence farming as a way of life and instead enter the labour market. This in turn has caused the growth of villages and larger urban centres such as **Oshakati**, **Ongwediva** and **Ombalantu** which function as part of the wider urban cash economy.

Namibia's governing party SWAPO emerged from the Owamboland People's Organization which was constituted in 1957, and originally dedicated to fighting the hated contract labour system. A breakdown of the traditional leadership system among four of the tribes left a political void which SWAPO stepped in to fill. Offering itself initially as the voice of the Owambo nation, the party eventually took the moral, political and military initiative for the whole country in launching the independence struggle against the South African government. Today SWAPO enjoys overwhelming support in the country as a whole and within the Owambo-speaking areas of the north draws over 90% of the vote.

Kavango The Kavango region stretching from Owamboland to the west as far as the Caprivi Strip in the east and bordered to the north by the Kavango River is home to five distinct tribal groups totalling around 140,000 people. Traditionally the five Okavango tribes – the **Geiriku**, **Shambiu**, **Mbunzu**, **Kwangai** and **Mbukushu** – followed a matrilineal system of leadership and inheritance, however, the growth of livestock farming by men has increased their economic and social status and stimulated a system of patrilineal ties of inheritance.

All of the five tribes live along the banks of the Kavango River and predominantly practise a subsistence economy made up of pastoralism, fishing and hunting. Fishing is a prime source of protein to the Kavango peoples and is practised by both men and women, who specialize in using funnel-shaped baskets to make their catch. Thanks to a rich store of wildlife, hunting has played an important part in the economy of the Kavango communities. However, today no game remains in the inhabited areas of the region and strict control is enforced over hunting in less densely populated areas.

Most Namibian wood carving originates in the Kavango area and objects such as masks, drums, stools are available in Windhoek curio shops. It is also not uncommon to see the carvers working and selling their products by the side of the road outside towns in the central and southern parts of the country.

Ethnic groups

Not to scale

Droughts and famine - the life of an old man

I am Tate Mwafangeyo, the oldest man in this village of Okalondo, Ongenga. I was born on the 4 April 1914, and I have lived here all my life. My wife died four years ago, and now I am living with my children and relatives.

I can remember my parents telling me of a very bad drought, during the time of King Naketo, who was king at the same time as Mandume. I was not yet born at this time. There was a very serious dry year which killed thousands of people. During this time people were forced to eat ombadwa, *which is cattle leather. When this food ran out, they turned to the insects, which also became scarce soon. There was no food and no water. Many people died, and their bodies were pulled to an* oshana, *far away in the bush. People were very weak, and there was not enough space or energy for digging graves. This period is called* Ondjala yo kapuka, *and many of our people and nearly all of our livestock died. Just before I was born came* Oshipuluka *(good rain). Those who survived the bad drought were very happy because the rain season brought frogs, birds,* ombidi, eembe, omwungo, *and so on. The people were on their feet again.*

Since I was born there have been several droughts, but none so bad as the one I have told you about. During this time people used to sacrifice their cattle for rain. When there was no rain they would go to King Nehale who lived in Angola. They went to him because rain came from the north. They would take him women of the Omulamba group and black cattle as a rain offering. If you took him these two offerings he would send you rain.

We also used to sing rain songs, but I cannot remember any of them now. What I can tell you are some words to use to promise rain: 'Xekulu yo mapongo, Ina yo mawila ndjila, Omapongo aha ka kwa te sha sho munhu' – 'Father of the refugees, mother of the starving, the refugees will not touch anybody's belongings.' This means that whenever there is rain there will be no stealing, because everybody will have something to eat.

In Oshiwambo we even have special names for those people born during rain. 'Ondula' means rain, and men who were born during the rain can be called Haidula, while women born during the rain are called Nadula.

As the population grows and more young people become educated, a gradual migration to the urban areas is taking place, although not on the same scale as with the Owambo. At the same time, stimulated by cross-border trade with Angola, the economy of the region is becoming more commodity and cash based, most visible in the regional capital Rundu.

Caprivi

Stretching from the Kavango region in the west to the Zambezi in the east, the narrow strip of land that constitutes the Caprivi region is home to the **Subia** and **Fwe** tribes, the latter including a number of Yeyi, Totela and Lozi communities. An estimated 92,000 people in all live in this well-watered, subtropical region which forms part of the northern Kalahari basin.

Historically the area has been dominated by the **Lozi** tribe from Zambia and the **Kololo** from South Africa. The more recent intervention of Europeans followed the agreement between Britain and Germany in 1890 which gave colonial authority over the land to the Germans, who only arrived, however in 1909.

The Lozi first conquered the area in the late 17th and early 18th century only to be ousted following the migration of southern Sotho tribes from South Africa in the wake of the Zulu wars in Natal. The existing Lozi customs were adapted to suit Sotho institutions in a so-called Kololo Empire – until a Lozi revolt in 1864 restored their control over the area.

Background

During the consecutive periods of Lozi and Kololo rule, Lozi was established as the *lingua franca* of the area and subsequently as medium of instruction in schools. Both Lozi and Kololo empires promoted patrilineal institutions making the patrilineal extended family the basic social unit.

Both Fwe and Subia practise a mixed economy including hunting, gathering, fishing, hoe-farming and pastoralism, with agriculture forming the backbone of the traditional economy. There are few urban centres asides from the regional capital Katima Mulilo and job opportunities outside subsistence farming are few and far between. Inevitably this is leading to many young people moving away from the land to look for work in urban areas in other parts of the country.

In recent years the population of the Caprivi has been hit very hard by the spread of HIV and AIDS and there is considerable concern over how this will effect the community as a whole.

Herero   Like the other **Bantu**-speaking tribes in Namibia, it is believed that the Herero originated in the great lakes region of East Africa, before migrating west and south. Initially settled in **Kaokoland** in the northwest of Namibia, the majority of Herero started a southward migration from the middle of the 18th century onward. By the time the first Europeans arrived in Namibia in the early part of the 19th century, the Herero were well established in the central areas of the country.

The second half of the 19th century saw virtual constant low-level warfare between the Herero and the Nama over the question of land and grazing rights for their cattle. Following the German occupation of Namibia late in the 19th century, more and more Herero land passed into the hands of the colonizers, leading to increasing discontent amongst the people.

Finally in 1904 the Herero rose up against the Germans in an attempt to claim back their tribal land. The final battle was fought at the Waterberg Plateau in August 1904 and in itself was not decisive. However, the subsequent retreat of the Herero into the *Omaheke* sandveld, in the east of the country, saw the deaths of thousands due to hunger and starvation. Defeat also brought about the further loss of traditional grazing lands and the displacement of the survivors into so-called homelands.

Traditionally, the Herero followed a semi-nomadic pastoral way of life, keeping large herds of cattle and following their cattle around in search of good grazing. However, unlike commercial farmers, the Herero have traditionally seen their cattle as an indication of wealth and status, not to be sold or slaughtered arbitrarily for food. Until relatively recently in fact, the Herero have largely remained outside of the formal labour market, preferring to focus on their livestock.

During the 20th century there has been a resurgence of Herero culture and former paramount Chief **Hosea Kutako** was a key figure in carrying the case for Namibian independence to the United Nations. One important expression of Herero identity is the annual 26 August Hero's Day parade in **Okahandja**, when the people march to the grave of their former leaders in order to pay respect to those fallen in battle. Some Herero women are also easily identified by the huge, colourful dresses and hats which they wear. These Victorian remnants of the influence of the 19th-century German missionaries' wives are nevertheless a symbol of pride to their wearers.

Himba   During the Herero-Nama conflict of the second half of the 19th century, the Herero still living in Kaokoland lost much of their cattle to marauding Nama bands. Those dispossessed of their cattle were forced into a hunter-gatherer way of life, considered an inferior way of existence to the pastoral Herero. This led to the branding of such people as *Tjimba* derived from *ondjimba-ndjimba* meaning an *aardvark* or digger of roots.

During the early years of this century groups of Tjimba-Herero who had fled into Angola, and other Hereros who had joined them there following the defeat at the hands of the Germans, united behind a Herero leader, **Vita**. Under his leadership, an effective fighting force operated in southern Angola, building up substantial herds of cattle. Following the German withdrawal from Southwest Africa after the First World War, Vita and many of his followers crossed back over the Kunene River into Namibia. Today their descendants form the bulk of the **Himba** and **Herero** population in Kaokoland.

Elevated to almost legendary status in Namibia, the **Himba** still live a more or less traditional existence, with their cattle as the centre of their lives. Largely eschewing westernization, they have managed to successfully live in balance with nature in the fragile Kaokoland, pursuing their old customs such as ancestor worship and the keeping of the sacred fire at the homestead.

Today, however, the Himba's independent way of life is being seriously challenged on a number of fronts. Like many traditional peoples the Himba are susceptible to the effects of strong alcohol; unscrupulous traders from both Namibia and Angola are currently spreading this curse to even the remotest Himba communities, while enriching themselves with Himba livestock in exchange for the alcohol. Until two years ago it was also feared that the proposed Epupa Dam scheme (see page 213, Kaokoland section) which is likely to finally break the Himba's geographic isolation from the rest of the country and introduce whole-scale modernization and westernization to that part of Kaokoland. This plan seems to have disappeared for the time being, and at present the biggest threat to the Himba appears to be people-spotting western tourists desperate for a glimpse of the nomadic past that all human being share!

Damara

Widely believed to be the oldest inhabitants of Namibia after the Bushmen and the **Nama**, and sharing a similar language and customs with the Nama, the precise origins of the Damara remain something of a mystery. Two conflicting theories suggest first that the Damara migrated from West Africa to Namibia, where they were subjected by the Nama people, and in this way acquired similar language and customs. An alternative theory suggests that the Damara evolved alongside the Nama in Botswana thousands of years ago, thereby explaining the similarities in language and culture, and simply migrated at a later date into Namibia.

By the beginning of the 19th century Damara communities were established throughout the central parts of Namibia, living by a mixture of hunting, livestock farming and limited crop cultivation. The Damara are also known to have been skilled smelters and workers of copper and it seems likely that they were engaged in trade with the Owambo to the north and the Nama to the south.

However, as tension over land issues grew during the 19th century, in particular between the Nama and the Herero, the Damara were squeezed out of many of the areas in which they were settled. Some became servants to the Herero and the Nama, others fled to the remote mountainous areas, earning them the name *Berg* or 'mountain' Damara.

Following the establishment of German colonial rule over Namibia, the first Damara 'reserve' was created in 1906 around the Okombahe area. This original area was enlarged upon the recommendations of the Odendaal Commission of Inquiry in the 1960s, when so-called tribal homelands were created for the different ethnic groups in Namibia. The Damara 'homeland' was established in the northwest of the country, from **Uis** in the south to **Sesfontein** in the north, and this remains a predominantly Damara area today.

Today the majority of the estimated 132,000 Damara community actually lives outside of this area, working in the towns of the central part of the country, such as

Windhoek, Okahandja, Swakopmund, Walvis Bay, Otavi and Tsumeb. Many Damara are today active in public life, notably the Prime Minister Hage Geingob and Labour Minister Moses Garoeb.

Nama Ethnically the Nama living in Namibia are descendants of **Khoisan** groups who have been living in southern Africa for many thousands of years. It is believed that the first Nama groups to arrive in Namibia did so about 2,000 years ago, having migrated first from Botswana.

Traditionally the Nama were semi-nomadic pastoralists who also continued to hunt and gather food from the veld. The various different clans shared the available grazing and water in southern and central Namibia, moving with their animals as need dictated. Although little is known of the precise relations between Nama and Bushmen, it is assumed that there must have been contact between the two groups, and even some social movement between them.

At the turn of the 19th century the first groups of Oorlam Namas started to cross the Orange River in search of land. These mixed race newcomers were generally Christians, having had extensive contact with white settlers in the Cape, and in most cases having lost their land to them. The Oorlams' contact with Europeans meant that they had acquired guns and horses and were consequently able to establish themselves in southern Namibia alongside existing Nama groups.

Although the first half of the 19th century saw significant conflict between the Nama and the Oorlams, by the end of the century the old differences had largely disappeared. Intermarriage and common enemies in the form first of the Herero and then the Germans had united the two groups so that today no differentiation is made between them.

In the 1890s, the famous Nama leader Hendrik Witbooi, was the first Namibian leader to see that differences between the various ethnic groups in the country were far less important than the struggle against the Germans. Together with other Nama leaders he led resistance to German rule in the south of Namibia during the 1904-07 war.

Like the Herero, the Nama suffered heavy losses during this period as a result of war and famine and their numbers declined significantly. In addition the loss of traditional land, a process which had begun during the 19th century, continued under German and then South African rule. During the apartheid era, the majority of the Nama-speaking population was confined to a tribal homeland southwest of **Mariental** and northwest of **Keetmanshoop**.

Today the majority of the Nama still live in the south of the country, although small groups, such as the **Topnaars** who live in the Kuiseb Canyon area, live in other parts of the country. Their main source of income is derived from livestock farming, especially cattle and goats, but the struggle for survival in the harsh environment of the semi-desert of the south of Namibia means that most Namas today still live a subsistence existence.

The estimated 80,000 Nama are famous for their poetry and singing, in the form of traditional praise poems and their church choirs, and these are an important form of modern-day Nama cultural expression.

San The San, or Bushmen as they are often called, are generally accepted to be the oldest indigenous inhabitants of southern Africa, and numerous examples of their rock art, dating back thousands of years, is to be found all over the sub-region.

Traditionally the San were skilled hunter-gatherers living in small independent bands with the family as the basic unit. Different bands had limited contact with each other, although individuals were free to come and go as they pleased, unhampered by possessions or fixed work responsibilities.

Although successful and well-adapted to their environment, about 300 years ago the San started to come under pressure both from migrating **Bantu** tribes and early European settlers. Regarded as cattle thieves and considered as more or less sub-human by these groups, the San were hunted down and forced off their traditional lands, the majority seeking the relative safety of the **Kalahari Desert** in Botswana and Namibia.

Today, the estimated 45,000 San living in Namibia live a marginalized existence on the fringes of mainstream society. Like other aboriginal peoples in Australia and North America, the loss of their land and traditional way of life has seriously undermined the San people's culture. Human rights groups in Namibia maintain that the San are seriously exploited and discriminated against by other ethnic groups in the country.

However, the San have not given up hope and there are groups who since independence in 1990 have been campaigning for the return of traditional hunting lands. In January 1997 a group of around 70 Hai/Om San demonstrated at the gates of Etosha National Park. The response of the authorities was to teargas and arrest these peaceful protestors, for which they were condemned by human rights groups and various opposition parties.

However, the future for the San in Namibia does not look good. They are unlikely to be granted significant tracts of land on which to return to their former way of life, and unless educational and employment opportunities can be provided for them, they will remain a poor and marginalized community.

Whites

The majority of the estimated 100,000 whites living in Namibia are of German and Afrikaner descent, with a small group of English speakers. The first Europeans to arrive in Namibia were missionaries travelling with Oorlam groups over the Orange River from Namaqualand. These were followed during the first half of the 19th century by traders and hunters who opened up the interior of the country for further European exploration.

Following the consolidation of German colonial rule towards the end of the 19th century, Europeans started to settle in larger numbers, most earning a living through trading and livestock farming. The discovery of diamonds and other minerals early this century attracted outside investment and led to further European control of the economy of the country.

The period of South African rule from 1917 until independence in 1990 saw the bulk of the viable farmland transferred into the hands of white farmers. Mineral rights were controlled by the multi-national European and American conglomerates and apartheid legislation ensured that all significant commercial activities were firmly placed in white hands.

Following independence, although political power has passed into the hands of the black majority, the bulk of viable commercial farmland is still in white hands. Likewise, most businesses in the towns of central and southern Namibia belong to whites and the majority of the private sector of the burgeoning tourist industry is also in white hands.

While many white people are making an effort to adapt to the realities of living in independent Namibia, an equal number still live as in the past, sticking exclusively to their own communities. Inevitably the barriers of the past will take time to be overcome but, with the integration of the education system, there is hope that the next generation of white Namibians, who have nowhere else to go, will participate fully in the wider society in their country.

Basters

The 39,000 strong Rehoboth Basters are the descendants of a group of Khoi-European mixed-race settlers who arrived in Namibia in 1869. After negotiations with the

Background

Herero and the Swartbooi Namas, the Basters bought and settled land in the Rehoboth area, where the majority earned a living through livestock farming.

During the apartheid era, the Basters managed to hold on to their land, enabling the community to retain a strong sense of its own identity; at independence a section of the Basters even called for the creation of a separate Baster homeland. The traditional leadership under former *Kaptein* or leader Hans Diergaardt was engaged in a series of court cases against the government concerning the rights to administer communal land in and around the town of Rehoboth. The matter was finally settled in 1996 with a Supreme Court ruling in favour of the government.

Recurrent drought over recent years has forced many Basters off the land to seek employment in Rehoboth and Windhoek. Today, despite the isolationism of some, the majority of Basters have entered the mainstream of Namibian society working in a wide range of trades and professions.

Coloureds Around 60,000 people in Namibia today regard themselves as 'Coloureds'. These people were originally of mixed European and African descent, but the vast majority today are born from Coloured parents. The apartheid reality of Coloured townships, Coloured schools and Coloured churches means that there is a strong sense of shared community and culture.

Afrikaans-speaking and urban-dwelling, the Coloured community is predominantly Christian and western oriented. Most Coloureds live in the central and southern parts of the country.

Tswana The Tswana make up the smallest ethnic group in Namibia, numbering around 9,000. Related to the Tswana in South Africa and Botswana, they are the descendants of a group who migrated to Namibia from South Africa during the 19th century. These people eventually settled in the east of the country between Aminuis and the Botswana border where they live predominantly as livestock farmers.

Land and environment

Geography

Namibia is located on the west coast of Africa between the 17th and 29th latitudes. The territory stretches from Angola and Zambia in the north to South Africa in the south; most of the eastern border is with Botswana. The total surface area is 824,269 sq km, nearly four times the size of the UK, or twice the size of California.

As you travel around the country you are likely to form the impression that the countryside is harsh and forbidding and that most of the country is either desert or semi-desert in appearance. If you do not like hot, dry and dusty countries then Namibia is not for you. There are only five perennial rivers, the Cuando, Kunene, Kavango and Zambezi in the north and the Orange River in the south, which forms the border with South Africa.

Regions

There are four distinct regions, although only the far north can be truly described as being green in appearance. The dominant feature is the **Namib-Naukluft deser**t which occupies almost a fifth of the total area. The desert varies between 80 and 120 km in width and stretches along the entire Atlantic coastline, a distance of approximately 1,600 km. This whole region receives less than 100 mm of rain per year. The central portion of the desert is an impassable mass of giant sand dunes which are one of the major tourist attractions.

The centre of the country is a semi-arid mountainous plateau, with the capital Windhoek located on this plateau. Most of the annual rains fall during the summer months when the plateau is covered with green grasslands and the occasional flowering acacia tree. The average elevation is 1,100 m, the highest mountains are the Brandberg (2,573 m) and the Moltkeblick (2,446 m) in the **Aus** range. Throughout the plateau are numerous dry, seasonal river courses, the signs of the ephemeral river that only flow for a few days each year if at all. Few ever drain into the ocean, the water disappearing in the sands of either the Namib or Kalahari deserts. The dramatic **Fish River Canyon** in the south of the country is evidence of the presence of a large body of water at some time in the distant past.

The southeastern area of the country is characterized by low-lying plains covered with scrub vegetation, typical of the Kalahari and Karoo regions of Botswana and South Africa.

The far north of the country is the only region which receives sufficient rainfall each year to sustain agriculture and a wooded environment. As you travel north of Etosha National Park the vegetation cover gradually increases and the overall landscape is more green than brown. The **Caprivi Strip** has some magnificent woodlands and lush riverine vegetation along with a wide variety of wild animals.

Climate

Namibia, like so many countries in Africa, eagerly waits for the first rains to fall every year. The country lies within the dry latitudes and depends upon the unpredictable movements of the climatic zones for its rainfall. These zones are known as the Inter-Tropical Convergence Zone (ITCZ), the Mid-Latitude High Pressure Zone (MLHPZ) and the temperate zone. Generally rains can be expected in areas dominated by the ITCZ or the temperate zone, whereas the MLHPZ is associated with little or no rainfall. The weather in the north of the country depends upon the southerly movement of the ITCZ, while in the extreme south the rains can be expected if the temperate zone pushes north into the MLHPZ. Predicting the movement of these climatic zones is the key to understanding Namibia's weather.

Background

Namibia is blessed with a climate in which the sun shines for more than 300 days per year, an important consideration for many holidaymakers. Most visitors will enjoy clear blue skies during their visit, and it is only during the height of the rainy season that you might encounter cloudy days. While these warm clear days are what most visitors are looking for it is important that you protect your skin from sunburn. The combined effect of latitude and altitude means that if you are fair skinned you will quickly burn without some form of protection – always wear a hat, sunglasses, apply sun-block on a regular basis and drink plenty of liquid throughout the day, preferably water. The warmest months are January and February, when the daytime temperature in the interior can reach 40°C. This will be far warmer than most visitors from the temperate latitudes will have experienced and clearly is not the weather to walk about in, especially without a hat or protection.

In general the rain season lasts from November to March, although during this period it might not rain for several weeks. However, by February most parts of the country should have received a significant proportion of their annual rainfall. Visitors to Namibia in April and May will see a country far greener than most would imagine or expect. The Caprivi region receives the most rainfall each year, the annual average for Katima Mulilo being over 700 mm. The isohyets run northwest to southeast, with total rainfall decreasing as you travel from the Caprivi towards the Karas region in the south. In a good year Lüderitz may receive 20 mm, which is insignificant when you take into account the high evapotranspiration rates. In a good year the first rain in the north may fall as early as October, this can cause havoc with the agricultural system if farmers plant their seed expecting the rains to continue. There is always the danger of planting too early with the young shoots of millet and maize emerging only to die from lack of water because the next rains don't fall until mid-November.

A quick glance at any map of Namibia will clearly show the entire coast to be desert. The three major coastal settlements all depend upon water piped from the interior for their survival. During the height of the summer, December, there is a mass exodus from the interior (especially Windhoek) to the coast and this is the peak tourist season for the coastal resort of Swakopmund. The reason is quite simple: local residents are looking to escape the heat. The cold Benguela ocean current has a modifying influence on the weather, although one negative aspect of the coastal climate is the frequent sea fogs which form when the cool ocean air mixes with the hot Namib desert air. It really can get very gloomy, but this fog is vital to the survival of plants and animals in the Namib desert. Do not be fooled into thinking the sun cannot harm you when there is a fog – the UV rays will still penetrate the mist and burn your skin.

The most pleasant weather in the interior is experienced during the autumn (April/May) and spring (August/September), when it tends to be neither too hot, nor too cold. Here the altitude has a modifying influence on temperatures.

A final point to remember when visiting Namibia is that more often than not the country may be suffering from a period of drought. Do not be wasteful with water, it is a valuable commodity which many people have to walk miles for each day. When you are camping or travelling in remote areas make sure you carry extra water with you – there are no guarantees of a clean source in the middle of the bush. Interestingly, rains over the last few years have been surprisingly good over most of the country, to the extent that Mariental – one of the driest and dustiest places in the south – experienced flooding!

Vegetation

While much of the Namibian landscape is characterized by deserts and mountains, the country extends far enough north into the tropical latitudes to have a varied range of plant life. The most interesting ecological area is the Namib desert where the diverse flora and fauna have had to adapt to a unique set of climatic conditions. Botanists from all over the world have visited the Namib to study some of the more unusual plants and the ways in which they cope with the hot and dry conditions. A good tour of the desert should include an introduction to some of these plants. This is also the only desert in the world where you can see elephant, lion and rhino.

Although a large proportion of the country is desert there are four distinct vegetation zones which together support more than 4,000 seed-bearing vascular plants, 120 different species of tree, over 200 endemic plant species and 100 varieties of lichen. These zones are loosely defined as follows: the tropical forests and wetlands along the banks of the perennial rivers in Kavango and Caprivi; the savanna plains with occasional trees in the Kalahari; the mountainous escarpment regions such as Kaokoland and Damaraland, which support a mixture of succulent and semi-succulent plants; and the low altitude coastlands and Namib desert.

Along the mountainous escarpment most of the plants are either arborescent, succulents or semi-succulents. The most common species are the **quiver tree**, or kokerboom (*Aloë dichotoma*), the spiky tall cactus-like plants known as *Euphorbia* and the **paper bark tree**, or *Commiphora*, which can be seen along the road between Sesfontein and Opuwo in Kaokoland. The vegetation mix in the Kaokoland is largely determined by physical and climatic factors. In the extreme north the Marienfluß and Hartmann valleys are covered with open grasslands with very few trees and shrubs. Further to the south a few more trees start to appear in the savanna, notably the **mopane** (*Colophospermum mopane*) and **purple-pod terminalia** (*Terminalia prunioides*). Along the Kunene River the dominant trees are **leadwood** (*Combretum imberbe*), **jakkalsbessie** (*Diospyros mespiliformis*) and **sycamore fig** (*Ficus sycamorus*). After the rains look out for the magnificent pink flowers of the **Boesmangif** (*Andanium boehmianum*), a creeper which is found on many of the larger trees. The palm trees along the river are **Makalani palms** (*Hyphaene petersana*), a common sight further east in Owamboland. In areas where there is slightly more rainfall there are a variety of flowering annuals which will cover the land with a carpet of colour for a couple of months. Most of these annuals are of the *Brasicaceae* and *Asteraceae* families.

The Kavango and Caprivi regions are the only areas where you will see large stands of forest. Most of the trees are deciduous so, like the rest of the country, the area looks at its best after the rains. Along the riverbeds you can expect to see mopane, the **palm** (*Hyphaene ventricosa*) and a couple of **reed** species on the flood plains, *Phragmites australis* and *Typha latifolia*. The woodland areas of the game reserves are dominated by *Terminalia* shrubs, *Boscia albitrunca*, *Bauhinia macrantha* and *Grewia*.

Along the edge of the Kalahari desert the sands gradually give way to trees and tall shrubs, although most of the vegetation is restricted to grasslands – *Stipagrotis* is the dominant grass. The most common flower is the **driedoring** (*Rhigozum trichotomum*).

As noted above, the Namib desert has the most interesting mix of plants in Namibia, many of which have been subjected to intensive studies. One of the most unusual of all plants is the *Welwitschia mirabilis*, a plant first seen by the white man in 1859. These plants are found in small groups inland from the coast at Swakopmund. Each plant has two long leaves which are often torn and discoloured. Using carbon dating they have been shown to live for over 1,000 years in the harshest of conditions. One of the oldest plants in the Namib is now protected by a fence but you can still get close to smaller plants. After the **welwitschia** it is the **lichens** which attract the greatest attention in the desert. The lichens are found on west facing slopes and surfaces where they are able to draw moisture from the sea fogs. If it were not for the fog the plants would have no source of water. They are now

Background

recognized as a vital component of the Namib environment and most areas are protected. Many of the animals rely upon the lichen as an important source of water after the fog has condensed on the plants. While they can survive long periods of drought they will quickly die when disturbed.

Visitors with a keen interest in the plants of Namibia will find the following publications helpful for background and identification purposes. *Namib Flora (86)*, P Craven & C Marais; *National List of Indigenous Trees (86)*, Von Breitenbach; *Trees of Southern Africa (77)*, KC Palgrave; *Waterberg Flora (89)*, P Craven & C Marais.

Precious stones, rocks and minerals

Every visitor to Namibia will at some point have read or perhaps been told something about the country that sparked their imagination and desire to see the place for themselves. For many holidaymakers it is the beauty and variety of the flora and fauna that initially tempts them to visit southern Africa – few return home disappointed. But Namibia can also prove to be an exciting and interesting destination for a much smaller interest group, for it is a country that has an outstanding assembly of precious and semi-precious stones as well as grand and spectacular rock formations. Throughout the Namib desert and the surrounding countryside there is a superb record of the events that took place millions of years ago as the landscape was formed and sculptured. The magnificent Fish River Canyon, the isolated Waterberg Plateau, the Spitzkoppe, Etosha Pan, the Naukluft Mountains, the Hoba Meteorite are just a few of the more popular sites. Namibia is often described as a geologist's paradise, and rightly so.

The few notes below are intended for the visitor who has never really taken an interest in rocks and gemstones, someone whose knowledge of semi-precious stones is confined to the jewellery which has been in the family for generations. One stone you are unlikely to be picking off the ground and carrying back home in the suitcase, is a **diamond**. Most of the diamonds are found in the south of the country around Lüderitz, in the Atlantic as well as on land (see page 315). When you look at a map of the Lüderitz district the **National Diamond Areas** can clearly be seen. This area is closed to the public and well patrolled as the diamond industry is an important component of the Namibian economy, and many of the diamonds are literally on the surface waiting to be picked up! Where there are diamonds you will also usually fine **garnets**, a dark maroon semi-precious stone. Along the Skeleton Coast the fine garnet sand can be sometimes seen on the dunes forming dark patterns.

If you set your sights on something a little less valuable then you may well stumble across a few small samples to take back home. The area around the northern town of Tsumeb has long been a popular mining region. Here you will find a wide variety of copper ores. One of the most beautiful semi-precious stones is **amethyst**, the deeper the violet in colour, the better the gem quality. This is a versatile stone which can be turned into rings, necklaces and broaches with great effect. Many stones are found around Omaruru and Otjiwarongo as well as the tiny town of Uis close to the Brandberg mountain. Further south is the small town of Usakos, where you may come across **tourmalin**, both blue and green varieties; elsewhere it occurs in red, pink, yellow and black. The uranium mine at Rössing had found **aquamarine** and elsewhere in the desert just inland from Swakopmund you are bound to come across outcrops of **rose quartz**, as well as some ancient rock formations which date back to the time when Africa and the Americas were one.

Where there is a town museum you are likely to come across a small display of locally found rocks and minerals. If you wish to collect pieces for your own collection, ask around until you find who the local specialist is – there is always someone. Always check with the local police station about access to the land, and once in the bush don't forget about the other more popular attraction – wild animals. Leopards tend to live in rocky regions. In Windhoek you can buy a geological map of the country which shows farm boundaries and mines as well as the major rock types. One final point to note is that in order to remove or possess **meteorites** or **fossils** a permit is needed from the government. Semi-precious stones can be picked off the land as long as you are not trespassing and have a good eye for small glinting stones.

Wildlife

The Big Nine

It is a reasonable assumption that anyone interested enough in wildlife to be travelling on safari in Africa is also able to identify the more well known and spectacular African animals. For example an **elephant** (*Loxodonta africana*) or a **lion** (*Panthera leo*) can hardly be confused with anything else, so they are not described in great detail here. It is indeed fortunate that many of the large and spectacular animals are also on the whole fairly common, so you will have a very good chance of seeing them on even a fairly short safari. They are often known as the Big Five. Unfortunately, no one agrees on quite which species constitute the Big Five! The term was originally coined by hunters who wanted to take home trophies of their safari. Thus it was that, in hunting parlance, the Big Five were **elephant**, **black rhino**, **buffalo**, **lion** and **leopard**. Nowadays the **hippopotamus** (*Hippopotamus amphibius*) is usually considered one of the Big Five for those who shoot with their cameras, whereas the buffalo is far less of a 'trophy'. Equally photogenic and worthy to be included are the **zebra**, **giraffe** and **cheetah**.

But whether they are the Big Five or the Big Nine these are the animals that most people come to Namibia to see. With the possible exception of the leopard, and the white rhino, you have an excellent chance of seeing all of these animals in Etosha National Park or in the parks along the Caprivi Strip. Namibia also has a number of privately owned guestfarms and game ranches which offer good game-viewing opportunities, but perhaps not the variety of wildlife that you will find in the larger national parks. Some of the private concessions represent the luxury top end of the game-viewing safari market; it is worth bearing in mind that when you pay top dollar there is far greater pressure on the operator to guarantee his guests see the Big Five or Big Nine. This takes something out of the thrill of game viewing when you know you are just as likely to see a rhino or a leopard as you are a family of impala. Yes you have the pleasure of seeing all these magnificent animals, but a lot of the thrill in looking for them at dawn or dusk has gone.

Of the more well known animals the only two that could possibly be confused are the leopard and the cheetah. The **leopard** (*Panthera pardus*) is less likely to be seen as it is more nocturnal and more secretive in its habits compared with the cheetah. It frequently rests during the heat of the day on the lower branches of trees. A good place for viewing leopard is *Tsaobis Leopard Nature Park* close to Otjimbingwe.

The **cheetah** (*Acinonyx jubatus*) is well known for its running speed. In short bursts it has been recorded at over 90 kph. But they are not as successful at hunting as you might expect with such a speed advantage. They have a very specialized build which is long and thin with a deep chest, long legs and a small head. But the forelimbs are restricted to a forward and backward motion which makes it very difficult for the cheetah to turn suddenly when in hot pursuit of a small antelope. They are often seen in family groups walking across the plains or resting in the shade. The black 'tear' mark on the face is usually obvious through binoculars. Any visit to a private game farm in Namibia should be rewarded with a sighting of cheetah as Namibia has the largest population of these animals in southern Africa not contained within national parks. The excellent *Okonjima Guestfarm*, 50 km from Otjiwarongo, is home to the Africat-Foundation; here guests are guaranteed to see cheetah and leopard in natural and artificial surroundings.

Elephants are awe-inspiring by their very size and it is wonderful to watch a herd at a waterhole. Although they have suffered terribly from the activities of war and poachers in recent decades they are still readily seen in many of the game areas, and you will not be disappointed by the sight of them. Everyone has their elephant tale. But it is the rhinoceros which has suffered the most from poaching. Both species are on the verge of extinction, and indeed if there had been no moves to save them during the last 20 years they probably would have gone from the wild by now. The **white rhino** (*Ceratotherium simum*) and the **black rhino** (*Diceros bicornis*) occurred naturally in Namibia. Although today you will find that in many of the reserves where you find them they have in fact been reintroduced. Their names have no bearing on the colour of the animals as they are both a rather nondescript dark grey. The name white rhino is derived from the Dutch word 'weit' which means wide and refers to the shape of the animal's mouth. The white rhino has a large square muzzle and this reflects the fact that it is a grazer and feeds by cropping grass. The black rhino, on the other hand, is a browser, usually feeding on shrubs and bushes. It achieves this by using its long, prehensile upper lip which is well adapted to the purpose.

The horn of the rhino is not a true horn, but is made of a material called keratin, which is essentially the same as hair. If you are fortunate enough to see rhino with their young you will notice that the white rhino tends to herd its young in front of it, whereas the black rhino usually leads its young from the front. The white rhino is a more sociable animal, and they are likely to be seen in family groups of five or more. Their preferred habitat is grasslands and open savanna with mixed scrub vegetation. The black rhino lives in drier bush country and usually alone. They will browse on twigs, leaves and tree bark. Visitors to Etosha National Park have a good chance of seeing rhino with their young at one of the three floodlit waterholes in the evening. It is worth staying up late one night to see these magnificent ancient creatures.

The **buffalo** (*Syncerus caffer*) was once revered by the hunter as the greatest challenge for a trophy. But more hunters have lost their lives to this animal than to any other. This is an immensely strong animal with particularly acute senses. Left alone as a herd they pose no more of a threat than a herd of domestic cattle. The danger lies in the unpredictable behaviour of the lone bull. These animals, cut off from the herd, become bad-tempered and easily provoked. While you are more likely to see them on open plains they are equally at home in dense forest. To see a large herd peacefully grazing is a great privilege and one to remember as you continue your safari. Not found in Namibia south of the so-called Red Line separating the communal grazing lands to the north from the commercial lands to the south, Mahango Game Reserve in the Caprivi Strip has a good record for sightings of herds of buffalo.

The most conspicuous animal of inland waters is the **hippopotamus** (*Hippopotamus amphibius*). A large beast with short stubby legs, but nevertheless quite agile on land. They can weigh up to four tonnes. During the day it rests in the water, rising every few minutes to snort and blow at the surface. At night they leave the water to graze. A single adult animal needs up to 60 kg of grass every day, and to manage this obviously has to forage far. They do not eat aquatic vegetation. The nearby banks of the waterhole with a resident hippo population will be very bare and denuded of grass. Should you meet a hippo on land by day or night keep well away. If you get between it and its escape route to the water, it may well attack. They are restricted to water not only because its skin would dry up if not kept damp but because the body temperature is regulated closely to 96.8°F. It is essentially an aquatic animal and needs to live in a medium where the temperature changes relatively slowly. Mudumu, Mamili and Mahango Game Parks all have family groups of hippo, if you are lucky you may also see them in the vicinity of Popa Falls restcamp.

The **giraffe** (*Giraffa camelopardalis*) may not be as magnificent as a full grown lion, nor as awe-inspiring as an elephant, but its elegance is unsurpassed. To see a small party of giraffe strolling across the plains is seeing Africa as it has been for millenia. You should note that both male and female animals have horns, though in the female they may be smaller. A mature male can be over 5 m high to the top of its head. The lolloping gait of the giraffe is very distinctive and it produces this effect by the way it moves its legs at the gallop. A horse will move its diagonally opposite legs together when galloping, but the giraffe moves both hind legs together and both forelegs together. It achieves this by swinging both hind legs forward and outside the forelegs. They have excellent sight and acute hearing. They are browsers, and can eat the leaves and twigs of a large variety of tall trees, thorns presenting no problem. Their only natural threat are lions who will attack young animals when they are drinking. Giraffe can be spotted both inside the game parks and in the communal lands of Damaraland and Kaokoveld.

The **zebra** is the last of the easily recognized animals. There are two common types in Namibia, **Burchell's zebra** (*Equus burchelli*) and **Hartmann's mountain zebra** (*Equus zebra hartmannae*). Burchell's zebra will often be seen in large herds, sometimes with antelope. You are most likely to see them in Etosha National Park. They stand 145-150 cm at the shoulder whereas Hartmann's mountain zebra are larger, standing 160 cm at the shoulder. Generally the latter only occur in mountainous areas close to the Namib desert. They are found in three isolated pockets: in Kaokoland and as far south as the Brandberg, along the escarpment to the south of the Swakop River and in the Huns Mountains close to the Fish River Canyon. As the name suggests they live on hills and stony mountains. They are good climbers and can tolerate arid conditions, going without water for up to three days. During the heat of the day they seek shade and keep very still, making spotting them more difficult. They are closely related to the Cape mountain zebra, but stand about 25 cm taller than the southern sub-species.

The first animals that you will see on safari will almost certainly be antelope. These occur on the open plains. Although there are many different species, it is not difficult to distinguish between them. For presentation purposes they have been divided into the larger antelopes which stand about 120 cm or more at the shoulder; and the smaller ones about 90 cm or less. They are all ruminant plains animals, herbivores like giraffe and the zebra, but they have keratin covered horns which makes them members of the family *Bovidae*. They vary greatly in appearance, from the small dik-diks to the large eland, and once you have learnt to recognize the different sets of horns, identification of species should not be too difficult.

The larger antelope

The largest of all the antelopes is the **eland** (*Taurotragus oryx*) which stands at 175-183 cm at the shoulder. It is cow-like in appearance, with a noticeable dewlap and shortish spiral horns present in both sexes. The general colour varies from greyish to fawn, sometimes with a rufous tinge, with narrow white stripes on the sides of the body. It occurs in herds of up to 30 in a wide variety of grassy and mountainous habitats. Even during the driest periods of the year the animals appear in excellent condition. Research has shown that they travel large distances in search of food and that they will eat all sorts of tough woody bushes and thorny plants.

Not quite as big, but still reaching 140-153 cm at the shoulder, is the **greater kudu** (*Tragelaphus strepsiceros*) which prefers fairly thick bush, sometimes in quite dry areas. You are most likely to see them in the northern areas of Etosha National Park and in the much smaller Mahango Game Park, although you have just as much chance of seeing one at dusk by the side of the road in central or northern Namibia. Although nearly as tall as the eland it is a much more slender and elegant animal altogether. Its general colour also varies from greyish to fawn and it has several white stripes running down the sides of the body. Only the male carries horns, which are very long and spreading, with only two or three twists along the length of the horn. A noticeable and distinctive feature is a thick fringe of hair which runs from the chin down the neck. Greater kudu usually live in family groups of not more than half a dozen individuals, but occasionally larger herds up to about 30 can be seen.

The **roan antelope** (*Hippoptragus equinus*) and **sable antelope** (*Hippotragus niger*) are similar in general shape, though the roan is somewhat bigger, being 140-145 cm at the shoulder, compared to the 127-137 cm of the sable. In both species, both sexes carry ringed horns which curve backwards, and these are particularly long in the sable. There is a horse-like mane present in both animals. The sable is usually glossy black with white markings on the face and a white belly. The female is often a reddish brown in colour. The roan can vary from dark rufous to a reddish fawn and also has white markings on the face. The black males of the sable are easily identified, but the brownish individuals can be mistaken for the roan. Look for the tufts of hair at the tips of the rather long ears of the roan (absent in the sable). The Roan generally is found in open grassland. Both the roan and the sable live in herds. Khaudum Game Reserve is home to the largest roan population in Namibia. There are also small herds in Etosha which were originally transported from Khaudum. Sable can be seen in the Waterberg Plateau Park as well as Khaudum and the Caprivi region; attempts to introduce them to Etosha have failed.

Another antelope with a black and white face is the **gemsbok** (*Oryx gazella*), which stands 122 cm at the shoulder. They are large creatures with a striking black line down the spine and a black stripe between the coloured body and the white underparts. The head is white with further black markings. This is not an animal you would confuse with another. Their horns are long, straight and sweep back behind their ears – from face-on they look V-shaped. The female also has horns but overall the animal is of a slightly lighter build. One of the lasting images of Namibia is a picture of a single gemsbok with the sand dunes of Sossusvlei as a backdrop. Visitors to Etosha will see large herds close to the waterholes, you will also see gemsbok in the Namib-Naukluft desert, western Damaraland and the Unaib Delta in the Skeleton Coast National Park.

The **wildebeest** or **gnu** (*Connochaetes taurinus*) is a large animal about 132 cm high at the shoulder, looking rather like an American bison in the distance. The impression is strengthened by its buffalo-like horns (in both sexes) and humped appearance. The general colour is blue grey with a few darker stripes down the side. It has a noticeable beard and long mane. They are often found grazing with herds of zebra. Blue wildebeest migrate into Etosha during the summer months in search of fresh grasslands, their numbers have been greatly reduced by the construction of game fences and attacks from predators around artificial water points.

The **common waterbuck** (*Kobus ellipsiprymnus*) stands at about 122-137 cm at the shoulder, it has a shaggy grey-brown skin which is very distinctive. The males have long, gently curving horns which are heavily ringed. There are two species which can be distinguished by the white mark on their buttocks. On the common waterbuck there is a clear half ring on the rump and round the tail. In the other species, the Defassa waterbuck, the ring is a filled-in white patch on the rump. Although they no longer occur in Mudumu National Park, due to hunting, herds of waterbuck can be seen in the remote marshlands and flood plains of Mamili National Park.

There are three other species of antelope that you can expect to see in the wetlands of Caprivi: red lechwe, sitatunga and puku. The **red lechwe** (*Kobus leche leche*) is a medium sized antelope standing at about 100 cm at the shoulder. They are bright chestnut in colour, with black markings on the legs. Only the males have horns. The horns are relatively thin, rising upwards before curving outwards and backwards forming a double curve. Only the sitatunga is known to favour the aquatic environment more than the lechwe. In the past herds of over 1,000 were recorded, but hunting and the destruction of habitat has seen their numbers fall to less than a tenth of the numbers 50 years ago. In Namibia you can still be sure of seeing lechwe along the Kavango or Kwando rivers in the Caprivi region. They tend to feed on grass and water plants, favouring water-meadows. As the river levels rise and fall so the herds migrate to the greenest pastures. All of the large cats as well as wild dog and hyaena prey upon the lechwe. They are unable to move fast on dry land, so when they feel threatened they will take refuge in shallow pools – if needs be, they are very good swimmers.

Puku (*Kobus adenota vardoni*) favour a similar habitat to the red lechwe, but you are only likely to see them in small numbers in Mamili National Park. They have a coat of golden yellow long hair and stand at about 100 cm at the shoulder. Their underparts are white and there are no black markings on the legs. The horns are thick and short with heavy rings, only the males have horns. They usually live in small groups of five to 10 animals, but during the mating season the males gather in groups and will strongly defend their respective territories.

The chances of spotting the **sitatunga** (*Tragelaphus sekei*) are rare since this species of antelope favours swampy areas where there are thick reed beds to hide in. It is the largest of the aquatic antelope standing at 115 cm at the shoulder. If you only catch a glimpse of the animal you can be sure it was a sitatunga if the hindquarters were higher than the forequarters. Their coat is long and shaggy with a grey brown colour, they have thin white stripes similar to those of the bushbuck. The horns are long, twisted and swept back. They have long hooves which are highly adapted to soft, marshy soils. When frightened they will enter the water and submerge entirely, with just their snout breaking the surface. This is a very shy antelope which few visitors will see, but if you spend some time at a quiet location by the river you may be rewarded with a sighting as they quietly move through the reedbeds. Mamili and Mahango are the best locations for viewing the sitatunga.

The **red hartebeest** (*Alcephalus caama*) stands about 127-132 cm at the shoulder. It has an overall rufous appearance with a conspicuous broad light patch on the lower rump. The back of their neck, chin, and limbs have traces of black. Small herds can be seen at Hardap Dam, Khaudum and Etosha National Park. The hartebeest has the habit of posting sentinels, which are solitary animals who stand on the top of termite mounds keeping a watch out for predators. If you see an animal on its 'knees' digging the earth with its horns then it is marking its territory – they are very territorial in behaviour. Their slightly odd appearance is caused by its sloping withers and a very long face. They have short horns which differ from any other animal, they are situated on a bony pedicel, a backward extension of the skull which forms a base.

Finally, you have a good chance of seeing the nyala on your travels. The **nyala** (*Tragelaphus angasi*) stands about 110 cm at the shoulder. Although large in appearance it is slenderly built and has a narrow frame. This is disguised, in part, by a long shaggy coat, dark brown in colour with a mauve tinge. The lower legs are a completely different colour, light sandy brown. When fully grown the horns have a single open curve sweeping backwards. Look out for a conspicuous white streak of hair along the back. Another feature which helps identification is a white chevron between the eyes and a couple of white spots on the cheek. The female is very different, firstly they are significantly smaller and they do not have horns. Their coat is more orange than brown in colour, the white stripes on the body are very clear.

Their numbers have been threatened in the past and their status has been one of endangered. You should consider yourself fortunate if you enjoy a clear sighting on safari. They like to live in dense bush and the 'savanna veld'. You will always find them close to water, which makes the task of finding them a little easier once you have located the waterholes. They are known to gather in herds of up to 30, but a small family group is more likely. One interesting aspect of their life is that they are almost exclusively browsers. Research has shown their diet to consist of wild fruits, pods, twigs and leaves. They will eat fresh young tender grass shoots after the first rains.

The smaller antelopes

The most well known of the antelope species in Namibia is the **springbuck** (*Antidorcas marsupialis*), or springbok, as it is called in Afrikaans. It stands 76-84 cm to the shoulder. It is the only gazelle found south of the Zambezi River. The upper part of the body is fawn and is separated from the white underparts by a dark brown lateral stripe. A distinguishing feature is a reddish brown stripe which runs between the base of the horns and the mouth, passing through the eye. When startled they start to 'pronk'. The head is lowered almost to the feet, the legs are fully extended with hoofs bunched together. Then the animal takes off, shooting straight up into the air for some 2-3 m, before dropping down and shooting up again as though it were on coiled springs.

The remaining common antelopes are a good deal smaller than those described above. The largest and most frequently seen of these is the **impala** (*Aepyceros melampus*) which stands 92-107 cm at the shoulder and is bright rufous in colour with a white abdomen. Only the male carries the long lyre shaped horns. Just above the heels of the hind legs is a tuft of thick black bristles, which are surprisingly easy to see as the animal runs. This is unique to the impala. Also easy to see is the black mark on the side of the abdomen in front of the back leg. They are noted for their graceful leaps which they make as they are running after being startled. You are most likely to see them in herds in the grasslands but they also live in light woodlands. They are the most numerous of the smaller antelope and no matter what the state of the veld they always appear to be in immaculate condition. During the breeding season male animals fight to protect, or gather, their own harem. It is great fun to come across such a herd and pause to watch the male trying to keep an eye on all the animals in the group. Young males may be seen in small groups until they are able to form their own harem. In parts of Etosha National Park you will see a distinct sub-species, the **black-faced Impala**, which as its name implies has a black streak on the face (aside from this it is identical in appearance to the common impala).

The **Bohor reedbuck** (*Redunca redunca*), which is often seen in the Caprivi game parks, stands 68-89 cm at the shoulder. The horns are sharply hooked forwards at the tip. Their general colour is described as reddish fawn, they have white underparts and a short bushy tail. It lives in pairs or small family groups. During the hottest time of day they will seek out shelter in reed beds or long grasses and are never far from water.

Another tiny antelope is the **oribi** (*Ourebia ourebi*), which stands around 61 cm at the shoulder. Like the reedbuck it has a patch of bare skin just below each ear, but that's where the similarities end. The oribi is slender and delicate looking. Its colour tends to be sandy to brownish fawn. Their ears are oval-shaped. Horns are short and straight with a few rings at their base. They live in small groups or as a pair. As the day-time temperatures rise, so the oribi seeks out its 'hide' in long grass or the bush. Like the reedbuck they never like to venture far from water. Mudumu National Park has a few family groups.

The last two of the common smaller antelopes are the bushbuck and the dik-dik. The **bushbuck** (*Tragelaphus scriptus*) is about 76-92 cm at the shoulder. The coat has a shaggy appearance and a variable pattern of white spots and stripes on the side and back. There are in addition two white crescent shaped marks on the front of the neck. The horns, present in the male only, are short, almost straight and slightly spiral. The animal has a curious high rump which gives it a characteristic crouching appearance. The white underside of the tail is noticeable when it is running. The Bushbuck tends to occur in areas of thick bush especially near water. They lie up during the day in thickets, but are often seen bounding away when disturbed. They are usually seen either in pairs or singly.

The **Damara dik-dik** (*Rhynchotragus kirki*) is so small it can hardly be mistaken for any other antelope, it only stands 36-41 cm high and weighs only 5 kg. In colour it is a greyish brown, often washed with rufous. The legs are noticeably thin and stick-like, giving the animal a very fragile appearance. The snout is slightly elongated which it wriggles from side to side, it has a conspicuous tuft of hair on the top of the head. Only the male carries the very small straight horns. The Damara dik-dik is considered to be the same species as Kirk's dik-dik which occurs in East Africa. What is so unusual is that there are no recorded sightings in between these two regions.

Although the antelope are undoubtedly the most numerous animals to be seen on the plains, there are others worth keeping an eye open for. Some of these are scavengers which thrive on the kills of other animals. They include the dog-like jackals, two species of which you are likely to come across in Etosha National Park (both are about 41-46 cm at the shoulder). The **side-striped jackal** (*Canis adustus*) is greyish fawn and it has a rather variable and sometimes ill-defined stripe along the side. The **black-backed jackal** (*Canis mesomelas*) is more common and will often be seen near a lion kill. It is a rather foxy reddish fawn in colour with a noticeable black area on its back. This black part is sprinkled with a silvery white which can make the back look silver in some lights. They are timid creatures which can be seen by day or night.

Other mammals

The other well known plains scavenger is the **spotted hyaena** (*Crocuta crocuta*), a fairly large animal about 69-91 cm at the shoulder. Its high shoulders and low back give it a characteristic appearance. It is brownish with dark spots and has a large head. Usually occurs singly or in pairs, but occasionally in small packs. Few people talk of the hyaena in a complimentary manner. This is as much to do with their gait as their scavenging habits. But they play an important role in keeping the countryside clean. When hungry they are aggressive creatures, they have been known to attack live animals and will occasionally try to steal a kill from lions. They always look dirty because of their habit of lying in muddy pools which may be to keep cool or alleviate the irritation of parasites. Both jackal and hyaena are occasionally spotted along the coast of the Skeleton Coast National Park where they scavenge for carrion and are common enough in Etosha and the other game parks.

Another aggressive scavenger is the **African wild dog** or **hunting dog** (*Lycaon pictus*). These creatures are easy to identify since they have all the features of a large mongrel dog. They have a large head and a slender body. Their coat is a mixed pattern of dark shapes and white and yellow patches, no two dogs are quite alike. The question is not what they look like, but whether you will be fortunate enough to see one as they are seriously threatened by extinction. In many areas of Namibia they have already been wiped out. The problem it seems is a conflict between the farmer and conservation. The dogs live and hunt in packs. They are particularly vicious when hunting their prey and will chase an animal until it is exhausted, then start taking bites out of it while it is still alive. Their favourites are reedbuck and impala. Unfortunately, these days the only chance you have of seeing wild dogs is in Kaudom – one of the least accessible areas for the average visitor.

A favourite and common plains animal is the comical **warthog** (*Phacochoerus aethiopicus*). They are unmistakable, being almost hairless and grey in general colour with a very large head with tusks and wart-like growths on the face. These are thought to protect the eyes as it makes sweeps sideways into the earth with its tusks, digging up roots and tubers. Often they kneel on their forelegs when eating. They frequently occur in family parties. When startled the adults will run at speed with their tails held straight up in the air followed by their young. Look out for them around the edges of waterholes as they love to cake themselves in the thick mud. This helps to keep them both cool and free of ticks and flies.

Background

Baboons

Baboons are a common sight on the trails in the park but are a real nuisance around the campsite, where they will steal anything you take your eyes off for a few seconds. Although still wary of people they will hang around a few metres away from your campsite and wait their moment. Their keen sense of smell means that should you leave anything tasty in your tent while you are hiking, you are likely to find your tent damaged and the edibles gone by the time you return. Although some visitors may be tempted to offer the odd morsel to vagrant baboons these animals soon become trouble makers around the campsite and consequently have to be shot.

In rocky areas, such as the Waterberg Plateau, look out for an animal that looks a bit like a large grey-brown guinea pig. This is the **dassie** or **rock hyrax** (*Heterohyrax brucei*), an engaging and fairly common animal. During the morning and afternoon you will see them sunning themselves on the rocks. They have the habit of always defecating in the same place, and where the urine runs down the rock face the latter can have a glazed appearance. Perhaps their strangest characteristic is their place in the evolution of mammals. Ancestors of the hyraxes have been found in the deposits of Upper Egypt of about 50 million years ago. The structure of the ear is similar to that found in whales, their molar teeth look like those of a rhinoceros. Two pouches in the stomach resemble a condition found in birds, and the arrangement of the bones of the forelimb are like those of the elephant. In spite of all these features it is regarded as being allied to the elephant!

You are likely to see two types of monkey on your travels, the vervet monkey and the Chacma baboon. Both are widespread and you are just as likely to see them outside a game reserve than in one. The **vervet monkey** (*Cercopithecus pygerythrus*) is of slim build and light in colour. Their feet are conspicuously black, so too is the tip of the tail. They live in savanna and woodlands but have proved to be highly adaptable. On your first visit you might think the vervet monkey cute. It is not, it is vermin and in many places treated as such. They can do widespread damage to orchards and other crops. On no account encourage these creatures, which can make off with your whole picnic, including the beers, in a matter of seconds.

The adult male **Chacma baboon** (*Papio ursinus*) is slender and can weigh up to 40 kg. General colour is a dark olive green, with lighter undersides. They never roam far from a safe refuge, usually a tree, but rocks can provide sufficient protection from predators. They occur in large family groups, known as a troop, and have a reputation for being aggressive where they have become used to man's presence.

Footnotes

12

380

Footnotes

Useful words and phrases

Afrikaans
Good morning!	Goeie more!
How's it going?	Hoe gaan dit?
Very well	Baie goed
Please	Asseblief
Thank you	Dankie
Goodbye	Totsies

Batswana
Hello	Dumela
How are you?	O kae?
Thank you	Ke a leboga
Goodbye	Sala sentle

Caprivi
I greet you!	Ma lumele sha!
Thank you	Ni itumezi
Please	Na lapela
Goodbye	Mu siale hande

Herero/Ovahimba
Are you well?	Perivi?
Yes, well.	Nawa
Thank you	Okuhepa
Goodbye	Kara nawa

Kavango
Hello!	Morokeni!
Thank you	Na pandura

Nama/Damara
How are you?	Matisa?
Thank you	Ayo
Good morning	Moro
Goodbye	Gaiseha

Owambo
Did you sleep well?	Wa lelepo nawa?
Yes!	Eee!
Well!	Nawa!
Thank you	Iyaloo
Good bye	Kalapo Nawa

San
How are you?	Am thai?
I am thirsty	Mem ari gu
I am hungry	Mem tlabe

Bus and train timetables

The following timetables provide a summary of the main luxury long-distance coach services and mainline railway services operating in Namibia – **Intercape** and **TransNamib**.

Intercape Mainliner Coach Services: runs luxury buses between Namibia and South Africa. Bookings can be made from their offices on 2 Gallilei St, Windhoek, T061-227847, F228285. Their Head Office is in Cape Town, 618 Belville 7535, T021-3864400, F3862488, info@intercape.co.za For further information on fares and times visit their website: www.intercape.co.za

TransNamib: although mainly a freight network, caters to passengers through its Starline Passenger Service, Private Bag 13204, Windhoek, T061-2982032, F2982495, paxservices@transnamib.com.na Further details of services and timetables can be found on their website: www.transnamib.com.na

Intercape Mainliner Coach Services

Capetown-Windhoek

	Out[1]	Return[2]
Cape Town[3]	0900	1300
Namibia Border Post	1900	0200
Grünau	2145	0030
Keetmanshoop	0001	2245
Mariental	0230	2015
Rehoboth	0415	1800
Windhoek (a)	0530	1700
Windhoek (b)	0600	1600

[1] Sun, Tue, Thu, Fri   [2] Sun, Mon, Wed, Fri
[3] Namibian Standard Time

Windhoek-Walvis Bay

	Out[1]	Return[2]
Windhoek (b)	0500	1700
Windhoek (a)	0600	1630
Okahandja	0700	1540
Karibib	1810	1430
Usakos	0900	1400
Swakopmund	1040	1215
Walvis Bay	1110	1130

[1] Mon, Wed, Fri, Sat   [2] Sun, Mon, Wed, Fri

Windhoek-Upington

	Out[1]	Return[2]
Windhoek (b)	1600	0600
Windhoek (a)	1700	0530
Rehoboth	1800	0415
Mariental	2015	0230
Keetmanshoop	2245	0001
Grünau	0030	2145
Karasburg	0100	2045
Namibia Border Post	0230	1930
Upington[3]	0530	1630

[1] Sun, Mon, Wed, Fri   [2] Sun, Tue, Thu, Fri
[3] Namibian Standard Time

Windhoek-Victoria Falls

	Out[1]	Return[2]
Windhoek (b)	1930	0300
Windhoek (a)	2000	0230
Okahandja	2100	0130
Otjiwarongo	2300	2345
Otavi	0015	2230
Tsumeb	0100	2145
Grootfontein	0215	2100
Rundu	0500	1815
Katima Mulilo	1230	1315
Victoria Falls[3]	1630	0900

[1] Fri, Mon   [2] Sun, Wed
[3] Namibian Standard Time

Windhoek (a) c/o Rev Michael Scott & Peter Muller Street
Windhoek (b) Intercape Office, 2 Galilei Street

TransNamib Train Services

Windhoek - Tsumeb - Windhoek

	Out[1]		Return[2]	
Windhoek	D	1745	A	0520
Okahandja	A	2010	D	0340
	D	2025	A	0330
Karibib	D	2300	A	0050
Kranzberg	A	2325	D	2355
	D	2345	A	2315
Omaruru	A	0110	D	2135
	D	0140	A	2040
Otijiwarongo	A	0420	D	1745
	D	0535	A	1500
Otavi	A	0755	D	1215
	D	0820	A	1145
Tsumeb	A	0940	D	1025

[1] Sun, Tue, Thu [2] Mon, Wed, Fri
Train no: **9966** Train no: **9913/15**

Walvis Bay - Tsumeb - Walvis Bay

	Out[1]		Return[2]	
Tsumeb	D	1030	A	0940
Otavi	A	1145	D	0820
	D	1215	A	0755
Otijiwarongo	A	1500	D	0535
	D	1630	A	0315
Omaruru	A	1940	D	0025
	D	2035	A	0005
Kranzberg	A	2200	D	2230
	D	2230	A	2220
Usakos	D	2255	D	2155
Arandis	D	0055	D	1945
Swakopmund	A	0210	D	1805
	D	0235	A	1750
Kuiseb	D	0350	D	1635
Walvis Bay	A	0400	D	1615

[1] Mon, Wed, Fri [2] Sun, Tue, Thu
Train no: **9901/12/13** Train no: **9900/07/66**

Windhoek - Walvis Bay - Windhoek

	Out[1]		Return[2]	
Windhoek	D	1955	A	0700
Okahandja	A	2155	D	0510
	D	2205	A	0450
Karibib	D	0040	A	0220
Kranzberg	A	0105	D	0135
	D	0130	A	0105
Usakos	D	0150	D	0045
Arandis	D	0345	D	2230
Swakopmund	A	0520	D	2045
	D	0530	A	2035
Kuiseb	D	0650	D	1920
Walvis Bay	A	0700	D	1900

[1] Daily except Sat [2] Daily except Sat
Train no: **9908** Train no: **9909**

Windhoek - Gobabis - Windhoek

	Out[1]		Return[2]	
Windhoek	D	2150	A	0425
Hoffnung	D	2300	D	0320
Neudamm	D	2340	A	0240
Omitara	A	0220	A	0000
	D	0215	D	0001
Witvlei	D	0400	A	2220
Gobabis	A	0525	D	2050

[1] Sun, Tue, Thu [2] Mon, Wed, Fri
Train no: **9903** Train no: **9904**

Upington - Keetmanshoop - Windhoek

	Daily[1]		Sun & Thu	
Upington			D	0500
Ariamsvlei			D	0855
Karasburg			D	1120
Grünau			D	1230
Keetmanshoop			A	1630
	D	1825		
Tses	A	2005		
	D	2010		
Asab	A	2105		
	D	2110		
Gibeon	A	2148		
	D	2150		
Mariental	A	2300		
	D	2350		
Kalkrand	D	0200		
Rehoboth	D	0355		
Windhoek	A	0620		

[1] Except Sat Train no: **9966**

Windhoek - Keetmanshoop - Upington

	Daily[1]		Wed & Sat	
Windhoek	D	1910		
Rehoboth	D	2145		
Kalkrand	D	2330		
Mariental	A	0120		
	D	0150		
Gibeon	A	0300		
	D	0301		
Asab	A	0340		
	D	0343		
Tses	A	0440		
	D	0441		
Keetmanshoop	A	0630		
			D	0850
Grünau			D	1310
Karasburg			D	1430
Ariamsvlei			D	1825
Upington			A	2130

[1] Except Sat Train no: **9907**

Index

Map index

Shorts

Advertisers

Footprint travel list

Footprint publish travel guides to over 120 countries worldwide. Each guide is packed with practical, concise and colourful information for everybody from first-time travellers to travel aficionados . The list is growing fast and current titles are noted below. For further information check out the website **www.footprintbooks.com**

Andalucía Handbook
Argentina Handbook
Bali & the Eastern Isles Hbk
Bangkok & the Beaches Hbk
Barcelona Handbook
Bolivia Handbook
Brazil Handbook
Cambodia Handbook
Caribbean Islands Handbook
Central America & Mexico Hbk
Chile Handbook
Colombia Handbook
Costa Rica Handbook
Cuba Handbook
Cusco & the Sacred Valley Hbk
Dominican Republic Handbook
Dublin Handbook
East Africa Handbook
Ecuador & Galápagos Handbook
Edinburgh Handbook
Egypt Handbook
Goa Handbook
Guatemala Handbook
India Handbook
Indian Himalaya Handbook
Indonesia Handbook
Ireland Handbook
Israel Handbook
Jordan Handbook
Laos Handbook
Libya Handbook
London Handbook
Malaysia Handbook
Marrakech & the High Atlas Hbk
Myanmar Handbook
Mexico Handbook
Morocco Handbook

Namibia Handbook
Nepal Handbook
New Zealand Handbook
Nicaragua Handbook
Pakistan Handbook
Peru Handbook
Rajasthan & Gujarat Handbook
Rio de Janeiro Handbook
Scotland Handbook
Scotland Highlands & Islands Hbk
Singapore Handbook
South Africa Handbook
South American Handbook
South India Handbook
Sri Lanka Handbook
Sumatra Handbook
Syria & Lebanon Handbook
Thailand Handbook
Tibet Handbook
Tunisia Handbook
Turkey Handbook
Venezuela Handbook
Vietnam Handbook

Also available from Footprint
Traveller's Handbook
Traveller's Healthbook

Available at all good bookshops

Updates

We try as hard as we can to make each Footprint Handbook as up-to-date and accurate as possible but, of course, things always change. Many people email or write to us – with corrections, new information, or simply comments. If you want to let us know about your experiences and adventures – be they good, bad or ugly – then don't delay; we're dying to hear from you. And please try to include all the relevant details and juicy bits. Your help will be greatly appreciated, especially by other travellers. In return we will send you details about our special guidebook offer. Why not contact us via our **website**:

www.footprintbooks.com
A new place to visit

alternatively email Footprint at:
nam3_online@footprintbooks.com

or write to:

Elizabeth Taylor
Footprint Handbooks
6 Riverside Court
Lower Bristol Road
Bath
BA2 3DZ
UK

www.footprintbooks.com
A new place to visit

Assisting you across Namibia

INSHORE SAFARIS
Box 2444,12th Road, Walvis Bay, Namibia
Tel: 264 64 202609, Fax: 264 64 202198
Email: info@inshore.com.na
Web: www.inshore.com.na

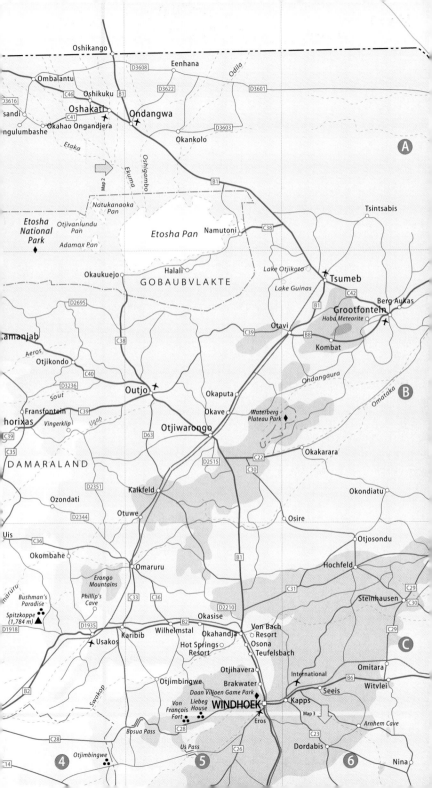

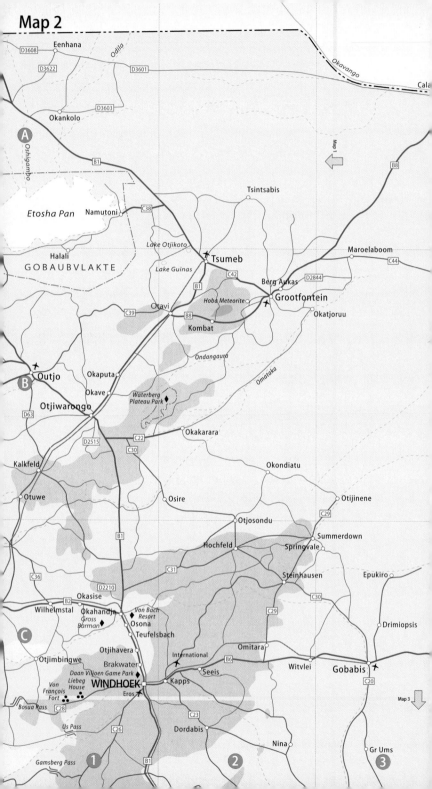

Map 2

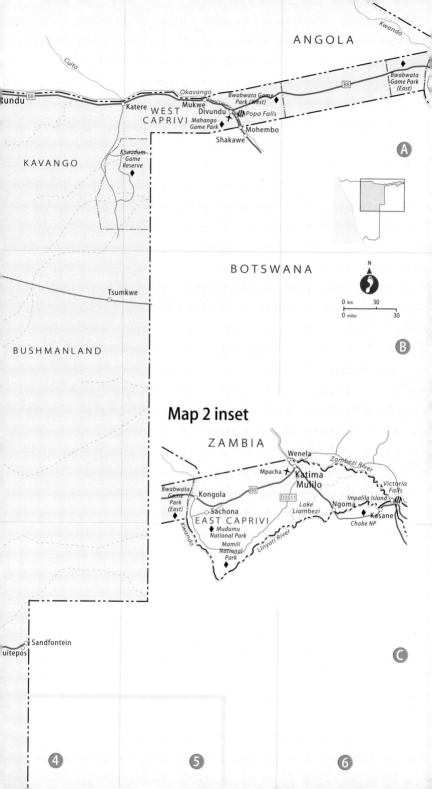

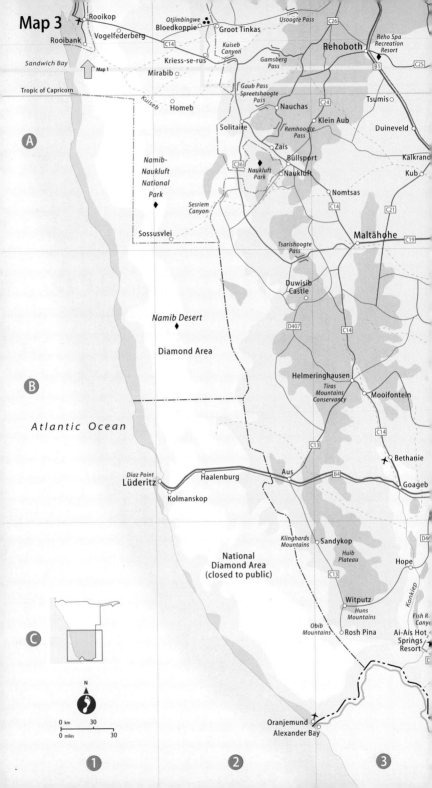

Map 3

Rooikop

Rooibank

Vogelfederberg

Otjimbingwe
Bloedkoppie

Groot Tinkas

Usoogte Pass

C26

Rehoboth

Reho Spa Recreation Resort

C14

Kuiseb Canyon

Kriess-se-rus

Gamsberg Pass

B1

C25

Sandwich Bay

Map 1

Mirabib

Kuiseb

Tropic of Capricorn

Gaub Pass
Spreetshoogte Pass

Nauchas

C24

Tsumis

Homeb

Solitaire

Klein Aub

Duineveld

A

Namib-Naukluft National Park

Remhoogte Pass

Zais

Büllsport

Kalkrand

C36

Naukluft Park

Naukluft

Kub

Sesriem Canyon

Nomtsas

C14

C21

Maltahöhe

C19

Sossusvlei

Tsarishoogte Pass

Duwisib Castle

Namib Desert

Diamond Area

D407

C14

B

Helmeringhausen

Tiras Mountains Conservancy

Mooifontein

Atlantic Ocean

C14

C13

Bethanie

Diaz Point

Haalenburg

Aus

B4

Goageb

Lüderitz

Kolmanskop

D4

Klinghards Mountains

Sandykop

Huib Plateau

Hope

National Diamond Area
(closed to public)

C13

Konkiep

Witputz

Huns Mountains

Fish R Canyo

Obib Mountains

Rosh Pina

Ai-Ais Hot Springs Resort

C

N

0 km 30

0 miles 30

Oranjemund
Alexander Bay

1

2

3

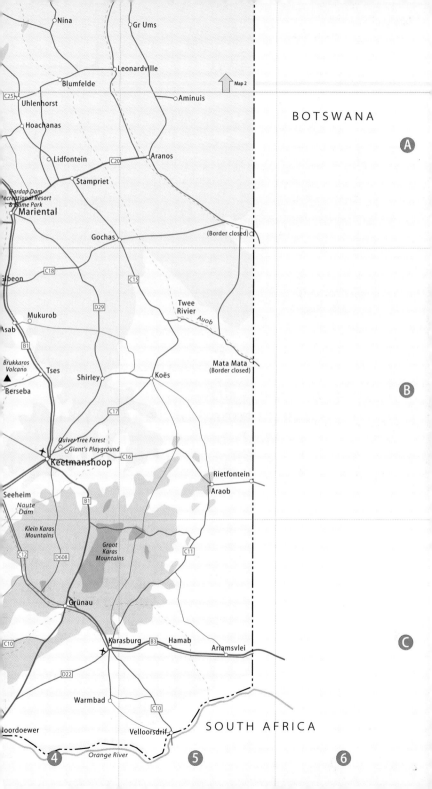

Acknowledgements

While we may all see the same things, it is often those around us who bring a place to life. Gordon would, accordingly, like to thank the following few people, without whom Namibia would not have been so rich, so fascinating, or so accessible:

Chris de Villiers of *Inshore Safaris*, Walvis Bay;
Uwe Kessler of the eponymous car hire firm;
Rob & Marianne of *Zebra River Lodge*;
Neville Neveling of the *Bush Pillow B&B*, Otjiwarongo;
all at *Out of Africa*, Otjiwarongo;
the father and son team at *S&T Motors*, Opuwo;
and Brummer's hospitality and kindness at *Epupa Camp* in northern Kaokoland.

Additionally, for technical support while on the move, David Baker, and for the appropriate kick starts and navigational guidance, Benji Donald and Katie Cowton.

Nick Santcross would like to thank the following: in Swakopmund and Walvis Bay, thanks to Nikolai and Katrien van Rooi for their incredible hospitality; to Chris at Pleasure Flights, the staff of the Cottage Maternity Hospital for Daniel's safe delivery, Nick at the Internet Cafe, Bruno and Kate Nebe for their expert advice, and friendship and enthusiasm; to Chris at Inshore Safaris for his time and of course the wonderful oyster tour. In Windhoek, Roberto and Monica Aceto once again provided a home from home, Jeanette Cross and Lazarus Jacobs for their wit and wisdom, Kessler Car Hire for their support throughout the trip and Mutaleni for her help in tracking down the latest on accommodation, bars and in places to be.

Nick Santcross

Nick Santcross was introduced to the delights of exploring the world at the tender age of 11 during a visit to Hong Kong. Since then, he has made a career of living and working around the developing world, starting with China and Ghana before arriving in Namibia in 1994. The first edition of the Namibia Handbook was written whilst Nick was working as an education advisor to the Namibian Ministry of Education. At this time he also managed to cement his relationship with the country by marrying Dia, a Rehoboth Baster. Nick and Dia's son Daniel was born in Swakopmund whilst they were researching the latest edition of the Namibia Handbook. They currently live and work in Bangladesh.

Gordon Baker

Gordon Baker's love affair with southern Africa is in the blood. His mother's family has lived and farmed in the Orange Free State for over 100 years. After numerous childhood holidays, extended periods of work in South Africa and holidays in the region, Gordon required little persuasion to work on the latest update of the Namibia Handbook. While this book represents his first foray into guide book writing, independent travel through 40 countries during the past 10 years provided the necessary background and driving over 16,000 km and visiting over 150 establishments the necessary detail to overhaul the material for this third edition.

Sebastian Ballard

Sebastian Ballard first visited Africa in 1973 and has been fortunate enough to travel extensively on this great continent. Aside from a couple of years of student poverty and a continuing flirtation with India, Sebastian has made a point of visiting Africa at least once a year. His most recent tour to South Africa, Namibia and Zimbabwe was his 40th visit. After studying African and Asian geography at university, Sebastian went to Mali in West Africa to carry out research into tropical agriculture. In 1995, the dream job was offered to him, to write a guide to southern Africa. Sebastian is author of the South Africa Handbook, the co-author of the Namibia Handbook, and a contributor to several other guides in the series.